SECOND EDITION

principles of
management
accounting

a south african perspective

Acknowledgements

The authors and publisher gratefully acknowledge permission to reproduce copyright material in this book. Every effort has been made to trace copyright holders, but if any copyright infringements have been made, the publisher would be grateful for information that would enable any omissions or errors to be corrected in subsequent impressions.

We are grateful to the Association of Chartered Certified Accountants (ACCA) for permission to reproduce past examination questions. These questions are the copyright of ACCA and are reprinted with the permission of ACCA. The suggested solutions in the solutions bank have been prepared by the authors unless otherwise stated.

We are grateful to the Chartered Institute of Management Accountants (CIMA) for permission to reproduce past examination questions. These questions are the copyright of CIMA and are reprinted with the permission of CIMA.

We are grateful to the South African Institute of Chartered Accountants (SAICA) for permission to reproduce past examination questions. These questions are the copyright of SAICA and are reprinted with the permission of SAICA.

SECOND EDITION

principles of management accounting
a south african perspective

Edited by SHELLEY-ANNE ROOS

CAROL CAIRNEY | RICHARD CHIVAKA | HENDRIK FOURIE | DEWALD JOUBERT
AHMED MOHAMMADALI HAJI | APPIE PIENAAR | LILLA STACK
JONATHAN STRENG | GARY SWARTZ | JOHN WILLIAMS

OXFORD
UNIVERSITY PRESS
SOUTHERN AFRICA

OXFORD
UNIVERSITY PRESS

Oxford University Press is a department of the University of Oxford.
It furthers the University's objective of excellence in research, scholarship,
and education by publishing worldwide. Oxford is a registered trade mark of
Oxford University Press in the UK and in certain other countries

Published in South Africa by
Oxford University Press Southern Africa (Pty) Limited

Vasco Boulevard, Goodwood, N1 City, Cape Town, South Africa, 7460
P O Box 12119, N1 City, Cape Town, South Africa, 7463

© Oxford University Press Southern Africa (Pty) Ltd 2014

The moral rights of the author have been asserted

First published 2008
Second edition published 2011

All rights reserved. No part of this publication may be reproduced, stored in
a retrieval system, or transmitted, in any form or by any means, without the
prior permission in writing of Oxford University Press Southern Africa (Pty) Ltd,
or as expressly permitted by law, by licence, or under terms agreed
with the appropriate reprographic rights organisation, DALRO, The Dramatic, Artistic
and Literary Rights Organisation atdalro@dalro.co.za. Enquiries concerning
reproduction outside the scope of the above should be sent to the Rights Department,
Oxford University Press Southern Africa (Pty) Ltd, at the above address.

You must not circulate this work in any other form
and you must impose this same condition on any acquirer.

Principles of Management Accounting: A South African Perspective 2e

ISBN 978 0 19 599868 9

Fifth impression 2014

Typeset in Palatino LT Std 9 pt on 11 pt
Printed on 70 gsm woodfree paper

Acknowledgements
Publishing manager: Alida Terblanche
Commissioning editor: Marisa Montemarano
Development editor: Lisa Andrews
Project manager: Janine Loedolff
Editor: Adrienne Pretorius
Typesetter: Baseline Publishing Services
Cover design: Oswald Kurten
Indexer: Adrienne Pretorius
Cover images: Gallo Images
Printed and bound by: Castle Graphics South (Pty) Ltd.

Unless otherwise indicated, certain questions and solutions are based on examination questions and solutions from
the University of Cape Town. The examination questions and solutions in their original examination form are the
sole copyright of the University of Cape Town. Adapted questions and solutions are copyright of the authors and/or
Oxford University Press.

The authors and publisher gratefully acknowledge permission to reproduce copyright material in this book.
Every effort has been made to trace copyright holders, but if any copyright infringements have been made,
the publisher would be grateful for information that would enable any omissions or errors to be corrected in
subsequent impressions.

Links to third party websites are provided by Oxford in good faith and for information only.
Oxford disclaims any responsibility for the materials contained in any third party website referenced in this work.

Abridged table of contents

Foreword xiii
Preface xiv
List of contributors..xv

1 Introduction to management accounting 1
2 Cost classification and behaviour 7
3 Cost estimation 37
4 Cost-volume-profit relationships 75
5 Absorption versus variable costing 101
6 Overhead allocation 139
7 Job costing 185
8 Process costing 209
9 Joint and by-product costing 247
10 Relevant information for decision-making 273
11 Decision-making under operational constraints 315
12 Budgets, planning and control 345
13 Standard costing 375
14 Performance management 449
15 Transfer pricing 487
16 Contemporary management accounting concepts 519
17 Competitive advantage 543

Glossary 595
Index 603

Contents

Foreword xiii
Preface xiv
List of contributors xv

CHAPTER 1   INTRODUCTION TO MANAGEMENT ACCOUNTING 1
Shelley-Anne Roos
Learning objectives 1
1.1   Introduction 1
1.2   Management accounting 1
1.3   Financial accounting versus management accounting 4
1.4   Levels of management information 5
1.5   Modern management accounting 5
References 6

CHAPTER 2   COST CLASSIFICATION 7
Carol Cairney (updated by Shelley-Anne Roos)
Learning objectives 7
2.1   Introduction 7
2.2   Cost behaviour 9
2.3   Assignment 17
2.4   Relevance 19
2.5   Function 22
2.6   Timing 27
2.7   Summary 28
Conclusion 28
Basic questions 29
Long questions 31
References 36

CHAPTER 3   COST ESTIMATION 37
Carol Cairney (updated by Shelley-Anne Roos)
Learning objectives 37
3.1   Introduction 37
3.2   Cost drivers 38
3.3   Scatter graph 40
3.4   High-low method 42
3.5   Least squares regression 44
3.6   Factors affecting the accuracy of cost estimation 52
3.7   Other means of estimating costs and predicting cost behaviour 53
3.8   Summary 53
Conclusion 54

Appendix 3.1: Learning curves 55
Basic questions... 67
Long questions 69
References... 73

CHAPTER 4   COST-VOLUME-PROFIT RELATIONSHIPS 75
John Williams
Learning objectives 75
4.1   Introduction.. 76
4.2   CVP analysis – the accountant's and economist's models 76
4.3   Break-even analysis 79
4.4   Sensitivity analysis 82
4.5   Break-even analysis with multiple products 89
4.6   CVP analysis assumptions and limitations... 92
4.7   Summary... 93
Conclusion 93
Basic questions... 94
Long questions 95
References... 100

CHAPTER 5   ABSORPTION VERSUS VARIABLE COSTING 101
Dewald Joubert, Ahmed Mohammadali Haji and Hendrik Fourie
Learning objectives 101
5.1   Introduction.. 102
5.2   Cost accounting concepts 102
5.3   The impact on profit if inventory levels change 109
5.4   Strengths and weakness of absorption and variable costing 121
5.5   Summary... 122
Conclusion 122
Basic questions... 124
Long questions 126
References... 132

Advanced reading: Integration section: Chapters 1 to 5 133
Shelley-Anne Roos
Integrated question 135

CHAPTER 6   OVERHEAD ALLOCATION 139
Carol Cairney (updated by Shelley-Anne Roos)
Learning objectives 139
6.1   Introduction.. 140
6.2   Volume- and value-based techniques 141
6.3   Allocation of support service department costs..................................... 151
6.4   Activity-based costing (ABC).. 159
6.5   Activity-based management and activity-based budgeting 167

principles of management accounting

6.6	Summary	167
Conclusion		168
Basic questions		169
Long questions		173
References		183

CHAPTER 7   JOB COSTING 185
Lilla Stack and John Williams

Learning objectives		185
7.1	Introduction	186
7.2	Job-costing objectives	186
7.3	The elements of cost in a job-costing system	186
7.4	Integrating the costing and financial accounting systems	195
7.5	Summary	200
Conclusion		200
Basic questions		201
Long questions		203
References		207

CHAPTER 8   PROCESS COSTING 209
Lilla Stack and John Williams

Learning objectives		209
8.1	Introduction	210
8.2	Calculations in a process costing system	211
8.3	Consecutive processes	233
8.4	Decision-making	234
8.5	Summary	236
Conclusion		237
Basic questions		238
Long questions		242
References		245

CHAPTER 9   JOINT AND BY-PRODUCT COSTING 247
Lilla Stack and John Williams

Learning objectives		247
9.1	Introduction	247
9.2	Cost accounting treatment of joint costs	249
9.3	Joint costs and International Accounting Standards	255
9.4	Joint costs in relation to decision-making	255
9.5	Summary	257
Conclusion		258
Basic questions		258
Long questions		261
References		266

Advanced reading: Integration section: Chapters 6 to 9 267
Shelley-Anne Roos
Integrated question 268

CHAPTER 10   RELEVANT INFORMATION FOR DECISION-MAKING 273
Dewald Joubert, Ahmed Mohammadali Haji and Hendrik Fourie
Learning objectives 273
10.1   Introduction 274
10.2   Understanding the concept of relevance 274
10.3   Decisions under conditions of certainty 278
10.4   Applying the concept of relevance to basic cost elements 292
10.5   Decisions under conditions of uncertainty 296
10.6   The pricing decision 301
10.7   Summary 305
Conclusion 305
Basic questions 306
Long questions 308
References 314

CHAPTER 11   DECISION-MAKING UNDER OPERATIONAL CONSTRAINTS 315
Appie Pienaar
Learning objectives 315
11.1   Introduction 316
11.2   Limiting factors 316
11.3   Make-or-buy decisions and scarce resources 322
11.4   Limiting factors and shadow prices 324
11.5   Linear programming: the graphical method 324
11.6   Shadow prices and linear programming 329
11.7   Linear programming: the simplex method 331
11.8   Linear programming in practice 334
11.9   Summary 335
Conclusion 336
Basic questions 336
Long questions 339
References 343

CHAPTER 12   BUDGETS, PLANNING AND CONTROL 345
Appie Pienaar
Learning objectives 345
12.1   Introduction 346
12.2   Objectives of budgets 346
12.3   Strategic, tactical and operational budgets 347
12.4   Responsibility for the budget 347
12.5   Determining the principal budgeting factor 348
12.6   The sequence in budget preparation 349

12.7	Production and related budgets	350
12.8	Cash budgets	351
12.9	The master budget	355
12.10	The role of ratio analysis and KPIs in the budgeting process	355
12.11	Alternative approaches to budgeting	355
12.12	Budgeting and probability theory	358
12.13	Preparing projections using historical data	359
12.14	Projecting sales	362
12.15	Budgetary control	363
12.16	Fixed and flexed budgets	363
12.17	Preparing a flexed budget	364
12.18	Impact of budgeting on the motivation of managers	365
12.19	Participation and performance evaluation	366
12.20	Negotiated style of budgeting	367
12.21	Continuous feedback on performance	367
12.22	The role of the management accountant in the budget process	368
12.23	Beyond Budgeting®	368
12.24	Summary	369
	Conclusion	369
	Basic questions	370
	Long questions	371
	References	374

CHAPTER 13 STANDARD COSTING 375
Jonathan Streng, Hendrik Fourie and Gary Swartz

	Learning objectives	375
13.1	Introduction	375
13.2	Standards and the interrelationship between standards and budgets	376
13.3	Standard costing and inventory valuation	377
13.4	Determination of cost standards	377
13.5	Calculation of variances	379
13.6	Reconciliation of actual profit to standard profit	396
13.7	Investigation of variances	397
13.8	Interpretation of variances	397
13.9	Possible causes of variances	399
13.10	Planning and operating variances	400
13.11	Revision of standards	402
13.12	Accounting entries	402
13.13	Balances in the variance accounts	410
13.14	Criticisms of standard costing	412
13.15	Variance analysis in modern mechanised environments	414
13.16	Standard costing in service organisations	415
13.17	Standard costing and benchmarking	415
13.18	Summary	416
	Conclusion	416

Appendix 13.1: Advanced standard costing concepts 417
Basic questions 428
Long questions 430
References 440

Advanced reading: Integration section: Chapters 10 to 13 441
Shelley-Anne Roos
Integrated question 442

CHAPTER 14 PERFORMANCE MANAGEMENT 449
Shelley-Anne Roos
Learning objectives 449
14.1   Introduction 450
14.2   Responsibility accounting 452
14.3   Centralised and decentralised organisational structures 455
14.4   Financial performance measures 458
14.5   Value-based management 468
14.6   Multidimensional performance measures 470
14.7   Agreeing on targets and rewarding performance 472
14.8   Not-for-profit and public sector organisations 473
14.9   Summary 473
Conclusion 474
Basic questions 475
Long questions 478
References 486

CHAPTER 15 TRANSFER PRICING 487
Shelley-Anne Roos
Learning objectives 487
15.1   Introduction 488
15.2   Decentralisation and transfer pricing 489
15.3   Principles of transfer pricing 489
15.4   Market price-based transfer prices 490
15.5   Cost-based transfer prices 491
15.6   Negotiated transfer prices 492
15.7   Resolving transfer pricing problems 495
15.8   Transfer of self-constructed assets 498
15.9   International transfers 498
15.10 Strategic and ethical considerations 500
15.11 Summary 500
Conclusion 501
Appendix 15.1: Determining transfer prices in perfect and imperfect markets 502
Basic questions 509
Long questions 511
References 517

principles of management accounting

CHAPTER 16 CONTEMPORARY MANAGEMENT ACCOUNTING CONCEPTS 519
Richard Chivaka and Shelley-Anne Roos
Learning objectives 519
16.1   Introduction 520
16.2   Theory of Constraints 520
16.3   Materials requirement planning (MRP) 526
16.4   Enterprise resource planning (ERP) 527
16.5   Just-in-time systems 528
16.6   Benchmarking 531
16.7   Summary 532
Conclusion 533
Basic questions 534
Long questions 538
References 542

CHAPTER 17 COMPETITIVE ADVANTAGE 543
Richard Chivaka and Shelley-Anne Roos
Learning objectives 543
17.1   Introduction 544
17.2   Porter's generic strategies 544
17.3   Activity-based management 545
17.4   Total quality management 547
17.5   Target costing 552
17.6   Life-cycle costing 555
17.7   Supply chain management 557
17.8   Value chain analysis 558
17.9   Summary 560
Conclusion 561
Basic questions 562
Long questions 563
References 567

Advanced reading: Integration section: Chapters 14 to 17 569
Shelley-Anne Roos
Integrated question 571

Suggested solutions to integration section questions 577
Shelley-Anne Roos
Integration section: Chapters 1 to 5 577
Integration section: Chapters 6 to 9 581
Integration section: Chapters 10 to 13 584
Integration section: Chapters 14 to 17 588

Glossary 595
Index 603

Foreword

Principles of Management Accounting: A South African Perspective is a long-overdue addition to the market of management accounting textbooks. For too long Higher Education institutions have had no alternative but to prescribe imported texts owing to the lack of a viable South African option. Students will now be afforded the benefit of understanding the key accounting concepts that underpin management decisions, as set and explained in the local context.

The book is clear and concise but provides sufficient theoretical underpinning and principles for students to understand the 'why' and not only the 'how'. Each chapter provides clear learning objectives and a short description of the relevance of the topic in practice. This provides students with a context to the topic, and will most definitely assist in the understanding of the principles discussed in each chapter. The South African references and examples are welcome, and provide a very useful framework for students to understand that management accounting is relevant and 'living out there'. Demonstrating that a subject 'lives out there' always adds to students' appreciation of the subject and the specific topic to be explained and discussed. Theory alone tends to be lost on students.

The South African economy and business in general is very dependent on sound financial management and management accounting, be it in the private or public sectors. It is clear from daily newspaper reports that there is a general lack of financial management and management accounting skills in South Africa. Though non-delivery or poor decision-making is partly to blame, it is often associated with low skills levels. A growing economy with sustainability as key driver will depend heavily on the principles explained in this book. *Principles of Management Accounting: A South African Perspective* will therefore be more than useful to practitioners as a source of reference on the underlying principles on a specific topic or to those who are not yet appropriately skilled in management accounting.

The book not only covers the relevant topics in management accounting – thus providing students with all the necessary principles in order to understand the basics of management accounting – but also provides insights into new developments in the field of management accounting, proving equally useful for those in private or public practice.

Henk Kriek

Deputy Vice-Chancellor: Finance
University of Johannesburg

Preface

This second edition of *Principles of Management Accounting: A South African Perspective* is the result of the collaborative effort of authors from several leading South African universities to produce an understandable yet comprehensive, principles-based management accounting textbook.

The book is unique in a number of ways. Firstly, the involvement of experienced lecturers from several different universities means the text is representative of the way in which management accounting is currently taught at South African universities. Secondly, it covers the topics that form the basis of almost any management accounting course (such as those followed by MBA students, or students studying towards a general business qualification who choose to include management accounting in their studies); yet it also very specifically aims to cover the management accounting syllabus of the South African Institute of Chartered Accountants (SAICA). In doing so, most aspects of the relevant papers' syllabi of the Chartered Institute of Management Accountants' (CIMA), as well as those of the Association for Certified Chartered Accountants (ACCA) are dealt with as well. Thirdly, the book was written by South Africans for South Africans, and gives preference to local examples, scenarios and business issues rather than international ones. Fourthly, the book aims to encourage students to integrate their knowledge of different management accounting topics, rather than to 'box' pieces of information inappropriately in their memories by viewing each topic in isolation.

The book has been structured in a manner that we hope will be most useful to its target readership. Every chapter lists the relevant learning outcomes to be achieved, followed by a brief introductory tutorial case study to illustrate the real-life need for the management accounting techniques that are to be discussed in the chapter. Numerous worked examples are integrated into the text of chapters throughout, and are used to explain the principles and provoke thinking about the topic, rather than merely to illustrate the calculations required. Each chapter ends with a brief summary, and an explanation of how the topics in that particular chapter link with those in other chapters in the book (to facilitate integration of knowledge). At the end of the text, a real-life tutorial case study with questions for class discussion is presented.

New to the second edition are integration sections, which tie together the knowledge gained in a number of chapters. These sections are specifically aimed at more advanced students preparing for higher-level exams.

Assessment opportunities provided include ten basic questions as well as five long questions at the end of each chapter. Answers to the basic questions, and suggested solutions to the long questions, are contained in the *Instructor's Manual*, which is on an accompanying compact disk made available to lecturers who prescribe this book. The second edition of the separate question book, *Principles of Management Accounting: The Question Book*, which includes questions based on all the topics covered in the various chapters in this book, is also available for purchase to accompany and support this textbook.

We would specifically like to thank our specialist technical proofreader, Birte Schneider, for her hard work and valuable contribution to this book.

Our hope is that this book will play a part in shaping competent, well-educated and well-informed management accountants. We hope that these management accountants will find themselves in influential business positions where they deliver quality information, resulting in optimal decision-making in the organisations that drive South Africa's economy forward.

Shelley-Anne Roos
July 2011

List of contributors

Editor
Shelley-Anne Roos (Chapters 1, 14, 15, 16 and 17, and some chapter updates)
BAcc (Stell), BAcc Hons (Stell), MPhil (Futures Studies) (Stell), CA(SA), ACMA

Shelley-Anne Roos has lectured at Stellenbosch University for over a decade, primarily preparing post-graduate students for the examinations of the South African Institute of Chartered Accountants (SAICA) and the Chartered Institute of Management Accountants (CIMA). Her research focuses primarily on performance management, and on the instruction of Management Accounting at tertiary level.

Other contributors
Carol Cairney (Chapters 2, 3 and 6)
BCom (UCT), PGDA (UCT), CA(SA)

Carol Cairney is a lecturer in Management Accounting and Finance in the Department of Accountancy at the University of Cape Town. She lectures in Management Accounting and Finance to final year post-graduate students preparing for the examinations of the South African Institute of Chartered Accountants (SAICA). She also lectures in Managerial Accounting on the MBA programme offered by the University of Cape Town Graduate School of Business, as well as on various other executive courses. Her research is in the area of cost allocation.

Richard Chivaka (Chapters 16 and 17)
PhD (UCT), MSc (Acc & Fin) (Manchester), BCom Hons (NUST)

Richard Chivaka is an Associate Professor in the Department of Accounting, and Deputy Dean (Research and Post-graduate Affairs) in the Faculty of Commerce at the University of Cape Town. His areas of specialisation are in cost management and supply chain management. He is the Programme Director for the Honours and Masters degree programmes in Strategic Cost Management. In addition to lecturing, Richard is also involved in post-graduate supervision, from Honours to PhD levels.

Hendrik Fourie (Chapters 5, 10 and 13)
CA(SA), BCom (cum laude)

Hendrik Fourie is a guest lecturer on various courses for professional accountants following the chartered accountancy route. He has a number of years' experience in investment banking.

Hendrik obtained his BCom degree cum laude and finished in a Top 10 position in Parts 1 and 2 of the SAICA national qualifying examination.

Ahmed Mohammadali Haji (Chapters 5 and 10)
BCom (Acc) (cum laude) (RAU), BCom Hons (cum laude) (RAU), CA(SA)

Ahmed Mohammadali Haji is a senior lecturer in the Department of Accountancy at the University of Johannesburg. His experience includes involvement in aspects of advanced financial management and advanced financial accounting. He lectures various postgraduate courses for professional accountants following the chartered accountancy route.

Ahmed is a CA(SA). He obtained his BCom Accounting and BCom Honours degrees cum laude, and achieved a Top 10 position in the SAICA national qualifying examination.

Dewald Joubert (Chapters 5 and 10)
BCom Hons (Acc)

Dewald Joubert is a senior lecturer and subject head in Management Accounting in the Department of Accountancy at the University of Johannesburg. He is a chartered accountant and lectures Management Accounting to prospective chartered accountants in their final year of studies. He also provides subject guidance through various programmes offered to candidates writing Part 1 of the national qualifying examination for chartered accountants.

Dewald is at present busy with his Masters degree in Financial Management.

Appie Pienaar (Chapters 11 and 12)
CA(SA), ACMA, MCom (Acc), BA (cum laude), BA Hons (Classical Greek), BD (cum laude).

Professor Appie Pienaar is an associate professor in Management Accounting at the University of South Africa (UNISA). He has a wide range of lecturing experience at various institutions, including the University of Pretoria, the University of Johannesburg, UNISA, Bond University and CIMA.

Appie is a qualified ACMA (in one of the papers, Financial Strategy, he obtained the highest mark worldwide).

Lilla Stack (Chapters 7, 8 and 9)
CA(SA), DCompt (UNISA)

Professor EM (Lilla) Stack is a professor in the Department of Accounting at Rhodes University and teaches mainly Taxation at post-graduate level, but has also been involved in teaching Management Accounting and Finance to aspiring chartered accounting students. Lilla has more than twenty years of teaching experience at UNISA and Rhodes University and has successfully supervised several PhD and masters students in tax. Her interests at present are mainly in the field of teaching research methodology to accounting students.

List of contributors

Jonathan Streng (Chapter 13)
  BCom (Acc) (cum laude), BCom Hons (Acc) (RAU), CA(SA)

  Jonathan Streng is a senior lecturer at the University of Johannesburg. He lectures Cost and Management Accounting and Financial Management to CTA students on Honours level, as well as to candidates preparing for their board exams on the Gauteng Board Course and Thuthuka repeaters programme. He has also lectured to MCom Business Management students on the MCom programme at the University of Johannesburg.

  Jonathan has been involved in various roles at SAICA including QE examination setting and marking, as well as university accreditation evaluations. Jonathan completed his BCom Accounting (cum laude) in 2003, obtained his BCom Accounting (Honours) in 2004 with the Rand Afrikaans University, and obtained a Top 10 position in Part 1 of the SAICA national qualifying examination in 2005. Jonathan completed his articles with PriceWaterhouseCoopers in 2007 in the metals and mining sector, working with clients such as Goldfields Ltd and SABMiller. He is currently finalising his thesis in completion of his Masters degree in International Accounting.

Gary Swartz (Chapter 13)
  CA(SA), MCom (Man Acc & Fin)

  Gary Swartz is a senior lecturer in the School of Accounting at the University of the Witwatersrand, Johannesburg. He is head of the Management Accounting and Finance division. Gary's experience includes involvement in both undergraduate and post-graduate levels preparing for the examinations of the South African Institute of Chartered Accountants (SAICA).

John Williams (Chapters 4, 7, 8 and 9)
  CA(SA), MCom, BSc (Inf Sys)

  John Williams is an associate professor in the Department of Accounting at Rhodes University. His experience includes a number of years as a finance and cost management consultant and as a lecturer in Management Accounting and Finance to undergraduate students.

Introduction to management accounting

chapter 1

Shelley-Anne Roos

LEARNING OBJECTIVES
By the end of this chapter, you should be able to:
1 Define management accounting.
2 Discuss the key elements of the definition of management accounting.
3 Distinguish between financial accounting and management accounting.
4 Explain the different levels in an organisation at which management accounting information is required.
5 Explain how reporting for financial accounting purposes differs from reporting for management accounting purposes.

1.1 Introduction

When students register for business courses at South African universities and colleges, one of the subjects on offer is called either 'Management accounting' or 'Cost accounting'. Even in post-graduate MBA courses in South Africa, one of these terms makes its way into the syllabus. The South African Institute of Chartered Accountants (SAICA) includes 'Management accounting' as one of the key elements in its syllabus and professional examinations. Many South African students study management accounting in order to obtain membership of the London-based organisation, the Chartered Institute of Management Accountants (CIMA), which focuses exclusively on professional management accountants. Management accounting principles also feature strongly in the syllabus of the Association of Chartered Certified Accountants (ACCA), another UK-based organisation that some South African students aspire to join.

What is management accounting, and why is it so important for business and accounting students to have a high-level understanding of it? This chapter introduces management accounting and provides an initial perspective on which the other chapters in the book build.

1.2 Management accounting

CIMA formally defines management accounting as follows:

> 'The application of the principles of accounting and financial management to create, protect, preserve and increase value for the stakeholders of for-profit and not-for-profit enterprises in the public and private sectors. Management accounting is an integral part of management. It requires the identification, generation, presentation, interpretation and use of information relevant to:
> • Inform strategic decisions and formulate business strategy
> • Plan long-, medium- and short-term operations

principles of management accounting

- » Determine capital structure and fund that structure
- » Design reward strategies for executives and shareholders
- » Inform operational decisions
- » Control operations and ensure the efficient use of resources
- » Measure and report financial and non-financial performances to management and other stakeholders
- » Safeguard tangible and intangible assets
- » Implement corporate governance procedures, risk management and internal controls.'

To understand this lengthy definition of management accounting, we need to focus on its individual parts. The subsections below discuss these parts in turn.

1.2.1 'The application of the principles of accounting and financial management ...'

As the name suggests, management accounting is a form of accounting. Accounting entails the communication of historical economic information to interested parties. But because the word 'accounting' is often immediately associated with the routine recording of debit and credit entries and the preparation of annual financial statements, care has to be taken to make a distinction between the disciplines of management accounting and financial accounting. This distinction is dealt with in section 1.5 below, and is fundamental to understanding the principles described in this book.

The definition also refers to the principles of 'financial management'. In most tertiary institutions in South Africa, the subject area of 'Management accounting' is divided into two parts. One may have a name such as 'Cost accounting' or 'Cost management', or may even go by the straightforward name of 'Management accounting'; while the other is likely to be called 'Financial management', 'Finance', or something similar. SAICA uses the terms 'Management decision-making' and 'Financial management' to describe the two parts.

This book does not deal with financial management as such, which is the part of the discipline that focuses specifically on how financial resources are best acquired and deployed. Instead, this book focuses on the pure 'management accounting' aspects, also often referred to as 'cost accounting', 'cost management', or even 'costing'. Because the aforementioned terms employing the word 'cost' do not embrace the full scope of the subject matter, we prefer the broader and more descriptive term 'management accounting', and have therefore used it in the title of this book.

1.2.2 '... to create, protect, preserve and increase value for the stakeholders ...'

Although most people would expect accountants to play some role in protecting and preserving value in an organisation, the fact that management accountants 'create' and 'increase' value may surprise some. Increasingly, management accountants are moving away from the stereotypical 'number-crunching', 'back-office' roles, and playing a crucial part in strategic decision-making within the organisation. Part of this change in focus may be due to advances in information technology that have resulted in tedious, repetitive tasks being automated, but much of it also has to do with the manner in which management accountants are educated and how they see their own roles in practice.

It is important to note that the definition refers to the delivery of value to 'stakeholders', not 'shareholders'. Stakeholders are any parties that have an interest in the organisation. It is therefore a much broader term than 'shareholders', which refers only to those with an equity stake in a company. While shareholders are indeed one of the primary user groups of financial accounting information, managers inside the organisation (who are included under the term 'stakeholders') are usually the primary (although not necessarily the only) users of management accounting information. Furthermore, it is a modern trend for businesses to focus their attention broadly on all stakeholders (which include, among many others, customers, suppliers, employees, the community, suppliers of capital, and even the natural environment), as it is increasingly believed that the long-term sustainability of organisations depends on this broader focus.

1.2.3 '… of for-profit and not-for-profit enterprises in the public and private sectors'

Although many of the techniques described in this book have their origins in a manufacturing environment, companies in the retail and services sectors have customised and employed them with great success. Management accounting techniques are even applicable beyond these profit-driven private sector companies. Some of the most welcome applications of the techniques are being experienced nowadays by not-for-profit and public-sector organisations, where the need for quality management information is high, and management information systems have traditionally been unrefined and ineffective. The CIMA syllabus in particular specifically emphasises application of the techniques in all types of environment.

1.2.4 The remaining part of the definition

In the last sentence of its definition of management accounting, CIMA calls it an 'integral part of management' and lists the different areas to which the information in a management accounting system is relevant. A shorter and more frequently encountered classification of the areas to which the information relates divides management activities into the three categories of planning, control, and decision-making. Although these three are valid categories to keep in mind when studying management accounting (as are the categories in the CIMA definition), management functions are very much intertwined and often almost indistinguishable in practice. In this book we have therefore not attempted to classify chapters or techniques according to categories, but have rather aimed to provide students with the principles that will enable them to fulfil these functions and/or to supply management accounting information for these functions.

Notice that the definition of management accounting does not limit it to either financial or quantitative information. This is because a well-designed, balanced management information system provides not only financial information (that which is measured in rands, such as the cost of a new production machine), but also non-financial information (that which is not measured in rands, such as the specifications of a new production machine). It also does not provide only quantitative information (that which is measured using numbers, such as how many units a machine can produce per hour), but also qualitative information (that which is not measured using numbers, such as the likely impact of automated production on staff morale).

1.3 Financial accounting versus management accounting

[Section 1.3 was based on material written by Ahmed Mohammadali Haji.]

Financial accounting involves the preparation of financial statements in line with prescribed standards to satisfy the needs of various external stakeholders of the organisation. Financial statement reporting originates from governance and stewardship principles: management is entrusted with shareholder funds, and consequently has to prepare a statement of account to shareholders on how those funds have been managed during a specified period in the past. Such statement of account is made publicly in the form of the company's published financial statements. In South Africa, companies issue financial statements once a year to comply with legal requirements, and listed companies report twice a year to comply with Johannesburg Securities Exchange (JSE) regulations. Financial statements have to comply with International Financial Reporting Standards (IFRS), which aim to obtain consistency in the manner in which organisations across the world report the financial consequences of past transactions and events.

Management accounting primarily deals with information for internal reporting purposes. It involves a combination of past information, together with future-orientated information, such as forecasts and budgets, to enable managers to perform their duties. This form of reporting is not governed by laws or reporting standards. Information is supplied according to the needs of the particular organisation, without having to comply with general standards for the sake of comparability with other reporting entities. The real nature of the transaction or event is therefore more likely to be retained and reported.

The aim of management accounting is simply to supply managers with relevant, quality information in a timely manner in order to enable them to take the best possible decisions.

The following table summarises the main differences between financial accounting and management accounting:

	Financial accounting	**Management accounting**
Target	Information primarily prepared for external users	Information primarily prepared for internal users
Time frame	Reports on past events	Includes past events, but focuses on information that enables decisions about the future
Framework	Complies with International Financial Reporting Standards (IFRS)	Not governed by laws or reporting standards
Depth	General purpose reporting	Specific purpose reporting
Focus	Organisation as a whole	Organisation as a whole or specific parts thereof (e.g. products, clients, and so on)
Frequency	Annually (semi-annually for companies listed on the JSE)	Determined by management needs

1.4 Levels of management information

Management accounting is about supplying relevant accounting and related information to managers. Therefore, the 'correct' management accounting information in terms of content, scope, presentation and timing depends on the purpose for which the information is required.

An organisation can be divided into three layers of management and decision-making. The lowest is the 'operational level', where day-to-day operations are executed and controlled. In a factory, for example, finished goods may be produced and accounted for daily. The process is controlled by the factory floor manager. In a bank, cheques are received from clients and accounted for every day, a process controlled by the head teller.

The middle level of an organisation is often called the 'tactical level', where mid-level managers control operations. For example, the Epping factory manager is in control of the whole Epping factory. The factory floor manager reports to him and he in turn reports to the company's head office. Similarly, the branch manager is in charge of the East London city centre branch of the bank. The head teller reports to her and she in turn reports to the bank's head office in Johannesburg.

The highest level of management and decision-making in an organisation is called the 'strategic level'. Executive directors and high-level managers take decisions and control operations at this level. This overall strategic function is usually performed at the headquarters of an organisation.

The characteristics of management accounting information differ at each level. Information that is required at operational level is typically specific, detailed, of limited scope, short-term-orientated, frequently required, and of a repetitive nature. At the tactical level, management accounting information needs are likely to be less specific and detailed than at the operational level, of broader scope, medium term-orientated, less frequently required (for example, weekly or monthly reports instead of daily ones) and of both a repetitive as well as an ad hoc nature. At strategic level, the information needs are likely to be broader, summarised rather than detailed, dealing with the organisation as a whole, long-term-orientated, of even lower frequency, and information needs of an ad hoc nature arise more regularly.

It is therefore imperative that students of management accounting are skilled in analysing the purpose for which information is required in a given scenario, and understand the importance of delivering the best information for the specific circumstance.

1.5 Modern management accounting

In the 1980s management accounting received much criticism from scholars and practitioners who believed that the discipline had lost its relevance. This was put on record in a book by Johnson and Kaplan, *Relevance Lost – the Rise and Fall of Management Accounting*. The authors expressed their concern that management accounting information was simply extracted from the organisation's financial accounting system (instead of being generated by an independent, purpose-made system), and that a lack of innovation had prevented management accounting from keeping up with changes in the environment. Because the book was highly regarded and received much publicity, many experts reacted to the criticism and have since made vast improvements to the discipline. The challenge, however, remains, in that management accountants should free themselves from the constraints of financial accounting systems, and continue to keep their work relevant to an ever-changing environment.

In the modern, highly competitive business environment, managers are increasingly aware of the quality and timeliness with which products and services should be delivered to clients. Similarly, management accountants are increasingly aware of the quality and timeliness with which information should be delivered to *their* 'clients' – the managers. Although management accounting is still primarily supplied to managers inside the organisation, there is also increasingly a tendency to disclose some of the information voluntarily to other stakeholders.

An effective management accounting system provides high-quality, timely information to the relevant persons. However, some consideration needs to be given to the cost of the system. Although advances in information technology have made the provision of information cheaper than ever, the cost of further refining an information system still needs to be weighed against the benefits that are likely to result from such refinement.

Tutorial case study

Two soon-to-be second year university students, Adam and Kanyi, are contemplating their studies. Adam is registered for a general BCom degree and is deciding whether he should take the subject Management Accounting. Kanyi, who is studying to become a chartered accountant, has noticed that Management Accounting is one of the compulsory subjects and is unsure what to expect.
1. Explain, in simple terms, what management accounting is.
2. Discuss how management accounting is different from one of the other subjects for which both students are registered, financial accounting.
3. Briefly outline the tasks for which you think a management accountant may be responsible. Use the different levels at which information is required in an organisation as a guide.

References

Eaton, G. 2005. *Management accounting: official terminology.* London: CIMA Publishing.
Johnson, HT & Kaplan, RS. 1987. *Relevance lost – the rise and fall of management accounting.* Boston, MA: Harvard Business School.

Cost classification

chapter 2

Carol Cairney (updated by Shelley-Anne Roos)

LEARNING OBJECTIVES

By the end of this chapter, you should be able to:
1 Understand the reasons for classifying costs according to each of the various cost attributes.
2 Classify costs according to the criteria set out in each of the cost categories.
3 Identify whether a cost is fixed, variable, mixed or step in nature.
4 Determine the total cost of an expense, for a given level of activity.
5 Identify which costs are to be allocated to the cost of inventory produced and which costs are expensed through the income statement.
6 Distinguish between direct and indirect costs and be aware of how these two types of costs are traced or assigned to cost objects.
7 Identify the kinds of costs that are relevant and not relevant to decision-making.

Shoprite Holdings and cost classification

In its 2010 annual report, *Shoprite Holdings* reported costs in its Group statement of comprehensive income with labels such as 'cost of sales', 'operating leases' and 'other expenses'.

Source: Shoprite Holdings Ltd 2010

These and other items form part of the limited information relating to costs that Shoprite Holdings is required to report publicly, according to financial accounting rules. Such information is not nearly enough for Shoprite's managers to take decisions and to control the operations of the organisation. The managers require management accounting information which contains much more detailed cost information. They study the attributes of the different costs and classify them accordingly. This allows them to add value to the organisation through informed management actions.

This chapter examines how costs behave and how they are classified.

2.1 Introduction

Key terms: assignment, cost behaviour, function, relevance, timing

This chapter introduces concepts that form the foundation of all of the management accounting tools and techniques that are discussed in this book. The title of this chapter, *Cost classification*, refers to the categorisation of financial information (with a focus on cost information) according to a number of different attributes that are of interest from a managerial perspective. The logical question that should arise at this point is: 'Why would we want to classify accounting information in a number of different ways? We already have the financial accounting classification – revenue or expense, asset, liability or equity – surely this is sufficient for management?' The answer is – no, it's not. Not by a long shot. But why not?

In order to understand why, for managerial purposes, viewing financial information from a financial accounting perspective is unhelpful, and why financial information actually needs to be considered from a number of different angles, we need to start by understanding what the management of an organisation is there to achieve. (The term 'management' in this context refers to all levels of management, but with particular emphasis on senior management, including an organisation's directors).

The objective of a profit-seeking organisation's management is to create and enhance shareholder value. In order to do this management needs to focus on maximising the value of the organisation itself. They do this by making *decisions* that increase the value of the organisation (such as which product and service ranges to introduce or discontinue, which departments and divisions to expand or close, which contracts and projects to accept or decline, and similar issues) and by *controlling* the actions of all the organisation's employees through financial mechanisms (such as performance evaluation and incentives) in such a way as to contribute to value creation.

Managers should seek to make decisions and control the organisation in such a way as to *increase the future cash flow* that the organisation is likely to generate. Managers view financial information from a number of perspectives that provide insight into the relationship between management's actions, and the value of the firm. These perspectives are based on the various attributes (characteristics) that cost information has, and comprise the following:

- Cost behaviour
- Assignment
- Relevance
- Function
- Timing.

These various perspectives are laid out below in section 2.1.1, and explained more fully in the remainder of this chapter. You will notice as we work through the explanations and examples that follow that many of these attributes are related, and an understanding of all of these aspects is required in order to determine how costs and revenues can be altered and managed.

2.1.1 Cost classification

For management accounting purposes the perspectives from which cost information is viewed are based on various characteristics:

- *Cost behaviour:* This deals with how a cost reacts to a change in sales volume, production volume, or any other activity level (for example, the number of machine set-ups). This chapter introduces four basic cost types: variable, fixed, step and mixed costs.
- *Assignment:* This is the tracing of costs to cost objects, such as products, services, projects, customers, departments, and divisions. Assignment is concerned with identifying the relationship between the cost and the object for which the total cost is calculated. Does the cost arise directly from producing and selling the product concerned? Or does the cost represent some resource that is drawn on by many aspects of the business? If this is the case, then the relationship between the cost object (the product, service, or business

unit, or any other relevant aspect) and the cost is less direct and more difficult to determine and trace. This chapter focuses on distinguishing between costs that are direct and costs that are indirect to the cost object. Chapter 6, *Overhead allocation* addresses in depth the problem of how to attach indirect ('overhead') costs to products.
- *Relevance:* It is important to identify costs and revenues that are affected or altered by a decision, as well as costs that are not altered by a decision. Costs and revenues should be taken into account in decision-making only to the extent that they are incremental (that is, to the extent that they will be changed by the decision). The basic principles of decision relevance are introduced in this chapter. Chapter 10, *Relevant costs for decision-making* explores these concepts more fully.
- *Function:* The presentation of cost information is done in accordance with the function of the cost within the entity. This aspect distinguishes, for example, between costs that are incurred in order to bring a product into a saleable location and condition, and costs that are incurred in order to support, but that are not directly related to, this function.
- *Timing:* This relates to the date and time period when a cost is recognised in the income statement.

In our discussion so far we have explained the need for classifying costs and analysing their behaviour from the perspective of the management team of a profit-seeking organisation operating in the private sector (in other words, an organisation that aims to make a profit from its operations). However, an understanding of cost classification and behaviour is just as important in public sector organisations (such as government departments) and in not-for-profit organisations (such as professional institutes or charities). In these cases there is usually an almost unlimited demand for the services of the organisation, but limited resources to supply the services. A thorough understanding of the organisation's costs helps managers to run the organisation efficiently.

2.2 Cost behaviour

Key terms: fixed costs, mixed costs, step costs, variable costs

Cost behaviour refers to how costs are affected by a change in sales volumes, production volumes, or other activity level (for example, the number of machine set-ups). This information is necessary in order to establish how changing production and sales levels will affect the organisation's profitability. Costs can be divided into four broad categories based on their relationship to changing activity levels: **variable costs, fixed costs, step costs** and **mixed costs**.

2.2.1 Variable costs

Variable cost increases (or decreases) in proportion with increases (or decreases) in the level of activity. Where the cost is related to production activities (for example materials costs), the total cost changes as *production volumes* change, while if the cost is related to sales (such as sales commission), the total cost changes as *sales volumes* change. Some costs may change in relation to another activity, for example set-up costs are likely to change in relation to the number of machine set-ups.

Example 2.1

Suppose one of the large South African universities decided to introduce a new course: a master's degree in management accounting. The number of students accepted on to the course each year is expected to vary from 15 to 20. The master's degree will require students to complete one year of course work, which includes writing and passing three term tests and one final exam. The university will supply each student with course notes and lecture notes. The cost of stationery (the cost of providing students with course and lecture notes, test and exam papers, and exam books) is R400 per student. In addition to writing tests and exams, students must also submit a thesis. Each student writing a thesis is supervised by a university lecturer, who is paid a supervisor's fee of R5 000 for each student supervised. Each thesis is marked by two markers. Each marker is paid R1 000 per thesis marked.

Required:
Calculate and discuss the variable and fixed cost components of the new master's degree.

All the costs described above are variable costs in respect of the number of students on the course. The variable cost per student is R7 400 (R400 + R5 000 + R1 000 × 2). These costs will increase directly with the number of students accepted onto the course. If only one student is accepted onto the course, then the total variable cost is R7 400, but if two students are accepted, the total variable cost increases to R14 800 (R7 400 × 2). The relationship between the total variable cost and the number of students can be plotted on a graph. Figure 2.1 shows the relationship between the total variable cost and the number of students accepted on the course, while Figure 2.2 shows the variable cost per student relative to the number of students on the course. Notice that while the variable cost varies in aggregate, the variable cost is constant per unit of the activity level (in this case, the number of students).

Figure 2.1 Variable cost graph: total cost

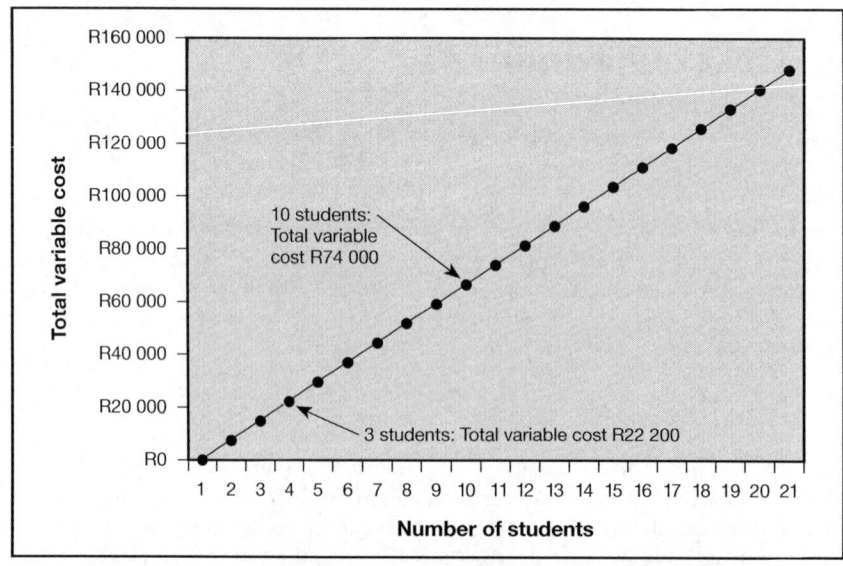

Figure 2.2 Variable cost graph: per student

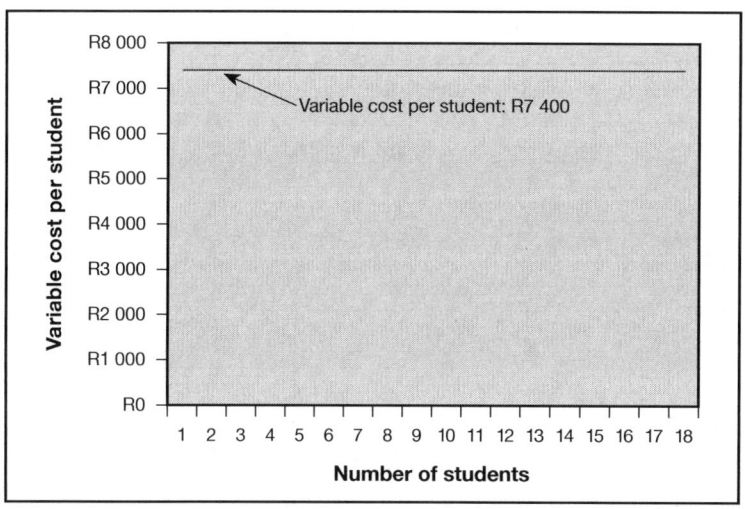

Economic considerations

Figure 2.3 Variable cost graph: activity level

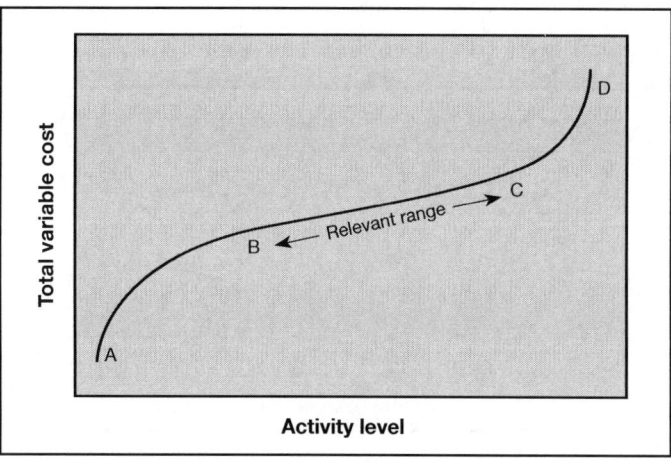

A perfectly linear relationship between the total variable cost and activity level existed in example 2.1, as shown in Figure 2.1. In many circumstances, such a perfectly linear relationship may not exist. Consider Figure 2.3. At low levels of activity (point A), an organisation may not benefit from economies of scale such as volume discounts and efficient use of resources, causing the variable cost per unit of activity to decrease initially with increasing activity levels (from A to B). Likewise, at high activity levels (C to D), where maximum capacity is approached, dis-economies may result from inefficiencies arising as a result of tired staff, overworked machinery, less flexibility owing to increased size, and other similar factors. For this reason, variable cost per unit increases in the C to D range as activity levels increase. However, a linear relationship between the activity level and total cost may well exist between these two extremes. This (B to C) is referred to as the relevant range – the range for which the linear relationship assumption is true.

principles of management accounting

2.2.2 Fixed costs

A fixed cost is a cost that in total is unresponsive to a change in activity. As a result, the cost per unit of activity would decrease as the activity level increased, and vice versa. The following example illustrates this.

Example 2.2

Other than the variable costs of running the course described in example 2.1, certain other costs must also be incurred in order for the course to be run. The class will be lectured by a retired professor who is no longer otherwise involved with the university and who will be paid R200 000 for the year to lecture up to 20 students exclusively. There will also be a number of guest lecturers, who will collectively be paid R10 000 for the year.

Required:
Calculate and discuss the variable and fixed cost components of the new master's degree.

All the costs in example 2.1 were variable in relation to the number of students, and the total variable cost was calculated to be R7 400 per student. The costs introduced to the scenario in example 2.2 are fixed costs, as these amounts will be incurred regardless of the number of students in the course (within a range of 0 to 20 students). Whether there are 15 students or 20 students in the class, the salary paid to the professor and guest lecturers remains at R210 000.

Figure 2.4 Fixed cost graph: total cost

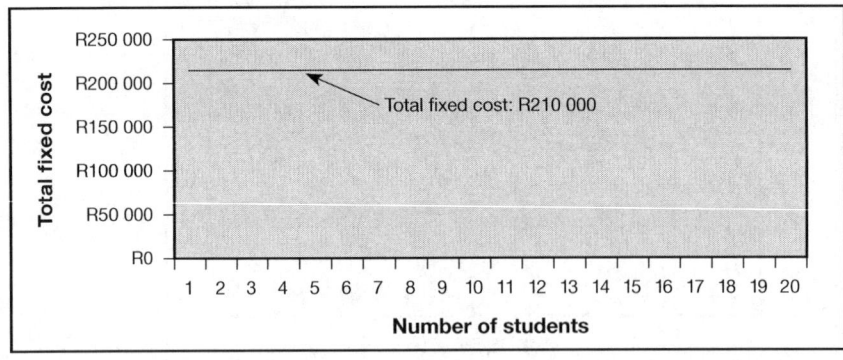

Figure 2.5 Fixed cost graph: per student

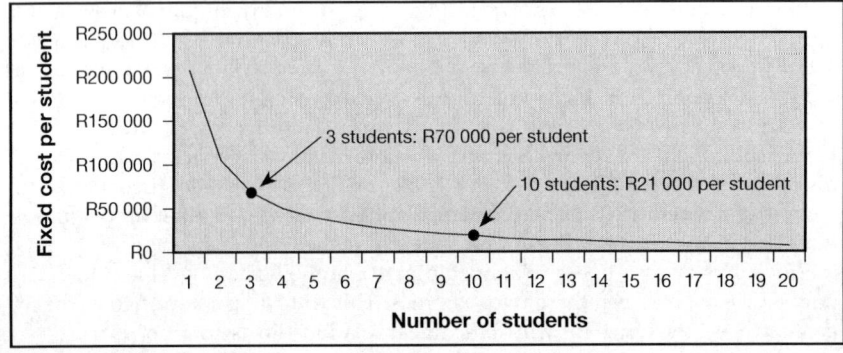

Notice that while the total fixed cost remains constant regardless of the number of students on the course, the fixed cost per unit of activity level (in this case the number of students) decreases as the number of students increases.

Economic considerations

The assumption that fixed costs remain unaltered regardless of the activity level is true only within the relevant range. Should the fixed costs relate to a machine or a factory building with a maximum capacity, if production volumes were to be increased beyond the capacity of the machine or building, then a second machine or building would have to be acquired, which would result in an increase of fixed costs. Referring again to the master's course example, if the course were to be expanded to more than 20 students, the professor would be paid more in terms of his contract, thereby increasing the total fixed costs.

Likewise, so-called fixed costs are fixed only for a specific period of time. The professor in the example above would probably not be paid R200 000 per year for as long as he is willing to lecture the class. Instead, it is likely that his fee will increase every year, perhaps in line with the university's general salary increase granted to staff. The professor's fee is 'fixed' only for the period under consideration, which is one year in this example. Although most management accountants make a habit of simply referring to a cost as 'fixed', strictly speaking we should phrase it more specifically by saying a cost is 'fixed for the period of (say) one year'. It follows that, in the long run, all costs are in fact variable in nature.

2.2.3 Step costs

A step cost is a cost that is available only in fixed allotments. It varies with the activity level, but in a stepwise manner, rather than in a perfectly linear fashion.

Example 2.3

In addition to the fixed and variable costs for the new master's course described in examples 2.1 and 2.2, the master's course will include a groupwork component whereby students will be required to submit projects in groups of no more than five students each. As a result, for every five students *or part thereof* accepted on to the course, marking costs will increase by R600.

Required:
Discuss the nature of the additional marking cost.

The additional R600 marking cost per 5 students (*or part thereof*) is a step cost. This can be plotted on a graph, as shown in Figures 2.6 and 2.7. As shown in Figure 2.6, marking costs for 3 students would be the same as marking costs for 5 students (R600). Any number of students from 6 to 10 would increase the marking costs to R1 200, and so on.

principles of management accounting

Figure 2.6 Step cost graph: total cost

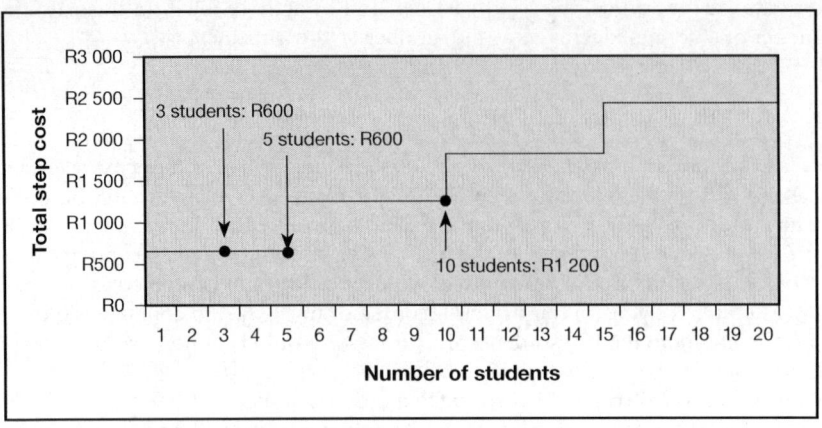

Figure 2.7 Step cost graph: per student

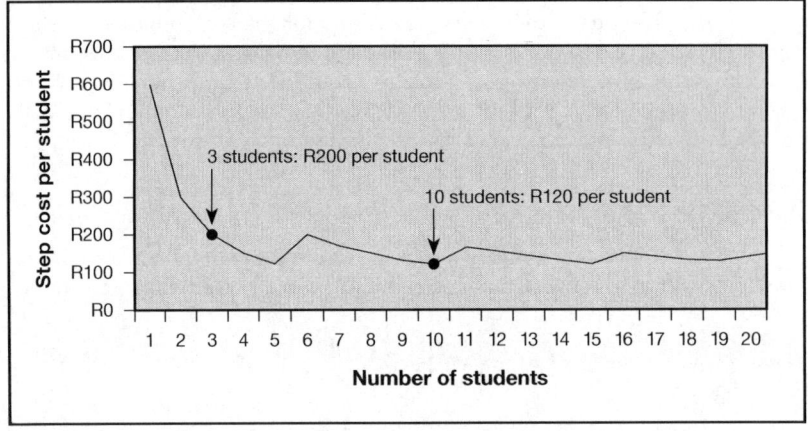

2.2.4 Mixed costs

A mixed cost is a cost that consists of two components, usually a variable and a fixed component. A typical example of a mixed cost is your monthly telephone account for a landline, or for a cellphone on contract. The telephone account is made up of a fixed component – the monthly line rental charge for a landline, or monthly contract fee in the case of a cellphone – as well as a variable component – call charges, which vary with the number and length of calls made. Another example of a mixed cost can be found in commercial property rental agreements. The rental charge paid by shopping centre tenants frequently consists of a fixed rental amount (usually based on floor area) as well as a variable portion calculated as a percentage of the tenant's monthly revenue. In order to determine how a mixed cost will respond to a change in activity level, the mixed cost must be split into its fixed and variable components. There are a number of approaches to splitting mixed costs, and these approaches are discussed in Chapter 3, *Cost estimation*.

Example 2.4

Consider the same university master's degree as in examples 2.1 to 2.3. In addition to the teaching and evaluation costs already discussed, there is one final cost with which the master's course will be charged: university administration charges. All courses offered by the university are expected to contribute towards the administrative costs of the university, which are significant. A few examples of administrative costs that the university bears on behalf of all faculties, departments and courses are: maintenance of facilities, cleaning, graduation, student records, technological infrastructure, research, and the finance function. These costs are not traced directly to courses, as this would be an incredibly expensive task which, in the view of the university, would have little benefit. Instead, all courses are charged a general fee that is calculated at R2 000 per course plus R500 per student.

Required:
Discuss whether the university administration charges allocated to the new master's degree can be described as a mixed cost.

The university administration charge is a mixed cost, as it has both fixed (course fee) and variable (charge per student) components. The mixed cost is plotted on a graph, as shown in Figures 2.8 and 2.9 below. Notice that the mixed cost graph (Figure 2.8) has the same shape as the variable cost graph (Figure 2.1), except that the intersection with the Y axis is not at zero as with the variable cost, but instead the line intersects the Y axis at R2 000, the amount of the fixed cost, just as a fixed cost graph does.

Figure 2.8 Mixed cost graph: total cost

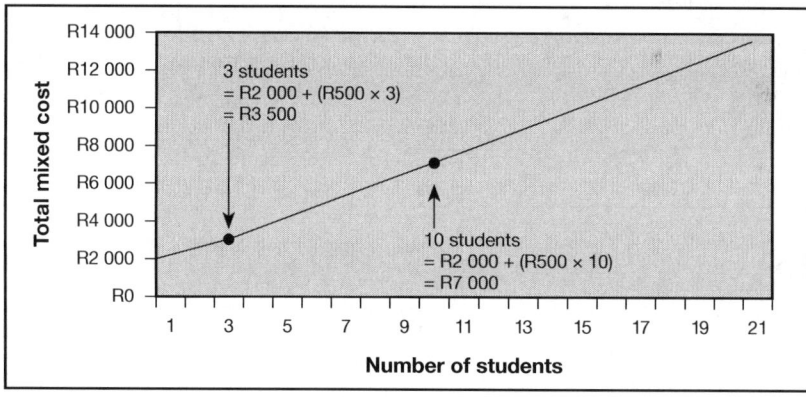

Figure 2.9 Mixed cost graph: per student

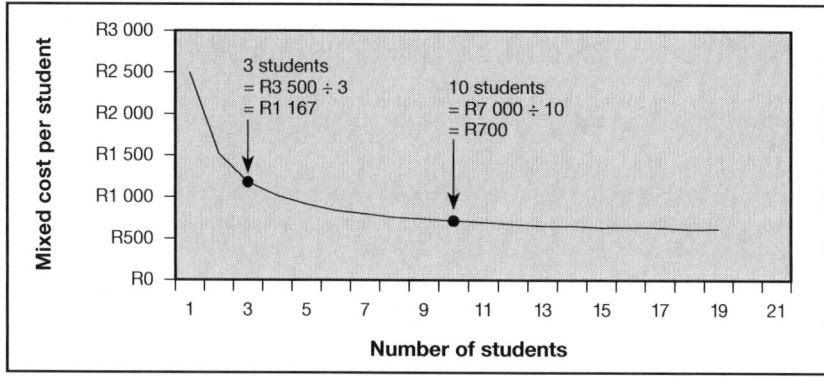

principles of management accounting

> ### Example 2.5
> Consider the same university master's degree as in the previous examples. In the first year that the course is run, 19 students are accepted onto the programme. Each student is charged a R20 000 course fee for the year.
>
> **Required:**
> Given all the cost information supplied in examples 2.1 to 2.4, draft an income statement for management accounting purposes for the course for the first year.

Taking all the available information into account, the income statement for management accounting purposes can be drawn up as follows:

Income statement for the master's course:

Revenue[1]	R380 000
Variable costs	
Stationery	(R7 600)[2]
Supervision	(R95 000)[3]
Thesis marking	(R38 000)[4]
Fixed costs	
Salary	(R200 000)
Guest lecturer fees	(R10 000)
Step cost	
Project marking fees	(R2 400)[5]
Mixed cost	
Administrative charges	(R11 500)[6]
Profit	R15 500

Notes:
1. R20 000 × 19 students
2. R400 × 19 students
3. R5 000 × 19 students
4. R1 000 × 2 markers × 19 students
5. R600 × 4 (that is, 19 students/5, and rounded up)
6. R2 000 + (500 × 19 students)

2.2.5 Application of cost behaviour principles

> **Key term:** analytical review

Earlier in this chapter it was noted that an understanding of cost behaviour is necessary for the majority of management accounting tools and techniques that are discussed in this text. In addition to this, cost behaviour principles are regularly used in certain audit procedures. Many students reading this text may find themselves in a position where they need to apply these principles in the context of an audit assignment.

Auditors carry out audit procedures in order to gain assurance that the financial statements of an organisation are free of material misstatement. Many types of procedures exist, one of which is **analytical review**. Auditors assess the reasonableness of the current year's figures by, among other things, comparing the current year's figures to the prior year's figures, after adjusting for expected changes. In adjusting prior year figures, some of the prior year's production costs may have to be adjusted for comparison if current year production volumes differ, while others may not. Other costs may be adjusted for changes in sales levels. Some costs may be changed for fluctuations in other activity levels, not just increases or decreases in production or sales volumes. In order to carry out this analytical review procedure, auditors need an understanding of the way that costs behave – are costs variable, fixed, step, or mixed?

They also need to understand what causes costs to change. What activities cause costs to vary? What causes these costs to be incurred in the first place? What underlying reason is there for these costs being expended? Similarly, managers frequently compare financial results line-by-line to the budget and to the prior year's figures, and therefore also need a thorough understanding of cost behaviour.

2.3 Assignment

Key terms: cost object, direct cost, indirect cost, tracing or allocating costs

Cost assignment refers to **tracing or allocating costs** to cost objects. A **cost object** is the item to which the cost is to be traced or allocated. Should an organisation intend to establish the cost of a service that it offers, then this service is the cost object. Likewise, if an organisation wishes to establish the cost of operating their human resources department, then the human resources department is the cost object. In general terms, a cost object could be a product, service, customer, project, job or activity that is carried out within the organisation, or division, department or any other organisational unit. Costs can be traced to cost objects with varying degrees of effort. In fact, it is the extent to which a cost can be feasibly traced to the cost object that determines whether that cost is classified as a **direct cost** (when it is economically feasible to trace to the cost object) or an **indirect cost** (when it is impossible or not economically feasible to trace to the cost object).

For example, suppose SAA wanted to determine the cost of a flight from Cape Town to London's Heathrow airport. The cost of the food served to passengers on that flight and the cost of the jet fuel used on the flight would be considered direct costs as these costs are easily traced to the flight. However, other costs associated with the flight may not be as easily traceable to the flight itself, such as the cost of maintaining the plane and expenses related to operating SAA's head office. These costs would be considered to be indirect costs should the organisation decide that accurately tracing these costs directly to this specific flight is either not possible, or not economically feasible.

Does this imply that indirect costs are then not assigned to cost objects? Not necessarily. Where it is not economically feasible to *trace* actual costs to cost objects, these indirect costs can be *allocated* to cost objects on some reasonable basis. A synonym for the word 'allocated' in this context is 'apportioned'. For instance, the monthly salary costs of the pilots and aircrew could be allocated to the flight based on the number of hours of flying time of the flight, relative to the number of hours the crew would normally fly in a month. Provided that there is some cause-and-effect relationship between the basis on which costs are incurred and the basis on which costs are allocated, the indirect costs assigned to the cost object will be a reasonably accurate reflection of the actual costs incurred.

> A synonym for indirect cost is overhead cost.

Example 2.6

Look at all the costs incurred to run the master's course, detailed in examples 2.1 to 2.4 above.

Required:
For costs appearing in the income statement, classify each cost as either a direct or indirect cost of the course.

The variable costs in this example, namely stationery, supervision and thesis marking, can all be classified as direct costs. The nature of these costs is such that they are all easily and readily traceable to the cost object (the master's course). The same holds true for the professor's salary and the guest lecturer fees (both fixed costs), as well as the project marking fees (a step cost). For all of these costs it is easy to determine how much will be spent solely as a result of offering the master's course.

Table 2.1 Summary of direct and indirect costs in example 2.6

Variable costs	
Stationery	Direct
Supervision	Direct
Thesis marking	Direct
Fixed costs	
Salary	Direct
Guest lecturer fees	Direct
Step cost	
Project marking fees	Direct
Mixed cost	
Administrative charges	Indirect

The administrative charges, however, constitute an indirect cost. This is because it is not easy to determine the extent of the resources relating to maintenance of facilities, graduation, student records, and similar matters that will be utilised by the course, as these resources are used only indirectly by the course, and as a result are very difficult to trace. Since tracing the costs to the cost object is not economically feasible, the university allocates a portion of these administrative costs to the course, based on a general formula that is used throughout the university. How was this general formula determined? At some point the finance director for the university most probably added up the total administrative costs that could not be easily traced to specific courses. He then possibly considered what the kinds of tasks were that the various administrative departments carry out on behalf of the numerous courses that the university offers, and noticed that some administrative costs would be the same regardless of the number of students on a course, while other costs would be driven by the number of students.

The finance director would then have divided the costs that did not fluctuate according to the number of students by the number of courses the university offered, to arrive at a cost of R2 000 per course. The costs that did indeed fluctuate according to the number of students would then have been divided by the total number of students at the university, in order to determine an average cost per student of R500. While this may not be 100 per cent accurate, clearly the university feels that the allocation is reasonable enough to provide a profit figure per course that is sufficiently reliable for their needs.

Note that it would be a mistake to assume that variable costs are always direct costs, or that fixed costs are always indirect. In fact, example 2.6 illustrated that fixed costs can indeed be direct costs. Similarly, it illustrated that variable costs can sometimes be indirect, like the variable position of administrative charges allocated.

Note that the classification of costs as variable, fixed, step or mixed can be accurate only:
1. Within the relevant range
2. Within a specified time period
3. In relation to a specific cost driver.

Requirements (1) and (2) above should be clear from section 2.2, while requirement (3) is discussed further in Chapter 6, *Overhead allocation*. The classification of costs as direct or indirect depends, however, on the cost object, as discussed in section 2.3.

2.4 Relevance

Key term: relevant cost

Relevant costing refers to determining the financial effect of a decision on the organisation. The financial effect is the overall increase or decrease in costs and revenues that will result from a decision to take a certain action. The key question that this topic addresses is: what costs and revenues should be taken into account in order to determine the financial impact on the firm of a decision that is under consideration?

The objective of a profit-seeking organisation's management team is to maximise shareholder value by making decisions that will *increase the future cash flows* of the organisation.

An organisation's value is the present value of all the future cash flows that the organisation is likely to generate. Management's decisions should be focused on increasing these future cash flows. Consequently, when we wish to determine the financial impact of a decision, what we wish to determine is the amount by which the decision is likely to change the value of the organisation.

In order to determine the financial impact of a decision, only differential, future cash flows should be taken into account.

principles of management accounting

In other words, a cost (or revenue) that is relevant and should be taken into account for decision-making purposes has three attributes. A **relevant cost** or revenue is:

- *A future cost (or revenue):* Since the value of the firm is determined by the future cash flows it will generate, only future costs and revenues have any effect on value. Besides, costs or revenues that have already been incurred cannot be changed by a decision, as they have already happened (such costs are referred to as 'sunk costs').
- *A differential cost (or revenue):* If a cost or revenue item will not be changed by the decision under consideration, then that cost is irrelevant from a decision-making perspective.
- *A cash flow:* A basic finance principle is that the value of an asset is the present value of the cash flows that the asset is likely to generate. Non-cash items (such as depreciation) that are created by accounting statements are irrelevant for establishing the financial effect of a decision on an organisation. (Depreciation refers to writing off the cost of an asset that has already been purchased. Regardless of the decision that is made, the asset has been purchased and the cash flow has already happened.)

Relevant costing is an extremely important principle. To ignore this principle and apply any other criteria to determine what costs and revenues should be considered or ignored for a decision, can result in a decision being made that appears to be profitable, but which will actually reduce the value of the firm. The financial accounting profit for a decision, and the relevant cost (or real financial impact) of the same decision, could be very different.

In order to understand the difference between accounting profit and the financial impact of a decision on a firm (relevant cost to a firm), consider example 2.7 below.

2.4.1 Relevant cost

Example 2.7

Refer again to the income statement that we drew up in example 2.5 for year one of the master's course. Assume that the following circumstances existed at the time that the decision needed to be made as to whether or not to launch the management accounting master's degree:

- Five of the 19 students would have taken the master's course in financial management, for which the course fee is R24 000 per student, if they had not been accepted onto the master's course in management accounting. The financial management master's course has been unable to fill these five positions with other students. The stationery, supervision and thesis costs per student are the same on both courses. No project-marking fees are incurred in the financial management course.
- Forty per cent of the stationery costs have already been incurred, as certain stationery had to be ordered months before the start of the financial year. The stationery was customised with the course name and year, and cannot be used by the university for other purposes. The stationery on the financial management course has not yet been ordered.
- Ninety-five per cent of the administrative charges allocated to the new master's course will be incurred by the university regardless of whether or not the new master's course is run.

Required:
Discuss whether the master's course should be run or not, and what the financial impact on the university would be if the course were to be offered in the upcoming academic year.

If the decision is based on the profit figure on the income statement that was drawn up in example 2.5, we will come to the wrong answer, which would be: 'Yes, the course should be offered, as the university will make a profit of R15 500.' This answer is incorrect, because it has not been made with reference to the amount by which the future cash flows of the university would change if the new master's course were to be introduced.

Working through the income statement (to identify the cash flows that would arise directly out of offering the course) and the additional information above (in order to identify any other reasons for the university's cash flows to change or remain unchanged), we are able to determine correctly the change in cash flow (that is, the financial impact of the decision to introduce the course). This correct answer is set out below.

The financial impact on the university as a whole of offering the management accounting master's course in the upcoming financial year is as follows:

Additional fee revenue received	
Fee revenue for the management accounting course	R380 000
Less: Fee revenue lost on the financial management course (5 × R24 000)	R120 000
Variable costs	
Stationery – 60% not yet incurred (R7 600 × 60%)	R4 560
Less: Cost saving on financial management course (5 students × R400 each)	R2 000
Supervision (14 extra students × R5 000 each)	R70 000
Thesis marking (14 extra students × R1 000 × 2 markers each)	R28 000
Fixed costs	
Salary	R200 000
Guest lecturer fees	R10 000
Step cost	
Project marking fees (assuming none on the financial management course)	R2 400
Mixed cost	
Administrative charges (5% × R11 500)	R575
Financial loss	(R53 535)

This is a very different picture. The course will have a negative financial impact on the university, despite the fact that the income statement for the course shows a profit.

The principle that we have applied in order to calculate the actual financial impact on the university gives rise to cost classification based on the relevance of the cost to the decision. They are discussed below.

2.4.2 Opportunity cost

Key terms: opportunity cost

An **opportunity cost** is the *best benefit forgone by taking the proposed course of action*. The best benefit is defined as the greatest profit option, or the least cost option. In this case the opportunity cost was the revenue that would be lost on the financial management course of R24 000 per student, if the new course were launched.

In this situation we also had a saving on opportunity cost – the saving on stationery costs on the financial management course for the five students accepted onto the management accounting course instead.

2.4.3 Differential cost

> **Key term:** differential cost

A **differential cost** is a cost that differs between two alternatives. Notice that in the case of supervision and thesis costs we took only the increase in thesis and supervision costs into account, as the other five students would have to be supervised regardless of which course they were on. The salary cost, guest lecturer fees, and project marking fees, as well as the five per cent of administrative charges which represents variable costs, are also differential costs, as they would be incurred only if the new master's course were to be introduced.

2.4.4 Sunk cost

> **Key term:** sunk cost

A **sunk cost** is a cost that has already been incurred and consequently cannot be altered by, and is therefore not relevant to, the decision. An example of a sunk cost is the 40 per cent stationery costs which have already been incurred, and which could not be saved if the course were not offered.

Relevant costing is discussed in more detail in Chapter 10, *Relevant costs for decision-making*.

2.5 Function

> **Key terms:** inventoriable costs, non-inventoriable costs

Function refers to the classification of costs in the financial statements in accordance with the function of the cost – or the purpose which the cost serves – within the organisation. Note that, unlike the other cost classifications we have made in this chapter, the 'function' classification focuses on financial accounting requirements (the requirements contained in international accounting standards) as opposed to focusing on management accounting principles. This is a matter of presentation, rather than an aid to management decision-making.

International Accounting Standard 1 (IAS 1) requires an entity to 'present an analysis of expenses using a classification based on either the nature of the expense, or their function within the entity, whichever provides information that is reliable and more relevant' (IAS 1 para 99). When costs are classified by function, they are divided, at a minimum, into **inventoriable costs** or **non-inventoriable costs**. Inventoriable costs are those that are included in inventory for financial accounting purposes, in other words, all costs required to be incurred in order to bring inventory into its present location and condition (IAS 2 para 10). Non-inventoriable costs are other operating costs and are often subdivided into selling costs (for example, sales commission) and administrative costs (for example, salary costs of accounting and bookkeeping staff).

In a manufacturing environment manufacturing costs are inventoriable, and these can be subdivided into three categories: direct materials, direct labour, and manufacturing overheads.

2.5.1 Direct materials

Direct materials are the physical inputs that can be traced in an economically feasible manner to the product that is manufactured. Materials that are considered to be indirect (that is, materials that cannot be traced to the product in an economically feasible manner such as, for example, the detergent used to clean production machinery) are classified as manufacturing overheads and allocated to the product on some basis (refer to manufacturing overheads below in 2.5.3).

2.5.2 Direct labour

Where it is economically feasible to trace the amount of labour that is physically expended on a product, such labour costs are considered to be direct labour costs. An example would be factory employees who work on only one product line, and where the amount of time that the workers spend working on each unit of that product is known. In contrast, it is usually not feasible to trace the amount of time spent on one unit of a product by the factory supervisors who do not work directly on the product, and may even supervise the manufacture of a number of product lines manufactured in the factory. The salary cost of the supervisors would typically be considered to be indirect labour costs, and classified as manufacturing overheads, again to be allocated to the product on some reasonable basis.

2.5.3 Manufacturing overheads

Key terms: fixed manufacturing overheads, variable manufacturing overheads

Manufacturing overheads comprise all manufacturing costs that are classified as indirect when the product is the cost object. These include indirect materials and indirect labour. Other examples of manufacturing overheads are water, electricity, rent, maintenance and depreciation, to the extent that these costs relate to the manufacturing process. Manufacturing overheads can be further sub-divided into **variable manufacturing overheads** and **fixed manufacturing overheads**. Maintenance may be a variable overhead if it varies in proportion to production volume changes. Depreciation and factory rental are examples of fixed overheads over relevant ranges of production volume.

Example 2.8

The detailed income statement of a South African manufacturer is presented below.

	R'000
Revenue	500 000
Salaries	
Factory (workers) [1]	61 000
Factory (management) [2]	55 000
Sales [3]	42 500
Human resources and payroll [4]	5 000
Accounting	10 000
Internal audit [5]	8 000
Directors	40 000
Security [6]	6 500
Engineers [7]	2 500
Depreciation [8]	
Factory equipment	10 000
Warehouse fixtures	2 500
Office fixtures and fittings	2 200
Forklifts	1 500
Delivery vehicles	1 600
Buildings	3 500
Purchases from creditors	
Raw materials	95 000
Spare parts for factory equipment [9]	7 000
Grease and lubricants for factory machinery [9]	2 900
Stationery for administrative use	2 100
Water and electricity [10]	
Factory	22 000
Warehouse	3 000
Office	4 000
Other	
Royalty [11]	10 000
Telephone (office) (fixed charges of R0,6m included)	3 500
Cleaning (office) ('flat rate' as per contract)	1 800
Entertainment (this amount is spent in every period)	600
Speeding fines (delivery)	180
Repairs (delivery) [12]	400
Repairs (factory equipment) [12]	6 500
External audit fee (as agreed per contract)	1 500
Advertising and marketing (this amount is spent in every period)	32 000
Profit	55 720

Chapter 2 Cost classification

Notes
1. Factory workers are paid on the basis of hours worked, in order to match labour hours to production requirements.
2. Factory management are permanent employees who are paid fixed salaries regardless of hours worked.
3. Sales staff remuneration includes commission of 5 per cent of revenue.
4. Sixty per cent of human resources and payroll time is spent on factory staff salaries and labour issues.
5. Thirty per cent of internal audit time is spent on factory controls and procedures.
6. Security guards are on the premises 24 hours a day, 7 days a week. Part of their responsibilities includes checking all goods that leave the premises are accompanied by an authorised despatch note.
7. An engineering team is permanently employed to monitor the factory equipment and perform routine maintenance on a regular basis.
8. All assets are depreciated on a straight-line basis over their useful lives expressed in years, except for delivery vehicles which are depreciated based on the number of kilometres travelled. The number of kilometres travelled is roughly proportional to production volumes. Three buildings exist on the premises – the factory building (depreciation of R1 400), the warehouse, in which raw materials are stored (R1 050), and the administrative building (R1 050).
9. The amount of part replacements and lubrication that machines require is directly proportional to number of operating hours. Operating hours are dependant on production volumes.
10. The water and electricity costs for the warehouse and office remain constant month on month, regardless of sales and production volume changes. R3m of the water and electricity requirements of the factory are unaffected by production requirements. The remaining amount and majority of the cost is directly affected by production volumes.
11. A royalty of 2 per cent of revenue is payable to the manufacturer's parent organisation for the use of patents and other copyright or protected material.
12. Repair costs vary directly with production quantities.

Required:
Analyse each of the costs in the income statement using the following categories:
- Manufacturing (state whether it constitutes direct materials, direct labour or overheads) or non-manufacturing
- Fixed or variable, with regard to production sales volume.

Below is a summary detailing the classification of each line item:

Table 2.2 Classification of income statement costs

	R'000	R'000	R'000	R'000	R'000	R'000	R'000
		Manufacturing			Non-manufacturing	Fixed	Variable
		Direct materials	Direct labour	Overheads			
Salaries							
Factory (workers)	61 000		61 000				61 000
Factory (management)	55 000			55 000		55 000	
Sales	42 500				42 500	17 500	25 000
Human resources and payroll	5 000				5 000	5 000	

principles of management accounting

	R'000	R'000	R'000	R'000	R'000	R'000	R'000
		Manufacturing			Non-manu-factur-ing	Fixed	Variable
		Direct materials	Direct labour	Over-heads			
Accounting	10 000				10 000	10 000	
Internal audit	8 000				8 000	8 000	
Directors	40 000				40 000	40 000	
Security	6 500				6 500	6 500	
Engineers	2 500			2 500		2 500	
Depreciation							
Factory equipment	10 000			10 000		10 000	
Warehouse fixtures	2 500			2 500		2 500	
Office fixtures and fittings	2 200				2 200	2 200	
Forklifts	1 500			1 500		1 500	
Delivery vehicles	1 600				1 600		1 600
Buildings	3 500			2 450	1 050	3 500	
Purchases from creditors							
Raw materials	95 000	95 000					95 000
Spare parts for factory equipment	7 000			7 000			7 000
Grease and lubricants for factory machinery	2 900			2 900			2 900
Stationery for administrative use (assumption: more stationery used at higher activity levels, therefore variable)	2 100				2 100		2 100
Water and electricity							
Factory	22 000			22 000		3 000	19 000
Warehouse	3 000			3 000		3 000	
Office	4 000				4 000	4 000	

	R'000	R'000	R'000	R'000	R'000	R'000	R'000
		Manufacturing			Non-manu-facturing	Fixed	Variable
		Direct materials	Direct labour	Over-heads			
Other							
Royalty	10 000						10 000
Telephone (office)	3 500				3 500	600	2 900
Cleaning (office)	1 800				1 800	1 800	
Entertainment	600				600	600	
Speeding fines (delivery)	180				180	180	
Repairs (delivery)	400				400		400
Repairs (factory equipment)	6 500			6 500			6 500
External audit fee	1 500				1 500	1 500	
Advertising and marketing	32 000				32 000	32 000	

2.6 Timing

Key terms: absorption costing, period cost, product cost, variable costing

Timing refers to when a cost is recognised as an expense in the income statement. A distinction is drawn between a **period cost** and a **product cost**. A period cost is a cost that is recognised as an expense immediately on being incurred, while product costs in an absorption costing system are absorbed in inventory and expensed only when the inventory is sold.

Under an absorption inventory costing system, manufacturing costs (in a manufacturing environment) are product costs, while non-manufacturing costs are period costs. Absorption costing is required by the international financial reporting standards (standard IAS 2).

IAS 2 requires that all costs required to get inventory into a saleable location and condition are included in inventory until that inventory is sold, at which point the costs are expensed as part of cost-of-sales. Examples of costs that would be regarded as necessary to get inventory into a saleable condition would be the following:
- *Manufacturing costs* (raw materials, all labour involved in the manufacturing process in any way, even the employees who work in the raw materials warehouse)
- *Overheads* (both fixed and variable, including typical expenses such as depreciation of factory and raw materials store equipment, electricity, water, rent of the buildings, and similar expenses)
- *Delivery costs* that were incurred to get the product to the location from where it is sold

- *Packaging costs*, if packaging was either necessary to get the product to the location from which it will be sold (for example, protective packaging) or if the product is sold in special packaging (for example, an attractive box).

Packaging and delivery costs incurred in getting the product from the location from which it was sold (for example, a sales branch) to the customer who purchased the product would not be included in the cost of inventory, as these were not incurred to get the product into a saleable condition and location. These costs were incurred after the sale of the product, in order to deliver the product to the customer.

An alternative inventory costing system that can be used instead of **absorption costing**, which is more useful for internal reporting and decision-making purposes, is **variable costing**. A variable costing system requires all fixed costs to be recognised as an expense in the period in which they are incurred.

Chapter 5, *Absorption versus variable costing* discusses these costing systems in detail.

2.7 Summary

This chapter introduced the numerous perspectives from which financial information is classified for the purposes of management decision-making and control.

Certain aspects of costs – such as behaviour, assignment, relevance, function and timing – are key considerations when analysing and interpreting accounting information for management purposes. An undiscerning use of financial accounting information may result in sub-optimal and counterproductive decisions being implemented. Management's primary mandate is to enhance shareholder value. It is for this reason that financial accounting rules are largely ignored for managerial purposes as they are of only limited relevance when it comes to analysing the feasibility of a decision, or the effectiveness of the controls that are put in place in order to encourage non-executive staff and managers alike to behave in the best interests of the organisation and its stakeholders.

Conclusion: Cost classification and other topics in this book

This chapter introduced several different perspectives from which cost and revenue information need to be considered in order for accounting information to be correctly interpreted and used for managerial purposes.

These concepts will be more fully developed and applied in the subsequent chapters in this text. The principles underlying decision-making are of central importance in managerial accounting, and these are examined more thoroughly in Chapter 10, *Relevant costs for decision-making* and Chapter 11, *Decision-making under operational constraints*. The issue of how to measure, trace and allocate indirect costs is explored in Chapter 6, *Overhead allocation*, while Chapter 5, *Absorption versus variable costing* analyses the issue of timing of measuring and recognising fixed costs (period or product cost), and answers the question of how absorption costing can distort decision-making and performance evaluation. Chapter 3, *Cost estimation* addresses the issue of how to generate the cost information if it is not readily available from existing sources inside the organisation.

Tutorial case study: Shoprite Holdings

Shoprite Holdings Ltd has a number of brands, one of which is the Shoprite chain of supermarkets. The Shoprite brand is one of the leaders in the South African food retailing sector. It is the mainstay of the group's operations and its biggest business by far.

Consider the following revision questions using your existing knowledge of the Shoprite retail brand. Identify what you would view as an example of an appropriate cost object in Shoprite, and answer the following questions in relation to the cost object you have identified.

Source: Shoprite Holdings Ltd 2010

1. Name one good example of a variable cost.
2. Name one good example of a fixed cost.
3. Discuss what factor is likely to determine the relevant range over which the fixed cost you named remains fixed.
4. Estimate the period over which the fixed cost you named is likely to remain fixed.
5. Name one good example of a step cost.
6. Name one good example of a mixed cost.
7. Name one good example of a direct cost.
8. Name one good example of an indirect cost.
9. Suggest a cost that is likely to be both variable and indirect, and one that is likely to be both fixed and direct.

Basic questions

BQ 1

If sales volume increases by 20 per cent, selling expenses increase by 15 per cent. What proportion of selling expenses was fixed at the initial sales volume, and at the final sales volume?

BQ 2

At a sales level of 10 000 units per month, the manufacturing overhead per unit is R3,30 per unit. If the sales level increases by 4 000 units, the manufacturing overhead per unit falls to R2,70. What is the variable manufacturing overhead per unit?

BQ 3

At a sales level of 10 000 units per month, the manufacturing overhead is R4,00 per unit. The next month the price of all manufacturing costs increases by 5 per cent. If the sales level increases by 4 000 units, the manufacturing overhead per unit falls to R3,48. What is the variable manufacturing overhead per unit?

BQ 4

The total manufacturing cost incurred during a year was R460 000, which comprises both variable and fixed costs in a ratio of 3 : 2 respectively, at a production level of 80 000 units. If a production level of 100 000 units is reached, a discount of 5 per cent is available on all variable costs. What will the total manufacturing costs be at a production level of 120 000 units?

BQ 5

The total manufacturing cost per unit was R10 at a production level of 90 000 units. If the production level increases to 111 000, total manufacturing costs will increase by 7 per cent. What is the variable manufacturing cost per unit?

BQ 6

Full capacity is 200 000 units. The direct labour cost is R10 per hour. 4 hours of labour time is required per unit. The current production level is 185 000 units. A large order for 40 000 units has been received. Staff will work overtime (at time and half) in order to create the additional capacity required to fill the order. What will the labour cost be for this order?

BQ 7

An organisation has 345 600 labour hours available to it each year (180 employees working 1 920 hours a year, who earn a salary of R60 000 per annum each). The organisation manufactures two kinds of units, Type 1 and Type 2. A Type 1 unit requires 3 labour hours to manufacture, while Type 2 requires 5 hours of labour time per unit. Both units incur other variable expenses at a rate of R25 per unit. The organisation already has orders for 44 000 and 39 000 Type 1 and Type 2 units respectively.

A large order for 6 000 Type 1 units and 4 000 Type 2 units has been received. The organisation is very excited, as the customer has a high profile in the industry and an association with this customer will enhance the organisation's image. As a result, staff will work overtime (at time-and-a-half) in order to create any additional capacity required to fill the order, if necessary. If the organisation accepts this order, by what amount will total manufacturing costs increase?

BQ 8

An organisation has the following total costs at two activity levels:

Activity level (units)	15 000	24 000
Total costs	R380 000	R470 000

Variable cost per unit is constant in this activity range but there is a step-up of R18 000 in the total fixed costs when the activity exceeds 20 000 units.

What are the total costs at an activity level of 18 000 units?
a) R404 000
b) R410 000
c) R422 000
d) R428 000

BQ 9

Which of the following should be classified as indirect labour?
a) Machine operators in a factory producing furniture
b) Lawyers in a legal firm
c) Maintenance workers in a power generation organisation
d) Lorry drivers in a road haulage company.

BQ 10
Equipment owned by an organisation has a net carrying amount of R1 800 and has been idle for some months. It could now be used on a six months' contract which is being considered. If not used on this contract, the equipment would be sold for a net amount of R2 000. After use on the contract, the equipment would have no saleable value and would be dismantled. The cost of dismantling and disposing of it would be R800. No dismantling cost will be incurred should the equipment be sold.

What is the total equipment cost relevant to the contract?
a) R1 200
b) R1 800
c) R2 000
d) R2 800

Long questions

LQ 1 – Intermediate (11 marks; 20 minutes)
Source: Adapted from UCT (Carol Cairney)

There are numerous types of operational decisions that need to be made on a regular basis within any organisation. Below are three scenarios that illustrate some of the most basic and typical decisions that are faced by organisations: introducing a new product, altering sales volumes, and considering new markets. These three scenarios are described in the context that most students would be familiar with: a large South African university.

Scenario 1
The accounting department of this university offers a number of highly successful post graduate degrees in accounting and financial management. The accounting department is considering introducing a new degree in this area, which is also expected to be highly successful. In order to prove to the university board that this course will be financially viable and will contribute towards the financial position of the university, a projected income statement has been drawn up for the course. The projected income statement shows that after deducting all the costs that would be attributable to the course (including everything from lecturers' fees and stationery to more general university resources such as electricity, maintenance, administration and student records) from the anticipated revenue, the course is expected to make a profit of R150 000.

Scenario 2
The manager of a breakfast and brunch bar on campus thinks that because of a larger student intake, there is a strong possibility that sales will double in volume in the next year. If sales volume doubles (assuming the mix of products sold stays the same), what is the most likely effect on the breakfast bar's profits?
a) As sales volume is expected to double, profit should double (approximately).
b) Profit should increase by more than 100 per cent (that is, profit should more than double).
c) Profit would increase by less than the increase in sales volume.
d) It is impossible to make any reasonable prediction without the numbers.

principles of management accounting

Scenario 3

All official university track tops and tog bags are made by an organisation called Official University Merchandise (Pty) Ltd (OUM). The student union has approached OUM on behalf of a group of students on financial aid, with respect to purchasing 100 track tops at a discounted price. The student union is able to pay R110 per track top. OUM understands that there is no other way that these students could ever hope to own a track top, as they cannot afford to buy them at the normal market price. OUM also understands that owning official university track tops will boost morale among these students, but has refused to sell these track tops at R110 as this would result in OUM making a loss and suffering a loss of profits overall. OUM has calculated a loss per top as follows:

Selling price	R110
Total manufacturing costs per top	(R130)
Loss per top	(R20)

REQUIRED	Marks
Based on the very limited information available, discuss the most likely financial consequence of each scenario. Ignore strategic and qualitative issues (they are important in decision-making, but you are not required to take them into account here).	11
TOTAL MARKS	**11**

LQ 2 – Intermediate (23 marks; 41 minutes)

Source: Adapted from UCT (Carol Cairney)

You are a university student doing vacation work at an audit firm, and you have been assigned to the audit of GreyLine Carriers Ltd.

GreyLine is a transport company specialising in the freighting of chemicals and commercial goods (for example fresh chickens). The company's head office is situated in Cape Town, while operations are carried out from the 11 branches (four in Gauteng, two in the Western Cape, two in the Eastern Cape, one in Durban and another two in the Northern Cape and Mpumalanga respectively). The company owns a fleet of approximately 300 trucks (2XX6 and 2XX7 models), and performs all its own maintenance and repairs from their purpose-built workshop in Durban.

Your task on the audit is to perform an analytical review of the income statement. The first-year clerk has given you the following instructions: 'Here's a copy of the 2XX6 and 2XX7 income statements. Go and chat to the financial director (FD) about the operations of the company for 2XX7. For each line item on the income statement, obtain reasons why that line item has changed from year to year. Then, for each line item, based on those reasons, recalculate the 2XX7 figure and see if the actual 2XX7 figures make sense and appear reasonable.'

You duly discuss the income statement with the FD, and obtain the following information:

- *Revenue:* In 2XX6 the total number of kilometres travelled and billed was 18 301 000 kilometres. This distance could be divided almost equally between chemical and commercial haulage. In 2XX7 the total number of kilometres travelled increased by 9 per cent. However, chemical haulage accounted for almost two thirds of the total number of kilometres travelled, as two large chemical contracts were won at the beginning of the year. The price per kilometre charged by GreyLine is 15 per cent higher for chemical haulage than for commercial work, owing to the hazardous nature of the cargo.

- *Salaries (drivers):* New safety regulations were promulgated at the beginning of 2XX7, whereby the number of hours drivers are allowed to drive continuously has been decreased significantly and the length of breaks has been increased. In order to prevent journey times from increasing (which would result in a loss of revenue), GreyLine hired 32 additional drivers at the beginning of 2XX7, and the average number of drivers employed for the 2XX7 year was 218. Drivers received salary increases of 7 per cent in that year.
- *Salaries (head office):* Head office staff received increases of 8,5 per cent in 2XX7. The number of staff at head office has remained constant for the last 3 years.
- *Salaries (maintenance):* Maintenance staff had to work overtime (at time and a half) this year, owing to increased maintenance required as a result of the increased proportion of chemical haulage (safety requirements require more frequent inspections and greater preventative maintenance on chemical haulage because of the increased cost of accidents, environmental damage, and similar issues). On average, staff worked 15 hours' overtime a month. No overtime was worked in 2XX6. Normal hours per month are 160 hours. Staff received 9 per cent salary increases in 2XX7 in recognition of their hard work.
- *Rental expense:* The rental expense is stipulated as follows in the rent agreement: A fixed lump sum (which will be increased by 10 per cent per annum), plus 1 per cent of revenue.
- *Depreciation:* The company replaced 30 per cent of the vehicles in 2XX7.
- *Other expenses:* Two thirds of 'other expenses' are fixed.

	2XX6 Actual R'000	2XX7 Actual R'000	2XX7 Recalculated R'000
Revenue	165 045	195 501	
Salaries (drivers)	22 281	28 968	
Salaries (head office)	18 155	19 700	
Salaries (maintenance)	8 252	10 200	
Fuel	17 825	20 886	
Licences	4 278	4 500	
Tyres	10 695	12 673	
Water	7 427	7 800	
Electricity	8 244	8 600	
Maintenance consumables	13 903	16 755	
Rent	2 971	3 403	
Depreciation	26 779	29 060	
Other	11 553	12 500	
Insurance	5 176	5 694	
Entertainment	1 476	1 700	
Profit	6 030	13 062	

principles of management accounting

REQUIRED	Marks
Recalculate the 2XX7 amount for each line item above, and comment on any large deviations noticed. Assume a threshold of R653 100. You may also assume an annual average inflation rate of 6,5 per cent, applicable to all expenses and income, except salaries.	23
TOTAL MARKS	23

LQ 3 – Intermediate (9 marks; 16 minutes)

Source: Adapted from ACCA paper 1.2

Pointdextre Ltd, which manufactures and sells a single product, is currently producing and selling 102 000 units per month, which represents 85 per cent of its full capacity. Total monthly costs are R619 000, but at full capacity these would be R700 000. Total fixed costs would remain unchanged at all activity levels up to full capacity. The normal selling price of the product results in a contribution to sales ratio of 40 per cent.

A new customer has offered to take a monthly delivery of 15 000 units at a price per unit 20 per cent below the normal selling price. If this new business is accepted, existing sales are expected to fall by one unit for every six units sold to this new customer.

	REQUIRED	Marks
(a)	For the current production and sales level, calculate: (i) The variable cost per unit (ii) The total monthly fixed costs (iii) The selling price per unit.	5
(b)	Calculate the net increase or decrease in monthly profit which would result from acceptance of the new business.	4
	TOTAL MARKS	9

LQ 4 – Advanced (9 marks; 16 minutes)

Source: Adapted from CIMA foundation level paper 2

The Management Accountant of J Ltd, a supplier of farm machinery components, is compiling the budget for next year.

Forecast sales for the first seven months of 2XX4 are as follows:

Month	Sales (units)
January	5 500
February	5 800
March	5 600
April	4 900
May	4 400
June	5 200
July	5 500

Other relevant information:
- Units held in inventory at the end of the month are maintained at 25 per cent of the following month's sales.
- Suppliers are paid two months after the inventory has been received.
- The purchase cost per unit is R7,20, increasing to R8,40 from April 2XX4.
- The warehouse section consists of 4 employees who each earn R950,00 per month, and a supervisor who earns R1 200,00 per month. A monthly bonus equivalent to 15 per cent of normal earnings is paid to everyone in the warehouse section if sales exceed 5 500 units per month. Normal wages are paid in the month in which they arise. Any bonus is paid one month after it is earned.

REQUIRED		Marks
(a)	Calculate the number of units the purchases in May will amount to.	3
(b)	Determine the amount that will be paid to suppliers in June.	3
(c)	Calculate the total cash paid for wages in April.	3
TOTAL MARKS		**9**

LQ 5 – Advanced (25 marks; 45 minutes)

Source: Adapted from Rhodes University (John Williams)

The following scenario and questions relate to the classification and behaviour of costs.

Barcon (Pty) Ltd has been manufacturing and selling Acron for many years. As at 31 December 2XX8, the organisation had 20 000 units of Acron in inventory, valued at the cost to manufacture these units, amounting to R200 000. One kilogram of materials costing R5 a kilogram is used in the manufacture of each unit of Acron, and the direct labour time required to manufacture one unit is 15 minutes, the labour cost being R4 per hour. The balance of the cost is made up of a variable cost element (30 per cent) and a fixed cost element.

REQUIRED		Marks
(a)	Calculate and discuss the elements of cost in one unit of Acron.	3
(b)	Discuss the behaviour of these elements of cost, in relation to increases (or decreases) in the volume of production.	6
(c)	During January 1999 a competitor placed a product on the market which is identical to Acron and which sells for R8 a unit, far less than the selling price of Acron (R14 a unit). The directors of Barcon (Pty) Ltd will discontinue the production of Acron and are considering two alternatives in relation to existing inventories of Acron: (i) To sell all the inventory on hand for R7,50 a unit, the distribution costs amounting to 20c a unit (ii) To convert Acron units into another product manufactured and sold by the organisation, Lacron. There are no competing products for Lacron, which has an unlimited market, costs R11 a unit to manufacture and 20c a unit to distribute, and sells at R16 a unit. Variable costs amounting to R8 a unit will be incurred in the conversion of Acron to Lacron. Advise the directors which of the two alternative courses of action to adopt in relation to the existing inventory of Acron, assuming that adequate facilities are available to convert Acron to Lacron.	16
TOTAL MARKS		**25**

References

SAICA (South African Institute of Chartered Accountants). 2010a. Statements of Generally Accepted Accounting Practice: IAS 1 (AC 101), *Presentation of financial statements (revised January 2010)*. Johannesburg: SAICA.

SAICA. 2010b. Statements of Generally Accepted Accounting Practice: IAS 2 (AC 108), *Inventories (revised January 2010)*. Johannesburg: SAICA.

Shoprite Holdings Ltd. 2010. *Annual financial statements: Shoprite Holdings Ltd and its subsidiaries as at June 2010*. [Online]. Available: <www.shopriteholdings.co.za/files/1019812640/Investor_Centre_Files/Annual_Reports/Annual-Report-2010/AnnualFinancialStatements.pdf > [27 March 2011].

Cost estimation

chapter 3

Carol Cairney (updated by Shelley Anne Roos)

LEARNING OBJECTIVES

By the end of this chapter, you should be able to:
1 Split mixed costs into fixed and variable components using both the high-low method and least squares regression.
2 Formulate a cost estimation equation based on the results of the high-low method and least squares regression calculations, and use the cost estimation equation to predict costs at various activity levels.
3 Interpret the r^2 statistic and be able to determine the extent to which a cause and effect relationship exists between the cost and the cost driver.
4 Indicate factors other than the extent of the relationship between the cost and the cost driver, that affect the accuracy with which costs can be predicted.
5 Apply learning curves to estimate costs.

MultiChoice and cost estimation

The following is an extract from the Chairman's review in the 2010 annual financial statements of *MultiChoice South Africa Holdings*, the satellite television operator behind DSTV.
'The coming year will see competitors entering the pay-television market, the first of which launched in May 2010, and our business will face several challenges.' The chairman proceeded to explain that, in the face of these challenges, MultiChoice will have to keep its focus on continuing to sell more DSTV subscriptions.

SOURCE: MultiChoice South Africa Holdings 2010

MultiChoice knows that it will face challenges when additional competitors enter the market. In order to plan for the next financial year and beyond, the company will need a thorough understanding of its costs. It will, for example, need to understand which costs vary according to the number of subscribers (costs that will decrease if some of its subscribers switch to competitors), and which costs are fixed irrespective of the number of subscribers.

This chapter examines the issues related to cost estimation, and helps us to realise how companies like MultiChoice can optimise their management team's decision-making if costs are properly understood.

3.1 Introduction

The previous chapter introduced the concept of cost behaviour, and described the manner in which four types of costs, variable, fixed, step and mixed costs, would react to changes in sales or production volumes or other activity levels. The previous chapter also indicated that an understanding of how a cost would behave given a change in activity level is necessary in order to predict the magnitude of costs in the future. Being able to predict costs with a reasonable degree of accuracy is necessary for decision-making and control purposes. In this chapter we discuss some of the methods, with particular emphasis on mathematical and statistical tools, which can be used to determine how a cost behaves. This provides information about the accuracy and predictability of the cause-and-effect relationship that exists between the cost and the variable that it is related to, and allows us to split composite (mixed) costs into their fixed and variable components.

The following cost estimation methods will be discussed:
- Scatter graph (a graphical approach)
- High-low (a mathematical approach)
- Least squares regression (a statistical approach), also referred to as linear regression.

> Most management accounting students would have completed at least a basic course in statistics. Parts of this chapter build on some of your knowledge of statistics, but the detailed theory is not repeated here. Your statistics textbooks and notes may be useful if you need to revise some of the technical terms and concepts.

3.2 Cost drivers

Key term: cost driver

When we refer to measuring costs, what we really mean is measuring how a cost will change in response to *a change in some activity*. For each cost, an activity needs to be identified that can be regarded as the **cost driver** of that particular cost. To what activity are we referring? The number of units sold? The number of units produced? Well, we could use these as cost drivers, or we could dig down to a lower level and use more specific activities that are carried out in the sales or production process. For instance, suppose an organisation carried out quality testing on a random selection of the items it produced. The cost of testing each unit could be calculated with reference to the total number of items produced by the factory (that is, the production of units is seen as the cost driver, and the variable cost is expressed per unit produced). It could also be calculated with respect to the number of items tested (that is, the number of items tested is seen as the cost driver, and the variable cost is expressed per item tested). In addition, if the items that the organisation produced are not all identical and different items require different amounts of inspection time, then the cost of testing could be determined in respect of the number of testing hours (rather than the number of items produced or tested).

What would you choose as your cost driver to measure the quality testing costs against? Would you calculate the cost per item produced, or per item tested, or per testing hour? You should be inclined to choose whichever cost driver you believe to be the most closely related to the cost itself. Or to put that another way, you should choose the cost driver that caused the costs to be incurred. You may argue that producing units doesn't cause the testing costs to be incurred, unless a fixed percentage of units is tested. Quality testing costs are caused by the number of units tested, so you can make a good case that to calculate the cost per unit tested, not per unit produced. However, if different items used different amounts of testing time, and if many of the costs are related to hours of use (such as labour costs), you would choose to calculate the testing cost per testing hour. In order to determine by how much the testing cost would increase in the next period, the organisation would have to estimate how many additional testing hours would be worked as a result of the additional production volumes that the organisation anticipates. The additional hours that are expected would then be multiplied by the testing cost per hour, in order to calculate the increase in testing costs in the next period.

Before mathematical or statistical techniques can be applied to a cost in order to calculate the variable and fixed components of that cost, consideration must be given to whether it is plausible (makes sense) that there is a relationship between the cost and the cost driver (in other words, that a change in the cost driver would cause the cost to change). Likewise, the extent to which this cost driver is able to influence the cost, and whether there are other factors that influence this cost, should also be considered. These two considerations are discussed in more detail below.

3.2.1 Plausibility of the cost driver

When we ask whether the selected activity represents a 'plausible cost driver' for a specific cost we mean, does it make sense that the cost would be significantly affected by changes in the selected activity? For example, suppose an airline wanted to investigate the cost implications of providing passengers with a complimentary newspaper on board each flight. The airline needs to establish the cost driver in order to predict the cost accurately. It is possible to calculate the cost of complimentary newspapers per kilometre travelled, but this would be meaningless as the number of kilometres travelled does not cause the cost to be incurred. Calculating the complimentary newspaper cost per passenger would be more meaningful. A plausible relationship exists between the number of passengers and the cost of providing them with newspapers. It is reasonable to expect the cost to increase as the number of passengers increases.

3.2.2 Extent to which the cost driver determines total cost

It is important to recognise that certain costs may be driven by more than one cost driver. Staying with the airline scenario, what is the cost driver of fuel costs? Jet fuel costs are affected by numerous factors, including:
- The distance that the aircraft flies
- The atmospheric pressure at take-off (less fuel is required for take-off in Cape Town than in Johannesburg owing to Cape Town's lower altitude)
- The weight of the passengers and their luggage
- Wind speed and direction.

While all of these factors play a role, the distance that the aircraft flies probably would have the most significant effect on the amount of jet fuel required for the flight. However, does the distance travelled determine such a great portion of the fuel cost that we can base our estimate of fuel costs on just this one variable, or do we also have to take into account the effect of a second cost driver (perhaps wind speed and direction) in order to build a reasonably accurate and reliable financial model?

Fortunately there are a number of methods available to help us to understand the relationship between costs and cost drivers.

principles of management accounting

3.3 Scatter graph

Key term: scatter graph

The **scatter graph** is a graphical method of cost estimation that plots various observations of costs against the activity level: cost is plotted in point form on the vertical (y) axis against the activity level on the horizontal (x) axis. The 'best guess' approach is then followed to fit a line to the points, and the line is extended to intercept the y-axis. In the scatter graph approach, the line is drawn onto the graph entirely according to one's own visual judgement. The intercept indicates the fixed cost portion (on the assumption that the intercept falls within the relevant range).

In reality, we cannot draw the conclusion that the intercept represents the fixed cost, as the observations on which the 'best guess' line is based are for only the activity levels falling within the relevant range of operations. If the level of operating activity increases above, or falls below, the relevant range, the new total cost figures at these points may not continue with the same linear relationship.

To predict a cost at a specific level of activity, a point is plotted (on the line drawn) at the relevant activity level (the x-value), and the predicted cost is read as the corresponding y-value. The scatter graph method is not very accurate, but it is useful to establish whether a linear relationship exists between cost and activity. What is the significance of the existence (or lack thereof) of a linear relationship? Simply put: the more linear the relationship between total cost and the activity level, the more reliable the cost estimate that is obtained when linearity is assumed.

The example below deals with telephone costs. The total cost of a monthly telephone account is driven by a number of factors, including the number of telephone calls made in that month and the length of each call. Which of these do you think determines the telephone expense for the month to a greater extent? If we wanted to predict next month's telephone account, on which cost driver would we rely more heavily?

Example 3.1

The total cost per month, total number of calls and total amount of talk time (in minutes) for a landline for 12 consecutive months is summarised below.

	Total cost (R)	Total number of calls	Total talk time in minutes
January	260,00	79	762,3
February	428,54	110	1 338,0
March	338,58	102	956,4
April	310,00	127	900,0
May	260,76	75	485,3
June	387,09	127	1 255,0
July	354,83	83	1 110,1
August	208,92	86	555,8
September	400,44	118	1 269,6
October	201,32	72	612,0
November	297,71	112	861,0
December	329,62	89	997,0

Chapter 3 Cost estimation

Required:
Use scatter graphs to determine which of the number of calls per month or the minutes talked per month has a stronger linear relationship with the total monthly telephone cost.

In order to answer this question we can draw two scatter graphs. Both graphs reflect the total monthly cost on the y-axis, but the first graph (Figure 3.1) reflects on the x-axis the total number of telephone calls per month as the cost driver, while the second graph (Figure 3.2) reflects the total number of minutes per month as the cost driver.

Figure 3.1 Total cost relative to number of calls per month

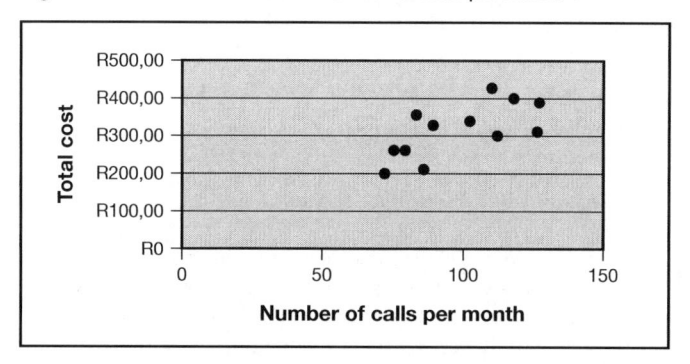

Figure 3.2 Total cost relative to number of minutes per month

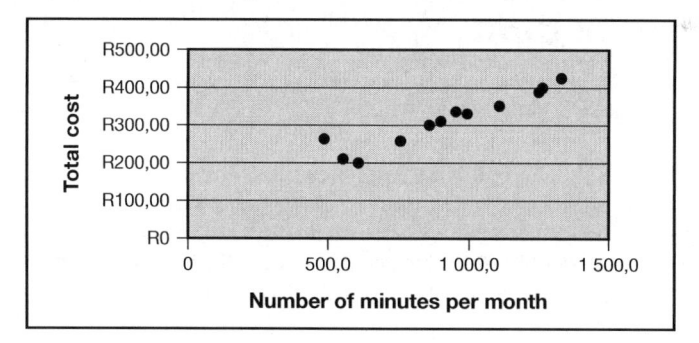

Notice that in both Figure 3.1 and Figure 3.2, the total telephone bill increases as the number of calls and talk time increases, although the relationship between the total telephone cost per month and number of minutes is significantly more linear than the relationship between the total monthly telephone cost relative to number of calls made per month. From the graphs it appears that the telephone expense is determined to a greater extent by the total duration of calls (number of minutes) than by the number of calls made.

The scatter graph can be used both to predict the total cost for a given level of activity, and to estimate the fixed and variable elements that make up the total cost. In order to do these two things, a line is fitted by inspection to the points that have already been plotted. This line is extended to intercept the y-axis (see Figure 3.3). The total cost at the y-intercept comprises only of the fixed cost component of the telephone cost, as the activity level at the y-intercept is nil, which means that the variable cost at this point is also nil. Reading off the graph, the fixed cost component of the monthly telephone expense is approximately R70. Compare this amount to the telephone account received from the service provider, which reflects the fixed cost at R87. The scatter graph method has not resulted in a perfectly accurate estimate of fixed costs, but this is not surprising as the scatter graph method is a rough approach to cost estimation.

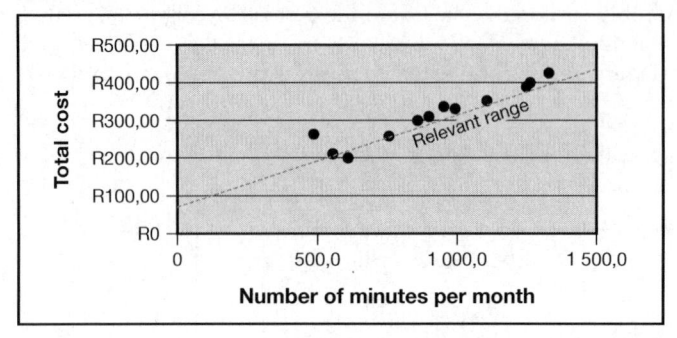

Figure 3.3 Total cost relative to number of minutes

Given that a telephone account has an easily determinable fixed and a variable component, you may wonder why the points on the graph do not form a neat, straight line that intercepts the *y*-axis precisely at the fixed cost amount and slopes steadily upwards in relation to the variable cost. We will first turn our attention to two further cost estimation techniques, and then discuss the reasons for these deviations in the section entitled 'Factors affecting the accuracy of cost estimation'.

3.4 High-low method

Key terms: high-low method, linear relationship

The **high-low method** is the mathematical approach which involves calculating the equation of a line to split a mixed cost into its variable and fixed components. Note that we are addressing the same linear relationship between cost and cost driver that we discussed under the scatter graph method, but the high-low method is an alternative method of estimating the line. The equation for a **linear relationship** is as follows:

$$y = mx + c$$

where:
- y is the total (aggregate) cost
- m is the gradient or slope of the line (and the variable cost per unit of the cost driver)
- x is the cost driver level
- c is where the line intercepts the *y*-axis (and therefore the fixed cost).

The above equation is referred to as a regression equation, in which y is called the dependent variable (because y is dependent on the value of x) and x is the independent variable.

Example 3.2

The same information regarding a monthly telephone account as in example 3.1 applies.

Required:
Use the high-low method to determine the variable and fixed cost portion of the monthly telephone account, and to derive an equation that explains the relationship between the two.

Table 3.1 Breakdown of annual cost and number of minutes

	Total cost (R)	Total talk time in minutes
January	260,00	762,3
February (the most talk-time minutes)	**428,54**	**1 338,0**
March	338,58	956,4
April	310,00	900,0
May (the least talk-time minutes)	**260,76**	**485,3**
June	387,09	1 255,0
July	354,83	1 110,1
August	208,92	555,8
September	400,44	1 269,6
October	201,32	612,0
November	297,71	861,0
December	329,62	997,0

We have already established that talk time, rather than the number of calls made, should be used as the cost driver, as a significantly more linear relationship exists in the case of the former. In order to employ the high-low method, we select the two points with the highest and lowest cost driver levels (all other points are disregarded at this stage). In this example, it means we have to select the month with the most minutes of talk time, and the month with the least minutes of talk time. From Table 3.1 we see that these months are February and May respectively.

Simultaneous equations can be used to determine the equation of the total cost line, which can then be used to predict the total cost at any activity level within the relevant range.

The following mathematical short cut can be used to calculate the variable cost per unit (the gradient or slope), eliminating the need for simultaneous equations:

$$m = \frac{\text{High-cost} - \text{Low-cost}}{\text{High-activity} - \text{Low-activity}}$$

$$= \frac{428{,}54 - 260{,}76}{1\,338{,}0 - 485{,}3}$$

$$= R0{,}19676 \text{ per minute}$$

This means that the variable cost (m in the equation) is R0,19676 per minute of talk time.

The fixed cost portion of the telephone expense can be calculated by replacing m in the formula with the variable cost per minute as calculated above, and then substituting the x and y co-ordinates of the highest or lowest data point. In the calculation of the fixed cost below we have chosen to use the data for February:

$y = mx + c$
$c = y - mx$
$ = \text{R}428{,}54 - (\text{R}0{,}19676 \times 1\,338)$
$ = \text{R}165{,}28$

The fixed cost is approximately R165 per month, and the complete equation is:
$y = 0{,}19676x + 165$

Figure 3.4 Shortcomings of using the high-low method

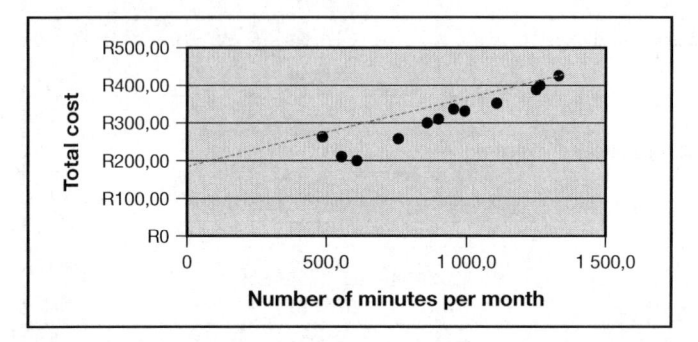

The line is fitted to the data using the data points at the highest and lowest activity levels. Disturbingly, the fixed cost that results is even further from reality (R165 as calculated, compared to R87 per the telephone account) than the rough scatter graph method employed earlier. This is a result of two major flaws that are inherent in this approach:
- Only two points are selected (no coverage of the population).
- These points are the extremes, and may not be representative of the population, or they may lie outside the relevant range.

Note that the high-low method is often used to split a mixed cost into its variable and fixed components. Where the relationship between the cost and the cost driver is perfectly linear (in other words, where the line is not merely an estimate as in example 3.2 above, but all the data points are genuinely on the line), the method results in a 100 per cent accurate split between the variable and fixed components. In such a situation, any two observations in the data set, not only the points with the highest or lowest cost driver value, can be used in order to calculate the variable and fixed cost components and all will yield the same result.

3.5 Least squares regression

Key terms: best fit line, least squares regression, regression error

Least squares regression is a statistical approach to establishing the equation of the line that *best fits* all of the data points provided. A **best fit line** is defined as the line that reduces the sum of the squares of the regression errors. (A **regression error**

is the distance between the line and the point/observation. Refer to Figure 3.5.) This is the most accurate of the three approaches, but the most tedious if the calculation is performed manually, as described in this section. The use of a computer software package greatly speeds up the process. This is described in the following section. In both instances the equation for the linear relationship is again as follows:

$$y = mx + c$$

where:
- y is the total (aggregate) cost
- m is the gradient or slope of the line (and the variable cost per unit of the cost driver)
- x is the cost driver level
- c is where the line intercepts the y-axis (and therefore the fixed cost).

Figure 3.5 Regression error

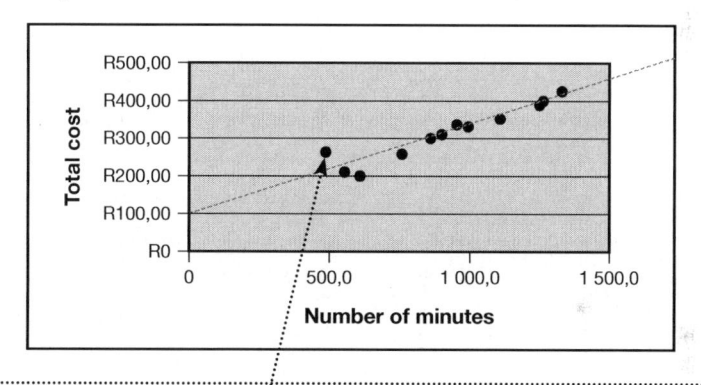

Do you notice the gap between this first dot and the regression line? The distance between the dot and the line is referred to as the regression error. Least squares regression generates a line that minimises the sum of the squares of all these gaps (errors). The line that results in the minimum sum of the squares of the regression errors is the line that best fits the data set.

3.5.1 Manual approach to determining the equation of the line

The gradient (slope) and intercept (the variable and fixed cost components of the formula respectively) can be found with the following two formulae:

To solve for the gradient or slope:

$$m = \frac{n(\text{sum}(xy)) - (\text{sum}x)(\text{sum}y)}{n(\text{sum}x^2) - (\text{sum}x)^2}$$

To solve for the intercept:

$$c = \frac{(\text{sum}y) - m(\text{sum}x)}{n}$$

n represents the number of observations.

principles of management accounting

Example 3.3

The same information regarding a monthly telephone account as in example 3.1 applies.

Required:
Manually apply least squares regression to determine the variable and fixed cost portion of the monthly telephone account, and derive an equation that explains the relationship between the two.

Again talk time, rather than the number of calls made, is used as the cost driver, as a significantly more linear relationship exists in the case of the former.

The total cost and cost driver can be tabulated as follows in order to facilitate working with the equations:

	Total cost (R)	Total talk-time in minutes		
	Y	X	YX	X²
January	260,00	762,30	198 198,00	581 101,29
February	428,54	1 338,00	573 386,52	1 790 244,00
March	338,58	956,40	323 817,91	914 700,96
April	310,00	900,00	279 000,00	810 000,00
May	260,76	485,30	126 546,83	235 516,09
June	387,09	1 255,00	485 797,95	1 575 025,00
July	354,83	1 110,10	393 896,78	1 232 322,01
August	208,92	555,80	116 117,74	308 913,64
September	400,44	1 269,60	508 398,62	1 611 884,16
October	201,32	612,00	123 207,84	374 544,00
November	297,71	861,00	256 328,31	741 321,00
December	329,62	997,00	328 631,14	994 009,00
Total	3 777,81	11 102,50	3 713 327,64	1 169 581,15

The above information can now be substituted into the regression formula.

Solve for the slope, m (that is, the variable cost per minute):

$$m = \frac{n(\text{sum}(xy)) - (\text{sum}x)(\text{sum}y)}{n(\text{sum}x^2) - (\text{sum}x)^2}$$

$$m = \frac{12(3\ 713\ 327{,}64) - (11\ 102{,}50)(3\ 777{,}81)}{12(1\ 169\ 581{,}15) - (11\ 102{,}50)^2}$$

m = R0,24298 per minute

The variable cost (m in the equation) is R0,24298 per minute.

Solve for y-intercept, c (that is, the fixed cost per month):

$$c = \frac{(\text{sum}y) - m(\text{sum}x)}{n}$$

$$c = \frac{(3\,777{,}81) - R0{,}24298(11\,102{,}50)}{12}$$

$$c = R90{,}01$$

The fixed cost (c in the equation) is R90,01 per month.

The linear equation that represents the relationship between the monthly telephone cost (y) and the number of minutes of talk time per month (x) is as follows:

> $y = R0{,}24298x + R90{,}01$

Notice that the fixed line rental cost per month as calculated using least squares regression is much closer to the actual fixed cost than the estimates we determined using the scatter graph and high-low methods. However, a difference between the actual (R87) and estimated (R90) fixed cost still exists. The reasons for this are discussed in section 3.6 below.

> Most students use a calculator to perform least squares regression calculations under exam conditions – it is unlikely that time restrictions will allow you to do the calculations manually. If the calculator that you are permitted to take into the exam room has statistical functions, please refer to the 'statistical calculations' or similarly named section of your calculator manual.

3.5.2 Computerised approach to calculating the equation of the line using Microsoft Excel®

> **Key terms:** coefficient of determination, correlation coefficient, normal distribution table, regression analysis, standard error

The section explains how to perform least squares regression with the use of Excel®, and also discusses two key pieces of statistical information that the Excel® analysis provides.

> The syllabi of professional accounting bodies require students to be capable of integrating IT skills with management accounting skills. The following example provides an opportunity for such integration.

Example 3.4

The same information as in example 3.1 regarding a monthly telephone account applies.

Required:
Apply the least squares regression technique using Microsoft's Excel® software to determine the variable and fixed cost portion of the monthly telephone account, and to derive an equation that explains the relationship between the two.

principles of management accounting

The data set (total cost and total talk time per month, for each month for which information is available) is set out in Excel®, as shown in Figure 3.6 below.

Figure 3.6 Setting out the data

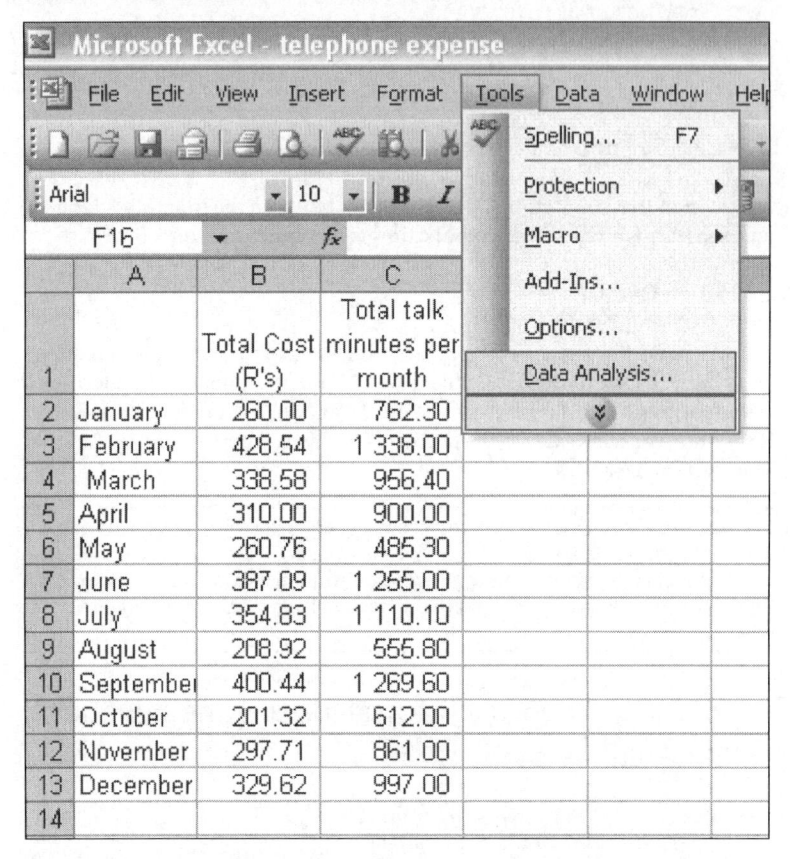

	A	B	C
1		Total Cost (R's)	Total talk minutes per month
2	January	260.00	762.30
3	February	428.54	1 338.00
4	March	338.58	956.40
5	April	310.00	900.00
6	May	260.76	485.30
7	June	387.09	1 255.00
8	July	354.83	1 110.10
9	August	208.92	555.80
10	September	400.44	1 269.60
11	October	201.32	612.00
12	November	297.71	861.00
13	December	329.62	997.00
14			

- Select the 'Data Analysis' tool from the 'Tools' menu option, as illustrated in Figure 3.6. If the Data Analysis tool is not available, follow the Microsoft Office® help options to install the menu item.
- The dialog box in Figure 3.7 appears. Select the 'Regression' option. A second dialog box appears into which you are required to input the data set (as in Figure 3.8). Click 'OK' once you have done this.
- The regression output appears in another sheet, as shown in Figure 3.9. You will notice that Excel® returns a fair amount of regression information. We will focus on just a few key statistics.

Chapter 3 Cost estimation

Figure 3.7 Selecting the regression data analysis tool

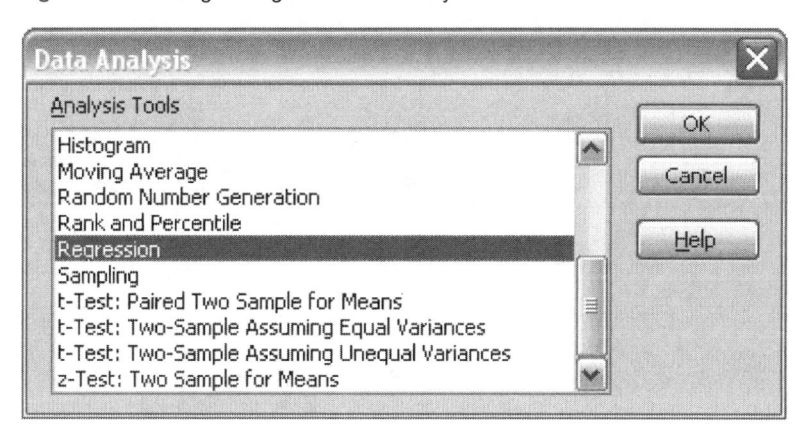

Figure 3.8 Inputting the data set

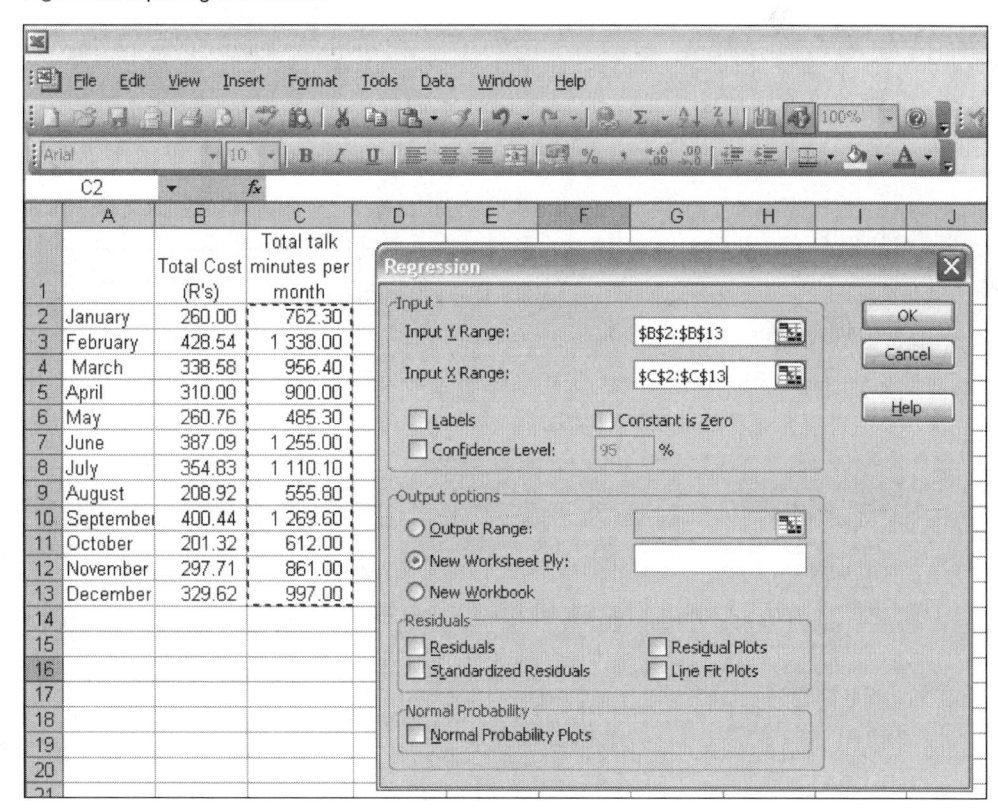

	A	B	C
1		Total Cost (R's)	Total talk minutes per month
2	January	260.00	762.30
3	February	428.54	1 338.00
4	March	338.58	956.40
5	April	310.00	900.00
6	May	260.76	485.30
7	June	387.09	1 255.00
8	July	354.83	1 110.10
9	August	208.92	555.80
10	September	400.44	1 269.60
11	October	201.32	612.00
12	November	297.71	861.00
13	December	329.62	997.00

49

principles of management accounting

Figure 3.9 Telephone expense calculated in Excel®

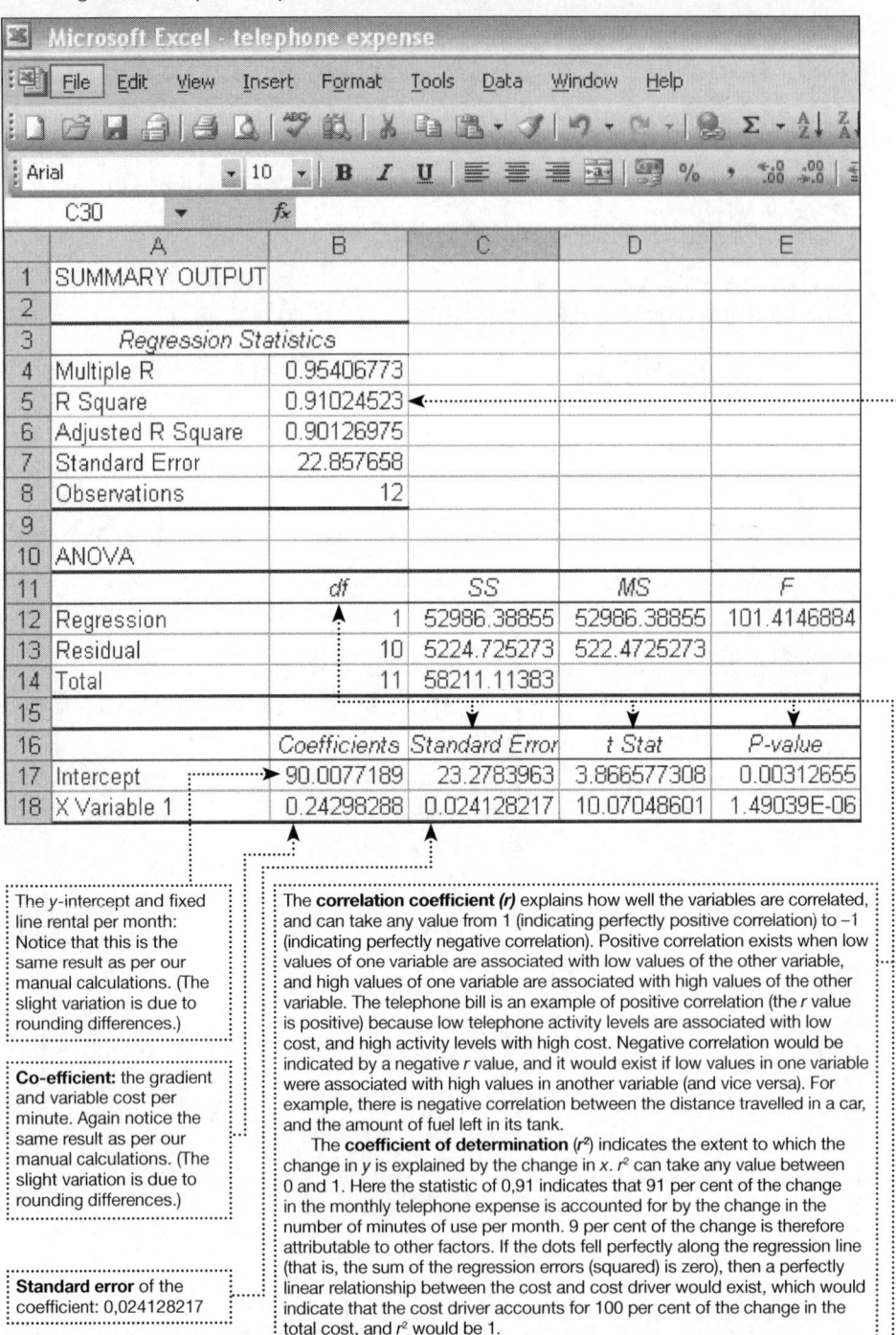

	A	B	C	D	E
1	SUMMARY OUTPUT				
2					
3	*Regression Statistics*				
4	Multiple R	0.95406773			
5	R Square	0.91024523			
6	Adjusted R Square	0.90126975			
7	Standard Error	22.857658			
8	Observations	12			
9					
10	ANOVA				
11		df	SS	MS	F
12	Regression	1	52986.38855	52986.38855	101.4146884
13	Residual	10	5224.725273	522.4725273	
14	Total	11	58211.11383		
15					
16		Coefficients	Standard Error	t Stat	P-value
17	Intercept	90.0077189	23.2783963	3.866577308	0.00312655
18	X Variable 1	0.24298288	0.024128217	10.07048601	1.49039E-06

The y-intercept and fixed line rental per month: Notice that this is the same result as per our manual calculations. (The slight variation is due to rounding differences.)

Co-efficient: the gradient and variable cost per minute. Again notice the same result as per our manual calculations. (The slight variation is due to rounding differences.)

Standard error of the coefficient: 0,024128217

The **correlation coefficient (r)** explains how well the variables are correlated, and can take any value from 1 (indicating perfectly positive correlation) to –1 (indicating perfectly negative correlation). Positive correlation exists when low values of one variable are associated with low values of the other variable, and high values of one variable are associated with high values of the other variable. The telephone bill is an example of positive correlation (the r value is positive) because low telephone activity levels are associated with low cost, and high activity levels with high cost. Negative correlation would be indicated by a negative r value, and it would exist if low values in one variable were associated with high values in another variable (and vice versa). For example, there is negative correlation between the distance travelled in a car, and the amount of fuel left in its tank.

The **coefficient of determination** (r^2) indicates the extent to which the change in y is explained by the change in x. r^2 can take any value between 0 and 1. Here the statistic of 0,91 indicates that 91 per cent of the change in the monthly telephone expense is accounted for by the change in the number of minutes of use per month. 9 per cent of the change is therefore attributable to other factors. If the dots fell perfectly along the regression line (that is, the sum of the regression errors (squared) is zero), then a perfectly linear relationship between the cost and cost driver would exist, which would indicate that the cost driver accounts for 100 per cent of the change in the total cost, and r^2 would be 1.

A brief explanation of the meaning and use of standard errors and t-stats is provided on the next page. The term 'df' indicates the 'degrees of freedom'. The significance of the number of degrees of freedom, as well as the statistical theory underlying the standard errors, t-stats and P-values, falls outside the scope of this book. Consult a statistics text book to learn more about these indicators.

The coefficient that is returned by the regression analysis (0,24298288 in the example above) is the best estimate possible of the variable cost, using the data available. In other words, the coefficient that is returned by the regression analysis is the best fit to the data that was used. Refer to the scatter graph that was originally plotted (Figure 3.2), which reflects the relationship between y (the total cost) and x (the total number of minutes (the cost driver)). Notice that the relationship between these two is not perfectly linear, and that regression errors exist. Because the relationship between cost and cost driver is not perfectly linear, it is impossible to say with 100 per cent certainty that the true value of the coefficient (the true variable cost per minute) is exactly 0,24298288.

While it is not possible to be 100 per cent confident that the true value of the coefficient is *one specific* number, it is possible to be confident, up to a certain level, of the true value of the coefficient, if the value of the coefficient is expressed as a range, instead of a discrete number. The standard error can be used to determine what the range needs to be, depending on the level of confidence that is required. *The higher the required level of confidence that the true coefficient lies in the range of numbers specified, the wider the range needs to be.*

This range is calculated by adding to and deducting from the coefficient determined by the regression analysis a certain number of standard errors of the coefficient. The more confident we want to be that the true value of the coefficient lies within the range, the wider the range needs to be, and the greater the number of standard errors that need to be added to and subtracted from the estimated coefficient. How many standard errors need to be added or subtracted for a certain probability level? This has been statistically determined, and for normal distributions, the **normal distribution table** is used. The normal distribution table can be found in statistics textbooks.

For the purposes of illustration, assume that we wish to determine a range within which we can be 95 per cent confident that the true value of the coefficient lies. We can see from a normal distribution table that to obtain a 95 per cent confidence level, 1,96 standard errors need to be added to and subtracted from the coefficient.

0,24298288 − (0,024128217 × 1,96) = 0,19569	< β <	0,24298288 + (0,024128217 × 1,96) = 0,29027

We are therefore 95 per cent confident that the true variable cost per minute lies between R0,19569 per minute and R0,29027 per minute.

T-stat

Key term: *t*-stat

The *t*-statistic (***t*-stat**) compares the size of the standard error of the coefficient to the size of the coefficient itself, in order to provide an understanding of the relative size of the standard error. It is calculated by dividing the coefficient by the standard error of the coefficient. In the example above, the *t*-stat of 10,07048601 (see Figure 3.9) is calculated as follows 0,24298288/0,024128217.

The *t*-stat therefore provides a relative measure of the standard error of the coefficient. This is useful, as the *t*-stat provides an indication of whether there is a statistically significant relationship between the dependent and independent variables. The larger the standard error of the coefficient relative to the coefficient itself, the smaller the *t*-stat, and the less meaningful the relationship between the dependent and independent variables. In the example above, the *t*-stat is in excess of 10, indicating that the standard error of the coefficient is quite small relative to the size of the coefficient, and that a statistically significant relationship exists between the number of minutes of talk time and the total cost of the telephone account.

3.6 Factors affecting the accuracy of cost estimation

Key terms: duration driver, intensity driver, multiple regression, transaction driver

A number of factors affect the accuracy with which costs can be estimated and predicted.

The first factor has already been raised. A cost may have multiple cost drivers. As an example, consider a monthly telephone account again: the number of telephone calls made; the amount of time spent on the phone; whether the telephone call is local, national, international or to a cellphone. The number of telephone calls is a specific kind of cost driver, known as a **transaction driver**. Transaction drivers measure the number of times an activity is performed. The amount of time spent on the phone is a type of cost driver referred to as a **duration driver**. Duration drivers recognise that the time spent performing an action may be influential in terms of driving costs. The third driver – the kind of call that is made – recognises that some types of calls make use of network resources more intensively than other types of calls. Local calls would place the least amount of demand on network resources, while national calls utilise greater quantities of bandwidth. This type of cost driver is referred to as an **intensity driver**. Costs with multiple cost drivers can be analysed using **multiple regression**, the detailed calculation of which falls outside the scope of this text.

A second factor is that a change in price or pricing structures of the cost may have occurred during the period. Suppose that, in an effort to reduce costs, the owner of the telephone decided to move to a structured billing plan, which would result in all calls made in off-peak time being free. There would be a change in the telephone account that is purely price related and has nothing to do with a change in the cost driver. This would result in a distortion of the variable and fixed-cost components calculated under any of the above methods. In such an instance, only telephone accounts after the pricing change should be considered in order to understand how costs will behave in future.

A third problem is that a linear relationship may not exist. The relationship may have step aspects to it, or the existence of efficiencies and inefficiencies at certain points may result in a curvilinear relationship between cost and cost driver (refer to the economists' curve described in Chapter 2, *Cost classification*). Direct labour cost, specifically, often has a non-linear relationship with production volumes, because labour efficiency may improve over time. 'Learning curves' are then used – these are discussed in Appendix 3.1.

Changes in technology, such as a switch from landline to cellphone, or switching from using a standard telephone line to using broadband for Internet access, is the fourth factor that can affect costs. A broadband line is often charged as a fixed amount each month with no variable cost component, where Internet usage over the dial-up telephone system may to a large extent have been a variable cost.

(Internet usage would have been billed based on time spent on the telephone line.) In a case such as this, the cost structure has changed from partially fixed, with a large variable cost component, to exclusively fixed.

Lastly, cut-off problems could exist between the periods over which the cost and activity respectively are recorded. A cut-off problem refers to the situation where the cost is for one particular period (for example, 1 January to 31 January), but the activity is reported for a slightly different period (for example, 3 January to 2 February). This often happens in organisations where cost information is generated by one system, and activity information is gathered from a different source. In our telephone example, a different kind of cut-off problem (or mismatch between billing and usage periods) could have arisen. If the telephone user had decided to switch from the old system of being billed – monthly in arrears – to another type of billing plan which is perhaps billed monthly in advance, this might result in an unusually large bill in the month of switching. Effectively, the switch-over month would represent a double bill. The increase in cost is a timing or cut-off issue, and has nothing to do with a change in usage.

3.7 Other means of estimating costs and predicting cost behaviour

Key term: historic cost data

In addition to the cost estimation methods discussed above, various other methods of cost estimation and prediction exist which may be useful in various circumstances. In situations where no **historic cost data** exists, the cost estimation could be carried out by means of an experimental approach. This is often referred to as a scientific or engineering approach, whereby a sample of activities is carried out, and the results are recorded and extrapolated over the full extent of the anticipated activities.

Alternatively, where historic cost information with which management is quite familiar is readily available, management may not feel it necessary to carry out graphical, mathematical or statistical analysis. Rather, a perusal of the accounting records, given a high level of familiarity with the detail of the accounts, may be sufficient to distinguish between the fixed and variable cost components of the total cost that is under analysis.

3.8 Summary

This chapter provides an introduction to some measurement techniques that can be used to calculate the variable and fixed components of a mixed cost, when these amounts are not already known. These techniques require an activity to be identified against which the cost can be measured, and the following linear equation is developed in order to assist the organisation with predicting future costs:

$$y = mx + c$$

where:
- y is the total (aggregate) cost
- m is the gradient or slope of the line (and the variable cost per unit of the cost driver)

- x is the cost driver level
- c is where the line intercepts the y-axis (and therefore the fixed cost).

This formula is valid only within the relevant range.

The relationship between costs and units can also be non-linear, as discussed in the appendix.

The most important criterion in selecting an appropriate cost driver is that there should be a plausible relationship between the cost and the cost driver. Furthermore, the relationship between the cost and the cost driver needs to be reasonably linear in order for the measurement techniques discussed in this chapter to be of use. In order to obtain a visual perspective as to whether a linear relationship exists between a cost and a selected activity, a scatter graph can be used. The observations of costs versus activity level can be plotted on a pair of axes in order to determine whether or not the points are linear.

The high-low method can be used to calculate the fixed and variable components of the total cost for a set of observations. The observations at the highest and lowest activity levels are used. High-low analysis is based on the assumption that any increase in total cost from one activity level to the other is due to the change in activity level, and by dividing the change in cost by the change in the activity level, the variable cost per activity can be determined. The shortcoming of this method is that only two observations are taken into account.

The least squares statistical method (whether performed manually, on a calculator, or in Excel®) is able to take all observation points into account. Further statistics can be computed to provide information on the reliability of the equation determined in this manner.

Potential shortcomings of all methods of analysis is that there may be more than one cost driver; price changes may have occurred in the cost; a linear relationship between cost and cost driver may not exist; changes in technology may have affected the cost or cost driver; or cut-off problems may have occurred.

Conclusion: Cost estimation and other topics in this book

Chapter 2, *Cost classification* introduced a number of different ways in which costs were classified for management accounting purposes. One of these classifications related to cost behaviour, with four types of costs being highlighted: variable, fixed, step and mixed costs. This chapter focuses on quantitative methods of identifying and calculating the variable and fixed cost components of a mixed cost. Such quantitative techniques are useful in budgeting, as discussed in Chapter 12, *Budgets, planning and control*. Management will find it necessary to apply some cost estimation technique when the relationship between the cost and activity to which it relates is not clear. The starting point for applying any quantitative technique is to identify the cost driver (or activity) that drives the cost under examination. The concept of cost drivers is further explored in Chapter 6, *Overhead allocation*. The appendix to this chapter deals with a non-linear relationship between cost and cost-driver. It examines the learning curve effect often encountered in direct labour costs.

Tutorial case study: MultiChoice

Consider again the example of the satellite television operator *MultiChoice*, introduced at the beginning of this chapter.
1. Give an example of a cost for which the number of subscribers could be a plausible cost driver.
2. Discuss whether the cost that you named would be likely also to have a fixed component, or whether it would be likely to be entirely variable.
3. Comment on whether MultiChoice's management accounting team could possibly make use of scatter graphs, the high-low method, or least squares regression to determine cost equations. Discuss what the relative advantages and disadvantages of the techniques would be.
4. If the management accountants did employ least squares regression, suggest a way around the tedious mathematical calculations that underlie this technique.
5. Determine what you think would be a possible example of a transaction cost driver, a duration cost driver and an intensity cost driver respectively, in MultiChoice.
6. Discuss what factors could affect the accuracy of estimations where cost estimation techniques have been employed by MultiChoice.

Appendix 3.1 Learning curves

[The author wishes to thank Birte Schneider for preparing this appendix on learning curves.]

Key terms: cumulative average–time learning model, cumulative doubling approach, experience curve, graph/schedule approach, incremental unit–time learning model, learning curve, learning curve index, learning rate, learning tempo, mathematical approach

Introduction

In the cost estimation methods and examples earlier in this chapter, we assumed a linear relationship between cost and cost driver. Sometimes this may not be true, particularly if we have (1) a new production process, (2) which is repeated and (3) which has large labour inputs – these are the *three requirements that need to be present before a learning process can take place*. In such a situation, as workers repeat the job, they become better at it and 'learn' to perform it more quickly. In other words, the labour efficiency increases. The time taken to produce each additional unit is therefore less than for the previous one, and the total labour costs (and related variable costs, where labour is the cost driver) increase at a relatively slower rate than the number of units produced. This relationship can be presented graphically as a curve, known as the learning curve.

The **learning curve** is a function that indicates how the number of labour hours per unit decreases as the number of units produced increases. Learning normally has the greatest impact on the first few units, and then the effect of the learning process decreases until, eventually, a point is reached where all possible learning has occurred and the curve flattens. This relationship is shown in exhibit 3.1.

principles of management accounting

Exhibit 3.1 Cumulative average time per unit

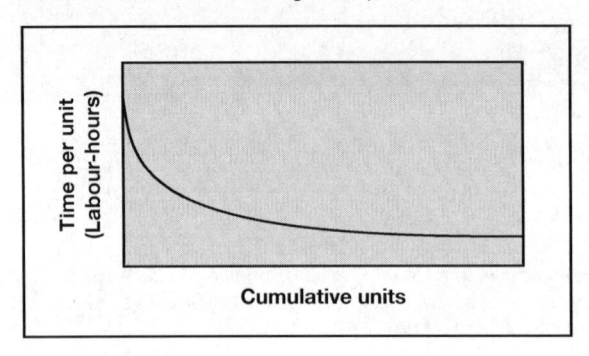

Exhibit 3.2 shows the impact on total production time. For each additional unit produced, the total time taken to produce all units increases by a smaller amount, resulting in a curve that flattens, but never becomes a line parallel to the *x*-axis (as each additional unit still takes some time to produce).

Exhibit 3.2 Cumulative total labour hours

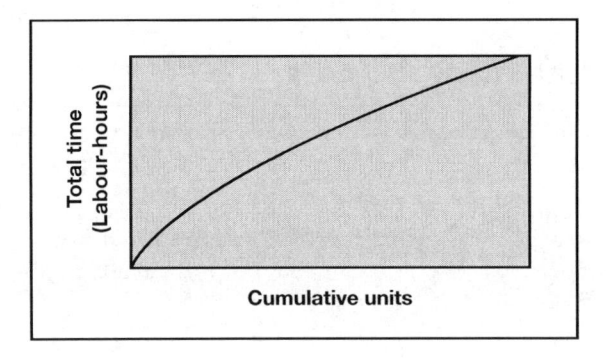

The **learning tempo** is defined as the percentage by which the labour time decreases each time the number of units doubles. The definition implies that, as time passes and workers' skills increase, more units have to be produced (for example, four units instead of two units) to achieve the same percentage decrease in labour time. Furthermore, the reduction in labour time becomes increasingly smaller in absolute terms, as the constant percentage is applied to an increasingly smaller amount. Appendix example 3.1 illustrates this.

Appendix example 3.1

ShadeConcepts manufactures umbrellas that are used outdoors by businesses such as restaurants to protect their customers from the harsh South African sun. It recently started manufacturing a new type of umbrella, the 'KerbCover', which provides shade for several tables at a time. It estimates that a learning tempo of 20 per cent will apply in the manufacturing process. The first unit took 10 hours to manufacture.

Required:
Calculate how long it is likely to take to manufacture the second and fourth units of the KerbCover.

If the first unit took 10 hours to produce, the second one will take 10 hours − (10 hours × 20%) = 8 hours. The fourth unit will take 8 hours − (8 hours × 20%) = 6,4 hours. If we calculate the absolute decrease in hours, it is 2 hours (10 hours − 8 hours) from the first to the second unit and only 1,6 hours (8 hours − 6,4 hours) from the second to the fourth unit. The way the learning tempo is defined therefore automatically captures the decreasing tempo of learning. This makes sense, as the more workers have learnt about manufacturing the new product, the less remains to be learnt. Eventually they will reach a point where they are manufacturing the umbrellas as quickly as possible, and very little further 'learning' will be possible.

It is generally assumed that learning occurs at a steady rate − the **learning rate**. This rate is defined as 100 per cent less the learning tempo, which was discussed above. Using the information in appendix example 3.1, the learning rate would be 80 per cent (100% − 20%). Most exam questions give the learning rate rather than the learning tempo. Synonyms for the learning rate are *rate of learning*, *learning curve* and *learning curve rate*.

It is important to note that a unit can refer to more than one product unit. If it refers to batches, the labour time per unit is obtained by dividing the total time needed to complete a certain number of batches by the number of units in the batch. Note that in such a case the situation must specifically be one where learning occurs according to batches of units (and not individual units) − calculations will be incorrect if batches are randomly created just to facilitate doubling and therefore calculation.

To illustrate a situation where learning occurs in batches, assume that ShadeConcepts, the organisation in appendix example 3.1, also manufactures smaller umbrellas for children's tables. These are manufactured in batches, with each batch containing six different animal-shaped umbrellas. Because the shape of each of the six umbrellas in a batch is unique, the effect of learning is felt only once an entire batch is complete. If it takes 10 hours to manufacture the first batch and the learning tempo is 20 per cent, it will take 8 hours (10 hours − 20%) to manufacture the next batch and 6,4 hours (8 hours − 20%) to manufacture the fourth batch. The labour hours per unit can now be calculated as 1,67 hours (10 hours per batch/6 units per batch) for the first batch and 1,5 hours (18 hours/12 units) for the total production of the first two batches.

The learning curve can apply to both direct labour cost and variable overhead cost, if the cost driver for overheads is direct labour hours (or a related measure such as labour costs).

Learning curves are not applicable only to the time taken to manufacture units in a factory setting. They can also be applied to white-collar work, such as the time it takes to make price and investment decisions, to schedule work, and to prepare budgets. They are also applied in the determination of standards, and in recent years have been applied to areas such as marketing, distribution and client services. In these settings the term **'experience curve'** is often used instead of 'learning curve'.

Incremental unit–time learning model and cumulative average–time learning model

The applicable learning rate can be modelled in one of two ways: the incremental unit–time learning model or the cumulative average–time learning model. The **incremental unit–time learning model** expresses the effect on the *additional time taken to produce the last unit* if the cumulative quantity of units doubles. The **cumulative average–time learning model** expresses the effect on the *cumulative average*

principles of management accounting

time per unit when the cumulative quantity of units doubles. The difference is best illustrated with an example.

> ### Appendix example 3.2
>
> ShadeConcepts' 'KerbCover' umbrella is being manufactured. It is estimated that a learning rate of 80 per cent is applicable. The first unit took 10 hours to complete.
>
> **Required:**
> Indicate the impact on the cumulative average time per unit, the total time taken to produce all units, and the incremental time taken to produce the last unit, if the applicable model is:
> a) An incremental unit–time learning model
> b) A cumulative average–time learning model,
>
> and the total number of units produced is two KerbCovers.

Under an incremental unit–time learning model, the additional time to produce the *second unit* is 8 hours (10 h × 80%). You will recognise this model as the one that was applied in appendix example 3.1. The total time it takes to produce both units is 18 hours (10 h + 8 h). To calculate the cumulative average time per unit, we must divide the total time it took to produce the units by the cumulative number of units produced: 18 h/2 units = 9 h per unit.

Under a cumulative average–time learning model, the cumulative average time for *each unit* produced would be 8 hours (10 h × 80%). The total time taken to produce both units would therefore be 8 h × 2 = 16 hours. Since we know that the first unit took 10 hours to produce, it will take 16 hours – 10 hours = 6 hours to produce the second unit.

From the above, it is clear that the time it takes to produce a given unit can differ significantly depending on whether an incremental unit–time or a cumulative average–time learning model applies.

The incremental unit–time learning model usually predicts a higher cumulative average time per unit than the cumulative average–time learning model (when the same learning rate is used in both models). The nature of the actual learning process that takes place in a given scenario determines which model is applicable.

As mentioned earlier in the chapter, correct costing information is necessary to facilitate decision-making. It is therefore important to determine whether a learning process does take place and which rate and model best approximate it. The enhanced information is useful in pricing and production decisions, as well as in performance evaluation.

> If a question does not state which learning curve model is applicable and does not give data from which this can be deduced, it is usually safer to assume that the cumulative average–time learning model applies. Be sure, however, to look thoroughly for clues in the question before you make this assumption.

Approaches

Now that the theory of learning curves has been explained, we turn our attention to the practical approaches to calculating learning curves. The following approaches have been developed to calculate the time needed to produce units (an additional unit, the average time per unit produced, or the total time needed to produce all units), or the learning rate:

- The cumulative doubling approach
- The graph/schedule approach
- The mathematical approach.

The cumulative doubling approach

The **cumulative doubling approach** can be used only if the problem involves the *doubling* of units or batches, as has been the case in our examples so far. It can therefore be applied, for example, if eight units are produced (as it involves the doubling from 1 to 2 to 4 to 8), but not to determine the effect if seven units are produced.

Appendix example 3.2 showed how this approach is used in calculating the following:
- The time needed to produce the last unit
- The average time per unit produced
- The total time needed to produce all units.

The same principles apply when more than two units are produced. Appendix example 3.3 illustrates this.

Appendix example 3.3

Assume the same information as for appendix example 3.2.

Required:
Calculate the time needed to produce the last unit, the average time per unit produced, and the total time needed to produce all units if eight KerbCover umbrellas are to be manufactured and:
a) An incremental unit–time learning model applies
b) A cumulative average–time learning model applies.

If the model is an incremental unit–time learning model, we can calculate the additional time it takes to produce the eighth unit. The calculation would be:

10 h × (0,8)^3 = 5,12 hours

As it is impossible to calculate the incremental time of the third, fifth, sixth and seventh units under the cumulative doubling approach, we cannot calculate the total time it takes to produce eight units or the cumulative average time per unit.

Let's now apply the cumulative average–time learning model. As the number of units produced doubles three times, the cumulative average time per unit produced would be: 10 hours × (0,8)^3 = 5,12 hours. The total time it takes to produce eight units therefore amounts to 5,12 hours × 8 = 40,96 hours. It is not possible to calculate the additional time taken to produce the last unit. The reason is that we do not know how long it took to produce seven units. We cannot calculate it using the cumulative doubling approach, as seven is not a doubling of units. We can merely state that it took an additional 30,96 hours (40,96 hours – 10 hours) to produce the *last seven* units, or an additional 15 to 36 hours (40,96 hours – (10 × 0,8^2 × 4 hours)) to produce the last four units.

The learning rate can be calculated using the cumulative doubling approach, if the cumulative average (or incremental average) times for the first and subsequent doubled units are given. Appendix example 3.4 shows the necessary calculations.

principles of management accounting

> ## Appendix example 3.4
>
> Assume that the following independent sets of information about ShadeConcepts' KerbCover umbrellas are available:
> - *Scenario A:* It takes 10 hours to produce the first unit and 6,4 hours to produce the fourth unit. An incremental unit–time learning model is applicable.
> - *Scenario B:* It takes 10 hours to produce the first unit and a cumulative average of 6,4 hours per unit to produce four units. A cumulative average–time learning model is applicable.
>
> **Required:**
> Calculate the learning rate for each of the independent scenarios A and B above.

First of all, we need to determine how many times the number of units produced doubles. Here it doubles twice, and the following formula is therefore applicable:

10 hours × $(y)^2$ = 6,4 hours, where y is the learning rate.

Solving for y, we obtain the following: $y = \sqrt{(6{,}4 \text{ hours} / 10)} = 0{,}8$. The learning rate is therefore 80 per cent (notice that this corresponds with the learning rate given in appendix example 3.2). The same calculation applies to both scenarios A and B. This implies that, if an incremental unit–time learning model applies, a learning rate of 80 per cent means it would take 6,4 hours to produce the fourth unit. However, if a cumulative average–time learning model applies, a learning rate of 80 per cent means it would take on average 6,4 hours to produce each of the four units, and a total of 25,6 hours.

Let's now assume that we are given the information that it took eight hours to produce the second KerbCover unit. For the second unit, the units produced doubled only once. If an incremental unit–time learning model applies, the learning rate can be calculated as follows:

10 hours × $(y)^1$ = 8, where y is the learning rate.

Solving for y, we find that the learning rate is 8 hours/10 hours = 80 per cent. Notice that this corresponds with the learning rate given in appendix example 3.2, where we used the 80 per cent learning rate to calculate that the second unit would take 8 hours to produce.

If a cumulative average–time learning model applies, the learning rate would be calculated as follows. First, we would need to calculate the cumulative average time per unit it takes to manufacture the two units: (10 hours + 8 hours)/2 = 9 hours. The learning rate is:

10 hours × $(y)^1$ = 9 hours.

Solving for y, we find that the learning rate is 9 hours/10 hours = 90 per cent.

Why does this 90 per cent differ from the 80 per cent learning rate given in appendix example 3.2? Because in that example it was shown that the second unit would take 6 hours (not 8 hours) to produce if a cumulative average–time learning model with a learning rate of 80 per cent applied. The information we were given in appendix example 3.2 was not that the second unit took 8 hours to produce, but rather that the learning rate was 80 per cent.

The graph/schedule approach

The **graph/schedule approach** is best illustrated by an example. Once again we can either determine the time needed to produce units (appendix example 3.5) or we can estimate the learning rate (appendix example 3.6).

Appendix example 3.5

As we know, ShadeConcepts also manufactures smaller umbrellas for children's tables. These are manufactured in batches, with each batch containing six different animal-shaped umbrellas. Because the shape of every one of the six umbrellas in a batch is unique, the effect of learning is felt only once an entire batch is complete. It took 10 hours to complete the first batch.

A learning curve of 80 per cent is applicable, and the organisation finds that a cumulative average–time learning model best describes the learning process.

Cumulative batches	1	1,25	1,5	2	2,5	3
Cumulative average hours per batch (expressed as % of time taken to produce the first batch)	100,00	93,07	87,76	80,00	74,46	70,21

Required:
Calculate the cumulative average time it takes to produce 15 children's umbrellas, and determine the necessary time to produce an additional three umbrellas once 15 umbrellas have already been produced.

The first step is to convert the required umbrellas into batches, as the model described above relates to batches (and not individual units):

15 umbrellas/6 umbrellas per batch
= 2,5 batches

Next we obtain the relevant cumulative average time percentage from the table and calculate the total time it takes to produce 15 umbrellas:

10 hours for the first batch × 74,46 per cent (read off the table) × 2,5 batches
= 18,62 hours

The last step is simply to divide the total time by the number of umbrellas produced:

18,62 hours/15 umbrellas
= 1,24 hours per umbrella

The time taken to produce an additional three umbrellas can be calculated by calculating the time it takes to produce 18 umbrellas and then deducting the time it takes to produce 15 umbrellas. 18 umbrellas are produced in three batches; therefore the total time it takes to produce them is:

10 hours for the first batch × 70,21 per cent × 3 batches
= 21,06 hours

principles of management accounting

We calculated above that it takes 18,62 hours to produce 15 umbrellas, and therefore the extra time to produce another 3 umbrellas is:

21,06 hours – 18,62 hours
= 2,44 hours

To estimate times when an incremental unit–time learning model is used, the table (or graph, if one has been given) needs to display the incremental time for the last unit at different numbers of cumulative units. To calculate information other than the additional time it takes to produce the last unit, the incremental times for all successive times must be provided (for 1, 2, 3,...). The reason is that these times must be added to obtain a total time and to be able to calculate a cumulative average time per unit.

Appendix example 3.6

ShadeConcepts is looking to launch a new type of umbrella, the StreetCafé. Each batch consists of 50 units. It takes 250 hours to manufacture the first batch and 195 hours to manufacture the third batch. The learning process is best approximated by an incremental unit–time learning model.

The management of ShadeConcepts suspects that the learning rate applicable to the manufacture of StreetCafé is somewhere between 80 per cent and 90 per cent. They have therefore determined the time it would take to produce the last batch for different numbers of cumulative batches at learning rates of 80 per cent and 90 per cent respectively, and summarised it in the table below.

Learning rate	Cumulative batches	1	1,5	2	3
80%	Hours for last batch (expressed as % of time taken to produce the first batch)	100	87,76	80,0	70,21
90%	Hours for last batch (expressed as % of time taken to produce the first batch)	100	94,02	90,0	84,62

Required:
Use the tables given to determine the applicable learning curve based on the information you have about the StreetCafé product line.

First, we need to express the time it takes to manufacture the third unit as a percentage of the time it takes to manufacture the first unit:

195 hours/250 hours × 100
= 78%

The time taken to produce the third batch, expressed as a percentage of the time taken for the first batch, is 70,21 hours for an 80 per cent curve and 84,62 hours for a 90 per cent curve. The appropriate learning curve will therefore be:

[(78 hours – 70,21 hours)/(84,62 hours – 70,21 hours) × (90%-80%)] + 80%
= 85,4 per cent

If the cumulative average–time learning model is used, the relevant table provided and the cumulative average time for three units given, we would proceed in the

Chapter 3 *Cost estimation*

same way. If the total time to manufacture three units is given, we would first need to calculate the cumulative average time and then continue as above.

The mathematical approach

In the mathematical approach, the following mathematical formula is used:

$$y = ax^b$$

where:
y = cumulative average time per unit (cumulative average–time learning model)
    OR time taken to produce the last unit (incremental unit–time learning model)
x = cumulative number of units produced
a = time taken to produce the first unit
$b = \dfrac{\log (\text{learning rate})}{\log (2)}$

As this approach can always be used (provided that the values for all but one variable are given or that the information for two formulas for all but two variables is given), it is the one most commonly used. Its main advantage is that its application is not limited to a doubling of units or to the cumulative units given in a table. Although you may often need to use this approach to solve problems, it may sometimes be quicker to use one of the first two approaches, if possible.

The formula can appear quite intimidating, especially because of its use of logarithms ('logs'). In appendix example 3.7 below, we show the log calculations to determine variable 'b' in the equation for the sake of completeness. However, in exam questions the value of 'b', which is also known as the learning curve index, will often be given.

Appendix example 3.7 shows how to estimate the various times given a cumulative average–time learning model and an incremental unit–time learning model.

Appendix example 3.7

ShadeConcepts' original umbrella was known as the ShadeMaster. Five years ago, when it was launched, it took 300 minutes to produce the first ShadeMaster and the applicable learning rate was 85 per cent. The organisation did not keep detailed records of how long it took to produce any subsequent units, or of the type of learning model applicable.

Required:
Calculate the additional time it probably took to produce the xth ShadeMaster, the cumulative total time to produce all ShadeMasters, and the cumulative average time per ShadeMaster, if the:
a) Incremental unit–time learning model applied
b) Cumulative average–time learning model applied.

Perform this calculation when a total of 1 to 16 ShadeMasters is produced (and therefore for the cumulative number of ShadeMasters of 1,2,3,...,16).

Exhibit 3.3 summarises the results if an incremental unit–time learning model was applicable. The time for the xth unit is obtained by using the formula. For example, for the second unit it would be:

$y = 300 \text{ minutes} \times 2^{[\log(0.85)/\log(2)]}$
  $= 255 \text{ minutes}$

principles of management accounting

Note that this answer can also be obtained by multiplying 300 minutes by 85 per cent. This is possible only because two is a doubling of units. The same would be applicable for the fourth unit (255 minutes × 85% or 300 minutes × $(0,85)^2$), but for the third unit we need to use the formula ($y = 300$ minutes × $3^{[\log(0,85)/\log(2)]}$).

Once this value is calculated for each of the cumulative number of units (x-values), it is easy to calculate the cumulative total time it takes to produce x units. The individual time for each of the units is added. It would therefore take 786,87 minutes (300 minutes + 255 minutes + 231,87 minutes) to produce three units.

Lastly, we can calculate the cumulative average time per unit, when x units were produced. The cumulative total time for x units (column 3) is divided by the cumulative number of units (x) (column 1). For example, it would have taken an average of 206,11 minutes (2 473,33 minutes/12) to produce each unit if a total of 12 units had been produced.

Exhibit 3.3 Incremental unit–time learning model

Cumulative number of units	Time for xth unit (in minutes)	Cumulative total time (in minutes)	Cumulative average time per unit (in minutes)
x	y		
(1)	(2)	(3)	(4) = (3)/(1)
1	300,00	300,00	300,00
2	255,00	555,00	277,50
3	231,87	786,87	262,29
4	216,75	1 003,62	250,91
5	205,70	1 209,33	241,87
6	197,09	1 406,42	234,40
7	190,10	1 596,52	228,07
8	184,24	1 780,75	222,59
9	179,22	1 959,97	217,77
10	174,85	2 134,82	213,48
11	170,98	2 305,80	209,62
12	167,53	2 473,33	206,11
13	164,41	2 637,74	202,90
14	161,58	2 799,33	199,95
15	158,99	2 958,32	197,22
16	156,60	3 114,92	194,68

Exhibit 3.4 summarises the results when the cumulative average–time model is applicable. The cumulative average time per unit is obtained by using the formula. For example, for two ShadeMasters it would be:

$y = 300$ minutes × $2^{[\log(0,85)/\log(2)]}$
$= 255$ minutes

Note that this answer can also be obtained by multiplying 300 minutes by 85 per cent. This is possible only because two is a doubling of units. The same would be applicable for four units (255 minutes × 85% or 300 minutes × $(0,85)^2$), but for three units we need to use the formula ($y = 300$ minutes × $3^{[\log(0,85)/\log(2)]}$).

Once this value is calculated for each of the cumulative number of units (x-values), it is easy to calculate the cumulative total time it takes to produce x units. The cumulative average time (column 2) is simply multiplied by the cumulative number of units (column 1). For example, for 5 units it would be:

205,7 minutes × 5 units
= 1 028,5 minutes

Lastly, we can calculate the additional time it takes to produce the xth unit. The cumulative total time for $x - 1$ units is subtracted from the cumulative total time for x units. To ascertain the time it would take to produce the 16th unit, we need to subtract 2 384,84 minutes (for 15 units) from 2 505,63 minutes (for 16 units) = 120,79 minutes.

Exhibit 3.4 Cumulative average–time learning model

Cumulative number of units	Cumulative average time per unit (in minutes)	Cumulative total time (in minutes)	Time for xth unit (in minutes)
x	y		
(1)	(2)	(3) = (1) × (2)	(4)
1	300,00	300,00	300,00
2	255,00	510,00	210,00
3	231,87	695,62	185,62
4	216,75	867,00	171,38
5	205,70	1 028,51	161,51
6	197,09	1 182,56	154,05
7	190,10	1 330,68	148,12
8	184,24	1 473,90	143,22
9	179,22	1 612,97	139,07
10	174,85	1 748,46	135,49
11	170,98	1 880,80	132,34
12	167,53	2 010,35	129,55
13	164,41	2 137,39	127,04
14	161,58	2 262,15	124,76
15	158,99	2 384,84	122,69
16	156,60	2 505,63	120,79

In appendix example 3.7, the learning curve index could have been given. In other words, the value of log [0,85]/log [2], which is –0,2345, could have been supplied as part of the question.

The mathematical approach can also be used to calculate the learning rate, the time taken to produce the first unit, or the cumulative number of units produced. The formula is simply solved for the required variable. Calculating the learning rate by using the mathematical approach is demonstrated in appendix example 3.8.

principles of management accounting

Appendix example 3.8

It takes 15 hours to produce the first unit and a total of 1 965,81 minutes to produce five units. It was found that a cumulative average–time learning model best describes the learning process.

Required:
Calculate the learning rate.

First of all, we need to ensure that we have all the necessary inputs for the formula. x is 5 units and a equals 15 hours. y needs to be calculated, by dividing 1 965,81 by 5 units. The resulting cumulative average time per unit is given in minutes, and must therefore be converted to hours by dividing by 60:

393,16 minutes/60 minutes per hour
= 6,55 hours

The formula must now be solved for b. By dividing by a, then taking the logarithm and finally dividing by $\log(x)$, we obtain the following formula:

$$b = \frac{\log(y/a)}{\log(x)}$$

For our example, the values are:

$$\frac{\log(6{,}55/15)}{\log(5)}$$

= –0,514829 (or –0,514573 if 6,55 hours is not rounded)

We now know b, which is:

$$\frac{\log(\text{learning rate})}{\log(2)}$$

= –0,514829.

So:

$$\log(\text{learning rate}) = b \times \log(2)$$

To find the learning rate we now need to perform the reverse operation of using the logarithm, which is to raise the term to the base 10. The base 10 and the logarithm on the left hand side of the equals sign in the equation directly above this paragraph will cancel each other out.

Therefore the learning rate:

$= 10^{b \times \log(2)}$
$= 10^{(-0{,}514829) \times \log(2)}$
$= 0{,}6999$
$\approx 0{,}70$

The applicable learning rate is therefore 70 per cent. It is important to note that it is necessary to keep as many decimal places as possible to ensure an accurate result.

Chapter 3 Cost estimation

> Note:
> Management accounting students may sometimes use financial calculators that do not have the 'log' function. However, most will have the 'ln' function and you can use 'ln' instead of 'log' if necessary. The mathematical equation $y = ax^b$ that is used in this chapter can be restated as $\ln y = \ln a + b \times \ln x$.
>
> If you were to use this restated formula in appendix example 3.8, you would end up with the equation:
>
> $b = \ln$ learning rate/$\ln 2$
>
> Therefore:
>
> $-0{,}514829 = \ln$ learning rate/$\ln 2$
>
> and
>
> $0{,}356852 = \ln$ learning rate
>
> Now look for the calculator function e^x, and apply it to 0,356852. The answer is 0,6999, which again indicates a learning rate of 70 per cent.

Basic questions

BQ 1

Source: Adapted from ACCA Paper 1.2

The following statements relate to the calculation of the regression line $y = a + bx$. Using the information in the formula below:

$$b = \frac{n(\text{sum}(xy)) - (\text{sum}x)(\text{sum}y)}{n(\text{sum}x^2) - (\text{sum}x)^2}$$

i) Sum(xy) is calculated by multiplying the sum of x by the sum of y.
ii) (Sum(x^2)) is not the same as (sum(x))^2.
iii) n represents the number of pairs of data items used.

Which statements are correct?
a) (i) and (ii) only
b) (i) and (iii) only
c) (ii) and (iii) only
d) (i), (ii) and (iii)

BQ 2

Source: Adapted from ACCA Paper 1.2

Which of the following correlation coefficients indicates the weakest relationship between two variables?
a) +0,9
b) −0,6
c) −0,8
d) −1,0

67

BQ 3

Source: Adapted from ACCA Paper 1.2

Regression analysis is being used to find the line of best fit ($y = a + bx$) from five pairs of data. The calculations have produced the following information:

Sum(x) = 129
Sum(y) = 890
Sum(xy) = 23,091
Sum(x^2) = 3,433
Sum(y^2) = 29,929

What is the value of a in the equation for the line of best fit (to the nearest whole number)?

a) 146
b) 152
c) 210
d) 245

BQ 4

Source: Adapted from ACCA Paper 1.2

Which of the following is a feasible value for a correlation coefficient?

a) +1,2
b) 0
c) –1,2
d) –2,0

BQ 5

Source: Adapted from ACCA Paper 1.2

The following statements relate to the calculation of the regression line $y = a + bx$, using the information in the formulae below:

i) n represents the number of pairs of data items used
ii) $(\Sigma x)^2$ is calculated by multiplying Σx by Σx
iii) Σxy is calculated by multiplying Σx by Σy

Formulae:

$$a = \frac{\Sigma y}{n} - \frac{b \Sigma x}{n}$$

$$b = \frac{n\Sigma xy - \Sigma x \Sigma y}{n\Sigma x^2 - (\Sigma x)^2}$$

$$r = \frac{n\Sigma xy - \Sigma x \Sigma y}{\sqrt{(n\Sigma x^2 - (\Sigma x)^2)(n\Sigma y^2 - (\Sigma y)^2)}}$$

Which statements are correct?

a) (i) and (ii) only
b) (i) and (iii) only
c) (ii) and (iii) only
d) (i), (ii) and (iii)

BQ 6

Source: Adapted from ACCA Paper 1.2

The correlation coefficient (r) for measuring the connection between two variables (x and y) has been calculated as 0,6.

How much of the variation in the dependent variable (*y*) is explained by the variation in the independent variable (*x*)?
a) 36%
b) 40%
c) 60%
d) 64%

BQ 7
Source: UCT (Carol Cairney)

For what purpose is the so-called 'high-low method' commonly used?

BQ 8
Source: UCT (Carol Cairney)

What does the *r*-squared (r^2) value mean in the context of a regression model?

BQ 9
Source: Adapted from CIMA P2

PT has discovered that when it employs a new test engineer, there is a learning curve with a 75 per cent learning rate that exists for the first 12 customer assignments. A new test engineer completed her first customer assignment in 6 hours. A cumulative average–time learning curve model applies.

How long should she take for her seventh assignment, to the nearest 0,01 hours?

Note: The index for a 75 per cent learning curve is –0,415.

BQ 10
Source: Adapted from CIMA P2

FH is an electronics company that has developed a new product for the video conferencing market. The product has successfully completed its testing phase and FH has now produced the first four production units. The first unit took 3 hours of labour time and the total time for the first four units was 8,3667 hours. A cumulative average–time learning curve model applies.

What is the learning curve improvement rate (learning rate), to the nearest 0,1%?

Long questions

LQ 1 – Intermediate (11 marks; 20 minutes)
Source: Adapted from CIMA Paper 3C

Each year, a large organisation which manufactures domestic electrical appliances pays its employees an annual bonus. The head accountant wishes to assess the effect of the previous year's bonus on the organisation's output for the following year.

principles of management accounting

Data relating to bonus paid (*as a percentage of annual salary*) and total output (*tens of thousands of units sold*) over an 8-year period are given in the following table:

Previous year's bonus (%)	0	1	2	3	4	5	6	7
Following year's output ('0000s)	3	6	14	15	20	18	24	25

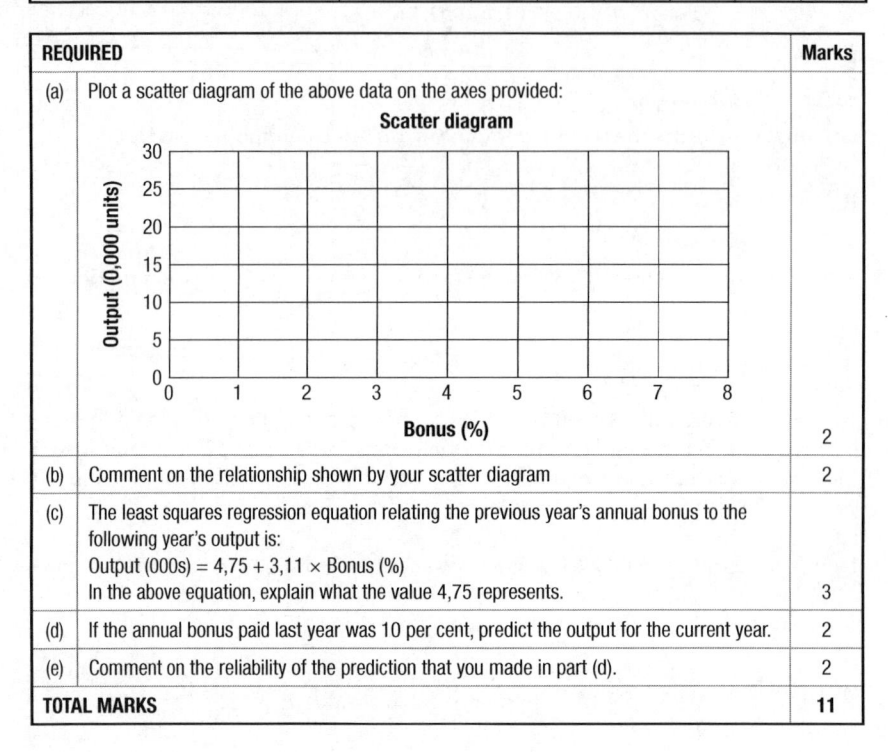

REQUIRED		Marks
(a)	Plot a scatter diagram of the above data on the axes provided: **Scatter diagram** [Graph with Output (0,000 units) on y-axis ranging 0 to 30, and Bonus (%) on x-axis ranging 0 to 8]	2
(b)	Comment on the relationship shown by your scatter diagram	2
(c)	The least squares regression equation relating the previous year's annual bonus to the following year's output is: Output (000s) = 4,75 + 3,11 × Bonus (%) In the above equation, explain what the value 4,75 represents.	3
(d)	If the annual bonus paid last year was 10 per cent, predict the output for the current year.	2
(e)	Comment on the reliability of the prediction that you made in part (d).	2
TOTAL MARKS		**11**

LQ 2 – Intermediate (10 marks; 18 minutes)

Source: Adapted from ACCA Paper 1.2

An organisation is seeking to establish whether there is a linear relationship between the level of advertising expenditure and the subsequent sales revenue generated.

Figures for the last eight months are as follows:

Month	Advertising expenditure	Sales revenue
	R'000	R'000
1	2,65	30,0
2	4,25	45,0
3	1,00	17,5
4	5,25	46,0
5	4,75	44,5
6	1,95	25,0
7	3,50	43,0
8	3,00	38,5
Total	26,35	289,5

Further information is available as follows:
∑ (Advertising expenditure × Sales revenue) = R1 055,875
∑ (Advertising expenditure)² = R101,2625
∑ (Sales revenue)² = R11 283,75

All of the above are given in Rmillion.

REQUIRED		Marks
(a)	On a suitable graph plot advertising expenditure against sales revenue or vice versa, as appropriate. Explain your choice of axes.	5
(b)	Using regression analysis, calculate a line of best fit. Plot this on your graph from (a).	5
TOTAL MARKS		**10**

LQ 3 – Advanced (10 marks; 18 minutes)

Source: Adapted from ACCA Paper 1.2

The management accountant at Josephine Ltd is trying to predict the quarterly total maintenance cost for a group of similar machines. She has extracted the following information for the last eight quarters:

Quarter number	1	2	3	4	5	6	7	8
Total maintenance cost (R'000)	265	302	222	240	362	295	404	400
Production units (000s)	20	24	16	18	26	22	32	30

The effects of inflation have been eliminated from the above costs.

The management accountant is using linear regression to establish an equation of the form $y = a + bx$ and has produced the following preliminary calculations:

∑ (total maintenance cost × production units)	=	R61 250m
∑ (total maintenance cost)²	=	R809 598m
∑ (production units)²	=	4 640m

REQUIRED		Marks
(a)	Establish the equation which will allow the management accountant to predict quarterly total maintenance costs for a given level of production. Interpret your answer in terms of fixed and variable maintenance costs.	7
(b)	Using the equation established in (a), predict the total maintenance cost for the next quarter when planned production is 44 000 units. Suggest a major reservation, other than the effect of inflation, that you would have about this prediction.	3
TOTAL MARKS		**10**

LQ 4 – Advanced (10 marks; 18 minutes)

Source: Adapted from CIMA P2

AVX CC assembles circuit boards for use by high technology audio video companies. Because of the rapidly advancing technology in this field, AVX CC is constantly being challenged to learn new techniques.

principles of management accounting

AVX CC uses standard costing to control its costs against targets set by senior managers. The standard labour cost per batch of one particular type of circuit board (CB45) is set out below:

Direct labour – 50 hours @ R10/hour = R500

The following labour efficiency variances arose during the first six months of the assembly of CB45:

Month	Number of batches assembled and sold	Labour efficiency variance (R)
November	1	Nil
December	1	170,00 Favourable
January	2	452,20 Favourable
February	4	1 090,65 Favourable
March	8	1 712,85 Favourable
April	16	3 425,70 Favourable

An investigation has confirmed that all of the costs were as expected except that there was a learning effect in respect of the direct labour that had not been anticipated when the standard cost was set.

REQUIRED		Marks
(a)	Calculate the monthly learning rates that applied during the six months.	6
(b)	Identify when the learning period ended and briefly discuss the implications of your findings for AVX CC.	4
Note: A cumulative average–time learning curve model applies.		
TOTAL MARKS		10

LQ 5 – Advanced (10 marks; 18 minutes)

Source: Adapted from CIMA P2

An organisation was planning to launch a new product. It had already carried out market research at a cost of R50 000 and as a result had discovered that the market price for the product should be R50 per unit. The organisation estimated that 80 000 units of the product could be sold at this price before one of the organisation's competitors entered the market with a superior product. At this time, any unsold units of the organisation's product would be of no value.

The organisation estimated the costs of the initial batch of the product as follows:

	R'000
Direct materials	200
Direct labour (R10 per hour)	250
Other direct costs	100

Production was planned to occur in batches of 10 000 units and it was expected that an 80 per cent learning curve would apply to the direct labour until the fourth batch was complete. Thereafter the direct labour cost per batch was expected to be constant. No changes to the direct labour rate per hour were expected.

The organisation introduced the product at the price stated above, with production occurring in batches of 10 000 units. Direct labour was paid using the expected hourly rate of R10, and the organisation began to review the profitability of the product.

The following schedule shows the actual direct labour cost recorded:

Cumulative number of batches	Actual cumulative direct labour cost
	R'000
1	280
2	476
4	809
8	1 376

REQUIRED		Marks
(a)	Calculate the revised expected cumulative direct labour costs for the four levels of output given the actual cost of R280 000 for the first batch.	4
(b)	Calculate the actual learning rate exhibited at each level of output.	3
(c)	Discuss the implications of your answers to (a) and (b) for the managers of the organisation.	3
TOTAL MARKS		10

References

MultiChoice South Africa Holdings (Proprietary) Limited. 2010. *Chairman's review. 2010 annual report to the shareholders of Phuthuma Nathi Investments Ltd*.

Cost-volume-profit relationships

chapter 4

John Williams

LEARNING OBJECTIVES

By the end of this chapter, you should be able to:
1. Discuss the purpose and usefulness of cost-volume-profit (CVP) analysis.
2. Explain how changes in activity levels, variable costs, fixed costs and selling price impact on an organisation's contribution margin and profit.
3. Understand the main differences between the economist's and accountant's model of CVP analysis.
4. Calculate the break-even point using the profit formula, the contribution margin formula, or a break-even chart.
5. Apply CVP analysis to a number of 'what if' scenarios.
6. Apply CVP analysis to multiple products and services and explain the impact that a change in the sales mix has on an organisation's contribution margin and profit.
7. Explain the limitations of CVP analysis.

SAA and cost-volume-profit relationships

The following statements were made by the chairperson of *South African Airways (SAA)* in the organisation's 2010 *Annual Report*:

> 'The global aviation industry endured what proved to be an exceptionally tough year ... Declining passenger numbers and a slow recovery from the effects of the global economic crisis posed serious challenges for all airlines. Despite these challenges, SAA managed to record positive financial results ... Prevailing market trends during the reporting period included dwindling passenger numbers, and a marked shift from premium to low-cost travel.'
>
> SOURCE: SAA 2010

Cost-volume-profit (CVP) analysis considers relationships between costs, volumes and profit. CVP analysis can be applied to answer many questions, such as:
- How many flight tickets does SAA need to sell to ensure that it does not make a loss?
- If the shift from premium air travel (as offered by SAA) to low cost air travel (as offered by SAA's low-cost competitors) continues, by how much can ticket sales drop before SAA makes a loss?
- What selling price per ticket does SAA need to charge to make a R900 million profit?
- If a five per cent decrease in the price per ticket is expected to increase sales volume by ten per cent, should such a price decrease be considered?
- Should a new model of aeroplane be purchased if it results in a reduction in fuel costs?

4.1 Introduction

Key term: cost-volume-profit ('CVP') analysis

This chapter explores how cost behaviour, production levels and sales volumes impact an organisation's profit. The interrelationship between activity levels, costs and an organisation's profits is commonly referred to as **cost-volume-profit ('CVP') analysis**.

4.2 CVP analysis – the accountant's and economist's models

Key terms: accountant's model, economist's model, relevant range

There are two main models for conducting CVP analysis – the **economist's model** and the **accountant's model**.

The economist's model recognises that the rate of change in total costs and total revenue is unlikely to remain constant as volumes change. This is illustrated in Figure 4.1 below. At low levels of activity it may not be possible to operate a production plant efficiently, resulting in total costs rising steeply. As production increases, it is possible to take advantage of production efficiencies, resulting in total costs rising less steeply. Once the level of activity exceeds the optimum production level for which a plant was designed, bottlenecks start occurring, plant breakdowns occur, and production schedules become more complex. This results in total costs rising more steeply once again.

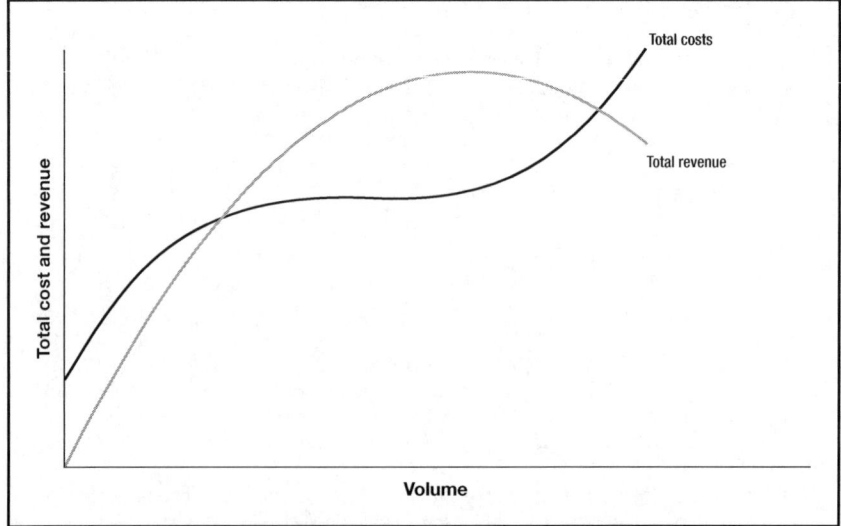

Figure 4.1 Economist's cost-volume graph

The economist's model also recognises that initially small reductions in selling price result in relatively large increases in sales volumes. However, as volumes increase, larger price reductions are required to increase sales volumes, and eventually the loss of revenue owing to price reductions exceeds that gained from increased volumes. As is the case with the relationship between production volume and total costs, it is unlikely that there will be a linear relationship between sales volume and total sales revenue. The relationship is more likely to be curvilinear.

The most significant difference between the economist's and accountant's model is the assumption underpinning the accountant's model that as volumes increase, the rate of change in both total revenue and total costs is constant (also known as a linear or straight line relationship). The accountant's model is illustrated in Figure 4.2 below.

Figure 4.2 Accountant's cost-volume graph

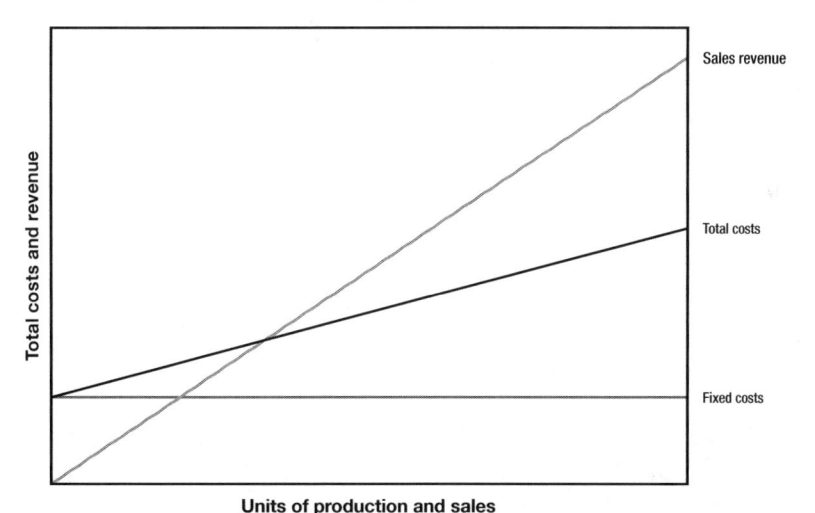

The effect of the linearity assumption on total revenue is that the selling price per unit remains fixed. In other words, the selling price per unit does not change with a change in the sales volume. The effect of the assumption on fixed costs is that total fixed costs remain the same regardless of the level of output. Total costs consist of both variable and fixed costs. We know from Chapter 2, *Cost classification* that total variable costs change in proportion to the change in levels of activity. Since we have now seen that with the accountant's model, total fixed costs remain constant and variable costs per unit remain constant, unlike total costs under the economist's model, total costs under the accountant's model have a linear relationship with levels of activity.

As a result of the linearity assumption, the accountant's model is unlikely to provide perfectly accurate results across all possible ranges of activity – selling prices may not remain fixed. For example, SAA has had to reduce the price of its domestic flights owing to new 'low cost' airlines entering into the market. It is also more likely that fixed costs will not remain fixed over all ranges of activity, but will rather increase in a stepwise manner (refer to Chapter 2 for a more detailed explanation of step costs) as output increases. If SAA needed to increase their fleet of aircraft significantly so that they could increase the number of flights, it is likely that they would also need to increase the number of aeronautical engineers that they employed to service and maintain their aircrafts. The increase in the number of aircraft and aeronautical engineers would result in an immediate increase in fixed costs, which would then remain constant until the next significant change in operating activity. The stepwise increase in fixed costs is illustrated as part of

Figure 4.3. Conversely, if SAA experienced a significant reduction in ticket sales and then reduced the size of their fleet, it is likely that there would be a number of redundancies, which would result in an immediate drop in fixed costs.

Since the accountant's model is unlikely to provide perfectly accurate results across all possible ranges of activity, one may be tempted to discard this model in preference for the economist's model. However, the accountant's model is simpler and easier to apply. To overcome the problem of a lack of linearity across all possible ranges of activity and therefore be able to apply the accountant's model with reasonable accuracy, the **relevant range** over which the model can be applied is identified for each scenario being considered. You may recall from Chapter 2 that the relevant range defines the range of activity over which the assumptions made concerning the behaviour of costs and revenue remain valid. The relevant range is illustrated in Figure 4.3 below.

Figure 4.3 Relevant range

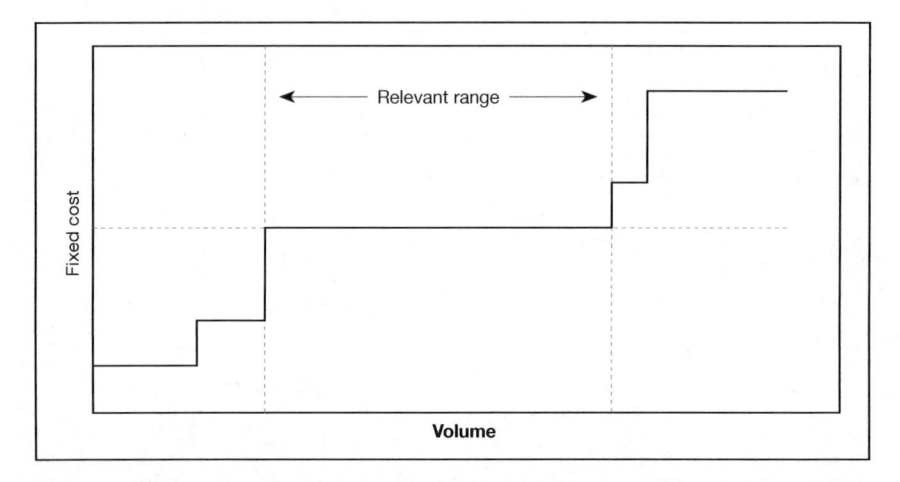

It is important to remember that if the level of output being considered falls outside this relevant range, the results obtained from the CVP analysis may not be accurate, and caution should be exercised in interpreting the results. Identifying the relevant range over which fixed costs remain constant also eliminates the difficulty of accounting for stepped fixed costs.

4.2.1 Variable versus absorption costing systems

You will see in Chapter 5, *Absorption versus variable costing* and Chapter 10, *Relevant costs for decision-making* that fixed costs are often irrelevant for short-term decision-making, and that variable costing systems isolate fixed and variable costs, treating all fixed costs as period costs. Since CVP analysis is a decision-making tool, it is useful to adopt a variable costing approach when performing CVP analysis.

You will see in Chapter 5 that when calculating profits using an absorption costing system, fixed manufacturing overheads are treated as a product cost, resulting in a portion of these overheads being included in inventory balances. The impact of this is that where the levels of production and sales differ, there will be a change in the inventory balance that will impact on the profit reported. This will distort the CVP analysis. In variable costing systems all fixed costs are treated as period costs, and no fixed manufacturing overheads are included in inventory balances. Differences between the level of production and sales will therefore not have an impact on profit, which is ideal for CVP analysis.

4.3 Break-even analysis

Key terms: break-even point, contribution

The most common application of CVP analysis is to perform a break-even analysis. The **break-even point** represents the level of activity where neither a profit nor a loss is made. In other words, this is the level of activity where total sales revenue equals total costs. There are three methods that can be applied to calculate the break-even point:
- The profit formula
- The contribution margin formula
- The break-even chart.

4.3.1 Profit formula

Simplistically stated, the profit made by an organisation in a period is calculated as the difference between total revenue and total costs. Total revenue and total costs are dependent on the number of units of products sold or services delivered, because CVP analysis assumes that volume is the only revenue and cost driver. Adopting a variable costing approach, the total costs incurred are split between fixed and variable costs. It is therefore possible to derive the following profit formula which forms the basis of all CVP analysis:

$$P = SPx - (FC + VCx)$$

In the above formula:
- P = profit
- SP = selling price per unit
- x = number of units sold
- FC = total fixed costs per annum
- VC = variable costs per unit.

Example 4.1

You are considering opening a new business selling lawnmowers. Currently you are considering selling only one make of lawnmower that you believe is the most popular. You have estimated that annual fixed costs will be R750 000, that variable costs will be R1 000 per unit, and that you could sell the lawnmowers for R2 500 each.

Required:
Using the profit formula, calculate:
1. The number of lawnmowers that must be sold to break even
2. The total sales value at the break-even point.

We can use the profit formula, $P = SPx - (FC + VCx)$, to calculate the number of lawnmowers that must be sold to break even. We know that an organisation breaks even when it makes neither a profit nor a loss, and P is therefore 0. From the information given in the question, the selling price (SP) is R2 500, fixed costs (FC) are R750 000 per annum, and variable costs (VC) are R1 000 per unit. Substituting these variables into the profit formula, it is possible to calculate the number of break-even units (x) as follows:

principles of management accounting

$$0 = 2\,500x - (750\,000 + 1\,000x)$$
$$0 = 2\,500x - 750\,000 - 1\,000x$$
$$1\,500x = 750\,000$$
$$x = 500$$

Therefore 500 lawnmowers must be sold in order to break even. The selling price of each lawnmower is R2 500 and since 500 lawnmowers must be sold, the total sales value at the break-even point is R1 250 000.

4.3.2 Contribution margin formula

> The term 'contribution' comes from 'contribute'. It is calculated as selling price less variable costs, and indicates how much each unit contributes towards covering fixed costs and making a profit.

An alternative method for calculating the break-even point is to use what is called the contribution margin approach. **Contribution** is calculated as the selling price less variable costs. Therefore, when the total contribution equals total fixed costs, the break-even point has been reached. The contribution margin formula is therefore expressed as:

$$\text{Break-even units} = \frac{\text{total fixed costs}}{\text{contribution per unit}}$$

or alternatively

$$\text{Break-even sales revenue} = \frac{\text{total fixed costs}}{\text{contribution margin ratio}}$$

$$\text{where the contribution margin ratio} = \frac{\text{contribution}}{\text{selling price}}$$

Example 4.2

Required:
The information is the same as in example 4.1. Calculate the break-even number of lawnmowers and break-even sales revenue using the contribution margin approach.

We are told that the total fixed costs are R750 000 per annum. We are not given what the contribution per unit is, but this can easily be calculated as:

Contribution per unit = selling price per unit − variable costs per unit
= R2 500 − R1 000
= R1 500

Substituting these values into the contribution margin formula, the number of lawnmowers that must be sold can be calculated as:

$$\text{Break-even number of lawnmowers} = \frac{\text{total fixed costs}}{\text{contribution per unit}}$$
$$= \frac{R750\,000}{R1\,500}$$
$$= 500 \text{ lawnmowers}$$

To calculate the break-even sales value, in addition to knowing what the total fixed costs are, we also need to know what the contribution margin ratio is. We have not been given the contribution margin ratio, but this ratio can be calculated as:

$$\text{Contribution margin ratio} = \frac{\text{contribution}}{\text{selling price}}$$

$$= \frac{\text{R1 500}}{\text{R2 500}} \text{ (calculated above)}$$

$$= 0{,}6$$

We can now calculate the break-even sales value as follows:

$$\text{Break-even sales value for lawnmowers} = \frac{\text{total fixed costs}}{\text{contribution margin ratio}}$$

$$= \frac{\text{R750 000}}{0{,}6}$$

$$= \text{R1 250 000}$$

This means that sales of R1 250 000 have to be achieved in order to break even.

4.3.3 Break-even chart

Key term: break-even chart

An additional approach that can be used to perform break-even analysis is to construct a **break-even chart**. The break-even chart depicts the break-even point graphically, and is therefore sometimes easier for non-financial managers to understand. The break-even chart for example 4.1 is shown below:

Figure 4.4 Break-even chart for example 4.1

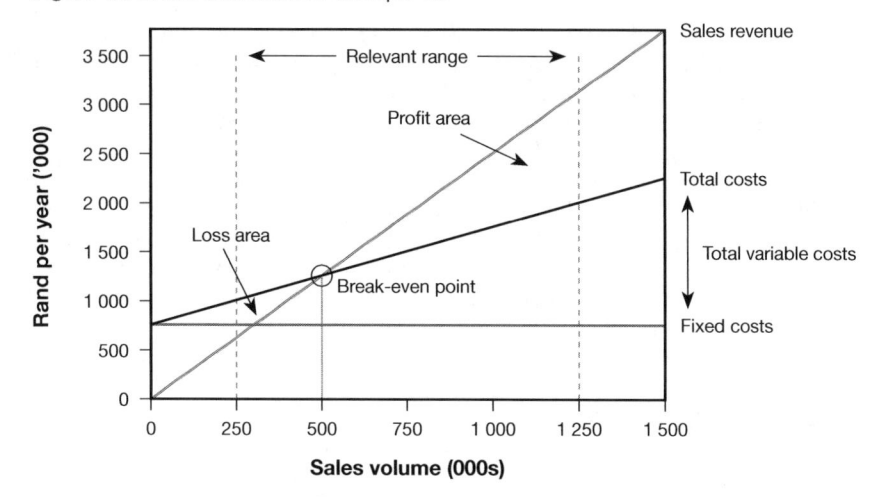

principles of management accounting

The vertical axis shows the rand values and the horizontal axis the output in units. From the graph you can see that three lines have been plotted: fixed costs, total costs and sales revenue. Since total fixed costs in terms of the accountant's model remain constant regardless of the levels of activity, the total fixed costs line remains parallel to the horizontal axis and meets the vertical axis at R750 000 (the amount of the fixed costs). Therefore, whether we sell no lawnmowers or 1 000 lawnmowers, we still expect the total fixed costs to remain at R750 000 per annum.

The total costs line can be plotted by determining what the total costs would be given any two activity levels. If no lawnmowers are sold, total costs comprise only the fixed costs of R750 000 per annum as there will be no variable costs (we therefore know that the total cost line will meet the vertical axis at R750 000, which is once again the amount of the fixed costs). Taking another activity level of, say, 1 500 lawnmowers, we can calculate the total costs as being R2 250 000 (R750 000 (fixed costs) + R1 500 000 (variable costs of R1 000 per lawnmower × 1 500 lawnmowers)). The total costs line can then be plotted by joining the two points: a sales volume of zero lawnmowers with a rand value of R750 000, and a sales volume of 1 500 lawnmowers with a rand value of R2 250 000.

Similarly, we can also plot the sales revenue line by determining what the sales revenue would be, given two activity levels. If no lawnmowers are sold, there is no sales revenue, and the sales revenue line meets the vertical axis at zero. If, say, 1 500 lawnmowers were sold, the sales revenue would be R3 750 000. Once again, the sales revenue line can be plotted by joining the two points: sales volume of zero lawnmowers with a rand value of zero, and a sales volume of 1 500 lawnmowers with a rand value of R3 750 000. It is also useful to depict the relevant range on the chart to serve as a reminder that outside of these activity levels, our assumption of linearity no longer applies, and our CVP analysis may no longer be accurate. The relevant range was not given in example 4.1, but a range of 250 to 1 250 lawnmowers has been assumed and indicated on the chart.

From the chart we can see that the break-even point is where the sales revenue line crosses the total costs line. By extending a vertical line from this point to the horizontal axis, we can see that the break-even point is 500 lawnmowers. Extending a horizontal line from the break-even point to the vertical axis reveals that the break-even point will result in sales amounting to R1 250 000.

The vertical distance (rand value) between the two lines to the right of the break-even point depicts the amount of profit that will be made for activity levels greater than the break-even number of lawnmowers, while the vertical distance (rand value) between the two lines to the left of the break-even point depicts the extent of losses that will be made for activity levels less than the break-even number of lawnmowers.

It is also possible to adapt the break-even chart to a profit-volume chart or a contribution chart that can then be used in the CVP analysis scenarios discussed in the remainder of this chapter. Constructing and interpreting the charts is, however, tedious and time consuming, and unless graphical representation of the scenarios is required, it is recommended that either the profit or the contribution margin formula be used for CVP analysis.

4.4 Sensitivity analysis

Key term: sensitivity analysis

In addition to being used in performing break-even calculations, CVP analysis can be a useful tool in performing **sensitivity analysis**. Sensitivity analysis indicates how sensitive one variable is to changes in another variable in the same model. In other words, 'what-if' questions are asked. This enables managers to assess the impact should any of the original variables within the CVP model change. This is useful in determining a range of possible outcomes, including an indication of the financial viability of alternative courses of action. Some of the more common forms of sensitivity analysis are illustrated in sections 4.4.1 to 4.4.5 below.

4.4.1 Amount of profit given a level of activity

Given an organisation's selling price, variable costs and fixed costs, it is possible to calculate the profit that will be made for any given level of activity within the relevant range. The calculations required are illustrated in example 4.3.

Example 4.3

Required:
Using the information given in example 4.1, calculate the profit that will be made if 750 lawnmowers are sold.

Using the profit formula $P = SPx - (FC + VCx)$, we know that in this scenario 750 units have been sold (x), the selling price (SP) is R2 500, fixed costs per annum (FC) are R750 000, and variable costs (VC) are R1 000. We can now calculate the profit that will be made (P) by substituting these values into the formula:

$$P = 2\,500 \times 750 - (750\,000 + 1\,000 \times 750)$$
$$= 1\,875\,000 - 750\,000 - 750\,000$$
$$= 375\,000$$

Therefore a profit of R375 000 will be achieved if 750 lawnmowers are sold.

It is also possible to calculate the profit that will be made by manipulating the contribution margin formula. The original formula was:

$$\text{Break-even units} = \frac{\text{total fixed costs}}{\text{contribution per unit}}$$

This is manipulated to:

$$\text{Units sold} = \frac{\text{total fixed costs + profit}}{\text{contribution per unit}}$$

The profit that will be made if 750 lawnmowers are sold can then be calculated as:

$$750 = \frac{750\,000 + P}{(2\,500 - 1\,000)}$$
$$750 = \frac{750\,000 + P}{1\,500}$$
$$750 \times 1\,500 = 750\,000 + P$$
$$1\,125\,000 - 750\,000 = P$$
$$P = 375\,000$$

This is the same as the profit calculated using the profit formula.

principles of management accounting

4.4.2 Target profits

Managers may have a specific target profit in mind that they want to achieve. CVP analysis can be used to calculate:
- The number of units of a product or service that must be sold to reach the target profit given the selling price per unit
- The selling price that must be charged to reach the target profit given the quantity of units that can be sold.

This form of CVP analysis is illustrated in example 4.4.

Example 4.4

Required:
Using the information given in example 4.1, calculate:
1. The number of lawnmowers that must be sold to achieve a profit of R150 000 (assuming that the selling price remains R2 500 per lawnmower)
2. The revised selling price that must be charged for each lawnmower if 750 lawnmowers are sold and a target profit of R450 000 is to be achieved.

Using the profit formula $P = SPx - (FC + VCx)$, we know that in this scenario P is the target profit of R150 000, the selling price (SP) is R2 500, fixed costs (FC) are R750 000, and variable costs are R1 000. Substituting these values into the formula, the required number of lawnmowers that must be sold is:

$$150\,000 = 2\,500x - (750\,000 + 1\,000x)$$
$$150\,000 = 2\,500x - 750\,000 - 1\,000x$$
$$1\,500x = 900\,000$$
$$x = 600$$

Therefore 600 lawnmowers must be sold to achieve a profit of R150 000.

The revised selling price that must be charged for each lawnmower if 750 lawnmowers are sold and a target profit of R450 000 is to be achieved can once again be calculated using the profit formula. In this scenario P is R450 000, the number of units sold (x) is 750, and fixed costs (FC) of R750 000 and variable costs (VC) of R1 000 remain unchanged. We can now calculate the selling price (SP) required as follows:

$$450\,000 = SP \times 750 - (750\,000 + 1\,000 \times 750)$$
$$450\,000 = 750SP - 750\,000 - 750\,000$$
$$750SP = 1\,950\,000$$
$$SP = 2\,600$$

Therefore a selling price of R2 600 per lawnmower must be charged to ensure that a target profit of R450 000 is reached on the sale of 750 lawnmowers.

The contribution margin formula can easily be manipulated so that it can be used to calculate the number of units that must be sold to achieve a target profit. Instead of needing to meet only the fixed costs with the contribution made, both the fixed costs and target profit must be covered by the contribution made.

In other words, the target profit is treated as if it is a fixed cost. The contribution margin formula is therefore adapted to:

$$\text{Target units} = \frac{\text{total fixed costs} + \text{target profit}}{\text{contribution per unit}}$$

The application of this adapted contribution margin formula is illustrated in example 4.5.

Example 4.5

Required:
With the information given in example 4.1, calculate the number of lawnmowers that must be sold to achieve a profit of R150 000 using the adapted contribution margin formula.

We know from example 4.1 that fixed costs per annum are R750 000, and in example 4.2 we calculated that the contribution per unit was R1 500. A target profit of R150 000 has been given for this scenario. Substituting these values into the adapted contribution margin formula, the number of units that must be sold to obtain a target profit of R150 000 can be calculated as follows:

$$\text{Target units} = \frac{\text{total fixed costs} + \text{target profit}}{\text{contribution per unit}}$$

$$= \frac{R750\ 000 + R150\ 000}{R1\ 500}$$

$$= 600 \text{ units}$$

Therefore 600 lawnmowers must be sold to achieve a profit of R150 000. This is the same answer we arrived at using the profit formula.

The contribution margin formula can also be manipulated to calculate the selling price required to achieve a target profit, given the number of units that can be sold. The manipulation required is, however, cumbersome, and the profit formula is therefore quicker.

4.4.3 Margin of safety

Key term: margin of safety

The **margin of safety** is a measure of the extent to which the current (or expected) level of sales can drop before a loss is incurred. The margin of safety can be useful to managers when they need to consider the impact of new competition, where there is a reduction in demand for products, or where there is uncertainty surrounding the exact level of expected sales, for example, when introducing a new product onto the market.

The margin of safety can be calculated as a percentage, as a total sales value, or in terms of the number of units of the product or service. The formulae for calculating the margin of safety are given below, but if you can remember that the margin of safety is simply the difference between expected sales and break-even sales, then it is not necessary to memorise these formulae.

principles of management accounting

$$\text{Margin of safety (percentage)} = \frac{\text{current sales} - \text{break-even sales}}{\text{current sales}} \times 100$$

Margin of safety (units) = current sales volume – break-even sales volume

Margin of safety (sales value) = current sales – break-even sales

OR

Margin of safety (sales value) = margin of safety units × selling price per unit

Note: These formulae can be used for calculating the margin of safety only in scenarios where there is only one product being sold or service being delivered. Multiple products and services are dealt with later in this chapter.

Example 4.6

In addition to the information given in example 4.1, assume that during the first year you expect to sell 750 lawnmowers.

Required:
Calculate:
1 The percentage by which expected sales could drop before a loss is incurred
2 The number of units by which expected sales could drop before a loss is incurred
3 The value by which expected sales could drop before a loss is incurred.

The percentage, number of units and value by which expected sales could drop before a loss is incurred is the margin of safety. The expected level of sales is 750 lawnmowers, and in example 4.1 we calculated that the break-even level of sales was 500 lawnmowers. The margin of safety, expressed as a percentage, can be calculated as:

$$\text{Margin of safety percentage} = \frac{750 - 500}{750} \times 100$$
$$= 33{,}3\%$$

Expected sales could therefore drop by 33,3 per cent before a loss would be incurred.

The number of units by which expected sales could drop before a loss would be incurred is simply the difference between the expected number of units and the break-even number of units. Expected sales could therefore drop by 250 lawnmowers (750 expected units – 500 break-even units) before a loss would be incurred.

Expected sales could drop by R625 000 before a loss was incurred. This is calculated by multiplying the margin of safety units of 250 by the selling price of R2 500. It could also be calculated as R1 875 000 (750 × 2 500 expected sales) – R1 250 000 (break-even sales computed above) = R 625 000.

4.4.4 Additional sales volume required to cover additional costs

Situations may arise where additional fixed costs per annum may be incurred. For example, an organisation may implement an advertising campaign to increase sales volumes. It is useful to use CVP analysis to calculate the additional sales volume required to cover the increased fixed costs per annum arising from the cost of the advertising campaign, in order to determine whether incurring the increased costs is warranted.

Example 4.7

In addition to the information given in example 4.1, you are now considering moving to larger premises. This would result in an increase of R60 000 per year in the fixed rental payable.

Required:
Calculate the additional number of lawnmowers that must be sold to cover the additional rental costs.

Either the profit or the contribution formula can be used in example 4.7 to calculate the additional number of lawnmowers which must be sold. Note that we are concerned only with the additional lawnmowers that need to be sold to cover the additional fixed costs that will be incurred. A profit (P) of zero is therefore chosen, and only the additional fixed costs (FC) of R60 000 are relevant, not the total fixed costs of R810 000 per annum (R750 000 existing + R60 000 additional). Variable costs (VC) remain R1 000 per lawnmower as the move to larger premises will not have any impact on variable costs. Substituting these values into the profit formula P = SPx − (FC + VCx), the number of additional lawnmowers that must be sold (x) can be calculated as follows:

$$
\begin{aligned}
0 &= 2\,500x - (60\,000 + 1\,000x) \\
0 &= 2\,500x - 60\,000 - 1\,000x \\
1\,500x &= 60\,000 \\
x &= 40
\end{aligned}
$$

Therefore 40 additional lawnmowers must be sold to cover the additional fixed rental payable of R60 000.

Using the contribution margin formula, fixed costs are R60 000 per annum and the contribution per unit is R1 500 (calculated in example 4.2). The number of additional lawnmowers that must be sold (x) can then be calculated as follows:

$$\text{Number of additional lawnmowers} = \frac{\text{R60 000}}{\text{R1 500}}$$

$$= 40 \text{ additional lawnmowers}$$

4.4.5 Reduction in selling price to increase sales volumes

An organisation may believe that by reducing its selling price, it may be able to increase its sales volumes and its overall profits. CVP analysis provides a useful mechanism to determine whether the increase in sales volumes is sufficient to offset the loss in sales revenue from the decrease in selling price.

principles of management accounting

Example 4.8

In addition to the information given in example 4.1, you are considering reducing the selling price per lawnmower to R2 250 as you believe this will increase the expected sales of lawnmowers from 750 lawnmowers to 850 lawnmowers.

Required:
Advise whether the revised selling price should be implemented.

The selling price that results in the greatest total contribution should be implemented. You will recall that the contribution per unit is the difference between the selling price and the variable costs per unit. Therefore, if the selling price per unit is R2 500, the contribution per unit is R1 500 (selling price of R2 500 less variable costs of R1 000) and the total contribution is R1 125 000 (R1 500 multiplied by the expected sales volume of 750 lawnmowers). However, if the selling price is R2 250, the contribution per unit is R1 250 (selling price of R2 250 less variable costs of R1 000). The total contribution is therefore R1 062 500 (R1 250 multiplied by the expected sales volume of 850 lawnmowers). The revised selling price would result in a decrease in contribution of R62 500 (R1 125 000 – R1 062 500) and should therefore not be implemented.

Alternatively, we can use the profit formula $P = SPx - (FC + VCx)$ to calculate what the expected profit under each scenario would be. The selling price resulting in the greatest expected profit should be implemented. We know from example 4.3 that the expected profit will be R375 000 if the selling price is R2 500 per lawnmower. If the selling price is R2 250, we are given that the number of lawnmowers sold (x) will be 850, and from example 4.1 we know that fixed costs (FC) will be R750 000 per annum and variable costs (VC) will be R1 000. The expected profit generated will then be:

$$\begin{aligned} P &= \text{R2 250} \times 850 - (\text{R750 000} + \text{R1 000} \times 850) \\ &= \text{R1 912 500} - \text{R750 000} - \text{R850 000} \\ &= \text{R312 500} \end{aligned}$$

Since the reduction in selling price would result in a R62 500 (R375 000 – R312 500) decrease in profit, the revised selling price should not be implemented.

Note: The decrease in contribution calculated using the contribution margin formula and the decrease in profit calculated with the profit formula is exactly the same. This is to be expected, as the difference between profit and the total contribution is the fixed costs. In this scenario, fixed costs are unaffected by the change in selling price and are therefore not relevant.

The scenarios detailed above deal with the most common situations to which CVP analysis can be applied. The same principles can be applied to many other variations that may arise.

Sensitivity analysis enables managers to assess the impact should any of the original variables within the CVP model change. This is useful because it recognises that there can be a range of possible outcomes. The use of computer software spreadsheet packages makes sensitivity analysis quick and easy to perform. Managers can ask 'what if' questions by changing one variable in the model at a time, and instantly see the impact of the change. Sensitivity analysis is a way of recognising that projected future outcomes are not guaranteed, and that all decisions are subject to a degree of risk and uncertainty. The more thoroughly managers consider the answers to questions such as 'But what would the profit be if 100 fewer units were sold?', the better informed their decisions will be.

4.5 Break-even analysis with multiple products

Key term: sales mix

Up to now the CVP analysis has been limited to situations where there is only one product being sold. Almost all organisations, however, have more than one product that they sell or more than one service that is delivered. It is therefore useful to extend CVP analysis to multiple products and services.

Each product or service may have its own break-even point as selling prices and cost structures are likely to be different for each product or service. A complication that often arises when using CVP analysis with multiple products and services is fixed costs that are not directly attributable to the products or services (common fixed costs). A few options on how to treat these common fixed costs can be considered. One option is to allocate the common fixed costs to the products and services. However, since the common fixed costs are not directly attributable to the products and services, any allocation is likely to be arbitrary. Arbitrary allocation of costs distorts decision-making and should therefore preferably be avoided. Another option is simply to ignore the common fixed costs. The problem with this approach is that the organisation may then not recover the common fixed costs, which is not sustainable in the long run. A third option, and the option most commonly used, is to use the organisation's **sales mix** to conduct the break-even analysis. An organisation's sales mix is the proportion in which its products and services are sold or delivered. A simple example is where an organisation sells 2 units of Product A for every 1 unit of Product B: the sales mix will be 2 : 1.

Using the organisation's sales mix, a weighted-average unit contribution margin is calculated. Applying the contribution margin formula, the break-even number of units for the sales mix is calculated by dividing total fixed costs per annum (directly attributable fixed costs for all the products and services plus common fixed costs) by the weighted-average contribution margin. The break-even point for each product or service can then be calculated using the proportion of each product in the sales mix. In the simple example used above, the break-even for Product A is $\frac{2}{3}$ and for Product B $\frac{1}{3}$ of the *total* number of break-even units calculated.

Example 4.9

This example follows on from the previous examples in this chapter. After successfully completing the first year of trading, you are now considering expanding your lawnmower business to include both a petrol and an electric model and also to include a garden service. The garden service will be offered on a monthly contract basis. These are the only three products or services the organisation provides.

The following estimates have been prepared for the following year:

principles of management accounting

	Electric lawnmowers	Petrol lawnmowers	Garden service	Total
Selling price per lawnmower/contract	R2 000	R2 500	R250	
Variable costs per lawnmower/contract	R850	R1 000	R100	
Contribution margin per lawnmower/contract	R1 150	R1 500	R150	
Directly attributable fixed costs (per annum)	–	–	R15 000	
Common fixed costs (per annum)				R810 000
Expected sales mix	3	2	1	

Required:
Calculate the break-even number of:
- Electric lawnmowers
- Petrol lawnmowers
- Garden service contracts.

Firstly, the weighted-average contribution margin must be calculated using the sales mix of 3 : 2 : 1. Electric lawnmowers contribute R3 450 (3 × R1 150), petrol lawnmowers R3 000 (2 × R1 500), and the garden service R150 (1 × R150). This results in a total contribution of R6 600 and a weighted-average contribution of R1 100 (R6 600 / (3 + 2 +1)).

Now that the weighted-average contribution has been calculated, the total number of break-even units can be calculated as:

$$\text{Break-even units} = \frac{\text{total fixed costs}}{\text{weighted-average contribution per unit}}$$

$$= \frac{R15\ 000 + R810\ 000}{R1\ 100}$$

$$= 750\ \text{units}$$

The break-even units for each product or service can now be calculated as:

	Break-even units	
Electric lawnmowers	375	(750 × 3/6)
Petrol lawnmowers	250	(750 × 2/6)
Garden service	125	(750 × 1/6)

Therefore, to break even, 375 electric lawnmowers, 250 petrol lawnmowers and 125 garden service contracts must be sold.

It is important to remember that since the break-even point for multiple products and services is dependent on the sales mix of those products and services, there will be different break-even points each time the sales mix changes. For the break-even analysis to be meaningful and reliable, it is vital for the sales mix to be predicted with reasonable accuracy. This may be difficult in some situations and care should therefore be exercised before performing CVP analysis on multiple products and services. The impact of a change in the predicted and the actual sales mix is illustrated in example 4.10.

Example 4.10

This example follows on from example 4.9. During the next year of trading, you were able to sell 400 electric lawnmowers, 200 petrol lawnmowers and 200 garden service contracts. You are delighted as the total combined sales of 800 lawnmowers and garden service contracts are in excess of the total number of break-even units that you had calculated at the start of the year. Taking this into account, and the fact that the actual selling prices and costs were as expected at the beginning of the year, you are expecting to have made a good profit.

Your delight is, however, short lived, as after preparing your year-end income statement, you realise that you have actually made a loss for the year.

Required:
1. Calculate the actual loss for year.
2. Explain how it is possible to have made a loss despite selling more than the total number of break-even units.

The loss for the year is:

	Electric lawnmowers	Petrol lawnmowers	Garden service	Total
	R	R	R	R
Sales				1 350 000
Electric lawnmowers (R2 000 × 400)	800 000			
Petrol lawnmowers (R2 500 × 200)		500 000		
Garden service contracts (R250 × 200)			50 000	
Variable costs				560 000
Electric lawnmowers (R850 × 400)	340 000			
Petrol lawnmowers (R1 000 × 200)		200 000		
Garden service (R100 × 200)			20 000	
Contribution margin	460 000	300 000	30 000	790 000
Directly attributable fixed costs (per annum)	–	–	(15 000)	(15 000)
Common fixed costs (per annum)				(810 000)
Loss				(35 000)

The fact that a loss has been made despite selling more than the break-even number of units can be explained by a change in the sales mix. The expected sales mix was 3 : 2 : 1, but the actual sales mix changed to 4 : 2 : 2 (400 electric lawnmowers : 200 petrol lawnmowers : 200 garden service contracts). Petrol lawnmowers have the highest contribution per unit, but their weight in the weighted-average contribution decreased from $\frac{2}{6}$ in the expected sales mix to $\frac{2}{8}$ in the actual sales mix. The weighted-average contribution per unit therefore decreased to (4 × R1 150 + 2 × R1 500 + 2 × R 150) / (4 + 2 + 2) = R7 900 / 8 = R 987,50, which is R112,50 less than the R1 100 computed in example 4.9 for the expected sales mix. Note that the difference between the budgeted and actual profit can simply be calculated by subtracting the contribution on the budgeted sales mix from the contribution based on the new sales mix. This would be the same as the sales mix variance, which is discussed in Chapter 13, *Standard costing*.

In multiple product and service scenarios, it may be useful to calculate a range of break-even points based on a few variations in sales mix so that managers can have a feel for the impact that a change in the sales mix may have.

4.6 CVP analysis assumptions and limitations

It is essential when preparing and interpreting CVP analysis that the underlying assumptions on which the information has been prepared are understood. If this is not the case, incorrect decisions may be made which could have serious consequences for an organisation. The most important assumptions are detailed below.

4.6.1 All other variables remain constant

The profit formula, contribution margin formula, and break-even chart approaches to CVP analysis assume that volume is the only variable that will cause a change in costs and sales revenues. Other variables are held constant.

4.6.2 Total costs and revenue are linear functions of output in the relevant range, which is definable

These assumptions have already been discussed in the introduction to this chapter. In practice, difficulties may be experienced in identifying the relevant range.

4.6.3 A single product exists or a constant sales mix can be predicted

It has been shown that where more than one product or service exists, it is necessary to calculate the break-even point using the sales mix. Changes in the sales mix may have a significant impact on the validity of the CVP analysis and therefore, if there are multiple products or services, it is necessary to assume that a constant sales mix can be predicted.

4.6.4 Profits are calculated on a variable costing basis or, if they are calculated on an absorption basis, the number of units produced equals the number of units sold

In the introduction to this chapter it was explained that it is preferable to use a variable costing system to calculate profits for CVP analysis to avoid profit distortions arising from differences between production and sales volumes. However, if an absorption costing system is used, assuming that the number of units produced equals the number of units sold will ensure that no profit distortions from differing production and sales levels arise. An assumption that inventory levels remain the same from year to year will have the same result. You will understand this better once you have studied Chapter 5, *Absorption versus variable costing*.

4.6.5 Costs can be split between fixed and variable costs

All of the CVP analysis methods (profit formula, contribution margin formula, and the break-even chart) require a distinction between fixed and variable costs. In practice, some costs may be semi-variable and it may be difficult to split these costs into their fixed and variable components. If the CVP analysis is to be valid, it is necessary for a reasonably accurate split to be made. This is where an activity-based costing system would provide more accurate cost information (see Chapter 6, *Overhead allocation*).

4.6.6 The analysis applies only to the short term

Fixed costs are likely to remain fixed only in the short term. The costs of providing an organisation's production capacity, for example, are a result of long-term planning and it is not easy to change these costs in the short term. However, in the longer term it is possible to increase production capacity by building new plants. Furthermore, other costs such as, for example, senior management salaries or property rentals cannot be altered in the short term. However, as an example, over a longer period, it is possible not to fill senior management positions when they become vacant.

Since we need to differentiate between fixed and variable costs to be able to perform a CVP analysis, it is necessary to limit the analysis to the short term. If a longer-term analysis is required, it will be necessary to reassess the split between fixed and variable costs.

After reading these assumptions, one may be tempted to discard CVP analysis as a useful tool, as it may seem highly unlikely that all the assumptions will always hold true. However, CVP is very useful in practice, as long as the results are correctly interpreted by someone who understands the assumptions.

4.7 Summary

In this chapter, CVP analysis has been shown to provide managers with a useful short-term planning tool.

The break-even point can be calculated using the profit formula, contribution margin formula, or a break-even chart. CVP analysis can also be applied to a number of 'what if' scenarios, including calculating target profits and pricing and volume decisions.

Where there are multiple products or services, using the sales mix to calculate a weighted-average contribution margin overcomes the problem of accounting for common fixed costs. Once the total break-even units have been calculated using the weighted-average contribution margin, the individual product or service break-even points can be determined using the sales mix ratios.

There are a number of underlying assumptions and limitations to CVP analysis. Understanding the impact of these assumptions and limitations is crucial to performing a valid and reliable CVP analysis. Only significant deviations from the assumptions are likely to have an impact on the validity and reliability of the analysis.

Conclusion: Cost-volume-profit relationships and other topics in this book

In order to apply CVP analysis, costs have to be classified as either fixed or variable. A thorough knowledge of Chapter 2, *Cost classification* is therefore required. One of the assumptions of CVP analysis is that a variable costing system is used. Should an absorption costing system be in use, the figures need to be restated on a variable costing basis. Chapter 5, *Absorption versus variable costing* addresses this. Restatement of figures on a variable costing basis is necessary, because fixed costs are often irrelevant for short-term decision-making, as discussed in Chapter 10, *Relevant costs for decision-making*. Sensitivity analysis using CVP principles is also a useful tool for decision-making and for assessing the impact of a decision on an organisation's risk.

principles of management accounting

Tutorial case study: Protea Hotels

The Balalaika Sandton hotel in Johannesburg's northern suburbs has 330 rooms and is owned by *Protea Hotels*, which operates hotels in eight African countries. The Balalaika Sandton has a four star grading, which means it is regarded as a hotel of superior quality by the Tourism Grading Council of South Africa. The price charged per guest per night depends on a number of factors. These include the room occupancy (single or sharing), the season, and whether the guest has a Prokard (Protea Hotels' loyalty card scheme). The price also depends on which type of room is chosen – the Balalaika Sandton has 18 executive suites, four deluxe rooms, eight two-bedroomed family suites, one one-bedroomed suite, 193 king-bedded rooms, 104 twin-bedded rooms, and two rooms with special amenities for physically challenged guests. As one might expect, Protea Hotels would like the Balalaika Sandton hotel to be as successful as possible. To ensure this, the company has to have a firm understanding of the relationship between cost (how much it costs to accommodate a guest per night), volume (how many guests sleep over), and profit (the amount of profit that the Balalaika Sandton can contribute to the group's bottom line).

Source: Protea Hotels 2011

1. Give examples of costs incurred at the Balalaika Sandton hotel which may be regarded by Protea Hotels as:
   a) Variable
   b) Fixed when a one-year time horizon is considered.
2. Discuss how Protea Hotels could use CVP analysis to quantify the impact on the profitability of the Balalaika Sandton hotel if a suggestion was made that the hotel should significantly cut back on the level of luxury offered to guests.
3. State what assumptions would need to be made in performing the CVP analysis in point 2 above, and explain what impact these assumptions could have on the analysis performed.
4. As mentioned, rooms are sold at different rates depending on a number of factors. Explain what impact this has on Protea Hotels' CVP analysis of the Balalaika Sandton hotel.

Basic questions

BQ 1

Is the break-even point:
a) Where total fixed costs per annum equal total variable costs?
b) Where total revenue equals total fixed costs per annum?
c) Where total costs equal contribution margin?
d) Where total fixed costs per annum equal contribution margin?

BQ 2

An organisation sells its only product for R100 per unit and has a variable cost ratio of 80 per cent. Total fixed costs are R200 000 per annum. What is the break-even point in units?

Note: 'Variable cost ratio of 80 per cent' means that variable costs are 80 per cent of the selling price.

BQ 3

Given the same information as for BQ2, what profit or loss will be made if 8 000 units are sold?

BQ 4

In addition to the information provided in BQ2, assume that expected sales are 15 000 units. What is the margin of safety percentage?

BQ 5

Given the following expected revenues and costs for the following year, how many units must be sold to generate a pre-tax profit of R700 000?

Selling price per unit	R500
Variable costs per unit	R150
Total fixed costs (per annum)	R350 000

BQ 6

Given the same information as for BQ5, what profit is made if one unit more than the break-even sales volume is sold?

BQ 7

Using the information provided in BQ5, how many additional units need to be sold to cover an increase in fixed costs of R175 000 per annum?

BQ 8

What is meant by CVP analysis, and how could such an analysis be useful?

BQ 9

What is the limitation of basic CVP analysis relating to an organisation's sales mix?

BQ 10

JB Limited manufactures and sells two products, J and B. The expected sales mix is 5 (J) : 3 (B). Total budgeted sales for the next year are R5 million. J has a contribution to sales ratio of 35 per cent and B 55 per cent. Budgeted annual fixed costs are R500 000. What is the budgeted break-even sales value?
a) 1 176 471
b) 1 233 767
c) 1 111 112
d) Can't be calculated with the information given.

Long questions

LQ 1 – Intermediate (20 marks; 36 minutes)

Source: Adapted from Rhodes University

This question consists of three related parts.

principles of management accounting

Part A *(7 marks; 13 minutes)*
Hawk Agricultural Enterprises (Pty) Ltd manufactures agricultural pumps. It recently introduced a new type of energy-efficient pump, which has the following unit cost structure:

	R	R
Selling price		275
Variable costs		150
Direct materials and components	70	
Direct labour	48	
Variable manufacturing overheads	17	
Variable selling expenses	15	
Contribution margin		125
Fixed costs		90
Fixed manufacturing overheads	80	
Fixed selling expenses	10	
Profit		35

The fixed overheads included in the unit cost of a pump are directly related to the manufacture and sale of this pump. The allocation of the overheads is based on the current sales level of 1 200 pumps per year.

REQUIRED	Marks
Calculate:	
(a) The break-even point in units; and	3
(b) The margin of safety percentage.	4
SUB-TOTAL (Part A)	**7**

Part B *(3 marks; 5 minutes)*
The directors are considering a new selling price of R268 per unit. The change in selling price will not result in any changes to fixed costs. The directors wish to maintain the existing profits but are unsure of how many additional units they will need to sell.

REQUIRED	Marks
Calculate how many additional units the organisation will have to sell in order to maintain the existing profits if the revised selling price is implemented.	3
SUB-TOTAL (Part B)	**3**

Part C *(10 marks; 18 minutes)*
As an alternative to reducing the selling price to R268 per unit, the directors are investigating whether or not to decrease the selling price to R260 per pump, anticipating that the sales volume will increase to 1 500 units. It is estimated that fixed manufacturing overhead costs will increase by 10 per cent as a result.

REQUIRED		Marks
(a)	Calculate: (i) Whether the annual net profit will increase, if the estimates are correct (ii) What the new break-even point (in units) will be, and (iii) What the new margin of safety percentage will be.	8
(b)	Advise the organisation whether it should decrease the selling price as proposed.	2
SUB-TOTAL (Part C)		10
TOTAL MARKS (Parts A, B and C)		20

LQ 2 – Intermediate (20 marks; 36 minutes)

Source: Adapted from Rhodes University

Carter Carriers (Pty) Ltd ('the company'), a company based in Port Elizabeth, manufactures and sells car rooftop carriers for fitting to cars and bakkies. The company produced its 2XX7 budget based on the assumption that they would be able to sell the carriers for R5 000 each. The variable cost of each canopy was projected at R2 500, and the annual fixed costs were budgeted at R1 250 000 (fixed costs accrue evenly during the year). The Company requires a profit of R3 000 000 for the year in order to meet its target return on capital.

The company normally expects its sales to rise during the second quarter of the year. However, the May management accounts show that sales volumes were not in line with expectations. During the first five months of the year variable costs were as projected, but at the budgeted price of R5 000, only 350 units had been sold.

To ensure that the company still meets its required profit of R3 000 000 for the year, the following mutually exclusive alternative plans of action have been developed:

a) *Reduce the selling price by 10 per cent*. The sales director believes that this will generate sales of 2 700 units during the remaining seven months of the year. Total fixed costs and variable costs per unit will not be affected and will remain as budgeted.

b) *Reduce variable costs per unit by 12,5 per cent through the use of less expensive raw materials*. Fixed costs will not be affected. This will allow the selling price to be reduced by 7,5 per cent. Based on the reduced selling price, the sales director believes that sales of 2 200 units will be achieved during the remaining seven months of the year.

c) *Reduce fixed costs by R125 000 per annum*. This will allow the selling price to be reduced by 5 per cent. Variable costs per unit will not be affected. Based on the reduced selling price, the sales director believes that sales of 2 000 units will be achieved during the remaining seven months of the year.

REQUIRED		Marks
(a)	If no changes are made to the selling price or cost structure, determine the number of units that the company must sell during the remaining seven months of the year in order to achieve: (i) Break-even, and (ii) The profit objective of R3 000 000 for the year.	5
(b)	For each of the three alternative plans of action: (i) Calculate the number of units required to be sold during the remaining seven months in order for the company to achieve its profit objective of R3 000 000 for the year (ii) Calculate the margin of safety percentage based on the sales director's estimates of projected sales volume for the remaining seven months for each of the three alternative plans of action, and (iii) Briefly comment on the level of risk perceived in each of the three alternative plans of action.	15
TOTAL MARKS		20

LQ 3 – Advanced (50 marks; 90 minutes)

Some businessmen have recently opened a petrol station called TAV Fillers. One grade of petrol is sold at R1,76 per litre. Variable charges – cost of petrol, delivery and excise duty – total R1,60 per litre. The fixed costs per month are as follows:

	R
Rent	10 000
Rates on business premises	5 000
Wages – five people on shifts	7 500
Wage-related costs	2 500
Electricity for continuous opening (24-hours)	1 500
Other fixed costs	740

After the first six months of opening, the average monthly sales achieved was 179 210 litres.

Owing to sustained pressure from commerce and industry, the government has recently announced measures to deregulate the petrol industry. In view of the government's announcements and in an attempt to improve performance, the businessmen are considering the following proposals:

Proposal 1
Allow customers to purchase petrol on credit. It is estimated that 50 per cent of average monthly sales (in litres) are to customers who would take advantage of this opportunity. They are expected to purchase exclusively from TAV in future and hence sales to these customers should increase by 30 per cent. Sales volumes to customers who do not take advantage of the credit facility are expected to remain unchanged. Additional costs arising from this proposal are anticipated to be:
i) Bad debts of 0,5 per cent of sales value in respect of customers who use the credit facility
ii) Fixed financing costs of R500 per month
iii) Fixed administrative costs of R1 000 per month.

What would be the average monthly profit if this proposal were implemented?

Proposal 2
Ideally, the businessmen would like a profit margin of 2 per cent on turnover. How many litres of petrol would need to be sold each month to achieve this profit margin, if the selling price was reduced by R0,02 per litre, sales commission of R0,01 per 10 litres was offered to petrol attendants, and R500 per month was spent on advertising? What would be the resulting profit?

Proposal 3
The possibility of only operating from 7am to 11pm is being considered. This earlier closing time is expected to result in a loss of sales of 25 000 litres on average each month. It is hoped that the saving in fixed costs resulting from a reduction in operating hours will enable the businessmen to achieve an average monthly profit of at least R3 000. Taking these new circumstances into account, what saving in monthly fixed costs is necessary to yield a profit of R3 000?

Note: Each proposal is independent of the other two.

REQUIRED		Marks
(a)	Before considering any of the proposals, calculate for the average month's performance the: (i) Profit (ii) Profit-Volume ratio (iii) Margin of safety percentage and explain its meaning.	11
(b)	Explain the purpose of a profit-volume graph and how the profit-volume ratio is represented in the graph.	4
(c)	Evaluate each proposal by answering the specific questions raised.	23
(d)	Comment briefly on each proposal.	12
TOTAL MARKS		**50**

LQ 4 – Advanced (20 marks; 36 minutes)

Source: Adapted from Rhodes University

You are a consultant, specialising in cost and management accounting. The managing director of a local organisation has asked for your advice on a certain matter. The management of the organisation, Credgro Limited, is in the process of investigating whether a decrease in the selling price of their product would increase sales and improve the profitability of the organisation. The organisation's former accountant (who has now disappeared) recommended a particular selling price and, based on this selling price, provided the following incomplete information in support of his recommendation:

Fixed costs	R1,2 million per annum
Variable costs	R20 per unit
Break-even point (in units)	120 000
Margin of safety	25%
Increase in sales volume	28%
Decrease in selling price	20%

REQUIRED		Marks
(a)	Calculate the selling price that the former accountant had recommended.	5
(b)	Calculate the original selling price and sales volume.	7
(c)	Explain whether you agree with the advice of the former accountant. Give reasons for your answer and state whether you would you make any other recommendations.	8
TOTAL MARKS		**20**

LQ 5 – Advanced (32 marks; 58 minutes)

A computer software company develops and sells three computer games, Gino, Dust and Elton. The combined sales of all the products in 2XX7 was 9 000 units and total fixed costs amounted to R726 000.

Other relevant data for 2XX7 were as follows:

	Gino	Dust	Elton
Sales price	R600	R500	R450
P/V Ratio	20%	30%	40%
Sales mix	5	1	4

Management expects sales in the current year to remain at 9 000 total units and there is no intention to change the selling price or cost structure. However, by reducing marketing expenditure on Gino and spending more on Dust and Elton, the Marketing Director believes that the sales mix can be changed to 2 : 3 : 5.

REQUIRED		Marks
(a)	For the organisation as a whole, calculate the P/V ratio, break-even sales and profit of each sales mix respectively, and advise management whether the proposed sales mix should be implemented or not.	19
(b)	Construct a profit-volume graph, drawing the average profitability line only of each sales mix on the same graph, thereby showing the respective break-even points.	10
(c)	Discuss why a profit-volume graph may be used in preference to a break-even or contribution chart.	3
TOTAL MARKS		32

References

Faul, MA, Du Plessis, PC, Van Vuuren, SJ, Niemand, AA & Koch, E. 1997. *Fundamentals of cost and management accounting*, Third edition. Durban: Butterworths.

Hilton, WH. 2002. **Managerial accounting: creating value in a dynamic business environment**, Fifth edition. Boston: McGraw-Hill.

Horngren, CT, Foster, G, Datar, SM & Uliana, E. 1999. *Cost accounting in South Africa: a managerial perspective*. Cape Town: Prentice Hall.

Protea Hotels. 2011. Protea Hotel Balalaika Sandton. [Online]. Available: <www.proteahotels.com/protea-hotel-balalaika-sandton.html> [24 February 2011].

SAA (South African Airways). 2010. *Chairperson's report. Annual report 2010*. Kempton Park: SAA.

Seal, W, Garrison, RH & Noreen, EW. 2006. *Management accounting*, Second edition. Berkshire: McGraw-Hill.

Wood, N & Skae, O. 2008. *Principles of management accounting: the question book*. Cape Town: Oxford University Press Southern Africa.

Ziemerink, T, Govender, B, Ambe, C & Koortzen, P. 2005. *Cost and management accounting*. Pretoria: Van Schaik.

Absorption versus variable costing

chapter 5

Dewald Joubert, Ahmed Mohammadali Haji and Hendrik Fourie

LEARNING OBJECTIVES
By the end of this chapter, you should be able to:
1 Explain how absorption and variable costing (respectively) are used in the context of reporting for financial and management accounting purposes.
2 Distinguish between the different income statement formats used under absorption and variable costing.
3 Calculate the impact of changes in inventory levels on profit calculated using absorption and variable costing, and reconcile the relevant profit figures.
4 Discuss the relative strengths and weaknesses of absorption and variable costing.

BHP Billiton and absorption costing

Absorption costing is used in statutory financial statements. In some instances, the term is specifically mentioned in the accounting policy notes of South African listed companies. Below is an extract from the accounting policies of *BHP Billiton*.

Inventories
Inventories, including work in progress, are valued at the lower of cost and net realisable value. Cost is determined primarily on the basis of average costs. For processed inventories, cost is derived on an absorption costing basis. Cost comprises cost of purchasing raw materials and cost of production, including attributable mining and manufacturing overheads.

Source: BHP Billiton Annual Report 2009

Reference is made in the excerpt above to 'costs being derived on an absorption costing basis'. This raises the question as to what absorption costing is. This chapter explores the concept of absorption costing, and contrasts it with another popular costing system called variable costing.

5.1 Introduction

Key terms: absorption costing, variable costing

Chapter 2, *Cost classification* introduces the cost behaviour of variable and fixed costs. The estimation of these is further discussed in Chapter 3, *Cost estimation*. This chapter describes the reporting of this information using two costing methods – **absorption costing** and **variable costing**. It further details the different profit figures which may arise under the two systems, the reconciliation of these profit figures, as well as the income statement format that is used for each system.

The chapter is concluded with a discussion on the arguments supporting the use of absorption costing over variable costing. The weaknesses of absorption costing are highlighted by discussing the arguments in support of variable costing. Overhead allocation is briefly discussed in this chapter and will be more broadly discussed in the chapter that follows. While this chapter focuses on allocating costs to inventory, the following chapter discusses overhead allocation with a wide application to business.

5.2 Cost accounting concepts

The management accountant of the 21st century is faced with many challenges. With the increasing pressures of globalisation leading to increased competition, the management accountant must have access to information of a high quality which is relevant and reliable to enable sound decision-making. This information must be obtained on a timely basis in order for the organisation to keep abreast of changing conditions.

As you have seen in Chapter 1, *Introduction to management accounting*, financial accounting reports are not sufficient to enable management accountants to perform their duties, and as a result management accountants require more information than purely financial accounting information.

Within the framework of these two disciplines of financial and management accounting, two cost accounting concepts/systems emerge:
- Absorption costing
- Variable costing.

Both the absorption and the variable costing systems entail inventory valuation. The difference between these concepts/systems is that absorption costing accumulates both variable and fixed inventoriable costs whereas variable costing accumulates only inventoriable variable costs (inventoriable costs are explained in Chapter 2, *Cost classification*). For purposes of absorption costing, fixed costs are allocated to units, or 'absorbed' into units – hence the name 'absorption costing'.

Broadly, absorption costing involves the accumulation and reporting of cost information within a format consistent with the accounting standards underlying financial accounting, which is aligned with the principle of matching income with expenses. Variable costing, on the other hand, involves the accumulation and reporting of cost information within a format that enables short-term planning, control, and decision-making.

For absorption costing purposes, as used in financial accounting, all costs directly associated with producing the inventory (regardless of whether they are fixed costs or variable costs) are included in the valuation of inventory. Remember that fixed costs are defined as costs that in total are unresponsive to a change in the level of activity, while variable costs are defined as those costs where the total cost increases or decreases in proportion to increases or decreases in the level of activity.

Under absorption costing, when an item is sold, the revenue associated with the sale of the inventory is recognised and the value of the inventory sold is expensed (typically in the 'cost of sales' line item). The profit figure therefore reflects the gain made out of the sale of the inventory after taking into account all expenses associated with it.

Allocating fixed overheads to inventory is justified as it ensures that cost of sales in the income statement and the inventory level on the statement of financial position reflect all the associated costs of the inventory (absorption costing is therefore sometimes referred to as 'full costing').

Absorption costing presents meaningful information, but may lead to incorrect decision-making owing to the inclusion of fixed costs in the valuation of inventory. These costs are often irrelevant (as they cannot be changed in the short term, and will be incurred regardless of what course of action is taken), and should be excluded from the decision-making process over the short term.

Variable costing is useful for short-term decision-making as it excludes fixed costs from inventory valuation – it treats these as expenses as and when they occur. This makes it easy to determine the incremental benefit from temporarily increasing sales – only the relevant information is taken into account as the fixed costs associated with this course of action remain constant.

The underlying cost information used for the two systems is the same, but the manner in which the information is reported differs.

5.2.1 Absorption costing

Key terms: fixed manufacturing overheads

Absorption costing involves the accumulation and reporting of cost information within a format which is consistent with the accounting standards underlying financial accounting. International Accounting Standard 2 (IAS 2) is the accounting standard governing inventories. Paragraph 10 of this standard defines the cost of inventories as including '… all costs of purchase, costs of conversion and other costs incurred in bringing the inventories to their present location and condition'. The costs of conversion are further explained in paragraph 12 as including 'a systematic allocation of fixed and variable production overheads that are incurred in converting materials into finished goods'.

From this paragraph, three key principles emerge. The first is that the cost of inventories should include 'a systematic allocation of fixed overheads'. This simply implies that *fixed overheads must be included in the cost of inventories*. The second principle relates to 'overheads that are incurred in converting materials into finished goods', which explains the type of fixed overheads to be included in the cost of inventories. *Fixed overheads incurred in converting materials into finished goods are called* **fixed manufacturing overheads**. Therefore fixed overheads must be split between manufacturing and non-manufacturing, and only the manufacturing component must be included in the cost of inventories.

Examples of fixed manufacturing and non-manufacturing overheads are given below:

Manufacturing	Non-manufacturing
Depreciation on factory machines	Depreciation on the sales representative's vehicle
Fixed electricity costs in the manufacturing plant	Fixed electricity costs in the administration building
Salaries of manufacturing staff	Salaries of administration staff

Fixed selling costs, fixed electricity costs in the administration building, and salaries of administration staff are costs incurred to effect the sale or carry out administrative functions, and are not costs incurred in 'bringing the inventories to their present location and condition' or 'costs incurred in converting materials into finished goods'. Consequently, these costs do not form part of the cost of inventories under IAS 2.

The third principle relates to 'a systematic allocation'. Fixed overheads are allocated to inventory. The process of allocation is explained in paragraph 13 of IAS 2, which requires fixed overheads to be allocated '... *based on normal capacity of the production facilities. Normal capacity is the production expected to be achieved on average over a number of periods or seasons under normal circumstances, taking into account the loss of capacity resulting from planned maintenance*'. Paragraph 13 of IAS 2 further states that '*unallocated overheads are recognised as an expense in the period in which they are incurred*'.

Now that we have discussed the activity level to be used when allocating fixed manufacturing overheads to inventory, we still need to discuss whether actual or budgeted costs should be used for this allocation. One may be inclined to use actual fixed manufacturing overheads. This practice, however, leads to some practical difficulties. Actual fixed manufacturing overheads will be known only after a specific period. However, we may already want to know the full cost of a product (which includes fixed manufacturing overheads) *during* the period. To overcome this practical problem, we may consider using actual fixed costs to calculate allocation rates on a monthly basis, but then the risk arises that there may be different cost allocations in different periods owing to seasonal fluctuations in production as well as different fixed manufacturing costs in different periods.

Instead, the allocation of fixed manufacturing overheads is preferably performed by taking *budgeted* fixed manufacturing costs for a period (normally a year) and dividing them by normal capacity. This allocation rate is then used for allocating fixed manufacturing overheads to inventory. The total fixed manufacturing overheads allocated to current production are referred to as allocated fixed manufacturing overheads. The difference between allocated fixed manufacturing overheads (allocation rate × actual production) and actual manufacturing overheads incurred in a specific period is then called an over- or an under-allocation. Over-allocation means that the allocation of fixed manufacturing overheads to inventory is more than the actual fixed manufacturing overheads incurred. Under-allocation means that the allocation of fixed manufacturing overheads to inventory is less than the actual fixed manufacturing overheads incurred. An over-allocation should be credited and an under-allocation should be debited to the income statement to ensure that actual manufacturing fixed costs are represented in the income statement. The absorbed fixed manufacturing overhead amount together with the over- or under-allocation will equal actual fixed manufacturing overheads.

It is worthwhile noting that paragraph 13 of IAS 2 further states that '*in periods of abnormally high production, the amount of fixed overhead allocated to each unit of production is decreased so that inventories are not measured above cost*'.

Chapter 5 Absorption versus variable costing

Applying the principles of IAS 2 relating to the cost of inventories and other costs that should be expensed, and using the cost information in example 5.1 below, the absorption costing income statement can be prepared.

Example 5.1

Information for the December 2XX0 financial year relating to Sweetz, a local manufacturer of chewable mints, is as follows:

Actual sales	980 000 @ 40 cents per mint
Actual number of mints produced in 2XX0	980 000 mints
Consisting of:	
Direct materials – raw gum	980 kilograms @ R20,00 per kilogram
Direct labour – wages	980 hours @ R50,00 per hour
Variable manufacturing overheads	1 960 machine hours @ R30,00 per hour
Budgeted fixed manufacturing overheads	R100 000
Normal capacity	1 000 000 mints per annum
Actual fixed manufacturing overheads	R105 000
Opening inventory for 2XX0	100 000 mints
Consisting of:	
Direct materials – raw gum	100 kilograms @ R20,00 per kilogram
Direct labour – wages	100 hours @ R50,00 per hour
Variable manufacturing overheads	200 machine hours @ R30,00 per hour
Total fixed manufacturing overheads allocated	R10 000
Closing inventory for 2X10	100 000 mints
Fixed selling costs	R25 000
Variable selling costs	5 cents per mint sold

Fixed manufacturing overheads are allocated on the basis of the number of mints produced. Inventory is valued on the first-in-first-out (FIFO) basis, which implies that closing inventory is valued at current year production cost (Chapter 7, *Job costing* describes FIFO inventory valuation in more detail).

Required:
Using the information provided above, prepare the income statement for Sweetz on an absorption costing basis.

principles of management accounting

The income statement can be presented as follows:

Table 5.1 Sweetz: Income statement for the year ending 31 December 2XX0, prepared on an absorption costing basis

		R'000	R'000	R'000
	Revenue (980 000 mints)			392
Manufacturing	Less: Cost of sales (980 000 mints)			(225,4)
	Opening inventory (100 000 mints) Direct materials (R2 000), Direct labour (R5 000), Variable manufacturing overheads (R6 000), and Fixed manufacturing overheads (R10 000)		23	
	Cost of production: (980 000 mints)		225,4	
	Direct materials	19,6		
	Direct labour	49		
	Indirect costs			
	Variable manufacturing overheads	58,8		
	Fixed manufacturing overheads Calculation: (100 000 mints/1 000 000 mints) × 980 000 mints	98		
	Less: Closing inventory (100 000 mints) Direct materials (R2 000), Direct labour (R5 000), Variable manufacturing overheads (R6 000) and Fixed manufacturing overheads (R10 000) Alternative calculation: (225 400/980 000 mints) × 100 000 mints		(23)	
	Gross profit			166,6
Non-manu-facturing	Under-allocation			(7)
	Less: Non-manufacturing variable costs (980 000 mints × 5 cents)			(49)
	Less: Non-manufacturing fixed costs			(25)
	Profit			85,6

All examples in this chapter disclose the over- or under-allocation of fixed overheads below the gross profit line. However, in financial accounting, the emphasis is on classifying manufacturing items separately from non-manufacturing items – in an income statement, the gross profit line separates manufacturing and non-manufacturing line items. It is therefore important to note that the over- or under-allocation can also be shown above the gross profit line as it can be seen as a manufacturing line item.

Gross profit is a measure of operating effectiveness, and in the example above, the R166 600 gross profit is arrived at by deducting cost of sales of R225 400 from revenue of R392 000. Fixed manufacturing overheads are included as part of the cost of production, and therefore form part of cost of sales. Notice that closing inventory is valued, in terms of fixed manufacturing overheads, using the *allocation rate calculated* and not the actual fixed manufacturing overheads. Because only the absorbed fixed manufacturing overheads amount forms part of inventory (R98 000), the difference between the actual fixed manufacturing overheads of

R105 000 and the amount of R98 000 must be adjusted in the income statement. An under-allocation of R7 000 (R105 000 – R98 000) is therefore debited to the income statement.

Non-manufacturing fixed costs of R25 000 are shown as a separate line item below the gross profit line on the income statement.

To summarise absorption costing:
- Absorption costing involves the accumulation and reporting of cost information within a format which is consistent with the accounting standards underlying financial accounting.
- Fixed manufacturing overheads are included in the cost of production, and consequently in opening and closing inventories. Fixed manufacturing overheads are taken into account in the cost of production and consequently in opening and closing inventory through a predetermined allocation rate.
- An over- or under-allocation is merely the difference between fixed manufacturing costs allocated and actual fixed manufacturing costs incurred, and is treated as a period cost in the income statement. The allocated amount together with the over- or under-allocation equals the actual fixed manufacturing costs incurred.
- Absorption costing emphasises the classification between manufacturing and non-manufacturing costs.
- 'Gross profit', which is revenue less cost of sales, is associated with the absorption costing reporting format.

5.2.2 Variable costing

Key terms: direct costing, marginal costing

Variable costing is the alternative form of accumulating and reporting cost information. It leads to reporting in a format that enables planning, control and decision-making. Variable costing is also known as **direct costing** or **marginal costing**. It is the reporting format preferred for management accounting. It utilises the same underlying cost information as absorption costing, but presents it in an alternative format.

The major distinguishing factor between variable costing and absorption costing is the treatment of fixed manufacturing cost.

Costs that are fixed for the duration of the period under review and cannot be altered are irrelevant to decisions pertaining to that period. Variable costing therefore supports such short-term decision-making as it does not 'absorb' fixed costs into the cost of the product.

Another distinguishing factor is that in a variable costing system, variable non-manufacturing cost is deducted higher up in the income statement, before arriving at the contribution (all variable costs have to be deducted before the word 'contribution' can be used). All fixed costs are deducted only after the contribution has been shown. The following example illustrates the variable costing income statement.

Example 5.2

Required:
Using the information in example 5.1, prepare the income statement for Sweetz on a variable costing basis.

The income statement can be presented as follows:

Table 5.2 Sweetz: Income statement for the year ending 31 December 2XX0, prepared on a variable costing basis

		R'000	R'000	R'000
Variable	Revenue (980 000 mints)			392
	Less: Cost of sales			(127,4)
	Opening inventory (100 000 mints) Direct materials (R2 000), Direct labour (R5 000), Variable manufacturing overheads (R6 000)		13	
	Cost of production:		127,4	
	Direct materials	19,6		
	Direct labour	49		
	Indirect costs:			
	Variable manufacturing overheads	58,8		
	Less: Closing inventory (100 000 mints) Direct materials (R2 000), Direct labour (R5 000), Variable manufacturing overheads R6 000) Alternative calculation: (127 400 mints/980 000 mints) × 100 000 mints		(13)	
	Less: Non-manufacturing variable costs (980 000 mints × 5 cents)			(49)
	Contribution			215,6
Fixed	*Less:* All fixed costs (actual manufacturing and non-manufacturing) (R105 000 + R25 000)			(130)
	Profit			85,6

The emphasis in variable costing is on reporting fixed costs separately from variable costs. The contribution line (R215 600 in this case), which is revenue less all variable costs, is specific to a variable costing system. All variable costs are reported in the income statement above the contribution line, while all fixed costs are reported below the contribution line. The fixed cost charge of R130 000 consists of R105 000 actual fixed manufacturing overheads and R25 000 non-manufacturing fixed costs. It is very important to note that there are no fixed overheads in opening and closing inventories, as all fixed costs (including fixed manufacturing cost) have been expensed in the income statement. Fixed costs are said to be treated as 'period costs' (that is, not part of the cost of inventory), as they are expensed in the period in which they arise.

Remember that direct costs are defined as those costs which are directly related to the cost object(s). Generally product direct costs are assumed to be variable. Given that they are directly attributable to a particular product (hence direct costs), it is assumed that an increase in the product volume will naturally lead to an increase in the cost. However, where the nature of the direct cost is such that it is fixed, it should be reported as a fixed cost below the contribution line.

Variable manufacturing and variable non-manufacturing costs are reported separately in the income statement. Variable non-manufacturing costs, for example, variable selling costs, are reported in the income statement only after the 'closing inventories' line has been brought in. This is because such costs are incurred on the units that have been sold, and not the units that have been produced.

To summarise variable costing:
- Variable costing involves the accumulation and reporting of cost information within a format that enables planning, control and decision-making.
- Fixed costs (manufacturing and non-manufacturing) are expensed in the income statement, and do not form part of opening or closing inventories. *Fixed costs are treated as period costs.*
- Variable costing emphasises the distinction between variable and fixed costs.
- 'Contribution', which is revenue less variable costs, is associated with the variable costing reporting format.

5.2.3 Similarities and differences between absorption and variable costing

- Both absorption and variable costing entail inventory valuation; therefore under both concepts only manufacturing costs can be allocated to inventory. Under both systems, non-manufacturing costs will be treated as period costs.
- The major distinguishing factor is the treatment of fixed manufacturing costs. Absorption costing accumulates both fixed and variable manufacturing costs to inventory. Variable costing accumulates only variable manufacturing costs to inventory. This is also the reason that these two systems may report different profit figures under certain circumstances. This will be discussed in the section that follows.

Before continuing, it is crucial to be entirely comfortable with what you have learnt in the chapter so far.

5.3 The impact on profit if inventory levels change

This section of the text addresses whether both absorption costing and variable costing report the same profit. Earlier it was stated that both costing systems utilise the same underlying cost information, but present the information differently. It is in fact the presentation that results in a change in profit in certain circumstances. The sections that follow explore this principle.

5.3.1 Scenario 1: No inventory

The fact that no inventory is held implies that all units produced were sold in the same period.

principles of management accounting

Example 5.3

Manufacturing information relating to Sweetz for the 2XX0 financial year is given below:

Sales	980 000 @ 40 cents per mint
Number of mints produced in 2XX0	980 000
Consisting of:	
Direct materials – raw gum	980 kilograms @ R20,00 per kilogram
Direct labour – wages	980 hours @ R50,00 per hour
Variable manufacturing overheads	1 960 machine hours @ R30,00 per hour
Budgeted fixed manufacturing overheads	R100 000
Normal capacity	1 000 000 mints per annum
Actual fixed manufacturing overheads	R105 000
Fixed selling costs	R25 000
Variable selling costs	5 cents per mint sold

Fixed manufacturing overheads are allocated on the basis of the number of mints produced. As in example 5.1, inventory is valued on the first-in-first-out basis.

Required:
Prepare income statements on both the absorption costing and the variable costing bases.

The absorption costing income statement looks as follows:

Absorption costing	R'000	R'000	R'000
Revenue			392
Less: Cost of sales			(225,4)
Cost of production		225,4	
Direct materials	19,6		
Direct labour	49		
Indirect costs			
Variable manufacturing overheads	58,8		
Fixed manufacturing overheads Calculation: (100 000 mints/1 000 000 mints) × 980 000 mints	98		
Gross profit			166,6
Under-allocation			(7)
Less: Non-manufacturing variable costs (980 000 mints × 5 cents)			(49)
Less: Non-manufacturing fixed costs			(25)
Profit			85,6

Given that there is no opening or closing inventory, there is no opening or closing inventory adjustment in cost of sales. This will be the case only when there is no opening inventory and production equals sales. Cost of sales comprises the cost of producing all the units that are to be sold. It was explained earlier that under an absorption costing system, the emphasis is on manufacturing versus non-manufacturing costs. Consequently cost of sales would consist of all variable and fixed manufacturing costs for the current year of production as all units produced were sold.

The fixed manufacturing overheads charged to this particular income statement amount to R105 000 (R98 000 absorbed and R7 000 under-allocation adjustment). It is evident that actual fixed manufacturing overheads of R105 000 are expensed in total in this particular income statement. The profit amounts to R85 600.

The variable costing income statement looks as follows:

Variable costing	R'000	R'000	R'000
Revenue			392
Less: Cost of sales			(127,4)
Cost of production		127,4	
Direct materials	19,6		
Direct labour	49		
Indirect costs:			
Variable manufacturing overheads	58,8		
Less: Non-manufacturing variable costs			(49)
Contribution			215,6
Less: All fixed costs (actual manufacturing and non-manufacturing) (R105 000 + R25 000)			(130)
Profit			85,6

As explained above, there are no opening or closing inventory adjustments to cost of sales in this specific example. Remember, under a variable costing system, the emphasis lies on separating variable and fixed costs. The apparent differences are that the cost of production under variable costing excludes fixed manufacturing overheads. That explains why the gross profit of R166 600 under absorption costing differs from the contribution of R215 600 under a variable costing system. The other difference is the fact that, under variable costing, variable non-manufacturing costs are reported at a higher classification level, that is, before contribution. This, however, is only a classification issue and does not affect the ultimate profit figures in any way.

So where are the fixed manufacturing overheads reported under a variable costing system? As we know, variable costing separates variable costs and fixed costs. The 'all fixed costs' amount of R130 000 is made up of R105 000 in actual manufacturing fixed costs and R25 000 in non-manufacturing fixed costs.

From example 5.3 the following is apparent:
- Absorption costing and variable costing classify the cost information differently. This leads to the following income statement figures being different: cost of production, gross profit (seen in an absorption costing income statement), and contribution (seen in a variable costing income statement).
- Although the classifications are different, the amount charged to the income statement for each cost element remains the same when there are no inventories. We refer to the costs as having expired when they are expensed to the income statement. *Therefore, we can conclude that regardless of whether an absorption costing or a variable costing system is used, all costs have been expensed to the income statement if there is no inventory.*

principles of management accounting

This explains why the profit figures are the same under both costing systems.

Example 5.3 illustrates that where there are no opening and closing inventories, absorption costing and variable costing report the same profit figure.

5.3.2 Opening inventory

With opening inventory introduced into the example, the income statements become more interesting. Consider example 5.4, where the information in the previous example has been amended to make provision for opening inventory.

Example 5.4

Manufacturing information for the 2XX0 financial year relating to Sweetz is given below:

Sales	980 000 @ 40 cents per mint
Number of mints produced in 2XX0	900 000
Consisting of:	
Direct materials – raw gum	900 kilograms @ R20,00 per kilogram
Direct labour – wages	900 hours @ R50,00 per hour
Variable manufacturing overheads	1 800 machine hours @ R30,00 per hour
Budgeted fixed manufacturing overheads	R90 000
Normal capacity	900 000 mints per annum
Actual fixed manufacturing overheads	R93 000
Opening inventory for 2XX0	80 000 mints
Consisting of:	
Direct materials – raw gum	80 kilograms @ R20,00 per kilogram
Direct labour – wages	80 hours @ R50,00 per hour
Variable manufacturing overheads	160 machine hours @ R30,00 per hour
Fixed manufacturing overheads	?
Fixed selling costs	R25 000
Variable selling costs	5 cents per mint sold

Fixed manufacturing overheads are allocated on the basis of the number of mints produced, and the overhead allocation rate is the same as in the previous year. Inventory is valued on first-in-first-out basis.

Required:
Prepare income statements on both the absorption costing and the variable costing bases.

The cost information from the previous example has been amended to accommodate opening inventory of 80 000 mints. It is important to remember that the value of the opening inventory will be different under each of the two costing systems. Let us consider the following extracts from the income statement reporting formats:

Chapter 5 Absorption versus variable costing

Absorption costing	Total R'000	Per unit R
Opening inventory:		
Direct materials	1,6	0,02
Direct labour	4	0,05
Variable manufacturing overheads	4,8	0,06
Fixed manufacturing overheads (Calculation: R90 000/900 000 = 0,10)	8	0,10

Variable costing	Total R'000	Per unit R
Opening inventory:		
Direct materials	1,6	0,02
Direct labour	4	0,05
Variable manufacturing overheads	4,8	0,06

Opening inventory in an absorption costing system comprises the cost of direct materials, direct labour, variable manufacturing overheads and fixed manufacturing overheads. In contrast, the value of opening inventory in a variable costing system consists of the same amount for direct materials, direct labour and variable manufacturing overheads, but excludes the fixed manufacturing overheads component.

Using this understanding, let us now prepare the absorption costing income statement.

Absorption costing	R'000	R'000	R'000
Revenue			392
Less: Cost of sales			(225,4)
Opening inventory:		18,4	
Direct materials	1,6		
Direct labour	4		
Variable manufacturing overheads	4,8		
Fixed manufacturing overheads	8		
Cost of production		207	
Direct materials	18		
Direct labour	45		
Indirect costs:			
Variable manufacturing overheads	54		
Fixed manufacturing overheads (Calculation: R0,10 × 900 000 mints)	90		
Gross profit			166,6
Under-allocation (R93 000 – R90 000)			(3)
Less: Non-manufacturing variable costs			(49)
Less: Non-manufacturing fixed costs			(25)
Profit			89,6

principles of management accounting

This income statement raises some questions: What is the total fixed manufacturing overheads charge to the income statement? How many years or periods of fixed manufacturing cost charge are included in the income statement?

The total fixed manufacturing overheads charge to the income statement is now R101 000. This consists of R93 000 (R90 000 absorbed fixed manufacturing costs and an under-allocation of R3 000) relating to fixed manufacturing overheads incurred in the current year, as well as fixed manufacturing overheads of R8 000 in opening inventories, which are carried forward from the previous period, when the inventories were produced. So not only are the current year's fixed manufacturing overheads expensed, but fixed manufacturing overheads which arose in the past when the opening inventories were produced are now being charged against revenues. The total fixed cost charge to the income statement is R126 000 (R101 000 relating to fixed manufacturing overheads and R25 000 for non-manufacturing fixed costs).

Using the same information, let us prepare the income statement on a variable costing basis:

Variable costing	R'000	R'000	R'000
Revenue			392
Less: Cost of sales			(127,4)
Opening inventory:		10,4	
Direct materials	1,6		
Direct labour	4		
Variable manufacturing overheads	4,8		
Cost of production		117	
Direct materials	18		
Direct labour	45		
Indirect costs:			
Variable manufacturing overheads	54		
			264,6
Less: Non-manufacturing variable costs			(49)
Contribution			215,6
Less: All actual fixed costs (R93 000 + R25 000)			(118)
Profit			97,6

With the introduction of opening inventory into the example, we have introduced additional costs for direct materials, direct labour and variable manufacturing overheads. These costs were also introduced when we prepared the income statement on an absorption costing basis. But concentrate on the 'all fixed costs' charge. The total fixed cost charge consists of R93 000 relating to current year actual fixed manufacturing overheads, and R25 000 relating to current year non-manufacturing overheads, the total being R118 000. This is R8 000 less than the total fixed cost charge in an absorption costing system. This R8 000 was written off as a period cost in the previous period under the variable costing system. This is summarised as follows:

	Absorption costing (R)	Variable costing (R)
Fixed manufacturing overheads in opening inventory	8 000	None
Current year actual fixed manufacturing overheads incurred	93 000	93 000
Current year non-manufacturing fixed costs incurred	25 000	25 000
Total fixed cost charge in current period	126 000	118 000
Profit	89 600	97 600

From the above it is clear that every cost item remains exactly the same except for fixed costs. In this scenario, under the absorption costing system, the total fixed cost charged to the income statement is higher than under a variable costing system, as the fixed cost charge includes fixed manufacturing overheads arising from prior periods of R8 000, which are included in opening inventories. The effect is that profit in an absorption costing system is lower than the profit in a variable costing system. The difference is exactly equal to the amount of fixed manufacturing overheads in the value of opening inventory, being R8 000.

From example 5.4 the following is apparent:
- When opening inventories are introduced, the profit under the absorption costing system usually differs from the profit under a variable costing system.
- The reason for the difference is that the total fixed cost charged in an absorption costing system differs from the total fixed cost charge in a variable costing system.
- This difference in fixed cost arises because opening inventories in an absorption costing system include fixed manufacturing overheads whereas in the variable costing system they do not.
- Variable manufacturing costs do not result in a profit difference as they are treated the same under both the absorption and the variable costing systems.
- Non-manufacturing costs (both fixed and variable) do not result in a profit difference as they are expensed in full under both the absorption and the variable costing systems.

When fixed manufacturing overheads are brought forward from previous periods, as we see in our example above with absorption costing, we say that previous costs have now expired (been expensed to the income statement) in the current period.

Example 5.4 illustrates that, where the number of units sold exceeds the number of units produced (implying opening inventories and a decrease in inventory levels), the absorption costing system will show a lower profit figure than the variable costing system.

Let us proceed to an example with closing inventory.

5.3.3 Closing inventory

The information from previous examples has been adapted to accommodate closing inventory of 220 000 mints in example 5.5.

principles of management accounting

Example 5.5

Manufacturing information for the 2XX0 financial year relating to Sweetz is given below:

Sales	980 000 @ 40 cents per mint
Number of mints produced in 2XX0	1 200 000
Consisting of:	
Direct materials – raw gum	1 200 kilograms @ R20,00 per kilogram
Direct labour – wages	1 200 hours @ R50,00 per hour
Variable manufacturing overheads	2 400 machine hours @ R30,00 per hour
Budgeted fixed manufacturing overheads	R120 000
Normal capacity	1 200 000 mints per annum
Actual fixed manufacturing costs	R125 000
Closing inventory for 2XX0	220 000 mints
Fixed selling costs	R25 000
Variable selling costs	5 cents per mint sold

Fixed manufacturing overheads are allocated on the basis of the number of mints produced, and inventory is valued on the first-in-first-out basis.

Required:
Prepare income statements on both the absorption costing and the variable costing bases.

Consider the following extracts:

Absorption costing	Total R'000	Per unit R
Closing inventory:		
Direct materials	4,4	0,02
Direct labour	11	0,05
Variable manufacturing overheads	13,2	0,06
Fixed manufacturing overheads (Calculation: R120 000/120 000 = 0,10)	22	0,10

Variable costing	Total R'000	Per unit R
Closing inventory:		
Direct materials	4,4	0,02
Direct labour	11	0,05
Variable manufacturing overheads	13,2	0,06

As discussed with opening inventory, the value of closing inventory under an absorption costing system includes fixed manufacturing overheads. The charges for direct materials, direct labour and variable manufacturing overheads are the same under both formats.

The income statement using absorption costing can be prepared as follows:

Absorption costing	R'000	R'000	R'000
Revenue			392
Less: Cost of sales			225,4
Cost of production:		276	
Direct materials	24		
Direct labour	60		
Indirect costs			
Variable manufacturing overheads	72		
Fixed manufacturing overheads (Calculation: R0,10 × 1 200 000 mints)	120		
Less: Closing inventory:		50,6	
Direct materials	4,4		
Direct labour	11		
Variable manufacturing overheads	13,2		
Fixed manufacturing overheads (Calculation: R0,10 × 220 000 mints)	22		
Gross profit			166,6
Under-allocation (R125 000 – R120 000)			5
Less: Non-manufacturing variable costs			49
Less: Non-manufacturing fixed costs			25
Profit			87,6

Notice the reference to fixed manufacturing overheads in three places. The first is in the cost of production, which comprises the absorbed costs relating to units produced in the current year of R120 000. The second reference is the under-allocation of R5 000. These two together reflect actual fixed manufacturing costs. The third reference to fixed manufacturing overheads occurs in closing inventory. This is shown as a negative amount of R22 000, the effect being that the fixed manufacturing overhead charge to the income statement is being reduced to R103 000.

As 220 000 mints in closing inventory were not sold, the corresponding costs of these units are not expensed, which is why there is a deduction from cost of sales. Absorption costing includes fixed manufacturing overheads in inventories, so a portion of the fixed manufacturing overheads, being R22 000, remains un-expensed at the end of the period. This is also referred to as the fixed manufacturing over-heads being unexpired (not expensed to the income statement) at the end of the period, and consequently capitalised to the statement of financial position as a current asset as part of inventories.

principles of management accounting

In contrast, the variable costing income statement is drawn up as follows:

Variable costing	R'000	R'000	R'000
Revenue			392
Less: Cost of sales			127,4
Cost of production:		156	
Direct materials	24		
Direct labour	60		
Indirect costs:			
Variable manufacturing overheads	72		
Less: Closing inventory:		28,6	
Direct materials	4,4		
Direct labour	11		
Variable manufacturing overheads	13,2		
Less: Non-manufacturing variable costs			49
Contribution			215,6
Less: All fixed costs (R125 000 + R25 000)			150
Profit			65,6

The 'All fixed costs' charge consists of actual fixed manufacturing costs of R125 000 and non-manufacturing fixed costs of R25 000 relating to the current year. This amount remains unaffected by inventories. Opening and closing inventory include no portion of fixed cost, and fixed costs expensed therefore consist of the total fixed cost charge incurred for the year.

The profits on the two income statements are different. The reason for this is that the total fixed cost charge under the absorption costing system is different from the total fixed cost charge in a variable costing system. Under the absorption costing system, a portion of fixed overhead is removed from the income statement by way of closing inventory. This is summarised as follows:

	Absorption costing (R)	Variable costing (R)
Current year fixed manufacturing overheads incurred	125 000	125 000
Fixed manufacturing overheads in closing inventory	(22 000)	None
Current year non-manufacturing fixed costs incurred	25 000	25 000
Total fixed cost charge	128 000	150 000
Profit	87 600	65 600

The difference in profit of R22 000 is explained by the fact that the total fixed cost charge in absorption costing is reduced by the amount of fixed manufacturing overheads of R22 000 which is included in closing inventory and capitalised to the statement of financial position.

Example 5.5 illustrates that, where production exceeds sales (implying that there are closing inventories and an increase in inventory levels), the profit under an absorption costing system will be higher than under a variable costing system.

From example 5.5 the following is apparent:
- When closing inventories are introduced, the profit under the absorption costing system usually differs from the profit under a variable costing system.
- The reason for the difference is that the total fixed cost charged in an absorption costing system differs from the total fixed cost charge in a variable costing system.
- This difference in fixed cost arises because closing inventories in an absorption costing system include fixed manufacturing overheads, whereas in the variable costing system they do not.
- Variable manufacturing costs do not result in a profit difference as they are treated equally under the absorption and the variable costing systems.
- Non-manufacturing costs (both fixed and variable) do not result in a profit difference as they are expensed in full under both the absorption and the variable costing systems.

5.3.4 Further discussion and conclusion on the effect of inventory on profit figures

All expenses (manufacturing and non-manufacturing) are dealt with under both the absorption and the variable costing systems. The only difference lies in the fact that the absorption costing system also includes a fixed manufacturing cost allocation in opening and closing inventory, whereas the variable costing system expenses the actual fixed manufacturing cost in the period in which it occurs. The result of any costs being capitalised to inventory in an absorption costing system is that these costs will be expensed only when these specific inventory items are sold. This is in line with the so-called 'matching principle' used in financial accounting, and helps us to understand why absorption costing is used for financial accounting purposes.

Variable manufacturing costs are treated in the same way under both systems – they form part of the inventory valuation and are expensed only when the inventory items are sold.

As only fixed manufacturing costs are treated differently in these two systems and the difference is in respect of inventory (opening and closing), the difference in profit figures reported must lie in the valuation of opening and closing inventory.

From what we've learnt so far, we may be inclined to assume that the profit figures reported will *always* be the same when the number of units produced is equal to the number of units sold. It is important to note that this is the case only when the amount of fixed manufacturing costs included in opening and closing inventory is the same. When the number of units produced equals the number of units sold but the amount of fixed costs absorbed into opening and closing inventory differs, the absorption and variable systems will not report the same profit figure. In practice it is highly likely that such a difference may exist – inflation causes budgeted fixed costs to increase, which is likely to result in a higher fixed cost allocation rate for the next period.

principles of management accounting

Table 5.3 summarises the relationships that have been explained in this section, on the assumption that fixed manufacturing cost per unit is the same for opening and closing inventory.

Table 5.3 Relationship between units produced and units sold

Units produced = units sold	Fewer units produced than sold	More units produced than sold
No change in inventory levels	Decrease in inventory levels	Increase in inventory levels
Absorption profit = variable profit	Absorption profit < variable profit	Absorption profit > variable profit

Profit figures reported under the absorption and variable costing systems will be different when:
- Production does not equal sales, and/or
- A different fixed manufacturing cost allocation rate was used for opening and closing inventory.

5.3.5 Reconciling absorption costing profit to variable costing profit

The process of reconciling absorption costing profits with variable costing profits should be fairly evident, assuming you have a good understanding of the principles explained so far.

In all the examples in the previous sections it has been pointed out that the difference in profit arises as a result of a change in the amount of fixed costs charged to the income statement.

In an absorption costing system, the amount of fixed cost expensed is driven by the current year's expense, the prior year's expense brought forward in opening inventories, and the expense deferred to future periods in closing inventories. In a variable costing system, only fixed costs relating to the current period are expensed.

The reconciliation process is simply a reversal of the fixed cost charge brought to the income statement through inventories. Using the cost information from example 5.4, this is done as follows:

	Notes	R'000
Absorption costing profit		89,6
Add: Fixed overheads in opening inventories	1	8
Less: Fixed overheads in closing inventories	2	0
Variable costing profit		97,6

Notes:
1. Fixed overheads in opening inventories are added back, as these were expensed in determining absorption profit, by inflating cost of sales.
2. Fixed overheads in closing inventories are deducted, as these were not deducted in determining absorption profit, resulting in a lower charge (with respect to closing inventories) to cost of sales than under variable profit. (Closing inventory was zero in example 5.4.)

Now let us recap what we have learnt in this section. We sought to address the impact of inventories on profit, and explained this impact using three scenarios.

In the first scenario, where we had no inventories, absorption profit was the same as variable profit. In the other two scenarios, where inventories were introduced, absorption profit differed from variable profit. We explained that the difference arose because of the movement in fixed costs. We also illustrated the reconciliation of absorption profit to variable profit.

5.4 Strengths and weaknesses of absorption and variable costing

We have learnt about both the absorption and variable costing methods, and should now consider which method is preferable. As the choice has an impact on the profit figure, the issue of which method is preferable becomes relevant.

Let us first look at the arguments for absorption costing. We will then counter-argue these with points in favour of variable costing.

5.4.1 Absorption costing

Inventory valuation

Absorption costing is the prescribed method for inventory valuation in terms of IAS 2. It is the method used for financial reporting purposes. As it is based on a global standard, it ensures consistency and comparability of financial information.

Emphasis on the importance of fixed costs

Unlike a variable costing system, which treats fixed costs as a period cost and potentially ignores them for decision-making purposes, absorption costing takes cognisance of the fact that fixed costs are a real cost, and should be considered for long-term decision-making, by absorbing overheads into the value of inventory.

5.4.2 Variable costing

Relevance for decision-making

Variable costing provides cost information which is relevant for decision-making purposes. In the short-term, fixed costs are irrelevant because they cannot be altered, and decisions should be based on cost information that changes in line with the decision. As variable costing treats all fixed costs as period costs, and therefore below the contribution line, it enables decisions to be made after considering only relevant cost information for the short term.

Variable costing also forms the basis of break-even analysis, which is discussed in Chapter 4, *Cost-volume-profit relationships*. The link between break-even analysis and variable costing is easily made when we take note of the principle that the variable costing profit is zero at break-even level.

Expired costs

Variable costing ensures that all fixed costs which relate to a period are expensed in the period in which they are incurred. In contrast, the absorption costing method would include fixed manufacturing overheads as part of inventories, and therefore some portion of fixed cost would be carried over to future periods. Variable costing facilitates decision-making in that expired or 'sunk' fixed costs are not carried forward.

Impact on profit

Under an absorption costing system, the relationship between sales volume and profit is camouflaged by changes in inventories. Profit is therefore a function of both sales volumes and production volumes, and the direct relationship between profit and sales volume is not clear. Under a variable costing system, the profit figure is a function of sales volume. Changes in sales volumes have a direct effect on the profit of the entity. An increase in the sales volume would result in a proportionate increase in the contribution, and consequently a movement in profit.

Performance measurement

Absorption costing can be subjected to manipulation through changes in inventories. Variable costing is therefore the preferred method for performance measurement purposes. We saw in the earlier sections that when closing inventory exceeded opening inventory, absorption costing showed a higher profit than variable costing. A manager who is being evaluated on the basis of profit has an incentive to show the highest profit possible, and one way of achieving such profits is by manipulating closing inventories. This is called 'window dressing': managers build up closing inventories at year-end (provided that the organisation has the spare capacity to do so), thereby transferring portions of fixed costs to future periods, and increasing current year profit.

5.5 Summary

In this chapter absorption costing and variable costing were introduced and their use for financial accounting and management accounting purposes was discussed. The underlying cost information remains the same, but absorption costing emphasises the distinction between manufacturing and non-manufacturing costs, while variable costing focuses on the separation of fixed and variable costs. The effect is that the two costing methods result in different income statement reporting formats.

Absorption and variable costing profits differ when production and sales levels differ from one period to the next, or a different manufacturing cost allocation is used for opening and closing inventory. Absorption costing profit is affected by changes in inventories, as a portion of fixed manufacturing overheads is carried forward in inventory. The over- or under-recovery of overheads is not the cause of the difference in profit between the two systems.

Absorption costing is used for financial accounting purposes, as required by IAS 2. Variable costing is usually preferred for management accounting purposes.

Conclusion: Absorption versus variable costing and other topics in this book

To understand the difference between absorption and variable costing, knowledge of the difference between fixed and variable costs, as explained in Chapter 2, *Cost classification*, is required. Chapter 4, *Cost-volume-profit* relationships assumed a variable costing system, as the analysis requires fixed costs to be treated as period costs. Chapter 6, *Overhead allocation* further explains how fixed overheads are allocated to inventory.

Chapter 10, *Relevant information for decision-making* explores the concept of relevance further and will aid in the illustration of why variable costing is useful in management accounting.

Tutorial case study: Chappies

Arthur Ginsburg is the creator of *Chappies*, the bubblegum that captured the youth of the 60s and 70s. It was an iconic South African sweet, recognised by everyone in its distinctive yellow wrapper with blue and red stripes.

In the mid-1930s, Ginsburg became the cost accountant of Chapelat while completing a BCom degree at the University of Witwatersrand. Chapelat manufactured expensive chocolates and toffees, but through a series of transactions found itself having to source a new product and new business.

Ginsburg looked around the market. 'I noticed that Wicks bubblegum was selling at a penny each. I wondered about making a gum that sells two for a penny.'

He experimented with a bubblegum base from the US. It came in square lumps of no particular colour – a greyish opaque mass. When heated, this base became malleable, after which it was put into a large metal container to be mixed. Flavouring and colourant were added, together with glucose and sugar.

From there the bubblegum went through an extruder, and came out in long strips. The strips were then sent through cutting and wrapping machines.

In the old days, 1 200 Chappies used to be produced every minute.

And how did Ginsberg come upon the name? 'While still in the initial experimental stage, I decided on an abbreviation of Chapelat, and that was Chappies,' says Ginsburg.

Chapelat was faced with many challenges. One of these was providing and reporting useful cost information. This was necessary to achieve Ginsburg's goal of 'making a gum that sells two for a penny'.

Source: Davie 2003

1 Discuss whether an absorption costing or variable costing income statement is likely to be seen as more appropriate for use by the management accounting team of the Chapelat company.
2 Discuss whether an absorption costing or variable costing income statement is likely to be seen as more appropriate for use by the financial accounting team of the Chapelat company.
3 If there were no opening inventory in 2XX6 but there was closing inventory, indicate whether you would expect absorption costing or variable costing to report the higher profit in 2XX6, and explain why the profits would differ.
4 If there were no opening inventory in 2XX6 and no closing inventory in 2XX7, discuss whether the cumulative profit over the two years would differ under absorption costing and under variable costing.
5 If a large order had been placed for Chappies and the minimum price to be charged for the order had to be determined, discuss whether the use of absorption costing or variable costing would be more appropriate in the calculation of the minimum price.
6 If the order in question 5 above is to be repeated every year, discuss whether and how your answer would change.
7 If Chappies under-allocated overheads in 2XX7, discuss whether this would further contribute to its absorption costing profit being different from its variable costing profit.
8 Discuss the relative advantages and disadvantages to Chappies of using an absorption costing versus a variable costing system.

principles of management accounting

Basic questions

BQ 1

The new management accountant of a company pointed out to one of the directors that all the company's management reports are traditionally drawn up on an absorption costing basis, and that he would like to make use of variable costing instead, where appropriate. What are the main differences between absorption and variable costing?

BQ 2

As an accountant, on what basis (absorption or variable costing) would you advise your clients to draw up income statements that are going to be used exclusively for financial reporting purposes? Give a reason for your answer.

BQ 3

In the Big Business company, the management accounting team prepare accounts on a variable costing basis each time senior management ask for information on which to base decisions. Why is variable costing useful for decision-making purposes?

BQ 4

The same set of accounts can be prepared on either an absorption costing or on a variable costing basis. Under what circumstances will absorption costing profit differ from variable costing profit, and why?

BQ 5

Most generally accepted alternative methods of calculation and presentation which accountants apply to figures have some strengths and some weaknesses. What are the advantages and disadvantages of the absorption and variable costing methods respectively?

BQ 6

What is the difference between over- and under-allocation?

BQ 7

Source: Adapted from CIMA P1

Summary results for Y Limited for March are shown below.

	R'000	Units
Sales revenue	820	
Variable production costs	300	
Variable selling costs	105	
Fixed production costs	180	
Fixed selling costs	110	
Production in March		1 000
Opening inventory		0
Closing inventory		150

Using variable costing, what was the profit for March?

a) R170 000
b) R185 750
c) R197 000
d) R229 250

BQ 8

Source: Adapted from CIMA P1

The following data relate to a manufacturing company. At the beginning of August there was no inventory. During August 2 000 units of Product X were produced, but only 1 750 units were sold. The financial data for product X for August were as follow:

	R
Materials	40 000
Labour	12 600
Variable production overheads	9 400
Fixed production overheads	22 500
Variable selling costs	6 000
Fixed selling costs	19 300
Total costs for X for August	109 800

What was the value of inventory of X at 31 August, using a variable costing approach?

a) R6 575
b) R7 750
c) R8 500
d) R10 562

BQ 9

Source: Adapted from CIMA P1

A company has a budget to produce 5 000 units of product B in December. The budget for December shows that for Product B the opening inventory will be 400 units and the closing inventory will be 900 units. The monthly budgeted production cost data for product B for December is as follows:

Variable direct costs per unit	R6,00
Variable production overhead costs per unit	R3,50
Total fixed production overhead costs	R29 500

The company absorbs overheads on the basis of the budgeted number of units produced. Assume that the absorption costing overhead rate has remained constant. What is the budgeted profit for Product B for December, using absorption costing?

principles of management accounting

a) R2 950 lower than it would be using variable costing
b) R2 950 greater than it would be using variable costing
c) R4 700 lower than it would be using variable costing
d) R4 700 greater than it would be using variable costing

BQ 10

Source: Adapted from CIMA P1

A company uses a standard absorption costing system. The fixed overhead absorption rate is based on labour hours.

Extracts from the company's records for last year were as follows:

	Budget	Actual
Fixed production overheads	R450 000	R475 000
Output	50 000 units	60 000 units
Labour hours	900 000	930 000

The under- or over-absorbed fixed production overheads for the year were:
a) R10 000 under-absorbed
b) R10 000 over-absorbed
c) R15 000 over-absorbed
d) R65 000 over-absorbed

Long questions

LQ 1 – Intermediate (30 marks; 54 minutes)

Source: University of Johannesburg archive

Auckland Company manufactures and sells a single product. Cost data for the product are as follows:

Variable costs per unit:

	R
Direct materials	6
Direct labour	12
Variable factory overheads	4
Variable selling and administrative costs	3
Total variable costs per unit	R25

Fixed costs per month:

	R
Factory overheads	R240 000
Selling and administrative costs	180 000
Total fixed costs per month	R420 000

The product sells for R40 per unit. Production and sales data for May and June, the first two months of operations, are as follows:

	Units produced	Units sold
May	30 000	26 000
June	30 000	34 000

Income statements prepared by the accounting department, using absorption costing, are presented below:

	May	June
	R	R
Sales	1 040 000	1 360 000
Less: Cost of goods sold:	780 000	1 020 000
Opening inventory	–0	120 000
Cost of goods manufactured	900 000	900 000
Goods available for sale	900 000	1 020 000
Less: Closing inventory	120 000	–0
Gross margin	260 000	340 000
Less: Selling and administrative expenses	258 000	282 000
Net income	2 000	58 000

REQUIRED		Marks
(a)	Determine the unit product cost under: (i) Absorption costing (ii) Variable costing.	5
(b)	Prepare income statements for May and June using the contribution approach (variable costing).	10
(c)	Reconcile the absorption costing and the variable costing net income figures.	5
(d)	Explain the influence of fluctuations in sales volumes on profits or losses realised under the absorption costing method and under the variable costing method.	5
(e)	Explain the difference between absorption and variable costing.	5
TOTAL MARKS		30

LQ 2 – Intermediate (23 marks; 41 minutes)

Source: Adapted from CIMA Stage 1 Accounting

The following data have been extracted from the budgets of ABC Limited, a company which manufactures and sells a single product.

	R per unit
Selling price	45,00
Direct materials cost	10,00
Direct wages cost	4,00
Variable overhead cost	2,50

Fixed production overhead costs are budgeted at R400 000 per annum. Normal production levels are thought to be 320 000 units per annum.

Budgeted selling and distribution costs are as follows:

Variable	R1,50 per unit sold
Fixed	R80 000 per annum

Budgeted administration costs are R120 000 per annum.

The following pattern for sales and production is expected during the first six months of 2XX3:

	January–March	April–June
Sales (units)	60 000	90 000
Production (units)	70 000	100 000

There is to be no inventory on 1 January 2XX3.

	REQUIRED	Marks
(a)	Prepare budgeted profit statements for each of the two quarters, in a columnar format, using: (i) Absorption costing (ii) Variable costing.	12
(b)	Reconcile the profits reported for the quarter from January to March 2XX3 in your answer to (a) above.	3
(c)	Write up the production overheads control account for the quarter to 31 March 2XX3, using absorption costing principles. Assume that the production overhead costs incurred amounted to R102 400 and the actual production was 74 000 units.	3
(d)	State and explain briefly the benefits of using variable costing as the basis of management reporting.	5
	TOTAL MARKS	23

LQ 3 – Advanced (22 marks; 40 minutes)

Source: Adapted from ACCA Level 2 Management Accounting

Note: A basic knowledge of Chapter 6, *Overhead allocation* is useful in answering this question.

The Miozip Company operates an absorption costing system which incorporates a factory-wide overheads absorption rate per direct labour hour. For 2XX0 and 2XX1 this rate was R1,50 per hour. The actual fixed factory overheads for 2XX1 were R600 000, and this amount would have been fully absorbed if the company had operated at full capacity, which is estimated at 400 000 direct labour hours. Unfortunately, only 200 000 hours were worked in that year, so that the overheads were seriously under-absorbed. Fixed factory overheads are expected to be unchanged in 2XX2 and 2XX3.

The outcome for 2XX1 was a loss of R70 000, and the management believes that a major cause of this loss was the low overheads absorption rate which had led the company to quote selling prices which were uneconomical.

For 2XX2 the overheads absorption rate was increased to R3,00 per direct labour hour, and selling prices were raised in line with the established pricing procedures, which involved adding a profit mark-up of 50 per cent onto the full factory cost of the company's products. The new selling prices were also charged on the inventory of finished goods held at the beginning of 2XX2.

In December 2XX2 the company's accountant prepared an estimated profit and loss account for 2XX2 and a budgeted profit and loss account for 2XX3. Although sales were considered to be depressed in 2XX1, they were even lower in 2XX2. Nevertheless, it seemed that the company would make a profit for that year. A worrying feature of the estimated accounts was the high level of finished goods inventory held, and the 2XX3 budget provided for a reduction in the inventory level at 31 December 2XX3 to the (physical) level existing as at 31 January 2XX1. Budgeted sales for 2XX3 were set at the 2XX2 sales level.

Production costs remained constant, and the ratio of variable to fixed inventoriable costs is unlikely to change. The FIFO method of inventory valuation was used.

The summarised profit statements for the three years to 31 December 2XX3 were as follows:

Summarised profit and loss accounts

	Actual 2XX1		Estimated 2XX2		Budgeted 2XX3	
	R	R	R	R	R	R
Sales revenue		1 350 000		1 316 250		1 316 250
Factory cost of goods sold		(900 000)		(817 500)		(877 500)
Opening inventory of finished goods	100 000		200 000		357 500	
Factory cost of production	1 000 000		975 000		650 000	
	1 100 000		1 175 000		1 007 500	
Less: Closing inventory of finished goods	(200 000)		(357 500)		(130 000)	
		450 000		498 750		438 750
Less: Factory overheads under-absorbed		(300 000)		(150 000)		(300 000)
		150 000		348 750		138 750
Administrative and financial costs		(220 000)		(220 000)		(220 000)
	Loss:	(70 000)	Profit:	128 750	Loss:	(81 250)

principles of management accounting

REQUIRED		Marks
(a)	Write a report to the board of Miozip explaining why the budget outcome for 2XX3 was so different from that of 2XX2 when the sales revenue was the same for both years.	6
(b)	Restate the profit and loss account for 2XX1, the estimated profit and loss account for 2XX2, and the budgeted profit and loss account for 2XX3 using variable factory costing for inventory valuation purposes.	8
(c)	Comment on the problems which may follow from a decision to increase the overhead absorption rate in conditions when cost-plus pricing is used and overheads are currently under-absorbed.	3
(d)	Explain why the majority of businesses use absorption costing systems while most management accounting theorists favour variable costing.	5
Note: Assume in your answers to this question that the value of the rand and the efficiency of the company have been constant over the period under review.		
TOTAL MARKS		**22**

LQ 4 – Advanced (22 marks; 40 minutes)

Source: Adapted from ACCA Level 2 Management Accounting

Mahler Products has two manufacturing departments, each producing a single standardised product. The data for unit cost and selling price of these products are as follows:

	Department A		Department B	
	R		R	
Direct materials cost		4		6
Direct labour cost		2		4
Variable manufacturing overheads		2		4
Fixed manufacturing overheads		12		16
Factory cost		20		30
Profit mark-up	50%	10	25%	7,50
Selling price		30		37,50

The factory cost figures are used in the department accounts for the valuation of finished goods inventory in both years. The department profit and loss accounts have been prepared for the year to 30 June 2XX5. These are given separately below for the two halves of the year.

Chapter 5 Absorption versus variable costing

Departmental profit and loss accounts for the year to 30 June 2XX5				
	1 July–31 December		1 January–30 June	
	2XX4	2XX4	2XX5	2XX5
	Department A	Department B	Department A	Department B
	R'000	R'000	R'000	R'000
Sales revenue	300	750	375	675
Manufacturing costs:				
Direct materials	(52)	(114)	(30)	(132)
Direct labour	(26)	(76)	(15)	(88)
Variable overheads	(26)	(76)	(15)	(88)
Fixed overheads	(132)	(304)	(132)	(304)
Opening inventory of finished goods	(60)	(210)	(120)	(180)
Closing inventory of finished goods	120	180	20	300
Administrative and selling costs	(30)	(100)	(30)	(100)
Profit	94	50	53	83

The total sales revenue was the same in each six-monthly period. However, in the second half of the year, the company increased the sales of Department A (which has the higher profit mark-up) and reduced the sales of Department B (which has the lower profit mark-up). An increase in company profits for the second six months was anticipated, but the profit achieved was R8 000 lower for the second half of the year than for the first half. The profit for Department A fell by R41 000, while the profit for Department B rose by R33 000. There has been no change in prices of inputs or outputs.

REQUIRED		Marks
(a)	Explain the situation described in the last paragraph. Illustrate your answer with appropriate supporting calculations.	14
(b)	Redraft the department profit and loss accounts using variable costing to value unsold inventory.	8
TOTAL MARKS		22

LQ 5 – Advanced (33 marks; 60 minutes)

Snoike (Pty) Ltd manufactures one type of product. The organisation uses an absorption costing system for both internal and external reporting purposes. Inventory is valued at budgeted cost per unit. Manufacturing overheads are absorbed on the basis of *units produced*, using a predetermined rate established at the *beginning* of the organisation's financial year. The latter runs from 1 July to 30 June. Management accounts are prepared on a quarterly basis.

You are the recently-appointed management accountant of Snoike (Pty) Ltd. Your predecessor resigned (under mysterious circumstances) while preparing the management accounts for the first two quarters of the financial year. The following is the only information you have to hand:

1. The previous management accountant determined the following budgeted costs of their product per unit, based on a budgeted normal operating capacity of 20 000 units produced and sold, per three-month period. It was assumed that this would remain unchanged for both quarters under review:

		R
Direct labour	(4 hours @ R20/hr)	80
Direct materials	(4 kg @ R15/kg)	60
Manufacturing overheads	(Variable and fixed)	?
Variable selling	(Per unit sold)	10
Fixed administration cost	(Per unit sold)	50
Total cost		?

131

principles of management accounting

2. It was determined that budgeted manufacturing overheads would be R 850 000 at a production level of 25 000 units.
3. The budgeted selling price per unit was determined by applying a mark-up of 20 per cent to the budgeted total cost. The actual selling price of R 288 per unit in each quarter was exactly as budgeted.
4. The unit variable manufacturing costs incurred in each quarter were exactly as budgeted.
5. The actual fixed manufacturing overheads incurred in each quarter and the actual units of production were as follows:

	1/7/2XX9 to 30/9/2XX9	1/10/2XX9 to 31/12/2XX9
Actual fixed manufacturing overheads	R620 000	R590 000
Actual production (units)	20 000	19 000

6. The actual selling and administration costs for each quarter were:

	1/7/2XX9 to 30/9/2XX9	1/10/2XX9 to 31/12/2XX9
Total fixed administration cost	As budgeted	5% higher than budget
Unit variable selling price	Unit cost as budgeted	Unit cost 10% lower than budget

7. Actual sales volume for each quarter was as follows:

	1/7/2XX9 to 30/9/2XX9	1/10/2XX9 to 31/12/2XX9
Actual sales (units)	Under budget by 3 000 units	Exceeded budget by 1 000 units

8. There was no opening inventory of raw materials, work-in-progress or finished inventory on 1/7/2XX9. There was no closing inventory of raw materials or work-in-progress at the end of either quarter.

REQUIRED		Marks
(a)	Using the organisation's normal basis of reporting, prepare the income statements for each quarter showing the actual financial results. (*Note:* Details of individual production costs are not required. Express the monetary figures in R'000. For example, R10 000 is 10 in R'000.)	15
(b)	Prepare the income statements for each quarter, showing the actual financial results according to variable costing principles, valuing inventory at the appropriate budgeted cost per unit.	10
(c)	Reconcile for each quarter the absorption costing profit to the variable costing profit.	2
(d)	Assume that the managing director said to you: 'I have compared the two sets of financial statements you have prepared for me. I am confused because the first set (that is, (a) above) shows a larger profit in the first quarter and a smaller profit in the second quarter when compared to the second set (that is, (b) above). Also I'm not happy about having two different sets of accounts. Why can't we have just one?'	
	(i) Explain to the managing director why the different sets of reporting methods derive different profit outcomes for each quarter.	3
	(ii) Express an opinion as to whether or not both reporting method should continue to be used by the organisation.	3
TOTAL MARKS		**33**

References

BHP Billiton. 2009. *Annual Report 2009*. 185.

Davie, L. 2003. *Chappies: A Jo'burg creation*, from the 'City of Johannesburg' web site. [Online]. Available: <www.joburg.org.za> [23 October 2006].

SAICA (South African Institute of Chartered Accountants). 2010. *IAS 2, Inventories (revised December 2009)*. Johannesburg: SAICA.

Advanced reading Integration section: Chapters 1 to 5

chapters 1 to 5

Shelley-Anne Roos

> The aim of this section is to integrate students' knowledge of Chapters 1 to 5, and to move students toward a more advanced, high-level understanding of the topics, the relationships between them, and the exam technique required.

Chapters 1 to 5 lay the foundation for your understanding of management accounting. Paradoxically, the depth of your understanding of the principles studied in these introductory chapters may largely determine your performance in other topics and in advanced exams. Let's discuss each chapter in turn to see how its content helps you to tackle complex management accounting questions.

Chapter 1, *Introduction to management accounting* is important reading for students who study management accounting for the first time. It is also fundamental to your understanding of advanced work. Higher-level questions usually feature a scenario with a large quantity of information, as well a set of requirements that test your practical insight into the particular organisation's situation. You will need to be very confident about the role of a management accountant – and the role of management accounting information – in order to approach the requirements in the correct way. For example, your answer may score poorly if you unwittingly apply financial accounting principles, because it may not give information appropriate for *management decision-making* purposes.

Chapter 2, *Cost classification* introduces the very important distinction between variable and fixed costs. The advanced student should have a thorough appreciation of the fact that, in the very long term, all costs are variable. This is because all costs can 'change' in the long run – consider, for example, where a factory's lease contract expires and is re-negotiated after a number of years, machine lease payments and depreciation charges change when they are replaced, staff salaries are adjusted, and so on. In other words, when we speak of 'variable' and 'fixed' costs, technically speaking we ought to specify the relevant period or cost object as well. For example, we should say the cost is 'fixed within a one-year planning period' or 'variable according to the number of units produced'. Try to use such full sentences in your mind when you think through examples and questions about variable and fixed costs. You will see that it helps you a great deal in more advanced questions, such as those on relevant costing (which is dealt with in Chapter 10, requires a thorough understanding of cost classification, and is often examined in professional examinations). Candidates who struggle to score well in difficult relevant costing calculations – and especially in discursive answers on the topic – often find that they lack an understanding of the basic principles of cost classification and behaviour.

Chapter 3, *Cost estimation* builds on your knowledge of cost classification. It illustrates how costs are split into their variable and fixed components. An

principles of management accounting

advanced question may, for example, require the use of the high-low method to separate variable from fixed costs. However, unlike basic questions on the topic, the advanced question's requirement is unlikely to directly stipulate the use of this method. The student will need to study the cost information in the scenario in-depth, and deduce from the requirement (which is likely to be something else entirely), that such a distinction has to be made before we can give a meaningful answer. In fact, we can formulate the following general guideline:

> To answer a question where a specific topic is not directly asked (an advanced question), we have to know the material more thoroughly than we need to know it when the topic is directly asked (a basic question). This is because the advanced question requires us to sense intuitively that it is necessary to process the information in a certain way before arriving at the answer.

Chapter 4, *Cost-volume-profit relationships* also relies heavily on your understanding of the distinction between variable and fixed costs. In addition it requires you to think about one of the very cornerstones of the business world: How many units do we need to sell, or how many customers do we need to serve, in order to earn a profit of Rx? It should not surprise you that almost any business proposition – whether it is a loan application at a bank, a proposed new venture, or a co-operative agreement with another organisation – will feature an in-depth study of the relationship between cost, volume and profit. This is because, bluntly put, it shows us whether things are likely to work out. Because advanced questions are designed to test whether you would make a good management accountant in practice, practical topics find their way into such questions in many different forms and are asked from a variety of different angles. Again, to judge when cost-volume-profit calculations are appropriate in an answer, you will have to understand the underlying principles thoroughly.

The differences between financial accounting and management accounting are highlighted in Chapter 5, *Absorption versus variable costing*. Absorption costing is appropriate for financial accounting purposes, because it gives the external user of financial statements a realistic indication of the value of the inventory sold and retained during the financial period. And because organisations apply absorption costing in the same prescribed way, external parties can easily compare financial results. The management of an organisation, however, is not an external party. Managers work inside the organisation to take decisions that improve the performance of the organisation – they need information that helps them to understand the impact of their decisions. Management accounting information is therefore compiled on a variable costing basis. As discussed in the paragraph on Chapter 1 above, an appreciation of the role of management accounting becomes more important in advanced questions.

Some of the aspects dealt with in Chapters 1 to 5 will now be integrated in an advanced question. The question used here comes from Part 1 of the SAICA qualifying examination, but it has been adapted for our purposes.

Because the question is meant to move you towards dealing with longer and more advanced questions, you have to approach it in a manner that will both save time and help you to write a quality answer. Apply the following technique:
- Read the question requirements first, to focus your thoughts on what will be required of you.
- Read the scenario and plan all of your answers.
- Answer the requirements in the given order, starting with requirement (a).

- *Apply* your answers to the specific organisation in the scenario – do not write general, theoretical answers.

Integrated question: Aqua Systems

Aqua-systems Ltd has two divisions. The Pumpworks division manufactures standardised electric water pumps for industrial use and the Agri-water division manufactures irrigation systems for agricultural purposes.

The normal production capacity of Pumpworks is 1 000 units per month, while an average of 970 units are sold. Pricing is based on a set mark-up as prescribed by Aqua-systems Ltd.

During a recent management meeting, the management of Aqua-systems Ltd reviewed the budgeted income statement of Pumpworks for April 2XX5. The manager of the Pumpworks division explained that the division was slowly but surely turning the corner. The division had improved its performance over the past three months and profitability should improve soon. In fact, the manager of Pumpworks indicated that the loss of the division had decreased and that it should reach a break-even position in five months' time.

However, the management of Aqua-systems Ltd is not convinced of this and they approach you, the management accountant of the company, to advise them on the likelihood that the Pumpworks division will return to profitability soon.

Pumpworks Division
Budgeted income statement for the month ending 30 April 2XX5

	Notes	R
Sales (970 units)		1 703 320
Less: Cost of sales		1 578 260
Opening inventory (24 casings @ R205 each)		4 920
Production cost (1 000 finished units)		1 622 000
Closing inventory (30 finished units)		(48 660)
Gross profit		**125 060**
Insurance claim	1	54 300
Sales and administration cost	2	(148 400)
Head office allocation	3	(173 580)
Loss for the month		**(142 620)**

Notes: Relevant information
1. During June 2XX4 the Pumpworks production facilities were damaged in a fire caused by an electrical fault. After initial problems with the insurance company, Aqua-systems Ltd received a letter from it shortly before the completion of the April budget to the effect that the amount of R54 300 had been awarded to the company for the damage.
2. Twenty-five per cent of sales and administration costs are variable.
3. Head Office overheads include a fee per water pump sold. The fee relates to a patent used on one of the components of the water pump. The budgeted April 2XX5 income statement projects the best unit sales ever. In its worst month, the Pumpworks division sold only 850 units, and head office overheads allocated amounted to R171 900.

principles of management accounting

The cost of the water pump components and related labour costs are set out below:

a) **Pipe connectors**

These units are bought from an external supplier. One connector is used per pump system. Pumpworks recently bought 250 pipe connectors at R20 each for use on the standard system. Although they cost the same as the connectors which were usually purchased, the units were the wrong size, and Pumpworks planned to return them to the supplier. However, the supplier offered Pumpworks a 50 per cent discount on the unit price for keeping the units. In anticipation of possible future contracts which might need smaller pumps, Pumpworks decided to accept the supplier's offer.

b) **Casings**

The 24 casings in inventory have been damaged, but can still be used if modified. The modification will cost R54 per casing in non-labour expenses and entail 30 labour minutes per casing. One casing is used per pump. Information on the 24 casings that are in inventory is as follows:

	R
Cost	205 each
Replacement cost	230 each
Net replacement value	225 each

c) **Impellers**

One set of impellers is used per pump. Pumpworks is able to manufacture 1 150 sets of impellers per month, at a total variable cost of R250 per set. It can sell spare sets of impellers at R370 per set. No impellers are currently in inventory. The total fixed cost for the production of impellers amounts to R132 000 per month, and represents depreciation on recently acquired machinery.

d) **Shafts**

Shafts are cut from standard steel bars. Each bar is cut into one shaft, and one shaft is used per pump. According to the inventory records, the total cost (excluding labour) amounts to R175 per shaft. Pumpworks has the capacity to cut 1 100 standard shafts per month. Depreciation and other fixed costs (excluding labour) related to this activity amount to R160 000 per month.

e) **Electric motors**

Electric motors are bought at R450 per unit. One motor is used per pump system.

f) **Labour**

- *Shaft cutting*: Shaft cutting labourers are highly skilled. They are paid R60 per hour and work 160 hours per month. Because of the high cost of training, all five of the shaft-cutting labourers are full-time employees of the company.
- *Casings*: A total of 13 labourers are employed in this section. Each labourer receives a salary of R5 000 per month and works 160 hours per month. Each standard casing takes two hours to manufacture. New casing casters can be trained at a cost of R5 000 per employee. The minimum employment period for these workers is three months.
- *Impellers*: Labour consists of full-time machine operators. Existing operators will be able to handle any expansion.
- *Assembly*: Labourers are paid R50 per hour to do the assembly. One pump system takes two hours to assemble. Assembly hours are not limited and can be adjusted as necessary.

Advanced reading Integration section: Chapters 1 to 5

Cost savings

As part of his attempts to return the division to profitability, the manager of the Pumpworks division recently asked Aqua-systems' new junior financial clerk to divide the cost of labour in the Pumpworks division into its variable and fixed components in order to investigate whether labour costs could be saved. The clerk is very confused about this request, because he has always thought that direct labour costs in a factory are always variable.

REQUIRED		Marks
(a)	Analyse and discuss the budgeted income statement for April 2XX5 and the detailed costs of Pumpworks, and: (i) Specifically comment on the statement by the manager of Pumpworks that the division is capable of returning to profitability within the next five months, and (ii) Suggest possible actions that could lead to profitability for the division.	30
(b)	Explain exhaustively whether the junior financial clerk's notion that 'direct labour costs in a factory are always variable' is true.	5
TOTAL MARKS		**35**

Discussion

A suggested solution to the question can be found at the back of the book. Once you have attempted the question and checked the solution, you may find the following discussion useful.

Requirement (a) is a two-part requirement. In part (i) you need to comment on whether the Pumpworks division is capable of returning to profitability within the next five months. Notice how the requirement gives you very little guidance in its wording to show you how to form an opinion. It leaves you to work through the large amount of information in the question, and to decide for yourself how you would be able to make such a judgement. This is a good example of a question where you have to be very confident about the contents of Chapter 5, *Absorption versus variable costing*. You have to sense – without being told – that the way in which the budget has been drawn up may not be a true representation of what is really going on in the division. The fact that closing inventory has increased over opening inventory, for example, makes the loss look smaller than it actually is. To rectify this, we need to calculate how much it costs to manufacture one pump. When we take this into account, together with the fixed costs of operating the business, we can determine whether there is any chance of making a profit under the present circumstances. The manager believes that the division can break even within five months. To comment on his statement, you need to use the information in the question to calculate the break-even point (as illustrated in Chapter 4, *Cost-volume-profit relationships*). Knowing what the break-even point is will allow you to comment on whether you think this is, in fact, a realistic target to reach within the next few months.

Also notice that you need to use the high-low method (as illustrated in Chapter 3, *Cost estimation*) to separate variable from fixed costs which were allocated by head office. Again, the question does not specifically mention the method – you have to realise that a variable costing approach is required in order to arrive at an appropriate answer, and this leads you to search for ways to distinguish between variable and fixed costs (the characteristics of variable and fixed costs were explained in Chapter 2, *Cost classification*).

Part (ii) of requirement (a) asks you to suggest ways in which the division could possibly return to profitability. You will not be able to give a sensible answer to part (ii) if you have not answered part (i) first – the answer to part (i) leads you to come up with the suggestions required in part (ii). Once you have performed the break-even analysis in part (i), you should realise that the formula used to calculate the break-even point is key to understanding how its result could be changed. Remember that in an advanced question you have to apply your answer to the scenario at hand. This means that as far as possible you should not write generic statements such as 'advertise more', 'cut costs' or 'manage the division better'. You can test the validity of what you write by asking yourself whether it would have been applicable to just about any company – if so, you're on the wrong track! Instead, follow your calculations from part (i), use the information given in the question, and write an answer that specifically helps *the Pumpworks division* to return to profitability based on its own unique set of circumstances.

Part (b) requires you to think through the basic distinction between variable and fixed costs, as discussed in Chapter 2, *Cost classification*. To score well, you should plan your answer before you start writing so that you approach it in a systematic way. The suggested solution may help you to make sure you have thought of all the relevant aspects. Again, you should use the information in the question as much as possible in your answer, together with the knowledge that you gained from doing direct labour cost calculations in part (a).

This may have been one of the first times that you have attempted an advanced question that was pitched at the highest professional exam level. If you had some trouble with it, be sure to work through the other three integration sections in this textbook as soon as you have had a chance to revise the relevant chapters. Most students who move from a basic to an advanced level of their management accounting studies find that they need to do two things: (1) revise and make sure that there are no knowledge gaps when it comes to the basic principles of each topic, and (2) pay attention to exam technique. As you may expect, both of these take a lot of time and practice, but are well worth the effort!

Overhead allocation

chapter 6

Carol Cairney (updated by Shelley-Anne Roos)

LEARNING OBJECTIVES
By the end of this chapter, you should be able to:
1 Accumulate and allocate overheads using volume-based, value-based, and activity-based techniques.
2 Allocate support service department costs using the direct, step down, repeated distribution, and simultaneous equation approaches.
3 Understand the background of both the traditional approach to overhead allocation and the activity-based costing (ABC) system.
4 Identify the characteristics of an organisation where ABC will be of most use.
5 Be proficient in ABC and be able to calculate cost driver rates and apply these in the costing of cost objects.
6 Discuss the context of the various uses of ABC.
7 Discuss the strengths and weaknesses of ABC.

The Gauteng Aids Programme and overhead allocation

The Gauteng province's Department of Health and Social Development has an Aids plan which sets out goals, strategic objectives, activities, service coverage targets and budgets. It is known as the *Gauteng Aids Programme*.

In April 2010 the Department launched an HIV counselling and testing campaign, which included health screening. The campaign was originally conducted in all of the province's clinics and hospitals, and later expanded to hostels, public transport hubs and shopping malls. In 2010 big events such as Worker's Day, the FIFA World Cup, and Women's Day were used as opportunities to encourage testing. HIV-positive people were enrolled in the anti-retroviral component of the programme.

However, the Department is simultaneously conducting a number of other programmes and providing a wide range of services. It is, for example, very concerned about the continuing prevalence of TB in the province.

How will the province determine the cost of its Aids Programme? The costs that are directly traceable to the programme, such as the cost of anti-retroviral drugs, can easily be identified. However, there are a number of other costs that may not be directly traceable to the programme. Clinics, for example, treat HIV, TB and numerous other illnesses. What portion of the overhead costs of running each clinic should be regarded as part of the cost of the Aids Programme? This chapter explains the allocation of overhead costs – those costs which are not directly traceable to a cost object.

According to the province, the Gauteng Aids Programme's services were costed for 2009 to 2014 using activity-based costing. Activity-based costing is a popular and sophisticated way of allocating overheads to cost objects, and is also discussed in this chapter.

Sources: Gauteng Province Department of Health and Social Development (2011); South African Government Information (2010)

6.1 Introduction

This chapter deals with the problem of how to allocate overheads to a variety of cost objects, ranging from products and services to departments and other business units.

Allocating overheads to products, services, and other business categories is a problem, because the relationship between the cost object (product, service, and so on) and how the overhead cost is incurred is not clear. As a result, there is no immediate or easy answer to the questions 'How much of the overhead cost should I allocate to a particular product?' or 'On what basis should overheads be divided between products?'

As already discussed in Chapter 2, *Cost classification*, for management accounting purposes, a distinction is drawn between direct costs and overhead (or 'indirect') costs. This distinction is based on the ease of traceability of the cost to the cost objects to which the costs relate. Direct costs are by definition easily *traceable* to the cost objects that they relate to. Overhead costs, on the other hand, are not traceable in an economically feasible way to the cost objects to which they relate. If an organisation wishes to attach these costs to products or services, then that organisation must devise some reasonable means of *allocating* these costs to the cost objects. In practice, a vast number of cost allocation approaches exist, which are usually customised to suit the purposes of the organisation by which they are used. While a great deal of variety may exist between systems, the basic considerations that should inform what kind of costing system would be the most suitable to the organisation are the same.

Before working through this chapter it is important to understand that there is no 'one size fits all' approach to cost allocation. Accounting information is used by a variety of different organisations, with diverse operations, product ranges and cost structures. In addition, accounting information is used for different purposes within an organisation, each with very different cost information needs. An obvious example of different cost information is the contrast between the requirements of the accounting standards with regard to financial reporting, and the information requirements of management when using it for internal purposes. Many readers of this text will be familiar with the requirements of the accounting standards, more specifically IAS 2, with regard to overhead allocation, and should be careful to note that these financial accounting requirements are not necessarily relevant or useful from a management accounting perspective.

It is the objective of management to manage the organisation in such a way that shareholder value is enhanced through the decisions that are taken by management, and by controlling the actions of the organisation's agents (employees). From a management accounting perspective, cost information should be presented in whatever way, and to whatever extent, is useful for the purpose of decision-making and control. Keeping this principle in mind, the focus of this chapter is to identify the basic techniques and principles on which overhead cost allocation systems are usually built, and highlight the core objectives that these basic techniques and systems are designed to meet.

While many different overhead allocation techniques exist, the basic techniques can be divided into two parts: (1) volume- and value-based techniques, and (2) activity-based overhead allocation techniques.

6.2 Volume- and value-based techniques

> **Key terms:** 'traditional' overhead allocation system, value-based overhead allocation system, volume-based overhead allocation system

A **volume-based overhead allocation system** refers to any method of allocating overhead costs that is based on some measure related to production or service volumes. A volume-based system is frequently referred to in the management accounting literature as a **'traditional' overhead allocation system**. The reason for this is that volume-based allocation systems originated at a time where production processes were simple and where very little complexity or variety existed in the product range (do you remember Henry's Ford's famous statement about his first Ford cars: 'You can have any colour you want, as long as it's black'?) There was not much variety in the Ford product range at that time.). As a result of the lack of variety in production process and product range, the organisation's various products tended to use resources very similarly. Adding up the organisation's total overheads and dividing this total overhead cost by one measure of volume (such as the total number of units produced, or the total number of labour hours worked, or other similar measures) was the method used in order to calculate a flat rate that was then applied to all of the organisation's products. This made sense and was a reasonably accurate method.

Another 'traditional' overhead allocation basis is that of relative sales values (a **value-based overhead allocation system**): overheads are allocated in proportion to the selling prices of products.

There are two basic considerations that apply to a traditional volume- or value-based overhead allocation system. The first consideration is the decision as to what volume or value measure should be used (should the overhead cost be calculated and allocated on the basis of units, or hours, or weight, and so on), and the second is the level of detail that is required in order to achieve a reasonably accurate allocation of costs.

6.2.1 Selecting an appropriate basis: volume and value-based measures

Volume-based measures

Where the products that the organisation produces, or services that the organisation supplies, are largely homogeneous, using the *number of units of output* as a volume measure may be appropriate. In other words, in order to determine the overhead cost of producing one unit of product, the organisation could simply take the total overhead cost incurred for the year, and divide this by the total number of units produced during the year. This method would result in every unit produced bearing exactly the same overhead cost. This would be appropriate where all the units produced were exactly the same, or at least very similar.

However, where the units differ in terms of how they are produced, an input measure such as labour hours or machine hours may be a more accurate measure of the overheads consumed by the various products. If one product takes more time and resources to produce than another, then allocating overheads in accordance with a measure that reflects the higher resource utilisation (such as the number of labour hours used by the product) is preferable to allocating the same amount of overheads to each product unit. The total overhead cost incurred during the year is divided by the total number of labour hours worked during the year, in order to determine the overhead cost per labour hour. Then, to establish the overhead cost of a particular product, the number of hours required to make that product are multiplied by the overhead cost per hour.

Value-based measures

Overheads are sometimes assigned to products or services on the basis of sales value (selling price). This reflects the belief that a product with a higher sales value has been more costly to produce. In other words, the assumption is that the relative sales value of products is representative of their relative cost of production. Where this assumption is false, value-based measures lead to the accounting cost of the item being different from its real cost, and therefore to potentially incorrect decision-making.

Notice that the above methods of overhead allocation do not actually measure the amount of overhead used to produce each type of product or service. They would be suitable in organisations where products or services are largely homogeneous. However, many organisations produce diverse products or services. There is also an increased trend towards customisation, giving customers more options from among which to choose. The production of products and carrying out of services are therefore often so complex in modern organisations that the use of volume- or value-related measures may not provide a good approximation of cost. This has given rise to the development of costing systems that are designed to measure the resource usage of products or services, in order to measure more accurately the overhead cost attributable to each. These kinds of costing systems are more complex and costly to operate. It is the responsibility of management to understand the resource demands of the various products or services that their organisation produces, and to select a cost allocation basis that adequately reflects the overhead cost associated with their respective demand for common resources.

6.2.2 Level of detail and accuracy

It is also important that management is able to apply judgement regarding the level of accuracy of the cost allocation system, given the set of circumstances that the business faces. Where different products or services consume overheads similarly, where overheads do not constitute a significant portion of the organisation's cost structure, or where competition is not particularly intense it may be adequate to operate a moderately accurate overhead allocation system.

Example 6.1

SA Paints manufactures a wide variety of paints. The managing director, Paul, has been comparing their profit margins. He wants to instruct sales staff to try to sell more of the paints with higher profit margins. If a particular line of paint is making a loss, he intends to stop manufacturing that paint altogether.

The cost of materials (which are added according to a paint 'recipe') can easily be traced to each type of paint. A transport company charges a set rate per drum of paint transported to SA Paints' customers for every kilometre travelled, so transport costs are also easily traced to each type of paint.

All other manufacturing costs, including labour, are difficult to trace directly to the paints manufactured. Labourers don't work directly on the paint itself, but instead spend their time on tasks such as setting up machinery, loading materials into the mixing pots, washing out the mixing pots, opening and closing seals, removing nozzles, and similar tasks. Labour is therefore not directly related to the number of litres of each type of paint produced. Labour is also not directly related to the time it takes to manufacture each type of paint. Some paints take longer than others to mix because the materials take longer to combine and settle.

Each type of paint is manufactured in the same batch size each time, but the batch size is different for each type of paint. Because there is limited warehouse space, less popular paints are produced in smaller batches. Paints that are in high demand are manufactured in large batches.

Below are the costs for two of the paints: Red Marine and Green Exterior. Both paints are sold in 20-litre drums. Red Marine Paint is produced in smaller batches than Green Exterior paint, which is more popular.

Product	Red Marine per 20-litre drum	Green Exterior per 20-litre drum
	R	R
Revenue	1 150,00	980,00
Direct costs	(310,50)	(272,40)
Materials	(276,00)	(243,00)
Transport	(34,50)	(29,40)
Revenue less direct costs	839,50	707,60

During the 2XX8 financial year 3 120 000 litres of paint were produced.

Income statement for SA Paints for the 2XX8 financial year

	R	
Revenue	156 000 000	
Direct costs	37 128 000	26% *
Direct materials (paint drums, raw materials, labels)	32 448 000	
Transport	4 680 000	
Manufacturing overheads	70 080 000	49% *
Factory rental	2 400 000	
Depreciation and maintenance	26 400 000	
Electricity and water	28 080 000	
Cleaning and machine set-up expenses	7 800 000	
Labour	5 400 000	

principles of management accounting

	R	
Profit after direct costs and manufacturing overheads	48 792 000	
Non-manufacturing overheads	34 752 000	25% *
Profit	14 040 000	

* Percentage of total costs of R141 960 000

Required:
Calculate the profit after direct costs and manufacturing overheads per drum of Red Marine paint and per drum of Green Exterior paint, allocating the manufacturing overheads on each of the following two bases in turn:
- On the basis of volume (total number of litres produced)
- On the basis of sales revenue.

To allocate overheads on the basis of volume, overheads per litre of paint have to be calculated. The total manufacturing overheads for the year were R70 080 000, and 3 120 000 litres were produced. Manufacturing overheads per litre produced amount to R22,46. For a drum containing 20 litres of paint, R22,46 × 20 litres = R449,20 is allocated. The cost of a drum of each type of paint can be summarised as follows:

Product per 20-litre drum	Red Marine	Green Exterior
	R	R
Revenue	1 150,00	980,00
Direct costs	(310,50)	(272,40)
Materials	(276,00)	(243,00)
Transport	(34,50)	(29,40)
Manufacturing overheads	(449,20)	(449,20)
Profit per drum	390,30	258,40
Profit percentage	33,9%	26,4%

To allocate overheads on the basis of sales revenue, overheads per rand of sales has to be calculated. Total manufacturing overheads of R70 080 000 are divided by sales revenue of R156 000 000. Manufacturing overheads per rand of sales revenue are R0,45. For a drum of Red Marine paint R1 150 (sales value) × R0,45 = R517,50 is allocated. For a drum of Green Exterior paint R980 (sales value) × R0,45 = R441 is allocated. The cost of a drum of each type of paint can be summarised as follows:

Product per 20-litre drum	Red Marine	Green Exterior
	R	R
Revenue	1 150,00	980,00
Direct costs	(310,50)	(272,40)
Materials	(276,00)	(243,00)
Transport	(34,50)	(29,40)
Manufacturing overheads	(517,50)	(441,00)
Profit per drum	322,00	266,60
Profit percentage	28%	27,2%

If the first allocation basis – that of litres – is used, the managing director gets the impression that Red Marine paint earns a healthy 33,9 per cent profit per drum, while Green Exterior paint earns 26,4 per cent. Just by changing the overhead allocation basis to sales revenue, the picture changes. Now it seems that Red Marine paint earns 28 per cent profit, while Green Exterior paint earns 27,2 per cent. Changing the overhead allocation basis can have a significant impact on the calculated product costs and the way products lines are regarded, especially in an organisation such as SA Paints, where a large portion of total costs (49 per cent) consists of manufacturing overheads.

> It is important to understand that SA Paints' overall profit is not affected by the method of overhead allocation that is used. It is only the allocation of overheads to the different types of paint (and therefore their relative profitability) that is affected by the method of overhead allocation chosen. However, costs may be saved in future periods (or profits may be improved as a result of better pricing of the paints) if management take better *decisions* based on a change in the overhead allocation base.

Example 6.2

The same information applies as in example 6.1.

Required:
1. Critically discuss the usefulness of allocating non-manufacturing overheads to products.
2. Calculate the profit per drum of Red Marine paint and per drum of Green Exterior paint when overheads (manufacturing and non-manufacturing overheads) are allocated on each of the following two bases in turn:
   - On the basis of volume (total number of litres produced)
   - On the basis of sales revenue.

The first requirement of this example asks us to discuss whether non-manufacturing overheads could be allocated to products. From an organisational perspective, in order to earn a profit, a product needs to earn sufficient revenue to cover not only the costs of manufacturing the product, but also storing, marketing and selling that product. However, while the relationship between the manufacturing overheads and individual units of product is not easy to trace, the relationship between the non-manufacturing overheads that the organisation incurs, and the individual units of product that are produced, is even more difficult to establish.

For the purposes of financial accounting only manufacturing overhead is allocated to products. Non-manufacturing overhead is expensed as a period cost in the income statement, as required by IAS 2. For management accounting purposes, however, management needs determine what allocation will yield the best management information.

In our SA Paints example, Paul needs to determine the relative profitability of the products that the organisation produces. Paul needs a per-product-unit profit figure that is reliable in the sense that it represents the financial impact on the organisation of selling one additional drum of each type of paint, or selling one less drum of each type. The costs that are allocated must be relevant to the decision he will be making (refer to section 2.4 in Chapter 2, *Cost classification* and Chapter 10, *Relevant costs for decision-making*).

The distinction between manufacturing and non-manufacturing overheads is not important from a decision-making perspective, and non-manufacturing costs may therefore be allocated if relevant.

The costs that Paul should not allocate to products are those that are not affected by the decision he faces, for example, audit fees.

The second requirement of this example asks that we again allocate overheads on the basis of volume and sales value in turn, as we did in example 6.1.

In the case of SA Paints, 'non-manufacturing overheads' consists of indirect costs that are incurred outside the manufacturing process. Total manufacturing (R70 080 000) plus non-manufacturing overheads (R34 752 000) amounts to R104 832 800. When divided by the total number of litres produced (3 120 000), the result is total overheads of R33,60 per litre of paint. For 20 litres, R33,60 × 20 litres = R672 in overheads is therefore allocated. The cost of a 20-litre drum of each type of paint can be summarised as follows:

Product per 20-litre drum	Red Marine	Green Exterior
	R	R
Revenue	1 150,00	980,00
Direct costs	(310,50)	(272,40)
Materials	(276,00)	(243,00)
Transport	(34,50)	(29,40)
Total overheads	(672,00)	(672,00)
Profit per 20-litre drum	167,50	35,60
Profit percentage	14,6%	3,6%

To allocate total overheads on the basis of sales revenue, overheads per rand of sales has to be calculated. Total overheads of R104 832 000 is divided by sales revenue of R156 000 000. Total overheads per rand of sales revenue is R0,67. For a 20-litre drum of Red Marine paint R1 150 (sales value) × R0,67 = R770,50 is allocated. For a 20-litre drum of Green Exterior paint R980 (sales value) × R0,67 = R656,60 is allocated. The cost of a 20-litre drum of each type of paint can be summarised as follows:

Product per 20-litre drum	Red Marine	Green Exterior
	R	R
Revenue	1 150,00	980,00
Direct costs	(310,50)	(272,40)
Materials	(276,00)	(243,00)
Transport	(34,50)	(29,40)
Total overheads	(770,50)	(656,60)
Profit per 20-litre drum	69,00	51,00
Profit percentage	6%	5,2%

On the first allocation basis in example 6.2, we allocate the same amount of overheads to each drum of paint. What this volume-based allocation implies is that every 20-litre drum of paint costs the same amount in overheads to produce and sell. However, some paints may use more labour time, more factory time and more warehousing space than others.

When sales revenue is used as the allocation basis, example 6.2 shows that more overheads are allocated to each drum of red paint than to each drum of green paint because red paint has the higher selling price. The underlying assumption is that a higher selling price reflects a larger amount of resources consumed. This is not necessarily true – the selling price is often a result of market forces rather than product cost.

Section 6.2.1 dealt with selecting an appropriate allocation basis. You may wonder whether SA Paints would arrive at a more equitable allocation of overhead if it based its allocation on the number of labour hours used in the manufacture of each type of paint.

The number of labour hours is one of the resources used to make and sell each product. By allocating overheads based on the number of labour hours put into the production of the product, the overheads would be allocated in accordance with how the product uses some of the organisation's resources to which the overheads relate. However, in this scenario, although red paint takes longer to manufacture and therefore takes up more factory time, it doesn't take up any more labour time than green paint. Furthermore, labour doesn't work directly on the paint. Most of the tasks that labour carries out are at a higher level and are more general tasks that apply to either a batch, or to the factory as a whole. In the SA Paints example, labour itself is an indirect cost that must be allocated to the different paints. Therefore, in this example,

principles of management accounting

using the number of labour hours as the basis on which overheads are allocated is unlikely to be any more accurate in allocating the overheads to the various types of paint in proportion to the actual resources the product uses.

Example 6.3

Consider the same information as in example 6.1.

Required:
Discuss the different perspectives with which SA Paints' auditors and its management team may regard the choice of overhead allocation base.

IAS 2 is the accounting standard that specifies what costs are to be included in inventory, and the statement also dictates the exclusion of certain costs from inventory. Paragraphs 12 and 13 of IAS 2 deal with the allocation of overheads to inventory.

There are three key points that should be noted:
- The purpose of IAS 2 is to specify what costs may be included in the inventory figure which is reported in the organisation's annual financial statements. It is a financial accounting statement with no bearing on management accounting, which is governed by management's information needs.
- The statement allows only manufacturing costs to be included in inventory. Non-manufacturing costs such as selling and administrative costs are not to be included in the inventory value reported on the statement of financial position.
- The statement requires costs to be allocated on a reasonable basis that reflects normal production volumes.

For statutory financial reporting purposes, the organisation's auditors would therefore be satisfied with any approach that allocates the manufacturing overheads at normal production volumes. Whether or not the amount of overheads allocated to a product reflects the amount of resources that are used to make that product is not an issue. Furthermore, the statement requires *all* manufacturing overheads to be allocated. The relevance of those costs to decision-making is not a consideration.

However, for management accounting purposes, the cost allocation in our SA Paints example is going to be used as a basis for a decision that will be aimed at increasing the organisation's profit. Note the difference here between the financial accounting objective and the management accounting objective. The financial accounting objective is to calculate the cost at which the inventory will be reflected at on the financial statements, before it is sold. The management accounting objective is to calculate the amount by which that product *contributes to profit* when the product is sold. These are two different objectives – for financial accounting purposes we would be trying to determine the costs incurred to manufacture the paint, and only the manufacturing cost should be considered. However, for decision-making purposes, Paul is trying to determine the ideal product mix by investigating how much each product contributes to profit. Therefore, as previously stated, all costs that are relevant to this decision ought to be taken into account.

Example 6.4

Consider the same information as in example 6.1.

Required:
Discuss the factors mentioned in the SA Paints example which indicate that a simple volume- or value-based overhead allocation method may not provide information that is reliable for the purposes of Paul's decision.

The following factors must be taken into consideration:
- *SA Paints' products do not all follow exactly the same production process, and as a result they use resources differently.* The paint is produced in batches, and a bigger batch is cheaper to produce per litre than a small batch (because activities such as set-ups and cleaning take place per batch). In many modern organisations product ranges are diverse, increasing the need for accurate overhead allocation.
- *Indirect costs (overheads) comprise a high percentage of total costs.* In fact, only 26 per cent of SA Paints' total costs are direct costs. Accurate allocation of overheads is very important in a situation where overheads are so significant. In many modern organisations, due to increased mechanisation, overhead costs are making up a larger and larger percentage of total costs, increasing the need for accurate overhead allocation.
- *SA Paints' profit margins are slim* (profit before tax is only 9 per cent of revenue). Slim profit margins mean that only a slim margin of error exists. A slight over-allocation of costs may result in profitable products seeming to be loss-making. Conversely, loss-making products may actually show a small profit, if costs are under-allocated by a small amount. As a result of globalisation, many organisations face fierce competition and small profit margins, increasing the need for accurate overhead allocation.

As with any management decision, the costs (in terms of tangible and intangible resources) of implementing a more sophisticated system should be weighed against the expected benefits of such a system. For an organisation such as SA Paints it may be beneficial to refine the costing system further by allocating overheads in a more sophisticated manner. The implementation of an activity-based costing system (ABC system) is an ideal way of addressing SA Paints' overhead allocation problems. This is discussed in section 6.4.

Plant-wide rate versus departmental rate

Key terms: departmental rate, plant-wide rate

The level of detail with which overhead costs are allocated to products can vary considerably. Overheads may be aggregated and allocated to products on one common basis, or costs may be aggregated and allocated at a departmental level. In other words, an organisation can decide either to determine a single overhead rate for the organisation in its entirety, commonly referred to as a **plant-wide rate**, or to have a **departmental rate** determined for each department.

A single plant-wide rate is determined by accumulating the total overheads incurred across the organisation, and dividing that by the allocation base that has been determined as the most suitable for the enterprise. As the use of a single average rate is applied to all products, the costs of each department is charged uniformly to all products. This approach ignores the fact that certain products may

principles of management accounting

use more of the resources of the different departments. This may even result in costs of certain departments being allocated to a product where that product does not use the resources of the department at all.

Where an organisation requires a more accurate cost allocation system, it would be preferable to calculate a rate per department, instead of a plant-wide rate.

Table 6.1 Comparison between plant-wide and departmental rate overhead allocation rates

Plant-wide overhead allocation rate	Departmental overhead allocation rate and cost centre overhead rate *
• A single overhead rate is calculated for the organisation as a whole	• Multiple overhead rates are calculated
• One allocation base is used	• A different allocation base can be used for different departments (labour hours, machine hours, number of employees, floor space, and so on)
• Overheads are assigned to products based on the total use of a single resource (allocation base) throughout the organisation	• Overheads are assigned to products based on the amount of resources used by the product in each department
Result: Overheads are averaged out between products	**Result:** Overheads are averaged out, but less extensively than if a plant-wide rate had been used

* Cost centre overhead rate is the same in concept as the departmental overhead rate, except that rates are calculated per cost centre, instead of per department. A cost centre may often be a sub-unit of a department.

Example 6.5 illustrates the difference between the use of a single plant-wide rate and the use of departmental rates to allocate overheads to products.

Example 6.5

SA Paints has divided its production process into three departments, each of which is responsible for one of the three steps required in producing a drum of paint. The first operating department, the colour-coding department, is used only where customers require a specific colour of paint that is not one of the standard colours. The mixing department is responsible for mixing the ingredients. The filling department is responsible for receiving the paint from the mixing department, filling the paint drums, printing and attaching the appropriate stickers, and packaging the drums on pallets for delivery.

For purposes of this example, assume that manufacturing overheads are allocated based on the number of direct labour hours.

The following information is supplied:

	Production departments			Total
	Colour-coding	Mixing	Filling	
Manufacturing overhead	R14 016 000	R35 040 000	R21 024 000	R70 080 000
Labour hours	66 000	237 600	136 400	440 000
Overhead allocation rate (manufacturing overhead divided by labour hours)	R212,36	R147,48	R154,14	R159,27
Red Marine:				
Labour hours per drum	0 hours	1,8 hours	1,2 hours	3 hours

150

> **Required:**
> Determine the manufacturing overhead cost to be assigned to one drum of Red Marine paint if:
> - A plant-wide overhead allocation rate is used
> - Departmental overhead allocation rates are used.

The overhead allocation rates were arrived at by dividing the relevant manufacturing overhead figure by the number of labour hours given. Using the plant-wide overhead allocation rate of R159,27, one can calculate that each drum of Red Marine paint will receive R159,27 × 3 labour hours = R477,81 in manufacturing overheads.

If departmental overhead allocation rates are employed instead of one plant-wide rate, a drum of Red Marine paint will receive overheads as follows:

	Production departments			
	Colour-coding	Mixing	Filling	Total for 1 drum
Departmental manufacturing overhead rate per hour	R212,36	R147,48	R154,14	
Labour hours per department	0	1,8	1,2	
Overhead to be allocated to 1 drum of Red Marine	R0 +	R265,46 +	R184,97 =	R 450,43

Notice that the manufacturing overhead cost per drum has changed from R477,81 to R450,43. Why has the cost diminished? The R447,81 was calculated by including the manufacturing overhead costs of all departments, including those incurred in the colour-coding department. However, as Red Marine paint is a standard paint, the colour-coding department is not used in order to produce this paint, and its manufacturing overheads should not have been included in the cost of the Red Marine paint. The plant-wide rate makes the basic assumption that the proportion of its total production time that each product spends in each department is the same across all products. This is clearly not the case where there is a difference in the production process of the various products, as in this example.

6.3 Allocation of support service department costs

> **Key terms:** production departments, support service departments

In example 6.5 all three departments are **production departments** – they are directly involved in producing paint. Support service departments, on the other hand, have no direct input into products, but instead support or 'service' the departments that do have direct input into products. Typical examples of **support service departments** are information technology and administration departments.

Support service departments' costs are allocated to the production departments before the departmental overhead allocation rate is calculated. The departmental overhead allocation rate of production departments is then applied to products, as already illustrated in example 6.5. The allocation of support service department costs can be performed in a number of ways. These are described below and then illustrated in example 6.6.

6.3.1 Direct approach

The direct approach requires management to allocate the support service departments' costs directly to production departments. This is often done in proportion to how the production departments make use of the resources of the support service departments. Organisations can also use other bases such as revenue. This approach ignores the fact that the support service departments may also be using each other's services. In reality support service departments may very well use each others' services. For example, in an organisation with an administration department and an information technology department, both of these departments are likely to use the services of the other. The direct approach may sometimes be preferred because of its simplicity. However, if support service departments consume a significant amount of each other's resources, the results will be less accurate than with other approaches.

> **Employing the direct approach (see Table 6.2 on page 155)**
> Under the direct approach, the costs of both support service departments are allocated to production departments only. The fact that the two departments also supply services to each other is ignored.

6.3.2 Step down approach (specified order of closing)

Here the fact that support service departments may use each others' services is taken into consideration to some extent. Support service departments are ranked in order of total costs, and the costs of the highest-ranking departments are allocated to production and other support service departments first and then 'closed off' (in other words, this department it is no longer available to receive any further costs). The process is repeated for the next ranked department, but costs accumulated in lower-ranked support service departments are not allocated to the higher-ranked support service departments that have already been closed off. A disadvantage of this technique is that, if lower-ranked departments use the higher-ranked departments' services, this fact is ignored.

> **Employing the step down approach (see Table 6.3 on page 155)**
> To employ the step down approach, the two support service departments first have to be ranked based on the total costs recorded in the departments. The administration department (R20 851 200) is ranked first and the IT department (R13 900 800) second. The costs of the administration department are therefore allocated first, the department is 'closed off' to prevent it from receiving any further costs (from the IT department), and the new higher total IT costs are then allocated to the production departments only.

6.3.3 Repeated distribution approach

The repeated distribution approach is an expanded version of the step down approach. Here, the fact that support service departments use each others' services is fully taken into account. The support service departments' costs are allocated to production departments and other support service departments, again starting with the support service department with the highest ranking, based on total cost.

There is no 'closing off', and support service departments can continue to receive costs from lower-ranked departments. This process is repeated for each support service department until the costs remaining in the support service departments are considered insignificant. This approach is more complicated and laborious, but renders the most accurate information of the three approaches discussed so far.

> **Employing the repeated distribution approach (see Table 6.4 on page 156)**
> Each support service department receives a portion of the costs of the other department. As under the previous approach, the departments are ranked and costs of the highest ranking department (administration) are allocated first, followed by that of the second-ranked department. Theoretically the allocation steps can be repeated infinitely, but in practice the process is stopped when the remaining unallocated costs are deemed to be immaterial. In Table 6.4, after four rounds of allocating administration costs and three rounds of allocating IT costs, the remaining amounts were no longer considered material.

6.3.4 Simultaneous equation approach

The simultaneous equation approach is based on the same principles as the repeated distribution approach. However, the problem is solved mathematically instead of through repetition. This approach requires total overheads for each support service department, including the costs of using other service departments, to be formulated as an equation. One equation is formulated per support service department. The unknown variables are then calculated by considering the equations simultaneously. Overheads are allocated to the production and service departments according to the equations. Unlike under the previous approach, the allocation is carried out only once. Although there are mathematical ways to solve many equations, if there are more than two support service departments, this becomes a rather complicated process and it is best done using computer software.

> **Employing the simultaneous equation approach (see Table 6.5 on page 158)**
> The first step is to present the costs of the support service departments as equations and to solve for the unknown variables:
> Let x = Total overhead costs of the IT service department
> Let y = Total overhead costs of the administration service department.
>
> | Then: | x = R13 900 800 + 0,25y | (1) |
> |---|---|---|
> | | y = R20 851 200 + 0,20x | (2) |
> | Therefore | x − 0,25y = R13 900 800 | (3) |
> | | −0,20x + y = R20 851 200 | (4) |
> | (3) × (4) | 4x − y = R55 603 200 | (5) |
> | (4) + (5) | 3,8x = R76 454 400 | |
> | | x = R20 119 578,95 | |
>
> Substitute x = R 20 119 578,95 for x in (1) above:
> R20 119 578,95 = R13 900 800 + 0,25y
> −0,25y = − R6 218 778,95
> y = R24 875 115,80

principles of management accounting

Example 6.6

The functions that give rise to SA Paint's R34 752 000 non-manufacturing overheads are carried out in two departments: information technology (IT) and administration. The IT department maintains the computer systems used by the three production departments and by the administrative department. The administration department is responsible for salary calculations, processing of invoices, and other administrative procedures for all three production departments, as well as the IT department. Of the total non-manufacturing overheads of R34 752 000, 40 per cent (R13 900 800) relate to the running of the IT department, and the remaining 60 per cent (R20 851 200) are incurred in the administration department.

Non-manufacturing overheads are allocated based on direct labour hours.

The following breakdown of departmental cost and resource information is supplied:

	Production departments			Support service departments	
	Colour-coding	Mixing	Filling	IT	Admin
Overhead cost per department	R14 016 000	R35 040 000	R21 024 000	R13 900 800	R20 851 200
Total labour hours per production department	66 000	237 600	136 400		
% use of IT department by other departments	10%	55%	15%		20%
% use of administration department by other departments	5%	35%	35%	25%	
Red Marine:					
Labour hours per drum	0 hours	1,8 hours	1,2 hours	0 hours	0 hours

Required:
Determine the overhead cost to be assigned to one drum of Red Marine paint under each of the following allocation approaches:
- Support service department costs are allocated to production departments *directly*.
- Support service department costs are allocated to production departments on a *step down basis*.
- Support service department costs are allocated to production departments on a *repeated distribution basis*.
- Support service department costs are allocated to production departments using *simultaneous equations*.

Tables 6.2 to 6.5 show the four approaches in turn.

Chapter 6 Overhead allocation

Table 6.2 Employing the direct approach

		Production departments		
		Colour-coding R	Mixing R	Filling R
Production overheads	A	14 016 000	35 040 000	21 024 000
Allocated IT costs	B	1 737 600	9 556 800	2 606 400
		(10/80)	(55/80)	(15/80)
Allocated administration costs	C	1 390 080	9 730 560	9 730 560
		(5/75)	(35/75)	(35/75)
Total overheads per production department	D = A + B + C	17 143 680	54 327 360	33 360 960
Total labour hours per production department	E	66 000	237 600	136 400
Departmental overhead rate per hour	F = D/E	259,75	228,65	244,58
Labour hours per drum of Red Marine paint	G	0	1,8	1,2

Total overheads per drum of Red Marine paint: R0 (colour-coding) + R411,57 (mixing) + R293,50 (filling) = R705,07

Table 6.3 Employing the step down approach

		Production departments			Service departments	
		Colour-coding R	Mixing R	Filling R	IT R	Admin R
Overhead costs	A	14 016 000	35 040 000	21 024 000	13 900 800	20 851 200
Allocated administration costs	B	1 042 560	7 297 920	7 297 920	5 212 800	−20 851 200
		(5/100)	(35/100)	(35/100)	(25/100)	
					19 113 600	–
Allocated IT costs	C	2 389 200	13 140 600	3 583 800	− 19 113 600	
		(10/80)	(55/80)	(15/80)		
						–

155

principles of management accounting

		Production departments			Service departments	
		Colour-coding R	Mixing R	Filling R	IT R	Admin R
Total overheads per production department	D = A + B + C	17 447 760	55 478 520	31 905 720		
Total labour hours per production department	E	66 000	237 600	136 400		
Departmental overhead rate per hour	F = D/E	264,36	233,50	233,91		
Labour hours per drum of Red Marine paint	G	0	1,8	1,2		

Total overheads per drum of Red Marine paint: R0 (colour-coding) + R420,29 (mixing) + R280,70 (filling) = R700,99

Table 6.4 Employing the repeated distribution approach

		Production departments			Service departments	
		Colour-coding R	Mixing R	Filling R	IT R	Admin R
Overhead costs	A	14 016 000	35 040 000	21 024 000	13 900 800	20 851 200
Allocated administration costs	B	1 042 560	7 297 920	7 297 920	5 212 800	−20 851 200
		(5/100)	(35/100)	(35/100)	(25/100)	
					19 113 600	–
Allocated IT costs	C	1 911 360	10 512 480	2 867 040	−19 113 600	3 822 720
		(10/100)	(55/100)	(15/100)		(20/100)
					–	3 822 720

156

Chapter 6 Overhead allocation

		Production departments			Service departments	
		Colour-coding R	Mixing R	Filling R	IT R	Admin R
Allocated administration costs (round two)	D	191 136	1 337 952	1 337 952	955 680	−3 822 720
		(5/100)	(35/100)	(35/100)	(25/100)	
					955 680	−
Allocated IT costs (round two)	E	95 568	525 624	143 352	−955 680	191 136
		(10/100)	(55/100)	(15/100)		(20/100)
					−	191 136
Allocated administration costs (round three)	F	9 556,80	66 897,60	66 897,60	47 784	−191 136
		(5/100)	(35/100)	(35/100)	(25/100)	
					47 784	−
Allocated IT costs (round three)	G	4 778,40	26 281,20	7 167,60	−47 784	9 556,80
		(10/100)	(55/100)	(15/100)		(20/100)
					−	9 556,80
Allocated administration costs (round four)	H	637,12	4 459,84	4 459,84	−	−9 556,80
		(5/75)	(35/75)	(35/75)		
					−	−
Total overheads per production department	I = A + B + C, and so on	17 271 596,32	54 811 614,64	32 748 789,04		
Total labour hours per production department	J	66 000	237 600	136 400		

principles of management accounting

		Production departments			Service departments	
		Colour-coding R	Mixing R	Filling R	IT R	Admin R
Departmental overhead rate per hour	K = I/J	261,69	230,69	240,09		
Labour hours per drum of Red Marine paint	L	0	1,8	1,2		

Total overheads per drum of Red Marine paint: R0 (colour-coding) + R415,24 (mixing) + R288,11 (filling) = R703,35

Table 6.5 Employing the simultaneous equation approach

	Production departments			Service departments	
	Colour-coding R	Mixing R	Filling R	IT R	Admin R
Overhead costs	14 016 000	35 040 000	21 024 000	13 900 800	20 851 200
Allocated administration costs	1 243 755,71	8 706 290,53	8 706 290,53	6 218 778,95	−24 875 115,80*
	(5/100)	(35/100)	(35/100)	(25/100)	
				20 119 578,95*	−4 023 915,80
Allocated IT costs	2 011 957,89	11 065 768,42	3 017 936,84	−20 119 578,95	4 023 915,80
	(10/100)	(55/100)	(15/100)		(20/100)
Total overheads per production department	17 271 713,68	54 812 058,95	32 748 227,37		
Total labour hours per production department	66 000	237 600	136 400		
Departmental overhead rate per hour	R 261,69	R 230,69	R 240,09		
Labour hours per drum of Red Marine paint	0	1,8	1,2		

Total overheads per drum of Red Marine paint: R0 (colour-coding) + R415,24 (mixing) + R288,11 (filling) = R703,35

* Refer to section 6.3.4 for the calculation of these amounts.

158

6.4 Activity-based costing (ABC)

> **Key terms:** activity-based costing, cost drivers, cost pool

Activity-based costing (ABC) is a popular and sophisticated form of overhead allocation. Overhead costs are assigned to cost objects based on the activities that drive those costs.

The activities that cause the overhead costs to be incurred are called **cost drivers**. Examples of cost drivers are the number of orders received, or the number of batches manufactured. Different costs that have the same cost driver are grouped together in what is known as a **cost pool**. The costs in each cost pool are then assigned to a cost object according to how much it makes use of the relevant cost driver.

Identify activities and group them into cost pools

Cooper developed a cost hierarchy that is helpful in guiding organisations on how to group activities. Activities are organised in four levels:

- *Unit-level activities:* These are performed each time a product is produced or a service is performed. These activities are also known as volume-related activities.
- *Batch-level activities:* These are performed each time a batch is handled or produced. An example is setting up the machine for each batch. Costs related to such activities are incurred in proportion to the number of batches handled. These costs behave as stepped fixed costs (refer to Chapter 2, *Cost classification*).
- *Product-level activities:* These activities relate to product or service lines and are incurred regardless of how many units are produced or how many batches are handled. The costs relating to these activities are incurred to maintain individual products and product ranges, from designing the product to marketing.
- *Facility-sustaining activities:* These activities are incurred to maintain the organisation in general. In the short term they are performed regardless of the number of units or batches produced and regardless of the number of different products produced. It is often difficult to identify a cost driver that represents the cause-and-effect relationship between the activity and the costs incurred. For this reason, facility-sustaining costs are usually not allocated to products.

Example 6.7

Consider again the example of SA Paints, which manufactures different paints. Raw materials such as pigment, a pigment vehicle, binder, solvents and additives are mixed in quantities ranging from 1 000 litres to 20 000 litres. Each time a batch of paint is produced, the machines have to be set up and cleaned. The paint is then canned and distributed.

The following activities are carried out by SA Paints:
- Researching a new shade of paint
- Cleaning of machines
- Setting up of machines
- Handling of raw materials and paint

principles of management accounting

> - Mixing (by machine)
> - Marketing of different paint types
> - Marketing of SA Paints' products in general
> - Rent and general plant-related expenses
>
> **Required:**
> Classify each of the activities according to Cooper's cost hierarchy, using a short-term planning horizon of one month.

Based on the information available to us, the following would be a reasonable classification:

Activity	Level
Researching new shades of paint	Product-level activity
Cleaning of machines	Batch-level activity
Setting up of machines	Batch-level activity
Handling of raw materials and paint	Unit-level activity
Mixing (by machine)	Unit-level activity
Marketing of different paint types	Product-level activity
Marketing of SA Paints' products in general	Facility-sustaining activity
Rent and general plant-related expenses	Facility-sustaining activity

Notice that SA Paints has identified eight activities in its operations, and these activities are now each regarded as a cost pool. The number of cost pools could be changed, however, according to preference. SA Paints could further refine its costing system by, for example, splitting up the 'marketing of different paint types' cost pool between a 'market research' cost pool and a 'promotion' cost pool (if it is possible and practical to record such costs separately). Or it could simplify its costing system by, say, grouping the 'cleaning of machines' cost pool and the 'machine set-up' cost pool together into a 'cleaning and set-up of machines' cost pool (if it is satisfied that it would be reasonable to apply the same cost driver to both).

The decision as to how many cost pools there should be is one that should be taken on a cost–benefit basis. In general, costs that are incurred at different levels of Cooper's cost hierarchy would not be grouped together into the same cost pool, as they would have very different cost drivers.

Identify cost drivers

A cost driver is identified for each cost pool. It is important for the cost driver to represent a cause-and-effect relationship between the activities in a cost pool and the cost incurred. There are three categories of cost drivers:
- *Transaction driver:* This is the most common type of cost driver and is based on the assumption that overhead costs are driven by the *number of times an activity is performed*. For example, if machine set-up costs in example 6.7 were found to increase in relation to the number of set-ups, this is a transaction driver and the cost driver would be identified as 'number of set-ups'.
- *Duration driver*: These cost drivers are used where the level of costs incurred is affected (driven) by the length of time that it takes to perform an activity. For example, it may take longer to research a new shade of one kind of paint than

of another kind of paint. In such a case the cost driver of the 'Researching new shades of paint' cost pool would be a duration driver, and could be described as 'research hours' or 'research time'.
- *Intensity driver:* This type of cost driver recognises that certain types of products may use resources more intensely than others. For example, some of SA Paints' products have proved to be more difficult to market than others – SA Paints' marketers call them 'complex' and 'simple' products. To market 'complex' products successfully takes three times more effort (for example, SA Paints sends an expert marketer to the customer). Products classified as 'complex' ought to carry three times the marketing costs of those classified as 'simple'. The 'marketing of different paint types' cost pool has an intensity cost driver, which can be called 'marketing classification'.

Calculate activity rates

Key term: practical capacity

The activity rate is expressed as, for example, R5 per order (where the number of orders is the cost driver), or R10 per machine set-up (where machine set-ups is the cost driver). This rate is calculated by dividing the total cost per activity cost pool by the organisation's capacity for that cost driver (in this case, its capacity for orders or machine set-ups for the period).

Under traditional volume- or value-based overhead allocation systems, this rate is calculated using *budgeted* overhead costs and a budgeted level of capacity. This can result in the cost of idle capacity being allocated to products or services. It also causes product cost instability: if the budgeted level of activity changes, so will the predetermined overhead rate, and consequently, the product cost fluctuates. ABC, however, uses **practical capacity** to calculate activity rates. Practical capacity is not a theoretical capacity and allows for normal downtime. It is also not necessarily the same as 'normal capacity' prescribed by IAS2 for financial accounting purposes, which is the average capacity over a number of periods (see Chapter 5, *Absorption versus variable costing*). ABC allocates overheads to products or services only to the extent that the product or service consumes resources. The remaining unallocated overheads represent the cost of idle capacity, and this cost is then treated as a period cost and expensed as part of cost of sales. The cost of idle capacity is important when making long-term decisions, as this cost can be eliminated by reducing capacity.

Assign costs to cost objects

The amount of overheads that is allocated to the cost object depends on how much use the cost object makes of the activity. Overheads are assigned by multiplying the activity rate by the number of activity measures for that specific cost object.

Example 6.8 below is used to illustrate two principles:
- The calculations necessary for ABC
- The differences and similarities between the traditional system and ABC.

It also considers the appropriateness of allocating certain fixed costs to product units.

Example 6.8

We continue the example of SA Paints, still assuming that SA Paints manufactures only two types of paint, Red Marine and Green Exterior. 39 000 drums of Red Marine and 117 000 drums of Green Exterior paint are normally produced and sold each year. Information regarding their manufacture is as follows:

	Red Marine	Green Exterior
Labour hours per drum	3,0	2,0
Machine hours per drum	2,0	1,0
Batch size (number of drums)	250	1 000

SA Paints has had time to consider the activities in example 6.7 above, and chose to group them into final cost pools as follows:

Cost pool name	Cost driver
Researching new shades of paint	Research time
Cleaning and set-up of machines	Number of machine set-ups
Handling of raw materials and paint	Labour hours
Mixing (by machine)	Machine hours
Marketing of different paint types	Marketing classification
Marketing of SA Paints' products in general	–
Rent and general plant-related expenses	–

The overheads for the 2XX8 financial year can be presented as follows, grouped according to activities:

	R
Manufacturing overheads	70 080 000
Cleaning and set-up of machines	7 800 000
Handling of raw materials and paint	5 400 000
Mixing (by machine)	12 960 000
Rent and general plant-related expenses	43 920 000
Non-manufacturing overheads	34 752 000
Researching new shades of paint	1 755 000
Marketing of different paint types	16 000 000
Marketing of SA Paints' products in general	16 997 000
Total overheads	104 832 000

Manufacturing overheads are currently allocated based on the number of labour hours at normal production levels. The organisation has a total practical capacity of 360 000 labour hours.

Below is a summary of the capacity of other cost drivers:

Cost driver	Practical capacity
Research time	500 hours
Number of machine set-ups	300 set-ups
Machine hours	240 000 hours

Research related to new shades of Red Marine paint (such as the 'Scarlet' and 'Tomato' shades) takes only half of the time that it takes to research new shades of Green Exterior paint (where customers are more concerned about using the right shade). Only 450 hours are normally spent on such research each year.

Marketing staff classify Red Marine paint as a 'complex' product to sell, while Green Exterior paint is regarded as 'simple'. Complex products incur three times the marketing costs of simple products. At present there is no unused marketing capacity.

Required:
Calculate the overhead costs that would be allocated per unit and in total for each product line, under the traditional system and under ABC at the normal production level.

The traditional allocation would be done as follows:

	Red Marine		Green Exterior		Total costs
	Total	Per unit	Total	Per unit	
Manufacturing overheads	23 360 000	598,98	46 720 000	399,32	70 080 000

Workings:
Number of labour hours based on normal production levels:
(39 000 drums × 3 hours) + (117 000 drums × 2 hours) = 351 000 hours

Overhead rate per labour hour: R70 080 000/351 000 hours = R199,6581 per hour

Per unit cost:	Red Marine	Green Exterior
Rate per hour	199,66	199,66
× Labour hours per unit	3	2
= Cost per unit	598,98	399,32

Manufacturing overheads for Red Marine paint: R598,98 per unit × 39 000 drums = R23 360 220 (or R23 360 000 if the rate per hour is not rounded)

Manufacturing overheads for Green Exterior paint: R399,32 per unit × 117 000 drums = R46 720 440 (or R46 720 000 if the rate per hour is not rounded)

principles of management accounting

In contrast, an activity-based approach would result in the following product costs:

	Red Marine	Green Exterior	Unused capacity	Total costs (R)
Allocated overheads:				
Manufacturing overheads				70 080 000
Allocated to products:	10 023 000	12 870 000	3 267 000	26 160 000
Cleaning and set-up of machines	4 056 000	3 042 000	702 000	7 800 000
Handling of raw materials and paint	1 755 000	3 510 000	135 000	5 400 000
Mixing (by machine)	4 212 000	6 318 000	2 430 000	12 960 000
Not allocated to products				43 920 000
Rent and general plant-related expenses	–	–	–	43 920 000
Non-manufacturing overheads				34 752 000
Allocated to products:	12 526 500	5 053 000	175 500	17 755 000
Researching new shades of paint	526 500	1 053 000	175 500	1 755 000
Marketing of different paint types	12 000 000	4 000 000	–	16 000 000
Not allocated to products:				16 997 000
Marketing of SA Paints' products in general	–	–	–	16 997 000
Total overheads				104 832 000

Workings:
Number of machine set-ups:
You can assume machines are set-up each time before a new batch is produced. Therefore:

Cleaning and set-up of machines: R7 800 000/300 batches = R26 000 per batch
- Red Marine paint: 39 000 drums/250 drums per batch = 156 batches
  156 batches × R26 000 per batch = R4 056 000
- Green Exterior paint: 117 000 drums/1 000 drums per batch = 117 batches
  117 batches × R26 000 per batch = R3 042 000
- Unused capacity: 27 batches (300 – 156 – 117) × R26 000 = R702 000

Handling of raw materials and paint: R5 400 000/360 000 hours = R15 per hour
- Red Marine paint: 39 000 drums × 3 hours per drum × R15 per hour = R1 755 000
- Green Exterior paint: 117 000 drums × 2 hours per drum × R15 per hour = R3 510 000
- Unused capacity: 9 000 hours [360 000 hours – (39 000 drums × 3 hours) – (117 000 drums × 2 hours)] × R15 per hour = R135 000

Mixing (by machine): R12 960 000/240 000 hours = R54
- Red Marine paint: 39 000 drums × 2 hours per drum × R54 per hour = R4 212 000
- Green Exterior paint: 117 000 drums × 1 hour per drum × R54 per hour = R6 318 000
- Unused capacity: 45 000 hours [240 000 hours − (39 000 drums × 2 hours) − (117 000 drums × 1 hour)] × R54 per hour = R2 430 000

Researching new shades of paint: R1 755 000/500 hours = R3 510 per hour
Of the 450 hours normally spent on research, 450 hours/3 = 150 hours are spent on Red Marine paint and 150 hours × 2 = 300 hours on Green Exterior Paint
- Red Marine paint: R3 510 per hour × 150 hours = R526 500
- Green Exterior Paint: R3 510 × 300 hours = R1 053 000
- Unused capacity: 50 hours (500 hours − 450 hours) × R3 510 = R175 500

Marketing of different paint types: R16 000 000/4 = R4 000 000
- Red Marine paint: R4 000 000 × 3 = R12 000 000
- Green Exterior paint: R4 000 000 × 1 = R4 000 000

Notice that the ABC costing method allocates both manufacturing and non-manufacturing overheads to products, while only manufacturing overheads were allocated under the traditional method.

Furthermore, notice that the ABC method allocated manufacturing overhead differently to the traditional method. Red Marine paint received R23 360 000 in manufacturing overheads under the traditional method, and R10 023 000 under ABC. However, the lower figure under ABC is mainly due to the fact that Rent and general plant-related expenses was not allocated under ABC because it was regarded as a facility-level activity. If we remove this from total manufacturing overheads and re-calculate the allocation to Red Marine paint under the traditional method, we find that only R8 720 000 [(R70 080 000 − R43 920 000)/351 000 hours × 3 hours × 39 000 drums] worth of unit and batch-level manufacturing overhead was allocated to Red Marine paint.

It is expected that ABC would allocate relatively more of these costs (R10 023 000 compared with R8 720 000) than the traditional method, to a lower volume product such as Red Marine paint. This is mainly because the traditional system does not recognise that Red Marine paint is produced in smaller batch sizes, which gives rise to additional costs. Under the traditional system, the high-volume product, Green Exterior paint, 'cross-subsidised' the Red Marine paint by carrying too large a portion of these costs. When ABC is first implemented, it is often found that low-volume products (such as Red Marine paint) receive more such costs than they had in the past. ABC highlights the activities that cause costs to be incurred (such as the number of machine set-ups). ABC aims to eliminate cross-subsidisation between products.

Facility-sustaining level costs were not allocated to products in the ABC calculation above as such costs will not be altered by any decision regarding a change in production (other than possibly to cease trading altogether). There is little purpose in allocating this cost to individual products based on machine hours, or batches, or business units, as these allocation bases would be arbitrary. Allocation based on space (and time) used is more realistic, but the allocation will be useful only if scope exists to alter these expenses, which is assumed not to be the case in the relevant time frame.

Table 6.6 A comparison between traditional allocation systems and ABC

Traditional: Departmental overhead rate and cost centre overhead rate	ABC
• Overheads are accumulated and assigned to products in accordance with organisational structure, (that is, departments or cost centres), based on the amount of resources used by the product	• Overhead costs are accumulated and assigned to products in accordance with activities, based on the amount of resources used by each product
• Multiple overhead rates can be calculated, one per department or cost centre	• Multiple overhead rates can be calculated, one per activity
• The allocation basis is usually based on some volume measure, and does not necessarily represent a cause-and-effect relationship between cost and allocation basis	• The allocation basis is referred to as a 'cost driver', as a cause-and-effect relationship exists between cost and allocation basis
• As the allocation basis is easily measured and because only a limited number of bases is used, the costing system is not prohibitively expensive to implement and operate	• Because of the extensive number of cost drivers that must be identified and measured, this costing system can be prohibitively expensive to implement and operate
• Overhead costs accumulated in service departments are allocated to production departments. A rate which is applied to products is then determined for each production department	• Overhead costs related to service activities are not allocated to production departments or activities first and then to the products. The cost driver for the service cost is used to allocate the service-related overhead directly to the products
Result: Overheads are averaged out between products. The overheads assigned to products may not be representative of the long-term cost savings if the product in question were not produced. Consequently this method of allocation does not support strategic or long-term decision-making	**Result:** The allocated overhead reflects the extent to which that product causes costs to be incurred. In other words, the overhead allocated represents the amount that could be saved in the long term if the product were not produced. Consequently this method of allocation supports strategic or long-term decision-making

Limitations of ABC

A drawback of ABC is that it can be expensive to implement. The process of gathering information and identifying activities can be time consuming and expensive. The benefit of implementing ABC is not always greater than its cost. This would be the case where the distortion in cost allocation created by a simpler (traditional) system is not significant, either because resources are consumed homogeneously, because overhead costs are insignificant, or because competition is not particularly intense and accurate costing is therefore not crucial.

The reliability of the cost information generated by an ABC system is undermined by certain impracticalities. As with any system, if the input is incorrect (the activity measures), the output will be incorrect. Worse yet is that if the system itself is faulty, the output will also be incorrect: the cost information is only as accurate as the accuracy with which the cost drivers have been identified. Many costs in reality have multiple cost drivers. Furthermore, facility-sustaining level costs are still left unallocated when ABC is used.

ABC can create a false impression of the relevance of overhead costs to decision-making. When making a decision, the timeframe and scope of the decision must always be considered. The impression can be created that all costs that are allocated to cost objects by ABC are variable in the short term, when some may, in fact, actually be stepped fixed costs or fixed costs that will not be affected by a small change in the cost driver. Stepped fixed costs can be saved in the short term, provided that the organisation is aware of and takes action on the information. However, fixed costs are normally determined by the capacity of an organisation and will change only if the organisation expands or downsizes its capacity. This can be done only in the long term (most costs are variable in the long term). ABC is therefore more suited to long-term decision-making rather than short-term decision-making.

6.5 Activity-based management and activity-based budgeting

Key terms: activity-based budgeting, activity-based management

When activity-based costing is used in an organisation, management becomes aware of how activities drive costs. It follows that management is likely to focus on minimising activities as far as is practical. This way of running an organisation is known as **activity-based management (ABM)**, which is discussed in more detail in Chapter 17, *Competitive advantage*. Furthermore, when budgets are drawn up, managers will budget for the number of activities (for example, the number of orders received or the number of machine set-ups) that they expect, and then calculate the budgeted costs from there. This is known as **activity-based budgeting (ABB)**. Budgeting is discussed in more detail in Chapter 12, *Budgets, planning and control*.

6.6 Summary

This chapter discusses the aspects that management should consider when choosing the method and level of detail with which overhead costs are allocated to products or services. Simple, volume- or value-based measures can be used with a reasonable degree of accuracy where the organisation's product range consists of products that use resources more or less homogeneously, overhead costs are proportionately small or where competition is not particularly intense. However, where a more accurate allocation of overhead costs is required, this is done with reference to the activities that cause the overhead costs to be incurred (activity-based costing).

Overheads should be allocated only to the extent that they are relevant to the decision that management is facing, or to control measures that management wishes to institute.

Just as traditional overhead allocation methods have disadvantages, ABC has limitations of its own. It is important to understand that, regardless of what method of overhead allocation is used, the total amount of overheads incurred by the organisation does not change. Different amounts of overheads may be allocated to cost objects depending on the basis used, but the total amount of overheads is not affected by a change in allocation. However, management may save overhead costs in future periods if they make better decisions because of their improved understanding of how costs behave. In addition, where selling prices are determined by applying a mark-up to cost, more realistic selling prices based on more accurate product costs may lead to improved profitability for the organisation.

Conclusion: Overhead allocation and other topics in this book

This chapter deals with the allocation of overheads to cost objects. The costs that ought to be assigned to a cost object in a given situation are the costs that are relevant to the decision at hand. A detailed understanding of what constitutes a relevant cost for decision-making can be obtained from Chapter 2, *Cost classification* (see section 2.4), and Chapter 10, *Relevant costs for decision-making*.

The appropriate manner in which to allocate overheads for management accounting purposes stands in contrast with the financial accounting approach to overheads allocation, namely absorption costing. The contrast is the result of the different objectives of the two disciplines. A detailed discussion of absorption costing can be found in Chapter 2, *Cost classification* (see section 2.6), Chapter 5, *Absorption versus variable costing*, and Chapter 13, *Standard costing* (see section 13.5.6).

An understanding of the basis on which overheads are allocated, which activities they respond to, and the varying extents to which they can be altered by various decisions, is necessary in all chapters in this book, and is relied on in particular in Chapter 7, *Job costing*, Chapter 8, *Process costing*, and Chapter 14, *Performance management* (see section 14.2.1 on controllability).

Finally, two concepts closely related to activity-based costing are activity-based management (ABM) and activity-based budgeting (ABB). ABM is discussed in Chapter 17, *Competitive advantage*, while Chapter 12, *Budgeting, planning and control* explains budgeting.

Tutorial case study: Gauteng Aids Programme

Refer to the information on the *Gauteng Aids Programme* at the beginning of this chapter, and perform the following tasks. (Because this case study deals with a public service rather than a manufacturing organisation, you may find the context challenging.)

1. Explain to what extent it would be appropriate to allocate the overheads of Gauteng's Department of Health and Social Development to its various programmes (such as the Aids Programme) using a volume-based measure, namely the number of patients treated.
2. Identify the cost objects in question 1 above.
3. Explain whether a value-based overhead allocation basis could be relevant in this scenario.
4. Give examples of cost pools that may possibly be used when the overhead costs of the Department of Health and Social Development are allocated to its various programmes (such as the Aids Programme).
5. Discuss in detail whether – in your opinion – a refined overhead-allocation system such as activity-based costing may be appropriate for allocating overhead costs to the Gauteng Aids Programme.

Basic questions

BQ 1

Source: Adapted from CIMA P1

X Ltd has two production departments, assembly and finishing, and two service departments, stores and maintenance.

Stores provides the following service to the production departments: 60 per cent to assembly and 40 per cent to finishing

Maintenance provides the following service to the production and service departments: 40 per cent to assembly, 45 per cent to finishing and 15 per cent to stores.

The budgeted information for the year is as follows:

Budgeted fixed production overheads:	
Assembly	R100 000
Finishing	R150 000
Stores	R50 000
Maintenance	R40 000
Budgeted output	100 000 units

At the end of the year, after apportioning the service department overheads, the total fixed production overheads debited to the assembly department's fixed production overhead control account were R180 000. The actual output achieved was 120 000 units.

What was the under- or over-absorption of fixed production overheads for the assembly department?

BQ 2

Source: Adapted from CIMA P1

CJD Ltd manufactures plastic components for the car industry. The following budgeted information is available for three of their key plastic components:

	W	X	Y
	R per unit	R per unit	R per unit
Selling price	200	183	175
Direct materials	50	40	35
Direct labour	30	35	30
Units produced and sold	10 000	15 000	18 000

principles of management accounting

The total number of activities for each of the three products for the period is as follows:

	W	X	Y
Number of purchase requisitions	1 200	1 800	2 000
Number of set-ups	240	260	300

Overhead costs have been analysed as follows:

Receiving and inspecting quality assurance	R1 400 000
Production scheduling and machine set up	R1 200 000

What is the budgeted profit per unit for each of the three products, using activity-based budgeting?

BQ 3

The total costs incurred in the invoice process department of a life insurance company was budgeted at R1 000 000 for the 2XX7 year, and R1 100 000 was actually spent during the year. All the costs incurred in this department are fixed costs. The only activity that this department caries out is the processing of invoices, and the company wishes to charge the costs incurred in this department, to the various business units for which the invoices are processed. The number of company invoices budgeted to be processed for the year was 20 000. The department actually processed 22 000 invoices during the year. The maximum number of invoices that could theoretically be processed by this department in one year is 26 000, but the practical capacity of the department is 25 000 invoices per annum.

What is the amount per invoice that the business units should have been charged, using ABC?
a) R40 per invoice
b) R44 per invoice
c) R50 per invoice
d) R55 per invoice

BQ 4

An information technology (IT) department is trying to determine the cost per page that should be charged to user departments. The IT department is responsible for managing the overall printing cost of the company, and the user departments are responsible for the amount of printing that they do. There are three significant costs associated with printing, and the budgeted costs for the year are as follows:

	R
Depreciation of printers	1 000 000 (Fixed cost)
Paper	2 000 000 (Variable cost)
Ink/toner	5 000 000 (Variable cost)

The total number of pages that the printers are capable of printing during the year (practical capacity) is 12 000 000 pages. The budgeted number of pages to be printed is 10 000 000 pages.

At what cost per page should the printing costs be allocated to the user departments, using ABC?
a) R0,67
b) R0,68
c) R0,78
d) R0,80

BQ 5

In order to determine the relative profitability of the products within an organisation's product range:
i) Manufacturing overheads can be allocated to products using ABC
ii) ABC cannot be applied to indirect costs that are non-manufacturing in nature (that is, non-manufacturing overheads)
iii) All manufacturing overheads should be included in the cost pools that are to be allocated to products.

Which of the above statements are true?
a) (i) and (iii)
b) (ii) and (iii)
c) (i) only
d) (ii) only

BQ 6

FluffyBunny (Pty) Ltd manufactures soft toys. Raw materials are imported in bulk (this is cheaper than purchasing smaller quantities at a time) and stored in one of several warehouses that it rents close to the factory. Raw materials are fetched from the warehouses as required, and loaded on to a laser cutting machine. 40 layers of fabric can be cut at a time. The number of units that are cut out of 40 layers of fabric varies, depending on the size of the toy (very small to very large) and width of the fabric. The toys are sewn and stuffed by employees who earn a monthly wage. The finished goods are then stored in the same warehouses in which raw materials are stored. The soft toys are of different sizes and remain in the warehouse for different lengths of time, depending on demand.

The following potential cost drivers have been identified:
- Number of m^2 of warehouse space
- Number of m^2 of warehouse space per day
- Number of materials and finished goods requisitions
- Number of materials movements
- Number of units of finished goods (that is, the number of toys)
- Labour time (sewing and stuffing)
- Number of cuts
- Cutting hours
- Factory hours

Which cost driver (from the list provided) would be the most appropriate for the following overhead costs associated with running the warehouses?
a) Maintenance of fluorescent overhead lights in the factory
b) Deprecation and maintenance of forklifts
c) Depreciation of computers, printers (for labels to stick on all raw materials and finished goods receipted into the warehouse) and scanning equipment (every item leaving or entering the warehouse must be scanned)

BQ 7

The same information as in BQ 6 applies.

Which cost driver (from the list provided) would be the most appropriate for the following overhead costs associated with running the warehouses?
a) Salaries of warehouse personnel
b) Rent of warehouse premises

BQ 8

The same information as in BQ 6 applies.

Which cost driver (from the list provided) would be the most appropriate for the following overhead costs associated with the manufacturing process? What concerns do you have regarding the use of the particular cost driver you have selected?
a) Electricity, depreciation, maintenance and salaries costs associated with the cutting of material
b) Electricity, depreciation, maintenance and salaries costs associated with the sewing and stuffing of toys
c) Factory rental

BQ 9

A company has three operational divisions, L, M and N, and two service departments (P and Q). R4m and R3m of overheads are incurred in service departments P and Q respectively. An analysis of the service departments records indicate that their services are used in the following proportions:

Service department	P	Q
Percentage use by other departments:		
L	20%	30%
M	25%	10%
N	40%	20%
P	–	40%
Q	15%	–

What amount of the service departments' overheads should be allocated to each of the three production departments under the direct approach?
a) L: R2 441 176   M: R1 676 471   N: R2 882 353
b) L: R1 700 000   M: R1 300 000   N: R2 200 000
c) L: R2 123 529   M: R1 829 412   N: R3 047 059

BQ 10

The same information as in BQ 9 applies.

What amount of the service departments' overheads should be allocated to each of the three production departments under the step down approach? Start by allocating the costs of the service department that renders the largest value of services to another service department.
a) L: R2 441 176   M: R1 676 471   N: R2 882 353
b) L: R1 700 000   M: R1 300 000   N: R2 200 000
c) L: R2 123 529   M: R1 829 412   N: R3 047 059

Long questions

LQ 1 – Intermediate (50 marks; 90 minutes)

Source: UCT (Richard Chivaka)

Cookwell manufactures household pots that bear the 'Proudly South African' logo. The organisation makes three different pots of the same size, namely copper, aluminium, and steel pots. Cookwell started making copper pots (CP) in 1980, taking advantage of cheap, high-quality copper which was imported from Zambia. It was the only organisation manufacturing and supplying copper pots to the South African market until 1990, when other organisations entered the market. The organisation introduced their aluminium pots (AP) and steel pots (SP) in 2XX0, both of which immediately became more popular than the copper pots. The organisation uses a full-cost-plus pricing method to calculate the selling prices for the three different pots. The current mark-up percentage is 20 per cent on cost. Currently, the most popular pot brand is the aluminium pot.

However, despite the popularity of the AP brand, and the organisation's traditional dominance in the CP market, the organisation's profits have significantly gone down since the introduction of the AP and SP brands. Competition in the SP market is fierce, and the organisation's competitors offer similar pots at lower prices. Also, the CP market is slowly slipping away as a result of the entry of other organisations since 1990. This is very confusing to the organisation's management, because every day the sales manager reports that retail shops are placing more orders for the AP, which should more than compensate for the loss of the CP market share.

Cookwell's Managing Director, who is very anxious to understand the source(s) of the huge profit reductions that the organisation has experienced since 2XX0, has convened an emergency meeting. Present in the meeting are the Managing Director, the production manager, the purchasing manager, the finance manager, the sales manager and the management accountant (you).

The organisation's production manager has produced the following information that relates to the three products for the current financial year.

	Copper pot	Aluminium pot	Steel pot
Labour hours per pot	1	⅔	1¾
Machine hours per pot	1	2	2½
Materials cost per pot	R20,00	R25,00	R45,00
Number of pots produced and sold	18 000	11 000	15 000

All direct factory employees are paid R60 per hour. The organisation's policy is to assign all production overheads using machine hours. The production manager indicates that the current recovery rate is R80 per machine hour. Using this overhead recovery rate, there is no under- or over-recovery of overheads.

After three hours of discussion and deliberation, the organisation's production manager suggests that the possible reason for the fall in the organisation's profits could be due to the costing system in use. The managing director takes the finance manager to task. He wants an informed response to the alleged weaknesses in the organisation's costing system. However, the finance manager is at a loss as to what could be wrong with the current costing system. The sales manager suggests that perhaps the management accountant (you), as a recent graduate from university, could offer insights into the matter. You then respond by suggesting the assignment

principles of management accounting

of costs using activity-based costing (ABC). The Managing Director is both excited and anxious. He wants you to demonstrate the impact that the application of ABC would have on the organisation's profitability.

Before the meeting ends, the production manager gives you a file that contains more information about the organisation's production overhead cost. Your analysis of the overheads yields the following information, as shown in Tables 1 and 2 below.

Table 1

	%
Set-up costs	40
Materials handling costs	20
Inspection costs	25
Machine-related costs	15
Total overheads	100

Table 2

	Copper pot	Aluminium pot	Steel pot	Total
Number of set-ups	150	300	250	700
Number of materials movements	200	450	560	1 210
Number of inspections	300	600	800	1 700

REQUIRED		Marks
(a)	Using the current overhead cost assignment method: (i) Calculate the unit product cost for each of the three pots. (ii) Calculate the selling price for each of the three pots.	8 3
(b)	Using activity-based costing (ABC): (i) Calculate the unit product cost for each of the three pots. (ii) Calculate the selling price that the organisation should be charging for each of the three pots.	29 3
(c)	Explain to the managing director of Cookwell why profits have been decreasing since 2XX0. Your explanation should refer to the calculations in parts (a)(i) and (ii) and (b)(i) and (ii) above.	7
TOTAL MARKS		50

LQ 2 – Intermediate (29 marks; 52 minutes)

Source: UCT (Peter Cramer)

Electrohealth (Pty) Ltd manufactures a diverse range of consumer electronic products aimed at the health-conscious market. The organisation has a solid brand image and a reputation for delivering high quality, reliable products.

The organisation has a new product development team that has the task of assessing opportunities in the organisation's market segment and proposing new products. Once the investigation of a new product has been approved in principle, including a proposed selling price, the design and engineering department determines draft product specifications, including production methods and materials specifications.

The new product development team has recently proposed the introduction of a new product, the XRunna, which it believes will be able to compete very successfully in the personal fitness market. The XRunna is planned to be a very compact and unobtrusive device to measure various items that are of importance to runners, including distance, heart rate, speed, acceleration and hydration factors. The XRunna will be sold at R250 per unit.

The Design and Engineering department has specified the following direct materials and labour in respect of the XRunna:
- Each unit will require one unit of Component A, which comprises the basic integrated circuitry that will be sourced from a supplier in Shanghai, China, at a landed cost of R40 per unit, calculated at the current exchange rate.
- Each unit will require two units of Component B, which will be sourced from the organisation's holding company in Japan at a landed cost of R15 per unit calculated at the current exchange rate.
- Other materials, including the rubberised housing and Velcro® strap, will be sourced locally at a cost of R30.
- Labour (skilled technicians) will be charged at R850 per hour of assembly time, which is 35 hours per batch of 1 000 XRunnas – see below.

Indirect costs will be allocated to the XRunna on the basis of ABC cost information. The XRunna will be manufactured in batches of 1 000 units. Activity requirements for 1 batch of XRunna are as follows:

Activity	Required for 1 batch of 1 000 units
Purchase ordering	2 purchase orders
Set-up time	5 hours
Assembly time	35 hours
Materials movement	3 movements
Inspection	3,5 hours

You have recently joined the organisation and have been co-opted to the new product development team as the financial representative. In preparation for an important meeting later today where you will be required to present a firm cost estimate in respect of the XRunna, you have been trying to locate the appropriate ABC information. You have established that the hard drive of the computer used by the previous management accountant has 'crashed' and cannot be accessed at present. Fortunately you have managed to obtain two documents containing all of the ABC information that you require. Unfortunately, coffee has been spilled over both documents and certain information is obscured. The first document (Doc 1) contains details of the total indirect costs, analysed by activity. The last two lines are unreadable, but you are confident that you can obtain the information you require from the second document (Doc 2) which contains details of the costing of another product – Product X – which was performed on the basis of the information contained in Doc 1. Note that Product X is manufactured in batches of 500 units.

principles of management accounting

The documents are as follows:

Doc 1: Total costs and activity levels

Activity	Total cost R	Cost driver description	Cost driver (total activity)
Purchase ordering	300 000	Number of orders	720
Machine set-ups	800 000	Set-up hours	400
Assembly*	2 500 000	Assembly hours	1 250
Materials movement	400 000	Number of m...	
Inspection	500 000		
Total indirect manufacturing costs	4 500 000		

(Coffee spill obscures part of the table)

Doc 2: Cost per unit of Product X

Item	Cost per unit R	Comment
Direct costs	100	
Direct materials	2...	
Direct labour		
Indirect costs		
Purchase ordering		
Machine set-ups		
Assembly	3...	
Materials movement	4	3 movements per batch
Inspection	2	2 inspection hours per batch
Total cost per unit	184	

(Another coffee spill obscures part of the table)

* Because of the nature of the product, it is extremely important that the components are properly embedded in the product's rubberised housing. The assembly process will therefore require the use of a variety of the robotic equipment that is present in the Electrohealth factory, in addition to the skilled technicians (referred to previously).

The indirect assembly cost is made up as follows:
- Sixty per cent of the total cost relates to power and maintenance of the various robotic equipment used in the Electrohealth factory. Maintenance is largely driven by operating hours, although the service intervals and costs vary from machine to machine.
- Forty per cent of the total costs relate to the factory rent, cleaning, lighting, factory managers' salaries, and other related expenses. These costs are allocated on a time-proportion basis, as various different products spend different amounts of time in the factory.

You have been advised that there is sufficient spare capacity within the organisation to accommodate the production of the XRunna. The organisation would like to earn a gross margin of 30 per cent.

Chapter 6 Overhead allocation

	REQUIRED	Marks
(a)	Calculate: (i) The cost driver rate for each activity. (ii) The current estimate of the actual cost to produce one unit of the XRunna.	17
(b)	Describe the key factors you think would have been taken into account in setting the organisation's target gross margin of 30 per cent.	2
(c)	The marketing manager has enquired why you are bothering with the ABC costing information. She has mentioned that in the past indirect costs have frequently been allocated on the basis of direct labour hours, and enquires why this would not be suitable for the purposes of estimating the cost of the XRunna. Briefly explain why the use of the ABC cost information may be preferable in this situation.	3
(d)	Discuss the shortcomings that may exist regarding the ABC cost allocation.	2
(e)	Discuss another risk that is evident in the costing of the XRunna, and action(s) that you think need to be taken to manage the risk.	3
	Format and presentation	2
	TOTAL MARKS	**29**

LQ 3 – Intermediate (20 marks; 36 minutes)

Source: Adapted from CIMA P1

F Ltd supplies pharmaceutical drugs to drug stores. Although the company makes a satisfactory return, the directors are concerned that some orders are profitable and others are not. The management has decided to investigate a new budgeting system using activity based costing principles to ensure that all orders they accept are making a profit.

Each customer order is charged as follows. Customers are charged the list price of the drugs ordered plus a charge for selling and distribution costs (overheads). A profit margin is also added, but that does not form part of this analysis.

Currently F Ltd uses a simple absorption rate to absorb these overheads. The rate is calculated based on the budgeted annual selling and distribution costs and the budgeted annual total list price of the drugs ordered.

An analysis of customers has revealed that many customers place frequent small orders with each order requesting a variety of drugs. The management of F Ltd has examined more carefully the nature of its selling and distribution costs, and the following data have been prepared for the budget for next year:

Total list price of drugs supplied   R8m

Number of customer orders	8 000	
Selling and distribution costs:	R'000	Cost driver
Invoice processing	280	See Note 2
Packing	220	Size of package – see Note 3
Delivery	180	Number of deliveries – see Note 4
Other overheads	200	Number of orders
Total overheads	880	

Notes:
1 Each order will be shipped in one package and will result in one delivery to the customer and one invoice (an order never results in more than one delivery).

2 Each invoice has a different line for each drug ordered. There are 28 000 invoice lines each year. It is estimated that 25 per cent of invoice processing costs are related to the number of invoices, and 75 per cent are related to the number of invoice lines.
3 Packing costs are R32 for a large package and R25 for a small package.
4 The delivery vehicles are always filled to capacity for each journey. The delivery vehicles can carry either 6 large packages or 12 small packages (or appropriate combinations of large and small packages). It is estimated that there will be 1 000 delivery journeys each year, and the total delivery mileage that is specific to particular customers is estimated at 350 000 miles each year. R40 000 of delivery costs are related to loading the delivery vehicles, and the remainder of these costs are related to specific delivery distance to customers.

Management has asked for two typical orders to be costed using next year's budget data, using the current method, and the proposed activity-based costing approach. Details of two typical orders are shown below:

	Order A	Order B
Lines on invoice	2	8
Package size	small	large
Specific delivery distance	8 miles	40 miles
List price of drugs supplied	R1 200	R900

REQUIRED		Marks
(a)	Calculate the charge for selling and distribution overheads for Order A and Order B using: (i) the current system, and (ii) the activity-based costing approach.	10
(b)	Write a report to the management of F Ltd in which you: (i) assess the strengths and weaknesses of the proposed activity-based costing approach for F Ltd, and (ii) recommend actions that the management of F Ltd may consider in the light of the data produced using the activity-based-costing approach.	5 5
TOTAL MARKS		20

LQ 4 – Advanced (35 marks; 63 minutes)

Source: UCT (Peter Cramer)

Azanian Bank Limited (AZBA) is a large South African commercial banking operation. The bank has three main business units, namely home loans, cheque accounts, and savings accounts. In addition, the bank has a corporate services department which houses the shared services, such as information technology, legal services, and accounting services, which support the operations of the business units.

AZBA is considering the introduction of a corporate finance division, aimed at the supply of corporate finance services to its existing corporate customer base, and hopefully to a growing number of new corporate customers. However, the bank's management have some concerns regarding the profitability of the existing operations, and would like these resolved before undertaking the development of a new business unit.

The three existing business units all earn a combination of fee and net interest income, much in line with the banking industry in general. The direct costs of each business unit include the salaries and related costs in respect of dedicated staff, depreciation of dedicated property, plant and equipment, bad debts written off and provided for, and all other costs which are directly traceable to the business unit. Traditionally, AZBA has determined the profitability of the business after re-allocating the corporate (or shared) costs to the three business units in proportion to the income (that is, the sum of fee and interest income) of each unit.

However, it has recently been suggested that this method of allocating the costs might be resulting in profit calculations which are a very poor reflection of the true profitability of the respective business units. In view of this, the bank's finance director has initiated a study based on the principles of activity-based costing. The results of this study are due to be presented at the bank's forthcoming board meeting, which is scheduled for one week from today. The consultant who originally prepared the data has unfortunately been taken ill, and will not be able to complete the analysis of the data, or to be present at the board meeting.

AZBA's board is eagerly awaiting the results of the ABC exercise, and the finance director does not consider postponement of the presentation as an option. The consultant, who is a recognised expert in the area of ABC in relation to the financial services industry, has left a file containing the data necessary to complete the exercise. The finance director is satisfied that the data is completely reliable, but does not have the time to complete the analysis herself. She has tasked you with the recalculation of the profits of the business units using the consultant's data, and the consideration of a few other points, in anticipation of questions the board might raise.

An exhibit reflecting the pertinent extracts from the consultant's files appears below. All of the information is complete, with the exception of the net income of the business units, which the consultant had left in a near-complete state.

Exhibit 6.1 Relevant extracts from consultant's files

Business unit	Current overhead allocation basis					
	Home loans	Cheque accounts	Savings accounts	Corporate services	Total
	R'000	R'000	R'000	R'000	R'000
Fees earned	820	1 996	705		3 521
Net interest income	10 000	6 000	4 000		20 000
Total income	10 820	7 996	4 705	0	23 521
Direct costs	3 246	3 198	941	9 400	16 785
Reallocation of costs					
Total costs					
Net income					

The corporate services costs comprise the following departments:

	R'000
ATM security and control	1 300
Legal services	1 200
Real estate services	1 600
IT services	3 400
Human resources	800
Accounting	1 100
	9 400

principles of management accounting

The corporate services costs have been traced to the activities specified as follows:

	Notes	R'000	Activity cost driver
ATM transaction logging		2 000	Number of ATM transactions
Pre-loan approval credit reviews		750	Number of loan applications processed
Bond applications processing		1 000	Number of bond applications processed
Overdraft management		250	Number of follow-up phone calls
New cheque accounts openings		550	Number of new cheque accounts
New savings accounts openings		350	Number of new savings accounts
Cash deposits and withdrawals		1 500	Number of cash transactions
Management of premises	1	1 700	Number of square metres of space occupied
Bad debt collection		1 300	Number of bad debt cases
		9 400	

Note:
1 Included in the premises management costs of R1 700 000 is R300 000 in refurbishment costs which arose because of re-branding by the home loan business unit. The remaining R1 400 000 costs are general property maintenance costs.

Activity cost drivers	Number of cost driver units per annum applicable to the business units			
	Home loans	Cheque accounts	Savings accounts	Total
Number of ATM transactions	20 000	80 000	150 000	250 000
Number of loan applications processed	6 000	8 000		14 000
Number of mortgage bond applications processed	4 000			4 000
Number of follow-up phone calls	1 000	1 500		2 500
Number of new cheque accounts		3 000		3 000
Number of new savings accounts			5 000	5 000
Number of cash transactions		278 000	22 000	300 000
Number of square metres of space occupied	3 000	16 000	6 000	25 000
Number of bad debt cases	800	2 000		2 800

	REQUIRED	Marks
(a)	Calculate the net income, after all direct and allocated costs, of the three business units, using AZBA's existing cost allocation basis.	4
(b)	Calculate the net income of the three units on an activity-based costing basis.	21
(c)	Comment briefly on the results of your two calculations and discuss why they may be of interest to AZBA's board. Recommend what action, if any, could be considered as a result of the information provided by the ABC exercise.	5
(d)	While the finance director is satisfied that the data presented in Exhibit 6.1 above is accurate, she asks you whether you have any reservations concerning the application of ABC to the corporate costs, the cost drivers identified, and whether there are any other issues concerning the activity-based costing exercise that the board should be made aware of. Comment on any reservations (or lack thereof) you may have in these areas.	5
	Round off all calculations to the nearest rand.	
	TOTAL MARKS	**35**

LQ 5 – Advanced (20 marks; 36 minutes)

Source: UCT (Carol Cairney)

Total Solutions Ltd is a large South African organisation which provides a wide range of financial services. Total Solutions has numerous operating divisions, each of which focuses on a single service line. Group Retirement Solutions (GRS) is the operating division that is responsible for managing organisation-specific pension and provident funds (an example of a typical fund that GRS might manage would be the 'University of Cape Town (UCT) Retirement Fund'). GRS manages 80 funds, with an average membership of 1 100 members per fund.

GRS charges each retirement fund a monthly administration fee of 1,5 per cent of the members' monthly retirement funding contributions (not contributions in respect of bank guarantees – see below). Members' contributions are based on a percentage of the member's salary (usually 15 per cent). The membership of the various funds administered by GRS ranges from funds that are dominated by low-income workers in the construction industry (average monthly contributions of R500 per employee), to funds dominated by higher income earners in more corporate environments (average monthly contribution of R1 600 per employee).

There is significant tension in the financial services industry regarding administrative fees charged to clients, and GRS is under pressure to keep administrative fees as low as possible. GRS is also mindful that they may need to be able to justify their fees to a regulatory body. As a result of these concerns, GRS has decided to perform an activity-based costing exercise in order to get a better insight into the cost of managing a pension (or provident) fund. The income statement for GRS, including information on actual activities performed, is presented immediately below. Additional information regarding the activities then follows.

Actual costs and income incurred by GRS for the 12 months ended 30 June 2XX6

	R	Actual number of activities performed for the year	
Administration fees collected	16 350 000		
Salaries [1]	13 900 000		
Quarterly AFS	2 650 000	320	AFSs prepared
Switching	350 000	7 900	Switches
Contributions – downloads and reconciliations	100 000	1 000	Downloads and reconciliations performed
Contributions – investing	7 400 000	1 020 000	Investing instructions carried out
Taking on new members	1 100 000	11 000	New members taken on
Retirement or resignation	1 400 000	9 000	Resignations/retirements
Death	900 000	1 400	Deaths
Telephone (variable)	660 000	75 000	Calls
Copying/printing/faxing/stationary (variable)	100 000	150 000	Pages
Entertainment	35 000	1	Annual staff party
Insurance/maintenance/cleaning [2]	500 000	5 000	Square metres
IT support [2]	880 000	5 000	Square metres
Profit	275 000		

Notes:
1 Salaries

Given that the bulk of administrative costs are labour related, GRS has divided the salaries expense according to the various activities carried out. This was easy enough to do, as GRS's employees (of which there are more than 150) are grouped according to these tasks. Included in the table below is a list and description of the core activities performed in managing a fund and the amount of time required to carry out each activity. In order to ascertain how long each activity takes to perform, employees were asked to estimate the amount of time they require to perform each activity listed below, and the average time per activity was calculated from these responses:

	Description of activities	Average hours per activity
1	**AFS** Preparing quarterly and annual financial statements for the fund	125 hours per AFS per quarter
2	**Taking on new members** Capturing the new member onto the system and setting up debit orders, and other similar activities	30 minutes per member
3	**Monthly contributions** *Downloads and reconciliations:* Receiving the members' monthly contributions *Investing* (in the members' preferred investment choice, or paid to the relevant bank in the case of housing guarantees) Note that two kinds of contributions are received: • Monthly retirement contributions, which are paid by all members of all funds • Housing guarantee contributions, which occur mainly in the lower-income funds Separate reconciliations and investments are carried out as for each kind of contribution	1 hour per fund per month 8 minutes per member per month
4	**Members exiting from the fund** Members can exit in one of three ways:	
	• **Retirement (at the stated retirement age)** The market value of the member's investment is disinvested and paid out	3 hours per retirement or resignation (Retirements and resignations are grouped together, as the same group of employees perform both tasks, which are very similar)
	• **Resignation** The employee leaves the employer and transfers to another pension fund	
	• **Death** This method of exiting a fund results in the most administration, given the extensive paperwork, and complexities involved in tracing the surviving beneficiaries	15 hours per death
5	**Switching** Once a year, members are given the option of changing their investment preferences	30 minutes per switch

Activities 2, 3 and 4 above are performed by Payclass 4 employees who earn R40 per hour, and activities 1 and 5 above are performed by Payclass 8 employees who earn R80 per hour. Both Payclass 4 and Payclass 8 employees are permanent employees who receive a fixed monthly salary.

2 Insurance, IT support, and similar costs

Insurance, maintenance and cleaning costs are all outsourced by Total Solutions to various suppliers, in terms of fixed annual contracts. These costs are allocated to every operating division based on a fixed rate per square metre of floor space. IT support costs relate to costs incurred by the IT support department, which are allocated on a per square metre basis to the various divisions. The argument for this simplistic allocation basis is that the various operating divisions have very similar IT needs, and the number of employees (and computers) per square metre are consistent between divisions.

REQUIRED		Marks
(a)	Calculate the annual activity-based charges per activity, as appropriate. Comment on the merit of applying ABC to the last three items (entertainment, insurance/maintenance/cleaning, and IT support).	10
(b)	The ABC exercise was intended to provide insight into cost and resource management, of which labour is the most significant. Discuss the concerns that arise regarding the labour costs (support your answer with an appropriate calculation(s)), and shortcomings that may exist regards the labour activity analysis (refer to Note 1).	7
(c)	Comment on the consequences of the current method of charging administration fees to the retirement funds, given the ABC information provided.	3
TOTAL MARKS		**20**

References

Cooper, R. 1990. 'Cost classification in unit-based and activity-based manufacturing cost systems'. *Journal of Cost Management*, 4–14, Fall.

Gauteng Province Department of Health and Social Development. 2011. *Gauteng Aids Programme*. [Online]. Available: <www.healthandsocdev.gpg.gov.za/Programmes/Pages/GautengAidsProgramme.aspx> [24 March 2011].

SAICA (South African Institute of Chartered Accountants). 2010. Statements of Generally Accepted Accounting Practice: IAS 2, *Inventories (revised January 2010)*. Johannesburg: SAICA.

South African Government Information. 2010. Media statement by Gauteng Health and Social Development MEC, Q Mahlangu. [Online]. Available <www.info.gov.za/speech/DynamicAction?pageid=461&sid=12584&tid=16608> [24 March 2011].

Job costing

chapter 7

Lilla Stack and John Williams

LEARNING OBJECTIVES

By the end of this chapter, you should be able to:
1. Explain the nature of a job-costing system and the type of organisations for which its use is appropriate.
2. Describe the procedure for recording the cost of materials issued for a particular job, including the FIFO, weighted average, and specific identification methods of pricing raw materials issues and inventory.
3. Explain how the total cost of labour and the hourly rate at which labour is charged to each job are determined, and how these costs are accounted for.
4. Calculate the cost of a job by assigning and allocating the various elements of cost to the job.
5. Prepare journal entries and general ledger accounts for a job-costing system.
6. Explain the difference between an integrated and an interlocking accounting system.

Easylife Kitchens and job costing

Easylife Kitchens has 23 showrooms located throughout South Africa, and factories in Johannesburg and Cape Town. The company designs custom-made kitchens suited to the particular physical kitchen area's size and shape, the customer's decorating preferences, and the budget. Easylife believes that the kind of person the customer is, what the kitchen will be used for, and the choices that the customer makes all ultimately determine the kitchen design. The process begins with a consultant performing a 'needs analysis' to determine the customer's specific requirements. This enables the consultant to suggest appliances, accessories and materials. An individual plan and design is then drawn up, and a quote is calculated based thereon.

SOURCE: *Easylife Kitchens* 2011

Since each kitchen is different and customers are able to customise their orders, it is quite likely that each order received for a kitchen will be unique. This means that the cost incurred by Easylife to fulfil each order is different. It is therefore necessary to determine the costs associated with each order so that the selling price of and the profit on each order can be determined. Job costing is a system of tracing and assigning costs to specific individual orders or 'jobs'.

7.1 Introduction

Key term: job costing

Job costing is used for accumulating costs and determining the price of the goods or services in situations where each product produced or service rendered ('job') differs from the next. Job-costing systems can be differentiated from process-costing and joint and by-product costing systems, which are used where a large number of similar items are produced (process-costing systems are discussed in Chapter 8, *Process costing*, and joint and by-product systems in Chapter 9, *Joint and by-product costing*).

A job-costing system is therefore a system designed to deal with the calculation of the cost of jobs, each of which is unique, requiring an input of differing quantities of materials, labour and allocated overhead cost.

A job can be anything from a multi-million rand bridge over a river to the restoration of an antique piece of furniture, or even the repair of a pair of shoes. Jobs are not restricted to tangible products, but include services. Examples of job-related services include the services of electricians, plumbers, garden services and television-repair services. Often with larger jobs, such as a contract to build a bridge or a toll road, it is also necessary to employ contract costing to determine the amount of revenue that should be recognised in each financial period. Contract costing, however, falls outside the scope of this textbook, and this chapter focuses on jobs which are completed in a relatively short period of time.

7.2 Job-costing objectives

When a car is collected from a vehicle repair shop, the client receives an invoice setting out the cost of the repairs. The repairs carried out on any particular car are likely to be different from the repairs carried out on other cars. In order to produce an accurate invoice, it is therefore necessary for the vehicle repair shop to have a costing system in place that can differentiate between the repairs carried out on different cars, and their associated costs.

A job-costing system enables a vehicle repair shop to:
- Determine the estimated costs for carrying out a particular repair job and provide a quote to a customer
- Determine the cost of sales to be recognised in a reporting period by accumulating the costs of each repair job undertaken during the period
- Budget for future costs and revenue and thereby exercise control over deviations of actual cost and revenues from the budget.

7.3 The elements of cost in a job-costing system

Each individual job undertaken by an organisation involves materials and labour, or machining, and collectively, an infrastructure in which to do the work. In the context of a vehicle repair shop, materials include the spare parts used and cleaning materials, labour includes the mechanics, while the infrastructure includes the repair shop building and the machinery used in repairing cars.

In Chapter 2, *Cost classification* the distinction between direct and indirect costs and overheads was made. Direct costs are those that can be traced to a cost object in a cost-efficient manner, while indirect costs are those that cannot. This distinction is important in job-costing systems. Spare parts used in repairing a car would be an example of direct materials, while the cleaning materials would be an example of indirect materials. Mechanics working on cars constitute direct labour, while indirect labour includes the cost of workers who move articles around, fetch and carry, or provide general assistance. Overhead costs consist of any indirect materials and indirect labour together with other overall infrastructure costs (the overall cost of the infrastructure relates to all activities undertaken that cannot be directly traced to individual jobs).

The costs involved in a job are therefore:
- Direct materials
- Direct labour
- Overhead cost, including indirect materials, indirect labour and infrastructural costs.

The allocation of overheads was discussed in Chapter 6, *Overhead allocation*. For a job-costing system, a commonly-used cost driver for the purposes of allocating overhead costs to individual jobs is direct labour. This is reasonable as each job is different and, to accommodate this, the intervention of labour is needed.

7.3.1 Determining the cost of materials

Key terms: job card

The materials needed for the jobs to be undertaken may be ordered as required (a just-in-time system, which is discussed in Chapter 16, *Contemporary management accounting concepts*) or kept in store until it is issued to a specific job. In a vehicle repair shop, for example, certain expensive parts are ordered as required, while other less costly items are kept in inventory. Irrespective of the inventory system, the materials used for each job together with the cost are recorded on a **job card**.

A simplified materials ordering and handling system is illustrated in Table 7.1.

Table 7.1 A materials ordering and handling system

Purchase requisition issued	When the inventory re-order point is reached, the storeman issues a purchase requisition to the purchasing department
	Note that the purchase requisition may automatically be generated if a computerised materials handling programme is used
Purchase order raised	The purchasing department then issues a purchase order to the appropriate supplier
Goods received note is issued	Once the order has been received, the storeman insects the goods and issues a goods received note
	The stores ledger account is updated for the receipt
Materials are issued	When materials are issued to a job, the workshop or factory foreman issues a stores requisition
	The issue of the materials is then recorded on the stores ledger account

principles of management accounting

The value at which materials are issued to the workshop can be determined in a number of ways:
1. Where materials or components are ordered as they are required, they are issued at actual cost. In most cases, the actual cost of materials, or a component, is simply the amount recorded on the purchase invoice. In other cases, a delivery charge or other charge, such as customs and clearing costs, may be reflected on the invoice and added to the cost of materials purchased. This additional charge would have to be allocated to all the items on the purchase invoice, either per item where all items cost the same, or in proportion to the cost of the items, where costs differ. The value-added tax charge reflected on the invoice would be excluded where the organisation is able to claim the tax as a value-added input tax deduction. Furthermore, some organisations add the cost of ordering and handling materials. They use activity-based costing to allocate materials ordering and handling costs to materials using the purchase price, size or volume of the materials as the cost driver.
2. Where items are ordered in bulk in advance of their use, the value at which they are issued would be calculated by one of the following methods: first-in-first-out (FIFO); weighted average; last-in-first-out (LIFO); specific identification; or standard costs. The LIFO method, where the issue price is assumed to be the cost of the last item purchased, is not acceptable for financial accounting purposes and this method will not be dealt with in further detail in this chapter, as it is also not particularly useful to management accountants. The other methods are discussed below.

The FIFO method of inventory valuation

Key term: FIFO

The **FIFO** method assumes that materials are issued in the sequence in which they were ordered, and assigns an issue price accordingly.

Example 7.1

At the beginning of the month, the inventory on hand in a vehicle repair shop was:

200 litre cans of motor oil @ R15,00 per can (purchased on the 20th day of the previous month)	R3 000
400 litre cans of motor oil @ R18,00 per can (purchased on the 25th day of the previous month)	R7 200

The first materials requisition is for 300 cans of motor oil to be issued for car repairs to be done during the particular day.

Required:
Calculate the value of the motor oil issued, as well as that of the remaining motor oil inventory, using the FIFO valuation method.

Using the FIFO method in example 7.1 to calculate the cost of the 300 cans of oil issued, the 200 cans purchased first at a cost of R15 per can are assumed to be issued first, followed by 100 cans (total of 300 cans issued less the 200 cans assumed to be issued first) at a cost of R18 per can. The total cost of the 300 cans issued is therefore R4 800 (200 cans × R15 per can plus 100 cans × R18 per can). Since all of the 200 cans on hand at the beginning of the month have been issued, the remaining inventory on hand at the end of the month will consist solely of 300 cans (400 on hand at the beginning of the month less 100 issued) at R18 per can, equal to a total value of R5 400.

The weighted average method of inventory valuation

Key term: weighted average

The **weighted average** method prices the inventory at an average price which is re-calculated each time materials are received.

Example 7.2

At the beginning of a month a vehicle repair shop had 10 clutch plates on hand at an average cost of R1 200 per clutch plate. The following receipts were issued during the month:

5 April	5 clutch plates costing R1 400 each received
7 April	9 clutch plates issued
15 April	10 clutch plates costing R1 300 each received

Required:
Calculate the value of the clutch plates issued on 7 April and the value of inventory on hand at the end of the month, using the weighted average valuation method.

In example 7.2, the cost of the clutch plates issued on 7 April will be the weighted average cost of the inventory on hand immediately prior to the issue. This cost is simply the total value of the inventory on hand immediately prior to the issue divided by the total number of clutch plates on hand immediately prior to the issue. The total value of inventory on hand immediately prior to the issue was R19 000 (opening inventory of 10 clutch plates multiplied by the average cost of R1 200 each, plus the receipt of 5 clutch plates on 5 April multiplied by the cost of R1 400 each). The total number of clutch plates on hand immediately prior to the issue was 15 (opening inventory of 10 plus the receipts of 5 on 5 April). Therefore the weighted average cost of the clutch plates issued on 7 April was R1 266,67 (R19 000 divided by 15) or a total of R11 400 (average cost of R1 266,67 × 9 clutch plates issued).

The value of inventory on hand on 7 April in Example 7.2 immediately after the issue of the clutch plates was R7 600 (R19 000 less R11 400). The value of inventory at the end of the month will therefore be R7 600 adjusted for any receipts or issues after 7 April but before the end of the month. During this period there was only the receipt of 10 clutch plates at R1 300 each. The value of inventory at the end of the month will therefore be R20 600 (R7 600 plus R1 300 × 10) and each clutch plate in inventory will have a weighted average cost of R20 600/16 = R1 287,50.

Specific identification

Key term: specific identification

The **specific identification** method values inventory at the specific price paid for each individual item. This method therefore requires each item of inventory to be identified, usually by purchase date and serial number.

principles of management accounting

> ### Example 7.3
> A friend of yours started a used car dealership last month. During her first month of trading the following vehicles were purchased and sold:
>
> *Purchases*
>
> | Registration: | Purchase price: |
> |---|---|
> | BBB 000 EC | R20 000 |
> | CCC 111 L | R80 000 |
> | DDD 222 MP | R120 000 |
> | FFF 444 NW | R100 000 |
> | NNN 888 GP | R200 000 |
>
> *Sales*
>
> | Registration: | Sales price: |
> |---|---|
> | CCC 111 L | R90 000 |
> | DDD 222 MP | R150 000 |
> | FFF 444 NW | R130 000 |
>
> **Required:**
> Calculate the cost of sales for the first month of trading as well as the value of closing inventory at the end of the month using the specific identification method.

The specific cost of each vehicle purchased and sold in Example 7.3 can be identified using the registration number of each vehicle. To calculate the cost of sales, it is necessary to add up the cost of the three specific vehicles sold: R80 000 (CCC 111 L) + R120 000 (DDD 222 MP) + R100 000 (FFF 444 NW), which equals R300 000. The first step in calculating the value of inventory at the end of the month is to identify which cars have not been sold. From the purchases and sales information given, we can tell that BBB 000 EC and NNN 888 GP have not been sold. This may be verified by physically checking that these were the cars on hand. The value of closing inventory is then the actual cost of each of these two vehicles, which is R220 000 (R20 000 paid for BBB 000 EC and R200 000 paid for NNN 888 GP).

Examples 7.1 and 7.2 featured a vehicle repair shop. If a specific identification system were implemented in a vehicle repair shop, this would mean that each part used in a repair would have to be specifically identified and traced to the job. In other words, if a car's silencer were replaced, the information system would have to be sophisticated enough to track exactly which silencer was used in a particular repair job. The cost of that specific silencer would be deducted from inventory, and it would be assigned to the particular repair job.

Standard costs

> **Key term:** standard cost

The materials pricing systems described above make use of actual costs. Many organisations which operate a standard costing system determine standard costs in advance and use these costs throughout the ensuing period. In these circumstances, the predetermined **standard cost** remains constant throughout the period and the cost accounting records are therefore usually maintained in terms of physical purchase and issue quantities only. At the end of the financial year, any variances between standard cost and actual cost have to be apportioned between the year's cost of sales and closing inventory, to ensure that inventories are valued in terms of financial accounting standards. Standard costs are dealt with in more detail in Chapter 13, *Standard costing*.

> ## Example 7.4
> At the beginning of the 2XX1 financial year a vehicle repair shop set the standard cost of oil at R17,50 per can. At the beginning of the current month 8 cans at R17,00 were in inventory, and a further 10 cans at R18,00 were purchased during the month.
>
> **Required:**
> Calculate the cost of oil for a job requiring 5 cans of oil.

In example 7.4, the cost of oil for a job requiring 5 cans of oil will be the standard cost of R17,50 per can multiplied by the 5 cans required, giving a total cost of R87,50.

Note that the standard cost is used instead of the actual purchase costs.

7.3.2 Determining the cost of labour

To calculate the cost of a job, the hourly rate of direct labour is required. The hourly rate of direct labour is determined by calculating the total cost of direct labour for a specific period and dividing this by the number of productive hours of direct labour available during the period.

It is not feasible to use actual direct labour costs and actual direct labour hours to set an hourly rate for direct labour, because the organisation would then have to wait until the end of the period before the hourly rate is known. Organisations therefore use the budgeted direct labour cost for the coming budget period and the estimated number of productive direct labour hours during the period to calculate the budgeted direct labour cost per unit of product or service. At the end of the financial year, any variances between the budgeted direct labour cost and the actual direct labour cost have to be debited or credited to cost of sales.

The wage system and the total cost of direct labour

> **Key terms:** cost to company, clock cards, time sheets

Organisations operate a payroll system to calculate the wage or salary payable to employees, using individual employee personnel records to determine the gross salary or wage, and **clock cards** or **time sheets** to record their presence at work.

The total budgeted cost of direct labour is needed in order to determine the hourly rate of direct labour. The total budgeted cost is the budgeted '**cost to company**'. This cost would include:
- The basic salary or wage of the employee concerned (before deducting contributions to funds)
- The organisation's share of contributions to the employee's pension fund, medical aid fund, unemployment insurance fund, trade union and, possibly, a group-life insurance fund
- Payments by the organisation to the Workmen's Compensation Fund and other tax levies based on the salary bill, such as the skills development levy.

principles of management accounting

Example 7.5

The following estimated direct labour costs were included in Joe's Vehicle Repair Shop's budget for the forthcoming year:

Basic salaries and wages (including employees' medical aid contributions)	R1 500 000
Bonuses	R150 000
Employer's contribution to UIF	R33 000
Employer's medical aid contributions	R67 000
Employer's pension fund contributions	R100 000
Skills development levy	R150 000

Required:
Calculate the total budgeted cost of direct labour.

The total budgeted direct labour cost for Joe's Vehicle Repair Shop in example 7.5 includes the estimated cost of bonuses, employer's contributions to UIF, medical aid and pension fund and the skills development levy payment, in addition to the basic salary and wages cost. The total direct labour cost is therefore R2 000 000 (R1 500 000 + R150 000 + R33 000 + R67 000 + R100 000 + R150 000).

Productive direct labour hours available

Key terms: productive hours, idle time

Employees are paid their wage or salary throughout the year, but are not productive throughout the year. They are entitled to take paid leave, they may be granted sick leave at full pay, and during each working day, there are times when they are not at the workbench (for example, during the regularly scheduled tea break). The organisation estimates the total number of **productive hours** for the budget period in order to calculate the hourly direct labour rate.

There may also be times when the labour force is idle. This could be due to a machine breakdown, strike action, waiting for materials, or no work to be done. These idle hours are usually recorded on an **idle time** card, and the costs written off as a period cost.

Example 7.6

The workshop manager at Joe's Vehicle Repair Shop has made the following estimation of direct labour hours that will be available during the forthcoming year:

Total paid labour hours	10 000 hours
Scheduled paid tea and lunch breaks	1 750 hours
Scheduled 'down time' for maintenance of hi-tech tuning machines	250 hours
Estimated idle time during which no work will be available	750 hours

Required:
Calculate the estimated number of productive direct labour hours available in the forthcoming year.

Since we are interested only in the number of productive direct labour hours, any hours during which no active work is expected should be excluded. Therefore, when calculating the number of productive direct labour hours available in example 7.6, the scheduled tea and lunch breaks, down time for scheduled maintenance and the idle time during which no work will be available must be excluded from the total hours available. The number of production direct labour hours is therefore 7 250 (10 000 – 1 750 – 250 – 750).

Once the total cost of direct labour and the productive direct labour hours for the period are known, the hourly rate of direct labour can be calculated as illustrated in example 7.7.

Example 7.7
Required:
Using the information given in examples 7.5 and 7.6, calculate the hourly cost of direct labour for Joe's Vehicle Repair Shop.

In example 7.5, the total direct labour cost was calculated as R2 000 000 and the total number of productive direct labour hours was calculated in example 7.6 as 7 250. However, if we want to write off idle time separately as a period cost, we need to calculate the rate based on productive direct labour hours (7 250 hours) plus the estimated idle time during which no work will be available (750 hours). The hourly cost of direct labour is therefore R250 (R2 000 000 divided by 8 000). Of this, R1 812 500 (R250 × 7 250) will be allocated to jobs and R187 500 (R250 × 750) will be written off as idle time. It is important to remember that since we need to have a direct labour rate to apply during the period, the *estimated* direct labour cost and *estimated* hours for the period are used. It is also important to note that if, for example, there were two additional hours of idle time while waiting for spare parts to arrive for a repair job (in other words, actual idle time is two hours more than estimated idle time), those hours would not be allocated to the job but would be recognised as a period cost.

Indirect labour

Some labour costs cannot be directly traced to a specific job, and these costs are known as indirect labour costs. The cost of indirect labour is usually debited to the overhead control account and allocated as part of the total overhead cost to individual jobs, using an appropriate cost driver. The allocation of overheads to jobs is discussed next.

7.3.3 Overhead expenses

The cost of each job includes an allocated overhead cost. Overhead costs usually consist of a variable component and a fixed component. The separation of total overhead cost into the variable and fixed elements was dealt with in Chapter 3, *Cost estimation*.

principles of management accounting

Variable overheads

The variable component may include materials and labour, which vary in relation to the volume of jobs worked on, but cannot be traced directly to individual jobs. In other words, variable overheads may include indirect materials and indirect labour. Variable overhead costs could also include the cost of power used for machines and similar costs. Chapter 6, *Overhead allocation* explored how appropriate cost drivers are selected and used to allocate variable overhead costs to each job.

Fixed overheads

Fixed overhead costs are costs that do not change within a specified period. In a vehicle repair shop, costs that are fixed in the short term could include the cost of establishing and maintaining the infrastructure of the workshop, rental paid (or property rates and insurance where the organisation owns the property), lighting and heating, insurance, the cost of supervision, and so on.

Some mechanism has to be used to allocate fixed overhead costs to individual jobs, to ensure that the total cost of each job carries its equitable share of the cost. In a job-costing system, the cost driver often used for this purpose is direct labour. Fixed costs are allocated either per direct labour hour or in relation to the labour cost charged to each job.

The budgeted overhead cost and the estimated number of cost-driver units (hours of direct labour, for example) during a particular period are used to set the overhead allocation rates, as the actual cost and the actual activity level will be known only after the end of the period. It is unlikely that the actual cost incurred during the period will be exactly the same as the budget or the standard set, and the variances between the actual cost and the budgeted or standard cost will have to be disposed of for financial accounting purposes. The estimated and the actual capacity level would also differ, and this would give rise to an under- or over-recovery of fixed overhead costs, which would also have to be disposed of for financial accounting purposes. The calculation of the under- or over-recovery of overheads and the manner in which they are disposed of for financial accounting purposes is discussed in Chapter 5, *Absorption versus variable costing*.

Example 7.8

The following overhead costs have been extracted from the budget of Joe's Vehicle Repair Shop for the forthcoming year:

Indirect materials	R50 000
Indirect labour	R400 000
Workshop rental	R250 000
Workshop cleaning	R75 000
Electricity	R25 000
Insurance	R20 000
Depreciation	R30 000

Overheads are allocated to jobs based on direct labour hours. A total of 8 500 productive direct labour hours are estimated to be available for the forthcoming year.

Required:
Calculate the overhead allocation rate for the forthcoming year.

The overhead allocation rate for example 7.8 can be calculated by dividing the total estimated overhead expenditure by the total estimated productive direct labour hours. The total estimated overhead expenditure is R850 000 (R50 000 + R400 000 + R250 000 + R75 000 + R25 000 + R20 000 + R30 000), and the total number of estimated productive direct labour hours is given as 8 500. The overhead allocation rate is therefore R100 per productive direct labour hour (R850 000/8 500).

7.4 Integrating the costing and financial accounting systems

Key terms: integrated accounting system, interlocking accounting system

The costing system may be fully integrated with the financial accounting system, making use of a number of control accounts (and possibly subsidiary ledger accounts) for this purpose. Such a system is called an **integrated accounting system**. Organisations may also make use of an **interlocking accounting system**. An interlocking system comprises two entirely separate accounting systems, running side-by-side, with only one control account linking the two systems.

7.4.1 Accounting entries for an integrated job-costing system

Materials, labour and overhead costs incurred during a reporting period are recorded in the control accounts via a series of journal entries. You should be familiar with the journal entries from your financial accounting studies and therefore detailed explanations of the journal entries have not been given, but an overview of the entries required is given in Table 7.2 below:

Table 7.2 Journal entries for an integrated job-costing system

Materials	Labour	Factory overheads

Purchase of materials:
Dr Stores ledger control
   Cr Accounts payable
	Payment of wages:
	Dr Wages control
	   Cr Bank
	   Cr PAYE
	   Cr UIF
	   Cr Pension
	   Cr Medical aid, and so on
		Purchase of indirect factory items:
		Dr Factory overhead control
		   Cr Accounts payable

		Depreciation of factory buildings and machinery: Dr Factory overhead control Cr Accumulated depreciation

Issue of direct materials to jobs:
 	
Dr WIP control
   Cr Stores ledger control
	Allocation of direct labour to jobs:
	
	Dr WIP control
	   Cr Wages control
		Allocation of factory overheads to jobs:
		Dr WIP control
		   Cr Factory overhead control

Issue of indirect materials:
 	
Dr Factory overhead control
   Cr Stores ledger control
	Allocation of indirect labour:
	
	Dr Factory overhead control
	   Cr Wages control
		Under- or over-allocation of factory overhead:
		Dr Factory overhead control
		   Cr Cost of sales

principles of management accounting

Note: The balance of the WIP account will consist of the cost of a number of jobs, unless the organisation is working on only one job.

Non-manufacturing overheads	Cost of sales and inventory valuation

Record costs incurred:
Dr Non manufacturing overheads control
    Cr Accounts payable
	Completion of jobs:
	Dr Finished goods inventory
	    Cr WIP control

	Invoicing of jobs:
	Dr Costs of sales
	    Cr Finished goods inventory
	Dr Accounts receivable
	    Cr Sales

Note: No closing journal entries have been shown. These would be the same as those covered in financial accounting texts.

7.4.2 Accounting entries for an interlocking job-costing system

With an interlocking accounting system, the costing accounts are maintained independently from the financial accounts, so a control account must be maintained in the costing accounts to record the corresponding entries that would have been recorded in the financial accounts if the systems had been integrated. This control account is commonly referred to as the 'cost control account' and ensures that the double entries are maintained in the costing accounts.

The journal entries for an interlocking job-costing system would be the same as for an integrated system shown in Table 7.2, except that entries in the Accounts payable, Bank, PAYE, UIF, Accumulated depreciation, and Accounts receivable accounts would be replaced with entries to the Cost control account.

Example 7.9

The following transactions occurred in Joe's Vehicle Repair Shop during July:
1. Materials amounting to R1 million were purchased.
2. Direct materials totalling R800 000 were issued to jobs.
3. Stores requisitions for indirect materials totalled R150 000.
4. Total wages of R2 million was paid. This consisted of wages paid to employees of R1 460 000, PAYE of R500 000 and UIF of R40 000. 80 per cent of the total wages paid related to direct labour, and the rest to indirect workshop labour.
5. Indirect workshop expenses of R250 000 were incurred.
6. Depreciation on workshop machinery amounted to R50 000.
7. Total overheads of R825 000 were allocated to jobs based on the overhead allocation rates.
8. Other overheads not directly related to repair vehicles of R200 000 were incurred.
9. Jobs with a total cost of R3 200 000 were completed.
10. Customers were invoiced a total of R4 000 000 for completed jobs. This represented a cost of R3 100 000.

Required:
Prepare general ledger T accounts for the above transactions assuming that the organisation uses:
a) An integrated system
b) An interlocking system.

Closing entries are not required.

The T accounts for the integrated system are summarised in Table 7.3 below. The purchase of the materials is recorded by debiting the Stores ledger control account and crediting the Accounts payable account. The issue of direct materials to jobs is recorded through a debit to the WIP account and a credit to the Stores ledger control account. Stores requisition for indirect materials is recorded via a debit to Workshop overhead control and a credit to the Stores ledger control accounts. The payment of wages to employees, PAYE, and UIF are recorded with a debit to the Wages control and credits to the Bank, PAYE, and UIF accounts. The 80 per cent portion of total wages paid to direct labour amounting to R1 600 000 (R2 million × 80%) will be allocated to work-in-progress, with a debit to the WIP account and a credit to the Wages control account. The remaining R400 000 (R2 million – R1 600 000) is allocated to the Workshop overhead account, as it relates to indirect overheads, with a debit to the Workshop overhead account and a credit to the Wages control account. As with the recording of indirect materials, indirect workshop expenses are recorded as a debit to Workshop overhead control, and, unlike indirect materials, a credit to Accounts payable.

The depreciation on workshop machinery represents an indirect cost and is therefore recorded through a debit to Workshop overhead control and a credit to Accumulated depreciation. The allocation of overheads to jobs is recorded by debiting WIP and crediting the Workshop overhead control account. Note that the difference between the workshop overheads actually incurred and the overheads allocated to jobs represents an under-recovery of overhead as more overhead expenses have been incurred than were allocated. The other overheads not directly related to the repair of vehicles are recorded in a separate control account, Non-repair-related overheads. When jobs are completed, the cost of the jobs completed is recorded by crediting WIP and debiting Finished goods. The cost of completed jobs invoiced to clients is recorded with a credit to Finished goods and a debit to Cost of services rendered. The invoice value of completed jobs invoiced is recorded with a debit to Accounts receivable and a credit to Sales.

Table 7.3 T accounts for an integrated system

		Stores ledger control (R'000)				
1	Accounts payable		1 000	2	WIP	800
				3	Workshop overhead control	150
	Balance b/d		50			
		Accounts payable (R'000)				
				1	Stores ledger control	1 000
				5	Workshop overhead control	250
				8	Non-repair-related overhead control	200
					Balance b/d	1 450

principles of management accounting

Work-in-progress (WIP) (R'000)					
2	Stores ledger control	800	9	Finished goods	3 200
4	Wages control	1 600			
7	Workshop overhead control	825			
	Balance b/d	25			
Workshop overhead control (R'000)					
3	Stores ledger control	150	7	WIP	825
4	Wages control	400			
5	Accounts payable	250			
6	Accumulated depreciation	50			
	Balance b/d *	25			
*Note that this represents an under-recovery of overhead.					
Wages control (R'000)					
4	Bank	1 460	4	WIP	1 600
4	PAYE	500	4	Workshop overhead control	400
4	UIF	40			
Bank (R'000)					
			4	Wages control	1 460
PAYE (R'000)					
			4	Wages control	500
UIF (R'000)					
			4	Wages control	40
Accumulated depreciation (R'000)					
			6	Workshop overhead control	50
Non-repair-related overheads (R'000)					
8	Accounts payable	200			
Finished goods (R'000)					
9	WIP	3 200	10	Cost of services rendered	3 100
	Balance b/d	100			
Accounts receivable (R'000)					
11	Sales	4 000			
Sales (R'000)					
			11	Accounts receivable	4 000
Cost of services rendered (R'000)					
10	Finished goods	3 100			

The T accounts for an interlocking system are summarised in Table 7.4 below. These T accounts are the same as for an integrated system shown in Table 7.3, except that entries in the Accounts payable, Bank, PAYE, UIF, Accumulated depreciation, and Accounts receivable accounts are replaced with entries to the Cost control account.

Chapter 7 Job costing

Table 7.4 T accounts for an interlocking system

Stores ledger control (R'000)					
1	Cost control	1 000	2	WIP	800
			3	Workshop overhead control	150
	Balance b/d	50			

Cost control (R'000)					
11	Sales	4 000	1	Stores ledger control	1 000
			4	Wages control (R1 460 + R500 + R40)	2 000
			5	Workshop overhead control	250
			6	Workshop overhead control	50
			8	Non-repair-related overhead control	200
	Balance b/d	500			

Work-in-progress (WIP) (R'000)					
2	Stores ledger control	800	9	Finished goods	3 200
4	Wages control	1 600			
7	Workshop overhead control	825			
	Balance b/d	25			

Workshop overhead control (R'000)					
3	Stores ledger control	150	7	WIP	825
4	Wages control	400			
5	Cost control	250			
6	Cost control	50			
	Balance b/d *	25			

*Note that this represents an under-recovery of overheads.

Wages control (R'000)					
4	Cost control (R1 460 + R500 + R40)	2 000	4	WIP	1 600
			4	Workshop overhead control	400

Non-repair-related overheads (R'000)			
8	Cost control	200	

Finished goods (R'000)					
9	WIP	3 200	10	Cost of services rendered	3 100
	Balance b/d	100			

Sales (R'000)					
			11	Cost control	4 000

Cost of services rendered (R'000)			
10	Finished goods	3 100	

199

principles of management accounting

7.5 Summary

Job costing is used in industries in the manufacturing sector, and examples include designing and installing security systems, restoring or repairing various types of asset, or producing articles to the specifications of the client – dressmaking and tailoring, furniture and upholstery, and innumerable others. Job-costing systems are also used in the service industry, and examples include the services of electricians, plumbers, carpenters, decorators, and many others.

Each job is unique and requires a different input of materials, labour and variable overhead. Each job carries its share of the overall fixed overhead cost of the organisation. A job-costing system is designed to provide the information necessary to allocate the correct cost to each job, to account for the cost of sales and the value of inventory, and to provide cost information for decision-making and for budgeting and control purposes.

Conclusion: Job costing and other topics in this book

Many of the concepts explained in this chapter can be applied when studying other topics. Determining the cost of materials and the issue price, determining the cost of and accounting for direct labour, and allocating variable and fixed overheads are actions that are also required for process costing (see Chapter 8); joint and by-products (discussed in Chapter 9); relevant costing (see Chapter 10); and standard costing (covered in Chapter 13).

Tutorial case study: Boeing

Boeing is an aircraft manufacturer based in the USA. Its aircrafts are used by South African Airways – which has 21 B737-800 aircraft in its fleet – and numerous other airlines across the world. According to its website, by July 2010 Boeing had received 279 orders for new aircraft in 2010. Of the 279 orders received, 27 were from unnamed customers and the remaining 252 from nineteen named customers. In addition to producing new aircraft, Boeing is also the world's leading seller of previously-operated aircraft. The company can modify aircraft configurations, enhance performance and improve cabin amenities according to the individual needs and preferences of their airline customers.

Sources: Boeing 2010 and SAA 2011

1. Discuss whether it would be appropriate for Boeing to use a job-costing system for accumulating the costs involved with each order.
2. Assume that Boeing did adopt a job-costing system. Working in pairs, prepare a written report which addresses each of the following requirements. Give reasons for your viewpoints, where relevant.
   a) Describe the procedure for recording the cost of materials used in manufacturing and assembling new aircrafts. Include examples of what materials you would expect to be used.
   b) Explain how the cost of the labour used in modifying previously owned aircrafts would be determined.
   c) Describe what overheads you would expect to be allocated to Boeing's jobs and how this allocation would be calculated.
   d) Identify what journal entries would be required to record the cost of materials, labour and overheads assigned to the jobs.

Basic questions

BQ 1

An organisation issues raw materials from inventory on the weighted average basis and uses this basis to value closing inventory. Using the following information, how would the closing inventory of material M be valued?

Date		Units	Unit cost R
01/07/2XX6	Opening inventory	500	2,00
25/08/2XX6	Purchases	1 000	2,15
31/08/2XX6	Issues	(1 200)	
30/11/2XX6	Purchases	1 500	2,04
15/01/2XX7	Issues	(1 000)	
31/03/2XX7	Purchases	1 000	1,87
30/04/2XX7	Issues	(1 500)	

BQ 2

What costs, other than the cost of the raw materials itself, are often incurred in respect of the *purchase* of raw materials, and how are these costs dealt with for cost accounting purposes?

BQ 3

There are two valuation methods most commonly used to price the issue from inventory of raw materials to individual jobs for cost accounting purposes. Describe the two methods and distinguish between them. Would either of these methods be appropriate for decision-making purposes and, if not, what method should be used?

BQ 4

How is the hourly cost of direct labour calculated? List the various labour-related costs that may be involved. How is each dealt with in calculating the hourly direct labour 'cost to company'?

BQ 5

An organisation uses productive direct labour hours to allocate indirect overheads to jobs. If the total estimated productive direct labour hours are 5 000 and the total estimated overheads are R1 million, what amount of overheads should be allocated to a job which took two direct labour hours?

BQ 6

Source: Adapted from Rhodes University

Assume that the organisation uses the weighted average method to issue raw materials to individual jobs. What will this stores ledger card look like if you fill in the missing information?

Date	Purchases (units)		R	Date	Issues (units)		R
April				April			
1	40	on hand	4 000,00				
4	140		15 400,00				
				10	90		??
12	60		7 200,00				
				13	100		??
16	??		??	21	70		??
26	200		20 000,00				
				27	80		??
				29	??		??
				30	90	on hand	9 191,74
	490		52 600,00		490		
May							
1	90	on hand	9 191,74				

BQ 7

Which of the following industries would not use a job-costing system, and why?
a) Construction
b) Petrochemicals
c) Shipbuilders
d) Custom-built furniture

BQ 8

Job 77 was started and completed on 3 December. The following details appeared on the job card:

Direct materials issues	R30 000
	R5 000
	R15 000
Direct labour	200 hours @ R100 per hour
Overheads	R50 per direct labour hour

The mark-up on Job 77 was 100% of cost.

What are the journal entries to record the above costs, the completion of Job 77 and the sale of Job 77?

BQ 9

The following information relates to a job-costing system:

	R
Direct materials issued	500 000
Indirect materials issued	100 000
Direct labour (1 000 hours)	1 000 000
Indirect labour	200 000
Depreciation of factory building and machinery	50 000
Other factory overhead	150 000
Factory overhead allocation rate (per direct labour hour)	50

What total amount should be credited to the Stores ledger control account?

BQ 10

The following information relates to a job-costing system:

	R
Direct materials issued	500 000
Indirect materials issued	100 000
Direct labour (20 000 hours)	1 000 000
Indirect labour	200 000
Depreciation of factory building and machinery	50 000
Other factory overhead	150 000
Factory overhead allocation rate (per direct labour hour)	25
Increase in work-in-progress balance	300 000

What total amount should be debited to the Finished goods account?

Long questions

LQ 1 – Intermediate (7 marks; 13 minutes)

Grandix Limited operates a job-costing system. Each job passes through two production departments, A and B, and two service departments, Purchasing and Packing. The budgeted overhead costs for the production and service departments for 2XX7 are as follows:

Production departments		Service departments	
A	B	Purchasing	Packing
R400 000	R500 000	R350 000	R250 000

Department A is machine intensive, while Department B is labour intensive. Overheads are therefore traditionally recovered in Department A on the basis of machine hours and Department B on the basis of labour hours. The overheads of service departments are allocated to production departments on the basis of estimated usage as follows:

	Department A	Department B
Purchasing	55%	45%
Packing	30%	70%

For 2XX7, a total of 80 000 machine hours and 50 000 labour hours have been budgeted for. One of the jobs completed during March 2XX7 was Job 100, which required 2 000 machine hours and 1 000 labour hours.

REQUIRED	Marks
Calculate the cost of overheads allocated to Job 100, using the traditional allocation method.	7
TOTAL MARKS	7

LQ 2 – Intermediate (7 marks; 13 minutes)

Robertsons Service Centre repairs all types of motor vehicle and has a highly trained team of motor technicians. The owner of the business is concerned because, despite the increase in turnover, the profits have not increased to the same extent. He suspects that the charge-out rate for skilled labour may be too low.

You are presented with the following information relating to the previous twelve months:

Extracts from the accounting records
- Gross basic wages paid: 10 technicians at R2 500 each, per week
- Income tax deducted from wages: R483,60 each, per week
- Employee contributions to a pension fund: 7,5 per cent of the gross basic wage, deducted from the weekly wage; the employer makes a further contribution of 7,5 per cent of the gross basic wage
- Employee contribution to a medical aid fund: R200 per week, deducted from the weekly wage. The employer makes a further contribution of R100 per employee per week
- Contribution to the Unemployment Insurance Fund: each employee and the employer contribute 1 per cent of the gross basic wage
- Contributions to the Workmen's Compensation Fund: the employer contributes R160 per month per employee to the fund
- Other levies based on gross basic wages paid: the employer contributes 3 per cent of gross basic wages.

Terms of employment
Employees work eight hours a day for five days a week. They are granted two weeks of fully-paid leave each year. In addition there are ten fully-paid public holidays during the year.

Productivity
Over the past twelve months, the records show that a total of 50 working days were lost owing to fully-paid sick leave and that, of the remaining available time, a 95 per cent productivity level was achieved as a result of unproductive time from scheduled tea breaks and normal maintenance requirements.

Details relating to the next twelve-month period

Wage negotiations with employees are expected to result in a basic wage increase of 5 per cent across the board. Medical aid contributions are expected to increase by 10 per cent and Workmen's Compensation insurance by 8 per cent.

REQUIRED	Marks
Calculate the hourly direct labour rate to be budgeted for for the coming twelve-month period.	7
TOTAL MARKS	7

LQ 3 – Advanced (20 marks; 36 minutes)

Source: Adapted from Rhodes University

Grahamstown Upholsterers received an order on 10 July 2XX7 to re-upholster a full living-room suite consisting of a three-seater couch, a two-seater couch and three easy chairs. The job estimate is based on the following requirements:
- 30 metres of imported velvet material
- 15 hours of direct labour at R20 per hour
- Variable production overhead costs allocated at R3,10 per metre of materials used
- Fixed production overhead costs allocated at R5,30 per direct labour hour.

The inventory account for the velvet materials to be used to re-upholster the furniture reveals the following information:

Date	Description	Metres	R
1 March 2XX7	Opening inventory	150	13 500
15 March 2XX7	Issued to workshop	60	
5 April 2XX7	Issued to workshop	40	
15 April 2XX7	Purchases	200	21 000
30 April 2XX7	Issued to workshop	80	
17 May 2XX7	Issued to workshop	70	
15 June 2XX7	Purchases	250	30 000
18 June 2XX7	Issued to workshop	90	

	REQUIRED	Marks
(a)	Calculate the issue price of the velvet for the purposes of calculating the cost of this job, using: (i) the FIFO method (ii) the weighted average method.	15
(b)	Determine the price for the order to re-upholster the lounge suite, assuming that Grahamstown Upholsterers issues materials at the weighted average price and applies a mark-up of 50 per cent on the selling price.	5
	TOTAL MARKS	20

LQ 4 – Advanced (10 marks; 18 minutes)

Source: Adapted from Rhodes University

You have been asked to price a special order for 100 ornamental wooden screens. You have been provided with the following information, in order to do so:

Wood:
The organisation issues its wood from the store to individual jobs on the FIFO basis. It has 400 kg of suitable wood in store at a stores price of R10,10 per kg. It has just placed an order to purchase 2 000 kg of wood at a cost of R9,95 per kg.

Each screen uses 10 kg of wood. In addition, the cost of sundry materials consumed in producing the screens amounts to R1,20 per kg of wood used.

Direct labour:
The organisation employs 20 craftsmen at a total cost to company of R235 200 per month. There are on average 20 working days in a month (of 8 hours a day). The organisation has just agreed to a 10 per cent increase in the basic wage (which amounts to an 8 per cent increase in the cost to company), with immediate effect.

Each screen takes 4 hours to produce. Because the order is urgent and the organisation is working at close to full capacity, the craftsmen have to work overtime to produce the whole order. The overtime rate is charged out at 1,5 times the normal rate.

Overheads:
Variable overhead costs amount to R5,00 per direct labour hour and fixed overhead costs amount to R2,00 per direct labour hour.

Mark-up on cost:
The organisation applies a mark-up sufficient to earn a gross profit percentage of 50 per cent.

REQUIRED	Marks
Calculate the amount to be quoted for the special order for the ornamental wooden screens.	10
TOTAL MARKS	10

LQ 5 – Advanced (12 marks; 22 minutes)
Source: Adapted from Rhodes University

One of the departments in a furniture factory restores antique furniture. The work is carried out by highly skilled workmen, using hand tools. As there are no direct materials involved, all the indirect materials are debited to the overhead account.

You have been asked by the director of the organisation to calculate the price to be charged for a job involving the restoration of an antique dining room suite. The dining room suite consists of a table, twenty-four chairs and two buffets. You are presented with the information set out below:

1 Factory overhead costs

The budgeted overheads for the factory *as a whole* for the year are:

	R
Rent, lighting, heating and cleaning	400 000
Factory supervisor's salary and the cost of his office administration	150 000

The furniture restoring department occupies 20 per cent of the floor space in the factory and employs five skilled workers and ten casual labourers. The total workforce in the factory amounts to 100 workers.

2 **Overhead costs of the furniture restoring department**

In addition to the overhead costs of the entire factory allocated to the department, it will incur the following budgeted overhead costs during the year:

	R
Indirect materials	50 000
Depreciation of tools and other fixed costs	80 000
Power	11 500
Wages of casual labourers	160 000

3 **Allocation of overhead costs**

All overhead costs are allocated on the basis of budgeted available skilled labour hours.

4 **Skilled labour costs**

The five skilled workmen earn R120 000 each per annum and each workman works, on average, 2 000 hours per year.

5 **The restoration job to be priced**

The factory foreman estimates that the restoration of the dining room suite will take 120 hours of skilled labour time.

6 **Mark-up**

The organisation uses a mark-up of 50 per cent on selling price in setting prices.

REQUIRED	Marks
Calculate the price to be charged for the job of restoring the antique dining room suite.	12
TOTAL MARKS	**12**

References

Boeing. 2010. Commercial airplanes and Orders and deliveries. [Online]. Available: <www.boeing.com/commercial/products.html> and <www.active.boeing.com/commercial/orders/index.cfm> [31 July 2010].

Easylife Kitchens. 2011. *Why choose Easylife?* [Online]. Available: <www.easylifekitchens.co.za> [24 February 2011].

South African Airways. 2011. *B737-800 Information.* [Online]. Available: <www.flysaa.com/Journeys/cms/ZA/flyingSAA/_categories/SAAFleet/B737-800_seat_plan.html> [24 February 2011].

Process costing

chapter 8

Lilla Stack and John Williams

LEARNING OBJECTIVES

By the end of this chapter, you should be able to:
1 Calculate:
   - The number of equivalent units produced during a particular period, and
   - The cost per unit incurred during a particular period.
2 Prepare a production cost statement reflecting the cost of finished goods and the cost of work-in-progress at the end of the period.
3 Calculate, account for and discuss the impact on cost of normal losses, abnormal losses, and abnormal gains in a process, during a particular period.
4 Understand the impact that the point in the process at which the units in process are inspected and losses in process identified has on:
   - The equivalent production costs
   - The unit cost, and
   - The production cost statement reflecting the cost of finished goods, closing work-in-progress, and abnormal losses or gains.
5 Discuss the difference between the weighted average method of valuing finished goods and work-in-progress, and the first-in-first-out (FIFO) method, and discuss when it is appropriate to use each method.
6 Discuss and account for the effect of the sale of scrap.

SAB and process costing

South African Breweries Limited (SAB) is the largest beverages company in South Africa, and one of the country's biggest manufacturers. The company operates seven breweries and 40 depots in South Africa, and has an annual brewing capacity of 3,1 billion litres. Its portfolio of beer brands includes Castle Lager, Hansa Pilsener, Carling Black Label and Grolsch.

Three of SAB's beer breweries are located in Gauteng and one brewery in each of Limpopo, KwaZulu-Natal, the Western Cape and the Eastern Cape. At these breweries, beer is produced in a process that consists of a number of steps: malting, mashing, lauretting, wort boiling, fermentation, maturation, filtration and packaging.

Source: SAB 2010

The batches of Castle Lager brewed during any given period go through the same brewing process, and each litre brewed is the same. It is therefore not necessary to accumulate costs individually for each litre of beer brewed during a given period. Instead, a process costing system can be used to accumulate the total costs incurred in the brewing process, and these total costs are then allocated to individual bottles of beer. This can be contrasted with the motor repair shop examples in Chapter 7, *Job costing*, where each individual job had to be costed separately, as each job was unique.

principles of management accounting

8.1 Introduction

> **Key term:** process costing

Process costing is a system used to determine the cost of a large number of identical product units produced in a continuous process. Each unit consumes an identical amount of variable and fixed cost. Unlike job costing systems, which trace and allocate costs to each unique job, process costing systems do not trace and allocate costs to individual product units. Costs incurred during a particular costing period are accumulated and allocated to all units produced during the period. The price of each unit produced during the costing period is then calculated as follows:

$$\text{Unit cost} = \frac{\text{Total cost}}{\text{Total number of units}}$$

The Chartered Institute of Management Accountants (CIMA) defines process costing as follows:

> 'The costing method applicable where goods or services result from a sequence of continuous or repetitive operations or process. Costs are averaged over the units produced during the period.' (CIMA 2000)

The types of cost involved in a process manufacturing system are the same as in any other mode of production: direct materials, direct labour, other direct costs and indirect overhead costs. Materials are introduced at the start of the process and, possibly, additional materials are added at a later stage in the process. The direct labour cost and the direct and indirect overhead costs are usually combined as 'conversion costs'. Labour and machinery may not work in unison, but may be applied at different stages of the process. A batch of products may be subjected first to manual processing and then progress through a mechanised processing stage. In this case, the two types of cost are allocated separately – labour costs as a separate cost category, and variable and fixed costs relating to the use of equipment as another cost category. The flow of costs in a simple process costing system is illustrated in Figure 8.1.

Figure 8.1 Flow of costs in a simple process costing system

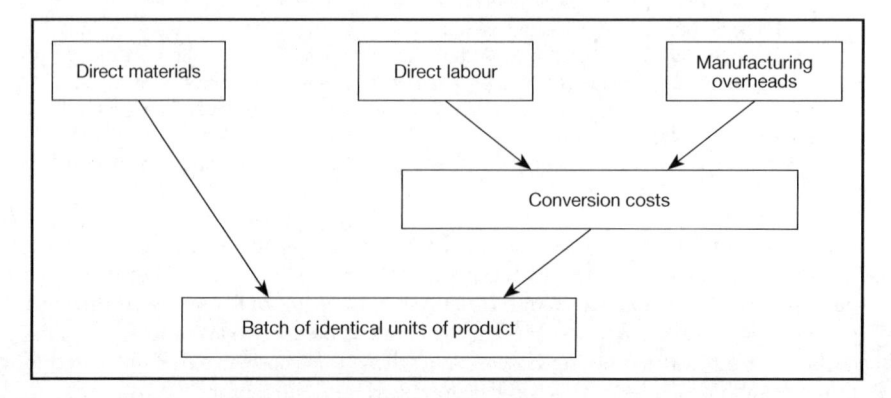

8.2 Calculations in a process costing system

The objective of a process costing system is to calculate the unit cost of the products produced during the period. Typically, the calculation of the unit cost is supported by three statements: the statement of equivalent production, the unit cost statement, and the production cost statement. The statement of equivalent production is used to calculate the number of units produced during the period. The unit cost statement calculates the average cost of producing one unit during the period, while the production cost statement reconciles the costs allocated to units during the period with the cost of production during the period.

The first example illustrates the most basic situation encountered in a process costing system.

Example 8.1

Details relating to ABC Ltd's production during November:

Units	Started and completed during November	20 000
Cost	Direct materials	R40 000
	Direct labour	R190 000
	Manufacturing overhead cost	R70 000

Required:
Draw up the following statements:
- Equivalent production
- Unit cost
- Production cost.

The equivalent production, unit cost and production cost statements for example 8.1 are given in Table 8.1. Note that the equivalent production statement reflects that 20 000 units were started (reflected in the input units column) in the process during November and 20 000 units were completed (reflected in the total column under output units). Note also that the total output is shown as the numbers of units that incurred materials and conversion costs during the period. The significance of this will become more evident once the complexity of work-in-progress has been discussed (refer to section 8.2.1 below).

The total materials, labour and overhead costs are reflected in the unit cost statement. Note that both labour and overhead costs form part of the conversion costs. The unit materials cost is calculated by dividing the cost of materials, R40 000, by the equivalent units processed, 20 000, as reflected in the 'materials' column in the statement of equivalent production. The unit conversion cost is calculated in the same way. The total unit cost (R15) is calculated by adding the unit materials cost (R2) to the unit conversion cost (R13). The total unit cost is not calculated by dividing the total cost by the total unit column. In this simple example the result would be the same (R300 000/220 000 = R15), but if the elements of cost were at different stages of completion or losses in the process were involved, the wrong result would have been obtained.

The production cost statement reflects that during the period, 20 000 units at a unit costs of R15 were completed and included in the finished goods inventory.

principles of management accounting

The total cost allocated to finished goods was R300 000 (20 000 units × R15 per unit). Note that the total cost reflected in the unit cost statement (R300 000) and the total of the production cost statement (R300 000) are the same, indicating that all costs have been accounted for.

Table 8.1 Equivalent production statement, unit cost statement and production cost statement for example 8.1

Equivalent production statement				
Input units		Output units		
		Total	Materials	Conversion
20 000	Started and completed	20 000	20 000	20 000
Unit cost statement		Total (R)	Materials (R)	Conversion (R)
Direct materials		40 000	40 000	
Direct labour		190 000		190 000
Manufacturing overheads cost		70 000		70 000
		300 000	40 000	260 000
Cost per unit		15,00	2,00	13,00
Production cost statement				R
Finished goods (20 000 units × R15)				300 000

8.2.1 Work-in-progress

Key terms: work-in-progress, equivalent full units

One of the main problems that arises in process costing systems is that, at the end of a costing period, some units may be only partially completed. These partially-completed units are referred to as **work-in-progress** (hereafter 'WIP'). As the WIP units are not fully completed, additional costs will be incurred in the following period to complete them. Therefore, if WIP units were treated as fully-completed units or were ignored in order to calculate a unit cost, it would mean that costs would not be accurately allocated. Incorrect inventory valuation would result.

The problem is solved by expressing partially-completed units as **equivalent full units**, using the percentage of completion. As an example, 5 000 litres of Castle Lager that has gone through 30 per cent of the process is expressed as being equivalent to 1 500 (5 000 × 30%) complete litres.

Closing work-in-progress

Example 8.2 introduces the complexity of the situation where there is work-in-progress. The statement of equivalent production, unit cost statement and production cost statement for this example are given in Table 8.2.

Example 8.2

Details relating to CDE Ltd's production during December:

Units	Started during December	14 000
	Completed	13 000
	Closing work-in-progress (75% complete)	1 000
	Note: This means that 1 000 unfinished units are in work-in-progress at the end of the period, and they are 75% complete.	
Cost	Direct materials	R14 000
	Direct labour	R55 000
	Manufacturing overhead cost	R27 500

The cost driver for overhead cost is direct labour hours, and all direct materials are added at the beginning of the process.

Required:
Draw up the following statements:
- Equivalent production
- Unit cost
- Production cost.

Table 8.2 Statement of equivalent production, unit cost statement and production cost statement for example 8.2

Equivalent production statement				
Input units		**Output units**		
		Total	Materials	Conversion
14 000	Started			
	Completed	13 000	13 000	13 000
	Closing work-in-progress (75% complete)	1 000	1 000	750
14 000		14 000	14 000	13 750

Unit cost statement	Total (R)	Materials (R)	Conversion (R)
Direct materials	14 000	14 000	
Direct labour	55 000		55 000
Manufacturing overheads cost	27 500		27 500
	96 500	14 0000	82 500
Per unit	7,00	1,00	6,00

Production cost statement		R	R
Finished goods (13 000 units x R7)			91 000
Work-in-progress:			
Materials (1 000 units × R1)		1 000	
Conversion (750 units × R6)		4 500	5 500
			96 500

As with example 8.1, the units started are reflected in the input units column of the statement of equivalent production. However, here the units started have to be split up in the output units column between the units that have gone through the whole process and were therefore completed (the 13 000 units) and those that are still in progress at the end of the period (the 1 000 units). It is important to note that since the 13 000 units have been through the whole process, they will have incurred the full materials and conversion costs and therefore the full 13 000 units are reflected in the materials and conversion columns.

The 1 000 unfinished units have incurred all of the direct materials costs, since direct materials are added at the beginning of the process. The full 1 000 units are therefore reflected under materials in the output units column. However, since the 1 000 units are only 75 per cent complete, they would have incurred only 75 per cent of the conversion costs, which is equivalent to 750 (1 000 × 75%) full units incurring the full costs. Therefore only 750 units are reflected under conversion in the output units column. In the same way as in example 8.1, the total of the input units column and the total of the output units column are the same, confirming that all units have been accounted for.

The materials, labour and overhead costs are recorded in the unit cost statement in the same manner as in example 8.1. Once again the unit materials cost (R1) is calculated by dividing the cost of materials by the equivalent units processed (obtained from the equivalent production statement), and the unit conversion cost (R6) is calculated in the same way. Remember that the total unit cost (R7) is calculated by adding the unit materials cost to the unit conversion cost. The total unit cost is *not* calculated by dividing the total cost by the total units column. As illustrated with this example, this would result in the incorrect total unit cost (R96 500/14 000 gives an incorrect answer of R6,89 instead of R7).

The production cost statement now reflects the cost allocated to WIP, in addition to the costs allocated to finished goods. Note that since a different number of equivalent WIP units has incurred materials and conversion costs respectively, a separate allocation of materials and conversion costs is required. Once again, the total cost reflected in the unit cost statement and the total of the production cost statement agree.

Opening work-in-progress

In example 8.3 which follows, incomplete units are brought forward from the previous reporting period, and there are unfinished closing work-in-progress units at the end of the current reporting period. As partly-completed units are brought forward from the previous period (and therefore also the costs which were incurred in the previous period on these units), it is necessary to stipulate the valuation method that is to be used.

In Chapter 7, *Job costing* it was noted that there are various inventory valuation methods: the weighted average method, the first-in-first-out (FIFO) method, the last-in-first-out (LIFO) method, specific identification, and standard costing. As noted in Chapter 7, the LIFO method is generally not particularly useful and is not an acceptable method for valuing inventory for financial reporting purposes. Specific identification is useful for job costing only, and will not be help us to value the large number of identical units encountered in a process costing system. Standard costing is dealt with in Chapter 13, *Standard costing*. The LIFO, specific identification, and standard costing valuation methods are therefore not considered further in this chapter. This leaves us with two valuation bases to consider: weighted average and FIFO.

The weighted average method merges opening work-in-progress units and costs with new units started during the accounting period and the costs incurred during the period, in order to calculate the unit cost and the cost of production for that period.

Therefore, under the weighted average method:
- Opening work in progress equivalent units are added to the units started during the current period
- The costs brought forward from the previous period are added to the costs incurred during the current period
- The total of the costs brought forward from the previous period and the costs incurred in the current period are divided by the total number of equivalent units for the period plus the opening WIP equivalent units in order to calculate the unit cost.

When calculating current period costs, the FIFO method takes into account only the units started during the current period. It accumulates the costs incurred in the current period to complete these units as well as the costs incurred to complete the equivalent units that were incomplete at the start of the period. The equivalent units that were incomplete at the start of the period and their associated costs are then added to the current period equivalent units and the current period costs, in drawing up the production cost statement. Notice that the choice of valuation method (weighted average cost versus FIFO) is relevant only when there is opening work-in-progress, because it determines the value of the units brought forward from the previous period. Where there is no opening work-in-progress, both methods result in the same valuation.

In example 8.3 the weighted average cost method is used, and example 8.9 illustrates the FIFO method.

Example 8.3

Details relating to XYZ Ltd's production during January:

Units	Opening work-in-progress (60% complete)	2 800
	Started during January	14 000
	Completed	14 680
	Closing work-in-progress (30% complete)	?
Cost	Opening work-in-progress:	
	Direct materials	R2 800
	Direct labour	R6 900
	Manufacturing overhead cost	R3 000
	Note: Notice that these costs were incurred in the previous period to bring the opening work-in-progress of 2 800 units to its 60 per cent stage of completion. The opening work-in-progress is processed further in the current period (40 per cent of the work is done in the current period), and the costs associated with their completion are included in the 'current period' costs below.	
	Costs incurred during the current period:	
	Direct materials	R14 000
	Direct labour	R51 996
	Manufacturing overhead cost	R30 000

principles of management accounting

> The cost driver for overhead cost is direct labour hours, and all direct materials are added at the beginning of the process. The company uses the weighted average method to value its inventory.
>
> **Required:**
> Draw up the following statements:
> - Equivalent production
> - Unit cost
> - Production cost.

The equivalent production, unit cost and production cost statements for example 8.3 are given in Table 8.3. As with the two previous examples, the units started during the current period are reflected in the input units column in the equivalent production statement. Since the opening WIP brought forward from the previous period is an input into the current period's process, these 2 800 WIP units are also reflected in the input units column. The question states that 14 680 units were completed in the period, so these units are recorded in the output units column. Once again, since these units would have gone through the whole process and incurred the full materials and conversion costs, the full 14 680 units are reflected under both materials and conversion in the output units column. Note that these completed units include units from the opening WIP (which still had to be finished in the current period) and units from those started in the period, but that all 14 680 units are now complete in terms of materials and conversion. The information given indicates that there is also closing WIP, but does not provide the number of units. Since we know that the total of the input and output columns should agree, the number of closing WIP units can be calculated. As with the treatment of closing WIP in example 8.2, the closing WIP units would have incurred the full materials costs (because all direct materials are added at the beginning of the process), but since they are only 30 per cent complete, they would have incurred only the equivalent of 636 units (2 120 units × 30%) in conversion costs.

In addition to recording the materials and conversion costs incurred in the current period in the unit cost statement, the costs that were incurred in producing the opening WIP in the prior period are also recorded in the unit cost statement. The total unit cost, materials unit cost and conversion unit cost are calculated in the same manner as in the two previous examples.

In the same manner as in example 8.2, the total costs allocated to finished goods and the materials and conversion costs allocated to closing WIP are recorded in the production cost statement.

Table 8.3 Statement of equivalent production, unit cost statement and production cost statement for example 8.3

Equivalent production statement				
Input units		**Output units**		
		Total	Materials	Conversion
2 800	Opening work-in-progress			
14 000	Started			
	Completed	14 680	14 680	14 680
	Closing work-in-progress (30% complete) – balancing figure	2 120	2 120	636
16 800		16 800	16 800	15 316

Unit cost statement	Total (R)	Materials (R)	Conversion (R)
Opening work-in-progress:			
Direct materials	2 800	2 800	
Direct labour	6 900		6 900
Manufacturing overheads cost	3 000		3 000
Current period cost:			
Direct materials	14 000	14 000	
Direct labour	51 996		51 996
Manufacturing overheads cost	30 000		30 000
	108 696	16 800	91 896
Per unit	7,00	1,00	6,00

Production cost statement		R	R
Finished goods (14 680 units × R7)			102 760
Closing work-in-progress:			5 936
Materials (2 120 units × R1)		2 120	
Conversion (636 units × R6)		3 816	
			108 696

8.2.2 Losses and gains in the process

Key terms: abnormal losses or gains, inspection, normal losses

A further problem that needs to be dealt with relates to losses in the production process. For example, the total volume of Castle Lager that is produced during the brewing process is likely to be less than the total quantities of water and other materials put into the process. It is necessary to differentiate between **normal losses** and **abnormal losses or gains**. Normal losses are expected or anticipated and arise when the process is running according to plan. Normal losses may arise from the anticipated shrinkage or evaporation of materials or from cut-off fabric that is discarded, such as wood shavings, metal filings, cloth discarded in the clothing industry, and so on. Abnormal losses or gains, on the other hand, arise where actual losses in the process differ from the anticipated (budgeted) losses. Examples of abnormal losses include losses arising from wastage, machine breakdowns or spillage. The process costing system has to provide for normal losses by incorporating such budgeted losses in the normal cost of production, but abnormal losses or gains are accounted for separately.

Where the actual losses during the production process exceed the planned losses, these are referred as abnormal losses. Likewise, where the actual losses during the production process are less than the planned losses, these are referred to as abnormal gains. Unlike normal losses, abnormal losses and gains are reflected separately in the production cost statement. Abnormal losses are written off as period costs, and abnormal gains are recorded as revenues in the costing income statement. How they are dealt with for financial accounting purposes in the annual financial statements will depend on the reason for their occurrence, as well as the monetary amount involved. If the amount involved is not material, the abnormal losses or

principles of management accounting

gains could be transferred to the overhead account and re-allocated as part of the over- or under-recovery of overheads. If the amount is material, separate disclosure may be required.

Losses are identified by **inspection** of the production output. Units are counted, measured or weighed and inspected for faults. Normally, inspection takes place at the end of the process, and example 8.4 illustrates this. However, inspections could also occur at a different point in the process, and this is illustrated in example 8.5.

Normal losses identified at the end of the process

Example 8.4 illustrates the impact of normal losses when the losses are identified at the end of the process. To simplify the illustration, no WIP and no abnormal losses feature in this example.

Example 8.4

Details relating to DEF Ltd's production during January:

Units	Started during January	3 000
	Anticipated normal losses – 10%	
	Inspection point – at the end of the process	
	No opening or closing work-in-progress	
	No abnormal losses or gains	
Cost	Direct materials	R6 000
	Conversion	R54 000

Required:
Draw up the following statements:
- Equivalent production
- Unit cost
- Production cost.

The equivalent production, unit cost and production cost statements for example 8.4 are given in Table 8.4. As the loss was discovered only at the end of the process, it affected all the units worked on during the period. Since the only units worked on during the period were the units started (there was no WIP), the normal loss units are calculated as being 10 per cent of the units started. These normal loss units are recorded in the output column of the equivalent production statement in order to balance the total of the input unit column and the total of the output unit column. The normal loss units are also extended across the materials and conversion columns to reflect that these units would have also incurred materials and conversion costs. Since the normal losses are considered to be a normal part of the process, the cost of the normal loss is included in the total cost of finished goods. This is also consistent with the requirements of IAS 2, *Inventories* and therefore with the requirements for financial reporting.

Table 8.4 Statement of equivalent production, unit cost statement and production cost statement for example 8.4

Equivalent production statement				
Input units		**Output units**		
		Total	Materials	Conversion
3 000	Started			
	Normal loss (10% × 3 000)	300	300	300
	Completed (balancing figure)	2 700	2 700	2 700
3 000		3 000	3 000	3 000

Unit cost statement	Total (R)	Materials (R)	Conversion (R)
Current period costs*	60 000	6 000	54 000
Per unit	20,00	2,00	18,00

Production cost statement			R
Finished goods:			60 000
2 700 units × R20		54 000	
Normal loss (300 units × R20)		6 000	

* Note that the total costs included in the production cost statement equal the total costs incurred during the period (as given in the information).

Losses identified before the end of the process

Example 8.5 illustrates two additional aspects that did not feature in the previous example: an inspection point at the 50 per cent stage of production, and closing work-in-progress at the end of the period. When working with losses before the end of the process, it is assumed that conversion costs are incurred evenly throughout the process (in other words, in this case, 50 per cent of conversion costs are incurred before the inspection point).

Example 8.5

Details relating to MNO Ltd's production during December:

Units	Started during December	12 000
	Anticipated normal losses – 5%	
	Inspection point – 50% stage of production	
	Completed	9 500
	Closing work-in-progress, 40% complete	2 000
Cost	Direct materials	R36 000
	Conversion costs	R47 475

All direct materials are added at the beginning of the process. Conversion costs are incurred evenly throughout the process.

Required:
Draw up the following statements:
- Equivalent production
- Unit cost
- Production cost.

The equivalent production, unit cost and production cost statements for example 8.5 are given in Table 8.5. The units started, completed units and closing WIP units are reflected in the equivalent production statement in the same manner as in example 8.2. The calculation of the loss units is based on the number of units that reached the inspection point at the 50 per cent stage of production.

In determining the number of units that reached the inspection point, it is important to determine whether any WIP units reached the inspection point during the current period. If they did, then the loss affected WIP as well. However, if the WIP units did not reach the inspection point in the current period, they should be excluded from the loss calculation. In example 8.5, closing WIP is 40 per cent complete, and since the inspection point is at the 50 per cent stage, the closing WIP units would not have passed through the inspection point where the loss occurred. The closing WIP units should therefore be excluded from the number of units reaching the inspection point. 10 000 units would have reached the inspection point (12 000 started less the closing WIP of 2 000 units). The normal losses are 500 units (10 000 units reaching the inspection point × 5% normal loss). These 500 normal loss units are reflected in the equivalent production statement in the same manner as in example 8.4 except that, since the inspection point is at the 50 per cent stage, only 50 per cent of the conversion costs will have been incurred. The equivalent normal loss units relating to conversion are therefore only 250 units (500 normal loss units × 50% completion at the inspection point).

The unit cost statement and production cost statement are drawn up using the same principles that were illustrated in examples 8.2 and 8.4. Note that the full cost of the normal loss has been allocated to finished goods. This is because work-in-progress has not yet reached the inspection point. If the work-in-progress had passed the inspection point in the current period, the normal loss would need to be pro-rated between finished goods and work-in-progress. This could be done on the basis of units or cost. In practice, the tedious allocation would automatically be done by process-costing software.

Note once again that when the equivalent production statement is drawn up, the input units column and the output units column both add up to 12 000 units. This is an indication that all units have already been accounted for, and it is therefore apparent that no abnormal losses or gains occurred. This is, however, not the case in the next example.

Table 8.5 Statement of equivalent production, unit cost statement and production cost statement for example 8.5

Equivalent production statement				
Input units		**Output units**		
		Total	Materials	Conversion
12 000	Started			
	Completed	9 500	9 500	9 500
	Normal losses	500	500	250
	Closing work-in-progress (40% complete)	2 000	2 000	800
12 000		12 000	12 000	10 550

Unit cost statement	Total (R)	Materials (R)	Conversion (R)
Current period costs	83 475	36 000	47 475
Per unit	7,50	3,00	4,50

Production cost statement		R	R
Finished goods:			73 875
9 500 units × R7,50		71 250	
Normal loss:		2 625	
Direct materials (500 units × R3,00)	1 500		
Conversion (250 units × R4,50)	1 125		
Closing work-in-progress:			9 600
Materials (2 000 units × R3,00)		6 000	
Conversion (800 units × R4,50)		3 600	
			83 475

Opening and closing work-in-progress and abnormal losses

Example 8.6 has opening and closing work-in-progress, normal and abnormal losses and an inspection point when the process is 60% complete.

Example 8.6

Details relating to PQR Ltd's production during January:

Units	
Opening work-in-progress on 1 January (80% complete)	2 000
Started during January	8 000
Anticipated normal losses – 10%	
Inspection point – 60% stage of production	
Completed	6 000
Closing work-in-progress, 40% complete	3 000

Cost	
Opening work-in-progress:	
Direct materials	R6 500
Conversion costs	R3 300
Current costs:	
Direct materials	R35 500
Conversion costs	R21 660

All direct materials are added at the beginning of the process. Conversion costs are incurred evenly throughout the process.

The weighted-average method is used for inventory valuation.

Required:
Draw up the following statements:
- Equivalent production
- Unit cost
- Production cost.

The equivalent production, unit cost and production cost statements for example 8.6 are given in Table 8.6. The opening WIP, new units started, completed units and closing WIP units are reflected in the equivalent production statement in the same manner as in examples 8.2 and 8.3. The calculation of the loss units is based on the number of units that reached the inspection point at the 60 per cent stage of production.

8 000 units started the process and since closing WIP was 40 per cent complete, only 5 000 units (8 000 started − 3 000 closing WIP) would have progressed past the 60 per cent inspection stage. In addition, since the opening WIP was 80 per cent complete, it would have passed through the inspection point in the previous period. These opening WIP units are therefore excluded from the current period normal loss calculation. A total of 5 000 units (8 000 started − 3 000 closing WIP) would have passed through the inspection point, and the normal losses are therefore 500 units (5 000 units reaching the inspection point × 10% normal loss). These 500 normal loss units are reflected in the equivalent production statement in the same manner as in examples 8.4 and 8.5. Once again note that since the inspection point is at the 60 per cent stage, only 60 per cent of the conversion cost would have been incurred on the normal loss units and therefore only 300 equivalent normal loss units (500 normal loss units × 60 per cent) are reflected in the conversion column.

In the previous example it was stated that there were no abnormal losses. In this example, it is important to determine whether there are any abnormal losses or gains. The easiest method is to see whether the input and output columns of the equivalent production statement balance without including abnormal losses. In example 8.6 it can be seen that if no abnormal losses are accounted for, the total input column of 10 000 units (2 000 units + 8 000 units) would not agree with the total output column of 9 500 units (6 000 units + 3 000 units + 500 units). Therefore there must have been 500 abnormal loss units (10 000 units − 9 500 units).

Similarly to normal loss units, when the abnormal loss was detected at the inspection point, these units had already received all of their materials, since materials are added at the beginning of the process. However, once the loss was detected, the units would not have been subjected to any further processing. The abnormal loss units are therefore 100 per cent complete in terms of materials (500 units of materials have been lost) and only 60 per cent complete in terms of conversion costs (500 abnormal loss units × 60% complete = 300 units of conversion costs have been lost).

The unit cost statement is drawn up using the same principles that were illustrated in example 8.3. The finished goods and closing WIP portions of the production cost statement are prepared in exactly the same manner as in example 8.5. However, note that an extra component is added for the costs that are allocated to the abnormal loss units. Since these losses are not expected and are not part of the normal process, the cost of the abnormal losses is accounted for separately. This cost is treated as a period cost in the profit and loss account. Notice that, as in example 8.5, the cost of the normal loss has been allocated to finished goods only. Once again, this is because neither opening nor closing WIP passed through the inspection point in the current period. If either or both opening and closing WIP had passed through the inspection point in the current period, the cost of the normal loss would need to be pro-rated across those units which had passed through the inspection point. As discussed above, this proration could be based on either units or cost.

Table 8.6 Statement of equivalent production, unit cost statement and production cost statement for example 8.6

Equivalent production statement				
Input units		**Output units**		
		Total	Materials	Conversion
2 000	Opening work-in-progress (80% complete)			
8 000	Started			
	Completed	6 000	6 000	6 000
	Closing work-in-progress (40% complete)	3 000	3 000	1 200
	Normal loss (10% × (8 000 units – 3 000 units))	500	500	300
	Abnormal loss (balancing figure)	500	500	300
10 000		10 000	10 000	7 800

Unit cost statement	Total (R)	Materials (R)	Conversion (R)
Opening work-in-progress	9 800	6 500	3 300
Current period costs	57 160	35 500	21 660
	66 960	42 000	24 960
Per unit	7,40	4,20	3,20

Production cost statement		R	R
Finished goods:			47 460
6 000 units × R7,40		44 400	
Normal loss:		3 060	
Materials (500 units × R4,20)	2 100		
Conversion (300 units × R3,20)	960		
Closing work-in-progress:			16 440
Materials (3 000 units × R4,20)		12 600	
Conversion (1 200 units × R3,20)		3 840	
Abnormal loss:			3 060
Materials (500 units × R4,20)		2 100	
Conversion (300 units × R3,20)		960	
			66 960

Normal and abnormal loss units sold as scrap

In many processes, loss units that are damaged or of unacceptable quality can be sold as second-grade units (if they are still functional), or as scrap. The income from the sale of these rejected units is dealt with as follows.

Normal loss units

Units which are within the planned normal loss limits and which are sold as second-grade units or as 'scrap' give rise to anticipated revenue. In other words, because the loss is 'normal', it is expected that such revenue will arise. The proceeds from such a sale are deducted from the cost of production for the period. This means that it is set off against the value of all inventory items that have passed through the inspection point.

Example 8.7

In addition to the information in example 8.5 (MNO Ltd), assume that loss units can be sold as scrap for R1,00 per unit.

Required:
Prepare the unit cost statement and the production cost statement.

The unit cost and production cost statements for example 8.7 are shown in Table 8.7. In example 8.5, there were 500 normal loss units and therefore the proceeds on the sale of loss units in example 8.7 would be R500 (500 units × R1). To account for revenue from the sale of normal loss units, the cost of finished goods and closing WIP reflected in the production cost statement are proportionately reduced by these proceeds. In example 8.5 it was noted that since the inspection point was at the 50 per cent stage and closing WIP was only 40 per cent complete, closing WIP would not have passed through the inspection point during the current period. Closing WIP therefore did not include any portion of the cost of the normal loss units. It would therefore be inappropriate to reduce the cost of closing WIP by any portion of the proceeds from the sale of the normal loss units. The cost of finished goods in the production cost statement is therefore reduced by the full proceeds from the sale of the normal loss units. Note that if WIP had passed through the inspection point during the current period, the proceeds from the sale of the normal loss units would be pro-rated across both finished goods and closing WIP. This pro-ration should be on the same basis on which the cost of the normal loss was pro-rated with regard to finished goods and closing WIP.

Table 8.7 Unit cost statement and production cost statement for example 8.7

Unit cost statement			
As for example 8.5			
Production cost statement	R	R	R
Finished goods			73 375
9 500 units x R7,50 (refer to example 8.5)		71 250	
Normal loss (refer to example 8.5)		2 625	
Direct materials (500 x R3,00)	1 500		
Conversion (250 x R4,50)	1 125		
Less: Sale of scrap (500 x R1,00)		(500)	
Closing work-in-progress (refer to example 8.5)			9 600
			82 975

Three other methods of dealing with the proceeds from the sale of normal loss units exist. Firstly, the proceeds could also be deducted from the input cost of materials, before the unit cost is calculated, particularly if the scrap consists mainly of materials. Two other methods are for the proceeds from the sale of scrap to be proportionally allocated to and deducted from *input costs* (both materials and conversion costs) on the basis of:
- The ratio of materials costs to conversion costs, or
- The ratio of equivalent materials units to the equivalent conversion units.

Note that these three methods work only when closing WIP has passed through the inspection point during the current period. If this is not the case, the value of closing WIP is incorrectly reduced by a portion of the proceeds from the sale of normal loss units. This is incorrect because in such a scenario, the value of closing WIP would be incorrectly understated. Closing WIP will not include any of the costs of normal losses, and its value should therefore not be reduced by any revenue from the sale of rejected units.

Abnormal loss units

The revenue from the sale of abnormal loss units is treated in a manner consistent with the way in which the cost of the abnormal losses was treated. Since the cost of abnormal losses is accounted for as a separate item in the production cost statement, the proceeds from the sale of these units should also be treated as a separate item. It is therefore simply deducted from the cost of the abnormal losses as reflected in the production statement. A simple example to illustrate this is to assume that the 500 abnormal loss units identified in example 8.6 are sold for R1 each. The R500 proceeds (500 units × R1 per unit) would then be deducted from the abnormal loss cost of R3 060 to reflect a net cost of R2 560.

Abnormal gain units

An interesting problem arises when there are abnormal gains in process. *An abnormal gain arises when the normal loss is smaller than anticipated.* Example 8.8 illustrates this situation.

principles of management accounting

Example 8.8

- Units started during the period: 1 000 units
- Units completed: 920 units
- Budgeted normal losses based on units started: 100 units
- Loss units can be sold as scrap at R3 per unit
- There is no opening or closing work-in-progress.
- The inspection point is at the end of the process.

Current costs are:
  Materials: R2 730
  Conversion: R4 050

Required:
Draw up the following statements:
- Equivalent production
- Unit cost
- Production cost.

Using the information above, we can calculate that an abnormal gain of 20 units [920 − (1 000 − 100)] exists. The equivalent production, unit cost and production cost statements for example 8.8 are provided in Table 8.8. The normal loss units are treated in the same manner as in examples 8.4 and 8.6 and the abnormal gain the same way as the abnormal losses in example 8.6, except that the abnormal gain is shown as a reduction in the number of units in the equivalent production statement and a reduction in cost in the production cost statement.

The full normal loss units are reflected in the equivalent production statement as this is the loss that is an expected part of the process and it should therefore be included in the cost of the process. The abnormal gain in the equivalent production statement reflects the reduction required to account for the net total losses of 80 units (1 000 units started − 920 units completed). The abnormal gain is therefore 20 units (100 units expected − 80 units actually lost).

It is important to note that the value of finished goods is increased by the cost of the expected normal loss of 100 units and since normal losses of 100 units were expected, it is necessary to reduce value of finished goods by the expected or 'normal' revenue of R300 on the sale of these 100 units as scrap, despite actual scrap sales being only R240 (actual loss of 80 units × R3). This effectively means that we need to account for an opportunity cost of R60 (20 units × R3). This opportunity cost reflects the fact that since the total losses were 20 units less than expected, the organisation has lost out on the scrap sales revenue of these 20 units. This opportunity cost is not reflected in the production cost statement but is treated as a period cost directly in the profit and loss section of the statement of comprehensive income.

Table 8.8 Statement of equivalent production, unit cost statement and production cost statement for example 8.8

Equivalent production statement					
Input units			**Output units**		
			Total	Materials	Conversion
1 000	Units started				
		Completed	920	920	920
		Normal losses (given)	100	100	100
		Abnormal gain (balancing)	(20)	(20)	(20)
1 000			1 000	1 000	1 000

Unit cost statement	Total (R)	Materials (R)	Conversion (R)
Current costs	6 780	2 730	4 050
Per unit	6,78	2,73	4,05

Production cost statement		R	R
Finished goods:			6 616
920 units × R6,78		6 238	
Normal loss: 100 units × R6,78		678	
Less: Proceeds on the sale of normal loss units (100 units x R3)		(300)	
Abnormal gain (20 units × R6,78)			(136)
			6 480

Process costing using the first-in-first-out (FIFO) method

The weighted average method of process costing has been used in all the examples up to this point. To recap, with the weighted average method, opening WIP units together with the related costs are simply added to the current month's production and costs, and the final cost calculated as an average. When the FIFO valuation method is used, opening WIP is assumed to be completed first, and these units are accounted for separately. Since only the equivalent units produced in the current year (started and completed units, as well as the equivalent units of opening and closing WIP produced in the current year) are accounted for in the materials and conversion output columns of the equivalent production statement, the opening WIP costs accumulated in prior periods are not included in the unit cost statement (as they would be under the weighted average method).

In IAS 2 paragraph 25, the use of the weighted average method as well as the FIFO method for valuing inventory is permitted. Both are therefore acceptable for financial accounting purposes. The weighted average method may, however, not necessarily be adequate for all decision-making problems.

Where there is no opening WIP it makes no difference whether the weighted average or the FIFO method of process costing valuation is used, as there are no opening WIP units or costs brought forward from the previous accounting period to account for. It also follows that, where opening WIP is too small to be material, the weighted average valuation method will be adequate for decision-making purposes.

principles of management accounting

Example 8.9 illustrates the FIFO method of inventory valuation in a situation where there is opening and closing WIP.

Example 8.9

Required:
Using the information in example 8.3, and assuming that XYZ Ltd uses the FIFO method to value its inventory, draw up the following statements:
- Equivalent production
- Unit cost
- Production cost.

The equivalent production, unit cost and production cost statements for example 8.9 are set out in Table 8.9. The opening WIP units and units started during the period are reflected in the input column of the equivalent production statement in the same manner as in example 8.3. However, in the output column with the FIFO method, we need to split the units completed during the year into those from opening inventory and those started and completed. Furthermore, only the equivalent units produced in the current year are included in the materials and conversion output columns. The 2 800 opening WIP units are therefore included in the total column, but since the opening WIP would have incurred the full materials costs in the prior period, there are no more materials costs incurred in the current period and therefore no equivalent units need to be reflected in the materials column. Since the opening WIP was 60 per cent complete, 40 per cent (100% – 60%) of the conversion costs are incurred during the current period, which is equivalent to 1 120 units (2 800 units × 40%). Therefore 1 120 units are reflected in the conversion column. Since the opening WIP units have been isolated, the remaining 11 880 units (14 680 total units completed – opening WIP of 2 800 units) that were completed during the period are shown. Since the 11 880 units would have gone through the whole process during the current period, the full number of units is reflected in all of the output columns. Closing WIP is calculated as in example 8.3.

Notice that in the unit cost statement only the current period costs are reflected under the FIFO method. This is due to the equivalent opening WIP units completed in the prior period not being included in the equivalent production statement. Since the opening WIP costs accumulated in the prior periods have actually been incurred, and are not included with current period costs in the unit cost statement, they are added to the cost of finished goods in the production cost statement. The total for the production cost statement is therefore R108 652. The difference of R12 656 between the total for the production cost statement and the total costs for the unit cost statement is due to the opening WIP costs of R12 700 and a difference of R44 as a result of rounding the conversion unit costs to R6,01.

Table 8.9 Statement of equivalent production, unit cost statement and production cost statement for example 8.9

Equivalent production statement				
Input units		**Output units**		
		Total	Materials	Conversion
2 800	Opening work-in-progress	2 800		1 120
14 000	Started			
	Started and completed (14 680 units – 2 800 units)	11 880	11 880	11 880
	Closing work-in-progress (30% complete) – balancing figure	2 120	2 120	636
16 800		16 800	14 000	13 636

Unit cost statement	Total (R)	Materials (R)	Conversion (R)
Current period costs:			
Direct materials	14 000	14 000	
Direct labour	51 996		51 996
Manufacturing overheads costs	30 000		30 000
	95 996	14 000	81 996
Per unit	7,01	1,00	6,01

Production cost statement		R	R
Finished goods:			102 710
Opening WIP costs (2 800 + 6 900 + 3000)		12 700	
Direct materials (11 880 units × R1)		11 880	
Conversion ((11 880 units + 1 120 units) × R 6,01)		78 130	
Closing WIP:			5 942
Materials (2 120 units × R1,00)		2 120	
Conversion (636 units × R6,01)		3 822	
			108 652

Example 8.10 illustrates both the weighted average and FIFO methods using one example.

Example 8.10

Details relating to KLM Ltd's production during January:

Units	Opening work-in-progress (40% complete)	1 000
	Started during January	10 000
	Anticipated normal losses – 10% (allocated on the relative number of units)	
	Inspection point – 80% stage of production	
	Closing work-in-progress (60% complete)	2 000
	Completed	8 100
Cost	Opening work-in-progress:	
	Direct materials	R4 000
	Direct labour and manufacturing overhead cost	R6 000
	Costs incurred during the current period:	
	Direct materials	R34 500
	Direct labour and manufacturing overhead cost	R142 400

Required:

1. Assuming that KLM Ltd uses the FIFO method to value its inventory, draw up the following statements:
   - Equivalent production
   - Unit cost
   - Production cost.

2. Assuming that KLM Ltd uses the weighted average method to value its inventory, draw up the following statements:
   - Equivalent production
   - Unit cost
   - Production cost.

The equivalent production, unit cost and production cost statements for example 8.10 are set out in Table 8.10. These have been prepared using the same principles described in examples 8.6 (for the weighted average method) and example 8.9 (for the FIFO method). This discussion therefore focuses mainly on the key differences between the two methods.

As illustrated in example 8.5, when calculating the normal loss units, it is necessary to determine the number of units which reached the inspection point during the current period. The inspection point is at the 80 per cent stage. Since opening WIP was 40 per cent complete, these units reached the inspection point in the current period. However, closing WIP was only 60 per cent complete and so would not have passed the inspection point. The number of units reaching the inspection point is therefore calculated as the 1 000 opening WIP units plus the 10 000 units started less the 2 000 closing WIP units, which equals 9 000 units. The normal loss units are therefore calculated by multiplying 9 000 by 10 per cent (900 units). Note that 100 (1 000 × 10%) of these units relate to opening WIP.

In Chapter 7, *Job costing*, it was noted that the FIFO method assumes that materials are issued in the sequence in which they were ordered and that therefore the issue price is assigned accordingly. Similarly, conversion costs are assigned to units in the sequence in which they were incurred. In addition, an underlying assumption of the FIFO method is that the first units issued to production will be completed first. Since the opening WIP units are processed further during the current period, costs assigned to these units when using the FIFO method will therefore consist of both the costs incurred on these units in prior periods as well as costs incurred to complete these units in the current period. In contrast, the units that were started and completed in the current period will incur costs only in the current period. It is therefore necessary for the opening WIP units to be isolated from the total number of units completed during the period. This enables the costs incurred in the prior period (which have been assigned to opening WIP) to be assigned to the opening WIP units only; and the costs incurred during the current period to be assigned to the further processing of opening WIP units, as well as to units started in the current period (and either completed or included in closing WIP). In contrast, when the weighted average method is used, there is no need to isolate opening WIP units as the weighted average of the prior period costs, and the costs incurred in the current period are simply assigned to all units processed during the period.

As a result of the need to isolate opening WIP units from the units completed during the current period when using the FIFO method, the 8 100 units completed during the current period (after normal losses have been deducted) are split into the 900 opening work-in-progress units (1 000 – 100 normal loss) and the remaining 7 200 units (8 000 × 90%), which were both started and completed in the current period. These units are reflected in the output columns of equivalent production statement using the same principles explained in example 8.9. Note the equivalent of 540 opening WIP units reflected in the conversion column. The opening WIP is only 40 per cent complete and therefore these units still need to complete the remaining 60 per cent of the process. No opening WIP units are reflected in the materials column as all the materials costs were incurred at the start of the process in the prior period (and will therefore be included in the opening WIP costs). When using the weighted average method, however, the full 8 100 units completed are reflected in the output columns of the equivalent production statement as there is no need to isolate the opening WIP from the total units completed.

Students may question why the full 8 100 units completed are reflected in the materials and conversion columns as it effectively means that the current period equivalent production statement reflects part of the process that was actually undertaken in a prior period. For the weighted average method, this is, however, correct. As explained above, when the weighted average method is used, the unit cost is calculated as the weighted average of both the prior period costs assigned to opening WIP and the costs incurred in the current period on processing all units. Since this calculation includes the costs of opening WIP in the unit cost statement, the equivalent production statement also needs to reflect the processing of opening WIP which took place in prior periods. The 8 100 units completed have incurred 100 per cent of both the materials and conversion costs and it is therefore correct to include all 8 100 units in both the materials and conversion columns.

When completing the unit cost statement using the FIFO method, it is necessary to isolate the cost of opening WIP units so that these costs are allocated to opening WIP units only and not to units started in the current period. Therefore, the cost of opening WIP is not included in the unit cost statement, but rather directly included under finished goods in the production cost statement. However, under the weighted average method, the cost of opening WIP is shown in the unit cost statement. This is consistent with the principles explained above, where the weighted average unit cost includes both the costs of opening WIP and the costs incurred in the current period.

One of the key differences between the weighted average and FIFO methods when completing the production cost statement is the allocation of the opening

principles of management accounting

WIP costs to finished goods. As explained above, the FIFO method excludes the cost of opening WIP from the unit cost statement, because the opening WIP units are isolated. These costs therefore need to be included as a separate line item in the production cost statement. Note that when using the weighted average method, the cost assigned to finished goods is simply the 8 100 units completed during the period multiplied by the weighted average cost. This is because under the weighted average method, it is not necessary to distinguish between opening WIP units and units that were started during the period, because a weighted average cost is simply applied to all units completed during the period. The normal loss can be allocated to finished goods and opening WIP based on the relative number of units. However, this is not necessary, as all of these units are included in finished goods. No normal loss is allocated to closing WIP as it did not pass through the inspection point.

The difference between the total costs assigned (to both finished goods and WIP) under the two methods in this example (R186 899,66 as opposed to R186 896) is simply due to rounding. However, the split of the total cost (the amount allocated to WIP versus the amount allocated to finished goods) will differ as a result of the different inventory valuation methods used.

Table 8.10 Statement of equivalent production, unit cost statement and production cost statement for example 8.10

Equivalent production statement – FIFO				
Input units		**Output units**		
		Total	Materials	Conversion
1 000	Opening WIP	900	–	540
10 000	Started			
	Started and completed	7 200	7 200	7 200
	Normal loss ((1 000 units + 10 000 units – 2 000 units) × 10%)	900	900	720
	Closing WIP	2 000	2 000	1 200
11 000		11 000	10 100	9 660

Unit cost statement – FIFO	Total (R)	Materials (R)	Conversion (R)
Current costs	176 900	34 500	142 400
Per unit	R18,157	R3,416	R14,741

Production cost statement – FIFO	R	R	R
Finished goods:			162 378,46
Opening WIP (R4 000 + R6 000)		10 000,00	
Materials (7 200 units × R3,416)		24 595,20	
Conversion ((7 200 units + 540 units) × R14,741)		114 095,34	
Normal loss:		13 687,92	
Materials (900 units × R3,416)	3 074,40		
Conversion (720 units × R14,741)	10 613,52		
Closing WIP:			24 521,20
Materials (2 000 units × R3,416)		6 832,00	
Conversion (1 200 units × R14,741)		17 689,20	
			186 899,66

Equivalent production statement – Weighted average				
Input units		**Output units**		
		Total	Materials	Conversion
1 000	Opening WIP			
10 000	Started			
	Completed	8 100	8 100	8 100
	Normal loss ((1 000 units + 10 000 units – 2 000 units) × 10%)	900	900	720
	Closing WIP	2 000	2 000	1 200
11 000		11 000	11 000	10 020

Unit cost statement – Weighted average	Total (R)	Materials (R)	Conversion (R)
Opening WIP	10 000	4 000	6 000
Current costs	176 900	34 500	142 400
	186 900	38 500	148 400
Per unit	R18,31	3,50	14,81

Production cost statement – Weighted average	R	R	R
Finished goods:			162 124
Completed (8100 units × R18,31)		148 311	
Normal loss:		13 813	
Materials (900 units × R3,50)	3 150		
Conversion (720 units × R14,81)	10 663		
Closing WIP:			24 772
Materials (2 000 units × R3,50)		7 000	
Conversion (1 200 units × R14,81)		17 772	
			186 896

Note that in the very long term, it does not matter whether the weighted average or FIFO valuation method is used, as the average unit costs would be virtually the same. The difference depends on the extent of the materials and conversion cost increases or decreases.

8.3 Consecutive processes

Up to this point, examples have dealt with only a single process. The manufacture of a product may, however, involve a series of consecutive processes where the output from the first process becomes the input for the next process (consider this chapter's introductory case study on SAB, for example). Each separate process is subject to its own calculation of costs, using the process costing system. This is illustrated in Figure 8.2.

principles of management accounting

Figure 8.2 Process flow in consecutive processes

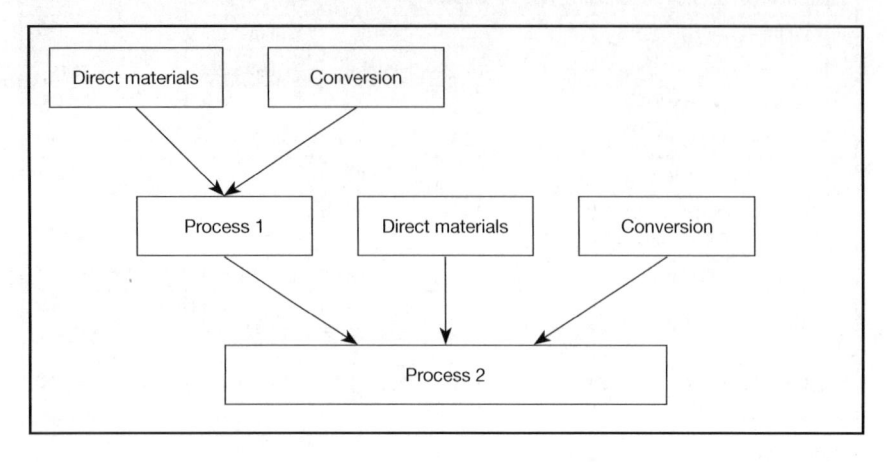

```
Direct materials ──┐       Conversion ──┐
                   ▼                    ▼
              ┌─────────┐
              │Process 1│   Direct materials   Conversion
              └────┬────┘         │                │
                   │              ▼                │
                   └──────► ┌──────────┐ ◄─────────┘
                            │ Process 2│
                            └──────────┘
```

The output from Process 1 becomes the input into Process 2, and so on. Further raw materials may also be added at any stage of any of the processes. The same process-costing principles still apply. Each of the consecutive processes is dealt with as a separate process for costing purposes. As the total cost of the finished goods from Process 1 constitutes an input cost for Process 2 (and so on if there are more than two processes), the cost of completed units in the final production statement combines the costs of all processes. If, for example, there are three processes, there may be three work-in-progress balances, one from each separate process. There may also be abnormal losses or gains from each process. These amounts would be allocated on some equitable basis for financial accounting purposes (as discussed earlier), but it may be necessary to disclose the amounts separately for management accounting purposes, in order to highlight them for further investigation.

8.4 Decision-making

The decisions that need to be taken based on process costing information may, for example, relate to issues such as the use of alternative (better or poorer quality) raw materials in the process, altering the proportions of skilled or unskilled labour, or the use of more efficient equipment. These decisions involve a change in cost as well as in production efficiency (possibly higher or lower 'normal' losses in process). Another type of problem may involve a decision as to whether units ought to be inspected at an earlier or later stage in the production process, or at multiple stages, affecting the costs relating to loss units. Example 8.11 illustrates one type of decision-making problem.

Example 8.11

Spartan (Pty) Ltd operates a process costing system in which anticipated losses of 10 per cent are identified by inspection at the end of the process. The budget for a four-week costing period is as follows:

Units started:	20 000 units
Units completed:	18 000 units

Production costs:

Raw materials	R360 000
Direct labour – variable	R720 000
Variable manufacturing overheads	R180 000
Fixed manufacturing overheads	R270 000

The cost driver for overhead cost is direct labour hours, and all direct materials are added at the beginning of the process. Conversion costs are incurred evenly throughout the process.

Spartan (Pty) Ltd is investigating whether it would be advisable to have two inspection points: one at the 40 per cent stage of completion and one at the end of the process. This system has been tested over a number of weeks and it has been established that 80 per cent of the losses can be identified at the 40 per cent stage of completion.

The fixed cost relating to the additional inspection point amounts to R15 000 during a four-week costing period.

Required:
Advise whether Spartan (Pty) Ltd should implement the additional inspection point at the 40 per cent stage of completion.

The advantage of having two inspection points, with 80 per cent of the losses being identified at the 40 per cent stage and 20 per cent at the 100 per cent stage instead of all of the losses being identified at the end of the process, is that loss units rejected at the 40 per cent stage will not incur any additional conversion costs after this point (that is, they will be rejected and not processed further). It is therefore necessary to determine whether the savings in conversion costs are greater than the increased cost of having two inspection points. In order to do this, we compare the costs incurred by having only one inspecting point with the costs incurred with the two inspection points. We then calculate the equivalent number of units under each of the scenarios. These calculations are shown in Table 8.11. The normal losses are calculated and reflected in the same manner as in example 8.4, but note that under the proposed inspection system, two calculations are required. The first is at the 40 per cent stage, and we know that 1 600 units will be identified at this stage (as 80 per cent of the total loss units of 2 000 will be identified at this stage). Since these units have incurred only 40 per cent of the conversion costs, this is equivalent to 640 units incurring 100 per cent of the conversion costs. 640 units are therefore reflected in the conversion column. However, since these units will have incurred the full materials costs, the full 1 600 units are shown in the materials column. The remaining 400 loss units will be identified at the end of the process, and since these loss units would have incurred the full conversion costs, the full 400 loss units are included in the conversion column.

It is now necessary to determine which costs will be affected by the change in the inspection system. Materials costs will remain the same, as materials costs are incurred at the start of the process before any inspection has taken place. Conversion costs will, however, change. In Table 8.11 we can see that under the proposed inspection system, an equivalent of 19 040 units have incurred conversion costs in comparison with 20 000 units under the current inspection system. Since only the variable portion of the existing conversion costs will be impacted by a change in volume (recall the definition of 'variable costs' in Chapter 2, *Cost classification*), we need to consider only the variable portion of the conversion costs.

This has been given as the direct labour cost of R720 000 and the variable manufacturing overhead cost of R180 000. This total variable conversion cost of R900 000 has been based on 20 000 units. The unit cost will therefore be R45 (R900 000/20 000) and the resulting savings in conversion costs from implementing the proposed inspection system will be R43 200 ((20 000 units – 19 040 units) × R45). This cost saving needs to be compared to the increased cost of the proposed inspection system of R15 000. There is therefore a net saving of R28 200 (R43 200 – R15 000), and if we base our decision solely on this quantitative analysis, the proposed inspection system ought to be implemented.

Table 8.11 Calculation of equivalent units for example 8.11

Current inspection system – Equivalent production statement					
Input units			Output units		
			Total	Materials	Conversion
20 000	Units started					
	Units completed		18 000	18 000	18 000
	Normal losses		2 000	2 000	2 000
20 000			20 000	20 000	20 000

Proposed inspection system – Equivalent production statement					
Input units			Output units		
			Total (R)	Materials (R)	Conversion (R)
20 000	Units started					
	Units completed		18 000	18 000	18 000
	Normal losses:				
		40% stage (80% × 2 000 units)	1 600	1 600	640
		100% stage	400	400	400
20 000			20 000	20 000	19 040

8.5 Summary

Process costing systems are designed to cost a large number of identical units, and stand in contrast to job costing systems as described in Chapter 7, *Job costing*.

The process costing systems discussed and illustrated in this chapter enable their users to:
- Calculate the average cost of the output generated by the process
- Apply either the weighted average or FIFO valuation methods for dealing with opening work-in-progress units
- Account for normal losses, abnormal losses and abnormal gains occurring during a specific costing period
- Account for the revenue arising from the sale of second-grade units or scrap
- Provide relevant cost information for the purposes of decision-making.

In conclusion to this chapter, it may be useful to summarise the principles applied in dealing with losses in a process costing system where there is opening and/or closing WIP.

Closing WIP units (in other words, units that are incomplete at the end of a period) should receive a share of the normal loss only if they passed through the inspection point in the current period. If they will pass the inspection point only in the next period, they will share in the normal loss in the next period.

Similarly, opening WIP units (in other words, units that were incomplete at the beginning of the period) share in the normal loss only if they passed through the inspection point in the current period. If they had already passed the inspection point in the previous period, they would already have shared in the normal loss in the previous period.

Conclusion: Process costing and other topics in this book

In the introduction to this chapter, we saw the differences between job costing systems, which were dealt with in Chapter 7, *Job costing*, and process costing systems.

Process costing systems are also closely linked to joint and by-products. Where more than one product is manufactured in a process, it is necessary to have a costing system to allocate that process costs between these products. Such costing systems are discussed in Chapter 9, *Joint and by-products*.

Furthermore, section 8.4 of this chapter links closely with issues regarding decision-making in organisations, as discussed in Chapter 10, *Relevant costs for decision-making*.

Tutorial case study: Simonsberg

Simonsberg is a cheese manufacturer in Stellenbosch in the Western Cape. It produces a number of cheeses that are readily available on South African supermarket shelves, including cream cheese, camembert and brie.

Simonsberg's production of brie started in 1979 when it purchased the Wechmarshof cheesery. Brie is a traditional French white rind cheese, which is milder and creamier than camembert. It is made from cow's milk. The curd to make brie cheese is obtained by adding rennet to raw milk and heating it. The cheese is then cast into moulds. The moulds are filled with several thin layers of cheese and drained for several hours. The cheese is then taken out of the moulds, salted, inoculated with cheese mould, and aged for a few weeks.

Source: Simonsberg 2011

1. Assess whether it is likely to be appropriate for Simonsberg to use a process costing system.
2. Discuss the impact of work-in-progress at the end of a financial year on the process costing calculations performed by Simonsberg.
3. Speculate about the factors that may influence a decision regarding the number of inspection points (if any) along the brie cheese making process.
4. Use the information given to discuss the kind of normal losses that occur when brie is produced, and how they should be treated in a process costing system.
5. Identify some examples of possible abnormal losses in a cheese factory, and explain how they would be accounted for in a process costing system.
6. Discuss whether you expect that Simonsberg would receive any revenue from the sale of second-grade cheese or scrap.
7. At a rather late stage in the brie-making process two new 'materials' – salt and cheese mould – are added. Explain in what respects a process costing system would differ because of these later additions from a process where all materials are added at the beginning of the process, as the illustrative examples in this chapter have assumed.

principles of management accounting

Basic questions

BQ 1

Source: Adapted from Rhodes University

The following information relates to two independent scenarios:

	Scenario 1	Scenario 2
Opening WIP – units	0	5 000
Opening WIP – % complete	n/a	50%
Additional input – units	10 000	10 000
Normal loss %	10%	10%
Closing WIP – 50% complete	2 000	2 000
Inspection point	100%	40%

For each of scenarios 1 and 2 respectively, what are the normal loss units?
a) 800
b) 1 000
c) 1 500
d) None of the above

BQ 2

Source: Adapted from Rhodes University

The following information relates to two independent scenarios:

	Scenario 1	Scenario 2
Opening WIP – units	0	5 000
Opening WIP – % complete	n/a	50%
Additional input – units	10 000	10 000
Normal loss %	10%	10%
Closing WIP – 50% complete	2 000	2 000
Inspection point	40%	75%

For each of scenarios 1 and 2 respectively, what are the normal loss units?
a) 800
b) 1 000
c) 1 300
d) None of the above

BQ 3

Source: Adapted from Rhodes University

The following information relates to two independent scenarios:

	Scenario 1	Scenario 2
Opening WIP – units	5 000	5 000
Opening WIP – % complete	40%	80%
Additional input – units	10 000	10 000
Normal loss %	10%	10%
Closing WIP – 50% complete	2 000	2 000
Inspection point	50%	75%

For each of scenarios 1 and 2 respectively, what are the normal loss units?
a) 800
b) 1 000
c) 1 200
d) 1 300
e) 1 500
f) 1 700
g) None of the above

BQ 4

Source: Adapted from Rhodes University

SA Manufacturers (Pty) Ltd operates a process costing system using the weighted average valuation method. The following information relates to one four-week costing period:
- Opening work-in progress   2 000 units

Materials costs	R9 000
Conversion costs (units are 40% complete)	R13 200

- New units introduced   12 000 units

Current costs:	
Materials costs	R54 700
Conversion costs	R192 832

- Units completed   10 600 units
- Closing work-in-progress
  (units are 60 per cent complete)   3 400 units

principles of management accounting

There were no losses in process, and all direct materials are added at the beginning of the process.

What will the statement of equivalent production, the unit cost statement and the production cost statement for the current costing period look like?

BQ 5

Source: Adapted from Rhodes University

Rhodes Limited presents you with the following (incomplete) equivalent production statement for the four-week costing period ending 26 January:

Equivalent production statement					
Input units			**Output units**		
		Total (R)	Materials (R)	Conversion (R)	
2 500	Opening work-in-progress (60% complete)				
15 000	Units started				
	Closing work-in-progress (50% complete)				
	Completed units	16 000			
17 500					

There were no losses in process, and all direct materials are added at the beginning of the process.

What are the missing figures in the statement of equivalent production, assuming that the company uses the weighted average method of inventory valuation?

BQ 6

Source: Adapted from Rhodes University

Using the same information as in BQ 5, what are the missing figures in the statement of equivalent production (for the current period's production), assuming that the company uses the FIFO method of inventory valuation?

BQ 7

Details relating to a certain process – Process Alpha – for the November costing period were as follows:

	Units
Opening work-in-progress (100% complete as to materials and 50% complete as to conversion)	500
New units introduced during the costing period	3 000
Units completed and transferred to finished goods inventory	2 700
Closing work-in-progress (100% complete as to materials and 70% complete as to conversion)	450
Normal losses – 10% of units reaching the 60% stage of completion	

Conversion costs are incurred evenly throughout the production process, while materials are introduced at the beginning of the process.

What will the statement of equivalent production look like in units if the weighted average method of inventory valuation is used?

BQ 8

Using the same information as in BQ 7, what will the statement of equivalent production in units (for the current period's production) look like if the FIFO method of inventory valuation is used?

BQ 9

Source: Adapted from Rhodes University

East London Paint Ltd produces industrial paint for use on heavy machinery. During processing, normal losses amount to 10 per cent of the raw materials input at the start of the process. There are no materials added at a later stage. These losses are identified halfway through the process and allocated based on the relative number of units. Most of the processing is done with equipment, so that machine hours are used as the cost driver for manufacturing overhead costs (which include fixed labour costs). No direct labour costs are incurred.

The following details relate to the month of April:

	R	Litres
Opening work-in-progress (40% complete)		10 000
Materials costs	16 500	
Overhead costs	6 060	
New materials introduced at the start of the process		50 000
Closing work-in-progress (60% complete)		5 400
Completed production		46 600
Current costs:		
Materials costs	69 900	
Overhead costs	77 826	

Conversion costs are incurred evenly throughout the production process.

Assuming that the company uses the weighted average method of inventory valuation, what will the statement of equivalent production, the unit cost statement and the production cost statement look like?

BQ 10

A company is constructing a submarine and an aircraft carrier for use by the navy. At the end of the reporting period, the submarine is 40 per cent complete, while the aircraft carrier is 66 per cent complete. Some materials used in their construction have been damaged and sold as scrap, but the damage was expected, and was regarded as a normal loss. To what extent are process-costing principles useful in this scenario?

Long questions

LQ 1 – Intermediate (11 marks; 20 minutes)

Source: Adapted from ACCA Certified Accounting Technician Exam P4

A company manufactures a product by means of two successive processes, Process 1 and Process 2. The following relates to the period just ended:

Process 2		
	Units	Cost (R)
Opening work-in-progress	Nil	Nil
Transfer from Process 1	2 160	22 032
Materials added		5 295
Conversion costs		8 136
Transfer to finished goods warehouse	1 950	
Closing work-in-progress	210	

The work-in-progress at the end of the period was 80 per cent complete with respect to materials added and 40 per cent complete with respect to conversion costs in Process 2.

REQUIRED		Marks
Calculate for the period the:		
(a)	Production cost per equivalent unit of the product	6
(b)	Value of the transfer to the finished goods warehouse	2
(c)	Value of the closing work-in-progress in Process 2.	3
TOTAL MARKS		**11**

LQ 2 – Intermediate (14 marks; 25 minutes)

Source: Adapted from ACCA Certified Accounting Technician Exam P4

600 tons of raw materials, costing R430 032, were input to a process during a period. Conversion costs totalled R119 328. Losses, in the form of reject product, are normally 12 per cent of input. Reject product is sold for R260,00 per ton.

521 tons of finished product passed inspection (which occurred at 100% completion) during the period. The remaining output was sold as reject product. There was no work-in-progress either at the beginning or the end of the period.

REQUIRED		Marks
For the period:		
(a)	Calculate the cost per unit of normal output.	8
(b)	Prepare the process account, including any abnormal losses/gains.	6
TOTAL MARKS		**14**

LQ 3 – Advanced (12 marks; 22 minutes)

Source: Adapted from ACCA Professional Papers Archive: Paper 1.2

Partlet Ltd makes a product that passes through two manufacturing processes. A normal loss equal to 8 per cent of the raw materials input occurs in Process 1 (inspection occurs at 100% completion), but no loss occurs in Process 2. Losses have no realisable value.

All the raw materials required to make the product are input at the start of Process 1. The output from Process 1 each month is input into Process 2 in the same month. Work-in-progress occurs in Process 2 only.

Information for last month for each process is as follows:

Process 1	
Raw materials input	50 000 litres at a cost of R365 000
Conversion costs	R256 000
Output to Process 2	47 000 litres
Process 2	
Opening work in progress	5 000 litres (40 per cent complete for conversion costs) valued at R80 000
Conversion costs	R392 000
Closing work-in-progress	2 000 litres (50 per cent complete for conversion costs)

	REQUIRED	Marks
(a)	Prepare the Process 1 account for last month, using FIFO.	5
(b)	Calculate in respect of Process 2 for last month: (i) The value of the completed output, and (ii) The value of closing work-in-progress.	5
(c)	If the losses in Process 1 were toxic and the company incurred costs in disposing of them safely, state how the disposal costs associated with the normal loss would have been recorded in the Process 1 account. No calculations are required.	2
	TOTAL MARKS	**12**

LQ 4 – Advanced (20 marks; 36 minutes)

Source: Adapted from CIMA P1 Pilot Paper

PQR Ltd is a chemical processing company. The company produces a range of solvents by passing materials through a series of processes. The first-in-first-out (FIFO) valuation method is used.

In Process 2, the output from Process 1 (XP1) is blended with two other materials (P2A and P2B) to form XP2. It is expected that 10 per cent of any new input to Process 2 (that is, transfers from Process 1 plus Process 2 materials added) will be immediately lost and that this loss will have no resale value. It is also expected that in addition to the loss, 5 per cent of any new input will form a by-product, Z, which can be sold without additional processing for R2,00 per litre.

No normal losses occur in Process 1.

principles of management accounting

Data from Process 2 for November was as follows:

Opening work-in-progress
Process 2 had 1 200 litres of opening work-in-progress. The value and degree of completion of this was as follows:

	R	% degree of completion
XP1	1 560	100
P2A	1 540	100
P2B	750	100
Conversion costs	3 790	40
	7 640	

Input
During November, the inputs to Process 2 were:

	R
XP1 5 000 litres	15 679
P2A 1 200 litres	6 000
P2B 3 000 litres	4 500
Conversion costs	22 800

Closing work-in-progress
At the end of November, the work-in-progress was 1 450 litres. This was fully complete in respect of all materials, but only 30 per cent complete for conversion costs.

Output
The output from Process 2 during November was:

Z	460 litres
XP2	7 850 litres

REQUIRED	Marks
Prepare the Process 2 account for November 2003, assuming that normal losses are allocated based on the relative number of units. By-product 2 is not separately valued, but is set off against XP2.	20
TOTAL MARKS	20

LQ 5 – Advanced (20 marks; 36 minutes)

Source: Adapted from CIMA P1

Part A *(12 marks; 22 minutes)*

M (Pty) Ltd produces 'Biotinct' in a lengthy distillation and cooling process. Base materials are introduced at the start of this process, and further chemicals are added when it is 80 per cent complete. Each kilogram of base materials produces 1 kilogram of Biotinct.

Data for October are:

Opening work-in-progress:	40 kg of base materials, which are 25 per cent processed	
Cost of opening work-in-progress:	Base materials	R1 550
	Processing	R720
Costs incurred in October:	Base materials (80 kg)	R3 400
	Conversion costs	R6 864
	Further chemicals	R7 200
Closing work-in-progress:	50kg of base materials, 90 per cent processed	
Finished output:	65 kg of Biotinct	

Under normal conditions there are no losses of base materials in this process. However, in October 5 kilograms of partially complete Biotinct were spoiled immediately after the further chemicals had been added. The 5 kilograms of spoiled Biotinct were not processed to finished goods stage and were sold for a total of R200.

REQUIRED	Marks
Using the FIFO method, prepare the process account for October.	12
SUB-TOTAL MARKS (Part A)	12

Part B *(8 marks; 14 minutes)*
One of the company's management accountants overheard the Managing Director arguing as follows, 'These process accounts are complicated to produce, and often conceal the true position. As I see it, the value of partly processed Biotinct is zero. In October we spent R17 464 and the output was 65 kg. So the average cost was R268,68 per kilogram, while the target cost is R170 (R40 for base materials, R70 for processing and R60 for further chemicals). These figures make me concerned about production efficiency.'

REQUIRED	Marks
Explain to the Managing Director any errors in the comment he has made, and discuss whether the data from the process account indicate that there has been production inefficiency.	8
SUB-TOTAL MARKS (Part B)	8
TOTAL MARKS (Parts A and B)	20

References

SAB (South African Breweries Limited). 2010. *Overview and Manufacturing*. [Online]. Available: <www.sablimited.co.za/sablimited/view/sablimited/en/page145?oid=111&sn=Detail&pid=145> [15 October 2010].

SAICA (South African Institute of Chartered Accountants). 2010. *IAS 2, Inventories (revised January 2010)*. Johannesburg: SAICA.

Joint and by-product costing

chapter 9

Lilla Stack and John Williams

LEARNING OBJECTIVES
By the end of this chapter, you should be able to:
1 Distinguish between joint and by-products, scrap and waste.
2 Account for the proceeds and costs relating to the sale or disposal of by-products, scrap and waste.
3 Allocate joint costs to joint products by applying the following methods:
   - Physical measures method
   - Market value at the split-off point
   - Relative market value of the final products (net realisable value)
   - Constant gross profit percentage method.
4 Discuss why the allocation of joint costs is not relevant for the purposes of decision-making.

Sasol and joint and by-product costing

Sasol Limited is an integrated energy and chemicals company with its headquarters in Rosebank, Johannesburg. Through unique proprietary technologies the company uses coal, oil and gas reserves to produce liquid fuels, fuel components and chemicals.

In Sasol's coal-to-liquids process at its Secunda plant, coal is converted, with the aid of heat, pressure, steam and oxygen, into a product called 'syngas', which is essentially a mixture of hydrogen and carbon monoxide. Once syngas is cooled, it yields tars, oils, pitches and associated products. Ammonia, sulphur and phenols are also recovered from the process.

Source: Sasol 2010

During the coal-to-liquids process, a number of costs are incurred by Sasol. A key question arises: how can these costs be optimally assigned to all the different products emanating from the process?

9.1 Introduction

Key terms: joint costs, joint process

A process costing system as discussed in Chapter 8, *Process costing* is used to calculate the average unit cost of identical products. In some processes more than one product is produced, such as Sasol's coal-to-liquids process mentioned above, which yields tars, oils, pitches, and so on. Such a process is referred to as a **joint process**, as more than one product is jointly produced by the same process.

principles of management accounting

The following diagram from the *Economic History of Europe* (Heaton 1948) provides a further illustration of the vast number of products derived from the raw material, coal, and further processing after the coal has been mined:

Figure 9.1 Coal's family tree

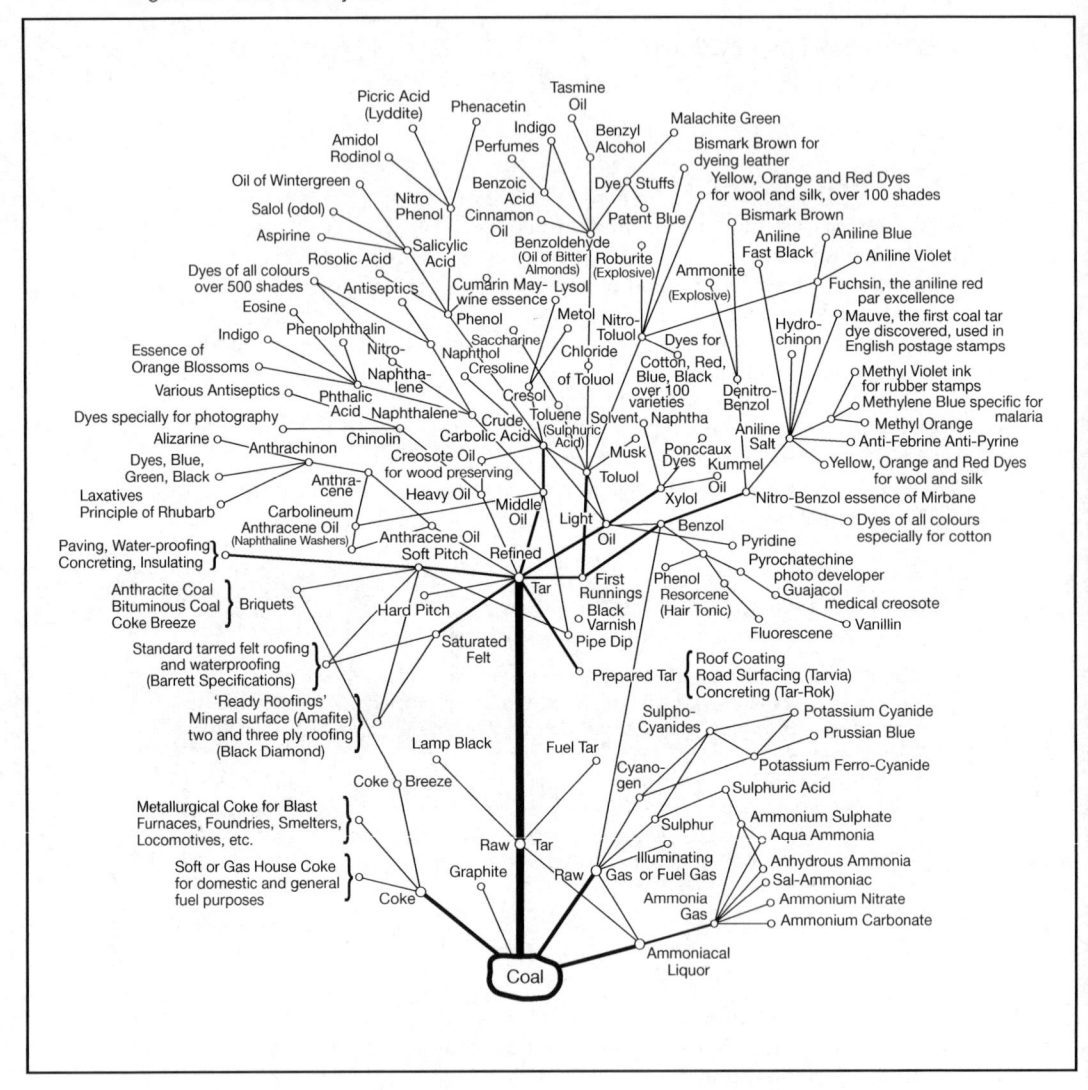

Source: Adapted from Heaton 1948

One of the main cost accounting problems arising from a joint process is how the costs (commonly referred to as **joint costs**) that are incurred before the joint products become separately identifiable should be assigned to the products emanating from the process. The materials and conversion costs accumulated during the joint process cannot be traced directly to the specific products as they relate to all the products. It is therefore necessary to have a method of allocating the joint costs in one or other equitable manner. Common methods of allocating joint costs are described in section 9.2 below. International Accounting Standards for joint costs are discussed in section 9.3.

In addition to the problem of how to allocate joint costs, it is also necessary to consider how to treat joint costs in decision-making scenarios, as often these costs are unavoidable costs and therefore irrelevant to the decision. The issue of joint costs and decision-making is discussed in more detail in section 9.4.

9.2 Cost accounting treatment of joint costs

Key terms: by-products, joint products, scrap, split-off point, waste

Joint costs need to be allocated to the products arising from a joint process to ensure a reasonable valuation of inventory. To determine the appropriate cost accounting treatment of the costs arising from a joint process, it is necessary to differentiate between joint products, by-products, scrap and waste. All four of these product types could arise from a joint process.

Joint products are two or more products produced simultaneously during the joint process which are distinguishable from each other only at the end of the joint process. The point at which joint products are distinguishable is referred to as the **split-off point**. In contrast to joint products, which have a significant sales value, a joint process may also give rise to one or more **by-products** which have a minor sales value in relation to the joint products.

In certain instances, the joint and/or by-products can be sold at the split-off point; in other cases further processing is required before the products can be sold. **Scrap** was discussed in Chapter 8, *Process costing*, but it may also arise from a joint process. Whereas a by-product is different from the original materials that went into the process, scrap consists of raw materials left over at the end of the process, which are still identifiable in the scrap. Note that, for a product to be classified as either a by-product or scrap, it must have some value (even if only a very small value). **Waste**, unlike a by-product or scrap, has no value. It may even have to be disposed of at a cost to the organisation.

To illustrate the distinction between the four different product types, consider an organisation that produces and packages meat for sale in supermarkets. The organisation slaughters cattle in its abattoir and further processes the meat in its processing facility. Two of the popular cuts obtained in this manner, T-bone steak and rump steak, are joint products in that they originate from the same joint process up to the point where they are separated. The same process also yields raw cattle hides that are further processed into low-quality leather goods in the organisation's tannery. Because the organisation is primarily focused on producing meat and the production of leather is incidental to its main business, it regards the low quality leather goods as by-products.

The organisation also earns a small amount of revenue from selling the less popular parts of the cattle carcass as tripe. The tripe is simply packaged in the meat processing plant – it requires no further processing before sale. The organisation regards the income from tripe sales as revenue generated through the sale of scrap. The remainder of the carcass that is of no use is removed from the meat processing plant and disposed of according to health regulations – it constitutes waste. The following table summarises the product characteristics:

principles of management accounting

Table 9.1 Summary of product types

Product	Value	Form (to distinguish by-products from scrap)	Example
Joint product	Significant sales value		T-bone and rump steak
By-product	Relatively smaller sales value	Different from the original materials	Leather
Scrap	Relatively small sales value	Raw materials still identifiable	Tripe
Waste	No sales value		Remaining parts of the carcass

Figure 9.2 illustrates a joint process.

Figure 9.2 A joint process

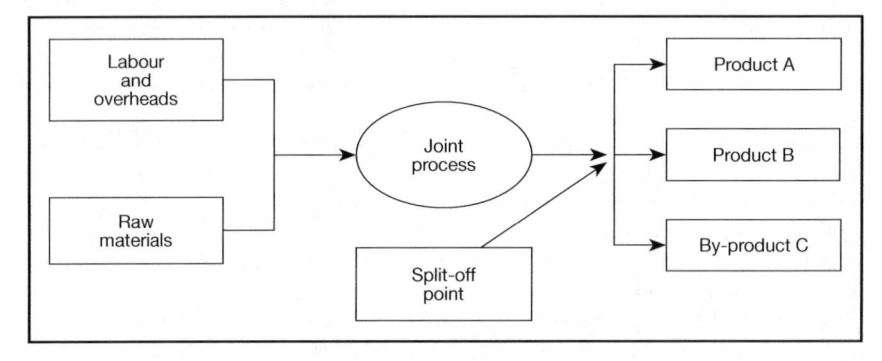

9.2.1 By-products

The main characterising features of by-products are the following:
- Their production arises incidentally as a result of producing the main product(s).
- They are not crucial to the commercial success of the organisation.
- Their production does not normally influence the selling prices of the main products.

Unlike joint products, by-products are therefore not allocated any of the joint costs. Where by-products have some sales value (either at the split-off point or after further processing), the sales value or the net sales value, after deducting the further processing costs, is deducted from the joint costs and in this way is allocated to the joint products. This treatment is illustrated in example 9.1 below.

Example 9.1

AmiNam (Pty) Ltd produces two products in a joint process, which also yields a by-product. The following details relate to a normal production run:

Joint costs:	
Direct materials	R150 000
Direct (variable) labour and overheads	R50 000
Fixed production overheads	R100 500
	R300 500

Chapter 9 Joint and by-product costing

Production at the split-off point:	Units
Joint product – Amm	20 000
Joint product – Namm	10 000
By-product – Tramm	500

At the split-off point, Amm can be sold at R10 and Namm at R30. Tramm requires further processing, during which additional variable costs of R2 per unit are incurred, before it can be sold at R3 per unit.

Required:
1 Describe the cost accounting treatment of Tramm.
2 Calculate the total joint costs of a normal production run.

In example 9.1, we can confirm that Tramm is a by-product as it has a total sales value of R1 500 (500 units × R3 per unit) which is relatively small in comparison with the total sales value of the joint products of R500 000 (20 000 × R10 + 10 000 × R30). Therefore Tramm will not be allocated any of the joint costs, but the proceeds on the sale of Tramm less the further processing costs will be off set against the joint costs of the process. The total joint costs will therefore be R300 000 (R300 500 given, plus further processing costs of R1 000 (500 × R2) less proceeds on the sale of the by-product of R1 500).

9.2.2 Scrap

The cost accounting treatment of scrap is exactly the same as that of by-products. No joint costs are allocated to the scrap and any proceeds on the sale of the scrap are set off against the joint process costs.

9.2.3 Waste

Similarly to by-products, waste is not allocated any joint costs. In addition, if there are costs involved in getting rid of waste, these should be added to the joint costs and allocated to the joint products. Note that there will not be any proceeds on the sale of waste, as by definition waste has no value. The treatment of waste is illustrated in example 9.2.

Example 9.2

In addition to the information given in example 9.1, assume that one production run of the joint process also usually yields 6 000 litres of toxic waste. The disposal costs of the toxic waste are R2 per litre.

Required:
1 Describe the cost accounting treatment of the toxic waste.
2 Re-calculate the total joint costs of a normal production run.

The toxic waste produced as part of the AmiNam process in example 9.2 will not be allocated any joint costs, and the R12 000 (6 000 litres × R2 per litre) disposal costs will be added to the joint costs. This will result in total joint costs of R312 000 (R300 000 calculated in example 9.1 plus R12 000 waste disposal cost).

As discussed and illustrated in Chapter 8, *Process costing*, where abnormal loss units were treated as a period cost, if there are abnormal waste units, the cost of disposing of the abnormal waste should not be treated as part of the joint costs but should be expensed in the profit and loss account as a period cost. A simple example to illustrate this is if a particular AmiNam production run yielded 6 500 litres of toxic waste. Because the process usually yields only 6 000 litres of toxic waste, the additional 500 litres would be treated as abnormal, and the cost of R1 000 (500 litres × R2 per litre) of disposing of these 500 litres would be expensed as a period cost. Once again, only the R12 000 costs of disposing the expected 'normal' waste would be added to the joint costs.

9.2.4 Joint products

It has already been seen that joint costs are not allocated to by-products, scrap or waste. In addition, since joint products are separately distinguishable only at the end of the joint process, joint costs cannot be directly traced to any of the products. It is therefore necessary to allocate the full joint costs to the joint products. This allocation can be made on the basis of physical units, sales value of products at the split-off point, net realisable value of the products (if further processing is required), or by means of a constant gross profit calculation. Each of these methods is based on a set of assumptions, has its own advantages and disadvantages, and is suitable in different circumstances. These four methods are discussed further below.

Physical measures

With the physical measures method, joint costs are allocated to joint products on the basis of the volume of output of each joint product. The method assumes that the benefit enjoyed by each joint product is in proportion to its volume of output and that therefore the cost per physical output unit is the same. This method is illustrated in example 9.3.

Example 9.3

Required:
Using the information given in examples 9.1 and 9.2, calculate the cost of each joint product using the physical measures method to allocate joint costs.

The total joint costs were calculated in example 9.1 to be R312 000. From the information given in example 9.1, we know that output is measured in terms of the number of units produced, and that a total of 30 000 units of Amm and Namm will be produced (20 000 + 10 000). The unit cost will be R10,40 (R312 000/30 000) and therefore the costs of Amm will be R208 000 (20 000 × R10,40) and Namm will be R104 000 (10 000 × R10,40).

The physical measures method is seldom an appropriate method of allocating joint costs. In the example above, output of both Amm and Namm could be measured in number of units. However, if the joint products emerge from the process in a different form, for example, a gas and a liquid, or a liquid and a solid, the physical measures used to measure the output would be completely different. It would not make sense to use this method if, for example, the joint process in the example yielded 20 000 *kilograms* of Amm and 10 000 *litres* of Namm.

A further disadvantage of the physical measures method is that where the market prices of joint products differ, allocating the same unit costs to all products could result in widely-varying product profitability. In addition, a further problem can arise whereby this method results in inventory being valued at an amount which is greater than its net realisable value. In example 9.3, each unit of Amm was valued at a cost of R10,40 per unit, but the selling price is only R10,00. For financial accounting purposes, unless it is written down to net realisable value, this valuation would not meet the requirements of the accounting standard IAS 2, which states: *'Inventories shall be measured at the lower of cost and net realisable value'* (SAICA 2010).

The physical measures method would therefore be suitable only where the outputs from a joint process are all measured in the same way (number of units, weight or volume) and where the selling prices are fairly similar.

Market values at the split-off point

The market values at the split-off point method allocate joint costs based on the estimated sales value of the joint products at the point where they first become separately identifiable. Example 9.4 illustrates this method.

Example 9.4

Required:
Using the information given in examples 9.1 and 9.2, calculate the cost of each joint product using the market values at the split-off point method to allocate joint costs.

The total joint costs were calculated in example 9.2 to be R312 000. From the information given in example 9.1, we can calculate that the market value of Amm is R200 000 (20 000 units × R10 sales price) and Namm is R300 000 (10 000 units × R30 sales price). This results in a total market value of the joint products amounting to R500 000 (R200 000 + R300 000). The joint costs allocated to Amm will therefore be R124 800 (R312 000 × R200 000/R500 000) and to Namm will be R187 200 (R312 000 × R300 000/R500 000).

If the products are actually sold at the split-off point, this method of allocating the joint costs results in each joint product making a profit and each having the same gross profit percentage. Unlike the physical measures method, this method can also be used for products that have different forms and significantly different selling prices. Inventory on hand would also be suitably valued. The method would not be suitable for products for which we are unable to determine the market value at the split-off point.

Net realisable value

Certain joint products require further processing. This may be either because they are not ready to be sold at the split-off point, or because further processing increases the profitability of the product. Where further processing takes place, joint costs may be apportioned in relation to the final selling price, less the cost of further processing (the relative market value or net realisable value). This method is illustrated in example 9.5.

principles of management accounting

Example 9.5

In addition to the information given in examples 9.1 and 9.2, if further variable processing costs of R6 per unit are incurred, Amm can be sold as a new product, Samm, at R18 per unit.

Required:
Assuming that the additional processing of Amm into Samm occurs, calculate the cost of each joint product using the net realisable method to allocate joint costs.

Once again the total joint cost of R312 000 calculated in example 9.2 is used. It is then necessary to calculate the net realisable value of the two joint products Samm and Namm. The net realisable value is calculated by deducting the additional processing costs from the final selling price. For Samm the net realisable value will therefore be R240 000 (20 000 units × [(R18 selling price – R6 further processing costs)]). Since no further processing of Namm takes place, the net realisable value for Namm will simply be the market value of R300 000 calculated in example 9.4. The total net realisable value of the joint products is therefore R540 000 (R240 000 + R300 000). Joint costs allocated to Amm (which later becomes Samm) will be R138 667 (R312 000 × R240 000/R540 000), while joint costs allocated to Namm will be R173 333 (R312 000 × R300 000/R540 000).

The main advantages of the net realisable value method are that inventory will always be recorded at an amount which is below its net realisable value (unless the total joint cost exceeds the total net realisable value), and that when allocating joint costs, the impact of further processing costs is taken into account. A disadvantage of this method, however, is as illustrated in example 9.5, where the gross profit percentages of the products are different. It could be argued that joint products produced by the same joint process should yield the same gross profit percentage and that, for this reason, the method is not suitable. For those who hold this view, the next method may be preferable.

Constant gross profit percentage

Some organisations believe it may be more reasonable to allocate joint costs in such a way that each joint product yields the same gross profit percentage. The constant gross profit percentage method assumes that the relationship between sales value and costs incurred for each of the joint products is the same. The constant gross profit percentage method is illustrated in example 9.6.

Example 9.6

Required:
Using the information given in examples 9.1, 9.2 and 9.5, calculate the cost of each joint product using the constant gross profit percentage method to allocate joint costs.

The starting point with the constant gross profit percentage method is to calculate the overall gross profit percentage for the joint products combined. The overall gross profit percentage is then used to calculate the gross profit for each joint product. The difference between the sales value and gross profit represents the total cost. Any further processing costs are deducted from total costs, leaving the joint cost allocation which will result in the constant gross profit percentage. In example 9.5, the combined sales revenue is R660 000 (20 000 units of Samm multiplied by the unit selling price of R18 plus 10 000 units of Namm multiplied by the unit selling price of R30), the joint costs are R312 000 (calculated in example 9.2), and the further processing costs are R120 000 (20 000 units of Samm × R6 per unit plus nil, as Namm isn't processed further). The overall gross profit percentage is therefore 34,6 per cent (R660 000 − R312 000 − R120 000)/R660 000).

Based on the sales values of R360 000 and R300 000, the gross profit for Samm and Namm will be R124 364 (R360 000 × 34,6 per cent) and R103 636 (R300 000 × 34,6 per cent) respectively. Total costs are therefore R235 636 (R360 000 − R124 364) for Samm and R196 364 for Namm (R300 000 − R103 636). The joint costs allocated to Amm (which later becomes Samm) will therefore be R115 636 (R235 636 − 120 000), and R196 364 will be allocated to Namm, which adds up to R312 000 in total. Note that the percentage was not rounded for the purpose of this calculation.

9.3 Joint costs and International Accounting Standards

IAS 2, *Inventories*, which is applied in South Africa in accordance with GAAP, prescribes the manner in which joint costs should be allocated when valuing inventories for financial reporting purposes. Paragraph 14 of IAS 2 is particularly relevant to the treatment of joint costs. Paragraph 14 states:

> 'A production process may result in more than one product being produced simultaneously. This is the case, for example, when joint products are produced or when there is a main product and a by-product. When the costs of conversion of each product are not separately identifiable, they are allocated between the products on a rational and consistent basis. The allocation may be based, for example, on the relative sales value of each product either at the stage in the production process when the products become separately identifiable, or at the completion of production. Most by-products, by their nature, are immaterial. When this is the case, they are often measured at net realisable value, and this value is deducted from the cost of the main product. As a result, the carrying amount of the main product is not materially different from its cost.'

From paragraph 14, it is clear that the treatment of joint costs when valuing inventories for financial reporting purposes is consistent with the management accounting treatment described in section 9.2 above (with the exception highlighted above of the physical measures method of allocating joint costs, which in some instances results in inventory being valued at an amount which is above net realisable value). While paragraph 14 does not specifically refer to 'scrap' and 'waste', the same treatment as for by-products can be applied, as these products by their nature are also immaterial.

9.4 Joint costs in relation to decision-making

The main purpose of allocating joint costs is for inventory valuation, but particular care in dealing with joint costs is required when considering decision-making scenarios. Even though some of the methods of allocating joint costs are more appropriate in some circumstances than other methods, each of the methods results in an arbitrary allocation of the costs. This is because it is impossible to trace the costs directly to any of the joint products.

principles of management accounting

Furthermore, joint costs that have, for example, been allocated to Amm are unavoidable if a special order is received for Namm (as illustrated in example 9.8 below). This is because in order for any of the joint products to be produced, all of the joint costs have to be incurred. Examples 9.7 and 9.8 illustrate the problem of joint costs in relation to decision-making.

Example 9.7

Required:
Using the information given in examples 9.1, 9.2 and 9.5, advise whether Amm should be further processed into Samm.

The joint costs of R312 000 are irrelevant to the decision as to whether Amm should be further processed as the costs will be incurred irrespective of whether Amm is sold at the split-off point or whether it is processed into Samm. It also does not matter what portion of the joint costs were allocated to Amm, because for purposes of the decision this is simply an arbitrary allocation of an irrelevant cost. Only the incremental revenue of R8 per unit (the selling price per unit of Samm less the selling price per unit of Amm) and the additional processing costs of R6 per unit are relevant to the decision. Since the incremental revenue of R8 per unit exceeds the incremental costs of R6 per unit, from a financial perspective, Amm should be processed into Samm.

Example 9.8

In addition to the information given in examples 9.1, 9.2 and 9.5, assume that the organisation receives a special once-off order to sell 1 000 units of Namm at a selling price of R25 000. Owing to the market for Amm, Samm and Tramm being saturated, the organisation currently has sufficient spare capacity to produce the additional units during the current production run.

Required:
Calculate the relevant net cost of the special order.

In order to produce the 1 000 additional units of Namm, the organisation will have to undertake the joint processing of both Amm and Namm, as the products emerge as distinct products only at the split-off point. The same joint processing costs will therefore be incurred irrespective of whether the additional units of Amm are required or not. Therefore the full additional joint process costs need to be considered when determining whether the once-off order should be accepted. It should be noticed that only additional variable joint process costs will be incurred. The organisation has sufficient spare capacity during its current production run and therefore no additional fixed costs will be incurred (the R100 500 existing fixed costs will be incurred irrespective of whether the once-off order is accepted). The additional variable joint processing costs will be R20 000 ((R150 000 direct materials costs plus R50 000 direct labour costs and variable overheads) divided by 10 000 units of Namm currently produced multiplied by 1 000 additional units of Namm).

Note that in this example the joint costs are relevant, because a decision has to be taken as to whether or not they should be incurred. However, how these joint costs are allocated to individual products (in other words which of the four methods in section 9.2.4 is used) remains irrelevant for decision-making purposes.

The organisation will also incur additional waste disposal costs on the additional waste that is produced. 10 000 units of Namm resulted in 6 000 litres of toxic waste, and therefore it is assumed that the additional 1 000 units of Namm will result in an additional 600 litres of toxic waste. The additional toxic waste disposal costs will be R1 200 (600 × R2).

Since the market for Amm, Samm and Tramm is saturated, no additional revenue can be earned from the sale of these products. It will therefore also make sense for the organisation not to process Amm further in Samm or to process the by-product Tramm further. No further processing costs will be incurred, and no income from the by-product can be set off against the joint processing costs.

The total relevant net costs of the special order will therefore be R21 200 (R20 000 variable joint process costs plus R1 200 cost of disposing the additional toxic waste). It should be noted that in arriving at this cost, it has been assumed that disposing of the additional units of Amm and Tramm will not cost the organisation anything.

As the total relevant costs are less than the income of R25 000, based on quantitative factors, the order should be accepted.

To summarise our discussion on the allocation of joint costs to products, it is important to emphasise specifically the arbitrary nature of all the allocation methods discussed in this chapter. The allocations are performed for accounting (specifically inventory valuation) purposes, and serve no other economic purpose. It should be clear from the examples above that the method chosen for the allocation of joint costs is irrelevant for decision-making purposes.

9.5 Summary

In some processes, different joint and by-products emerge from the production process. Costs that are incurred up to the point where the joint and by-products become separately identifiable (the split-off point) are not directly attributable to any individual product and must be allocated on a logical and fair basis. The products which emerge may take on different forms (solids, liquids or gases) or may have very different potential market prices. Some joint products can be sold at the split-off point; others require further processing or have a higher market value if processed further.

There are four methods that can be used to allocate joint costs that are incurred up to the split-off point: the physical measures method, the method based on market values at the split-off point, the net realisable value method, and the constant gross profit percentage method. Each of these methods has advantages and disadvantages and may be applicable only in particular circumstances, and all of the methods are used purely for product-costing purposes and not for decision-making.

By-products have a minor sales value (either at the split-off point or after further processing) and the proceeds from their sale are deducted from the joint costs before the costs are allocated to joint products. Unlike by-products, scrap is not processed, and the raw materials are still identifiable. Any proceeds from its sale are also deducted from joint costs before their allocation. Waste may result from the joint process and there may be a cost involved in the disposal of waste. This cost is added to the joint costs before allocation.

For decision-making purposes relevant costs, not allocated costs, are important. This principle is discussed further in the following chapter, *Relevant costs for decision-making*.

Conclusion: Joint and by-product costing and other topics in this book

In Chapters 7 and 8 we differentiated between a costing system that would be required to assign costs in scenarios where each product manufactured or service delivered was unique (in Chapter 7, *Job costing*) on the one hand, and the system required where masses of identical products were produced from a process (in Chapter 8, *Process costing*) on the other hand. Joint and by-product costing is similar to process costing except that joint and by-product costing systems need to be able to allocate the process costs to more than one type of product produced during the process, these products being separately identifiable only at the end of the joint process.

Tutorial case study: Sasol

The coal-to-liquids process of *Sasol Limited* was introduced in the beginning of the chapter. In another of Sasol's processes, the company, through its joint venture with Natref oil refinery located in Sasolburg, refines crude oil to produce petrol, diesel, jet fuel and illuminating paraffin, as well as ethylene and propylene feedstock, fuel oil, bitumen, sulphur and carbon dioxide.

Source: Sasol 2010

In small groups, prepare a short presentation that covers the following points:
1. Discuss the characteristics you would need to take into account in determining whether the products refined in the Natref oil refinery are joint products, by-products, scrap or waste.
2. Explain how the cost accounting treatment differs for each category of product discussed in 1 above.
3. Suggest which of the four methods for allocating joint costs you believe is most appropriate to Sasol.
4. Indicate which production costs would most likely be relevant to Sasol in any decision-making scenarios they might wish to consider.

Basic questions

BQ 1
What is the difference between accounting for a process that produces batches of identical products and for a process from which different joint and by-products emerge?

BQ 2
How does the method of allocation of joint costs affect decision-making where joint and by-products are concerned?

BQ 3
Anka Limited manufactures two raw materials used in the manufacture of perfumes – A and K – in a joint process. These raw materials are then subject to further processing into perfumes – A to produce Anne, and K to produce Karen. The following statement was drawn up for September:

Chapter 9 Joint and by-product costing

Details	Anne R	Karen R	Total R
Joint costs	1 300 000	1 300 000	2 600 000
Further processing costs	500 000	600 000	1 100 000
Production costs	1 800 000	1 900 000	3 700 000
Closing inventory	(360 000)	(475 000)	(835 000)
Cost of sales	1 440 000	1 425 000	2 865 000
Gross profit	360 000	75 000	435 000
Sales	1 800 000	1 500 000	3 300 000

The joint costs were allocated on the basis of the market value at the split-off point. Management believes that the joint costs should be allocated on the basis of the net realisable value.

If joint costs are allocated on the basis of the net realisable value, what would the joint cost allocated to Anne be?
a) R1 376 471
b) R1 300 000
c) R1 444 444
d) R1 536 364
e) None of the above

Show your workings.

BQ 4

In addition to the information given in BQ3, management has recently found a market for a by-product of the joint process – 'Smell'. The following information for September relates to this by-product:

Sales value of the production of 'Smell'	R200 000
Further processing costs required to make the by-product marketable	R100 000

What will the joint costs to be apportioned to the joint products now be?
a) R2 500 000
b) R2 600 000
c) R2 300 000
d) R2 400 000
e) None of the above

Show your workings.

BQ 5

Using the information provided in BQ 3 and BQ 4, what is Anne's gross profit/(loss) as reflected in the income statement for September?
a) R100 000
b) Loss R100 000
c) R50 000
d) R0
e) None of the above

Show your workings.

BQ 6

In a joint process, expenses incurred before the split-off point are:

Labour and overheads (conversion costs)	R125 000
Raw materials	R175 000

The joint products manufactured are:

Alpha	2 000 units
Beta	4 000 units
Charlie	6 000 units

How would the joint costs be allocated using the physical measures method?

BQ 7

In addition to the unit and cost information provided in BQ 6 above, assume that:
- Product Alpha sells at R60,00 per unit.
- Product Beta sells at R75,00 per unit.
- Product Charlie sells at R30,00 per unit.

How would the joint costs be allocated using the market value at the split-off point method? What is the gross profit from each joint product?

BQ 8

In addition to the information relating to costs and units provided in BQ 6 and BQ 7, assume:

	Further processing cost R	Sales value if products are further processed R	Net realisable value R
Product Alpha	120 000	300 000	180 000
Product Beta	90 000	450 000	360 000
Product Charlie	30 000	90 000	60 000
	240 000	840 000	600 000

How would the joint costs be allocated using the net realisable value method? What is the gross profit arising from each joint product?

BQ 9

Using the same information as provided in BQ 6, BQ 7 and BQ 8, how would the joint costs be allocated using the constant gross profit method of allocation?

BQ 10

Joint production costs of R1 000 000 are incurred in producing products M and N, which can be sold as follows at the split-off point:

| Product M: | 50 000 units at R16 per unit |
| Product N: | 50 000 units at R 8 per unit |

If additional processing costs of R60 000 are incurred on Product N after the split-off point, it can be processed into Product P and sold at R10 per unit. Each Product N renders one unit of Product P.

Should the additional processing of Product N take place?

Long questions

LQ 1 – Intermediate (10 marks; 18 minutes)

Source: Adapted from Rhodes University

Envoy (Pty) Ltd produces two products, En and Voy, in a joint process. During a standard four-week period, the following particulars apply:

| Joint costs | R500 000 |

Production:

| En: 60 000 units which sell at R22,00 each |
| Voy: 40 000 units which sell at R9,00 each |

The joint costs consist of:

Direct materials	R100 000
Direct labour	R200 000
Fixed production overheads	R200 000

Envoy (Pty) Ltd presently operates at 80 per cent of its capacity. The market for En is saturated.

The organisation receives a special order for 4 000 units of Voy, to be delivered within the following four-week period, at a selling price of R8,00 each.

REQUIRED	Marks
Advise whether or not the organisation should accept the special order.	10
TOTAL MARKS	**10**

principles of management accounting

LQ 2 – Intermediate (12 marks; 22 minutes)
Source: Adapted from Rhodes University

1 The following information relates to 4 products produced following a joint process:

	Output (litres)	Sales price (per litre)
Product 1	200 000	R40
Product 2	250 000	R48
Product 3	45 000	R2
Toxic waste	5 000	–

2 Inputs into the process were:

	Input (litres)	Cost (per litre)
Raw materials 1	300 000	R15
Raw materials 2	200 000	R50

3 Product 3 incurs additional processing costs of R40 000 before it can be sold at R2 per litre.
4 It costs the organisation R100 per litre to dispose of the toxic waste.
5 Toxic waste of 0,5 per cent of input is considered normal.

REQUIRED		Marks
(a)	Calculate the total process costs for the joint process.	8
(b)	Assuming that joint costs are allocated based on the market value of the joint products, calculate the joint costs that should be allocated to each product.	4
TOTAL MARKS		12

LQ 3 – Advanced (23 marks; 41 minutes)
Source: Rhodes University

Part A *(13 marks; 23 minutes)*
Hunters Lodge (Pty) Ltd operates a game farm and a hunter's retreat for local and foreign clients. In addition to its other sources of revenue, the organisation slaughters and processes the animals which hunters have shot. The game farm has a wide variety of antelope, but kudu are the most popular with hunters. The joint process of slaughtering the animal which has been shot results in the following products:
- Horns, which are then subject to a further process to make them suitable for trophy purposes for the hunters and sold at R1 500 for a pair of horns
- Meat which is suitable for biltong and, after processing into biltong on the farm, is sold at R50 per kilogram
- Meat which is sold to local butchers at R20 per kilogram
- Hides, which are also subject to further processing on the farm and are sold to various customers at R40 each
- Scraps, hooves and bones, which are transported to the vulture-feeding grounds on the farm, at a cost of R14 per carcass.

Joint costs incurred in the slaughter and cutting up of a carcass are as follows:

| Variable costs, including casual labour: | R1,00 per kilogram |
| Fixed cost, allocated per kilogram (excluding the cost of the animal): | R1,20 per kilogram |

Further processing costs are as follows:

	Horns R	Biltong R	Hides R	Total R
Variable costs:				
Per animal		25,00	5,00	30,00
Per kilogram		5,00		5,00
Fixed costs:				
Per animal		10,00	1,00	11,00
Per kilogram		0,50		0,50

An average male kudu weighs 200 kilograms on average, yielding the following:
- A pair of horns, weighing 10 kilograms
- Biltong meat, weighing 30 kilograms
- Fresh meat, weighing 40 kilograms
- A hide, weighing 40 kilograms
- Scraps and bones, weighing 80 kilograms.

A male kudu has a cost for inventory purposes of R1 000.

REQUIRED	Marks
Calculate the profit derived from processing a kudu carcass, as well as the profit derived from each of the joint products. Allocate the joint costs in the most appropriate manner.	13
SUB-TOTAL (Part A)	13

Part B *(10 marks; 18 minutes)*
An American tourist wants to shoot an additional five kudus to buy the horns as trophies to take back as gifts for friends. In addition to the information given in Part A:
- The market for hides and fresh meat is saturated. The hides and fresh meat can be disposed of with the scraps, hooves and bones at no additional cost (that is, the cost of disposal remains R14 per carcass).
- If the kudus were sold at an auction, the owner of the business would make a profit of R1 500 on each kudu.

REQUIRED	Marks
Calculate the minimum selling price for which a pair of horns should be sold to the tourist.	10
SUB-TOTAL (Part B)	10
TOTAL MARKS (Parts A and B)	23

LQ 4 – Advanced (14 marks; 25 minutes)

Source: Adapted from Rhodes University

Miro Limited produces four products, M, A, N and U as part of a joint process. The following information has been extracted from the organisation's financial and production records for May 2XX7:

Product	Units produced	Units sold	Sales revenue* (R'000)
M (joint product)	1 500	1 000	3 000
A (join product)	2 000	2 000	1 000
N (waste – see note 1)	200	–	–
U (by-product)	500	450	100
	4 200	3 450	4 100

* The sales revenue column refers to the sales revenue from units produced (not sold) during the year.

The following costs relating to the manufacture of the four products were incurred during May 2XX7:

	R'000
Direct costs	1 500
Overheads	450
Waste disposal costs (see note 1)	200
	2 150

Starting from June 2XX7, the organisation is planning on processing Product A further, as it will result in a better quality product and therefore a 25 per cent increase in the sales price. Further processing costs, all variable, of R50 per unit will be incurred.

Notes:
1. During the month production difficulties were experienced resulting in an additional 50 units of N being produced. These 50 units are included in the 200 units of N produced, but should be treated as abnormal. The disposal costs of the 50 units are included in the R200 000 waste disposal costs given above.
2. There were no opening inventories at the beginning of May 2XX7.
3. Miro uses the sales value at the split-off point method of apportioning joint costs.

REQUIRED		Marks
(a)	Calculate the value of closing inventory at the end of May 2XX7 for financial reporting purposes.	10
(b)	Ignoring the impact of the abnormal waste units, but assuming the rest of the production and financial information given for May 2XX7 can be used to estimate future costs and revenues, recommend whether the further processing of Product A should be undertaken.	4
TOTAL MARKS		14

LQ 5 – Advanced (25 marks; 45 minutes)

Source: Adapted from Rhodes University

Green Plastics Limited operates two processes that produce two joint products (Alpha and Beta), a by-product (Charlie) and a product, called Delta, which is treated as scrap.

During a standard month:

1. 10 000 kilograms of raw materials at a total cost of R1 million, 10 000 labour hours at an average cost of R50 per hour, and 50 000 machine hours at a cost R10 per hour are input into a joint process. The joint process yields 2 000 kilograms of Alpha, which is sold at the split-off point for R1 000 per kilogram, 7 000 kilograms of unprocessed Beta, and 1 000 kilograms of Delta, which is sold for R100 per kilogram.
2. The unprocessed Beta then undergoes further processing during which 1 000 kilograms of raw materials B costing a total of R5 million, 1 000 labour hours at an average cost of R100 per hour, and 10 000 machine hours at a cost of R40 per hour are input. This process yields 6 000 kilograms of Beta, 1 500 kilograms of Charlie, and 500 kilograms of waste. Beta sells for R2 000 per kilogram and Charlie for R500 per kilogram, but the waste costs R500 per kilogram to dispose of.

During March 2XX7:

1. The production of Alpha, unprocessed Beta, and Delta were at the normal levels for a standard month. Costs and revenues were also at the normal levels for a standard month.
2. The inputs into and costs incurred in the second process were at the normal levels for a standard month, except that the organisation could not purchase any raw material B. A new raw material, material C, was purchased as an alternative. Material C cost the same as material B, but it resulted in only 5 500 kilograms of Beta and 1 250 kilograms of Charlie, and the waste increased to 1 250 kilograms. The organisation expects to be able to switch back to raw material B in April 2XX7.

The organisation uses the physical measures method to allocate joint costs.

	REQUIRED	Marks
(a)	Calculate the cost per kilogram of Alpha, Beta, Charlie and Delta for March 2XX7.	17
(b)	Calculate the cost of any abnormal losses for March and state how they should be treated.	4
(c)	Comment on the acceptability of Green Plastic Limited's use of the physical measures method to allocate joint costs.	4
	TOTAL MARKS	**25**

References

Heaton, H. 1948. *Economic History of Europe*, Revised edition. New York: Harper & Row.

SAICA. 2010. Statements of Generally Accepted Accounting Practice: IAS 2, *Inventories (revised January 2010)*. Johannesburg: SAICA.

SASOL. 2010. Welcome to Sasol and Sasol facts. [Online]. Available: <www.sasol.co.za/sasol_internet/frontend/navigation.jsp?navid=1&rootid=1&pnav=sasol&cnav=sasol> and <www.sasol.co.za/sasol_internet/downloads/Sasol_Facts_2010_1274875069088.pdf> [1 August 2010].

Advanced reading Integration section: Chapters 6 to 9

chapters 6 to 9

Shelley-Anne Roos

> The aim of this section is to integrate students' knowledge of Chapters 6 to 9, and to move students toward a more advanced, high-level understanding of the topics, the relationships between them, and the exam technique required.

As you already know from earlier chapters in this book, a thorough understanding of how costs behave is fundamental to management accounting. When assigning costs to a cost object, the first step is to assign those costs that are directly traceable. This is usually fairly straightforward. For example, we can quite easily determine that each plastic bucket that we manufacture uses 500 grams of plastic and 5 minutes of direct labour time (the cost of which we can then easily assign to each bucket). The more complex question, however, is how we assign those costs that are not directly traceable to the cost object – those costs that are regarded as overhead costs (for example, the monthly water bill of the plastic goods factory). Because overhead costs cannot be *traced* to cost objects in an economically feasible manner, they have to be *allocated*. Chapter 6 deals with overhead allocation. Overheads can be allocated in a number of ways, and some decisions will have to be made in order to choose the optimal overhead allocation in a given scenario. As with any management accounting topic, these decisions should be guided by how the information will be used – the optimal allocation under the circumstances is the one that will provide the best management information. The choice between a simple volume-based allocation system and a more sophisticated system such as ABC, as well as the choice regarding the number of cost pools used, therefore depends on the circumstances.

Chapter 7, *Job costing* is applicable in situations where products or services are unique and consume resources differently. The appropriate amount of costs relating to materials, labour and overheads is assigned to each individual job. Notice that you need to understand the previous chapter on overhead allocation in order to apply job costing, because while direct costs are traced to each individual job, overhead costs are also assigned to each individual job according to the chosen overhead allocation method.

In contrast with job costing, process costing applies in situations where many identical units progress through the same process and consume resources in an identical manner. Chapter 8, *Process costing* describes how the cost of materials as well as the cost of labour and overheads ('conversion costs') is assigned to units in a process costing system. Because all units are identical, each unit carries the same amount of direct and overhead costs. It is important to understand that the valuation method applied, namely the weighted average or the first-in-first out method, affects only the *value* placed on inventory. The physical units are the same, regardless of how they are valued.

Chapter 9, *Joint and by-product costing* is applicable only in certain limited situations. There has to be a process that results in more than one end-product. It is usually not difficult to determine which costs are to be assigned to which products

principles of management accounting

once the products have become separately identifiable. Rather, the question is how the costs, that were incurred *before* the products became separately identifiable are to be allocated to the different products in a meaningful manner. These costs are called joint costs, and their treatment depends largely on whether products are regarded as joint products or by-products.

A question that appeared in Part 1 of SAICA's qualifying exam a number of years ago has been used as a basis for setting the question that follows below. It integrates some important aspects of Chapters 6 to 9, and you should be ready to attempt it now.

In an advanced question like this one, it is important to understand exactly what is expected of you. You therefore need to read the question requirements very carefully. In order to save time, you should read the requirements *before* you read the scenario – this will enable you to be alert to relevant information when you read the scenario and will focus your thoughts while you are reading. Once you have finished reading through the scenario, you should finalise your answer plan. Plan your answers to *all of the requirements* before writing out any of the formal answers – this will ensure that you don't accidentally write an answer in the wrong place. Once your plans are in place, you can start writing the formal answer to requirement (a), followed by (b), (c) and (d), in the logical order. When you plan and write your answers, make sure that you are applying your thoughts to the particular scenario. At a high academic or professional level you are unlikely to earn marks for regurgitating theory, or for writing answers that – although they may contain facts – are not directly relevant to the case at hand.

Integrated question: Chem (Pty) Ltd

Chem (Pty) Ltd is a manufacturer of liquid fertiliser. The company was established in 1993 and has expanded over the years to become a niche player in the South African fertiliser market. Chem (Pty) Ltd is highly specialised and manufactures only one finished product.

The financial manager of Chem (Pty) Ltd has recently completed the draft budget for the financial year ending 31 March 2XX5 with significant input from production and sales personnel. The abridged income statement of this draft budget, which will shortly be presented to the board of directors of Chem (Pty) Ltd for approval, is set out below:

Chem (Pty) Ltd
Draft budget for the year ending 31 March 2XX5
Abridged income statement

	Notes	R'000
Revenue	1	27 060
Raw material costs	2	(8 140)
Labour	4	(3 060)
Variable manufacturing overheads:		(5 526)
Delivery costs	5	1 386
Water and electricity	4	1 080
Waste disposal costs	6	1 800
Other overheads	4	1 260
Fixed manufacturing overheads:		(5 440)
Depreciation on plant and machinery		1 450
Depreciation on transport fleet		750
Repairs and maintenance of plant		1 820
Repairs and maintenance of transport fleet	5	550
Other overheads		870
Closing inventory:		880
Finished product	2	440
Work-in-progress	3	440
Gross profit		5 774
Non-manufacturing overheads	7	(3 200)
Profit before interest and tax		**2 574**

Notes

1 Chem (Pty) Ltd is budgeting to sell 33 000 litres of finished product at an average price of R820 per litre.

2 Planned production for the 2XX5 financial year is 35 000 litres of finished product. There will be no inventory at the end of March 2XX4 as the company will shut down the plant for two weeks before year-end. Chem (Pty) Ltd shuts down the plant every three years to enable external contractors to perform major preventative maintenance on the plant.

    Raw materials are added at the start of the production process. The company produces 1 litre of finished product for every 1,1 litre of raw material input. The loss occurs immediately after the raw materials have been added. The financial manager is uncertain how closing inventories should be recorded in the budget. Chem (Pty) Ltd has historically adopted variable costing to determine product costs and to value inventory for budgeting and planning as well as management accounting purposes.

    The company is considering a change to an absorption costing basis in the 2XX5 financial year. This will result in management accounts being prepared on a basis that is consistent with information contained in the annual financial statements. No adjustments have yet been made in the budgeted income statement with regard to the change in costing basis. Closing finished product and work-in-progress inventories in the budgeted income statement reflect only the estimated raw materials costs associated with producing inventories.

    Raw materials costs recorded in the above income statement are based on an average cost of R200 per litre of raw materials introduced into the production process. Production involves one process by means of which raw materials are converted into the finished product.

principles of management accounting

3 Work-in-progress at 31 March 2XX5 is budgeted to consist of 2 000 litres of 50 per cent-complete finished product. The budgeted income statement incorporates the variable costs associated with producing the budgeted work-in-progress at 31 March 2XX5.
4 Labour and other conversion costs are incurred evenly throughout the production process.
5 Chem (Pty) Ltd sells finished products to consumers from its premises, and customers can opt to have the goods delivered free of charge. Chem owns a fleet of tankers that delivers finished products to customers. Delivery costs in the draft budget represent forecast variable costs of operating the tanker fleet. The budgeted repairs and maintenance costs of R550 000 are consistent with prior years. The company does not have workshop facilities and outsources the repair and maintenance of tankers.
6 The production process generates effluent water, which has to be removed from the premises, treated, and recycled. An independent waste disposal company is contracted to perform these tasks.
7 Non-manufacturing overheads include all other overheads budgeted for the 2XX5 financial year.

Possible new venture

Research by Chem (Pty) Ltd has shown that its liquid fertiliser does not always have the maximum potential fertilising impact on farmers' crops. The two main reasons for this are that the fertiliser is not necessarily stored under ideal conditions by agents and farmers, and that the optimal procedure for the treatment of soil is often not followed. To increase the effectiveness of the product, Chem (Pty) Ltd is considering offering a service whereby the company itself transports the product directly from the factory and applies it to the soil on behalf of farmers. The optimal application of the fertiliser is very dependent on the type of crop to be cultivated, as well as on the specific soil and weather conditions.

This possible new service is still in an early planning phase, and is not reflected in the draft budget for the year ended 31 March 2XX5. The financial manager has heard that the directors are considering a new venture, and has remarked to a colleague, 'Whatever it is that they are planning, I will apply absorption costing to it and use exactly the same costing system that is used for the fertiliser. It will be too confusing and time consuming to operate two different costing systems in the same company.'

REQUIRED		Marks
(a)	Recalculate the budgeted profit before interest and tax of Chem (Pty) Ltd for the financial year ending 31 March 2XX5, incorporating the necessary changes to value closing inventories on an absorption costing basis.	16
(b)	Explain what impact it would have on the value of liquid fertiliser if the production process had, instead of generating effluent water, generated another useful product with a sales value of R50 per litre. You are not required to calculate a revised value for liquid fertiliser.	5
(c)	Critically discuss the financial manager's intention to apply exactly the same costing system to the possible new venture as is used for liquid fertiliser.	5
(d)	Recommend whether it would be appropriate for Chem (Pty) Ltd to make use of activity-based costing.	4
TOTAL MARKS		**30**

Discussion

A suggested solution to this question can be found at the back of the book. Once you have attempted the question and checked the solution, you may find the following discussion useful.

Part (a) requires you to apply absorption costing – notice how this builds on your knowledge from Chapter 5, *Absorption versus variable costing*. The profit before interest and tax in the draft budget was calculated by valuing closing inventory (finished goods as well as work-in-progress) on a variable costing basis. The information states that closing inventory in the draft budget reflects only raw materials costs (see note 2). To change to an absorption costing basis, all relevant costs – including relevant variable *and* fixed overheads – will have to be included in the value of inventory. We are fortunate that there is no opening inventory at 1 March 2XX4, so we can focus on revaluing closing inventory only.

In this question, process costing is required to value (or rather, to revalue) inventory. We can recognise this because we know that process costing is relevant where masses of identical units (in this case, litres of liquid fertiliser) move through the same production process and consume an identical amount of resources. However, if you have simply applied logic to your answer, you may have scored well in part (a) without expressly realising that process costing was applicable. Unfortunately, in the feedback that the SAICA examiner gave after the exam, it was noted that many candidates performed poorly in part (a). If you look through the suggested solution, you are likely to agree that part (a) called for some rather basic numerical calculations. Instead, it was the integration of the principles of absorption costing and process costing that may have caused some difficulty. It was also necessary to think about the treatment of waste, as discussed in Chapter 9, *Joint and by-product costing*.

Part (b) tests your understanding of the principles dealt with in Chapter 9, *Joint and by-product costing*, albeit in a context that requires you to think from an unusual angle. You are not required to value joint or by-products. Instead, you have to think through the impact of the emergence of a joint or by-product on the value of a main product. The requirement also highlights the fact that, in practice, whether a product is treated as a joint or a by-product is by no means a clear-cut decision. It depends on your subjective judgement regarding the significance of the product's sales value.

Parts (c) and (d) require you to discuss whether specified alternative costing systems may be applicable. The function of the management accountant is to provide the best quality of relevant information for decision-making purposes. It follows that the management accountant should be able to justify not only why information (such as cost and budget information) is compiled in a certain why, but also why it is *not* compiled in a different way.

Note the wording in part (c). 'Critically discuss' does not mean that you should necessarily disagree with the manager outright – it calls for a balanced ('critical') discussion of what you feel is valid and invalid about his statement. It would have been easier to answer part (c) if you had addressed the requirements in the logical order, because then you would likely already have thought about the principles of process costing to answer part (a). In part (c) you need to assess the applicability of process costing in a different line of business. It is not enough to know that it is not the ideal costing system for the proposed service – you have to be able to explain *why* this is the case.

Part (d) tests whether you have considered the purpose of activity-based costing – if you did not have a thorough understanding of the fact that it is simply a sophisticated way of allocating overhead costs to products and services, and that such allocation would be required only if there were more than one non-identical product or service, you would not have scored well here. The suggested solution to part (d) may aid your understanding of activity-based costing principles.

It is important that you notice how all the answers in the suggested solution are *applied* to the scenario – they are not answers that you could have copied from any textbook or from any similar question, because they deal very specifically with the circumstances of Chem (Pty) Ltd.

Advanced questions often call for more discussion than lower-level questions do – you should not even be surprised if some advanced questions require significantly *more* discussion than calculation. In this question, the answer to part (a) required numerical calculations, while parts (b) to (d) mostly required discussion. However, this distinction is by no means a characteristic that you can count on. The next integration section in this book features a question where a synthesis of calculation and discussion is necessary to fulfil the individual requirements. You may have realised by now that, the more advanced the question, the less you can afford to have boundaries in your mind that limit either the integration of topics, or your approach to answers, to specific pre-conceived categories. The advanced student operates at a level where it is assumed that all the 'textbook' knowledge has been studied and thought through. This knowledge is now tested in a manner that calls for the reasoned, balanced response that would be required if the question had genuinely been posed in a boardroom situation.

Relevant information for decision-making

chapter 10

Dewald Joubert, Ahmed Mohammadali Haji and Hendrik Fourie

LEARNING OBJECTIVES

By the end of this chapter, you should be able to:
1 Distinguish between long-term and short-term decisions.
2 Understand the concept of relevance, and its various elements, and distinguish between relevant and irrelevant information.
3 Calculate the relevant costs of special order, make-or-buy and closing-down decisions.
4 Apply the concept of relevance to the basic cost elements of materials and labour.
5 Discuss qualitative factors to be considered in evaluating a particular decision.
6 Calculate the relevant cost of a decision, where one or more cost elements are uncertain.
7 Understand the pricing decision and what it entails.

The FIFA World Cup 2010 and relevant costs for decision-making

South Africa hosted the *FIFA World Cup* in 2010. The South African Government had to make a decision to host this prestigious event before they entered the bidding process, which was successfully won by South Africa in 2004.

What does a country need to consider before they decide to host such an event?

Firstly, some costs are relevant to the decision. The infrastructure development costs were significant for South Africa. New stadiums had to be built and existing infrastructure such as stadiums, airports, the railway network, and telecommunications and broadcast technology had to be upgraded. Other costs included security expenses, as well as money spent by provinces and local municipalities in order to host this event.

Secondly, the event generated income, because of the money spent by the thousands of tourists who visited South Africa during the FIFA World Cup 2010.

Thirdly, there are qualitative factors. We have to acknowledge that this decision was not a simple mathematical calculation of what South Africa expected to pay for hosting this event versus what it expected to receive from tourists during this period. There were many other considerations, such as:
- New infrastructure could lead to future investment in South Africa and also improve the lives of citizens.
- South Africa could be seen as a country that can deliver, improving perceptions about South Africa and the rest of Africa.
- Future tourism to South Africa could potentially benefit.
- Nation-building could result through uniting the nation behind one goal.
- On the downside, if a major undesirable event were to occur while the whole word was watching, this could generate significant negative publicity internationally.

Source: FIFA World Cup South Africa 2010

These are just some of the considerations that would have needed to be taken into account. This chapter focuses on decisions like these, and introduces a quantitative framework in order to evaluate such decisions. Qualitative factors are of the utmost importance and are also discussed.

10.1 Introduction

This chapter focuses on the decision-making aspect of the management accountant's role.

Broadly, the management accountant is exposed to two types of decisions in the normal course of business. These are long-term and short-term decisions. Long-term decisions typically are decisions that have a timeframe exceeding one year. They are often characterised by large capital investments, the benefits of which accrue over a period of more than one year.

In this chapter you will learn to consider decisions based on differential cash flows: only the costs and revenues that differ between the alternatives are relevant and are taken into consideration.

Because all costs and revenues, even those that are considered fixed in the short term, can be changed in the very long term, short-term relevant costing principles are not particularly useful for long-term decisions.

The focus in this chapter is on short-term decisions. The short-term decisions to be covered are:
- Special orders
- Make-or-buy decisions
- Closing down of a part of the business.

This chapter will also discuss the pricing decision with reference to the short as well as the long term.

Optimisation, which entails the optimal use of scarce resources, is also a short-term decision. However, this topic will be covered in Chapter 11, *Decision-making under operational constraints*.

Before moving onto the decisions referred to above, it is very important that you understand key terminology associated with short-term decisions, and are able to apply these concepts to basic cost items and revenue. These will now be covered in the section that follows.

10.2 Understanding the concept of relevance

Key terms: opportunity cost, relevance, sunk costs

10.2.1 What is relevance?

The concept of **relevance** has already been introduced in Chapter 2, *Cost classification*. Costs and revenues differ in various scenarios. Information is relevant to a decision when the *information differs* between alternative courses of action evaluated. By contrast, information is irrelevant to a decision when the *information remains the same* regardless of the course of action taken.

Chapter 10 Relevant information for decision-making

Consider the information in example 10.1 below:

Example 10.1

It is the end of January, and Jo Tshabalala is busy contemplating whether he should travel to work using his car (from Pretoria to Johannesburg, and back) or by Gautrain for the month of February. He has determined that a weekly Gautrain ticket will cost him R100. Jo already has one non-refundable weekly ticket that will expire in one month. He purchased it a few months ago for R75, and he cannot sell it to someone else. If he decides to travel by train, he now needs to purchase only three more tickets for the three remaining weeks in the month. In order to travel by car, he has calculated that fuel amounting to R200 will be needed for the month. Jo uses his car for private purposes as well. Insurance for his car for a month amounts to R150, and will not increase if he uses the car to go to work.

Employees who arrive by train enter the building at the platform entrance of the building, while employees who arrive by car enter at the parking lot entrance. Jo has to swipe a magnetic card to record his entry every morning, and for security reasons the system does not allow persons to enter through different entrances during the same calendar month.

Required:
Advise Jo as to whether he should travel to work by car or Gautrain in February. Discuss which information is relevant or irrelevant for purposes of his decision.

Example 10.1 is a simple decision that requires the identification of relevant and irrelevant information. This requires an understanding of the concept of relevance. The following exhibit best illustrates the concept of relevance, and serves as a guide to assist you in identifying relevant and irrelevant information:

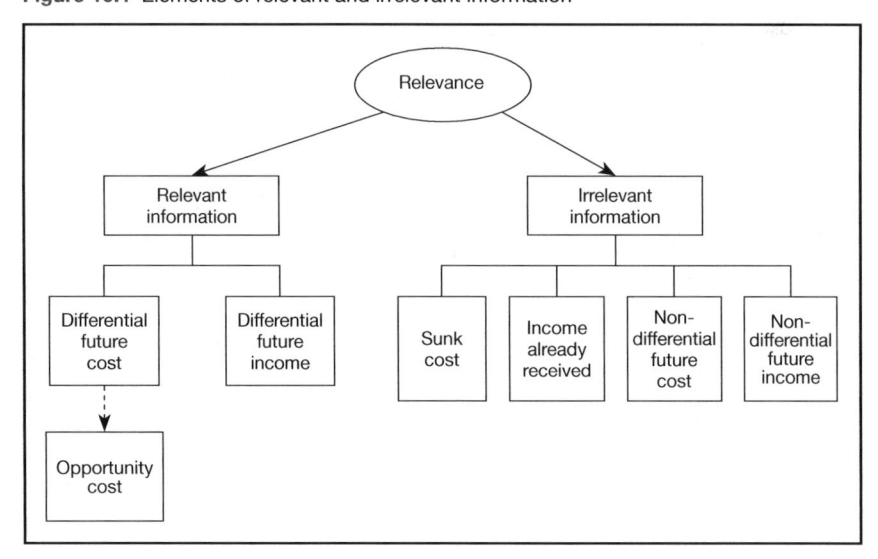

Figure 10.1 Elements of relevant and irrelevant information

```
                          Relevance
                         /         \
              Relevant              Irrelevant
              information           information
             /        \           /    |    |    \
    Differential  Differential  Sunk Income Non-  Non-
    future       future         cost already differential differential
    cost         income              received future future
      |                                      cost   income
      ↓
  Opportunity
  cost
```

Relevant information versus irrelevant information

The fundamental difference between relevant and irrelevant information, as mentioned above, comes down to whether the information differs between courses of action evaluated.

275

In example 10.1, the decision is whether Jo should travel to work by car or by Gautrain for the month of February. Because of the office entrance system, Jo cannot use a combination of car and train travel in the same month. There are therefore two possible courses of action considered in this decision:
- Travel by car
- Travel by Gautrain.

Applying the fundamental difference between relevant and irrelevant information, if the cost or income information is the same for travel by car or Gautrain, then it would be irrelevant. However, if the cost or income information differs for travel by car or Gautrain, then it would be relevant.

Elements of relevant and irrelevant information

A future cost and future income can be relevant or irrelevant, as depicted in Figure 10.1 above. This is a very important point, and care must be taken not to draw a conclusion that *all* future costs or income are relevant. A future cost or income can be irrelevant when the future cost or income remains the same regardless of the course of action followed in a decision. In example 10.1, the insurance cost of R150 is a future cost. However, it is a future cost that will be incurred regardless of whether the car or Gautrain options are followed. As Jo uses his car for private purposes as well, if he chooses to travel by Gautrain, he would still have to insure his car. He would therefore incur the insurance cost whether he travels to work by car or by Gautrain, and the insurance cost would be irrelevant for the purposes of the decision. One could also argue that the R150 is unavoidable regardless of Jo's decision, because he needs to insure his car for private use anyway. Unavoidable costs are irrelevant as they need to be incurred irrespective of the course of action taken.

In contrast, the fuel cost of R200 is also a future cost. But it will be incurred only if Jo travels to work by car. It will not be incurred if he travels by Gautrain. Given that the cost information differs between the courses of action, the fuel cost of R200 is relevant to the decision. One could also argue that the R200 would be avoidable if Jo travels by Gautrain. Costs which are avoidable when a certain course of action is taken are relevant. Avoidable costs are therefore relevant and unavoidable costs are irrelevant.

Now let us look at the cost of the weekly ticket. Jo already has one weekly ticket in his possession, and needs to purchase only a further three if he chooses to travel by Gautrain.

The first issue that arises is whether the R75 cost of the first ticket has any relevance to this decision. The R75 cost of the first ticket is referred to as a sunk cost in management accounting. It is a cost that Jo incurred in the past, and can also be called a past cost. **Sunk costs** are costs that were incurred in the past or costs that were committed to in the past and that can no longer be avoided or changed, regardless of what course of action is taken.

For decision-making purposes, sunk costs are always irrelevant. How do we reach this conclusion? Jo incurred a cost of R75 prior to this decision. Whether Jo travels by car or by Gautrain, he would still incur the cost of R75. The cost was incurred in the past, and a future decision would not have an impact on the cost of the past; therefore it is irrelevant.

Figure 10.1 shows, among other things, the link between irrelevant information and sunk costs. Take specific note that sunk costs have no link to relevant information. This should be obvious from the discussion above, as sunk costs are *always* irrelevant for decision-making. The same logic applies to income that has already been received, or that will be received regardless of what course of action is taken.

Now let us turn our attention to the remaining three weekly tickets that Jo has to purchase. As Jo has yet to purchase these, they represent future costs. As mentioned above, future costs can be relevant or irrelevant. As Jo would purchase these tickets only if he were to travel by Gautrain, we can conclude that the cost of the remaining three weekly tickets would be relevant.

Below is a summary of the cost information in example 10.1:

Travel by:	Car	Gautrain
Relevant items:		
Ticket – three weekly tickets	–	R300
Fuel	R200	–
Irrelevant items:		
First weekly ticket	R75[1]	R75[1]
Insurance	R150[2]	R150[2]

Notes:
1 This cost was incurred in the past, and a future decision will have no impact on it.
2 This cost will be incurred if Jo travels to work by car, and will still be incurred if he travels to work by Gautrain, as he uses the car for private purposes as well. The cost is irrelevant to the decision because it does not differ between the two alternatives.

Future cost versus opportunity cost

In example 10.1, Jo uses his car for private purposes as well. Fortunately, Jo's car was available to be used for travel to work as well. This is usually referred to as spare capacity. We say that Jo had spare capacity with respect to the use of his car, and was able to use it for travel to work.

A situation could arise where Jo's car is not available, for example if Jo's brother pays Jo to use the car on weekdays at exactly the times that Jo has to travel to work and back. One of the options available to Jo would be to hire an additional car. This would represent a future cost, and would be a future cost that would be relevant to the decision. In management accounting terms we could say that Jo would be obtaining additional capacity.

But now let us make the scenario even more interesting. Jo may be unable to obtain additional capacity – perhaps Jo does not have money available to hire another car. In management accounting terms, we would say that Jo has capacity constraints, and that capacity is now limited.

A capacity constraint is identified by comparing resources available versus resources required. Whenever the resources available are less than resources required, a capacity constraint exists. This chapter will explore the impact on relevant costs when a capacity constraint exists. Chapter 11, *Decision-making under operational constraints* will further examine the impact capacity constraints will have on choosing products or services which will utilise the scarce resource in the most profitable manner.

Let us return to our example. Jo is experiencing a capacity constraint, and there is no future cost in the form of hiring costs in such a situation. The problem that Jo now has is one of opportunity costs. Jo must decide whether he should forgo the money that his brother pays for the use of the car, in order to use the car himself to travel to work. **Opportunity cost** is the net income forgone by not choosing the alternative option. In our example, the money Jo's brother would have paid him for the month of February is the opportunity cost. This opportunity cost would be relevant to his decision.

Opportunity cost arises when capacity constraints exist, which means additional capacity cannot be acquired, and is therefore scarce. At this point, it is also very important to realise that there would be no future cost in respect of the capacity (this should be obvious, as additional capacity cannot be acquired), and this future cost would be replaced by an opportunity cost. This is depicted by the dotted line in Figure 10.1 between future cost and opportunity cost. The opportunity cost would then be relevant to the decision. It is important to understand the concept of an opportunity cost, and its relationship to relevance.

Now that you understand the concept of relevance and its various elements, we will move on to applying this concept to the three types of short-term decisions mentioned in part 10.1.

10.3 Decisions under conditions of certainty

Firstly, we will commence this discussion by assuming that the variables within a decision are known with certainty. This is done for purposes of simplicity, but it should be apparent that decisions taken in practice are characterised by a high degree of uncertainty, and these uncertainties need to be dealt with. The use of probability distributions to assist in making decisions under conditions of uncertainty will be discussed later in this chapter.

In this section of the text, we will address three types of decisions:
- Special order decisions
- Make-or-buy decisions
- Decisions regarding closing down a part of the business.

Please note that, while these are three decision-types that occur frequently, you should also be able to apply your minds in a similar manner to any other decision you may encounter.

It is very important to note that decisions cannot be taken on the basis of a quantitative assessment only. When decisions are made you should first identify all relevant information by identifying all factors that differ between the alternatives. This relevant information obtained is then examined in detail. Quantifiable information is quantified as accurately as possible, while information which cannot be accurately quantified will be carefully considered. Relevant information which cannot be accurately quantified is referred to as being a qualitative factor. Qualitative factors, such as the strategic importance of the decision, are therefore relevant information which should be considered and should not be seen as less important.

10.3.1 Special order decisions

Key term: special order decision

The **special order decision** is *generally* characterised by an organisation that is approached by an external party:

Chapter 10 Relevant information for decision-making

- To supply a similar product to its existing product line in a different market
- To modify the existing product to suit the needs of the external party.

More importantly, special orders are intended to be 'once-off', and this aspect is the main reason that they would fall within the ambit of a short-term decision. Should the special order become repetitive, the focus changes, making it a strategic issue, and the organisation would need to take into account the long-term consequences of such an order, including issues surrounding whether the order should become part of the permanent product line of the organisation.

Let us begin with a simple example of a special order in example 10.2 below.

Example 10.2

Bubbles Galore Ltd is a manufacturer of bubblegum. Their available production capacity for a month amounts to 1 000 000 units of bubblegum, while sales are only 800 000 units in a month. Bubblegum is sold at R4 per unit.

At the end of December a leading toy manufacturer approaches Bubbles Galore to supply 150 000 units of bubblegum, which will have to be modified in size in order to fit into their newest toy – the bubble ship. The toy manufacturer has offered a total contract price of R450 000 for delivery in January. The variable cost of the special bubblegum will be the same as normal bubblegum, except that an additional R75 000 will be incurred for the modification. The variable cost of normal bubblegum is R1 per unit. Fixed costs for the Bubbles Galore facility amount to R300 000 per month.

Required:
Assess whether the toy manufacturer's order ought to be accepted.

Quantitative issues

Example 10.2 clearly illustrates the important special order characteristic of spare capacity. During a month, Bubbles Galore has spare capacity of 200 000 (1 000 000 – 800 000) units of bubblegum. Bubbles Galore is approached by an external party to fulfil a special order of 150 000 units.

As the concept of relevance is inextricably related to the various courses of action available in a decision, the starting point with any type of decision-making question is to fully understand the decision. By this, we are implying that you should fully understand the different courses of action available in a decision. Remember, information is relevant to a decision when the information differs for alternative courses of action evaluated.

The decision above involves determining whether it is worthwhile for Bubbles Galore to accept the special order. There are two courses of action in this decision:
- Accept the special order.
- Do not accept the special order.

Remember from Figure 10.1 that future costs and income can be relevant or irrelevant, while sunk costs and income already received are always irrelevant. The second step is therefore to identify all the future costs and income, and then to test whether they differ between the different courses of action.

From the information above, we can extract the following future costs and income for the month of January:
- Normal sales of 800 000 units per month amounting to R3 200 000 (800 000 × R4)
- Special order sales of 150 000 units for the month, with a contract price of R450 000
- Variable cost of normal sales of R800 000 (800 000 × R1)
- Variable cost of special order sales of R150 000 (150 000 × R1) plus additional R75 000 for modification = R225 000
- Fixed cost for the Bubbles Galore facility of R300 000 per month.

Let us now assess the relevance of each of the items above:

	Notes	Accept the special order	Do not accept the special order
Relevant items:			
Special order sales of 150 000 units	1	R450 000	–
Variable costs of special order sales	2	(R225 000)	–
Total relevant income		R225 000	–
Irrelevant items:			
Normal sales of 800 000 units per month	1	R3 200 000	R3 200 000
Variable costs of normal sales	2	(R800 000)	(R800 000)
Fixed cost for the Bubbles Galore facility	3	(R300 000)	(R300 000)

Notes:
1. Bubbles Galore will receive the R450 000 only if it accepts the special order. If it does not accept the special order, it will not receive the R450 000. The special order sales are therefore relevant to the decision. In contrast, Bubbles Galore will continue to sell its 800 000 units regardless of whether the special order is accepted or not. The sales proceeds of R3 200 000 will therefore be irrelevant to this decision.
2. Bubbles Galore will incur the variable costs of R225 000 only if it fulfils the special order. It will not incur this cost if it does not accept the special order. The variable costs of special order sales of R225 000 are therefore relevant to the decision. In contrast, the variable costs of normal sales of R800 000 will be incurred regardless of whether the special order is accepted or not. This cost of R800 000 is therefore irrelevant to this decision.
3. The fixed cost of R300 000 for the Bubbles Galore facility is fixed, and incurred for the production capacity of 1 000 000 units. As this cost is fixed, it will not change in the short term, and will therefore be incurred regardless of whether the special order is accepted or not (the very nature of a fixed cost is such that it cannot be altered within the decision-making timeframe). This makes the cost irrelevant.

On the basis of relevant items above, Bubbles Galore will receive an additional income of R450 000 and will incur an additional cost of R225 000 if it accepts the special order. This yields a net additional (incremental) benefit of R225 000 from accepting the special order. On a purely quantitative basis, Bubbles Galore should accept the special order.

Chapter 10 Relevant information for decision-making

> For interest's sake, let's assume we did not know that Bubbles Galore could earn R450 000 from the special order. We could then say that Bubbles Galore should accept this special order only for a minimum special order price of R225 000. At this special order price, they would be in the same position as before, that is, neither worse nor better off than before. Now, let us assume that Bubbles Galore requires a profit of at least R100 000 on this special order. The minimum order price that Bubbles Galore would then accept would be R325 000 (R225 000 + R100 000). When the special order price is unknown and Bubbles Galore is required to determine a selling price, the scenario is referred to as short-term pricing (refer to section 10.6.4 later in this chapter).

To come to a final decision, Bubbles Galore has to consider qualitative factors such as whether their workforce has sufficient skills to fulfil the special order to an acceptable standard, and whether they are willing to accept the risk of litigation if small children accidentally swallow the bubblegum placed inside the toy.

This was a simple illustration of a special order. In practice, special orders are complicated as a result of further issues arising with respect to spare capacity. In example 10.2 above, Bubbles Galore had spare capacity of 200 000 units, which was sufficient to accommodate the special order of 150 000 units.

- What if the special order was for 250 000 units? More capacity would need to be obtained in order to fulfil the order. The question that now arises is whether the cost of the additional capacity is relevant.
- Further problems arise if the special order was for 250 000 units and more capacity could not be obtained within the decision-making timeframe. What would the implication be in that situation?

Let us answer these questions using the illustrations in examples 10.3 and 10.4.

Example 10.3

The information is the same as in example 10.2, except that the order is for 250 000 units instead of 150 000 units, and additional production capacity of 150 000 units can be obtained at a cost of R100 000 per month. This cost for additional capacity remains R100 000 regardless of how many additional units are actually produced.

The contract price is R750 000, and modification variable costs increase proportionately. They therefore amount to R125 000.

Required:
Assess whether the toy manufacturer's order ought to be accepted.

Let us commence by looking at the spare capacity. We can prepare the following table to depict the availability of capacity for both courses of action:

Capacity	Accept the special order Units	Do not accept the special order Units
Available	1 000 000	1 000 000
Normal sales	(800 000)	(800 000)
Special order	(250 000)	–
(Short)/Spare	(50 000)	200 000

principles of management accounting

From the table above, you need to take note of some important facts:
- Bubbles Galore is able to maintain its normal sales level of 800 000 units under both courses of action.
- In order to accommodate the special order, Bubbles Galore will have to incur a future cost of R100 000 to extend its production capacity. This cost would be incurred only if the special order is accepted. This cost is therefore relevant to the decision. Furthermore, earlier we illustrated the link between a future cost and an opportunity cost. We said that if there is a future capacity cost, then there would be no opportunity cost, and this situation is an example of this concept. The organisation can incur a future cost of R100 000 to extend its capacity, and thereby avoid the sacrifice of any normal sales (opportunity cost).

Once again, after identifying the courses of action in the decision, and the future costs and income, we can prepare the following schedule:

	Notes	Accept the special order	Do not accept the special order
Relevant items:			
Special order sales of 250 000 units	1	R750 000	–
Variable costs of special order sales	1	(R375 000)	–
Fixed costs for extension of the capacity by 150 000 units	4	(R100 000)	–
Total relevant income		**R275 000**	–
Irrelevant items:			
Normal sales of 800 000 units per month	2	R3 200 000	R3 200 000
Variable costs of normal sales	2	(R800 000)	(R800 000)
Fixed cost for the 1 000 000 unit facility	3	(R300 000)	(R300 000)

Notes:
1. The special order sales of R750 000 would be received only if the special order were accepted. This makes the R750 000 relevant to the decision. The same applies to the variable costs of R375 000 ((R1 × 250 000 units) + R125 000).
2. In contrast, the normal sales and its variable costs of R3 200 000 and R800 000 respectively would continue regardless of whether the special order was accepted or not. This makes these items irrelevant to the decision.
3. The fixed cost for the existing 1 000 000 unit production facility would be incurred, regardless of whether the special order was accepted or not. This makes this cost irrelevant to the decision.
4. Bubbles Galore would need to extend its production facility only if it accepted the special order. The cost of R100 000 would therefore be incurred only if the special order were accepted. This makes the cost relevant. Note that the entire cost is relevant as it has to be incurred as a whole, regardless of the fact that only 50 000 units of the extra 150 000 units are needed.

On the basis of the relevant items above, Bubbles Galore will receive an additional income of R750 000 and will incur additional costs of R475 000 if it accepts the special order. This yields a net additional (incremental) benefit of R275 000 from accepting the special order. On a purely quantitative basis, Bubbles Galore should accept the special order.

In example 10.3 above, Bubbles Galore was able to obtain additional capacity of 150 000 units at R100 000. What happens if additional capacity cannot be obtained within the decision-making timeframe? Consider the information in example 10.4 below.

Example 10.4

The information is the same as in example 10.2, except that the order is for 250 000 units instead of 150 000 units, and additional production capacity cannot be obtained within the decision-making timeframe.

The contract price is R750 000 and modification variable costs increase proportionately. They therefore amount to R125 000.

Required:
Assess whether the toy manufacturer's order ought to be accepted.

Once again, we commence by looking at the spare capacity. We can prepare the following table to depict the availability of capacity for both courses of action:

Capacity	Accept the special order Units	Do not accept the special order Units
Available	1 000 000	1 000 000
Normal sales	(800 000)	(800 000)
Special order	(250 000)	–
(Short)/Spare	(50 000)	200 000

In this illustration, Bubbles Galore has not been able to extend its production facility. There is therefore no future cost in this regard. Now where does Bubbles Galore obtain 50 000 units in order to satisfy the special order? It has only one choice, and that is to sacrifice 50 000 units of its normal sales. This decision is not ideal, and will have several qualitative considerations, which will be discussed later. It has the effect that without the special order, Bubbles Galore would sell 800 000 normal sales units, and with the special order, it would sell 750 000. Normal sales (and their related costs) now become relevant to the decision. With the sacrifice of 50 000 units, Bubbles Galore would lose sales amounting to R200 000 (R4 × 50 000 units), but at the same time save variable costs of R50 000 (R1 × 50 000 units), thereby yielding a loss of R150 000. This is the contribution yielded by the 50 000 units ([R4 – R1] × 50 000). The opportunity cost is therefore the contribution lost through not selling the 50 000 units.

After identifying the courses of action in the decision, and the future costs and income, we can prepare the following schedule:

	Accept the special order	Do not accept the special order
Relevant items:		
Special order sales of 250 000 units	R750 000	–
Variable costs of special order sales (R1 × 250 000 + R125 000)	(R375 000)	–
Normal sales (750 000 × R4); (800 000 × R4)	R3 000 000	R3 200 000
Variable costs of normal sales (750 000 × R1); (800 000 × R1)	(R750 000)	(R800 000)
Total relevant income	**R2 625 000**	**R2 400 000**
Irrelevant items:		
Fixed cost for the 1 000 000 unit facility	(R300 000)	(R300 000)

principles of management accounting

On the basis of relevant items above, Bubbles Galore will receive a total income of R2 625 000 if it accepts the special order and R2 400 000 if it does not accept the special order. Accepting the special order would mean that Bubbles Galore is quantitatively better off by R225 000. On a purely quantitative basis, Bubbles Galore should accept the special order.

A simpler approach

For examples 10.2 to 10.4, we have used a more thorough and detailed approach in order to introduce the concepts of relevance and irrelevance. However, there is a simpler approach we can follow to assess whether a special order should be accepted. This is expressed in terms of the following function:

> **Incremental benefit of a special order = Additional income from accepting the special order – Additional costs that will be incurred if the special order is accepted**

The additional income and additional costs represent the difference between the 'accept the special order' course of action and the 'do not accept the special order' course of action. Using this, we can reach the following conclusion:

Additional income	Sales of special order
Additional costs	Variable costs of special order
	Difference in fixed costs
	Opportunity costs

Applying this to the information in example 10.4, we can calculate the following:

Additional income	Contract price		R750 000
Additional costs	Variable costs of special order		(R375 000)
	Difference in fixed costs		–
	Opportunity costs [1]		(R150 000)
Incremental benefit			R225 000

Note:
1. Here the opportunity cost is calculated as the lost contribution arising from lost sales. Bubbles Galore had to sacrifice 50 000 units of normal sales, for which it would have earned a contribution of R3 per unit (R4 sales – R1 variable costs). There is therefore a total opportunity cost of R150 000.

The incremental benefit amounts to R225 000, which is the same conclusion that was reached using the more detailed approach earlier. The more detailed approach is called the total approach where a calculation is performed for both the options considered (accept/do not accept). The simpler approach is called the incremental approach as it entails only one calculation of what happens incrementally (assuming we accept).

Qualitative issues

It has been stressed that decisions should not be made on the basis of a quantitative assessment only, and that qualitative issues should also be considered. Some qualitative issues that could arise are discussed below.

Sometimes special orders are sold at a slightly cheaper price than normal sales, and concerns arise regarding competitors' reactions, as well as those of existing customers, should they hear about the cheaper price. The long-run implication of the lower price must therefore be considered.

If the special order is to be exported, international trade issues including potential 'dumping' allegations could arise. The term 'dumping' refers to the practice where products are exported at a price which is below the price the exporter charges in its home market. The practice is often opposed by those who believe that local businesses and labourers in the receiving country suffer negative consequences owing to unfair international competition.

Issues may arise regarding the sacrifice of existing sales in order to accommodate the special order, as in example 10.4. In the quantitative assessment, the opportunity cost would have been quantified, but the effect of the lost sales must be assessed on a permanent level with respect to the impact on customer goodwill, and damage to reputation.

As mentioned earlier, the idea with a special order is that it should be once-off. However, the possibility of repeat orders must be considered. Also, sometimes a special order may not initially yield a positive quantitative assessment, but the organisation may see the order as an opportunity to penetrate a new market. In such cases, the special orders are accepted, with a view to improving other lines of business in the long run.

The fact that spare capacity is 'committed' must also be considered. Generally, organisations maintain a level of safety capacity, in the event of break-downs and similar contingencies. However, with special orders, this safety capacity could be committed, and the impact in the case of a breakdown or similar event must be considered.

In a decision regarding the acceptance of a special order, both quantitative analysis (the calculation of relevant costs) and a thorough assessment of qualitative factors ought to be taken into consideration.

Now that we have discussed the quantitative and qualitative issues with regard to special orders, we move on to the next type of decision: the make-or-buy decision.

10.3.2 Make-or-buy decisions

Key terms: make-or-buy decision, outsourcing decision

The **make-or-buy decision**, also known as the **outsourcing decision**, entails evaluating the costs of manufacturing a component internally in contrast to acquiring it from an external party (outsourcing). Once again, quantitative and qualitative factors must be taken into account before a decision is made.

principles of management accounting

Let us begin with the illustration in example 10.5.

Example 10.5

Manyane CC operates a lodge and conference centre in the Limpopo Province. Management is currently evaluating the possibility of outsourcing the catering at the lodge. They have prepared the following cost schedule, and have also expressed the costs on a per head basis (based on current levels of 5 000 heads):

	R	Cost per head (R)
Cost of meals	250 000	50
Catering labour	125 000	25
Variable catering overheads	100 000	20
Fixed catering overheads	80 000	16
Total	555 000	111

A catering organisation has offered to do the catering at an all-inclusive price of R85 per head. Catering will be done at the lodge. Should Manyane accept the catering organisation's offer, 40 per cent of the catering labour can be released, with no retrenchment costs. The other 60 per cent will be transferred to other parts of the organisation where they can be productively employed. These positions will not be created if the organisation does not outsource.

Fixed catering overheads comprise of an allocation of the rental for the eating areas that Manyane pays to the landlords of the lodge.

Assume that all figures are annual.

Required:
Assess whether the catering ought to be outsourced.

Quantitative issues

On an initial quantitative level, it appears that the organisation should accept the catering organisation's offer of R85 per head, as it is significantly lower than the current costs of R111 per head. However, such a decision cannot be made without distinguishing between relevant and irrelevant information.

As mentioned earlier, the starting point of any decision must be to understand fully the various courses of action available within a decision. In this decision, we are evaluating two possible courses of action:
- Providing meals in-house (the 'make' option)
- Utilising a catering organisation (the 'buy' option).

The second step is to identify the future costs and future income, under each alternative, when catering for 5 000 people. The third step is to assess the relevance of each future cost and income. The table below summarises the future costs and income, as well as their relevance and irrelevance:

	Notes	Make R	Buy R
Relevant items:			
Cost of meals	1	250 000	–
Labour (40%)	2	50 000	–
Variable catering overheads	1	100 000	–
External catering fees (R85 × 5 000)	3	–	425 000
Total relevant costs		**400 000**	**425 000**
Irrelevant items:			
Labour (60%)	2	75 000	75 000
Fixed catering overheads	4	80 000	80 000

Notes:
1 The cost of meals will be incurred if Manyane chooses to provide its own meals. However, should they choose to outsource, this cost will not be incurred (and will therefore be saved). As the future cost differs between the two courses of action, it is relevant to the decision. The same applies for variable catering overheads.
2 If Manyane chooses to provide its own meals, it will incur R125 000 in labour cost. However, if Manyane chooses to outsource, it will continue to incur labour costs amounting to R75 000 (R125 000 × 60%) relating to the employees that it transfers to elsewhere in the organisation. The amount of R75 000 is therefore irrelevant, as it will be incurred in both courses of action. The remaining R50 000 is relevant, as it will be incurred only if the 'make' option is chosen.
3 External catering fees of R425 000 (R85 × 5 000 people) will be incurred only if the 'buy' option is chosen. This makes this cost relevant.
4 Fixed catering overheads relate to the rentals paid for eating areas at the lodge. Both courses of action would require the use of the eating areas. Furthermore, the nature of a fixed cost is such that it is fixed for the duration of the planning horizon. It is therefore irrelevant.

After performing a relevant cost assessment, the external catering option comes out as being the more expensive of the two options, which is contrary to the initial assessment. This emphasises the importance of relevant costs and the correct calculation thereof. Before a final conclusion can be reached, certain qualitative aspects must also be considered.

Qualitative issues

In example 10.5 the decision involves a significant degree of reliance on an external party to perform the catering and consideration should be given to:
- The reputation of the external caterer
- The quality of meals provided by the external caterer
- The ability of the external caterer to deliver catering on time
- The financial stability of the external caterer, and their ability to handle an order of this size
- The service level agreement with the external caterer, and
- Other relevant factors.

principles of management accounting

Another consideration that may be relevant in the South African context is whether the catering organisation is accredited for Black Economic Empowerment (BEE) purposes.

As staff may be released or retrenched in example 10.5, staff-related issues such as trade union involvement and loss of existing staff morale are also factors that need to be considered.

10.3.3 The closing-down decision

In the closing-down decision, an organisation evaluates whether it should close down a particular line of business, product line, or even an entire division. Once again, both quantitative and qualitative factors must be taken into account.

Although closing-down decisions are regarded as being short-term decisions, the consequences of closing down are very often of a long-term nature. Closing-down decisions therefore carry long-term consequences. However, these consequences are addressed through qualitative factors. The long-term quantitative consequences of closing down fall outside the scope of this text.

Many organisations close down a line of business, product line or division on the grounds that it is not 'performing adequately'. This could be a mistake if the organisation bases this decision on the division's performance, as depicted by an absorption costing income statement. In the chapter on absorption costing (Chapter 5, *Absorption versus variable costing*), it was stressed that variable costing is often more appropriate for decision-making. Should the financial information be based on absorption costing, your first reaction should be to realise that such an income statement probably needs to be restated on a variable costing basis in order to reflect the information in a relevant form.

There are multiple approaches available to determine whether a division should be closed down. We will address two of these approaches. Consider the following illustration in example 10.6.

Example 10.6

Nongoma Ltd operates two manufacturing sites, one in Johannesburg and one in Richards Bay. Given the poor performance of the Richards Bay division, the organisation is evaluating whether it should close down the division. The following income statements are available for the latest financial year:

	Johannesburg	Richards Bay
	R'000	R'000
Sales	130 000	50 000
Less: Costs		
Direct materials	45 000	25 000
Direct labour	20 000	15 000
Salaries	25 000	20 000
Rental of premises	10 000	5 000
Allocated fixed costs	9 000	4 000
Profit/(loss)	21 000	(19 000)

Nongoma Ltd's cost accountant has determined that, should the Richards Bay division be closed down, the following factors must be taken into account:
- Seventy-five per cent of salaries would be saved and retrenchment costs of R1 000 000 incurred. Staff making up the remaining 25 per cent of the salary bill will be accommodated in the Johannesburg division. These positions will not be created if the Richards Bay division is not closed down.
- The Richards Bay premises are leased in terms of a contract that cannot be cancelled in the short term.
- Head office costs are allocated on the basis of sales.
- Sales cannot be transferred to the Johannesburg office.

Required:
Assess whether the Richards Bay division ought to be closed down.

Quantitative issues

On an initial quantitative level, it appears that Nongoma Ltd should close down the Richards Bay division, as it is making a loss of R19 million per annum. However, such a decision cannot be made without distinguishing between relevant and irrelevant information, and considering the overall impact on the organisation.

As mentioned earlier, the starting point of any decision must be to understand fully the various courses of action available. In this decision, we are evaluating two courses of action:
- Close down the Richards Bay division.
- Do not close down the Richards Bay division.

The second step is to identify the future costs and future income, under each alternative. The secret to closing down a division is not to focus on a divisional level, but rather to view the decision and its impact on the overall organisational level. In evaluating the 'close down' course of action, the organisation should therefore ask itself what future costs it will incur, and what future income it will receive. The answer to these questions is that it would incur future costs and earn future income relating to operating the Johannesburg division, and also incur future costs relating to the Richards Bay division that could not be saved after closing down.

In evaluating the 'do not close down' course of action, the organisation should once again ask itself what future costs it will incur, and what future income it will earn. In this case, it will incur future costs relating to operating the Johannesburg and Richards Bay divisions, and will also earn future income from both these divisions.

We now need to assess the relevance of each future cost and income. Once again, this is done by analysing which of these costs and income differ between the courses of action. The example below will be performed on the total approach. The table below summarises the future costs and income, as well as their relevance and irrelevance:

	Notes	Close down	Do not close down
		R'000	R'000
Relevant items:			
Richards Bay sales	1	–	50 000
Richards Bay direct materials	2	–	(25 000)
Richards Bay direct labour	2	–	(15 000)

principles of management accounting

	Notes	Close down R'000	Do not close down R'000
Relevant items:			
Richards Bay salaries (75% × R20 000)	3	–	(15 000)
Retrenchment costs	4	(1 000)	–
Total relevant costs		**(1 000)**	**(5 000)**
Irrelevant items:			
Johannesburg profit	5	21 000	21 000
Richards Bay salaries (25% × R20 000)	6	(5 000)	(5 000)
Richards Bay rental	7	(5 000)	(5 000)
Head office allocated costs	8	(4 000)	(4 000)

Notes:
1 Richards Bay sales would be earned only if the division is kept open. If the division is closed down, Nongoma Ltd would lose these sales. Therefore the sales figure of R50 million is a future income that is relevant.
2 Direct materials and direct labour of the Richards Bay division would be saved if the Richards Bay division is closed down. However, they will be incurred if the division is kept open. The variable costs are therefore also relevant to the decision.
3 Seventy-five per cent of the salaries would be saved (avoided) if the division were closed down. However, if the division is kept open, this amount would be incurred. Therefore, this amount is relevant to the decision.
4 Retrenchment costs of R1 million would be incurred only if the division is closed down, and not if the division is kept open. This makes this cost relevant to the decision.
5 The Johannesburg division would continue to operate regardless of the course of action followed with respect to the Richards Bay division. Therefore this division would continue to earn its sales of R130 million, and still incur R109 million in costs, regardless of which course of action is followed with respect to the Richards Bay division. However, if the Richards Bay division is closed down, the Johannesburg division's costs will increase as a result of the higher salary bill. This is discussed in point 6 below.
6 Should the Richards Bay division be closed down, 25 per cent of the cost of its salaries will be incurred in the Johannesburg division. If the Richards Bay division is kept open, 25 per cent of the salaries cost would be incurred in this division. Regardless of which division it is incurred in, the fact of the matter is that from Nongoma's point of view, the cost is being incurred irrespective of which course of action is followed, and the cost is therefore irrelevant to the decision.
7 As the rental costs cannot be avoided in the short term, they would still be incurred if the Richards Bay division is closed down. As the costs are incurred regardless of the course of action followed, they are irrelevant for the purposes of the decision.
8 Head office costs are allocated on the basis of sales. As far as the information indicates, the decision being taken will simply change the basis of the allocation, but not the actual cost. The head office cost is therefore irrelevant to the decision.

Total relevant costs of closing down are less (by R4 million, to be exact) than the relevant costs of keeping the Richards Bay division open. Therefore, on a quantitative basis, it would be better to close down the division.

A simpler approach

We can also reach the same conclusion using an alternative approach, the incremental approach. This approach is really the difference between the 'close down' and 'do not close down' courses of action. This difference is costs saved (avoidable costs), income lost and additional costs incurred, if the division is closed down.

The following expression can be used to assess whether it is worthwhile to close down the division (incremental approach):

> **Incremental benefit = Costs saved from closing down – income lost from closing down – additional costs incurred in closing down**

Using this method, the costs saved from closing down the Richards Bay division would be:

	R'000
Richards Bay direct materials	25 000
Richards Bay direct labour	15 000
Richards Bay salaries (75%)	15 000

The income lost from closing down the Richards Bay division would be:

	R'000
Richards Bay sales	(50 000)

The additional costs incurred in closing down the Richards Bay division would be:

	R'000
Retrenchment costs	(1 000)

The incremental benefit, which is the net of all of the above, is R4 million. Based on this, we can interpret the incremental benefit by saying that Nongoma Ltd will save R4 million if the Richards Bay division is closed down. You will notice that this R4 million is exactly the same as the difference between the relevant costs of R1 million relating to the closing down and R5 million relating to keeping the division open, which we calculated earlier using the total approach. Therefore we can conclude that when we save (avoid) more costs than what we lose in revenue, it makes economic sense to close down.

Qualitative issues

As with any decision, we cannot conclude a discussion of the closing-down decision without considering the qualitative issues around such a decision.

- Firstly, closing down a business, product line or division entails discontinuing the manufacture and marketing of a particular product in a particular location or industry. This raises concerns about the market's reaction to such a decision.
- Secondly, there are several staff-related issues arising from a closing-down decision. There may be trade union issues that need to be considered – staff may go on strike, for example. The quantitative aspect of retrenchment costs have been taken into account, but the effect of disruptions on existing operations must be noted. The fact that certain staff members have been retrenched may raise concerns among the existing staff as to the security of their own jobs, and this would have an impact on staff morale, and ultimately the quality of the final product.
- Finally, the closing decision would have an impact on the organisation's regular customers. Concerns may arise regarding the provision of after-sales service, and the issues around the honouring of guarantees and warranties. There may be considerations regarding the loss of customer goodwill, and the resulting impact on the reputation of the organisation. This could have subsequent effects on the other product lines and business of the organisation.

These are just some of the considerations worthy of note, and attention must be given to the specifics of every situation.

Notice that you could also consider adding a particular line of business, product line, or even an entire division. Once again, both quantitative and qualitative factors must be taken into account. This decision would entail the consideration of future income and costs. If incremental future income exceeds incremental future costs it would make economic sense to add this particular line of business, product line or division. It is also important to note that, similarly to the closing down decision, this decision affects the long term and should therefore be considered through qualitative factors.

10.4 Applying the concept of relevance to basic cost elements

So far our discussion has been focused on the concept of relevance, introducing the various elements underlying relevance, and discussing the thought process for the different types of decisions. This part of the text addresses some of the challenges you may experience in calculating a relevant cost. We will look at these with specific reference to materials and labour.

10.4.1 Materials

To put the challenges into perspective, let us think back to the special order decision. A special order may require a particular type of material that is used in the manufacture of another product. What would the consequences and the future costs be if the organisation used that material? Or perhaps the special order utilises a material that the organisation already has in inventory. What would the future cost of that material be for purposes of the special order?

Let us illustrate these concepts. Consider the information in example 10.7:

Example 10.7

Amandla Ltd manufactures hair care products for sale to the retail market. A Zimbabwe-based organisation has approached Amandla with a special order for a product which is different from current products sold by Amandla. In order to meet the order, Amandla will have to use certain raw materials, some of which are in inventory. The following schedule summarises the materials required, as well as those which are in inventory:

Materials code	Note	Quantity required	Quantity in inventory	Last cost price (R) per litre	Replacement value (R) per litre	Scrap value (R) per litre
AAA	1	100 litres	–	8	10	7
BBB	2	50 litres	50 litres	5	6	2
CCC	3	25 litres	30 litres	20	30	15
DDD	4	10 litres	15 litres	35	40	20

Notes:
1. AAA is used in the manufacture of Amandla's hair dye product. There is no shortage in supply of AAA.
2. BBB was purchased a few months ago in order to fulfil another special order. The special order was cancelled. Amandla had no other use for this material, and intended to sell it for scrap.
3. CCC is used in the manufacture of Amandla's hair shampoo product. There is no shortage in supply of CCC.
4. DDD is used in the manufacture of Amandla's hair conditioner product. One litre of DDD is used per 5 litre bottle of hair conditioner. There is currently such a serious shortage in supply of DDD that it is impossible to obtain in the short term. Amandla's hair conditioner product sells for R60 per 5 litre bottle, and incurs a variable cost (including the cost of DDD @ R35 per litre) of R50 per 5 litre bottle.

Required:
Determine the relevant costs related to the special order received.

Based on the information supplied in example 10.7, we can draw the following conclusions:

Materials code	Reason	Future cost/ Opportunity cost
AAA	AAA is not in inventory. Therefore it will have to be acquired for the purposes of the special order at R10 per litre. The relevant future cost is therefore R10 per litre × 100 litres = R1 000	Future cost = R1 000
BBB	BBB is in inventory. The cost price of R5 per litre is a sunk cost and is therefore irrelevant. BBB could have been sold as scrap. This means that there is an opportunity cost of R2 per litre × 50 litres = R100 (the income from the sale as scrap that is forgone). Note that, if BBB is used for this order, it would not have to be replaced into inventory (Amandla does not need BBB for any other purpose). The opportunity cost of R100 is therefore the only relevant cost.	Opportunity cost = R100
CCC	CCC is in inventory. The cost price of R20 per litre is a sunk cost and is therefore irrelevant. CCC is also used in Amandla's hair shampoo product. This means that any CCC litres used for the special order will have to be replaced. The replacement cost is R30 per litre × 25 litres = R750	Future cost = R750

principles of management accounting

Materials code	Reason	Future cost/ Opportunity cost
DDD	DDD is in inventory. The cost price of R35 per litre is a sunk cost and is therefore irrelevant. DDD is also used in Amandla's hair conditioning product. This means that any DDD litres used for the special order ought to be replaced. However, replacement is not possible owing to scarcity. This means that, unlike CCC above, DDD does not have a relevant replacement cost (and the R40 per litre is therefore irrelevant). However, the fact that units of DDD in inventory are required to fill the special order now means the hair conditioner cannot be manufactured. The opportunity cost of not being able to sell hair conditioner has to be calculated.	Opportunity cost = R450 (see calculation below)

Calculation of opportunity cost

Calculate the opportunity cost on the contribution lost method:

Lose external sales	(R60)
Save variable costs	R50
Contribution lost	(R10)
Additional variable costs (scarce resource)	(R35)
Total opportunity cost	(R45)

OR Calculate the opportunity cost on the sales lost method:

Lose external sales	(R60)
Save variable costs*	R15
Total opportunity cost	(R45)
* The cost of DDD will not be saved, as it is being used in the special order. Only R15 (other variable costs) will be saved.	

One litre of DDD is used per hair conditioning product. Therefore ten 5-litre bottles of the hair conditioning product will have to be sacrificed. The opportunity cost is 10 bottles × R45 = R450.

10.4.2 Labour

For the purposes of this discussion, it is important to distinguish between the variable cost component and the fixed cost component of labour.

Variable labour

When labourers are paid on an hourly basis and can be sourced and dismissed as and when needed, their wages constitute a variable cost. With this type of labour, there should be no idle capacity, as it is expected that the correct amount of labour would be obtained as and when needed. In a special order that requires the use of such labourers, generally the future cost would be the cost per hour multiplied by the number of hours required for the special order. This assumes that we are able to source sufficient labourers in order to fill the special order within normal business hours. However, situations could also arise where overtime is required, or where labourers who ordinarily work on other products of the organisation are required to work on the special order.

Fixed labour

In the case of salaried staff, the monthly salaries paid represent a fixed labour cost. Skilled higher-level staff usually receive salaries. Regardless of the actual number of hours worked, they receive their fixed salaries. Therefore, it is possible that such labour can be under-utilised, and that spare capacity may exist.

The same is true of wage workers who have a contractual agreement with the organisation and cannot be sourced and dismissed at will.

Let us apply these principles to the information in example 10.8.

Example 10.8

Amandla Ltd manufactures hair care products for sale to the retail market. A Zimbabwe-based organisation has approached Amandla Ltd with a special order for a product which is different from current products sold by Amandla. In order to meet the order, Amandla will have to use certain types of labour, all of which are currently either already employed or readily available. The following schedule summarises the labour hours required, as well as the availability thereof:

Type	Cost	Hours required for special order
Unskilled type A	R50 per hour	500
Unskilled type B	R75 per hour	700
Unskilled type C	R100 per hour	300
Semi-skilled	R40 000 per month	1 000
Skilled type D	R80 000 per month	600
Skilled type E	R120 000 per month	300

- Unskilled type A labour can be sourced and dismissed as needed. There is no limitation on the maximum number of labourers available.
- Unskilled type B labour can be sourced and dismissed as needed. A maximum of 500 normal hours are available for the special order; thereafter staff are prepared to work overtime at a 50 per cent premium on the normal rate.
- Unskilled type C labour can be sourced and dismissed as needed, but these workers are in short supply. Overtime is not an option. The labourers are currently being used on a hair shampoo production line. This production line generates a contribution (excluding the cost of labour) of R125 per type C labour hour.
- Semi-skilled labourers receive a fixed salary. 1 200 hours are available for the special order.
- Skilled type D labourers receive a fixed salary. Only 500 hours are currently available for the special order. An additional staff member can be employed at R20 000, which will make an additional 200 hours available.
- Skilled type E labourers receive a fixed salary. Only 100 hours are available for the special order, and this type of labour is in short supply. Hours can be freed up by reducing the scope of the hair conditioner production line, which currently yields a contribution of R175 per type E labour hour.

Required:
Determine the relevant future and opportunity cost related to the special order received in respect of each type of labour.

Let us look at the future cost of each type of labour in example 10.8 above.
- *Unskilled type A* is a variable cost, as it can be sourced as and when needed. As there is no limitation, the future cost would be R25 000 (R50 × 500).
- *Unskilled type B* is a variable cost. 500 normal hours are available, which means 200 are short. However, overtime is available. Therefore the future cost would be R60 000 ((500 normal hours × R75) + (200 × R75 × 1,5 overtime hours)).
- *Unskilled type C* is a variable cost, but in short supply. Overtime is not an option; therefore there is no future cost. This triggers an opportunity cost. The opportunity cost would be R37 500 (300 × R125).
- *Semi-skilled labour* is a fixed cost, but sufficient hours are available for the special order. As the cost is fixed, there is no relevant future cost.
- *Skilled type D* is a fixed cost. 100 hours are short, and an additional staff member will have to be employed. Therefore the future cost amounts to R20 000. As these types of employee receive a fixed salary, the R20 000 will have to be paid, regardless of how many additional hours are actually needed. There is no relevant future cost for the 500 hours currently available, as they constitute spare capacity.
- *Skilled type E* is a fixed cost. 200 hours are short, and there is no alternative supply. Therefore there is no future cost, and an opportunity cost is triggered. The opportunity cost will be R35 000 (200 × R175).

10.5 Decisions under conditions of uncertainty

In the previous sections we introduced three types of decisions, and then moved on to discuss the relevance of materials and labour. In these discussions we assumed that the variables in the decision were known with certainty. However, decisions in practice involve a large degree of uncertainty regarding the costs that will be incurred or the income that will be received, and this section of the chapter looks at techniques in order to quantify and account for this risk and uncertainty.

10.5.1 Probabilities

The likelihood that an event will occur is known as its probability, and this is normally measured on a scale of 0 to 1 (which can also be expressed as 0 per cent to 100 per cent). For example, the weatherman refers to a 20 per cent chance of rain occurring in Gauteng. What does this mean? The event is rain, and the probability of rain is 20 per cent (or 0,2). A probability of 0 would mean that there is no likelihood of the event occurring, while a probability of 1 (or 100 per cent) implies that the event will definitely occur. There are two outcomes in our simple example – rain will occur versus rain will not occur.

When we are dealing with a number of mutually exclusive possible outcomes for an event, each with a probability of occurrence, the sum of all the probabilities equals 1 (or 100 per cent). In our simple rain example above, the probability of rain occurring is 0,2 (or 20 per cent), and the probability of rain not occurring is 0,8 (or 80 per cent).

This information can be presented in a probability distribution. A probability distribution is a list of all possible outcomes associated with a particular event, and the probability attached to each outcome. The probability distribution for our rain example is as follows:

Event: Rain

Outcome	Probability
Rain will occur in Gauteng	0,2
Rain will not occur in Gauteng	0,8
	1,00

Probability distributions are useful in management decisions, since they allow management to consider not only the outcomes in a particular decision, but also the probabilities attached to each outcome. Consider the information in example 10.9:

Example 10.9

An organisation is contemplating whether it should manufacture hair shampoo or body soap. A research survey yields the following probability distribution for the profit that can be made from each product in the first year:

Event: Make hair shampoo

A Outcome (profit)	B Probability
R100 000	0,05
R110 000	0,25
R120 000	0,40
R130 000	0,20
R140 000	0,10
Total	**1,00**

Event: Make body soap

Outcome (profit)	Probability
R80 000	0,15
R110 000	0,10
R120 000	0,40
R140 000	0,10
R150 000	0,25
Total	**1,00**

Required:
Determine whether the organisation ought to manufacture hair shampoo or body soap. Base your decision on the expected outcome only.

principles of management accounting

The expected value for each alternative can be calculated as follows:

Event: Make hair shampoo

A	B	A × B
Outcome (profit)	Probability	Weight
R100 000	0,05	R5 000
R110 000	0,25	R27 500
R120 000	0,40	R48 000
R130 000	0,20	R26 000
R140 000	0,10	R14 000
Total	1,00	R120 500

Event: Make body soap

Outcome (profit)	Probability	Weight
R80 000	0,15	R12 000
R110 000	0,10	R11 000
R120 000	0,40	R48 000
R140 000	0,10	R14 000
R150 000	0,25	R37 500
Total	1,00	R122 500

The probability distribution in example 10.9 shows that there is a five per cent chance that a profit of R100 000 will be yielded if the organisation manufactures hair shampoo. We can also add together probabilities and say that there is a 70 per cent chance (40% + 20% + 10%) that profits will be R120 000 or more, and a 30 per cent chance (5% + 25%) that profits will be less than R120 000. We can do a similar calculation for the body soap product, and say that there is a 75 per cent chance (40% + 10% + 25%) that profits will be R120 000 or more, and a 25 per cent chance (15% + 10%) that profits will be less than R120 000.

10.5.2 Expected values

Expected values are calculated by weighing each of the outcomes (profits in example 10.9) by its related probability. This yields a single value, which is often referred to as the 'expected value'. The Chartered Institute of Management Accountants (CIMA) defines an expected value as the *'financial forecast of the outcome of a course of action multiplied by the probability of achieving that outcome. The probability is expressed as a value ranging from 0 to 1'*.

Statistically, the expected value is therefore the weighted arithmetic mean of the possible outcomes. The expected values for the products in example 10.9 are R120 500 for hair shampoo and R122 500 for body soap.

A profit of R120 000 has the highest chance of occurring for both products (it has a 40 per cent chance of occurring for hair shampoo, and the same for body soap). However, if the events were to be repeated numerous times in the long run, it is expected that a R120 500 profit would result from manufacturing hair shampoo and a R122 500 profit from body soap.

Management would be inclined to choose to manufacture body soap owing to its higher expected value. However, management should also note that there is a 15 per cent chance that profits for body soap could be only R80 000. The hair shampoo product has only a five per cent chance of a lower profit of R100 000. So it appears that the body soap product has the higher expected value, but may carry a higher risk.

10.5.3 Decision trees

So far in this chapter we have concentrated on uncertainty in one variable – in example 10.9, future profits were uncertain. However, in practice the outcome of one event may be dependent on the outcome of another. In such circumstances a decision tree may be employed.

A decision tree diagram consists of several branches to reflect the various choices, events and possible outcomes for a decision. A decision tree is intended to depict all the possible outcomes and the probability of each. Let us explain the workings of a decision tree using an illustration in example 10.10:

Example 10.10

Coega Ltd is an oil drilling organisation operating on the east coast of South Africa. They are currently contemplating the drilling of a new site.

Coega will have to drill 30 metres into the ground in order to establish whether oil lies below. This will cost R1 000 000 per drill. Experts say that there is a 60 per cent chance of finding oil. If oil is found, demand is uncertain, and the following probability distribution will apply for the different demand levels:

Demand	Probability	Profit/(Loss) (drilling expense has not been deducted)
High	0,3	R11 000 000
Medium	0,3	R7 000 000
Low	0,4	(R500 000)

Required:
Employ a decision tree to advise whether Coega should drill for oil at the new site.

In example 10.10, it should be clear that there are two uncertain variables:
- Existence of oil
- Demand.

Furthermore, a dependency exists between the variables. The demand for oil will need to be considered only if oil exists. Therefore, a decision tree is required.

We can prepare a decision tree for example 10.10 as follows:

Figure 10.2 Decision tree for example 10.10

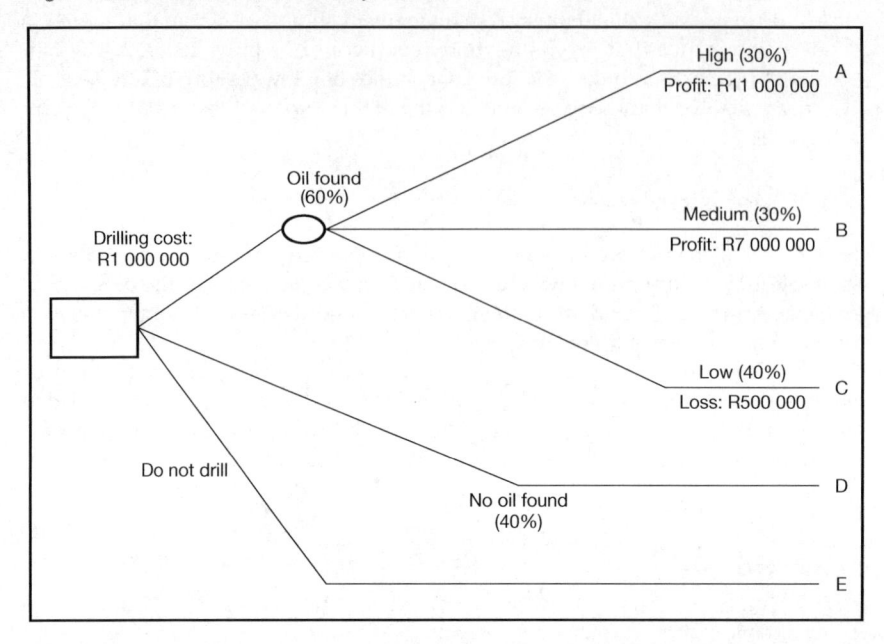

```
                                                              High (30%)
                                                              Profit: R11 000 000    A

                              Oil found
                               (60%)
                                                              Medium (30%)
   Drilling cost:                                             Profit: R7 000 000     B
   R1 000 000

                                                              Low (40%)
                                                              Loss: R500 000         C

       Do not drill
                                                                                     D
                                  No oil found
                                    (40%)
                                                                                     E
```

Take note of the use of boxes and circles in the decision tree. The boxes indicate a point where a decision needs to be taken. For example, a decision needs to be taken whether the drilling should proceed or not. In contrast, a circle reflects a point where an event occurs, the outcome of which is uncertain. The organisation has no control over the outcome, and probabilities are attached to do the different outcomes that flow from the event.

Also take note of the fact that demand is dependent on oil being found: Coega would not be concerned about the level of demand if oil were not found. Therefore, we can calculate the joint probability of oil being found AND demand being high by multiplying the probability of oil found (60 per cent) by the high demand probability of 30 per cent, which amounts to a joint probability of 18 per cent. We can calculate a joint probability of 18 per cent for the oil found and medium demand combination, and a joint probability of 24 per cent for oil found and low demand. Using these probabilities, we can prepare the following probability distribution for each decision and its related expected value:

Decision: Drill

Outcome	Probability	Net cash inflow	Expected value (R)
A: Oil found and high demand	0,18	R11 000 000 – R1 000 000 = R10 000 000	1 800 000
B: Oil found and medium demand	0,18	R7 000 000 – R1 000 000 = R6 000 000	1 080 000
C: Oil found and low demand	0,24	R500 000 – R1 000 000 = (R1 500 000)	–360 000
D: No oil found	0,40	(R1 000 000)	–400 000
Total	1,00		2 120 000

Decision: Do not drill

E: Expected value = R0

Take note that the total of all probabilities for the *drill decision* is equal to 1. Using these probabilities, we can calculate an expected value of R2 120 000. Remember, the expected value is not a guaranteed profit, but rather represents the long-run average profit that would result if the actions were performed many times over. If the organisation does not drill, the expected value is zero. Given the expected value, the decision should be accepted as it yields an expected net cash inflow of R2 120 000. However, the organisation must take specific note that there is a 64 per cent (Outcome C's 24% + Outcome D's 40%) chance of a loss arising, and only a 36 per cent (Outcome A's 18% + Outcome B's 18%) chance that a profit will arise. Therefore, the ultimate decision will be based on the organisation's appetite for risk.

10.6 The pricing decision

This chapter focuses on the decision-making aspect of the management accountant's function. We have already addressed short-term decision making. The management accountant's role, however, also includes the pricing decision, which simply entails the process of deciding on the best selling prices for organisations' products or services. It affects almost all organisations as all their products or services must be priced. The pricing decision is of the utmost importance, as the selling price directly affects the performance, and ultimately the value, of an organisation.

It is important to understand what effect this decision has on the profitability of an organisation. Gross profit is sales less cost of sales (product costs). In order to improve the gross profit percentage of an organisation either the selling price must be increased, or the cost of sales (product costs) must be reduced. Gross profit will also increase in absolute terms when either the selling price or the sales volume increases. Sales volume can be increased through several actions taken. One of these techniques is to reduce the selling price of a product or service. A reduced selling price may increase demand and although this would have a negative impact on the gross profit percentage, it may lead to an increased gross profit in absolute terms. It is evident that the correct sales price affects not only the gross profit percentage but also gross profit in absolute terms.

This section will look first at the difference between a price taker and a price setter. We will then discuss the impact of selling prices on the demand for products and services. The difference between cost-plus pricing and target costing will be explored. The pricing decision differs over the short and long term. This difference will be explored further, and finally a number of pricing strategies will also be briefly discussed.

10.6.1 Price takers versus price setters

Key terms: price setter, price taker

Organisations can be classified, in terms of their products or services, as either a **price setter** or a **price taker**. A price taker's product or service price is largely determined by market supply and demand. These products or services are normally not differentiated in the market, and the organisation's product or service is as good as its competitor's. Organisations selling commodities (for example, agricultural products such as maize) are usually price takers, as prices are set by the market.

In contrast, a price setter organisation is in a position to set the price for its product or service. Normally this will be the case where the organisation is the market leader, or it has a product which is significantly different from what is available on the rest of the market (there is low competition). For example, DSTV in South Africa can be considered a price setter (even with the entrance of competitors into this market, it remains the market leader for the time being).

10.6.2 Price elasticity

Key term: price elasticity

Price elasticity refers to the price versus demand relationship of a specific product or service. Generally speaking, as the selling price of a product or service is increased, the demand decreases. If the selling price of a product or service is decreased, the demand usually increases. Consider the automotive industry as an example: there are generally significantly more affordable cars on our roads than expensive cars. This is the case because lower selling prices result in higher demand.

Now that we are familiar with the price versus demand relationship, let us investigate this relationship further for a specific product or service. In the case of some products or services, there is little or no impact on demand when the selling price changes – we say that the demand for these products or services is inelastic. When there is a significant impact on demand when the selling price of a product or service changes, we say that the demand for these products or services is elastic. An example of an inelastic product is luxury items such as 'brand name' clothes. The demand is not significantly affected by the selling price. An example of an elastic product is bread: if the selling price is increased by one supplier, demand decreases significantly, because the customer is likely to buy bread (or a similar product) from another supplier. In practice, no product or service is completely inelastic, as this would mean that any price could be charged without reducing demand. It's rather a question of *how* elastic the product or service is, and how this information can best be used when making a pricing decision.

An organisation estimates and calculates which combination of selling price and unit sales (demand) will maximise contribution. Fixed costs – those that are fixed over the timespan of the pricing decision – are ignored, as they are irrelevant.

10.6.3 Cost-plus pricing versus target costing

Key terms: cost-plus pricing, target cost, target costing

Cost-plus pricing is a simple yet widely used method of pricing. It involves accumulating product costs and then adding a profit margin to determine the selling price. Accumulating product costs is also known as inventory valuation and can be done using variable or absorption costing (refer to Chapter 5, *Absorption versus variable costing*).

The principle behind using inventory valuation as a starting point for determining a selling price is to ensure that all costs incurred that relate to the product or service are recovered. Although this method ignores many other important considerations, it can often be a valuable starting point to the pricing decision. Some practical difficulties with cost-plus pricing are that it is difficult to decide on the profit margin, and that the resulting calculated selling price may not be the optimal selling price in the market.

Target costing, on the other hand, starts by first determining the selling price that will be accepted by the market. In other words, the selling price is determined by performing market research, taking into account estimated market share, assumed market demand, growth opportunities, and so on. After the selling price is determined, the required profit margin is deducted (again, it may be difficult to decide on an appropriate profit margin). The amount remaining after this deduction is then referred to as the target cost. The organisation proceeds by designing and re-designing the product or service as best it can in an effort to produce it within the target cost.

Note that, very often, organisations that use target costing base their decisions on medium- to long-term projections. They may not make a profit in the short term, but may be willing to accept such losses, because over time they are expecting significant cost savings owing to economies of scale and the learning effect (which means that, in theory, every unit produced should cost slightly less than the previous one).

In conclusion: the cost-plus approach starts with the cost and calculates the selling price, whereas target costing starts with the selling price and calculates the target cost.

Target costing is also discussed in Chapter 17, *Competitive advantage*.

10.6.4 Short-term pricing

Key term: short-term pricing

Organisations may encounter short-term, once-off, special order decisions from time to time. When this situation occurs, short-term relevancy principles (as already discussed in this chapter) should be applied (refer to example 10.2). A price setter would most likely need to determine the selling price of such a short-term special order (this is referred to as **short-term pricing**), and it is important to apply relevancy principles to ensure that the organisation covers at least all relevant costs. A price taker's customer would most likely indicate what price it is willing to pay for the special order, and the price taker would then decide whether it ought to accept this special order or not. In essence, this is not a pricing decision but rather an accept-or-reject decision.

10.6.5 Long-term pricing

Key term: long-term pricing

Short-term pricing is relevant to once-off special orders. When deciding on a selling price of a once-off special order, we therefore ignore fixed costs, as we argued their irrelevance. The reality, however, is that fixed costs must be covered over the long term in order to be profitable. Therefore, when deciding on a selling price for products or services over the long term, an organisation must ensure that all costs relating to these products or services are covered. All costs must be covered by sales revenue irrespective of whether these costs are fixed or variable in nature. This is known as **long-term pricing**.

When considering an organisation as a whole, it is evident that sales must cover all the expenses the organisation incurs in order to ensure a profit is made. It is important to track all these expenses to specific products or services in order to price them accurately. If too few costs are allocated to a product and cost-plus pricing is used, there is a risk of making a loss, as prices may be set too low. If too many costs are allocated and cost-plus pricing is used, the risk arises that the selling price could be set too high and potential sales may be lost. It may be impractical for all costs to be allocated to specific products or services, but to ensure profitability, the organisation's total costs must be lower than the total sales revenue.

Activity-based costing can be used as a tool to allocate overhead costs accurately to products or services (refer to Chapter 6, *Overhead allocation*).

10.6.6 Pricing strategies

> **Key terms:** loss leader, penetration pricing, premium pricing, price skimming, pricing strategies, product bundling, product differentiation

The pricing decision does not involve only mathematical calculations – customer behaviour should also be considered. Various **pricing strategies** exist which can assist organisations in their pricing decisions. A number of these strategies are briefly explained below:

Price skimming

Price skimming entails setting a high initial price while the product or service is new on the market and while certain customers are willing to pay this high price. As this market becomes saturated, the price is reduced to attract the more price-sensitive customers.

Premium pricing

A **premium pricing** strategy entails the setting of a high selling price to encourage a favourable perception of the product or service amongst customers. This strategy relies on the perception that expensive products are of a better quality.

Penetration pricing

Penetration pricing entails a low initial selling price in order to quickly enter the market and to build up market share. This strategy is normally adopted when substitute products or services exist. The price may be increased later when the product or service is well-established in the market.

Loss leader

A **loss leader** is a product or service sold at a very low price (sometimes below cost) to attract customers in the hope that they will buy other profitable goods. This pricing strategy is often followed by supermarkets, or by the manufacturers of items such as razors for shaving (the razor is often reasonably priced in order to 'hook' the customer, who must then repeat-purchase specific razor blades that fit the razor. The company primarily makes its profit on the blades).

Product bundling/optional extras

Product bundling entails bundling multiple products or services and then selling them together. The reasoning behind this is that customers feel they receive good value for money, so they buy more products. This pricing policy is widely used in the fast food industry (for example, a special price for a meal consisting of a burger, chips and a soft drink).

Product differentiation

In order to sell a product or service, the offering must either be competitively priced, or must be different from that offered by competitors. Making a product or service different from the ones already on the market is called **product differentiation**. When a product or service is not different from other products available on the market, an organisation could end up being a price-taker and as a result not have much pricing power. Differentiation could ensure more pricing power by allowing an organisation to move towards becoming a price setter. A product or service can be differentiated in many ways, such as offering a different level of quality, different features, a different level of sales or after-sales service, and so on. Note that in a differentiation strategy, the emphasis is on making the product or service *different*. Also refer to Chapter 17 for a discussion on Porter's generic strategies.

10.7 Summary

The most important principle underlying decision-making is that only costs and income that differ between alternatives are relevant. This chapter illustrated this principle in three frequently-encountered situations, but it can be applied in other decision-making scenarios as well. The chapter also addressed the problem of inputs into a decision often not being known with certainty in practice. The last part of the chapter addressed the importance of the pricing decision for the management accountant.

Conclusion: Relevant costs for decision-making and other topics in this book

Because management accountants supply information to facilitate management's decision-making, the issue of relevant costs and relevant income is key to many aspects of their work. Relevant information principles are frequently examined by professional bodies, because they are key to understanding management accounting, and easily integrated with other topics.

principles of management accounting

> **Tutorial case study: Tendering in the pharmaceutical industry**

Manufacturers of pharmaceutical products in South Africa, such as *Enaleni* and *Adcock Ingram*, have seen unprecedented growth, despite strict regulation of the pharmaceutical industry by the government.

Let's assume that one of these manufacturers is tendering for a sizeable government order for the production of antiretroviral drugs, something that has not been done by the organisation in the past.

The organisation runs a very lean operation, with limited excess capacity. In order to fulfil the government order, they may have to cease production temporarily of certain over-the-counter drugs.

Fixed overheads are low (they rent factories in low-cost regions, such as parts of the Eastern Cape), and the majority of the labour force is permanently employed, as this works out cheaper in the long run than using temporary labour.

Assume that the management of the organisation manufacturing pharmaceuticals is not too concerned about having to cease production temporarily of certain over-the-counter drugs, as they believe that customers will continue to buy the drugs, even though they may be unavailable for a few weeks. As an alternative, they could expand an existing factory, and use the capacity created to focus on special government tenders.

From a regulatory perspective, the organisation would have to appoint a supervisor accredited by the Medicines Control Council, and ensure that they meet the appropriate empowerment criteria. Given the social impact of antiretroviral drugs, government has promised certain tax incentives in future for producers of these drugs, such as accelerated 'wear-and-tear' allowances on equipment.

1. Describe how you would go about assessing whether you agree with management's decision to cease production temporarily of certain over-the-counter drugs.
2. Discuss how the temporary halting of production of certain over-the-counter drugs may impact on the pricing of the government tender.
3. Discuss how the expansion of the factory should be evaluated, and whether this is a long-term or a short-term decision.
4. Discuss whether management should consider discontinuing a portion of the existing product lines to create capacity in order to focus exclusively on government tenders.
5. Speculate on what qualitative factors government might consider in awarding the tender.
6. Discuss whether the tax incentives proposed, but not yet enacted, are a relevant factor to consider in the decision regarding the government tender.

Basic questions

BQ 1

What is the difference between relevant costs and irrelevant costs?

BQ 2

How would you go about deciding between two investments with different returns and risks? Explain your understanding of the measures of risk and return. *(You need some knowledge of statistical measures carried over from previous chapters to answer this question.)*

BQ 3

What are the differences and similarities between quantitative and qualitative relevant information?

BQ 4
How can uncertainty be taken into account in short-term decisions?

BQ 5
What is an opportunity cost, and how does it arise?

BQ 6
Source: Adapted from ACCA Paper 1.2

An organisation wants to purchase a new machine for R150 000 to perform a contract. The machine will cost R25 000 to instal and will have a scrap value of R10 000 in 5 years. It is depreciated on the straight-line basis over 5 years.

What is the relevant cost of the machine for the contract?
a) R140 000
b) R150 000
c) R165 000
d) R175 000

BQ 7
Source: Adapted from ACCA Paper 1.2

i) Materials can never have an opportunity cost, while labour can.
ii) The annual depreciation charge is not a relevant cost.
iii) Fixed costs will have a relevant cost element if a decision causes a change in the total expense.

Which statements are true?
a) (i) and (ii) only
b) (i) and (iii) only
c) (ii) and (iii) only
d) (i), (ii) and (iii)

BQ 8
Source: University of Johannesburg Archive

A company is considering a contract which will require, among other inputs, 50 kilograms of material M. Eighty kilograms of material M, which were purchased for R1,60 per kilogram, are in inventory. The replacement price of M is R1,75 per kilogram. The material is in inventory as a result of a buying error, and the company has no other use for it. If not used on this contract, it could be sold for R1,20 per kilogram.

What is the relevant cost of the material to be used in this contract?

BQ 9
Source: Adapted from ACCA Paper 1.2

An organisation's skilled labour, which earns R8 per hour, is fully utilised in manufacturing the following product:
- Selling price R60 per unit
- Variable cost R35 per unit (R20 skilled labour and R15 other costs)

The organisation considers a contract requiring 90 skilled labour hours. No other skilled labour is available.

What is the relevant skilled labour cost for the contract?
a) R720
b) R900
c) R1 620
d) R2 160

BQ 10

Source: Adapted from ACCA Paper 1.2

An organisation considers a contract that requires two types of materials, T and V.

	Required for project	In inventory	Original price	Current price	Re-sale price
T	500 kg	100 kg	R40 per kg	R45 per kg	R44 per kg
V	400 kg	200 kg	R55 per kg	R52 per kg	R40 per kg

Material T is regularly used. Material V is no longer used and has no alternative use in the business.

What is the total relevant cost of materials for the project?
a) R40 400
b) R40 900
c) R43 400
d) R43 900

Long questions

LQ 1 – Intermediate (22 marks; 40 minutes)

Source: University of Johannesburg archive

The management of Computer Development Limited is considering marketing a new application software package. The package will also include a hardware portion in the form of a graphic monitor. The costs associated with this project are as follows:
i) Development costs of R200 000 with a 70 per cent chance of success.
ii) Manufacturing costs:
   - Management could service the existing machinery (carrying amount R Nil and remaining life 14 years) which could manufacture the hardware at a cost of R1 000 000. The variable costs per package which will be offered for sale will in this case amount to R2 000 per package.
   - Otherwise, they could invest in new machinery (which also has an expected life of 14 years) at a cost price of R2 000 000. However, the difference lies in the fact that the variable costs per package will now amount to only R1 000.
iii) Marketing information
   - Management is considering a selling price of R6 000 per package.
   - The following information was obtained through market research:

Condition of economy	Sales volume (number of packages)	Probability of selling at a price of R6 000 per package
Boom phase	1 000	40%
Recovery phase	500	40%
Recession	50	20%

REQUIRED	Marks
Advise the management of Computer Development Limited, by means of a decision tree, on whether or not they should undertake the project. *(Note:* Management wishes to write off the cost price of the machinery completely within the first year of production.)	22
TOTAL MARKS	22

LQ 2 – Intermediate (25 marks; 45 minutes)

Source: Adapted from CIMA Stage 1 Operational Cost Accounting

You have received a request from EXE Ltd to provide a quotation for the manufacture of a specialised piece of equipment. This would be a one-off order, in excess of normal budgeted production. The following cost estimate has already been prepared:

		Note	R
Direct materials:			
Steel	10 m² at R5,00 per m²	1	50
Brass fittings		2	20
Direct labour:			
Skilled	25 hours at R8,00 per hour	3	200
Semi-skilled	10 hours at R5,00 per hour	4	50
Overhead	35 hours at R10,00 per hour	5	350
Estimating time		6	100
			770
Administrative overheads at 20% of production cost		7	154
			924
Profit at 25% of total cost		8	231
Selling price			1 155

Notes:
1. The steel is regularly used, and has a current inventory value of R5,00 per m². There are currently 100 m² in inventory. The steel is readily available at a price of R5,50 per m².
2. The brass fittings would have to be bought specifically for this job. A supplier has quoted the price of R20 for the fittings required.
3. The skilled labour is currently employed by your organisation and paid at a rate of R8,00 per hour. If this job were undertaken it would be necessary either to work 25 hours overtime, which would be paid at time plus one half, or to reduce production of another product which earns a contribution of R13,00 per skilled labour hour.
4. The semi-skilled labour currently has sufficient paid idle time to be able to complete this work.

5 The overhead absorption rate includes power costs which are directly related to machine usage. If this job were undertaken, it is estimated that the machine time required would be ten hours. The machines incur power costs of R0,75 per hour. There are no other overhead costs which can be specifically identified with this job.
6 The cost of the estimating time is made up of the four hours taken by the engineers to analyse the drawings and determine the cost estimate given above.
7 It is the policy of the organisation to add 20 per cent to the production cost as an allowance against administration costs.
8 This is the standard profit added by your organisation as part of its pricing policy.

REQUIRED		Marks
(a)	Prepare, on a relevant cost basis, the lowest cost estimate that could be used as the basis for a quotation. Explain briefly your reasons for using each of the values in your estimate, and/or show the calculation.	12
(b)	There may be a possibility of repeat orders from EXE Ltd which would occupy part of normal production capacity. Discuss the factors that need to be considered before quoting for this order.	7
(c)	When an organisation identifies that it has a single production resource which is in short supply, but is used by more than one product, the optimum production plan is determined by ranking the products according to their contribution per unit of the scarce resource. Using a numerical example of your own, reconcile this approach with the opportunity cost approach used in part (a) above. (*Note:* Candidates who have already studied Chapter 11 will find this requirement easier.)	6
TOTAL MARKS		25

LQ 3 – Intermediate (20 marks; 36 minutes)

Source: University of Johannesburg Archive

Klipfontein Construction CC produces metal drums that the mines use to move equipment. The organisation's normal production volume is 3 000 units, which is also its budgeted monthly sales.

Information with regard to June 2XX0:

Production volume	3 000 units	4 000 units
Manufacturing costs per unit:	R	R
Materials	100	100
Variable labour	150	150
Variable overheads	50	50
Fixed overheads allocation rate	120	120
Total marketing costs	570 000	620 000

Additional information:
- The normal selling price per unit is R740.
- Marketing costs are composed of a monthly contract fee and a commission fee charged for every unit sold locally. These are payable on *all* local orders.
- The production capacity of the company is 4 000 units.
- Actual fixed overheads were equal to budgeted fixed overheads
- The organisation does not hold an inventory of finished goods.

Foreign market proposal

The CC has an opportunity to enter a foreign market in which price competition is strong. Klipfontein is keen to follow up this opportunity because the foreign market demand occurs at a time of year when local demand is at its lowest. An order for 1 000 units is being sought, but this order will need to be priced below the normal market price to be competitive. For this order there will be an additional cost of R75 per unit for shipping. Klipfontein will have to pay an agent's fee of R4 000 if the order is accepted. They will also need to buy a wrapping machine for wrapping the units before shipping. The cost of the wrapping machine will be R300 000 and it will be sold after completion of the order for an estimated amount of R280 000.

Business Forum special order

On 10 June 2XX0, the Johannesburg Business Forum requests the supply of 1500 units to re-stock the mines for a 30 June 2XX0 delivery. They are willing to pay R600 per unit.

REQUIRED		Marks
(a)	Assume that the foreign market proposal can be contracted at a selling price of R600 per unit. Advise whether Klipfontein Construction CC should accept the Business Forum special order or the foreign market order, assuming that they are mutually exclusive.	10
(b)	Market research indicates that the sales volume is likely to increase from 3 000 units to 4 000 units if the selling price is reduced from R740 to R650 per unit.	
	(i) Calculate the margin of safety as well as the total contribution under both of these price-volume relationships. (Ignore the foreign market proposal as well as the Business Forum special order.)	8
	(ii) By referring to your calculation in (i) above, comment on the selling price on which Klipfontein ought to decide. (Ignore the foreign market proposal as well as the Business Forum special order.)	2
TOTAL MARKS		20

LQ 4 – Advanced (28 marks; 50 minutes)

Source: University of Johannesburg Archive

Umdoni Ltd currently publish, print and distribute a range of catalogues and instruction manuals. The management have now decided to discontinue printing and distribution and concentrate solely on publishing. Nongoma Ltd will print and distribute the range of catalogues and instruction manuals on behalf of Umdoni Ltd commencing either at 30 June 2XX0 or at 30 November 2XX0. Nongoma Ltd will receive R65 000 per month for a contract which will commence on either 30 June 2XX0 or 30 November 2XX0.

The results of Umdoni Ltd for a typical month are as follows:

	Publishing (R'000)	Printing (R'000)	Distribution (R'000)
Salaries and wages	28	18	4
Materials and supplies	5,5	31	1,1
Occupancy costs	7	8,5	1,2
Depreciation	0,8	4,2	0,7

Additional information:

Further information relating to the possible closure proposals is as follows:

i) Two specialist staff from the printing department will be retained at their present salary of R6 500 each per month in order to liaise with Nongoma Ltd. One further staff member will be transferred to publishing to fill a staff vacancy through staff turnover, anticipated in July. This staff member will be paid at his present salary of R3 000 per month, which is R100 more than that of the staff member who is expected to leave. On closure, all other printing and distribution staff will be made redundant and paid an average of two months' salary in redundancy pay.

ii) The printing department has a supply of materials (already paid for) which cost R18 000 and which will be sold to Nongoma Ltd for R10 000 if closure takes place on 30 June 2XX0. Otherwise the material will be used as part of the July 2XX0 printing requirements. The distribution department has a contract to purchase pallets at a cost of R500 per month for both July and August 2XX0. A cancellation clause allows for non-delivery of pallets for July and August at a one-off cancellation fee of R300. Non-delivery for August only will require a cancellation fee payment of R100. However, if the purchase contract of the pallets is honoured and not cancelled, Nongoma Ltd has agreed to purchase them from Umdoni Ltd at a price of R380 for each month's supply which is available. Pallet costs are included in the distribution material and supplies cost stated for a typical month.

iii) Company expenditure on apportioned occupancy costs to printing and distribution will be reduced by 15% per month if the printing and distribution departments are closed. At present, 30% of printing and 25% of distribution occupancy costs are directly attributable costs which are avoidable on closure, whilst the remainder are apportioned costs.

iv) Closure of the printing and distribution departments will make it possible to sub-let part of the building for a monthly fee of R2 500 when space is available.

v) 'Printing plant and machinery' in total has an estimated net carrying amount of R48 000 at 30 June 2XX0. It is anticipated that it will be sold at a loss of R21 000 on 30 June 2XX0. If it is sold on 30 November 2XX0, the prospective buyer will pay R25 000.

vi) The net carrying amount of distribution vehicles at 30 June 2XX0 is estimated as R80 000. The vehicles could be sold to the original supplier for R48 000 on 30 June 2XX0, or the original supplier could purchase the vehicles on 30 November 2XX0 at a price of R44 000.

REQUIRED		Marks
(a)	Advise Umdoni Ltd whether the printing and distribution departments should ideally be closed on 30 June 2XX0, or on 30 November 2XX0.	14
(b)	Explain the approach that Umdoni's management ought to have followed in determining whether or not to close the printing and distribution departments.	3
(c)	Explain what factors, other than financial factors, Umdoni ought to have considered in the decision as described in part (b).	5
(d)	Briefly comment on the extent to which you agree with the following statements: (i) 'As a rule, fixed costs are irrelevant to decision-making.' (ii) 'ABC information is used for decision-making purposes.'	3 3
TOTAL MARKS		**28**

LQ 5 – Advanced (20 marks; 36 minutes)

Source: Adapted from CIMA P2

H, a printing company, uses traditional absorption costing to report its monthly profits. It is seeking to increase its business by winning work from new customers. It now has the opportunity to prepare a quotation for a large organisation that currently requires a new catalogue of its services.

A technical report on the resource requirements for the catalogue has been completed at a cost of R1 000, and its details are summarised below:

Production period
It is expected that the total time required to print and despatch the catalogue will be one week.

Material A
10 000 sheets of special printing paper will be required. This is a paper that is in regular use by H and the company has 3 400 sheets in inventory. These originally cost R1,40 per sheet, but the current market price is R1,50 per sheet. The resale price of the sheets held in inventory is R1,20 per sheet.

Material B
This is a special ink that H will need to purchase at a cost of R8 per litre. 200 litres will be required for this catalogue, but the supplier has a minimum order size of 250 litres. H does not foresee any other use for this ink, but cannot sell it, and will therefore hold the surplus in inventory. H's inventory policy is to review slow-moving items regularly. The cost of any inventory item that has not been used for more than 6 months is accounted for as an expense of the period in which that review occurs.

Direct labour
Sufficient people are already employed by H to print the catalogue, but some of the printing will require overtime working owing to the availability of a particular machine that is used on other work. The employees are normally paid R8 per hour. The order will require 150 hours of work, and 50 of these hours will be in excess of the employees' normal working week. A rate of R10 per hour is paid for these overtime hours. Employees are paid using an hourly rate with a guaranteed minimum wage for their normal working week.

Supervision
A supervisor will take responsibility for the catalogue in addition to her existing duties. She is not currently fully employed and receives a salary of R500 per week.

Machinery
Two different types of machine will be required. Machine A will print the catalogue. This is expected to take 20 hours of machine time. The running cost of machine A is R5 per hour. There is currently 30 hours of unused time on machine A per week that is being sold to other printers for R12 per hour. Machine A cannot operate after hours.

Machine B will be used to cut and bind the catalogue. This machine is being used to full capacity in the normal working week and this is why there is a need to work overtime. The catalogue will require 25 machine hours, and these machines have a running cost of R4 per hour.

Dispatch
There will be a delivery cost of R400 to transport the catalogue to the customer.
Fixed overhead costs
H uses a traditional absorption costing system to attribute fixed overhead costs to its work. The absorption rate that it uses is R20 per direct labour hour.

Profit mark-up
H applies a 30 per cent mark-up to its costs to determine its selling prices.

REQUIRED		Marks
(a)	To assist the management of H in preparing its quotation, prepare a schedule showing the relevant costs for the production of the catalogue. State clearly your reason for including or excluding each amount that has been provided in the above scenario.	15
(b)	Explain how the use of relevant costs as the basis of setting a selling price may be appropriate for short-term pricing decisions but may be inappropriate for long-term pricing decisions. Also discuss the conflict between reporting profitability within a traditional absorption costing system and the use of relevant cost-based pricing.	5
TOTAL MARKS		20

References

Eaton, G. 2005. *Management accounting official terminology.* London: CIMA Publishing.
Fifa World Cup South Africa. 2010. *Government preparations for the 2010 FIFA world cup.* [Online]. Available: <sa2010.gov.za/en/highlights – 2010> [20 April 2011].

Decision-making under operational constraints

chapter 11

Appie Pienaar

LEARNING OBJECTIVES

By the end of this chapter, you should be able to:
1 Understand the concept of contribution per limiting factor.
2 Apply linear programming to resolve contribution maximisation problems where there are two or more scarce resources.
3 Calculate shadow prices.
4 Interpret the final table of a simplex tableau.
5 Evaluate the use of linear programming.

> **McCain and decision-making under operational constraints**
>
> The food manufacturer *McCain* sells a range of frozen foods. Its South African operations are managed from its offices in Bedfordview, Johannesburg. One of McCain's standard supermarket product lines is bagged frozen potatoes, and it also uses potatoes as an ingredient in other products such as its frozen cottage pies and 'veggie fingers'. In the third quarter of 2010, South Africa experienced a potato shortage as a result of adverse climatic conditions which had affected local crops. McCain South Africa struggled to find enough fresh potatoes which met the company's specifications for processing. It tried to procure suitable potatoes from its global network, but Europe was experiencing drought at the time and the North American farmers had not yet harvested their crops. McCain announced that, despite its efforts, shortages were likely to persist in South Africa for a few months. The company promised to keep exploring possible solutions to address the problem and to minimise any negative consequences to customers.
>
> *Source: Fin24 2011*

McCain faced what is known as an operational constraint. In this case study, the constraint is a scarce resource, namely potatoes. A key question that arises is how the company could best make use of the limited amount of potatoes that it does have available. Should McCain spread its limited potato inventory across the different product lines that make use of potatoes so that at least some units of each product line are manufactured? Should the company rather package as many frozen potatoes as they can, or perhaps manufacture as many cottage pies or veggie fingers as possible? The principles in this chapter help organisations such as McCain to make the most sensible decisions when faced with operational constraints.

11.1 Introduction

In every organisation it may be possible to find a constraining factor, some barrier preventing it from unimpeded growth and expansion. Very often this constraining factor is the market demand for the organisation's products or services, which can be partially addressed by implementing more effective marketing techniques. This scenario falls outside the scope of this chapter. However, other factors such as a shortage of manpower, limited machine capacity, or scarce raw materials may also be constraining factors. In the medium to long term, these problems can usually be overcome by, for example, appointing more staff, purchasing another machine, or importing raw materials.

In the short term, however, while more sustainable solutions are being sought and implemented, the organisation will have to manage the constraining factors to the best of its ability.

Alternatively, an organisation may find itself in a position where there is a temporary capacity constraint, such as when a once-off special order has been received. If there is insufficient capacity to meet the order, a choice has to be made as to whether it ought to be accepted at the expense of normal production.

Whatever the cause of the constraint, management has to decide which products or services should receive preference. From a purely financial perspective, preference ought to be given to those products or services that utilise the scarce resource(s) in the most profitable manner.

11.2 Limiting factors

11.2.1 A single limiting factor

Key terms: constraint, limiting factor

A **limiting factor** or **constraint** is a scarce resource of which there is a limited supply and which affects the ability of the organisation to earn profits.

As already mentioned, examples of limiting factors are:
- Shortage of manpower, for example skilled labour
- Limited machine capacity
- Scarce raw materials, for example some metal ores.

Example 11.1

Mary Craven produces two products, pillows and duvets, from the down that she gets from the geese on her Karoo farm.
Contribution per unit is as follows:

	Pillow R	Duvet R
Selling price	300	1 000
Direct labour at R25 per hour	(50)	(200)
Goose down at R100 per kg	(100)	(300)
Other fabrics	(40)	(200)
Variable overheads at R15 per labour hour	(30)	(120)
Contribution	80	180

Owing to a lack of poultry farming activities in the area, the availability of goose down is limited to 300 kg per month. The monthly demand for Mary's products is 240 pillows and 150 duvets.

Required:
Determine the product mix that would maximise Mary's contribution.

Our first reaction may be to argue that duvets have a higher contribution per unit than pillows (R180 compared to R80) and that Mary should therefore focus her effort on the production of duvets. We can see that one duvet requires 3 kg of goose down (R300/R100/kg). If only duvets were produced, she would be able to produce 100 duvets per month (300 kg down available/3 kg per duvet). Mary's total contribution would be R18 000 per month (100 duvets × R180 contribution).

However, we cannot simply focus on the contribution per unit alone. We need to establish to what extent a product consumes the specific scarce resource.

If Mary, for example, opts to produce 240 pillows in order to satisfy the total monthly demand and then use the remaining 60 kg [(300 kg – (R100/R100/kg) × 240)] to produce a further 20 duvets (R60kg/3kg per duvet), she could increase the total contribution as follows:

	R
Contribution from 240 pillows (240 × R80)	19 200
Contribution from 20 duvets (20 × R180)	3 600
	22 800

Owing to their economical use of the scarce resource, the preferential production of pillows results in a contribution of R22 800 instead of R18 000. Profit is therefore maximised when the maximum possible number of pillows is manufactured.

The calculation to determine the more profitable of the two products is as follows:

	Pillow R	Duvet R
Contribution	80	180
Kg down used	1	3
Contribution per kg down used	80	60
Ranking	1	2

Profit is optimised by producing the maximum number of pillows (240 pillows) and using the remaining down to produce 20 duvets. Pillows have the *highest contribution per limiting factor*.

A more formal approach to the above is as follows:
- Firstly, confirm that the limiting factor is something other than sales demand. This is done by comparing to the resources available the total raw materials (or other resources) required to satisfy the total demand. If there is an unlimited demand for the organisation's products, resources would be the limiting factor(s).

principles of management accounting

	Kg
Down needed (240 pillows × 1 kg) + (150 duvets × 3 kg)	690
Down available	(300)
Shortfall	390

- Secondly, calculate the contribution per limiting factor. This is done by dividing the contribution that each product renders by the amount of scarce resources used. The products are then ranked in the order of how economically they use the scarce resource.

    Pillows: R80/1 kg = R80/kg Ranking: 1
    Duvets: R180/3 kg = R60/kg Ranking: 2

- Lastly, we determine the optimum sales mix. Production of the product with the most economical use of the scarce resource should be maximised, so 240 pillows should be produced. If there is still some of the scarce resource left unused after the full market demand for the most economical product has been met, the remaining resources can now be used to produce the rest of the products in descending ranking order.

After 240 pillows have been produced, there will be left:

300 kg – (240 pillows × 1 kg) = 60 kg
Number of duvets that can be produced: 60 kg/3 kg = 20 duvets.

Example 11.2 illustrates the situation where a short-term opportunity exists to increase profits by taking on a special order. However, in order to meet the resources requirements of the order, production of one of the products normally produced will have to be reduced.

Example 11.2

Consider the information in example 11.1. In addition, Mary Craven has recently received a request from Simple Linen to supply them with customised pillows. Simple Linen will buy the pillows at R360 each. The additional costs of customising the pillows will be R4 per pillow. The order is for 80 pillows which must be delivered within the next month.

Required:
Discuss the changes to production that Mary will have to make if she decides to accept the order, and determine whether Mary should take on this new project.

Only 300 kg of goose down is available. If Mary accepts the order, she has to cut down on regular production.

The goose down presently used is the whole of the 300 kg (240 kg for pillows and 60 kg for duvets, as previously calculated). The special order requires 80 kg of goose down. There is therefore a shortfall of 80 kg of goose down.

This shortfall must be sourced from somewhere. In this case more goose down cannot be purchased. The only way to get extra goose down is to cut back on the production of existing products. In example 11.1 we saw that duvets have the lowest contribution margin per kilogram of goose down.

Mary will therefore cut back on duvets first. However, cutting back on duvets frees up only 60kg (20 duvets) of goose down. She will also need to cut back on 20 pillows to free up the additional 20kg needed.

The production changes that Mary has to make if she accepts the order are therefore to produce only 220 pillows per month (240 less 20) and no duvets. In light of this, is it a good idea to accept the order at all? In the previous example we found that Mary would normally earn a contribution of R22 800 per month. The order earns her a contribution of R10 880 [(R360 − R50 − R100 − R40 − R30 − R4) × 80], plus R17 600 on the 'normal' pillows (R80 × 220). This total contribution of R28 480 is larger than R22 800, and – based on relevant costing principles (see Chapter 10, *Relevant costs for decision-making*) – Mary should accept the order. In reality, she would also have to consider qualitative factors before making a decision.

11.2.2 Two potentially limiting factors

Where there is more than one scarce resource, each of the resources should be tested to see whether it is, indeed, a limiting factor. If only one scarce resource is truly a limiting factor, the product or service with the higher contribution per limiting factor should be produced. If the sales demand for that product has been met and there is still some of the scarce resource left, the second product or service should be produced.

Let's see what happens when there are two scarce resources.

Example 11.3

JamChut manufactures two products, jam and chutney. Both products require both labour and machine hours in their manufacture. Variable labour cost amounts to R30 per labour hour, and variable machine-related overhead costs are R60 per machine hour. There are only 5 000 labour hours and 4 600 machine hours available each month.

The products consume the scarce resources as follows:

	Labour hours	Machine hours
Jam	30 minutes	30 minutes
Chutney	50 minutes	20 minutes

The demand for the products is limited to 6 000 containers of jam and 4 500 containers of chutney per month. The contribution earned is R55 per jam container and R65 per chutney container.

Required:
Determine the optimal product combination to be manufactured each month.

The time required in order to produce enough containers to fill the maximum demand for jam and chutney is as follows:

	Labour hours	Machine hours
Jam (6 000 × 0,5 hours); (6 000 × 0,5 hours)	3 000	3 000
Chutney (4 500 × 50/60 hours); (4 500 × 20/60 hours)	3 750	1 500
Total hours required	6 750	4 500
Hours available	5 000	4 600
(Shortfall)/Excess	(1 750)	100

principles of management accounting

In this example there are two scarce resources. However, our calculation above has shown that only one of them (labour hours) is a limiting factor. There are enough machine hours available to meet the maximum demand for both jam and chutney.

This means that, in order to determine the optimal product combination, we need to maximise the contribution per labour hour:

	Jam	Chutney
Contribution per container	R55	R65
Contribution per labour hour (R55/0,5 hours); (R65/50 min × 60 min)	R110	R78
Ranking	1	2

The contribution is maximised when the maximum demand for jam is met and the remaining available labour hours are then used to produce chutney. JamChut should therefore produce 6 000 containers of jam, which will use 3 000 labour hours (6 000 containers × 30 minutes). This leaves 2 000 hours (5 000 – 3 000) for the production of chutney. In the remaining 2 000 labour hours, JamChut can produce 2 400 containers of chutney (2 000 hours × 60 minutes/50 minutes).

At this production mix, JamChut earns a contribution of R330 000 from jam (6 000 containers × R55) and R156 000 from chutney (2 400 containers × R65). This gives a total contribution of R486 000 per month.

Notice that there are machine hours left over when this optimal mix is produced. The production of 6 000 containers of jam and 2 400 containers of chutney uses only 3 800 machine hours ((6 000 containers × 0,5 hours) + (2 400 containers × 0,333 hours)). This leaves 800 machine hours unutilised (4 600 available – 3 800 used).

Example 11.4 now sketches a similar situation to that in example 11.3, but introduces a special order into the scenario. The company will have to decide whether and how to cut back on regular production in order to accommodate the special order.

Example 11.4

Consider the information in example 11.3. JamChut has been approached by Extreme Chicken, a fast food franchise, to produce a special chilli chutney for the franchise's tenth birthday celebration. Extreme Chicken wants to order 1 000 containers of the chutney, on which JamChut will earn a contribution of R70 per container. Producing the chilli chutney will require the same number of labour and machine hours as the regular chutney.

Required:
Discuss the changes JamChut will have to make if it decides to accept the order, and determine whether JamChut should in fact accept this order.

We know from example 11.3 that there are two scarce resources: labour hours and machine hours. We must again establish whether these resources are limiting factors, this time taking the special order into account.

	Labour hours	Machine hours
Total available	5 000	4 600
Currently being used (from example 11.3)	(5 000)	(3 800)
(Shortfall)/Excess without special order	0	800
Special order (1 000 × 50/60 hours); (1 000 × 20/60 hours)	(833)	(333)
(Shortfall)/Excess with special order	(833)	467

Again, we find that only labour hours are a limiting factor. In order to make labour hours available for the special order, we will therefore first reduce the production of the product with the lowest contribution per labour hour. In example 11.3 we calculated that this product was chutney. To make 833 labour hours available for the production of chilli chutney, JamChut has to reduce the number of regular chutney containers manufactured by 1 000. It will now manufacture only 1 400 (2 400 – 1 000) containers of regular chutney. All 6 000 containers of jam (see example 11.3) will still be manufactured.

Is it worth it to reduce the number of regular chutney containers in order to manufacture chilli chutney? In example 11.3 it was found that JamChut would normally earn a contribution of R486 000 per month. It can now earn a contribution of R70 000 on the special order (1 000 containers × R70) plus R330 000 on jam (6 000 × R55) plus R91 000 (1 400 × R65). This gives a total contribution of R491 000 per month, which is more than the regular R486 000. Based on relevant costing principles only, JamChut should accept the order. In reality, it would also have to consider qualitative factors before making a final decision.

In example 11.5 we introduce two scarce resources that are both limiting factors. Now the contribution per limiting factor for both resources needs to be considered. Where there are multiple limiting factors and the contribution per limiting factor of each of them ranks the products in the same order, products should be produced according to this unanimous ranking.

Example 11.5

Consider the information in example 11.3 again, but take into account that JamChut now uses re-sealable containers for its chutney. The new bottling process means it now takes 45 minutes of machine time to produce a container of chutney.

Required:
Determine the optimal product combination to be manufactured each month.

The time required in order to produce enough containers to fill the maximum demand for jam and chutney is as follows:

	Labour hours	Machine hours
Jam (6 000 × 0.5 hours); (6 000 × 0,5 hours)	3 000	3 000
Chutney (4 500 × 50/60 hours); (4 500 × 45/60 hours)	3 750	3 375
Total hours required	6 750	6 375
Hours available	5 000	4 600
(Shortfall)/Excess	(1 750)	(1 775)

In this example there are two scarce resources, and our calculation has shown that both of them are limiting factors.

This means that, in order to determine the optimal product combination, we need to maximise the contribution per labour hour *and* the contribution per machine hour.

principles of management accounting

We know from example 11.3 that jam has the higher contribution per labour hour. The contribution per machine hour is as follows:

	Jam	Chutney
Contribution per container	R55	R65
Contribution per machine hour (R55/0,5 hours); (R65/45/60 hours)	R110	R87
Ranking	1	2

In addition to having the highest contribution per labour hour, jam also has the highest contribution per machine hour. In order to optimise production, jam should therefore get preference over chutney.

JamChut should therefore produce 6 000 containers of jam, which will use 3 000 labour hours (6 000 containers × 30 minutes) and 3 000 machine hours (6 000 containers × 30 minutes). This leaves 2 000 labour hours (5 000 – 3 000), and 1 600 machine hours (4 600 – 3 000) for the production of chutney. In the remaining 2 000 labour hours JamChut can produce 2 400 containers of chutney (2 000 hours × 60 minutes/50 minutes), but in the remaining machine hours JamChut can produce only 2 133 containers of chutney (1 600 hours × 60 minutes/45 minutes).

The optimal production mix is therefore 6 000 containers of jam and 2 133 containers of chutney per month.

In example 11.5 there are two limiting factors (labour hours and machine hours), and both happened to give the same ranking for the products: both indicated that jam should be given preference. If, however, the two limiting factors were to give conflicting rankings (for example, if jam had the highest contribution per labour hour while chutney had the highest contribution per machine hour), linear programming would be required in order to solve the problem. Linear programming is discussed in section 11.5.

11.3 Make-or-buy decisions and scarce resources

Where an organisation purchases from a third party goods or services that the organisation had previously made itself, this is called 'outsourcing'. The outsourcing decision was previously discussed in Chapter 10, *Relevant costs for decision-making*, but limiting factors were not considered in detail.

In a situation where an organisation considers outsourcing work to make up a shortfall in its own in-house capacity, the difference between the cost of outsourcing and the cost of in-house manufacturing has to be determined for each product. The product for which outsourcing is the least costly when compared to in-house manufacturing, per unit of scarce resource, is the one that should be prioritised for outsourcing.

Example 11.6

Naledi Aviation Electronics manufactures three electronic components, K, L and M, using the same equipment for each. Its final product, Product X, uses one of each component. Naledi has a contract for the production of 12 000 units of Product X for the next year.

Process hours and variable cost pertaining to the three components can be summarised as follows:

	Processing time (hours)	Total variable cost R
1 unit of K	2	45
1 unit of L	3	30
1 unit of M	4	36
Assembly		24
		135

Only 72 000 hours of processing time will be available during the year. The manufacturing of the components can also be outsourced, and a competitor has quoted the following prices for supplying components:
- K: R53
- L: R48
- M: R56

You may assume that Product X generates a large enough contribution to be profitable whether its components are manufactured or bought in.

Required:
Advise Naledi whether they should make use of the competitor's services, and if they do, which components should be bought in.

Total machine hours required to do all production in-house:

12 000 × (2 + 3 + 4) = 108 000 hours
Available: 72 000 hours
36 000 hours should therefore be outsourced.

The aim should be to minimise the extra variable costs of outsourcing per unit of the scarce resource saved.

	K	L	M
	R	R	R
Variable cost of purchasing	53	48	56
Variable cost of internal production	45	30	36
Extra cost of purchasing	8	18	20
Production hours	2	3	4
Cost per production hour saved if manufacturing in-house	4	6	5

The most economical production plan would be to outsource the production of component K and to give priority to component L for in-house production.

The optimal production plan is therefore to produce all 12 000 units of L internally, as well as 9 000 units of M. This will utilise the full capacity of 72 000 hours (12 000 units of L × 3 hours + 9 000 units of M × 4 hours). The remaining 3 000 units of M and 12 000 units of K should be bought in.

11.4 Limiting factors and shadow prices

> **Key term:** shadow price

In certain cases where there are scarce resources, it may be possible to acquire additional units of the scarce resource, but at a cost higher than that of the original units. If, for example, scarce labour generates a contribution of R20 per hour, management would be prepared to pay up to R20 extra per labour hour if they can acquire additional labour. R20 is then referred to as the 'shadow price' of labour.

> A **shadow price** is the increase in value which would be created by having available one additional unit of a limiting resource at the original cost.

Example 11.7

A paint factory produces two specialised products, roof paint and varnish, which earn a contribution of R36 and R48 per 5 litre container respectively. Both products require a scarce, imported sunlight protector, UV-40. Roof paint requires 0,5 litres of UV-40 per container, and varnish requires 1,5 litres of UV-40. Only 20 000 litres of UV-40 are available per month. The potential demand is 25 000 containers of roof paint and 15 000 containers of varnish per month.

Required:
Determine the optimum production schedule as well as the shadow price of UV-40.

Roof paint renders a contribution of R72 per litre of UV-40 (R36/0,5 litres), and varnish R32 (R48/1,5 litres). The maximum amount of roof paint should therefore be produced, and the balance of the available UV-40 should be used for varnish.

Producing 25 000 containers of roof paint takes 12 500 litres of UV-40. The remaining 7 500 litres of UV-40 is then used to produce 5 000 units of varnish. The total contribution is R1 140 000 (25 000 × R36 + 5 000 × R48).

Now, let us assume that there were an additional 1,5 litres of UV-40 available. That would enable the factory to produce one additional container of varnish, earning an additional contribution of R48. The shadow price of UV-40 is therefore R32 per litre, the additional contribution (R48) divided by the number of litres required (1,5 litres).

Note that the shadow price relates only to the additional contribution that can be earned by having available one extra unit of the scarce resource. The original cost of the scarce resource is specifically excluded from the shadow price. See sections 11.6 and 11.7 for further discussion of shadow prices.

11.5 Linear programming: the graphical method

11.5.1 Introduction

Linear programming is used where an organisation faces more than one limiting factor, and where the contribution per limiting factor does not suggest production preference for a specific product. One product may, for example, be more profitable in its use of scarce raw materials, while another product may be more profitable in its use of scarce labour hours.

There are two linear programming techniques. The first, the graphical method, can be used only where there are only two products for which contribution per limiting factor does not suggest a production preference.

This implies that, where an organisation produces more than two products, all the products' contributions per limiting factor should be calculated to see whether any products can be eliminated because they perform worst (or best) in terms of contribution per limiting factor for all of the scarce resources. Linear programming can then be applied if this process of elimination results in only two products remaining.

However, if more than two products remain for which contribution per limiting factor does not suggest a production preference, the second linear programming technique – the simplex method – is required. This method is discussed in section 11.7 of this chapter.

11.5.2 Steps in the graphical method

A linear programming problem can be solved by applying the following steps:
1. *Define the variables.* The variables are the two products or services produced.
2. *Establish the objective function.* The objective is to maximise the total contribution of the two products or services.
3. *Establish the limiting factors.* All scarce resources should be tested to see whether they are limiting factors.
4. *Determine and rank the contribution per limiting factor.* This step is done to establish whether there are conflicting rankings between the two products or services. If one is ranked higher than the other in its consumption of all limiting factors, linear programming is not required.
5. *Draw a graph of the constraints for which linear programming is required.* The limiting factors should be expressed as algebraic equations and presented on a graph.
6. *Establish the feasible region.* The feasible region can visually be detected on the graph.
7. *Determine the optimal production mix.* This is done by means of solving the intersection of the two simultaneous equations that will maximise the organisation's contribution.

Example 11.8

Details of Vashumi's two products are as follows:

	Unit cost	X	Y
Raw materials used	R50/kg	3 kg	5 kg
Labour hours required	R100/hour	4 hours	2 hours
Processing time required	R40/hour	2 hours	2 hours

principles of management accounting

Contribution per product has been determined as follows:

	X	Y
	R	R
Selling price	810	700
Raw materials	(150)	(250)
Labour	(400)	(200)
Processing time	(80)	(80)
Contribution	180	170

During the period under review, raw materials are limited to 18 000 kilograms, labour to 17 000 hours, and processing time to 16 000 hours. The demand for the period for product X is 4 000 units and for product Y 3 000 units.

Required:
Determine the optimal number of units of Product X and Product Y respectively that ought to be manufactured during the period under review.

The linear programming steps can be applied to the problem as follows:

Step 1: Define the variables

Let x be the number of units of Product X.
Let y be the number of units of Product Y.

We do not at this stage know how many units of Product X and Product Y should be manufactured, therefore both of these are unknown variables.

Step 2: Establish the objective function

The objective is to maximise the combined contribution of Product X and Product Y. Therefore:

$$180x + 170y = \text{Max}$$

Again, although we are uncertain how many units of each product should be manufactured, the aim is to maximise the total contribution. This equation is not a fixed line on a graph, but the gradient can already be determined.

Step 3: Establish the limiting factors

Possible limiting factors can now be formulated and represented as algebraic equations.

	Required	Available	(Shortfall)/ Excess
Raw materials:			
X (4 000 units × 3 kg)	12 000		
Y (3 000 units × 5 kg)	15 000		
	27 000	18 000	(9 000)

Labour:			
X (4 000 units × 4 hours)		16 000	
Y (3 000 units × 2 hours)		6 000	
		22 000	17 000	(5 000)
Processing time:			
X (4 000 units × 2 hours)		8 000	
Y (3 000 units × 2 hours)		6 000	
		14 000	16 000	2 000

Raw materials and labour are the only limiting factors, because there is a shortfall of both. Processing time is not a limiting factor as the current capacity is adequate to satisfy the total demand for Vashumi's products.

Product X uses 3 kilograms of raw materials per unit, while Product Y uses 5 kilograms per unit. A maximum of 18 000 kilograms of raw materials are available. The number of Product X units manufactured multiplied by the raw materials per unit, plus the number of Product Y units manufactured multiplied by the raw materials per unit, should therefore not exceed 18 000. The equation for raw materials can be formulated as:

Raw materials $3x + 5y \leq 18\,000$

Similarly, the equation for labour is:

Labour $4x + 2y \leq 17\,000$

The demand for Product X is limited to 4 000 units, while it is limited to 3 000 units for Product Y. The limiting factors are therefore stated as follows:

Demand $x \leq 4\,000$
 $y \leq 3\,000$

It would be illogical to produce negative quantities of either of the products. We can therefore add a 'non-negativity' limiting factor, which specifies that the value of both x and y should be greater than zero:

Non-negativity $x, y \geq 0$

Step 4: Determine and rank the contribution per limiting factor

	X	Ranking	Y	Ranking
Raw materials	R180/3 kg = R60	[1]	R170/5 kg = R34	[2]
Labour	R180/4 hours = R45	[2]	R170/2 hours = R85	[1]

Product X produces a higher contribution per kilogram of raw materials, while Product Y has a higher contribution per labour hour.

Ranking the contribution per limiting factor is an important step. Linear programming is not required if a specific product is more profitable than another, taking into account its consumption of all of the scarce resources. For example, if Product Y had produced the highest contribution per unit of raw materials and labour, we would simply have given priority to the production of Product Y.

principles of management accounting

Step 5: Draw a graph of the limiting factors for which linear programming is required

The equations are:

Raw materials	$3x + 5y \leq 18\,000$	(1)
Labour hours	$4x + 2y \leq 17\,000$	(2)
Processing time	$2x + 2y \leq 16\,000$	(3)
Demand	$x \leq 4\,000$	(4)
	$y \leq 3\,000$	(5)
Non-negativity	$x, y \geq 0$	
Objective function	$180x + 170y = M$ (Max)	(6)

Figure 11.1 Graph illustrating limiting factors in example 11.8

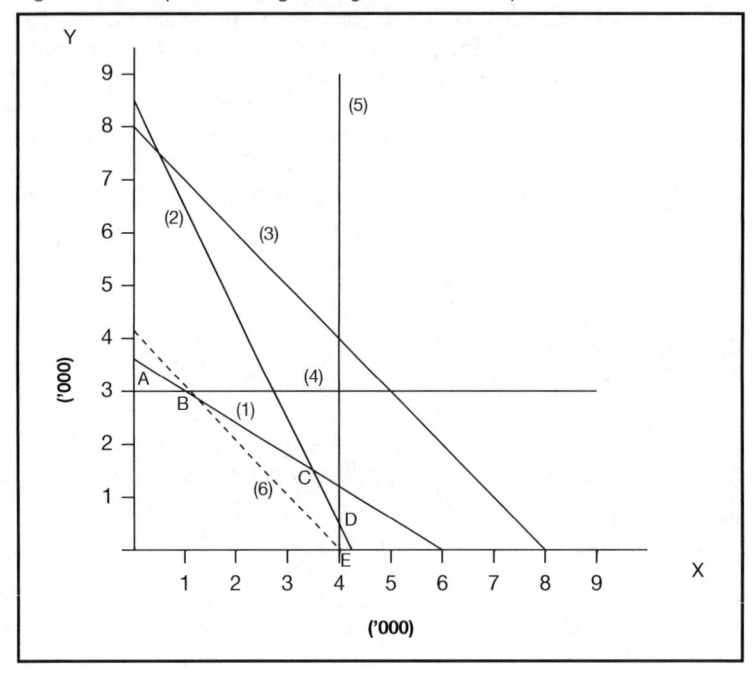

Step 6: Establish the feasible region

The feasible region includes all possible solutions to the linear programming problem, and is represented by the area ABCDE on the graph; it is the area that falls within all of the constraints.

The optimum solution can now graphically be found by shifting the objective function (the dotted line on the graph, determined in Step 2) away from the zero point, maintaining its gradient. The last possible intersection that it moves through before leaving the feasible region represents the optimum solution. This is point C.

Step 7: Determine the optimal production mix

The optimal production mix is at point C on the graph, which is where:

$3x + 5y \leq 18\,000$

and

$4x + 2y \leq 17\,000$ intercept

These two equations should now be solved simultaneously:

Simultaneous equations:

[1] $3x + 5y \leq 18\,000$
[2] $4x + 2y \leq 17\,000$

[1] × 2 $6x + 10y \leq 36\,000$ (3)
[2] × 5 $20x + 10y < 85\,000$ (4)
[4] − [3] $14x + 0 = 49\,000$
            $x = 3\,500$

Substitute in [1] $10\,500 + 5y = 18\,000$
                      $y = 1\,500$

Therefore $x = 3\,500$ units and $y = 1\,500$ units

The optimum product combination is therefore to manufacture 3 500 units of Product X and 1 500 units of Product Y. This product combination will render a total contribution of R885 000 ((3 500 units of X × R180) + (1 500 units of Y × R170)).

We can test the answer by also calculating the contribution at points A, B, D and E. If they are all less than at point C (which they are), we have chosen the correct intercept.

11.5.3 Slack

If a resource is scarce but not a limiting factor at the optimal solution, there will be what is known as 'slack'. This means that there will be some units of that particular scarce resource left unutilised when the optimal mix of products or services is produced. In the above example, processing time is not a limiting factor. After producing 3 500 units of X and 1 500 units of Y, there will be 6 000 process hours left unutilised [16 000 − ((3 500 × 2) + (1 500 × 2))].

11.6 Shadow prices and linear programming

11.6.1 Calculating the shadow price: adding one unit to the available limited resource

As mentioned in section 11.4, the shadow price of a limiting factor is the increase in contribution that would be created by having available one additional unit of the limiting factor at its original cost.

For example, the shadow prices of raw materials or labour can be calculated as follows: add 1 unit to the available kilograms of raw materials (or the number of labour hours) and calculate the new optimal mix. The difference between the new contribution (at the new optimal mix), and the previous contribution gives the shadow price of the resource in question.

principles of management accounting

This can be illustrated by following on from the previous example:

Shadow price of raw materials:	Shadow price of labour:
$3x + 5y \leq 18\ 001$	$3x + 5y \leq 18\ 000$
$4x + 2y \leq 17\ 000$	$4x + 2y \leq 17\ 001$
Therefore (determined by following the linear programming steps):	Therefore (determined by following the linear programming steps):
$x = 3\ 499{,}8571$ units	$x = 3\ 500{,}3571$ units
$y = 1\ 500{,}2857$ units	$y = 1\ 499{,}7857$ units
New contribution: R885 022,86	New contribution: R885 027,86
Previous contribution: R885 000	Previous contribution: R885 000
Shadow price of raw materials: R22,86 per kg	Shadow price of labour: R27,86 per hour

Note that we should *not* use rounding when we calculate shadow prices. The more decimals we include in the calculation, the more accurate the shadow price that we calculate.

The original cost of raw materials was R50 per kg. The shadow price of R22,86 means that the organisation can pay up to R72,86 per kilogram for additional raw materials. Likewise, the maximum it can pay for additional labour is R127,86 (R100 + R27,86) per hour.

11.6.2 Calculating the shadow price: alternative method

There is an alternative method of determining the respective shadow prices of raw materials and labour. This can be achieved by relating the resources used for a particular product to the contribution generated by those resources.

In the example above, each kilogram of raw materials and each labour hour contribute to the total contribution of a product. 3 kilograms raw materials and 4 labour hours generate a contribution of R180 for Product X. Likewise 5 kilograms of raw materials and 2 labour hours generate a contribution of R170 for Product Y.

The question is now: how much of the total contribution of a product is made up by each kilogram of raw materials and by each labour hour respectively? This contribution made by a single kilogram of raw materials or a single labour hour is its shadow price and is an unknown variable that can be determined.

Let the shadow price of raw materials and labour be R and L respectively. Therefore we can say:

In respect of Product X: $3R + 4L = 180$
In respect of Product Y: $5R + 2L = 170$

Solving the simultaneous equations:

$R = R22{,}86$
$L = R27{,}86$

11.7 Linear programming: the simplex method

> Some management accounting syllabi require students to know the simplex method. Check your syllabus guidelines to see whether you should study section 11.7.

11.7.1 Introduction

This section deals with the use of the simplex tableau to solve linear programming problems. Simplex tableaux can be used to solve linear programming problems where more than two products and/or resources (decision variables) are involved. In this chapter the basic principles of the method are illustrated, with the emphasis on the interpretation of the final tableau.

11.7.2 The principles of the simplex method

The first three steps of the simplex method are similar to the graphical method. Continuing with example 11.8 above, Vashumi (Pty) Ltd, we followed the following steps:

Step 1: Define the variables

Let x be the number of units of X that should be produced and sold.
Let y be the number of units of Y that should be produced and sold.

Step 2: Establish the objective function

Maximum contribution (M) = $180x + 170y$, subject to the constraints below.

Step 3: Establish the constraints

Raw materials	$3x + 5y \leq 18\ 000$
Labour hours	$4x + 2y \leq 17\ 000$
Processing time	$2x + 2y \leq 16\ 000$
Non-negativity	$x, y \geq 0$

Step 4: Introduce slack variables

Key term: slack variable

In the simplex method, so-called 'slack variables' have to be introduced in order to eliminate any possible inequalities. One slack variable is used for each constraint.

A **slack variable** represents the amount of a scarce resource that is left unused after the optimal production mix has been achieved.

Let a be the quantity of unused raw materials
     b be the number of unused labour hours
     c be the number of unused processing time

We can now express the original constraints as equations:

Raw materials	$3x + 5y + a = 18\ 000$
Labour hours	$4x + 2y + b = 17\ 000$
Processing time	$2x + 2y + c = 16\ 000$

The equation for raw materials above is derived as follows: 3 kilograms multiplied by the number of units of Product X produced, plus 5 kilograms multiplied by the number of units of Product Y produced, plus any unused raw materials (denoted by 'a'), equals 18 000 kilograms (the maximum raw materials available).

The equations for labour hours and processing time are derived in a similar manner.

Step 5: Express the objective function as an equation

With regard to the objective function, the convention is to express the function in the same format as the constraints, that is, with the unknown variables x and y on the left side of the equation. This means that $M = 180x + 170y$ is restated as:

$$M - 180x - 170y = 0$$

Step 6: Derive the final tableau

Once the above steps have been carried out, the actual calculation involves deriving a series of simplex tableaux that eventually result in the final tableau. Because commercially available computer spreadsheet packages are usually employed to perform the tedious calculations involved, these steps are not explained here.

Step 7: Interpret the final tableau

When the objective function and the constraints for our Vashumi example (example 11.8) are processed by a computer spreadsheet package that performs the simplex method's calculations, the following final tableau is produced by the software.

Variables in solution	x	y	Processing time c	Raw materials a	Labour hours b	Solution column
X	1	0	0	−0,1429	0,3571	3 500
Processing time	0	0	1	−0,2857	−0,2857	6 000
Y	0	1	0	0,2857	−0,2143	1 500
Solution row	0	0	0	22,8571	27,8571	885 000

The final tableau holds important management accounting information, and is interpreted as follows:

- The solution row at the bottom indicates the shadow price of each of the limiting factors. The available processing time has not all been used at the optimal production mix, and therefore the processing time column has a shadow price of zero in the solution row. Raw materials and labour hours have been fully utilised at the optimal production mix, and their respective shadow prices (that is, the amount by which the contribution of R885 000 in the solution column would increase if one additional unit of that resource became available) are shown in the solution row. The shadow price of raw materials (denoted by a) is R22,8571 per kg, so the contribution would increase by R22,8571 if one extra kilogram of raw materials could be made available at its normal variable cost of R50 per kg. Similarly, the contribution would increase by R27,8571 if one extra hour of labour time could be made available at its normal cost of R100 per labour hour.
- The solution column on the right indicates that, at the optimal production mix, 3 500 units of Product X and 1 500 units of Product Y are produced,

resulting in a contribution of R885 000. At this optimal production mix, 6 000 hours of processing time remain unused (this also re-affirms that the shadow price for processing time is zero, as shown in the solution row – there are still 6 000 hours of unused processing time available when the optimal product mix is produced).

Sensitivity analysis

The information in the raw materials and labour hours columns (the columns for the two limiting factors) of the final tableau facilitates an analysis of the optimal production mix, and the effect of an increase in any of the scarce resources. We can also use the information to determine the maximum amount of a scarce resource to obtain before we encounter the next constraint.

In the example above, the following would happen *if we had one additional kilogram of raw materials available* (refer to the raw materials column):
- The number of Product X that should be produced to obtain the optimal mix would decrease by 0,1429 units to 3 499,8571 units (3 500 less 0,1429).
- The number of Product Y that should be produced to obtain the optimal mix, would increase by 0,2857 units to 1 500,2857 units (1 500 plus 0,2857).
- An additional 0,2857 hours of processing time would be used up, and only 5 999,7143 hours of processing time would remain (6 000 less 0,2857).
- As already discussed, contribution would increase by R22,8571 (the shadow price of raw materials, as seen in the solution row) to R885 022,8571 (R885 000 plus R22,8571). Note that 0,2857 additional units of Product Y increases contribution by 0,2857 × R170 = R48,5714. However, we would then also produce 0,1429 fewer units of Product X, which would reduce total contribution by 0,1429 × R180 = R25,7143. The net effect is an increase of R22,8571, as shown in the tableau.

Since the demand for Product Y is limited to 3 000 units, there is a limit to the additional raw materials that Vashumi would be interested in purchasing. This limit can be calculated as follows:

	Units
Market demand for Product Y	3 000
Current production of Product Y	(1 500)
Potential additional units of Product Y	1 500

For every kilogram of raw materials purchased additionally, the optimal number of units of Product Y will increase by 0,2857 units. The maximum additional amount of raw materials to be purchased is therefore 1 500/0,2857 = 5 250,2625 kilograms.

Following the logic above, similar interpretations can be made for the labour hours column.

Purchasing additional resources at a premium above the normal cost

As already stated, each additional unit of a scarce resource that becomes available increases contribution by the shadow price for that resource. We can therefore add the shadow price to the original cost of the scarce resource to determine the maximum amount that can be paid for additional resources.

In the example above, the maximum price for raw materials would be the original cost of R50 per kg plus the shadow price of R22,8571, giving R72,8571. A similar calculation would apply for labour cost.

11.8 Linear programming in practice

11.8.1 Introduction

Situations where organisations have only two products or services with two scarce resources may seem to be rather theoretical and not exactly representative of real-life situations. However, the principles of linear programming remain as relevant as ever.

11.8.2 Practical application of linear programming

Budgeting

Typical scarce resources in the South African business environment include the following aspects:
- It may be difficult to obtain financing for capital equipment, especially for start-up organisations. Fluctuating interest rates increase the risk for organisations with excessive debt capital, preventing these organisations from acquiring all the capital equipment required for optimal production.
- High costs of importing raw materials and other manufacturing resources into South Africa, and the volatility of the local currency compared to the major currencies, have a significant impact on the viability of local manufacturing. An organisation relying on local (and sometimes scarce) resources usually bears less risk than companies relying on imported resources.
- The shortage of skilled labour owing to the so-called 'brain drain' over the past decades has led to certain skills being in great demand. Inevitably organisations operating in service-related industries have to be selective in terms of the work they take on.

All of the above will have a significant impact on the budget-setting process, and may require the use of linear programming principles to determine optimum product mixes.

Maximum payment for additional resources

The concept of shadow prices is an important indicator of the maximum amount that should be paid to acquire additional resources that are in short supply.

Capital investment appraisal

Where funds are limited and different projects compete, the concept of linear programming can be used to determine capital investment priorities over longer periods.

Computer packages

The fact that there are computer packages that are specifically aimed at solving linear programming problems is an indication that there is practical use for this technique. An example of such a package is the Excel Solver Add-in®. In MS Excel®, click Tools, and then click Add-Ins. Solver Add-in® is one of the options available.

11.8.3 Limitations of linear programming

Linear programming enables us to choose the most profitable mix of products or services when faced with scarce resources. However, in addition to short-term profits, qualitative factors should be considered.

For example, it may sometimes be strategically important to offer a product or service that is less profitable, because we suspect that it may lead the customer eventually to purchase our more profitable products or services. Similarly, we may wish to sell new, less profitable ones because the new products ensure long-term survival of the business. These are examples of valid qualitative arguments that may override purely quantitative decisions.

The linear programming methodology may provide acceptable answers for a given situation. This situation, for example, the scarcity of raw materials or labour, may, however, change overnight, rendering the solution outdated. To be effective, linear programming principles should be applied continuously, which may not be practical.

It is not always possible to identify exactly which resources will be in short supply, and to what extent. Figures such as market demand for a certain product and the availability of production resources are based on estimates and these estimates may prove to be incorrect.

11.9 Summary

Chapter 10, *Relevant costs for decision-making* dealt with everyday decisions faced by an organisation. This chapter addresses the particular situation where decisions are taken under operational constraints. From a purely financial perspective, the optimal product or service mix is the one that maximises contribution per limiting factor. The same principle of maximising contribution per limiting factor also applies in situations where special orders are considered.

Where there are multiple limiting factors but products or services rank in the same order when the contribution per limiting factor is calculated for each resource, linear programming can be avoided. However, where ranking differs, linear programming is necessary. Linear programming can be done using either the graphical or the simplex method.

The shadow price of a scarce resource is the increase in contribution created if one additional unit of the scarce resource becomes available at the original cost.

Conclusion: Decision-making under operational constraints and other topics in this book

This chapter introduced the concept of contribution per limiting factor, and how to apply this principle to resolve maximisation problems where there are two or more scarce resources. It relied heavily on the principles studied in Chapter 10, *Relevant costs for decision-making*.

In order to calculate the contribution derived from the sale of a product, the concept of variable cost needs to be understood. Variable costing is discussed in Chapter 5, *Absorption versus variable costing*.

The necessity to determine optimal product mixes is an integral part of budgeting. Budgeting is discussed in more detail in Chapter 12, *Budgets, planning and control*.

Tutorial case study: Zevenwacht estate

Zevenwacht estate on the Stellenbosch Wine Route has 200 hectares under vineyards. The region is ideally situated for the growing of wine grapes. Zevenwacht's south- and south west-facing vineyards are protected from the heat of summer afternoons by the Bottelary Hills and cooled by the sea breezes blowing in from nearby Table Bay and False Bay. The estate has varied soils, which have been planted with both red and white grape varietals. The estate produces a wide variety of red and white wines in its cellar.

Source: Zevenwacht 2011

1. Each time aged vineyards are removed and the soil is replanted, Zevenwacht has to decide which variety of grape to plant and how much of each should be planted. Discuss the limiting factors that may apply to Zevenwacht's wine production.
2. If Zevenwacht had the opportunity to rent land from an adjacent farming operation in order to plant more vineyards, discuss how it could calculate the maximum price per hectare that it would be willing to pay for the land.
3. Assume that Zevenwacht wishes to produce only two wines (and therefore plants only these two varietals): Chenin blanc and Sauvignon blanc. Outline and discuss a seven-step method that could be employed to find the optimal production mix.
4. Discuss how the limitations of linear programming might apply to Zevenwacht if it used this method to determine its optimal production mix. Specifically mention qualitative factors that may cause Zevenwacht to take a different decision from that suggested by linear programming.

Basic questions

BQ 1

An accounting organisation is currently assisting a large number of clients with the completion of their tax returns. Which of the following are probable factors limiting income?
a) Lack of computers
b) Lack of suitably qualified accounting staff
c) Lack of secretaries assisting with administration

BQ 2

An organisation produces two components, G and H, in two processes: Process 1 has a maximum capacity of 4 000 hours per week, while Process 2 is limited to 10 000 hours. Component G requires 6 minutes per unit in Process 1 and 12 minutes per unit in Process 2. Component H requires 9 minutes in Process 1 and 21 minutes in Process 2.

What are the equations pertaining to Process 1 and Process 2 for linear programming purposes?

BQ 3

A game farmer has to decide about the mix of antelope on his new farm. The size of the farm is 1 200 hectares (ha). The farmer has only R3 million available to invest in antelope, and is considering a mix of impala and sable antelope.

Sables cost R75 000 each and require 12 ha per animal. Impala cost R1 200 each and require 4 ha per animal.

What are the equations pertaining to possible limiting factors for linear programming purposes?

BQ 4

An organisation has determined that its limiting factors are:

Raw materials: $14A + 8B \le 308\,000$
Labour: $0{,}3A + 0{,}7B \le 15\,850$

It has also determined that the optimal product mix can be found at the intersection of these limiting factors.

What is the organisation's optimum product combination of Product A and Product B?

BQ 5

Source: Adapted from CIMA P2

The following details relate to ready-made meals prepared by a food processing company:

Ready-made meal	K R/meal	L R/meal	M R/meal
Selling price	5,00	3,00	4,40
Ingredients	2,00	1,00	1,30
Variable conversion cost	1,60	0,80	1,85
Fixed conversion costs*	0,50	0,30	0,60
Profit	0,90	0,90	0,65
Oven time (minutes)	10	4	8

* The fixed conversion costs are general fixed costs that are not specific to any type of meal.

principles of management accounting

Each of the meals is prepared using a series of processes, one of which involves cooking the ingredients in a large oven. The availability of cooking time in the oven is limited, and because each of the meals requires cooking at a different oven temperature, it is not possible to cook more than one of the meals in the oven at the same time.

What is the most profitable and the least profitable use of the oven?

	Most profitable	Least profitable
a)	Meal K	Meal L
b)	Meal L	Meal M
c)	Meal L	Meal K
d)	Meal M	Meal L

BQ 6

AB Pharmaceutical Ltd manufactures sleeping pills that require 0,2 grams of a scarce ingredient, ZZ, per dose. The contribution per dose is R6. The cost of ZZ is currently R80 per gram.

What is the shadow price per gram of ZZ?
a) R6
b) R30
c) R80
d) R110

BQ 7

A tax consultancy firm employs a foreign tax specialist at a monthly salary of R60 000. On average, the specialist is able to book 120 hours per month to clients. The specialist's charge-out rate to clients is R1 800 per hour. The specialist does not have the capacity to handle the total workload, and the firm is considering contracting in the services of another specialist on an hourly basis.

What is the shadow price of tax consulting hours?

BQ 8

Match the following concepts with their definitions. Write the concept next to the letter which matches its definition.

Concepts: Slack, limiting factor, non-negativity, shadow price

a) A scarce resource of which there is a limited supply that affects the profitability of the organisation
b) The increase in value which would be created by having available one additional unit of a limiting resource at its original cost
c) Units of a resource that are unutilised once the optimal product combination has been determined
d) A constraint that should be included when formulating linear programming solutions to ensure that the answer makes sense in operational terms and that we do not end up with negative production quantities

BQ 9

The following information pertains to Products K and L:

	K	L
Contribution per unit	R10	R12
Raw material Z per unit	2 kg	3 kg
Monthly demand	2 000 units	3 000 units

The availability of raw material Z is limited to 7 000 kg per month. What is the product combination that will optimise the total monthly contribution?

BQ 10

Source: Adapted from CIMA MA Decision Making Exam

An organisation produces two products, Product X and Product Y. The standard variable costs per unit of the products are as follows:

	X	Y
	R	R
Materials (R3 per kg)	15	12
Other variable costs	45	50
Total variable costs	60	62

The management accountant determined the optimal production plan by using graphical linear programming. He noticed that the optimal plan was given at ANY point on the line indicating the limiting factor for materials.

If the selling price of Product X is R100, what is the selling price of Product Y?

Long questions

LQ 1 – Intermediate (10 marks; 18 minutes)

Source: Adapted from CIMA P2

A bakery produces three different-sized fruit pies for sale in its shops. The pies all use the same basic ingredients. Details of the selling prices and unit costs of each pie are as follows:

	Small R per pie	Medium R per pie	Large R per pie
Selling price	3,00	5,00	9,00
Ingredients	1,80	2,40	4,60
Direct labour	0,40	0,50	0,60
Variable overhead	0,30	0,50	0,80
Weekly demand (pies)	200	500	300
Fruit (kg per pie)	0,20	0,30	0,60

The fruit used in making the pies is imported and the bakery has been told that the amount of fruit that they will be able to buy for next week is limited to 300 kg.

principles of management accounting

The bakery has established its good name by baking its pies daily using fresh fruit, so it is not possible to buy the fruit in advance.

REQUIRED	Marks
Determine the mix of pies to be made and sold in order to maximise the bakery's contribution for next week.	10
TOTAL MARKS	10

LQ 2 – Intermediate (25 marks; 45 minutes)

AB Organix (Pty) Ltd manufactures, among its many organic health products, two basic suntan cream products. The cream consists of two ingredients, Cream A and Cream B, both imported from Italy, which are manually mixed and sold as an environmentally friendly alternative to the many suntan lotions available in the market.

Details pertaining to Cream UV-20 and Cream UV-40 are as follows:

	UV-20	UV-40	Cost
Selling price	R50 per litre	R60 per litre	
Cream A required per litre	0,4 litres	0,2 litres	R10 per litre
Cream B required per litre	0,6 litres	0,8 litres	R15 per litre
Labour (litres mixed in a 6 hour shift)	60 litres	40 litres	R40 per hour
1 litre bottle (can be recycled)	1 bottle	1 bottle	R1 per bottle

Market demand for UV-20 is estimated at 30 000 litres a year, and for UV-40 at 20 000 litres. The availability of Cream A is limited to 3 000 litres a year, and Cream B to 8 000 litres a year. There are two labourers, and they can effectively work 1 200 hours a year each.

REQUIRED		Marks
(a)	Determine the product mix that will optimise AB Organix's contribution.	22
(b)	Determine the shadow price of Cream A, Cream B and labour.	3
TOTAL MARKS		25

LQ 3 – Intermediate (7 marks; 13 minutes)

Source: Adapted from CIMA MA Decision Making Exam

PQ Ltd produces three products, A, B and C, from two processes. The slack variables for Process 1 hours, Process 2 hours and the maximum demand for Product A are $s4$, $s5$ and $s6$ respectively.

The contribution per unit for each of the products is as follows:

    Product A   R400
    Product B   R200
    Product C   R100

The following linear programming solution has been determined in order to maximise contribution for the forthcoming period.

	A	B	C	s4	s5	s6	Solution
B	0	1	0,833	0,333	0	−0,667	506,667
s5	0	0	0,333	−0,667	1	−1,667	586,667
A	1	0	0	0	0	1	200
Z	0	0	*	66,667	0	266,667	181 333,33

* This box has deliberately been left blank.

REQUIRED		Marks
(a)	If the organisation could increase production time in process 1 by 10 hours, determine what the increase in total contribution would be.	4
(b)	If eight additional units of Product C were produced, determine what the change in total contribution would be.	3
TOTAL MARKS		7

LQ 4 – Advanced (25 marks; 45 minutes)

David Masikela produces two different types of wooden decorative toys in his factory, toy cars and toy soldiers. The production process consists of sawing, assembling and finishing.

David buys his wood at R100 per m^3. There is an unlimited supply of wood. The weekly capacity of the sawing department is 600 labour hours, while the assembling and finishing departments are limited to 1 200 labour hours each.

David has a market for 300 toy cars and 375 toy soldiers per week.

The profit per toy is as follows:

	Car R	Soldier R
Selling price	250,00	200
Direct materials	38,50	55,25
Wood	36,00	53,00
Other	2,50	2,25
Direct labour	71,00	45,25
Sawing department	15,00	8,25
Assembling department	30,00	24,00
Finishing department	26,00	13,00
Variable overheads	19,20	16,00
Fixed overheads	7,20	6,00
Profit	114,10	77,50

principles of management accounting

The cost of labour per department is as follows:

	R/hour
Sawing department	10
Assembling department	12
Finishing department	13

REQUIRED		Marks
(a)	Determine the combination of cars and soldiers that will optimise total contribution, taking into account the limiting factors.	20
(b)	Calculate how much David should be prepared to pay per hour if additional labour can be obtained for the sawing department. Also state the shadow prices of all types of labour.	5
TOTAL MARKS		25

LQ 5 – Advanced (10 marks; 18 minutes)

A university accounting lecturer recently signed an agreement with the finance department of one of the provincial governments to provide additional lectures to their CTA students, all of whom are correspondence students studying through Unisa. The agreement stipulates that a total of twenty 3-hour lectures (five lectures per subject) should be presented for the next year on Saturday mornings for a total amount of R51 000.

The lecturer has prepared his quotation as follows:

	No of lectures	Duration per lecture (hours)	Total lecture hours	Rate per hour R	Total R
Management accounting	5	3	15	750	11 250
Taxation	5	3	15	900	13 500
Auditing	5	3	15	750	11 250
Financial accounting	5	3	15	1 000	15 000
					51 000

The agreement stipulates that the lecturer is allowed to involve his colleagues, provided that he ensures that a proper standard of lecturing is maintained.

The lecturer has wide experience lecturing in management accounting, but will have to do considerable preparation for the other three subjects. He estimates the preparation time required as follows:
- Management accounting: 1 hour preparation per lecturing hour
- Taxation: 4 hours' preparation per lecturing hour
- Auditing: 3 hours' preparation per lecturing hour
- Financial accounting: 5 hours' preparation per lecturing hour.

Owing to work commitments, the lecturer has only 180 hours available for both lecturing and preparation for the year, and therefore decides to involve some of his colleagues to assist him. They are prepared to lecture at the following rates:
- Management accounting, taxation and auditing: R500 per lecture hour.
- Financial accounting: R800 per lecture hour.

It would not pose any problems should the lecturer decide to outsource only a portion of a specific subject.

REQUIRED	Marks
Advise the lecturer with regard to a plan that will optimise his income from lecturing.	10
TOTAL MARKS	**10**

References

Fin24. 2011. 'SA hit by potato shortage'. [Online]. Available: <www.fin24.com/Business/SA-hit-by-potato-shortage-20100802> [24 January 2011].

Upchurch, A. 1998. 'Management accounting principles and practices'. *Financial Times*. London: Pitman Publishing.

Zevenwacht. 2011. 'Zevenwacht cellars & vineyards'. [Online]. Available: <www.zevenwacht.co.za/zw_cellarsvineyards.html > [3 March 2011].

Budgets, planning and control

chapter 12

Appie Pienaar

LEARNING OBJECTIVES

By the end of this chapter, you should be able to:
1. Explain the objectives of budgeting.
2. Explain the concept of a principal budgeting factor.
3. Discuss the steps in the budgeting process.
4. Prepare a production budget.
5. Prepare a cash budget.
6. Explain alternative approaches to budgeting, including incremental budgeting, zero-base budgeting and rolling budgets.
7. Apply projection techniques such as the high-low method and regression analysis in preparing a budget.
8. Discuss the concepts of fixed and flexed budgets.
9. Discuss the difference between imposed, participative and negotiated budgets.
10. Discuss the motivational impact of budgets.
11. Explain the rationale behind the concept of Beyond budgeting®.

African Barrick Gold and budgets, planning and control

African Barrick Gold has four gold mines in northwest Tanzania. Although the company is listed on the the London Stock Exchange, it announced that it would be seeking a listing on the JSE because most of its top management and management operations are based in Johannesburg.

During 2010 African Barrick Gold lowered its original production target for 2010. Its revised target was to produce 716 000 ounces of gold. In the end it missed the revised target as well, producing only 700 934 ounces during the year. This was primarily due to unforeseen output difficulties at its Buzwagi mine. Despite its lower production in 2010, profit – which was expected to be $204,8m – exceeded expectations and was reported as $218,1m in the financial statements. The main reason for the favourable profit was the high gold price as a result of a weaker dollar and global economic uncertainty.

The difficulties at the Buzwagi mine have reportedly been resolved, and the company expected to produce between 700 000 and 760 000 ounces of gold in 2011. However, the price of gold showed a downward movement early in 2011.

Source: Miningmx.com 2011

principles of management accounting

Estimating production volumes and fluctuations in the gold price are two of the many difficulties that African Barrick Gold encounters in its budgeting process. Budgeting affects everyone. From the individual who is concerned about making it through the month to the next payday, to the large company with its formal planning and forecasting framework, we all have to sit down and plan our financial future.

12.1 Introduction

Budgets are used in financial planning and are drawn up by a diverse range of individuals and organisations, all of whom feel the need to plan ahead.

A budget has the following characteristics:
- It is future-orientated.
- It aims to achieve a predetermined goal or objective.
- It is expressed in quantifiable terms.

This chapter deals with various issues pertaining to budgeting, financial planning and forecasting.

12.2 Objectives of budgets

Key term: sales budget

The characteristics of budgets mentioned above provide an indication of the main objectives of budgeting, which are as follows:
- *Budgets facilitate the achievement of an organisation's strategic and tactical objectives.* Divisional budgets should be prepared in such a manner that they contribute towards the achievement of the vision of the organisation as a whole.
- *Budgets compel planning.* The preparation of a budget forces a manager to sit down and think ahead, not just about the next day or the next week, but the next year or even longer. Without this process, managers may become too focused on the short term, neglecting important long-term and medium-term planning.
- *Budgets promote the co-ordination of activities.* The purchasing department, for example, cannot plan future purchases of raw materials without knowing the production department's requirements. The production department will not know how many units to produce unless they receive a **sales budget** from the marketing or sales department. Budgets such as the capital expenditure budget and the human resources budget will, in turn, be influenced by the requirements of the production department.
- *Budgets promote communication in the organisation.* Staff and management working in different business units are brought into contact with each other because of the budgeting process, improving communication. Budget guidelines are also used by senior management to communicate their vision and plans for the organisation to the rest of the staff.
- *Budgets provide a framework for control and responsibility accounting.* A typical budget system will require the organisation to be divided into responsibility centres, with departmental managers assuming responsibility for income and expenses in their departments. Performance evaluation is based on a

comparison of pre-determined budgets to actual performance. Investigating variances between actual results and budgeted results is an important means of control in an organisation.
- *Budgets serve as a framework for authorisation of decisions within the organisation.* Significant expenditure is often not authorised unless it has been properly motivated and budgeted for. Budgets prevent unplanned, spur-of-the-moment decisions about expenditure which could later impact on profitability.
- *Budgets provide a basis for performance evaluation.* Many organisations base their performance reward system on the achievement of budgeted results. Failure to meet budgeted targets could also be the cause for action against an employee.
- *Budgets provide motivation for employees to improve their performance.* Working towards a common goal may be beneficial to team spirit and meeting this goal provides a sense of personal achievement. It is important for budgets to be set at the appropriate level to achieve the desired motivational effect. Budgets set too leniently or too stringently may have an adverse effect on employees.

12.3 Strategic, tactical and operational budgets

Key terms: operational budgets, strategic budgets, tactical budgets

In the context of general business control, we distinguish between the strategic, tactical and operational levels of planning, control and decision-making. When preparing a budget, we need to ensure that the budget period (the length of time to which the budget relates) agrees with the specific business requirements for which the budget will be used.

Strategic budgets will usually be for a long period, perhaps between three years and 15 years. The scope will also be much less detailed than in the case of operational budgets. In some industries in today's fast-paced business world, budgets that cover too long of a planning horizon may be of little use – if such budgets are set (for example, to seek long-term funding), they may contain low levels of detail and revisions are inevitable. **Tactical budgets** are usually prepared for periods of between one and three years, or even as many as five, while **operational budgets** are prepared for a single financial period, usually a year or less. Quarterly, monthly and daily budgets are also examples of operational budgets. These budgets are more detailed in terms of numbers and deadlines, and because the planning horizon is shorter it is easier to budget accurately.

12.4 Responsibility for the budget

12.4.1 The budget committee

A large organisation preparing a budget will usually have a budget committee which assumes overall responsibility for the co-ordination and administration of the whole budget process. The budget committee issues the budget manual or guidelines. The budget manual is a collection of instructions setting out general guidelines, procedures to be followed, deadlines and responsibilities.

12.4.2 Responsibility for preparing budgets

In most organisations, functional managers assume responsibility for the budgets in their functional departments. Examples of these are the following:

Functional manager	Area of responsibility
• Sales manager • Production manager • Purchasing manager • Human resources manager • Cost centre managers	• Sales budget • Production budget • Materials purchases budget • Human resources budget • Respective cost centre budgets, for example IT, accounting, administration

12.5 Determining the principal budgeting factor

Key term: principal budgeting factor

Before starting with the preparation of the budget, it is important to identify the **principal budgeting factor**: the factor that restricts output. There is little use, for example, in preparing very favourable sales forecasts when the organisation has limited production capacity and a lack of funds to expand the production capacity. The most likely principal budgeting factors are the following:

- *Sales demand*. In most organisations sales demand will be the principal budgeting factor, setting the level of production, purchases and other supporting activities. In most cases it will be possible to overcome other obstacles preventing growth, as long as the market for the organisation's products exists.
- *Availability of raw materials*. Certain industries depend on the availability of scarce raw materials. All products may be sold in the market (at reasonable prices) but growth is hampered by the availability of raw materials. In this case the budget will primarily be guided by the amount of raw materials that can be acquired during the budget period.
- *Machine capacity*. In some organisations a lack of machine capacity and the inability to expand machine capacity may be limiting factors preventing growth in the short term. Machine capacity is then the principal budgeting factor that influences how other factors will be budgeted for.
- *Availability of cash and sources of funding*. Organisations that lack ready access to cash resources such as owners' capital or bank debt will be limited because they cannot build up adequate inventory levels, provide sufficient credit facilities to customers, or invest in additional equipment. In such a situation the limitations on cash and funding are the principal budgeting factors.

12.6 The sequence in budget preparation

In a normal manufacturing concern, the following budgeting steps would apply:
1 *Identify the principal budgeting factor.* In most organisations, as discussed above, the principal budgeting factor will be the sales demand for the organisation's products. Should this be the case, the next logical step is to prepare the sales budget.
2 *Prepare the sales budget.* Information regarding potential sales for the budget period are sourced from the marketing department, while the history of the organisation's past sales provide good indicators of what could be expected for the future.
3 *Prepare the production budget.* The number of units to be produced is budgeted, taking into account the desired sales budget and closing inventory levels as well as the level of opening inventory.

Example 12.1

A furniture company selling office chairs wishes to maintain an inventory level of 100 chairs as buffer inventory. At the end of the previous period they maintained a level of 80 chairs. Expected sales for the next year amount to 850 chairs. They lose an average of 5 chairs a year as a result of theft.

Required:
Prepare the company's production budget for the current period.

The production budget is determined as follows:

	Units
Expected sales	850
Add: Units lost due to theft	5
Add: Desired closing inventory	100
Less: Opening inventory	(80)
Production required	875

Once the production budget has been set, the next step is to budget for production resources:
- *Budget for production resources.* Production resources include the usage of raw materials, process time (machines and equipment), and labour.
- *Raw materials purchases budget.* Purchases of raw materials are budgeted after considering the expected production requirements, the desired raw materials closing inventory level, the level of opening inventory and expected scrap or wastage.
- *General overheads costs budget.* General overheads include aspects such as factory rental, salaries of supervisors, electricity, depreciation and cleaning.
- *Overhead absorption rates.* The cost accountant can now calculate overhead absorption rates based on the overhead costs budgeted and the appropriate cost drivers. These may involve traditional cost drivers such as budgeted machine hours or labour hours, or an activity-based approach may be followed.

principles of management accounting

- *Administrative expenditure budget.* This budget will include all supporting activities such as IT- related expenditure and the accounting function.
- *Cash budget.* The cash budget is an important part of the process, as it will ensure that the organisation avoids situations where it has insufficient cash. Having excess cash on hand is also detrimental to profitability, as the returns on cash balances are usually considerably lower than on other investments.
- *Capital expenditure budget.* Taking into account future production requirements, the organisation has to decide about investment in long-term capital assets such as equipment. These decisions are influenced by the production capacity required, the cash outlay of new equipment and the required rate of return on assets.
- *Master budget.* The master budget is a summary of all of the individual functional budgets discussed above, and culminates in budgeted financial statements, which include a statement of financial position, a statement of comprehensive income, and a statement of cash flows.

Note that, should the principal budgeting factor be identified in step one as something other than sales, the second step will not be to prepare the sales budget. Instead, the budget in which the principal budgeting factor is addressed will be prepared in step two, followed by the rest of the budgeting steps.

12.7 Production and related budgets

Key terms: production budget, raw materials purchases budget

The interaction between the sales budget, the **production budget** and the **raw materials purchases budget** can be illustrated through the following example.

Example 12.2

Tshwane Curios CC purchases unprocessed wood and then reworks it into ornaments for resale to tourists at popular tourist destinations such as Table Mountain and the Kruger National Park. Selling prices are directly related to the physical size of the ornaments and are expressed in terms of kilograms sold.

The sales budget for the period September to November is as follows:

	September	October	November
Sales in kg	2 000	2 400	2 500

- The basic raw materials cost R200 per kilogram of wood.
- Raw materials scrap is 20 per cent of raw materials input.
- The target month-end raw materials inventory level is 600 kilograms plus 20 per cent of the raw materials required for next month's budgeted production.
- The target month-end inventory level for finished goods is 800 kilograms plus 20 per cent of the next month's budgeted sales.

Required:
Calculate the budgeted raw materials purchases for September.

To budget for September's raw materials purchases, the calculation is as follows:

	August kg	September kg	October kg
Required finished goods inventory:			
Base inventory	800	800	800
+ 20% of next month's sales	400	480	500
Required closing inventory	1 200	1 280	1 300
Sales for the month		2 000	2 400
		3 280	3 700
Less: Opening inventory		(1 200)	(1 280)
Required finished goods production		2 080	2 420
+ 20% losses of input raw materials		520	605
Raw materials for production *		2 600	3 025
Required materials inventory:	1 120	1 205	
Base inventory	600	600	
+ 20% of next month's requirement	520	605	
		3 805	
Less: Opening inventory		(1 120)	
Required materials purchases		2 685	

* 2 080 kg/80% and 2 420 kg/80%

The budgeted raw materials purchases cost for September is 2 685 kg × R200 per kilogram = R537 000. Note that the raw materials purchases are influenced by the production requirements as well as the required opening and closing inventory of raw materials. Production, in turn, is influenced by expected sales as well as the required opening and closing finished goods inventory levels.

12.8 Cash budgets

Key term: cash budget

12.8.1 Drawing up a cash budget

When a **cash budget** is drawn up, two aspects in particular have to be kept in mind:
- Only cash flow items are reflected in a cash budget. Non-cash items such as depreciation or provisions do not affect the cash budget.
- The period in which the cash flow is recorded is the period in which the cash flow takes place. We ignore the period in which the transaction is to be recorded for accounting purposes.

Example 12.3

Levubu Farmers' Co-op has prepared the following budget for the period September to December:

	September R	October R	November R	December R
Sales	70 000	80 000	100 000	90 000
Cost of sales	(38 500)	(44 000)	(55 000)	(49 500)
Salaries	(6 500)	(6 500)	(7 000)	(7 000)
Other expenses	(8 000)	(7 000)	(6 500)	(7 000)
Profit	17 000	22 500	31 500	26 500

Notes:
- Sixty per cent of sales are for cash. Forty per cent of sales are to debtors who pay a month later.
- Closing inventory should be 30 per cent of the next month's sales demand. This policy has been in place for the whole of the period under review.
- Trade creditors are paid in the month after the purchase has been made. No other inventoriable costs are incurred. The same applies to creditors for expenses other than purchases. All other expenses are on credit.
- Included in expenses is an amount of R1 500 for depreciation on office equipment.
- Salaries are paid in the month to which they relate.
- Labour is paid in full by the end of the relevant month. Labour costs and expenses are treated as period costs in the profit-and-loss account.
- The organisation will sell a second-hand bakkie for R25 000, and will make an accounting profit of R3 500 on the sale of the vehicle. This has not been included in the budget above. Although the sale agreement was signed in October, the buyer has arranged to settle the amount in November.
- The organisation declared dividends of R10 000 in October, payable on 12 November.

The opening cash balance for October was R5 000.

Required:
Prepare a cash budget for October and November.

The following is the cash budget for October and November. The workings indicated next to amounts are explained in more detail below.

	October R	Workings	November R	Workings
Receipts				
Receipts from customers	76 000	(W1)	92 000	(W2)
Sale of vehicle			25 000	(W3)
	76 000		117 000	

Chapter 12 Budgets, planning and control

	October R	Workings	November R	Workings
Payments				
Trade creditors	40 150	(W4)	47 300	(W4)
Salaries	6 500		7 000	
Expense creditors	6 500	(W5)	5 500	(W5)
Dividends	–		10 000	
Total payments	53 150		69 800	
Receipts less payments	22 850		47 200	
Opening balance	5 000		27 850	
Closing balance	27 850		75 050	

Workings:

W1: Receipts from customers in October are calculated as 60 per cent of October sales plus 40 per cent of September sales:
(60% × R80 000) + (40% × R70 000) = R76 000

W2: Receipts from customers in November are calculated as 60 per cent of November sales plus 40 per cent of October sales
(60% × R100 000) + (40% × R80 000) = R92 000

W3: The accounting profit on the sale of an asset does not represent a cash flow. The only cash flow related to this transaction is the cash received for the vehicle.

W4: The amounts provided in the budged do not represent actual purchases in a particular month, but the cost of sales in that month.

Purchases in a particular month will depend on the opening inventory for the month, units sold and the required closing inventory: Purchases = Cost of sales + closing inventory – opening inventory. Purchases in September, payable in October, can be calculated as follows:

	R
September cost of sales	38 500
Less: Opening inventory in September (30% of September cost of sales)	(11 550)
Add: Closing inventory (30% of October cost of sales)	13 200
	40 150

Likewise, purchases in October, payable in November, can be calculated as follows:

	R
October cost of sales	44 000
Less: Opening inventory in October (30% of October cost of sales)	(13 200)
Add: Closing inventory (30% of November cost of sales)	16 500
	47 300

W5: Expenses in September, October and November are paid a month later. The cash amount payable excludes depreciation as this is not a cash item.

12.8.2 Management action based on cash budgets

A cash budget is one of the most important planning tools used by an organisation. It shows the cash effect of all plans made within the budgetary process. After a cash budget has been drawn up, the net position could point to an anticipated short-term cash surplus, a long-term cash surplus, a short-term cash deficit, or a long-term cash deficit. Both insufficient and excessive cash balances are undesirable – the goal is to have just the desired amount of cash on hand. Insufficient cash can threaten the survival of the business, while excess cash can usually be employed in a more profitable manner. Table 12.1 lists the management action that could be taken based on the budget in each scenario in order to avoid the anticipated insufficient or excess balances:

Table 12.1 Management action based on various scenarios in the cash budget

Cash position predicted by cash budget	Appropriate management action	Additional benefit gained through action taken in case of surplus
Short-term deficit	Obtain cash by doing one or more of the following: • Arrange with suppliers to pay them later • Encourage debtors to pay sooner by offering early settlement discounts • Arrange a bank overdraft • Postpone capital expenditure • Postpone dividend payments (if not yet declared) • Reduce inventory levels	
Long-term deficit	Obtain cash by doing one or more of the following: • Raise long-term finance (for example bank loan) • Sell unused assets (for example land) • Issue equity	
Short-term surplus	Eliminate surplus by doing one or more of the following: • Pay creditors early • Grant credit to customers • Invest in interest-bearing short-term securities	• Receive early settlement discount • Increase sales • Receive interest income
Long-term surplus	Eliminate surplus by doing one or more of the following: • Invest in capital equipment • Expand business operations • Diversify into other business areas	• Increase production capacity • Increase earning potential • Increase earning potential, decrease risk

12.9 The master budget

Key term: master budget

When all the functional budgets and the cash budget have been prepared, they are summarised and a budgeted statement of financial position, a statement of comprehensive income, and a statement of cash flows are prepared. This **master budget** provides the overall picture of the planned performance for the budget period.

12.10 The role of ratio analysis and KPIs in the budgeting process

Key term: key performance indicator

A **key performance indicator** (KPI) is a metric used to quantify the performance an organisation aims to achieve. This could relate to actual financial results, budgeted financial results or other quantitative data.

Typical financial key performance indicators relate to areas such as:
- Profitability (return on capital employed (ROCE), gross profit margin, growth in turnover)
- Management effectiveness (asset turnover, debtors' collection period, inventory turnover, creditors' payment period)
- Liquidity (current ratio, quick ratio)
- Solvency (gearing ratio, debt ratio)
- Investor ratios for listed organisations (EPS, dividend cover).

An organisation that has, for example, set out in its objectives that it wants to achieve an ROCE of 20 per cent or a quick ratio of 1 : 1 should now apply these ratios to the budgeted financial statements to determine whether its financial planning supports these key performance indicators.

12.11 Alternative approaches to budgeting

12.11.1 Incremental budgeting

Key term: incremental budgeting

Incremental budgeting is the term used for the traditional approach to budgeting where the previous period's results are used as a basis for the budget. These figures are then adjusted for inflationary increases as well as increases and decreases in budgeted volumes to determine expected income and expenditure.

principles of management accounting

> ## Example 12.4
> KL Division produces a single product. Information for the current year (given on the last day of the year) is as follows:
> - Number of units produced: 3 400 units.
> - Total production cost: R425 000.
> - Sixty per cent of production costs are estimated to be fixed, and the balance is variable according to the number of units produced.
> - The inflation rate is 8 per cent per annum.
>
> **Required:**
> Determine the budgeted cost of KL Division if it expects to increase production to 4 100 units in the next financial year.

In the current year 3 400 units were produced. The total production costs of R425 000 consist of R170 000 in variable costs (R425 000 × 40%) and R255 000 in fixed costs (R425 000 × 60%). Variable production costs are therefore R50 per unit (R170 000/3 400).

In the next financial period 4 100 units will be produced. The variable production costs are budgeted to increase to R54 per unit (R50 + 8 per cent inflation). Total variable production costs are therefore budgeted to be R221 400 (R54 × 4 100 units), while fixed costs are budgeted at R275 400 (R255 000 + 8 per cent inflation). The total production cost in the budget is R496 800 (R221 400 variable + R275 400 fixed).

12.11.2 Zero-base budgeting

> **Key terms:** decision package, zero-base budgeting

Zero-base budgeting (ZBB) is an approach to budgeting which rejects the principle of incremental budgeting. Instead, it advocates that a budget should be prepared from 'scratch', or zero. Every item in a budget has to be specifically justified in order to be included.

Typical questions that should be asked when a zero-base approach is followed are the following:
- Should this expense and the activity that it relates to be performed at all?
- How much should the activity cost?
- What is the level of activity required?

Zero-base budgeting involves the following three stages:
- Each discrete, stand-alone organisational activity is called a **decision package**. The organisation's decision packages should be identified and described. To identify whether an activity is independent enough to qualify as a decision package, one should ask whether the activity can be outsourced or abandoned without materially affecting another activity.
- Decision packages are then evaluated and ranked in order of importance.
- Resources are allocated accordingly.

12.11.3 Relative advantages of zero-base budgeting over incremental budgeting

- Zero-base budgeting challenges the current way of doing things. Incremental budgeting simply preserves the status quo by adding an inflation factor to current expenditure and adjusting for volume changes.

- Zero-base budgeting facilitates the identification and removal of unnecessary activities and expenditure. Incremental budgeting does not question whether the activities undertaken are necessary, and is therefore unlikely to lead to such changes.
- Where activities undertaken are deemed to be necessary, zero-base budgeting compels employees to question wasteful expenditure. Incremental budgeting may lead to an inflation-based increase in the budget for such expenditure.
- Zero-base budgeting leads to greater staff involvement, which may lead to greater job satisfaction and more motivated staff.
- The identification of decision packages provides in-depth insight into the organisation's operations, while incremental budgeting can be undertaken with a very superficial knowledge of the organisation.
- Starting from a zero base forces staff to stay up to date with the latest developments in the organisation's environment. For example, management has to be informed regarding best industry practices in order to know whether some activities are necessary. Incremental budgeting is less likely to force managers to study the organisation's environment.
- Zero-base budgeting can be very advantageous to service departments where output is sometimes difficult to identify or quantify. Examples of service departments are finance, information technology and human resources. Incremental budgeting to a large extent depends on output, as seen in example 12.4.

12.11.4 Disadvantages of zero-base budgeting compared with incremental budgeting

- Incremental budgeting is less likely than zero-base budgeting to result in radical changes to operations, which makes for a more stable organisational environment.
- Zero-base budgeting can be very time-consuming, while incremental budgeting is a simpler process that requires less effort.
- Zero-base budgeting is more complicated than incremental budgeting and could require management skills which the organisation may not possess. The identification and ranking of decision packages, for example, can be difficult and may even result in arbitrary allocations.
- Information systems may be inadequate to provide the information required to identify decision packages and to rank them for purposes of zero-base budgeting, making incremental budgeting a more viable option in the short term.

12.11.5 Rolling budgets

Key terms: continuous budget, rolling budget

A **rolling budget** is also known as a **continuous budget**. A rolling budget is prepared on a regular basis for the next year or other short-term period. The organisation therefore continuously updates the existing budget. Cash budgets are usually prepared on a rolling basis.

Example 12.5

A not-for-profit organisation draws up quarterly budgets for one year in advance on a rolling basis. It is now nearly the end of quarter 1 of the 2XX8 calendar year, and it is time to update the rolling budget.

Required:
Explain for which period the organisation should now be budgeting.

The organisation prepares its quarterly budgets one year in advance. This means that at the beginning of quarter 1 of 2XX8, the organisation had four quarters' worth of budgets prepared: January to March 2XX8, April to June 2XX8, July to September 2XX8 and October to December 2XX8.

Now that the quarter January to March 2XX8 is nearing its end, the organisation has to add on another quarter's budget in order to keep the budget rolling for the one-year planning period. To ensure that a year's worth of budgets is available, it now needs to prepare the budget for January to March 2XX9 (quarter 1 of the 2XX9 calendar year). It will also revise the budgets for the three remaining quarters of 2XX8.

The main advantage is that rolling budgets ensure that planning is done on a continuous basis and not only once a year. Variances between actual and budgeted figures are also more meaningful as budgets are constantly reviewed and updated.

The major disadvantage of rolling budgets is probably the time required to prepare them properly.

12.12 Budgeting and probability theory

Key term: probability theory

The concept of expected values may be used where there is a great degree of uncertainty about future events. This is referred to as the **probability theory**.

Example 12.6

Assume that an ice cream vendor's sales depend on the weather at the Durban beachfront. If the weather is fine, sales in the budget period are expected to be an average of about 300 ice creams per day. If there is rainy weather, sales are expected to drop to only 60 ice creams per day. A long-term statistical analysis of the weather has indicated that the chance of rain for any given day is on average 20 per cent.

Average daily sales for the budget period can be forecast as follows:

	Units	Probability
Fine weather	300	80%
Rainy weather	60	20%
		100%

Required:
Calculate the vendor's expected daily sales for the budget period.

Note that, when expressed as percentages, the probabilities assigned to mutually-exclusive events must add up to 100 per cent. In this case, the 80 per cent average chance of sunny weather and the 20 per cent average chance of rain add up to 100 per cent. To determine the expected daily sales the probabilities are multiplied by the expected outcomes, and the results are added together.

The expected daily sales are therefore (300 ice creams × 80 per cent) + (60 ice creams × 20 per cent) = 252 ice creams per day. This can now be used in the budget, taking all other relevant information into account as well.

12.13 Preparing projections using historical data

Key term: projections

Projections are an important aspect of the budgeting process. The Chartered Institute of Management Accountants defines projection as 'an expected future trend pattern obtained by extrapolation', which is based on the notion that past events can serve as an indication of what will happen in the future.

Note that some of the projection techniques in this section require a basic knowledge of statistics. Although this chapter discusses the techniques in the context of their usefulness for budgeting, students who require further explanation are advised to consult statistics textbooks and resources for a comprehensive explanation.

In this section we briefly revisit some of the techniques learnt in Chapter 3, *Cost estimation*.

12.13.1 Projections using the high-low method

Key term: high-low method

One technique frequently used in projections is the so-called **high-low method**, which was discussed in Chapter 3, *Cost estimation*. The method is best illustrated by use of an example.

Example 12.7

The manager of a factory is trying to budget maintenance costs for July. The results for the past six months to be used as a basis are as follows:

	Machine hours	Cost R
January	18 300	48 300
February	17 900	47 100
March	21 200	53 900
April	14 800	41 100
May	16 200	43 800
June	18 500	48 700

principles of management accounting

> The factory manager expects that, based on the required production for July, the number of machine hours for July will be 17 500 hours.
>
> **Required:**
> Determine the expected maintenance cost for July, using the high-low method.

The month with the highest level of activity is March, and the month with the lowest level of activity is April. The high-low method calculates the difference between the costs in these two months, as well as the difference between the two cost driver values (hours in this example) for the two months.

	Hours	R
Highest month – March	21 200	53 900
Lowest month – April	14 800	41 100
Difference	6 400	12 800

This enables us to surmise that the increase in maintenance cost (R12 800) must be a variable cost, and can be ascribed to the increase in machine hours worked (6 400 hours).

The variable cost per machine hour is therefore R12 800/6 400 hours = R2 per hour.

Now the variable cost per hour can be applied to either the high or the low figure, in order to determine the fixed portion of the cost:

High: R53 900 (total cost in March) – (21 200 hours × R2) (variable cost in March)
= R11 500 (fixed cost in March)

Or:

Low: R41 100 (total cost in April) – (14 800 hours × R2) (variable cost in April)
= R11 500 (fixed cost in April).

The fixed cost per month is therefore R11 500.

The projected total maintenance cost for July is (17 500 hours × R2) + R11 500
= R46 500.

12.13.2 Linear regression analysis

Key terms: least squares method, linear regression analysis

When applying **linear regression analysis**, the end result that we are trying to achieve is to 'fit' the historical information available to us into a formula where we can distinguish between the variable and fixed portions. This information can then assist us to forecast what the total cost will be when there is a new level of activity in the future. The formula we refer to is the following:

$y = a + bx$

where:
- y, the dependent variable = total cost
- x, the independent variable = the units of activity
- a, the intercept of the line on the Y axis = the fixed cost
- b, the gradient of the line = the variable cost per unit of activity

Linear regression analysis is also known as the **least squares method**.

The above regression equation for a straight line can be found from the following two equations by solving for a and b. In these equations, n = the number of observations.

$\Sigma y = na + b\Sigma x$
$\Sigma xy = a\Sigma x + b\Sigma x^2$

Example 12.8

The information from example 12.7 applies.

Required:
Calculate the expected costs for 17 500 maintenance hours.

When applying the information from example 12.7, the data can be expressed as follows:

	Machine hours x	Cost (R) y	R'000 x^2	R'000 xy
January	18 300	48 300	334 890	883 890
February	17 900	47 100	320 410	843 090
March	21 200	53 900	449 440	1 142 680
April	14 800	41 100	219 040	608 280
May	16 200	43 800	262 440	709 560
June	18 500	48 700	342 250	900 950
	106 900	282 900	1 928 470	5 088 450

Solving for a and b in the two formulae provided above by means of the simultaneous equation method, we find:

282 900 = 6a + 106 900b
5 088 450 000 = 106 900a + 1 928 470 000b

Therefore:

a = 11 234,26

and

b = 2,01585

principles of management accounting

The expected costs for 17 500 maintenance hours would therefore be:

$y = 11\ 234{,}26 + (2{,}01585 \times 17\ 500) = R46\ 512$

The above can also be calculated using the statistical function on a financial calculator. MS Excel® also has a 'forecast' function which applies linear regression analysis.

12.13.3 Other methods for preparing projections using historical data

Two other methods for preparing projections based on historical data should be mentioned here: scatter diagrams and correlation.
- *Scatter diagrams.* Under this method of cost estimation, cost and corresponding activity are plotted on a graph known as a scatter diagram. A line of best fit is then drawn through the middle of the plotted points. This is not a very accurate method, but it provides a visual indication of the correlation between past activities and their related costs. The technique is discussed in Chapter 3, *Cost estimation*.
- *Correlation.* The degree of association between two variables such as cost and activity is referred to as correlation. Correlation is discussed in Chapter 3, *Cost estimation*.

12.14 Projecting sales

As previously explained, the first budget drawn up is usually the sales budget. It is therefore important for management to try to determine what future sales will be. They can do this in one of the following ways:
- Obtain information on future sales from the organisation's sales personnel.
- Conduct market research.
- Apply mathematical methods and techniques, such as those discussed in section 12.13.

12.14.1 Regression and projections

When regression analysis is used for estimating sales, the years (or days or months) become the x variables in the regression formulae by numbering them from 1 upwards. This is illustrated in example 12.9.

Example 12.9

The following historic sales information for an organisation is available:

Quarter	1	2	3	4	5	6	7
Sales of B ('000 units)	674	770	737	800	894	858	923

Required:
Estimate how many units will be sold in quarters 8 and 9 respectively.

The forecast sales for quarters 8 and 9 can be determined by employing regression analysis. Using the regression formulae shown in section 12.13, let the quarter be x and the corresponding sales y.

Quarter x	Sales (R) y	x^2	xy
1	674	1	674
2	770	4	1 540
3	737	9	2 211
4	800	16	3 200
5	894	25	4 470
6	858	36	5 148
7	923	49	6 461
28	5656	140	23 704

Solving for a and b in the two regression formulae provided above by means of the simultaneous equation method, we find:

$$5656 = 7a + 28b$$
$$23\,704 = 28a + 140b$$

Therefore:

$$a = 653{,}71429$$

and

$$b = 38{,}571429$$

The expected number of units that will be sold is therefore:

$y = 653{,}71429 + (38{,}571429 \times 8) = 962$ units in quarter 8
$y = 653{,}71429 + (38{,}571429 \times 9) = 1\,001$ units in quarter 9

12.15 Budgetary control

Budgetary control is the process of comparing actual results to budget results and, if there are significant undesirable variances, taking corrective action in an attempt to prevent these variances from recurring. Budgetary control is the cornerstone of good internal control.

12.16 Fixed and flexed budgets

Key terms: fixed budget, flexed budget

Fixed budgets are not affected by changes in activity levels, for example, the volume of units produced. Instead, a **fixed budget** is drawn up for a specific activity

principles of management accounting

level (for example, production of 400 000 units). A fixed budget is useful to gain an overall picture of the business plan, but as a control measure it often fails, especially when actual activity levels vary from budgeted activity levels.

Let us assume total production cost according to a fixed budget amounts to R40 million. Actual production costs turn out to be R43 million. Using a fixed budget approach, we have to conclude that the organisation has overspent its production budget, which is seemingly a negative outcome. However, if we assume that the original budget was to produce 400 000 units at R100 each, and the organisation ended up producing 440 000 units at a total cost of R43 million, then it performed better than expected. At R100 per unit we would logically expect production cost to be around R44 million. To prevent the wrong conclusion from being drawn, we need a flexed budget.

Flexed budgets are based on variable costs per unit, and can therefore easily be adjusted when actual activity levels differ from budgeted activity levels. A **flexed budget** is designed to change according to changes in activity levels (see the next section for more details).

12.17 Preparing a flexed budget

A flexed budget is prepared by separating expected fixed costs from expected variable costs. Fixed costs are not affected by different activity levels. Variable costs, however, increase in line with increasing activity levels, and the flexed budget should be adjusted accordingly. This can best be explained by means of an example.

Example 12.10

A review of past information has revealed the following costs for FG (Pty) Ltd for production levels of 8 000 and 10 000 units per month:

	8 000 units R	10 000 units R
Direct materials	360 000	450 000
Maintenance	54 000	60 000
Factory rental	56 000	56 000

Required:
Prepare cost budgets for production levels of 11 000 units, 11 500 units and 12 000 units per month.

Using the high-low method, we can calculate that the variable cost for direct materials is R45 per unit, with no fixed cost. The variable portion can be determined as follows: (R450 000 − R360 000)/(10 000 units − 8 000 units) = R45 per unit.

Maintenance consists of a fixed and a variable portion. Again, using the high-low method we determine that the variable maintenance cost is R3 per unit, while the fixed portion is R30 000. The variable portion is determined as follows: (R60 000 − R54 000)/(10 000 units − 8 000 units) = R3 per unit. The fixed portion is calculated by subtracting the variable cost from the total cost: R54 000 − (8 000 × R3) = R30 000 or R60 000 − (10 000 units × R3) = R30 000.

Factory rental is not affected by the production level and will remain fixed at R56 000.

The flexed budget will be as follows:

	11 000 units R	11 500 units R	12 000 units R
Direct materials (× R45)	495 000	517 500	540 000
Variable maintenance (× R3)	33 000	34 500	36 000
Fixed maintenance costs	30 000	30 000	30 000
Factory rental	56 000	56 000	56 000
	614 000	638 000	662 000

12.18 Impact of budgeting on the motivation of managers

Key term: budgetary slack

Managers may be negative towards the budget-setting process for various reasons:
- Some may lack the necessary numerical skills and technical knowledge to prepare a budget properly, leaving them with a sense of inadequacy.
- It may be a very busy period and they may find it difficult to make time for preparing a budget.
- Managers may not be aware of the importance of preparing a budget, failing to understand the bigger picture and senior management's long-term strategy for the organisation.
- Managers may have the perception that the budget will be used as a punitive device if they fail to meet targets, with the result that they could attempt to build slack into their forecasts. **Budgetary slack** is built into a budget when a manager intentionally overestimates expenses or underestimates expected income in order to meet set targets more easily.
- Managers may perceive the budget process as a bureaucratic exercise and attempt to get it out of the way as effortlessly as possible. This is often done by simply adding an inflation factor to past budgets.

Once the budget has been set, the following performance-related problems may be encountered:
- Managers may have an attitude of doing just enough to meet the set targets without trying to *beat* the targets. In certain cases where managers have already met the target, they may attempt to apply smart accounting to carry some of the surplus profits over to the next budget period, ensuring that it will be easier to meet the next budgeted target as well.
- In governmental organisations a budgeted expense is sometimes seen as an amount that has to be spent. There are two reasons for this: firstly, it is often feared that the budget for that particular expense item may be reduced by the government in the next budget period and allocated to a different department. Secondly, public opinion could turn against the organisation if it becomes known that tax money earmarked for specific purposes is not being spent as

promised. 'Use it or lose it' is a phrase often heard in these organisations. The result is that there is often wasteful expenditure in the few months before the end of the budget period.
- Managers may find it difficult to interpret control reports (reports that show how actual results deviated from budgeted figures) because of a lack of financial training.
- In cases where control reports are not prepared timeously, such information loses its value and managers may be more likely to ignore it.
- Managers may resist the budgetary control process if they feel that they have not had control over either the budget-setting exercise or the variances between the budgeted and actual results. In Chapter 14, *Performance management*, the importance of measuring someone's performance based only on factors over which they have control is discussed in more detail.

Notwithstanding the potential negative aspects above, the setting of targets (as done during a budgeting process) is an extremely powerful motivating force in the minds of managers. Budgets provide a way of communicating at the beginning of a period what is expected of the entity and its managers during the period, as well as a means of measuring actual performance against these expectations at the end of the period.

12.19 Participation and performance evaluation

Senior management may adopt different approaches with regard to the extent to which they allow line managers to be involved in the budgeting process.

On the one hand, we find an autocratic style, where the budget is imposed from the 'top down' (in other words, imposed by senior management) on the line manager. We say that an 'imposed' style of budgeting is employed. The underlying philosophy is that budgets ought to be set in line with strategic plans for the organisation as a whole, and that senior management is in the best position to do so.

On the other hand, there is a more democratic management style, where line managers are encouraged to participate in the budget-setting process – a 'participative' budgeting style is employed. The underlying philosophy is that participation in the budgeting process increases the motivation of managers to meet their targets.

Although the participative style is popular in modern organisations, both styles have advantages and disadvantages.

12.19.1 Potential relative advantages of imposed budgets over participative budgets

- When imposed budgets are used, it is easy for senior management to ensure that the budget is in line with the overall long-term business strategy.
- It is easier to ensure co-ordination between different business units when imposed budgets are used, because senior management sets the budget and they have a better view of the organisation as a whole, compared to line managers.
- Senior management may be in a position to make better decisions than line managers owing to their experience and knowledge, a fact that favours imposed budgets.
- Imposed budgets can be set in a shorter period of time, because senior managers can complete the task without having to wait for 'bottom up' inputs

from line managers. This means that the budget may be more accurate, as the budgeting process can start later and the budget can therefore be based on more recent information.
- When budgets are imposed 'top-down', line managers are not involved in the budgeting process, which means they do not have the opportunity to build in any budgetary 'slack' (in other words, they cannot deliberately set budgets for themselves that are easy to attain).

12.19.2 Potential relative disadvantages of imposed budgets compared with participative budgets

- When budgets are imposed, line managers could be dissatisfied and feel that their position in the organisation does not receive the necessary recognition. This could lead to a lack of 'buy-in' from these line managers.
- Line managers often have a better understanding and more experience of the operations of their divisions because of their active involvement. This insight is not applied when budgets are imposed from the top.
- The budgeting process could be seen as an opportunity to gain ideas from line managers about ways of improving the operation of their units. This opportunity is not exploited when budgets are imposed.
- Because senior management is not always in touch with the detail of the circumstances faced by a specific unit, they may impose unachievable budgets which could in turn impact negatively on the motivation of line managers.

12.20 Negotiated style of budgeting

It is important to note that a participative style of budgeting does not necessarily imply that line managers set 'bottom up' budgets that are unconditionally accepted by senior management. If this were the case, there would be no way for senior management to ensure that the organisation is steered in the direction of its strategic objectives. Instead, budgets are usually the result of a process of negotiation between line managers and senior management.

Senior management will usually communicate their ideas and aspirations for the organisation to line managers, and from there the budget is negotiated until both parties are satisfied that the budget is challenging, yet achievable.

The major drawback of negotiated budgets is that they take considerable time to prepare.

The major advantage is that the resulting budgets will probably be very realistic and are therefore likely to be accepted by all the parties involved.

12.21 Continuous feedback on performance

The organisational unit for which the budget is set needs to receive regular feedback on how it is performing, both because line managers require time to take corrective action when unfavourable feedback is received, and because line managers could be motivated by favourable feedback.

Feedback should adhere to the following principles:
- Information should be communicated to a line manager who is in a position to take corrective action. It should focus on those income and expenditure items falling within the scope of the manager's control.

- Feedback reports should highlight significant variances so that managers can focus their attention on exceptions (this is called *exception reporting*). It means that not every negligible budget variance is highlighted for attention, but rather that pre-set limits determine when a variance is large enough to require the attention of line managers (and their actions are followed up on by senior management).
- Reports should be clear and understandable.
- Reports should be as accurate as possible.
- Reports should be timely. Note that the more time management spends on ensuring accuracy, the less timely the reporting will be. A balance therefore has to be struck between the quality and the timeliness of reports.

12.22 The role of the management accountant in the budget process

The management accountant in an organisation has an important role to play in improving the quality of the budgetary control system.

The management accountant needs to have regular contact with line managers and should make time to discuss control reports with them. The meaning and implication of information in these reports should be explained to line managers, keeping accounting jargon to the minimum.

Special care should be taken with the content and outlay of the control report drawn up by the management accountant to ensure that the information is clear and understandable. He or she needs to ensure that information contained in reports is both accurate and timely. Accuracy is, of course, vital, and reports should be timely so that line managers do not act on out-dated information.

12.23 Beyond Budgeting®

The Beyond Budgeting® Round Table, an independent research body, is often in the news, and suggests that traditional budgeting should be done away with. Their criticism of traditional budgeting includes the following:
- Budgets are time consuming and expensive.
- Budgets provide poor value to users.
- Budgets fail to focus on shareholder value.
- Budgets can be too rigid and prevent fast response.
- Budgets protect rather than reduce costs.
- Budgets stifle product and strategy innovation.
- Budgets focus on sales targets rather than customer satisfaction.
- Budgets are divorced from strategy.
- Budgets reinforce a dependency culture.
- Budgets lead to unethical behaviour.

Beyond Budgeting® advocates adaptive management processes as opposed to fixed annual budgets. It believes that managers should rather focus their attention on the generation of cash than on control over expenditure. Furthermore, the organisation calls for a move away from traditional centralised organisational hierarchy to a more devolved network where individuals assume responsibility for their own actions.

12.24 Summary

Although the scope of the budget is usually medium to short term, the budget is part of the long-term strategic planning process of an organisation. It is a practical tool for setting objectives in the short to medium term, and to maintain control over the organisation's efforts in achieving these objectives. Other advantages of budgeting include the fact that it facilitates performance measurement, motivation, communication, and co-ordination of activities.

Cash budgets deal with cash flows only, and disregard accounting entries.

Some frequently-encountered budgeting techniques include incremental budgeting, zero-base budgeting, and rolling budgets. Some of the projection techniques discussed in Chapter 3, *Cost estimation* are particularly useful for budgeting purposes.

Conclusion: Budgets, planning and control and other topics in this book

This chapter introduced the objectives of budgets and the different types of budgets. One of the major objectives of budgets is to provide a framework for control and responsibility accounting. The importance of control and responsibility accounting is discussed further in Chapter 14, *Performance management*.

An integral part of budgeting is the setting of predetermined targets and standards. This is very closely related to the concept of standard costing, which is discussed the next chapter, Chapter 13, *Standard costing*. In Chapter 13 we will learn that one of the objectives of standard costing is to facilitate the budgeting process.

Some of the projection techniques discussed in Chapter 3, *Cost estimation* are particularly useful in the budget-setting process.

Tutorial case study: Capital Harvest

Capital Harvest provides finance to farmers and other agricultural enterprises, primarily in the Western Cape. By the end of December, the company draws up an annual budget detailing the budgeted income and expenditure per month for the next financial year. This budget is submitted to shareholders for approval. The shareholders do not require the submission of any further budgets during the year.

In turn, Capital Harvest negotiates a budget with each one of its bankers. The bankers are responsible for managing existing loans and for expanding the company's business by finding additional suitable opportunities where loans can be granted. Extensive discussions take place between Capital Harvest and each of its bankers which may result in modifications. Once all parties are satisfied with the final budget, it is formally approved.

When Capital Harvest prepares its annual budget, the first figure it estimates is the rand value of loans to be granted to clients during the financial year. Most of its expenses are fixed in the short term and are easy to budget. For the remaining items, the company primarily bases its budget on the previous year's results.

1. Discuss the reasons that Capital Harvest's shareholders may require the company to submit a budget each year, despite the fact that it takes up a great deal of management time.
2. Speculate whether the budget submitted to its shareholders by Capital Harvest is likely to be of a strategic, tactical or operational nature.
3. Identify the principal budgeting factor for Capital Harvest.

principles of management accounting

> 4 Advise Capital Harvest as to whether it ought to prepare a cash budget in addition to the annual budget, even though this is not required by its shareholders.
> 5 Discuss the key performance indicators that you think may be specifically important in the industry in which Capital Harvest operates.
> 6 Evaluate whether Capital Harvest uses an incremental or a zero-based approach to budgeting.
> 7 Advise Capital Harvest as to whether it ought to make use of rolling budgeting during the financial year, even though this is not required by the shareholders.
> 8 Discuss to what extent projection techniques may assist Capital Harvest in its budgeting process.
> 9 Discuss the style of budgeting that Capital Harvest seemingly follows in relation to its bankers.

Basic questions

BQ 1
Name five of the most important objectives of budgeting.

BQ 2
What is the function of a budget manual?

BQ 3
Which type of planning in the left column matches the budget period in the right column?

• Tactical planning	• Long-term
• Operational planning	• Medium-term
• Strategic planning	• Short-term

BQ 4
Who in the organisation is likely to be responsible for preparing the following aspects of the budget?
- Materials purchases budget
- Production budget
- Sales budget
- Budget guidelines
- Fixed overhead absorption rate

BQ 5
What are three possible principal budget factors (factors that could determine the volumes and amounts that should be budgeted)?

BQ 6
What three actions could management consider in order to alleviate a short-term cash deficit?

BQ 7
What is a master budget?

BQ 8
The following figures represent a factory's production figures and related production costs for the past seven months. The cost accountant has to prepare a production budget for the next five months. Budgeted production is 25 000 units per month. Using the high-low method, what are the expected fixed and variable production costs, and the amount to be included in the budget for production costs?

	Production (units)	Production cost R
January	20 500	366 000
February	23 200	398 000
March	26 800	441 900
April	26 000	432 650
May	29 100	469 200
June	22 300	388 000
July	25 500	425 600

BQ 9
What is the difference between an incremental budget and a zero-base budget?

BQ 10
What is the meaning of the term 'coefficient of determination' (r^2)?

Long questions

LQ 1 – Intermediate (15 marks; 27 minutes)
KC Ltd purchases raw materials and then reworks them into a product for resale. Budgeted sales are as follows:

	October	November	December
Sales in units	27 000	31 000	35 000

- The basic raw materials cost R6 per kilogram.
- A completed sales unit requires 2 kilograms of raw materials input.
- The target month-end raw materials inventory level is 15 000 kilograms plus 20 per cent of the raw materials required for next month's budgeted production.
- The target month-end inventory level for finished goods is 5 000 units plus 20 per cent of the next month's budgeted sales.

REQUIRED	Marks
Calculate the budgeted raw materials purchases for October.	15
TOTAL MARKS	15

principles of management accounting

LQ 2 – Intermediate (15 marks; 27 minutes)

Raps (Pty) Ltd operates a supermarket. Purchases are sold at cost plus 40 per cent. The following budgeted figures are available:

	Sales R	Salaries R	Other expenses R
March	280 000	18 000	22 000
April	308 000	18 000	24 000
May	350 000	19 000	24 000
June	364 000	19 000	28 000

- It is management policy to have sufficient inventory on hand at the end of each month to meet half of the next month's sales demand.
- Creditors are paid in the month after the purchases are made or the expenses incurred. Salaries are paid at the end of each month.
- Expenses include monthly depreciation of R8 000.
- Eighty per cent of sales are for cash; 20 per cent of sales are on one month's credit. No bad debts are incurred.
- The organisation will pay a dividend of R90 000 in April and will buy equipment costing R30 000 for cash in May. The opening cash balance at 1 April is R20 000.

REQUIRED	Marks
Prepare a cash budget for April and May.	15
TOTAL MARKS	15

LQ 3 – Intermediate (10 marks; 18 minutes)

JD Ltd has established the following key metrics in order to assess profitability in the budgetary plans for the forthcoming budget period:
- Return on capital employed = 25 per cent.
- Profit margin = 10 per cent.
- Contribution to sales ratio = 40 per cent.

Extracts from JD's master budget are as follows:

	R million
Budgeted statement of financial position:	
Non-current assets	3 500
Current assets	3 780
Current liabilities	2 320
Budget income statement:	
Revenue	6 980
Contribution	2 560
Profit from operations	990

REQUIRED	Marks
Assess whether senior management would approve the budget in terms of the key metrics.	10
TOTAL MARKS	10

LQ 4 – Advanced (15 marks; 27 minutes)

Fastflow (Pty) Ltd prepared the following budget for the month of October:

Budgeted production and sales (units)	25 000
	R
Sales	450 000
Raw materials	(187 500)
Labour	(76 000)
Total overheads	(125 000)
Budgeted profit	61 500

Labour is regarded as a fixed cost, as all employees earn a fixed salary per month regardless of their efficiency.

The budget for total overheads for September was R110 000, and the budgeted production 20 000 units.

The actual results for October were as follows:

Actual production and sales (units)	27 000
	R
Sales	472 500
Raw materials	(202 500)
Labour	(77 000)
Total overheads	(127 600)
Actual profit	65 400

Actual total overheads consisted of fixed costs of R52 000 and the remaining overhead costs varied with production.

REQUIRED	Marks
Prepare a flexed budget statement comparing budgeted profit to actual profit for October. Calculate all variances.	15
TOTAL MARKS	15

LQ 5 – Advanced (15 marks; 27 minutes)

The production director of a local mine has been asked to assist with the preparation of the budget for the next two years, specifically with reference to the size of the labour force required to produce the set targets of 10 000 tonnes and 12 000 tonnes of mineral for the next two years respectively.

Production information for the past eight years is as follows:

Year	1	2	3	4	5	6	7	8
Tonnes mined	9 500	11 500	14 000	12 800	9 300	7 600	6 500	8 500
Labour force	2 280	2 710	3 230	2 970	2 240	1 910	1 690	2 110

REQUIRED	Marks
Using linear regression analysis (the least squares method), determine the number of workers required to mine respectively (a) 10 000 tonnes and (b) 12 000 tonnes of mineral for the next two years.	15
TOTAL MARKS	15

References

Eaton, G. 2005. *Management accounting official terminology*. London: CIMA Publishing.
Miningmx.com. 2011. *African Barrick beats expectations*. [Online]. Available: >www.miningmx.com/news/gold_and_silver/African-Barrick-beats-expectations.htm> [11 March 2011].
Upchurch, A. 1998. 'Management accounting principles and practices'. *Financial Times*. Pitman Publishing.

Standard costing

chapter 13

Jonathan Streng, Hendrik Fourie and Gary Swartz

LEARNING OBJECTIVES
By the end of this chapter, you should be able to:
1. Understand the purpose of a standard costing system.
2. Explain how standards are set in a standard costing environment and the design of a standard costing system.
3. Explain how a standard costing system works.
4. Calculate variances (labour, materials, overhead, and revenue).
5. Reconcile actual profit to budgeted profit.
6. Investigate and identify the causes of variances, and interrelationships between variances.
7. Prepare journal entries to record standard costs and variances.

> **Managers and standard costing**
>
> Investors can monitor the performance of South Africa's large manufacturers by following the movements in the *Industrial 25* index, which reflects how the share prices of our country's industrial giants behave, given the myriad factors than impact on their value. But behind every company share that makes up the index, there are layers of managers analysing their respective companies' performance in much more detail – studying why the company's results differed from what they had anticipated, what factors contributed to each line item on the monthly management accounts not being as expected, and investigating why these variances occurred.

Standard costing offers a way of analysing performance in as much detail as is required by management, by investigating the specific factors that caused actual results to differ from planned/budgeted results. Standard costing is, however, not only an effective performance management and budgetary control technique, but also a tool for inventory valuation as well as providing valuable information for management decision making and internal control. This chapter explains how a standard costing system works.

13.1 Introduction

Key terms: variance analysis

In Chapter 12, *Budgets, planning and control*, we learnt about the budgeting process. If we have a budgeted set of results which shows an anticipated profit of R100 000 for a month, it means very simply that the total expected revenues exceed the total expected costs for the month by R100 000. However, assume that after receiving the actual results for the month, a loss of R50 000 is reported. Therefore, in total, there is a R150 000 (R100 000 + R50 000) discrepancy in terms of profit between what we had anticipated and what actually happened. If we were asked to analyse the actual results compared to the budget and determine the reasons for the poor performance, we would clearly require more detailed information. We would need to understand how revenues fell short of the budget, and/or which costs were more than budgeted. Was it perhaps overhead expenses that were out of control that caused the poor results? This process of analysing in detail the reason for actual performance differing from planned performance is called variance analysis. Where costs were saved or revenues exceeded the budget as a result of better performance, favourable variances will result. Poor performance indicated by cost overruns or lower than budgeted revenues results in unfavourable (also called 'adverse') variances.

Variance analysis is critical because once the root causes of the difference between planned and actual results have been identified, corrective action needs to be taken so that performance can be improved, and so that the same mistakes are not repeated. Performance measurement is therefore essential to the survival of organisations. This chapter focuses on planning, control and measurement of performance using standard costing.

Standard costing systems are widely used in practice because they:
- Provide a prediction of future costs and revenues that can be used for planning purposes and decision-making
- Provide information for performance evaluation
- Assist in the identification of problem areas and areas where attention and action is required within the business
- Provide information for inventory valuation purposes for both management reporting and financial reporting functions
- Provide inputs into the budgeting process.

Standard costing systems are traditionally found in the manufacturing industry, but are equally useful in any organisational context where meaningful standard prices and input quantities can be determined.

13.2 Standards and the interrelationship between standards and budgets

Before going further, it is essential that you clearly understand the meaning of a 'standard' and the difference between standards and budgets. Note that a budget is usually a 'total' concept, for example, 'the budgeted direct labour cost in total of Division A for the month is R300 000'. Standards, on the other hand, usually refer to the individual cost objects or units that comprise the total budget. So, for example, 'the standard labour cost of one unit of Product X is R100'. In this example, the standard cost for labour refers to the R100 making up the cost of labour for each unit manufactured. From this information, we can deduce that there were 3 000 labour hours budgeted for the month in total (3 000 hours x R100 = R300 000).

Although the standard cost for labour of one unit of Product X was R100 as per the example, 'standards' can be further broken down into their price and quantity components. In other words, suppose that labourers are expecting to be paid R25 per hour. This 'R25 per hour' would be referred to as the price standard for labour. From this, it is easy to infer that each unit of Product X takes 4 hours to manufacture (R100 per unit divided by R25 per hour). Therefore, '4 hours per unit' would be referred to as the quantity (or 'volume') standard for labour. The standard cost (R100 per unit) is therefore a product of the standard price (R25 per hour) multiplied by the standard quantity (4 hours per unit). If either the actual price or actual quantity of labour input is different from the price and quantity standards anticipated, a variance will exist.

These same principles can be applied to all input costs, such as labour (discussed above), as well as materials and both variable and fixed manufacturing overheads. In addition to standards for input costs, it is possible to determine standards for sales as well as for non-manufacturing costs.

13.3 Standard costing and inventory valuation

International Financial Reporting Standards ('IFRS') allow the use of standard costing for inventory valuation for external reporting purposes. IAS 2, the IFRS accounting standard dealing with inventory, states that valuing closing inventory at standard cost per unit is a suitable alternative to valuing it at actual cost per unit, but specifies that the standard costs should 'approximate actual' and that standards should 'be regularly revised in light of current conditions'. We will come back to the accounting treatment of a standard costing system later under section 13.12, but for now it is important to realise that if an organisation is operating a standard costing system, it means that closing inventory of finished goods will be valued at the end of each reporting period at the standard manufacturing cost per unit (that is, the sum of the unit's standard materials, labour, variable and fixed manufacturing overhead cost per unit).

13.4 Determination of cost standards

Standard prices and input quantities are set in advance before actual results are known. In setting price standards, an organisation should take factors such as suppliers' quotations, price seasonality, volume discounts available and market prices into account. In setting quantity standards, factors such as the quality of material and labour, the wastage expected, time and motion studies, learning curve effects, skills levels of staff, and idle time expected should be considered by the organisation.

Two approaches can be used to determine standards, firstly, the use of historic records, and secondly, engineering studies.

13.4.1 Historic records versus engineering studies

Historic records

Historic records provide a starting point for the development of standards, because they contain the prices and input quantities that were recorded in previous financial periods. This is very similar to the incremental budgeting method discussed in Chapter 12, *Budgets, planning and control*.

principles of management accounting

There are, however, a number of potential disadvantages when standards are based on the prices and input quantities recorded in a prior period:
- Historic records have been affected by any efficiencies or inefficiencies experienced in the past.
- Using historic records can promote the use of averages, resulting in standards being set midway between past 'good' and 'bad' performances, rather than striving for best practices.
- Historic records do not reflect subsequent changes in the organisation or its environment (such as, for example, the introduction of a just-in-time system). Clearly, in such circumstances variances based on prior performance are unlikely to provide adequate benchmarks for managers to strive for.

Basing standards on historic records is usually time- and cost-effective, but because of the potential disadvantages listed above, it may result in less desirable standards than those obtained through engineering studies.

Engineering studies

Engineering studies, such as time-and-motion studies and business process re-engineering, include a detailed study of each operation, and careful specifications are created for each cost item. Best practices are sought, focusing attention on finding the best combination of resources, production methods, and quality. There are many similarities between this method and the principles of zero-base budgeting as discussed in Chapter 12, *Budgets, planning and control*. Although engineering studies encourage organisations to strive constantly for better levels of performance by setting standards based on the most effective execution of the value chain, it is more costly than merely basing standards on historic records.

To set standards, organisations use either historic records or engineering studies, or a combination of the two, and adjust for any factors that may need to be taken into consideration. Ideally, standards should not be affected by historic inefficiencies, and should take into account any expected changes in the organisation and its environment.

13.4.2 Level of difficulty

Key terms: achievable standards, basic standards, ideal standards

Irrespective of whether historic records are used as a starting point or whether engineering studies are performed to set standards, management will need to decide how lenient or strict they would like to be when it comes to the setting of standards. For example, they have the option of setting so-called **ideal standards** – standards that represent perfect working conditions, with absolutely no allowance for spoilage or inefficiency. However, while **basic standards** that are too slack may fail to motivate employees to improve performance, ideal standards may be seen as unattainable and may also result in demotivating employees if they believe that their bonuses are based on budgets that are impossible to achieve.

The solution is often to set **achievable standards** – standards that are not too slack, but which represent normal working conditions and allow for a certain level of expected spoilage and inefficiency under normal conditions.

13.5 Calculation of variances

As mentioned, a standard costing system essentially compares the standards set at the beginning of the period to the actual performance during the period, yielding favourable and unfavourable variances on which management can be assessed and improvements can be made.

These variances are of little use if not recorded, evaluated, and acted upon where necessary. After the variances have been calculated, the relevant managers deemed responsible for the variances should be consulted to determine the cause of each significant variance and corrective action should be taken as necessary.

13.5.1 The static budget variance, volume variance and flexed budget variance

> **Key terms:** flexed budget variance, price variance, quantity variance, static budget variance, volume variance

You will recall that a budget is an aggregate or total estimate of results for the organisation that is used for planning purposes. The original overall budget is usually in the form of a static budget, which reflects the budgeted sales and production volumes. A comparison of the static budget profit with the actual profit at the end of the period yields the total budget variance – this is called the **static budget variance**. This variance represents the difference between the profit or loss as originally planned at the budgeted level of output, and the profit or loss actually made.

In order to analyse the static budget variance further, we have to determine which part of the variance is as a result of the change in production levels (as it is unlikely that *precisely* the planned level of output was achieved) and which part of the variance is as a result of a change in the expected price or quantity of the underlying inputs.

For us to do be able to do this, the original budget has to be adjusted to reflect the actual level of production for the period in question. The original static budget, adjusted for actual production levels, is called the flexed budget. You may recall this from Chapter 12, *Budgets, planning and control*, where static versus flexed budgets were discussed.

'Flexing the budget'

The principle of flexing the budget prior to evaluating the the results of an organisation is extremely important. Although this is normally a principle that is taught along with standard costing, it is a crucial principle that can be applied beyond the boundaries of standard costing.

Take the example of a factory foreman who works in a pen factory. The standard usage of plastic materials input per pen is 0,1 kilograms per pen. Based on a planned production level given by top management of 100 000 pens, the procurement division ordered 10 000 kg (100 000 pens x 0,1 kg) of plastic in order to meet expected production demand. At the end of the period, owing to unanticipated sales orders received for pens, 120 000 pens were manufactured. If it were determined that the factory actually used 11 000 kg of plastic instead of the budgeted 10 000 kg, would it be correct for top management to reprimand the factory foreman for using more plastic than budgeted?

The answer is clearly 'No!' Of course more plastic would be used, because more pens were produced! In fact, if the factory had used the 'correct' amount of plastic per pen, it would have consumed 12 000 kg of plastic (120 000 pens x 0,1kg). The factory in fact saved costs by using on average less plastic per pen manufactured.

This example highlights the importance of first 'flexing the budget' prior to performance evaluation, by revising our expectations based on the actual level of activity achieved. The actual activity level is the figure that drives the flexed budget and all the variance calculations that will follow.

principles of management accounting

This process of 'flexing the budget' is achieved by re-preparing the budget, now basing the amounts on the *actual* activity levels achieved (not the budgeted levels). Note, however, that although the flexed budget depicts the ACTUAL activity levels achieved, the input costs will still be based on the standard costs per unit (that is, standard price and standard quantities) originally determined at the beginning of the period.

The difference between the static budget profit and the flexed budget profit represents the variance owing to the difference between planned and actual activity levels – this is called the **volume variance**.

The difference between the profit as shown in the flexed budget and the actual profit represents the variance as a result of changes in the expected price or quantity of the underlying inputs – this variance is called the **flexed budget variance**.

Example 13.1

Specialised Cycles is a manufacturer of a racing bicycle, the Madone XXI, which it sells to cycling retail stores within South Africa. The organisation purchases components and raw materials for the bicycle from various suppliers, and uses semi-skilled labour to manufacture the frames, and skilled labour to assemble the bicycle. The organisation has fixed costs relating to the factory and head office infrastructure.

The following budget has been prepared for the month of October:

Static budget	October budget
Units produced and sold	1 000
Revenue	R5 500 000
Raw materials (carbon fibre for frame manufacture)	(R1 000 000)
Components	(R2 000 000)
Semi-skilled labour	(R500 000)
Skilled labour	(R300 000)
Variable overhead	(R100 000)
Factory fixed overhead	(R400 000)
Head office overhead (fixed)	(R100 000)
Budgeted profit	R1 100 000

The actual results for the month of October are as follows:

Actual results	October actual
Units produced	1 300
Units sold	1 200
Revenue	R6 840 000
Raw materials (carbon fibre for frame manufacture)	(R1 495 000)
Components	(R2 431 000)
Semi-skilled labour	(R716 300)

Actual results	October actual
Skilled labour	(R414 700)
Variable overhead	(R95 000)
Factory fixed overhead	(R650 000)
Head office overhead (fixed)	(R155 000)
Closing inventory (100 bicycles)	R430 000 *
Profit	R1 313 000

* In a standard costing environment, the closing inventory is valued at the *standard* manufacturing cost per bicycle multiplied by the closing inventory of 100 bicycles i.e. (R1 000 000 + R2 000 000 + R500 000 + R300 000 + R100 000 + R400 000)/1 000 bicycles = R 4 300 per bicycle × 100 bicycles = R430 000.

Assume that there was no bicycle inventory on hand at the beginning of month of October. In addition, there was no opening or closing inventory of raw materials or components.

Required:
Analyse the variance between the static budget and the actual results for October in as much detail as the information permits.

It is clear from comparing the actual budget to the static budget that the organisation has performed better than expected by delivering R213 000 additional profit. This represents the total variance between the static budget profit and the actual profit, and can be summarised as follows:

Static budget variance
= Actual profit – Static budget profit
= R1 313 000 – R1 100 000
= R213 000 F

The variance is favourable because more profit was made than anticipated, and is therefore denoted by an F. Unfavourable variances are usually denoted by a U.

Favourable and unfavourable (also called 'adverse') variances

Note that, from an exam technique perspective, it is important to get into the habit of always writing 'favourable' or 'unfavourable' (or 'F' or 'U') next to each variance. In standard costing exam questions, not only the amount of a variance, but also its classification ('F' or 'U'), usually counts for marks. To a management accountant in practice, this becomes even more important: one has to interpret and report whether each variance has had a positive ('favourable') or negative ('unfavourable') impact on the organisation.

Be aware that 'unfavourable' variances are sometimes also referred to as 'adverse' variances, denoted by the letter 'A'.

Do not 'study' when a variance is favourable or unfavourable, for example, 'when the first figure is larger than the second figure in the equation, the calculator returns a positive number and thus the variance is favourable'. This leads to incorrect answers, because cost and revenue variances differ, and it does not aid an understanding of the underlying principles. Always use logic to decide on the nature of a variance, for example, 'because the actual profit in October was larger than the budgeted profit, the variance was favourable', or 'because more material was used than the standard amount, the variance is unfavourable'.

principles of management accounting

At the end of October, we know that 1 300 units were actually produced and 1 200 actually sold by Specialised Cycles during the month instead of the planned 1 000 units of sales and production. It appears that much of the additional profit earned is due to the additional 200 units sold resulting in additional revenue, but at the same time, most of the input costs also exceeded the budget. For example, the cost of skilled labour was R414 700 instead of R300 000. In order to determine what the impact of the higher-than-anticipated production and sales levels were on skilled labour and all the other input costs, the static budget needs to be flexed by increasing the number of budgeted units produced to 1 300 units and the number of budgeted units sold to 1 200 units, in other words, the same as the actual activity levels that were achieved. In order to flex the budget, we first need to convert variable costs into 'per unit' costs.

Exhibit 13.1 Specialised Cycles: flexed budget for October

Flexed budget	Budgeted	Actual
Units sold	1 000	1 200
Units produced	1 000	1 300
	Amounts per unit (budget / units)	Flexed budget (per unit × units produced)
Revenue	R5 500	R6 600 000 *
Raw materials (carbon fibre for frame manufacture)	R1 000	(R1 300 000)
Components	R2 000	(R2 600 000)
Semi skilled labour	R500	(R650 000)
Skilled labour	R300	(R390 000)
Variable overhead	R100	(R130 000)
Factory fixed overhead	Fixed	(R520 000)
Head office overhead (fixed)	Fixed	(R100 000)
Closing inventory		R430 000
Profit		R1 340 000

* Note that sales values are flexed based on the actual number of units sold, whilst manufacturing cost line items are flexed using the actual number of units of production.

Note the difference in treatment between the factory fixed overhead and the head office fixed overhead in the flexed budget. Remember that we learnt in Chapter 5, *Absorption versus variable costing* that fixed manufacturing overheads are allocated to inventory in an absorption costing environment using a fixed overhead allocation rate, and these costs are 'absorbed' into the income statement based on the actual production levels. The amount of fixed manufacturing overheads absorbed (that is, expensed) into the income statement will therefore vary with production levels. Even though this may seem strange as we know that fixed manufacturing overheads are still fixed and should not vary with activity, remember that this is rectified in the actual results through the over or under absorption so that the net amount expensed to the income statement equals the actual fixed manufacturing overheads incurred during the period.

However, non-manufacturing (head office) overheads are still treated in an absorption costing system as a period cost and are expensed in full. The amount of non-manufacturing overheads expensed to the income statement therefore does not vary with production levels.

If we compare the flexed budget to the actual results for October we find that, although the organisation did well in selling an additional 200 units, the actual profit was R27 000 less than the profit in the flexed budget (in other words, R27 000 less than the profit that 'should have been made' based on the actual activity levels that took place of 1 300 units produced and 1 200 units sold).

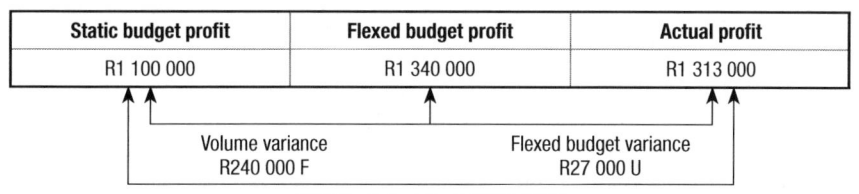

Static budget profit	Flexed budget profit	Actual profit
R1 100 000	R1 340 000	R1 313 000

Volume variance R240 000 F

Flexed budget variance R27 000 U

Static budget variance R213 000 F

Notice that, throughout this chapter, we determine total variances and then break them into progressively smaller parts to investigate further the cause of each variance – in practice, this is exactly how a standard costing system helps management to determine the precise reasons for the difference between the financial outcomes they had planned for the organisation, and what actually took place.

The volume variance shows that, had Specialised Cycles sold an additional 200 units at the standard cost, they should have made an additional R240 000 in profit. However, the flexed budget variance shows an unfavourable variance of R27 000 – profit was lower by this amount because of either higher input costs or lower selling prices of bicycles in the market, leaving us with a higher profit of only R213 000 (R240 000 – R27 000). At this point we do not know what factors specifically caused profits to be lower than they should have been at a production level of 1 300 and sales level of 1 200. Was the skilled labour less efficient? Was the unskilled labour more expensive per hour than we initially expected? Were fixed factory overheads higher than anticipated? Did we use more materials than expected? Did materials cost more than anticipated? Did competition for bicycles cause us to drop our selling prices in order to retain our market share?

In order to answer these questions, we need to drill down further into the R27 000 unfavourable flexed budget variance by breaking the flexed budget variance into the parts comprising of each of the revenue and cost items in the operating budget. The next exhibit illustrates a line-by-line analysis of the flexed budget variance.

Exhibit 13.2 Line-by-line analysis of flexed budget variance

Flexed budget variance by line item	Flexed budget	October actual	
Units produced	1 300	1 300	
Units sold	1 200	1 200	
	Flexed budget (standard per unit × actual units produced)	October actual	Flexed budget variance
Revenue	R6 600 000	R6 840 000	R240 000 F
Raw materials (carbon fibre for frame manufacture)	(R1 300 000)	(R1 495 000)	(R195 000) U
Components	(R2 600 000)	(R2 431 000)	R169 000 F
Semi-skilled labour	(R650 000)	(R716 300)	(R66 300) U
Skilled labour	(R390 000)	(R414 700)	(R24 700) U

principles of management accounting

Flexed budget variance by line item	Flexed budget	October actual	
Variable overhead	(R130 000)	(R95 000)	R35 000 F
Factory fixed overhead	(R520 000)	(R650 000)	(R130 000) U
Head office overhead (fixed)	(R100 000)	(R155 000)	(R55 000) U
Closing inventory (100 bicycles)	R430 000	R430 000	
Profit	R1 340 000	R1 313 000	(R27 000) U

The exhibit illustrates the breakdown of the variance into each of the line items comprising profit. However, at this point we still do not know whether each of the variances was caused by a difference in the price or in the quantity of the input – a variance can result from an input costing more or less than expected (**price variance**), or using more or less of the input than expected (**quantity variance**). We therefore need to drill down further into each of the variances.

The flexed budget variance for each line item shown can be broken up into its price and quantity variance components using two basic formulae. The basic formula for a *price variance* is:

> **(Actual price x Actual quantity) – (Standard price x Actual quantity)**

The basic formula for a *quantity variance* is:

> **(Standard price x Actual quantity) – (Standard price x Standard quantity)**

Although it is never advisable to memorise formulae, but rather to understand the principle behind the topic that you are studying, these formulae do help in an exam situation to ensure you calculate the relevant price and quantity variances correctly. Note that there are a few exceptions to the rule where these basic formulae will *not* work, and these exceptions will be indicated in the text below.

Example 13.2

Consider the following information relating to Specialised Cycles in addition to that already given in example 13.1.

Specialised Cycles produces only one type of bicycle (the Madone XXI), with a standard selling price of R5 500 to cycle retailers. The organisation manufactures each bicycle frame from carbon fibre. Each frame requires 2,5 metres of carbon fibre, and each metre costs R400. The bicycle components are purchased as a set from the component manufacturer. Each bicycle requires one set costing R2 000 each. Semi-skilled labour is used in the manufacturing process, and four hours of labour are required at a cost of R125 per hour. Skilled labour is then used to fit all of the components onto the frame, and to apply final finishes to the bicycle. Two hours of skilled labour are required, at a standard cost of R150 per hour.

Variable overheads and fixed overheads are incurred in the manufacturing process. The appropriate cost driver for variable and fixed overheads has been identified as semi-skilled labour hours. The variable overhead rate is R25 per hour and the fixed overhead allocation rate is R100 per hour.

Required:
Calculate the standard revenue and standard cost of each input per bicycle.

Chapter 13 Standard costing

Exhibit 13.3 Calculation of standard revenue and standard cost of each input per bicycle

Flexed budget standard costs			October actual
Units produced			1 300
Units sold			1 200
	Calculation	Standard cost per bicycle	Flexed budget (per unit × units produced)
Revenue	R5 500	R5 500	R6 600 000
Raw materials (carbon fibre for frame manufacture)	2,5 m × R400	R1 000	(R1 300 000)
Components	1 set × R2 000	R2 000	(R2 600 000)
Semi-skilled labour	4 hours × R125	R500	(R650 000)
Skilled labour	2 hours × R150	R300	(R390 000)
Variable overhead	4 hours × R25	R100	(R130 000)
Factory fixed overhead	4 hours x R100	R400	(R520 000)
Head office overhead (fixed)			(R100 000)
Closing inventory (100 bicycles)			R430 000
Profit		R1 200	R1 340 000

Note: The last column has been inserted to illustrate how the standard cost per bicycle can be used to calculate the flexed budget. Notice that the flexed budget is the same as previously shown. Again it is crucial to notice that the flexed budget is based on the **standard prices** and **standard quantities** for each line item, multiplied by the actual activity levels.

So far we have analysed the static budget variance into its volume variance and flexed budget variance components, and we have calculated the flexed budget variance for each line item in totality. Remember that the flexed budget variances are crucial for performance measurement purposes, as these compare what actually happened to what should have happened given the actual activity levels that the organisation operated at. We cannot evaluate the performance of a manager by comparing his performance to the static budget as this leads to incorrect conclusions regarding the manager's performance. In order to do a further analysis, we need to break up the variances into price and quantity variance components.

13.5.2 Revenue variances

Key terms: revenue variance

To calculate the sales price variance, we must isolate the effect that the difference between the actual and standard prices has had.

Example 13.3

Consider the information relating to Specialised Cycles given in the previous examples.

Required:
Calculate the sales price variance.

principles of management accounting

The organisation budgeted a sales price of R5 500 per bicycle. However, the actual results for October reflected a price of R5 700 (R6 840 000/1 200 bicycles).

Exhibit 13.4 Sales price variance

Actual price	Actual quantity		Standard price	Actual quantity	
R5 700	× 1 200	= R6 840 000	R5 500	× 1 200	= R6 600 000

Sales price variance R240 000 F

The difference in sales volume of 200 units (the difference between the actual sales of 1 200 bicycles and the budgeted sales of 1 000 bicycles) has already been reflected in the volume variance calculated in example 13.1. Now that we are discussing revenue variances, we can call the volume variance already calculated the 'sales volume variance'. Specialised Cycles therefore has a favourable sales volume variance of R240 000 (calculated in example 13.1) and a favourable sales price variance of R240 000 (calculated in example 13.3, or as 200 units × R1 200 profit per unit in example 13.2).

In example 13.1 we calculated the sales volume variance at profit level, comparing the standard profit per unit at the actual and budgeted sales volumes. We could, however, also have calculated the sales volume variance at contribution level or at sales price level. For example, at sales price level the sales volume variance is:

Exhibit 13.5 Sales volume variance at sales price level

Standard sales price	Actual quantity		Standard sales price	Static budget quantity	
R5 500	× 1 200	= R6 600 000	R5 500	× 1 000	= R5 500 000

Sales volume variance calculated at sales price level
R1 100 000 F

Although sales volume variances can be calculated at any one of the three levels discussed above, sales volume variances that are calculated at sales price level ignore the fact that selling decisions impact on profit. It could be more appropriate to calculate the variance at contribution or at profit level. Contribution level would be most appropriate where variances are calculated to reconcile the actual and standard profit *if a variable costing system is used*. In Table 13.1 under section 13.6, a reconciliation is given. Notice that the sales volume variance used there for Specialised Cycles is calculated at profit level because Specialised Cycles is using an absorption costing system. Profit level is most appropriate where variances are used to reconcile absorption costing profits (refer to Chapter 5 for more on absorption and variable costing), as in the Specialised Cycles example.

> If the sales volume variance can be calculated using either sales price, contribution or profit, how will the books balance? It is important to note that input ('cost') variances are recorded in the accounts, because in a standard costing system inventory is valued at standard cost. However, revenue variances are calculated for informational purposes only, giving us more flexibility to choose the calculation that yields the best management information.

If the sales volume variance is calculated at sales price level (which is the level at which the sales price variance is calculated), the combination of the two give the total sales variance: the total variance between actual sales and the static budget. The total sales variance differs from the total cost variances for materials, labour and variable overhead, in that it represents the whole spread from actual results to the static budget. The cost variances represent only the spread between actual results and the flexed budget. In the remainder of this chapter, look at how the cost variances in this chapter are derived by 'drilling down' from example 13.1. You will see that it is the flexed budget variance for each line item that is further split up.

To sum up our revenue variances example: Specialised Cycles received R1 340 000 more sales revenue than originally budgeted for. The analysis shows us that the higher-than-budgeted price of R5 700 at which the bicycles were sold had contributed to the higher revenue along with the fact that 200 more bicycles were sold than had originally been budgeted for.

Exhibit 13.6 Sales variances at sales price level

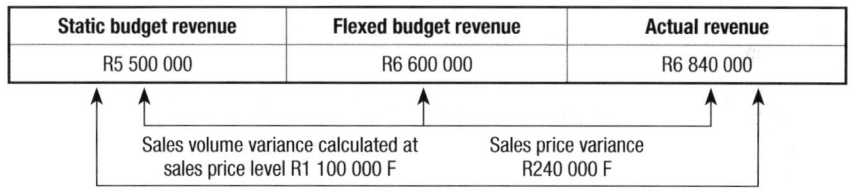

Static budget revenue	Flexed budget revenue	Actual revenue
R5 500 000	R6 600 000	R6 840 000

Sales volume variance calculated at sales price level R1 100 000 F

Sales price variance R240 000 F

Total sales variance R1 340 000 F

Where more than one product is sold, the sales volume variance can be further analysed into sales mix and sales quantity variances, and the sales quantity variance further broken down into market size and market share variances. These are discussed in the appendix to this chapter.

13.5.3 Direct materials variance

Key term: direct materials variance

The total **direct materials variance** is calculated as the difference between the total actual costs of the materials and the total standard cost of the materials as shown in the flexed budget. This variance can be broken down into two components – a price variance and a quantity variance (also called a 'usage variance').

The *price variance* is the difference between the actual quantity of the materials at the actual price, and the actual quantity of the materials at the standard price. This variance expresses the difference between what the actual quantity of materials actually cost, and how much the actual quantity of the materials should have cost had we acquired it at the pre-determined standard price.

The usage or *quantity variance* is the difference between the actual quantity of the materials at the standard price, and the standard quantity of the materials at the standard price. This variance expresses the difference between the quantity of materials actually used, and the quantity that should have been used in accordance with the standard. It expresses this difference in terms of the standard price per unit: the effect of the actual price on the total materials variance has already been recorded in the price variance.

principles of management accounting

Example 13.4

Consider the information relating to Specialised Cycles given in the previous examples.

In October the organisation purchased and used 2 990 m of carbon fibre at a total cost of R1 495 000 in producing the bicycle frames.

Required:
Analyse the raw materials (carbon fibre) variance in as much detail as the information permits.

Remember that no opening or closing inventory of raw materials exists (example 13.1). Therefore, the entire 2 990 metres was used for October production.

The direct materials variance for raw materials can be split into a price and a quantity variance as follows:

Exhibit 13.7 Direct materials: raw materials variances

Actual price	Actual quantity		Standard price	Actual quantity		Standard price	Standard quantity	
R500	× 2 990 m	= R1 495 000	R400	× 2 990 m	= R1 196 000	R400	× 3 250 m	= R1 300 000

R299 000 U
Price variance

R104 000 F
Quantity variance

Total raw materials (carbon fibre) variance R195 000 U

This has helped us to gain a more in-depth understanding of the reasons behind the total direct materials variance of R195 000 U. The fact that we paid too much for materials had a negative impact of R299 000, while the fact that we used materials more sparingly than budgeted had a positive impact of R104 000.

Example 13.5

Consider the information relating to Specialised Cycles given in the previous examples.

A new supplier of components was used as their price per component set was discounted to R1 700 per set. A total of 1 430 sets were purchased and used.

Required:
Analyse the components variance in as much detail as the information permits.

The calculation for the direct materials variance for components is as follows:

Exhibit 13.8 Direct materials: components variances

Actual price	Actual quantity		Standard price	Actual quantity		Standard price	Standard quantity	
R1 700	× 1 430 sets	= R2 431 000	R2 000	× 1 430 sets	= R2 860 000	R2 000	× 1 300 sets	= R2 600 000

Price variance
R429 000 F

Quantity variance
R260 000 U

Total components variance R169 000 F

Note that the calculations for the component variance follow the same logic as those for the raw materials variance above. The fact that we paid less per unit for components had a positive impact of R429 000, while the fact that more components were used than should have been used on 1 300 bicycles had a negative impact of R260 000.

In our Specialised Cycles example, all raw materials and components purchased in October were used in production in October. In practice, more materials could have been purchased than were actually issued to production and used in the manufacturing process, resulting in the excess materials and components being carried forward in closing inventory at the end of the month. In such a situation we may wonder whether the direct materials price variance ought to be calculated at the time of purchase based on the quantity of material purchased, or at the time of use, based on the quantity of material issued to production. The choice is a policy decision and either one is acceptable in practice. It is recommended that the direct materials price variance be calculated at the time of purchase based on the quantity purchased, because the earlier we calculate a variance, the sooner corrective action can be taken based on the variance (if action is required). In addition, calculating the materials price variance at the time of purchase removes the price variance from the raw materials account with the effect that all raw material inventories are held in the accounting records at standard cost.

13.5.4 Direct labour variance

Key term: direct labour variance, mix and yield variances

The same approach that was followed to calculate the direct materials variance is used to calculate the **direct labour variance**. The total direct labour variance is calculated as the difference between the total actual costs of the direct labour, and the standard cost of the direct labour per the flexed budget. This variance can also be broken down into two components: a price variance and a quantity variance. In the case of direct labour, the price variance is sometimes called the 'rate variance' and the quantity variance is usually called the 'efficiency variance'.

The *price (or rate) variance* is the difference between actual quantity (generally measured in hours) of the direct labour at the actual price of the labour, and the actual quantity of labour at the standard price. This variance tells us the difference between what we actually paid for the actual quantity of the labour, and how much we should have paid for the actual quantity of labour if we had acquired it at the pre-determined standard price.

The *quantity (or efficiency) variance* is the difference between the actual quantity of the direct labour at the standard price, and the standard quantity of the direct labour at the standard price. This variance tells us the difference between how much labour we actually used, and how much labour we should have used in accordance with the standard. It expresses this difference in terms of the standard price per unit of labour.

principles of management accounting

Example 13.6

Consider the information relating to Specialised Cycles given in the previous examples.

At Specialised Cycles semi-skilled labourers are used in the frame manufacturing process, while skilled labourers are used to assemble the frames and components into a complete bicycle.

In October the semi-skilled labourers worked for 4 940 hours, and the skilled labourers worked for 2 860 hours. Following union negotiations, both semi-skilled and skilled workers were paid at a rate of R145 per hour.

Required:
Analyse the direct labour variances in as much detail as the information permits.

Semi-skilled labour variances are determined as follows:

Exhibit 13.9 Semi-skilled labour variances

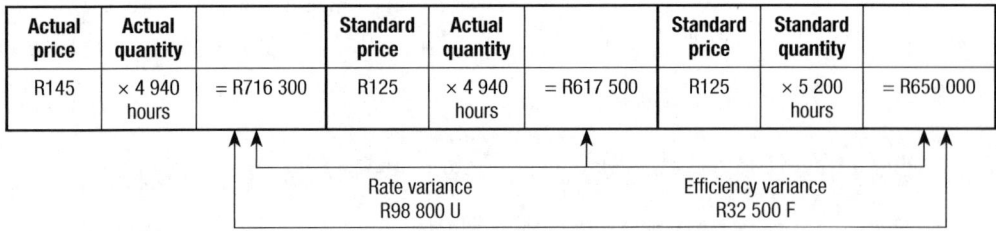

Actual price	Actual quantity		Standard price	Actual quantity		Standard price	Standard quantity	
R145	× 4 940 hours	= R716 300	R125	× 4 940 hours	= R617 500	R125	× 5 200 hours	= R650 000

Rate variance R98 800 U

Efficiency variance R32 500 F

Total semi-skilled labour variance R66 300 U

Skilled labour variances are determined as follows:

Exhibit 13.10 Skilled labour variances

Actual price	Actual quantity		Standard price	Actual quantity		Standard price	Standard quantity	
R145	× 2 860 hours	= R414 700	R150	× 2 860 hours	= R429 000	R150	× 2 600 hours	= R390 000

Rate variance R14 300 F

Efficiency variance R39 000 U

Total skilled labour variance R24 700 U

The total actual cost of labour for October was more than expected based on the standard for both semi-skilled and skilled labour. Semi-skilled labour had an unfavourable variance of R66 300 (the higher hourly rate paid had a negative impact of R98 800, while the fact that fewer hours than expected were worked in terms of output produced (higher efficiency) had a positive impact of R32 500). Skilled labour had an unfavourable variance of R24 700 (the lower hourly rate paid had a positive impact of R14 300, while the fact that more hours than expected were worked in terms of output produced (lower efficiency) had a negative impact of R39 000).

In our Specialised Cycles example, the two types of direct materials (raw materials and components) are not interchangeable – in other words, each bicycle has to have carbon fibre (the raw material) and components, and the one cannot be substituted for the other. Similarly, there has been no indication that the two types of labour (semi-skilled and skilled) used by Specialised Cycles can be interchanged, as the semi-skilled labourers, who are involved in the manufacture of the frames, perform a function independent to the skilled labourers, who are responsible for the assembly of the bicycles. However, in situations where more than one type of material is used and the materials are interchangeable to some extent, or where more than one type of labour is used and the labour types are interchangeable, the mix of inputs used in a particular period may differ from the standard. In such a circumstance we can further analyse the materials or labour quantity variance (whichever is applicable) into **mix and yield variances**. These are discussed in Appendix 13.1.

13.5.5 Variable overhead variance

Key term: variable overhead variance

We can perform an analysis similar to the ones for materials and labour above in order to learn more about the **variable overhead variance**. The total variable overhead variance is calculated as the difference between the total actual costs of variable overhead, and the standard cost of variable overhead as reflected in the flexed budget. This variance can also be broken down into two components – a price variance and a quantity variance. In the case of variable overhead, the price variance is usually called the 'spending variance' and the quantity variance is usually called the 'efficiency variance'.

Example 13.7

Consider the information relating to Specialised Cycles given in the previous examples.

Specialised Cycles incurs certain costs (such as the use of cleaning materials, among others) that are directly related to the number of semi-skilled labour hours spent in the frame manufacturing process. These costs make up the 'variable overhead' cost category.

Required:
Analyse the variable overhead variances in as much detail as the information permits.

The variable overhead variances are determined as follows:

Exhibit 13.11 Variable overhead variances

Actual price	Actual quantity		Standard price	Actual quantity		Standard price	Standard quantity	
R19,23	× 4 940	= R95 000	25	× 4 940	= R123 500	25	× 5 200	= R130 000

Spending variance
R28 500 F

Efficiency variance
R6 500 F

Total variable overhead variance R35 000 F

principles of management accounting

Notice that the number of actual hours and standard hours used in the calculation are those related to semi-skilled labour. This is because Specialised Cycles' variable overhead varies according to semi-skilled labour hours. Also notice that the actual price of variable overhead per semi-skilled labour hour was not given – it is calculated by dividing the actual variable overhead cost for October (R95 000) by the actual quantity of semi-skilled labour hours worked in October (4 940). The standard price of variable overhead was given as R25 per hour in example 13.2, but if it had not been given, it could be calculated using the same logic: R100 000/(4 × 1 000) hours = R25.

The lower spending per labour hour had a positive impact of R28 500, and the fact that fewer than expected semi-skilled labour hours (the cost driver) were worked also had a positive impact to the extent of R6 500.

13.5.6 Fixed overhead variances

Key terms: fixed overhead variances, production volume variance, spending variance

Fixed overheads are a significant expense in many organisations in the modern context. Mechanised manufacturing operations lead to large overhead expenditure. Service organisations are also renowned for high levels of overhead costs.

The area of **fixed overhead variances** is one where you cannot use the 'basic formulae' for price and quantity variance as referred to earlier in the chapter. The reason for this is simply that fixed costs are inherently different by nature to variable costs and revenues, which fluctuate with activity. Therefore, it is very important that you pay close attention to this section in order to ensure that you are comfortable with the differences in the calculations for fixed overhead variances.

For *non-manufacturing* fixed overheads, the variance calculations are simple. The variance is calculated as the difference between the budgeted expense and the actual expense. The variance is a price variance, and is also referred to as a **spending variance**.

However, *manufacturing* fixed overhead variances are more complicated than *non-manufacturing* fixed overheads variances when an absorption costing system is used. This is explained further below.

Variable costing system

You learnt in Chapter 5, *Absorption versus variable costing* and Chapter 6, *Overhead allocation* that under a variable costing system, fixed overheads are treated as a period cost (that is, they are expensed in the period incurred). There is therefore no allocation of fixed manufacturing overheads to inventory as in an absorption costing system. For this reason, the flexed budget amount for fixed manufacturing overheads under a variable costing system would not look the same as in our previous examples (where an absorption costing system was assumed).

What amount do you think the flexed budget would show for 'Factory fixed overheads' in our Specialised Cycles example if a variable costing system had been assumed? If you said R400 000, you are absolutely correct! Why do you think this is so? Remember that in an absorption costing system, so-called 'allocated' fixed manufacturing overheads are allocated to the income statement by taking the allocation rate and multiplying this by the actual production figures, which results in the amount expensed being affected by production volumes. This does not, however, happen in a variable costing system, where the total amount is expensed regardless of production activity, and therefore the flexed budget amount for 'factory fixed overheads' should look identical to the amount in the static budget.

As for all other cost variances, the total fixed manufacturing overhead variance is calculated as the difference between the expense as shown in the flexed budget, and the actual expense incurred for the period. Under a variable costing system, there is only a price variance (in the case of overheads, a price variance is usually called a 'spending variance'). The total difference between the static budgeted fixed overhead (which equals the flexed budgeted fixed overhead in a variable costing system) and the actual fixed overhead is therefore the 'spending variance'.

There is never an efficiency variance for fixed overheads in a variable costing system, and the total fixed overhead variance is therefore not split up into a price and a quantity component. This is because under a variable costing system, as discussed, fixed manufacturing overheads are treated as a period cost, and are not absorbed to the income statement based on activity levels and therefore do not change with volume levels.

Absorption costing system

In the case of an absorption costing system, the fixed manufacturing overheads are absorbed into the income statement based on the actual production that takes place. Even though fixed manufacturing overheads are fixed in nature, the amount that is allocated to the income statement therefore varies with production, as discussed above. For this reason, when we are using an absorption costing system, there is a price variance as well as a quantity variance. We call the price variance a 'spending' variance, and we call the quantity variance a **production volume variance**.

The price or 'spending' variance is calculated in the same way as under a variable costing system, and is simply the difference between the static budgeted expenditure and the actual expenditure incurred.

The quantity or production volume variance is the difference between the static budgeted expenditure and the flexed budgeted expenditure. Remember, in an absorption costing system, the flexed budgeted expenditure is not the same as the static budgeted expenditure. In an absorption costing system, the flexed budgeted expenditure represents fixed overhead allocated to products (or services, in a service organisation). To determine the amount of fixed overhead allocated, the budgeted fixed overhead allocation rate (as calculated in Chapter 5, *Absorption versus variable costing*) is multiplied by the standard quantity of the fixed overhead allocation base for the actual number of products produced (or services delivered).

This principle is best demonstrated with an explanatory example, as follows:

Example 13.8

Consider the information relating to Specialised Cycles given in the previous examples.

Specialised Cycles operates an absorption costing system. Fixed manufacturing overheads are absorbed as part of the cost of bicycles and allocated to the income statement on the basis of semi-skilled labour hours.

Required:
Analyse the fixed overhead variances for Specialised Cycles in as much detail as the information permits.

The calculation of the two fixed overhead **spending variances** is as follows:

Factory fixed overhead variance
Actual fixed overhead − Static budget fixed overhead
R650 000 − R400 000
= R250 000 U Spending variance

Head office fixed overhead variance
Actual fixed overhead − Static budget fixed overhead
R155 000 − R100 000
= R55 000 U Spending variance

The calculation of the fixed overhead quantity or 'production volume' variance is as follows:

Factory fixed overhead quantity variance
The budgeted figure for fixed factory overhead for October was R400 000. The production volume variance is the difference between this amount and the fixed factory overhead allocated to bicycles in October.

Factory fixed overheads are allocated based on semi-skilled labour hours. To determine the fixed factory overhead allocated to bicycles, the budgeted fixed factory overhead rate should therefore be multiplied by the budgeted semi-skilled labour hours for the actual number of bicycles produced in October.

- The budgeted fixed factory overhead rate is the budgeted fixed factory overhead of R400 000 divided by the number of semi-skilled labour hours that the static budget makes allowance for, therefore:
R400 000 / (4 hours × 1 000 units) = R100 per semi-skilled labour hour.
- The budgeted semi-skilled labour hours for the actual number of bicycles produced in October is 4 hours per bicycle multiplied by 1 300 bicycles produced in October. Therefore 5 200 semi-skilled labour hours are budgeted for (note that this equals the number of semi-skilled labour hours in the flexed budget).
- Fixed factory overheads allocated are therefore R100 × 5 200 hours = R520 000 (note that this equals the factory fixed overhead per the flexed budget).

The quantity (or production volume) variance for fixed factory overheads is therefore:

R400 000 (static budget) − R520 000 (flexed budget/allocated) = R120 000 F

Head office overhead quantity variance
None.

> *You should notice the following from the above example:*
> - There is only a spending variance for the head office overhead, and not a quantity variance. This would be true regardless of whether the entity is operating a variable costing system or an absorption costing system.
> - There is a spending variance and a production volume variance for the factory fixed overhead in an absorption costing system. If a variable costing system was in operation, there would be only a spending variance, which would be calculated in exactly the same way as in this example (that is, R250 000 U).

- The production volume variance in this example is favourable. This may seem odd, as the static budget expenditure is less than the flexed budget expenditure (which is based on actual activity levels). The reason it is favourable can be explained as follows: more fixed overheads were absorbed, because more bicycles were produced than were budgeted for. Specialised Cycles therefore made better use of their capacity by producing more bicycles than originally budgeted for, and the average fixed cost per bicycle is therefore proportionately less.
- The sum of the spending variance and the production volume variance is R130 000 U (R250 000 U – R120 000 F). This equals the difference between the amount in the absorption costing flexed budget (R520 000, as in example 13.1) and the actual results for October of R650 000 (that is, R520 000 – R650 000 = R130 000 U).
- Finally, you should take note that R130 000 U is also the under-recovery of fixed overheads that you would have calculated for Specialised Cycles as discussed in Chapter 5, Absorption versus variable costing. The under-recovery equals the difference between the absorbed factory fixed overheads of R520 000 and the actual factory fixed overheads incurred for October of R650 000 (that is, R520 000 – R650 000 = R130 000 under-recovery).

The factory overhead variances can be summarised as follows:

Exhibit 13.12 Summary of factory fixed overhead variances for example 13.8

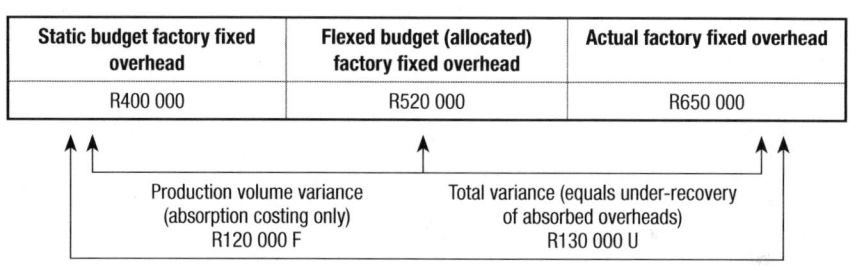

Static budget factory fixed overhead	Flexed budget (allocated) factory fixed overhead	Actual factory fixed overhead
R400 000	R520 000	R650 000

Production volume variance (absorption costing only) R120 000 F

Total variance (equals under-recovery of absorbed overheads) R130 000 U

Spending variance (variable and absorption costing) R250 000 U

Note that the production volume variance can be further split for management purposes into so called 'fixed overhead efficiency' and 'fixed overhead capacity' variances. Furthermore, the fixed overhead capacity variance can also be split between a pure capacity variance and a calendar variance. A calendar variance would arise if there are either more or fewer working days available in a calendar period, causing our total hours of capacity available in a year to change. This would happen if, for example, the government declared a public holiday that was not anticipated, causing our total expected operating hours available for a period to decrease.

Most variances (labour, materials, overheads, and revenue) can be broken down further and even further in a similar manner to that described. We will deal with some of these later in the appendix to this chapter. However, there is almost no limit to the extent to which management could choose to break down variances further for performance management and control purposes. This is, however, beyond the scope of this chapter.

The production volume variance exists only in an absorption costing system, a system which is usually kept for the purpose of complying with financial accounting rules for inventory valuation. As you have learnt in previous chapters, absorption costing usually holds limited informational value for management accountants. Similarly, the resultant production volume variance is of limited use to management accountants. It simply shows the over- or under-recovery of fixed factory overheads in a standard absorption costing system. This over- or under-recovery may, however, be closely monitored by senior managers for financial accounting purposes, because it affects the organisation's income statement.

13.6 Reconciliation of actual profit to standard profit

A standard costing system results in a reconciliation between the actual operating profit and the budgeted operating profit. The reconciling items take the form of each of the variances that have been calculated. The reconciliation also provides a consolidated view of all of the variances, which is important because of the interdependence of the variances of the different cost categories. The reconciliation for Specialised Cycles is presented in Table 13.1, on the assumption that an absorption costing system is used.

Table 13.1 Standard costing reconciliation

	Sub-variances R	Reconciliation R	
Static budget profit		1 100 000	
Volume variance at profit level		240 000	F
Sales price variance		240 000	F
Raw materials			
– Price variance	299 000 U		
– Efficiency variance	104 000 F	(195 000)	U
Components			
– Price variance	429 000 F		
– Efficiency variance	260 000 U	169 000	F
Semi-skilled labour			
– Rate variance	98 800 U		
– Efficiency variance	32 500 F	(66 300)	U
Skilled labour			
– Rate variance	14 300 F		
– Efficiency variance	39 000 U	(24 700)	U
Variable overhead			
– Spending variance	28 500 F		
– Efficiency variance	6 500 F	35 000	F
Fixed overhead variances			
– Factory overhead spending variance	250 000 U		
– Factory overhead production volume variance	120 000 F		
– Head office overhead spending variance	55 000 U	(185 000)	U
Actual profit for October		1 313 000	

13.7 Investigation of variances

Key terms: cost-benefit model, rule of thumb model, statistical models

Once variances have been calculated, it is necessary for the organisation to decide which of these variances ought to be investigated further. In most cases, not all variances, but only those that meet a pre-determined set of criteria, will warrant further investigation.

Cost variance investigation models in the accounting literature include the **rule of thumb model**, based on arbitrary criteria, the **cost-benefit model**, based on investigation costs and corrective benefits, and **statistical models**, based on statistical analysis.

13.7.1 Rule of thumb models

This process is a subjective one where management uses previous experience and its knowledge of the business to identify problem areas. Management may choose to investigate all variances larger than a specified rand amount as these are likely to have the most financial impact on the organisation. Another option is that variances can be expressed as a percentage of the standards set, and all variances greater than a given percentage can be investigated. In some circumstances management may choose to investigate even small variances of a certain kind (if management know that they are critical performance indicators to the organisation), and to apply value criteria to other variances that they regard as less critical.

Real-time systems may allow managers to detect such variances earlier, and to take corrective action to prevent any further losses, or to capitalise on any savings.

13.7.2 Cost-benefit models

A second approach would be to use a cost-benefit approach. Management would determine the cost of investigating a specific variance, measured against the benefit that is likely to be obtained from taking corrective action. Statistical models can be developed to weigh up the costs and benefits of investigation.

13.7.3 Statistical models

Accounting literature includes a number of statistical models based on probabilities that can be used in variance investigation. Such models typically assume two states of a system are possible, either in control, or out of control. If such a model labels a variance as 'in control', then the fluctuation is regarded as being within acceptable limits, and no further investigation is made. If a variance is labelled 'out of control', the variance is investigated further and corrective action is taken.

13.8 Interpretation of variances

Once a variance has been flagged for investigation, it is important for it to be correctly interpreted. One of the factors that should routinely be considered is whether the standards themselves may have been inappropriately set or may have become outdated which resulted in large variances. It may be discovered that the standards themselves caused the variances because they are erroneous and have to be adjusted in future reporting periods. Another consideration is whether the actual

principles of management accounting

values were accurately recorded. If both of these factors fail to explain the variance and it is an unfavourable one, further action needs to be taken to address the problem and to prevent it from recurring. However, especially before any accountability is assigned for unfavourable variances, the variances have to be interpreted with the utmost care by a knowledgeable person.

Note that favourable variances – not only unfavourable ones – may also require further investigation. For example, if an organisation calculates a favourable sales price variance (which means that products were sold above the standard price per unit), this may be seen in a negative light by management if the organisation's mission and marketing strategy is to target discount shoppers. There is also a good chance that a favourable price variance in this case may result in an unfavourable sales volume variance, especially if the organisations products are price elastic and sensitive to changes in their sales prices. Furthermore, any favourable revenue or input variances need to be investigated to show management what 'went right' and how it can be built upon in future.

Example 13.9

Consider the information relating to Specialised Cycles given in the previous examples.

In the Specialised Cycles factory, the components purchases manager is responsible for purchasing raw materials, while the production manager is responsible for the production process. In October the components purchases manager bought cheaper components than usual from a new supplier. The production manager used more than the standard number of components in the production process, because a number of the component sets purchased in October were damaged in the assembly process. There was no opening or closing inventory of components.

Required:
Discuss how the two managers performed with reference to the variances calculated.

You will recall that we have already calculated a R429 000 favourable price variance for components, and a R260 000 unfavourable quantity variance for components. Our first impression is that the components purchases manager has performed well, because the variance over which he had control (that is, the price variance) was favourable, and that the production manager has performed poorly, because the variance over which he had control (that is, the quantity variance) was unfavourable. However, we notice that after cheaper component sets had been purchased, some sets were damaged. When we discuss this variance with the production manager, we may learn that the components purchased were of a lower quality (and therefore cheaper), which resulted in the damaged components and ultimately in his having to use extra components in the production process. The unfavourable efficiency variance may therefore be due to the inferior components purchased by the components purchases manager, and are not necessarily due to wastage or inefficiency by the production manager. This is a good example of why it is important to analyse variances properly, to look for possible interrelationships between variances, and to interpret them with care. In this example it would have been erroneous and unfair to blame the production manager for the entire unfavourable components efficiency variance.

In our Specialised Cycles example, it is possible that the management accountant may in the end have a discussion with the two managers together, and talk about the fact that although the inferior components resulted in an unfavourable efficiency variance, the savings made on purchasing the lower grade components outweighed this negative variance, resulting in a net favourable components variance of R169 000. Furthermore, the managers may indicate that damaged components can be sold, further contributing to the organisation as a whole being better off when the lower quality components are purchased. Unless there is a specific qualitative reason for using high-quality components (for example, the organisation may not want to risk the reputation of the brand name by using low quality components in the bicycles), the managers may then agree to revise the standards for price and efficiency to reflect that they will in future use the cheaper, lower-quality components, and allow for some damaged sets.

The above is just one example of an investigation into the causes of a variance. Reasons for variances are likely to vary between organisations, depending on the nature of their operations, product, and environment. For example, transport companies are likely to have large cost variances as the oil price fluctuates, affecting the cost of petrol or diesel. Such variances are beyond the control of the transport companies, and proper corrective action may be in the form of raising prices to pass the price increase onto customers. Manufacturing organisations may have significant variances when the quality of their raw materials is compromised. The appropriate corrective action may be to discuss quality with suppliers, or to change suppliers. Some common general causes of variances follow in section 13.9 for illustrative purposes. Note that each circumstance is different and that, in a test or exam situation, you need to analyse the scenario given in the question. These are merely a few basic ideas (and by no means a complete list) to assist students in thinking through the possible causes of variances.

13.9 Possible causes of variances

13.9.1 Inflationary effects

- *Cost variances:* Prices and labour rates may increase year on year owing to inflationary pressures acting on the economy. This could affect all price variances. In addition, imported or exported goods would be impacted by currency fluctuations.
- *Revenue variances:* Remember that there is normally an inverse relationship between sales prices and sales volumes. This relationship is known as price elasticity. Higher sales prices resulting from inflation may impact negatively on sales volumes. Some industries are more exposed to price elasticity than others.

13.9.2 Materials-related effects

- *Quality of materials:* Lower-grade materials may be available at a discounted price, resulting in a favourable materials price variance, but more may be used because of the inferior quality (resulting in an unfavourable material usage variance). This may also affect the labour efficiency variance, as more time may be spent because of the inferior quality of the materials.
- *Inventory losses:* Spoilage may arise from theft or damage caused by careless handling, resulting in unfavourable materials usage variances. Insufficient care of perishable materials or the obsolescence of non-perishable materials may result in spoilage and additional costs, resulting in unfavourable materials usage variances.

principles of management accounting

- *Inventory management:* Poor inventory planning and production scheduling may result in an organisation running out of materials and supplies, forcing it to make rush purchases. This may result in the organisation not purchasing at optimal prices (for example, no volume discounts) or purchasing from alternative suppliers who have inventory available. Suppliers may also charge premiums for emergency deliveries. This would result in unfavourable materials price variances.

13.9.3 Labour-related effects

- *Quality of staff:* Staff not properly trained may be less expensive (resulting in a favourable labour rate variance), but may be less efficient or make more mistakes than properly-trained staff (resulting in an unfavourable labour efficiency variance). They may even waste or damage more materials, resulting in unfavourable materials usage variances. Well-qualified staff may cost more (resulting in an unfavourable labour rate variance), but may work faster, resulting in a favourable labour efficiency variance.
- *Experience levels:* As a result of the learning curve effect, staff who are experienced are likely to perform a task more efficiently, resulting in a favourable labour efficiency variance (if standards have not yet been revised accordingly).
- *Capacity:* Should there not be enough labour available, existing labour may be overworked or hurried, which could lead to mistakes. Overtime compensation, which is normally paid at a premium (resulting in an unfavourable labour rate variance), may not be sufficient to motivate workers in such circumstances (resulting in an unfavourable labour efficiency variance).
- *Relationship factors:* Industrial action (such as strikes or go-slows) as well as incentives (or lack thereof) can have a significant impact on the efficiency of labour in a manufacturing environment, and can therefore impact the labour efficiency variance.
- *Work environment:* Machinery which workers use may break down, or workers may take a long time initially to get used to new equipment. Both of these factors may show up as an unfavourable labour efficiency variance.

The above ought to help you think through some of the reasons why variances could occur. However, in a test or exam you should analyse the scenario given, and use it to find the possible reasons for the variances under those particular circumstances.

13.10 Planning and operating variances

Key terms: operating variance, planning variance

As part of their investigation of variances, senior management may sometimes wish to separate individual variances into 'planning' and 'operating' components, creating a so-called **planning variance** and an **operating variance**. The planning component represents the difference between the standard, and how the standard would have been set if management had knowledge of future events at the time of setting that standard. The planning component typically isolates the effect of something that has fallen outside a manager's control and for which he would not be held accountable, such as an unforeseen event. The operating component is the remaining part of the variance for which a manager would typically be held accountable.

Look at the following example:

Example 13.10

Consider the information relating to Specialised Cycles given in the previous examples.

It has already been stated that, in October, the organisation purchased and used 2 990 m of carbon fibre at a total cost of R1 495 000 in producing the bicycle frames. The direct materials price variance that resulted from this was unfavourable in the amount of R299 000. Specialist Cycles' purchases manager is concerned that he will receive a poor performance review. He has informed his superior that there was an unforeseen general 10 per cent increase in the cost of carbon fibre owing to a temporary shortage in the entire industry.

Required:
Calculate a planning and an operating variance to form an opinion as to whether the purchases manager performed poorly in terms of the direct materials price variance for carbon fibre.

Earlier in the chapter the direct materials price variance for carbon fibre was calculated as follows:

Actual price	Actual quantity		Standard price	Actual quantity	
R500	× 2 990 m	= R1 495 000	R400	× 2 990 m	= R1 196 000

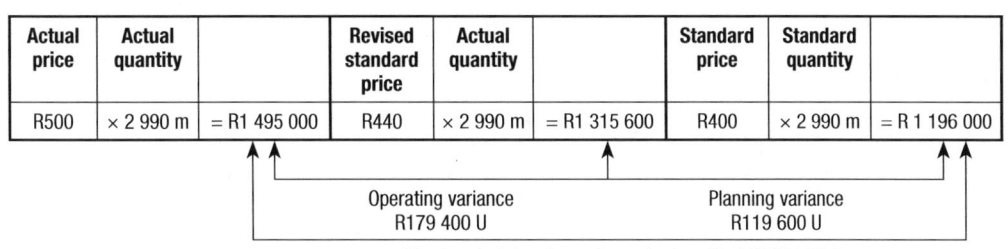

Direct materials price variance (carbon fibre)
R299 000 U

However, given the information about the general carbon fibre price increase, we can argue (with hindsight) that the standard for October would have been set 10 per cent higher if the information had been known at the time of setting the standard. The price variance can therefore be analysed as follows:

Exhibit 13.13 Analysis of price variance

Actual price	Actual quantity		Revised standard price	Actual quantity		Standard price	Standard quantity	
R500	× 2 990 m	= R1 495 000	R440	× 2 990 m	= R1 315 600	R400	× 2 990 m	= R1 196 000

Operating variance R179 400 U Planning variance R119 600 U

Direct materials price variance (carbon fibre) R299 000 U

From the above analysis it is clear that, although the general price increase had a negative effect of R119 600, the purchases manager would still be accountable for the largest part of the unfavourable variance. This is because, even if the standard had been set 10 per cent higher, there would still have been an unfavourable variance of R179 400. If the remaining variance is regarded as material and flagged for investigation, such investigation will bring to light whether this operating variance may have been the result of poor purchasing decisions.

13.11 Revision of standards

It is important for standards to be revised on a regular basis. In practice, this is often done once a year. However, it may be necessary to revise standards more frequently if, for example, a company imports a significant portion of its raw materials and the rand is volatile. In this case, more frequently revised standards may yield materials price variances that are more useful for control purposes.

Another example of where standards should be revised occurs when there is a change in the nature of the activities of the organisation. Consider, for example, an organisation implementing a radically new production system. The implementation of such a system will have a material affect on the organisation's operations. Some attributes of the new system may be better-trained staff, more expensive multi-skilled staff, more expensive and higher-quality inventory, improved production organisation, less production downtime, less waste, and so on. The implementation of such a system will therefore no doubt result in a number of variances if standards are not revised beforehand.

If standards are outdated, the variances that are calculated become less useful from a performance management perspective. In addition, outdated standards mean inaccurate budgeting and planning as well as management decision-making. Moreover, outdated standards cannot be used for financial accounting inventory valuation purposes, because IFRS (as discussed earlier) requires standards to be 'regularly revised in light of current conditions'.

Inaccurate inventory valuation as a result of outdated standards in a standard costing system can lead to inaccurate pricing decisions if the organisation bases selling prices on a sales markup above cost price, which could have serious implications for the organisation. If, for example, an organisation prices its products too low, this may result in the organisation not recovering the costs incurred in manufacturing the product. On the other hand, if an organisation prices the product too high, it may lose customers to competitors who are able to offer more competitive prices to the market.

Note that, while standards that are infrequently revised are prone to becoming outdated and irrelevant, it is just as unhelpful to revise standards too often. Standards should not be revised so frequently that we get the impression that they are changed every time a significant variance occurs – this defeats the purpose of a standard costing system. In general, a good guideline is that standards should be revised whenever the previous standards are outdated or no longer relevant or reflective of the current business environment.

13.12 Accounting entries

International Financial Reporting Standards (IFRS) specify that inventory valuations based on standard costs may be used for reporting purposes (provided that the standard costs approximate the actual costs, that they are current, and that they are attainable). If standard costing is used for the valuation of inventory, all inventory will be carried forward from the previous year at the previous year's standard costs, and all inventory carried into the following year will be carried at the current year's standard cost (assuming all the previous year's inventory has been disposed of).

IFRS also specifies that 'abnormal amounts of wasted material, labour or other production costs' should be treated as an expense (that is, not included as part of the cost of closing inventory). This is an important concept, because assuming that all standards were up to date and approximating actual costs, the variances calculated should in theory represent abnormal wastage that occurred. Variances should therefore normally be expensed. However, if the standard costs do not approximate actual costs, the variances may not represent abnormal wastage, in which case the inventory may need to be restated, by apportioning the variances between cost of goods sold, work-in-progress, and closing inventory. This apportionment of variances is referred to as 'pro-rating' of variances, which is discussed further in section 13.13.

Note that even though inventory is held in the accounting records at standard cost, accounting standards and IFRS still require inventory to be measured at the lower of 'cost' or 'net realisable value'. In the case of a standard costing system, 'cost' would be the standard cost of inventory. If the net realisable value of inventory is lower than the standard cost, a write-off of inventory would therefore be necessary.

We will now consider the accounting entries required to record the costs in the accounting records using a standard costing system. We will use a system which records all inventories (raw materials, work-in-progress and finished goods) at standard cost. Any variances (differences between standard and actual) will be debited or credited to the relevant accounts, as shown below. In such a system, cost of sales, work-in-progress and finished goods are reflected at standard costs. Variances are transferred to the income statement separately. What you should note when working through the journal entries is the general principle, that price variances are normally isolated and journalised at the time the expense is incurred (for example, purchase of material, payment of labourers, and so on), whereas quantity variances are normally isolated and journalised at the time of transfer into work-in-progress (that is, when materials are transferred into the production process, when labourers are used in the production process, and so on).

Example 13.11

Consider the information relating to Specialised Cycles given in the previous examples.

As previously stated, 1 300 bicycles were produced in October and 1 200 bicycles were actually sold. Therefore, there were 100 bicycles in closing inventory at month end.

Required:
Prepare the standard costing journal entries for Specialised Cycles for October.

Notice that the organisation will transfer 100 bicycles (1 300 produced less 1 200 sold) as inventory into the next accounting period. These bicycles should be reflected at the standard manufacturing cost in the accounting records.

Raw materials

The organisation purchased and used 2 990 m of carbon fibre at a total cost of R1 495 000. The accounting entries are as follows:

Dr		Raw materials control account	R1 196 000	
Dr		Raw materials price variance	R299 000	
	Cr	Creditors' control account		R1 495 000

principles of management accounting

The raw materials are recorded in the inventory control account at standard cost, and the price variance is allocated to a variance account (called 'Raw materials price variance').

To produce the bicycles at standard cost, 3 250 metres of carbon fibre would be required at a standard cost of R 1 300 000 in total. As only 2 990 metres were used, there is a favourable variance of 260 metres. When raw materials are issued to the production department (that is, to work-in-progress), the following entry is recorded:

Dr		Work-in-progress	R1 300 000	
	Cr	Raw materials usage variance		R104 000
	Cr	Raw materials control account		R1 196 000

In the example, all materials that were purchased were used in production. If more was purchased than was required, the raw materials purchased and not used would be carried forward in the raw materials account at standard cost.

Components

The organisation purchased and used 1 430 component sets at a total cost of R2 431 000. The accounting entries are as follows:

Dr		Components control account	R2 860 000	
	Cr	Components price variance		R429 000
	Cr	Creditors' control account		R2 431 000

The components are recorded in the inventory control account at standard cost, and the price variance is allocated to a variance account, which will be transferred to the income statement. To produce the bicycles at standard cost, 1 300 component sets should be required. As 1 430 component sets were actually used, there is an unfavourable variance of 130 component sets. When component sets are issued to the production department the following entry is recorded:

Dr		Work-in-progress	R2 600 000	
Dr		Components usage variance	R260 000	
	Cr	Components control account		R2 860 000

In the example all component sets purchased were allocated to production. If more were purchased than required, the component sets purchased and not used would be carried forward in the components control account at standard cost.

Semi-skilled labour

During the month a total of 4 940 hours were worked by semi-skilled employees at a total cost of R716 300. The accounting entries are as follows:

Dr		Wages control account	R617 500	
Dr		Wage rate variance – semi-skilled	R98 800	
	Cr	Wages accrued		R716 300

The wages are recorded in the wages control account at standard cost, and the rate variance is allocated to a variance account (called Wage rate variance – semi-skilled). To produce the bicycles at standard cost, 5 200 semi-skilled labour hours should be required. As only 4 940 hours were actually billed, there is a favourable variance of 260 hours. The wages are therefore transferred to the work-in-progress account as follows:

Dr		Work-in-progress	R650 000	
	Cr	Semi-skilled labour efficiency variance		R32 500
	Cr	Wages control account		R617 500

Skilled labour

During the month a total of 2 860 hours were worked by skilled employees at a total cost of R414 700. The accounting entries are as follows:

Dr		Wages control account	R429 000	
	Cr	Wage rate variance – skilled		R14 300
	Cr	Wages accrued		R414 700

The wages are recorded in the wages control account at standard cost, and the rate variance is allocated to a variance account (called 'Wage rate variance – skilled'). To produce the bicycles at standard cost, 2 600 skilled labour hours should be required. As 2 860 hours were actually billed, there is an unfavourable variance of 260 hours. The wages are therefore transferred to the work-in-progress account as follows:

Dr		Work-in-progress	R390 000	
Dr		Skilled labour efficiency variance	R39 000	
	Cr	Wages control account		R429 000

Variable overheads

Variable overhead cost is driven by semi-skilled labour hours. During the month semi-skilled labour worked for 4 940 hours and the total variable cost incurred was R95 000.

Dr		Variable overhead	R123 500	
	Cr	Variable overhead spending variance		R28 500
	Cr	Creditors control account		R95 000

The variable overheads are recorded at standard cost, and the spending variance is allocated to a variance account (called 'Variable overhead spending variance'). To produce the bicycles at the standard input quantity, 5 200 semi-skilled labour hours should be required. As actual semi-skilled labour hours amounted to 4 940, there is a favourable variance of 260 hours. Therefore, the transfer of variable overheads to work-in-progress looks as follows:

Dr		Work-in-progress	R130 000	
	Cr	Variable overhead efficiency variance		R6 500
	Cr	Variable overhead		R123 500

Fixed overheads

The two fixed overhead variances will be treated differently. As we are using an absorption costing system, the manufacturing related overheads will be allocated to inventory. Non-manufacturing related overheads will be treated as a period cost and expensed in the period incurred. Fixed overhead cost is allocated based on semi-skilled labour hours. During the month, semi-skilled labour worked for 4 940 hours. Remember that the allocation rate is R100 per semi-skilled labour hour.

When the costs are incurred, the following journal entries will be processed:

Factory fixed overhead

Dr		Factory fixed overhead	R400 000	
Dr		Factory fixed overhead spending variance	R250 000	
	Cr	Bank/Creditors		R650 000

Head office overhead (fixed)

Dr		Head office overhead	R100 000	
Dr		Head office overhead spending variance	R55 000	
	Cr	Bank/Creditors		R155 000

The factory fixed overheads are recorded at standard cost, and the spending variance is allocated to a variance account (called Factory fixed overhead spending variance). To produce the bicycles at the standard input quantity, 5 200 semi-skilled labour hours should be required (1 300 bicycles x 4 hours each). Fixed overheads would therefore be allocated to production based on the standard number of hours that would be required to manufacture the actual number of bicycles produced.

Dr		Work-in-progress	R520 000	
	Cr	Factory fixed overhead production volume variance		R120 000
	Cr	Factory fixed overhead		R400 000

Revenue

The organisation sold 1 200 of the 1 300 bicycles in inventory at a selling price of R5 700 each. Total revenue received in cash sales was R6 840 000. The remaining 100 bicycles are still in inventory at the end of the month, and should be recorded in inventory at standard cost. The first entry we need to record is the sales of the 1 200 bicycles. Note that unlike the cost variances, sales are not recorded at the 'standard amount', but rather brought to book at actual amounts. It follows that sales variances are not recorded in the accounts. This is because standard costing is essentially an inventory valuation technique – revenue variances are calculated for decision-making purposes only.

Chapter 13 Standard costing

Dr		Bank	R6 840 000	
	Cr	Revenue		R6 840 000

The next step is to transfer the completed bicycles from the work-in-progress account to the finished goods account. In the example all 1 300 bicycles manufactured were completed, and therefore there was no work-in-progress at the end of the month. We therefore transfer the entire balance on the work-in-progress account to the finished goods account. All 1 300 bicycles will be transferred at standard cost. If there were bicycles that had not been completed at the end of the month, the costs relating to these that had been allocated from the various cost categories, depending on the level of completion, would be left in the work-in-progress account at standard cost. They would be transferred out of the account only once complete in the following month.

Dr		Finished goods inventory	R5 590 000	
	Cr	Work-in-progress (R4 300* × 1 300)		R5 590 000

* R4 300 = standard manufacturing cost per unit (R1 000 [raw materials] + R2 000 [components] + R500 [semi-skilled labour] + R300 [skilled labour] + R100 [variable factory overheads] + R400 [fixed factory overheads])

Finally, we need to transfer the costs of the bicycles that have been sold from the finished goods inventory account to the income statement. We therefore transfer the standard cost of 1 200 bicycles, leaving the cost of 100 bicycles in the finished goods inventory account at standard cost, effectively carrying the inventory items of R430 000 into the following month. If the 100 bicycles are sold in that month, their costs will be transferred to the income statement cost of goods sold line item at that time.

Dr		Cost of sales	R5 160 000	
	Cr	Finished goods inventory (R4 300 × 1 200)		R5 160 000

The journal entries are summarised in the general ledger accounts as per exhibit 13.14 below:

Exhibit 13.14 General ledger accounts for Specialised Cycles for October

	R		R
Raw materials control account			
Creditors control account	1 196 000	Work-in-progress	1 196 000
Components control account			
Creditors control account	2 860 000	Work-in-progress	2 860 000
Wages control account			
Wages accrued (semi-skilled)	617 500	Work-in-progress (semi-skilled)	617 500
Wages accrued (skilled)	429 000	Work-in-progress (skilled)	429 000
	1 046 500		1 046 500

	R		R
Variable overheads			
Creditors control account	123 500	Work-in-progress	123 500
Factory fixed overheads			
Bank/Creditors	400 000	Work-in-progress	400 000
Head office overheads			
Bank/Creditors	100 000	Profit and loss	100 000
Work-in-progress			
Raw materials (control account and usage variance)	1 300 000	Finished goods inventory	5 590 000
Components (control account and usage variance)	2 600 000		
Wages (semi-skilled) (control account and efficiency variance)	650 000		
Wages (skilled) (control account and efficiency variance)	390 000		
Variable overhead (control account and efficiency variance)	130 000		
Factory fixed overhead (control account and production volume variance)	520 000		
	5 590 000		5 590 000
Finished goods inventory			
Work-in-progress	5 590 000	Cost of sales	5 160 000
		Closing balance	430 000
	5 590 000		5 590 000
Cost of sales			
Finished goods inventory	5 160 000	Profit and loss	5 160 000

Chapter 13 Standard costing

	R		R
Variances			
Raw materials price variance	299 000	Raw materials efficiency variance	104 000
Components efficiency variance	260 000	Components price variance	429 000
Wage rate variance (semi-skilled)	98 800	Semi-skilled labour efficiency variance	32 500
Skilled labour efficiency variance	39 000	Wage rate variance (skilled)	14 300
Factory fixed overhead spending variance	250 000	Variable overhead spending variance	28 500
Head office overhead spending variance	55 000	Variable overhead efficiency variance	6 500
		Factory fixed overhead production volume variance	120 000
		Profit and loss	267 000
	1 001 800		1 001 800
Revenue			
Profit and loss	6 840 000	Bank	6 840 000
Creditors control account			
Closing balance	4 021 000	Raw materials (control account and price variance)	1 495 000
		Components (control account and price variance)	2 431 000
		Variable overhead (control account and spending variance)	95 000
	4 021 000		4 021 000
Wages accrued			
Closing balance	1 131 000	Wages control account (semi-skilled) (control account and rate variance)	716 300
		Wages control account (skilled) (control account and rate variance)	414 700
	1 131 000		1 131 000
Bank			
Revenue	6 840 000	Factory fixed overhead (control account spending variance)	650 000
		Head office overhead (control account spending variance)	155 000
		Closing balance	6 035 000
	6 840 000		6 840 000

principles of management accounting

The next step would be to draft the income statement. The profit is reflected below:

Exhibit 13.15 Specialised Cycles: Income statement for the month of October

	R	R
Revenue (net of price and volume variance)		6 840 000
Less: Cost of sales		(5 160 000)
Less: Unfavourable variances		(1 001 800)
Raw materials price variance	(299 000)	
Components efficiency variance	(260 000)	
Wage rate variance (semi-skilled)	(98 800)	
Skilled labour efficiency variance	(39 000)	
Factory fixed overhead spending variance	(250 000)	
Head office overhead spending variance	(55 000)	
Add: Favourable variances		734 800
Raw materials efficiency variance	104 000	
Components price variance	429 000	
Semi-skilled labour efficiency variance	32 500	
Wage rate variance (skilled)	14 300	
Variable overhead spending variance	28 500	
Variable overhead efficiency variance	6 500	
Factory fixed overhead production volume variance	120 000	
Less: Head office overheads		(100 000)
Actual profit		1 313 000

You should notice that this profit reconciles to the profit calculated in the Specialised Cycles examples that we have been using from the start of the chapter (see example 13.1).

13.13 Balances in the variance accounts

At the end of each period, the balances on the variance accounts are either expensed in the period by transferring them to the income statement as period costs (as was done in section 13.12 above), or if material, the variances could be capitalised to the cost of inventory by allocating them between work-in-progress, finished goods inventory, and cost of sales. If standards are up to date and variances are not material, they are likely to represent period over-efficiencies and in-efficiencies, and therefore the suggested treatment is to charge them to the period (directly to profit and loss). This is considered to be an appropriate treatment as inventory should be valued on a normal activity basis, and should not include short-term, non-recurring fluctuations as such fluctuations may affect the organisation adversely from a strategic and pricing perspective.

If, however, standards are not considered to be up to date, or if fluctuations are material or are likely to continue, the accounting records prepared with standard costing are not a true reflection of the economic reality of the transactions that occurred. Large variances that are written off to the income statement may result in inventory being either overstated or understated. Overstated inventory that has been left unadjusted could cause the costs in the income statement to be understated, resulting in an overstated profit. If material, this could be misleading to users of the financial statements. As mentioned, accounting standards generally require restatement in such circumstances. Consideration should be given to updating standards for future periods, and the variances for current periods should be re-allocated to the relevant accounts (work-in-progress, finished goods inventory and cost of sales). The net effect of reallocating such variances would be to allocate a portion of the variance to inventories instead of directly to profit and loss, providing a better estimate of the actual value of inventory and a better reflection of profit for the period.

As mentioned in section 13.12, pro-rating – a combination of the two approaches – can also be used, reallocating to the cost of inventory some variances considered to meet the criteria, and expensing other variances which are considered to reflect efficiencies and inefficiencies. Various methods of pro-rating are suggested in modern texts.

Example 13.12

Consider the information relating to Specialised Cycles given in the previous examples.

It has already been established that the total semi-skilled labour variance was R66 300 U. This was partly because Specialised cycles paid these labourers more per hour, resulting in an unfavourable rate variance of R98 800. This was offset by the fact that the labourers were more efficient in their work, which resulted in a favourable efficiency variance of R32 500.

Assume that it was discovered that the wage increases were due to a permanent increase in the legislative basic wage rate in terms of the Basic Conditions of Employment Act 75 of 1997. On the other hand, it was discovered that the increased efficiency was because all semi-skilled labourers worked through their lunch break for the month of October in order to meet production demands owing to a tight deadline for an order of bicycles that had come in.

Required:
Discuss the accounting treatment of the variances for semi-skilled labour, and journalise the resulting effect.

The efficiency variance in example 13.12 appears to be short-term over-efficiency by semi-skilled labourers. It does not appear that the standard should be changed in future, as we cannot expect labourers to work through lunch on a permanent basis in order to be more efficient in a day's work. Therefore, this appears to be an 'abnormal' non-recurring factor, and should therefore not impact on the cost of inventory. This variance should be treated as an expense and charged directly to profit and loss.

The rate variance, however, appears to be a permanent change in the standard price for semi-skilled labour. It is not due to a short-term fluctuation in the rate, such as an exceptional overtime payment. Therefore, on the assumption that the variance is material, it appears that the rate variance should be allocated to the cost of inventory. In future, Specialised Cycles would change the standard rate for semi-skilled labour in order to reflect the change.

principles of management accounting

The journal entries would be as follows:

Dr		Variance control	R32 500	
	Cr	Profit and loss		R32 500

The above journal entry reflects the transferring of the efficiency variance for semi-skilled labour out of the variance control account, and charging the amount directly to the income statement.

Dr		Cost of sales	R91 200	
Dr		Finished goods	R7 600	
	Cr	Variance control		R98 800

The above journal entry reflects the transfer of the rate variance out of the variance control account, and the allocation of this amount to the cost of inventory. Note that the split between cost of sales and finished goods inventory is calculated as (1 200/1 300 × R98 800 = R91 200) for cost of sales and (100/1 300 × R98 800 = R7 600) for finished goods inventory. This is because the efficiency variance must be allocated to the units of production which caused the variance, which were 1 300 units of production for the month of October. Of these 1 300 units, 1 200 have already been sold, and the variance relating to these units must therefore be allocated to cost of sales. Further, of the 1 300 units, 100 are still on hand and so the pro rata portion of the variance that relates to these 100 units must be allocated to finished goods inventory.

13.14 Criticisms of standard costing

Standard costing has not kept pace with the changing complexity of operations and cost structures

Standard costing has been in use since the start of the industrial revolution – an environment very different from that of today. These days, products are more complex. Direct labour no longer comprises the major cost category in many manufacturing organisations and production runs are shorter, yet standard costing has remained largely unchanged. When manufacturing complexity increases, the investigation of and assignment of responsibility for variances become very difficult and require a great deal of diligence and care. A complex manufacturing process generally involves a higher level of investment in specialised equipment, leading to a shift in the composition of the cost base to a more fixed cost structure, which makes standard costing less relevant (the analysis of a fixed cost variance is relatively straightforward).

Standard costing encourages dysfunctional behaviour

A further argument against the use of standard costing is that it emphasises financial performance measures that tend to motivate managers to manage the short-term financial results rather than the processes that add value and contribute to the organisation's long-term profitability.

For example, types of dysfunctional behaviour encouraged by a standard costing system include:

- *Creating excess direct materials* (because buying in bulk can have a positive impact on the materials price variance)
- *Using many different suppliers* (because shopping around can have a positive impact on the materials price variance)
- *Buying low-quality materials* (because they are often cheaper and have a positive impact on the materials price variance)
- *Creating excess inventory* (in an absorption costing system, this has a positive effect on the production volume variance).

All of these problems are indicative of a traditional 'push' system rather than a just-in-time type or 'pull' system driven by demand. This has the effect of de-emphasising quality and promoting competitive behaviour among employees and production department managers. From the perspective of the just-in-time philosophy, this behaviour creates waste and promotes non-value adding activities (see Chapter 16, *Contemporary management accounting concepts*).

Standard costing does not incentivise good performance

Another criticism of standard costing is that it emphasises the achievement of a pre-determined standard – once this standard has been reached, the system does not effectively incentivise additional improvements. Target costing is superior in this regard.

Weighing the benefits of standard costing

In defence of standard costing, we can argue that it provides a powerful planning device and a macro performance-monitoring system that allows middle and upper-level managers to see the big picture on a periodic basis. The correct implementation of a standard costing system is the key to overcoming the criticisms mentioned above. If other non-financial performance measurements are used in conjunction to guide and evaluate lower level managers, then standard costing can still play an important role in the overall management of the organisation, even in a just-in-time environment. From this perspective, it is just a matter of developing a balanced system that does not overemphasise any particular aspect of performance, takes non-financial factors and a variety of measures into account, and does not emphasise performance over the short term to the detriment of the organisation over the long term.

We should always bear in mind that standard costing was designed as an internal, not an external, control measure. Performance measurement systems ought to consider the impact of customers, competitors and other external factors in addition to the internal cost control measures implemented – this is further discussed in Chapter 14, *Performance management*.

Surveys have indicated that the majority of manufacturing firms use some form of standard costing. It is important to recognise and remember that where people are involved, performance measurement systems measure behaviour, but also simultaneously *influence* behaviour.

Standard costing as a control system is best used at the middle-management level as an overall monitoring device where monthly aggregated actual costs are compared with estimates of what these costs should have been. Standard costing can create problems if it is used as a way to micro-manage in a top-down fashion, particularly for organisations which adopt the bottom-up, employee empowerment, self-managed team concepts associated with just-in-time and the theory of constraints (see Chapter 16, *Contemporary management accounting concepts*).

13.15 Variance analysis in modern mechanised environments

Impact of cost drivers

We have concentrated up to now on a costing system where overheads are mainly driven by labour hours. When looking at a highly mechanised and automated factory environment, a similar standard costing exercise can be used. Some pre-determined basis is used to apply the overhead to production. However, in a highly mechanised environment, we must give particular thought to the 'cost driver.' The cost driver is the factor that is viewed as causing costs to be incurred within an organisation. In the examples above, direct labour hours were viewed as the primary cost driver and the basis for assigning overheads. Labour hours may not be the most significant cost driver in a mechanised setting. Machine hours, number of set ups, time in production, or number of assembly steps could each provide a potentially logical base for allocating overhead (refer to Chapter 6, *Overhead allocation*).

These types of drivers are also typically used in an activity-based costing environment, and it is important to remember that fixed overheads can be driven by an array of drivers in a manufacturing environment. Although the Specialised Cycles example assumed that semi-skilled labour hours were the cost driver, any other basis may be considered more appropriate. The principles behind the calculations as discussed in this chapter will, however, remain the same. Therefore, in our Specialised Cycles example, variable overheads might have been allocated based on, say, machine hours instead of direct labour hours. The variable overhead efficiency variance would then have measured the difference between machine hours spent versus machine hours that should have been spent, given the output (instead of comparing labour hours).

'McDonaldisation'

In modern businesses, many organisations have produced homogeneous products, for example, motor manufacturers which mass produce standard models, chassis, engines, and so on. The pinnacle example in this regard is McDonalds, a company often associated with the concept of uniform operations and efficiency. Its standardised machinery, uniform packaging, pre-cut cheese, bread, burger patties, and even pre-prepared phrases such as 'Welcome to McDonalds' and 'Have a nice day' make for a uniform and standardised operation in every aspect. In such environments, it is easier to set pre-defined standards as there is uniformity within the product and service specifications. This uniformity leads to potentially greater efficiency and cost savings. If the operations are uniform and can be forecast with a high degree of accuracy, it also makes it easier to assess the performance using standard costing. From a customer's perspective, this 'McDonaldisation' phenomenon is often welcomed, as customers know what to expect from what they are buying, leading to reassurance and brand recognition.

Despite its distinct advantages and efficiencies, the modern business environment can lead to demotivation among staff who feel the work is dull and boring, and can frustrate innovation or creativity from workers.

13.16 Standard costing in service organisations

There are a number of characteristics of service organisations that make them quite different from manufacturing organisations. Service organisations are renowned for being fixed overhead-intensive in their cost structures, particularly in respect of a large salary bill (examples are airlines, financial services, telecommunications service providers, audit services, and so on). In service environments, the 'product' is intangible and is not a physical object. In addition, the product cannot be stored (for example, in the case of a vacant seat on an aeroplane, if the seat is not sold today, it cannot be booked into inventory and sold tomorrow). Services are also normally heterogeneous, in that the service could vary each time it is delivered (for example, the same hairdresser does not necessarily cut the same style identically every time). For these reasons, standard costing is often considered more difficult to apply within the service environment.

There are some interesting applications of standard costing within service environments, for example, in the health care industry, the accountancy profession, and even the retail sector.

In the health-care environment, the so-called Diagnostic Related Group system has been implemented, whereby medical conditions have been classified into hundreds of groups (referred to as DRGs), which are expected to have similar hospital resource requirements – the premise being that similar medical conditions require the same or similar health care treatment. In such a way, the attempt is made to 'standardise' health care. This system enables health-care providers to standardise their resources in terms of medication, patient treatment, consultancy services, and wards or beds required, as well as for medical insurance claims purposes. Of course, critics of this system argue that health care is about providing patient care and not about applying standardised treatments.

In the accountancy profession, for example, the effects of changing the staff mix (such as articled clerks, audit managers, and audit partners) required to complete a certain task can be analysed using mix and yield variances. Mix and yield variances are discussed further in the appendix to this chapter.

13.17 Standard costing and benchmarking

In a competitive business environment, organisations strive for a competitive advantage. One way to achieve this is through the use of benchmarking, which is the process of comparing your own organisation's performance to another organisation considered to be the market leader in the industry. Benchmarking can also involve comparing performance internally between departments, or even against hypothetical 'best-practice'. Refer to Chapter 16, *Contemporary management accounting concepts*.

An organisation can choose to set its standards at the benchmark levels, meaning variances will show the difference between actual performance and the 'best-in-business' performance benchmark.

13.18 Summary

This chapter introduced the usefulness of standard costing as a performance management tool, a planning and decision-making tool, and an inventory valuation technique. The chapter also described how price and usage variances for labour, materials, overheads, and revenue are calculated. When variances are deemed material, they are investigated in order to evaluate past performance and improve future performance. It is important to understand how variances are recorded in the accounts, but it is also important to understand the interpretation of variances and the shortcomings of a standard costing system.

In the appendix to this chapter, we investigate some more advanced standard costing concepts such as further revenue variances, as well as mix and yield variances. In addition, we further analyse the labour efficiency variance through the idle time variance.

Conclusion: Standard costing and other topics in this book

In Chapter 12, *Budgets, planning and control*, the practice of budgeting as a means of controlling operations was discussed. Note that standard costs are effectively a 'per unit' budget: they express how much one unit of a product or service ought to cost according to pre-determined standards.

In the next chapter (Chapter 14, *Performance management*), the concept of evaluating performance based on performance measurement systems (such as standard costing systems) is explored further.

Chapter 5, *Absorption versus variable costing* and Chapter 6, *Overhead allocation* were critical to the discussions in this chapter. Specifically, the choice between variable and absorption costing affects the manufacturing fixed overhead variance. The total manufacturing fixed overhead variance equals the over- or under-recovery of fixed manufacturing overheads.

In Chapter 16, *Contemporary management accounting concepts* and Chapter 17, *Competitive advantage*, some techniques are discussed that clash, in principle, with the traditional standard costing approach, because they place a strong emphasis on value creation. These include just-in-time systems, activity-based management, and value chain analysis. Chapter 16 also discusses benchmarking, a concept that can be used in conjunction with standard costing, as explained in section 13.17.

> **Tutorial case study: Murray & Roberts Foundries Group**
>
> The summary of a project conducted by the South African supply chain process consulting company, Volition, in 2005 reads as follows:
>
> 'The *Murray & Roberts Foundries Group*, situated in Brits and Port Elizabeth, manufactures and supplies a variety of engine blocks and other automotive parts to numerous local and international original equipment manufacturers. The costing system implemented at the Murray & Roberts Foundries Group was a hybrid of job-order costing and standard costing – with most of the emphasis on standard costing and variance analysis. The implementation of the costing system resulted in an accurate bill of materials, and provided product costing and the ability to measure and highlight materials, labour and overhead variances.'
>
> *Source: Volition 2005*

1. From the information above, explain what benefits the Murray & Roberts Foundries Group could gain from its standard costing system.
2. Discuss considerations on which the Murray & Roberts Foundries Group and their consulting company might have based the standards.
3. Suggest how the Murray & Roberts Foundries Group might decide which variances to investigate further.
4. Name some possible causes if the Murray & Roberts Foundries Group reports a favourable direct materials price variance.
5. Name some possible causes if the Murray & Roberts Foundries Group reports an unfavourable direct labour efficiency variance.
6. Name some possible causes if the Murray & Roberts Foundries Group reports an unfavourable variable overhead spending variance.
7. Advise the Murray & Roberts Foundries Group on how frequently the standards ought to be revised.
8. Discuss potential problems that the Murray & Roberts Foundries Group may encounter when implementing a standard costing system, especially considering the mechanised nature of its operations.

Appendix 13.1: Advanced standard costing concepts

The Specialised Cycles example in this chapter has up to this point dealt with an organisation that produces and sells only one product (the Madone XXI bicycle) that is manufactured using specific direct materials and direct labour. In this appendix we will extend our analysis by adding multiple products, resulting in different possible mixes of product sales. We will also add different possible direct materials inputs, resulting in different possible mixes of direct materials. Adding such complexity will result in new variances that can be calculated: sales mix and sales quantity variances; and direct materials mix and direct materials yield variances. When discussing the sales quantity variance we will also introduce market share and market size variances.

Revenue variances: sales mix and sales quantity variances

Key terms: sales mix variance, sales quantity variance

Organisations do not necessarily produce and sell only one product as does Specialised Cycles, the organisation used in the examples in this chapter so far. Organisations may produce and sell a number of different products (or deliver a number of different services), supply various models with different specifications, and perhaps manufacture complementary or even unrelated products. Such products may also each have different gross margins. In such an environment, changes in the sales price or quantity of one product may impact on the sales of the organisation's other products, either positively or negatively, thereby affecting the profitability of the organisation as a whole. In these types of scenarios, it is therefore important to extend our standard costing analysis of revenue variances by further breaking up the sales volume variance into sales mix and sales quantity variances.

principles of management accounting

The **sales mix variance** measures the impact from the actual sales mix being different from the standard sales mix (in other words, relatively more or less of a product was sold compared with the others, than the organisation had planned), and the **sales quantity variance** measures the impact of the actual sales volume being different from the planned volume, while holding the sales mix constant at the standard level. Like the sales volume variance discussed in section 13.5.2, these further variances can be calculated at sales *price* level, *contribution* level, or *profit* level.

Appendix example 13.1

In order to illustrate sales mix and quantity variances, the Specialised Cycles example in this chapter will now be extended by adding an additional product offering to the organisation, the Saneone XXI, a lower specification bicycle, which is priced lower than the Madone XXI and will compete directly for sales with the Madone XXI. The marketing strategy of the organisation is to sell the Madone XXI bicycle to elite athletes who are willing to spend extra to get a higher specification bicycle, and to sell the Saneone XXI to less serious price-sensitive riders who want the exclusivity of the brand, but do not need the superior specification.

The Madone XXI information has already been given earlier in this chapter.
The Saneone XXI bicycle is produced from a mixture of carbon fibre and aluminium.

These two raw materials are interchangeable to some extent – in other words, the one can be substituted for the other to a certain extent. The aluminium is cheaper to use, although it is heavier, making the bicycles heavier when more aluminium is used. The Saneone XXI division decided to use relatively more carbon fibre compared with aluminium in their raw materials mix in October to try to keep the Saneone XXI bicycles as light as possible. There were no work-in-progress or completed Saneone XXI bicycles in opening or closing inventory for October. The sales details for the month of October are as follows (note that the budgeted sales figures of Madone XXI are different from the example in the chapter):

Exhibit 13.16 Sales details for October

Product	Number of bicycles	Sales price per unit R	Total sales R	Contribution per unit R	Total contribution R
October actual					
Madone XXI	1 200	5 700	6 840 000	1 736,92	2 084 308
Saneone XXI	900	3 600	3 240 000	900	810 000
	2 100		10 080 000		2 894 304
October budget					
Madone XXI	1 500	5 500	8 250 000	1 600	2 400 000
Saneone XXI	500	3 800	1 900 000	1 000	500 000
	2 000		10 150 000		2 900 000

Required:
Calculate revenue variances in as much detail as the information permits.

At first glance it appears as if the organisation has performed better than expected by selling an additional 100 bicycles in total. It appears that the sales of Madone XXI have under-performed by 300 bicycles (1 500 unit sales budgeted compared with 1 200 unit sales actually made), and that the Saneone XXI has over-perfomed by 400 units (500 unit sales budgeted compared with 900 unit sales actually made). It appears as if the decision to use more carbon fibre in the Saneone XXI bicycle has stimulated sales of the Saneone XXI (900 bicycles sold compared to budget of 500), possibly because of the lighter weight frame due to less aluminium in the mix that attracted customers to this model of bicycle. It also appears that the increased popularity and demand for the Saneone XXI bicycle arises from a decrease of the sales price from the budgeted R3 800 to R3 600 per unit.

> *Note:* You will remember in that revenue variances can be calculated at price level, contribution level or profit level. In the example in the chapter, under an absorption costing system, the sales volume variance was demonstrated at price level, and it was mentioned that calculating the sales volume variance at profit level would also be appropriate (this was also demonstrated through the 'volume variance' in example 13.1).
> In order to illustrate the calculation of sales variances at contribution level, for this example only, assume that a *variable* costing system is operated by Specialised Cycles. In this example we will then show the calculation of sales variances at sales price and at contribution level.

The sales price and quantity variances are calculated as follows:

Exhibit 13.17 Sales price variance

	Actual sales price	Actual sales quantity			Standard sales price	Actual sales quantity		Sales price variance
Madone XXI	R5 700	× 1 200	= R6 840 000	less	R5 500	× 1 200	= R6 600 000	= R240 000 F
Saneone XXI	R3 600	× 900	= R3 240 000	less	R3 800	× 900	= R3 420 000	= (R180 000) U
Total			R10 080 000				R10 020 000	R60 000 F

Exhibit 13.18 Sales volume variance at sales price level

	Standard sales price	Actual sales quantity			Standard sales price	Standard sales quantity		Sales volume variance
Madone XXI	R5 500	× 1 200	= R6 600 000	less	R5 500	× 1 500	= R8 250 000	= (R1 650 000) U
Saneone XXI	R3 800	× 900	= R3 420 000	less	R3 800	× 500	= R 1900 000	= R1 520 000 F
Total			R10 020 000				R10 150 000	R130 000 U

The combined effect of the sales price and sales volume variances can be summarised as follows:

Sales price variance	R60 000 F
Sales volume variance at sales price level	R130 000 U
Static budget variance at sales price level	R70 000 U

principles of management accounting

Note that R70 000 equals the total difference between budgeted sales and actual sales (R10 080 000 – R10 150 000).

The sales volume variance can also be calculated at contribution level under a variable costing system.

Exhibit 13.19 Sales volume variance at contribution level

	Standard contribution	Actual sales quantity			Standard contribution	Standard sales quantity		Sales volume variance
Madone XXI	R1 600 *	× 1 200	= R1 920 000	less	R1 600 *	× 1 500	= R2 400 000	= (R480 000) U
Saneone XXI	R1 000	× 900	= R900 000	less	R1 000	× 500	= R 500 000	= R400 000 F
Total			R2 820 000				R2 900 000	R80 000 U

* Contribution per unit = sales price per unit – variable costs per unit. You should check that you can calculate the standard contribution given for the Madone XXI bicycle from the information in the previous examples in the chapter related to Specialised Cycles (R1 600 = R5 500 sales price – R1 000 raw material – R2 000 components – R500 semi-skilled labour – R300 skilled labour – R100 variable overheads). The contribution information for the Saneone XXI is specific to this example only.

The sales price variance arises from the difference between the actual sales price and the standard sales price, using actual quantities. The sales volume variance (as shown here at contribution level) reflects the difference between the actual and the budgeted sales volumes, using the standard contribution, in other words, what the net effect on the contribution of the company is due to selling more or fewer bicycles. There is an unfavourable sales volume variance of R80 000 at contribution level, which is unexpected, considering that the total sales volume of the two products was more than expected by 100 units (2 100 actual bicycle sales compared with 2 000 budgeted bicycle sales). This unfavourable variance has occurred because there were proportionately fewer than expected sales of one product (the Madone XXI), and proportionately more than expected sales of the other product (the Saneone XXI). The overall effect of this in rands was negative. To understand this, our next step is to break the sales volume variance down further and explore the mix and quantity variances of these sales. The sales mix variance at contribution level is as follows:

Exhibit 13.20 Sales mix variance at contribution level

	Standard contribution	Actual sales mix	Actual sales quantity			Standard contribution	Standard sales mix*	Actual sales quantity		Sales mix variance
Madone XXI	R1 600	× 1 200 / 2 100	× 2 100	= R1 920 000	less	R1 600	× 1 500 / 2 000	× 2 100	= R2 520 000	= (R600 000)
Saneone XXI	R1 000	× 900 / 2 100	× 2 100	= R900 000	less	R1 000	× 500 / 2 000	× 2 100	= R525 000	= R375 000
Total				R2 820 000					R3 045 000	R225 000

* Notice that this column calculates the percentage of each type of bicycle that should have been sold according to the standard mix. 1 500 out of 2 000 bicycles (75%) should have been Madone XXI, while 500 out of 2 000 bicycles (25%) should have been Saneone XXI.

Only 57,1 per cent (1 200/2 100 = 57,1%) of the bicycles actually sold were Madone XXI, compared with the budgeted percentage of 75 per cent (1 500/2 000). Because Madone has the higher standard contribution (R1 600 compared with Saneone's R1 000), this has resulted in a negative total sales mix variance.

Next we compare the actual quantity at standard mix to the standard quantity at standard mix to determine the sales quantity variance component of the sales volume variance. The sales quantity variance shows us the effect of the sales quantity having been different from the planned quantity. To isolate this aspect, the sales mix is held constant in the calculation. We expect this variance to be favourable, as we know that in total 100 more bicycles were sold than planned. The sales quantity variance is as follows:

Exhibit 13.21 Sales quantity variance at contribution level

	Standard contribution	Standard sales mix	Actual sales quantity			Standard contribution	Standard sales mix	Standard sales quantity		Sales quantity variance
Madone XXI	R1 600	× 1 500 / 2 000	× 2 100	= R2 520 000	less	R1 600	× 1 500 / 2 000	× 2 000	= R2 400 000	= R120 000 F
Saneone XXI	R1 000	× 500 / 2 000	× 2 100	= R525 000	less	R1 000	× 500 / 2 000	× 2 000	= R500 000	= R25 000 F
Total				R3 045 000					R2 900 000	R145 000 F

This combined effect of the sales mix and sales quantity variances can be summarised as follows:

Sales mix variance at contribution level   R225 000 U
Sales quantity variance at contribution level R145 000 F
Sales volume variance at contribution level   R80 000 U

Splitting the sales volume variance into a sales mix variance and a sales quantity variance has allowed us to see how a shift in the relative mix of products (Madone XXI from a planned 75 per cent to 57,1 per cent, and Saneone XXI from a planned 25 per cent to 42.9 per cent) and a shift in the actual quantity of sales (2 100 – 2 000) has affected profitability. The sales mix variance has shown that because the mix of bicycles moved towards the Saneone XXI, which has a lower contribution than the Madone XXI, an unfavourable variance has arisen. The sales quantity variance, in turn, has indicated the effect of having sold 100 bicycles more in total, given the planned mix of products.

Although the total Saneone XXI sales have made more profit than expected, this has been at the expense of Madone XII sales, which has resulted in lowered profitability for the organisation as a whole because Saneone XXI has a lower contribution than Madone XXI. Because of this difference in contribution, from a purely quantitative perspective, the organisation should actually have attempted to maximise sales of the Madone XXI.

principles of management accounting

Market share and market size variances

Key terms: market share variance, market size variance

Should the required information be available, the sales quantity variance can be further divided into a **market share variance** and a **market size variance**. These variances reflect whether the organisation has achieved greater sales by capturing a larger share of the market, or whether the organisation has increased (or decreased) sales because of an increase (or decrease) in the total market size.

Appendix example 13.2

The information on Specialised Cycles given in the chapter and in appendix example 13.1 still applies. In addition, the following information is available:
 The total budgeted industry sales was 20 000 bicycles for the month of October, and the actual industry sales volume for October was 14 000 bicycles.

Required:
Calculate the market share and market size variances at contribution level for October.

The organisation planned to have a 10 per cent market share (2 000 total budgeted bicycle sales by Specialised Cycles / 20 000 total budgeted industry sales), but in fact had an actual market share of 15 per cent (2 100 / 14 000).

The market share variance is as follows:

Exhibit 13.22 Market share variance

Standard average contribution per unit*	Actual market share	Actual market size			Standard average contribution per unit	Budgeted market share	Actual market size		Market share variance
R1 450	× 15%	× 14 000	= R3 045 000	less	R1 450	× 10%	× 14 000	= R2 030 000	= R1 015 000 F

* This is calculated as the total budgeted contribution for October (see appendix example 13.1) of R2 900 000 divided by 2 000 (the total number of bicycle sales budgeted for October).

The market share variance is favourable, because Specialised Cycles managed to capture a larger share of the market than planned.

Exhibit 13.23 Market size variance

Standard average contribution per unit*	Budgeted market share	Actual market size			Standard average contribution per unit	Budgeted market share	Budgeted market size		Market size variance
R1 450	× 10%	× 14 000	= R2 030 000	less	R1 450	× 10%	× 20 000	= R2 900 000	= (R870 000) U

The combined effect of the market share and market size variances can summarised as follows:

Market share variance at contribution level	R1 015 000 F
Market size variance at contribution level	R870 000 U
Sales quantity variance at contribution level	R145 000 F

Note that we have continued to calculate these variances at contribution level to show how they together make up the sales quantity variance (which was calculated at contribution level). However, you may prefer to calculate the market share and market size variances at sales price level instead.

The market share variance indicates the effect of the actual market share of 15 per cent being higher than the planned 10 per cent, resulting in a favourable variance of R1 015 000. It indicates that management performed well in a difficult (declining) market, by capturing more market share. Meanwhile, the market size was smaller than anticipated (20 000 compared with 14 000 units), resulting in an unfavourable market size variance of R870 000. Such a variance would presumably be largely outside the control of management, as it affects the entire industry. The net variance is R145 000, which is the sales quantity variance we have already calculated.

Production mix and yield variances

Key term: Mix variance, yield variance

In this chapter we have investigated direct materials price and usage variances. In many industries there are several direct materials that are interchangeable that combine to make a product. Notice that our Specialised Cycles example in this chapter, where only the Madone XXI was manufactured, featured (as far as materials were concerned) only direct raw materials (carbon fibre) and components. These were not interchangeable – carbon fibre could not be substituted in any way for any of the components, or the other way around. However, now that we have introduced the Saneone XXI bicycle the frame of which is made of a mixture of carbon fibre and aluminium that can be interchanged to some extent, the issue of direct materials mix and yield variances arises. The Saneone's frame can have varying combinations of carbon fibre and aluminium, with the same product, a Sameone XXI bicycle frame, being produced. The aluminium is cheaper than carbon fibre, but is inferior in the production of bicycles as it is heavier. A lighter bicycle usually performs better. There is therefore a trade-off between a more expensive raw material (carbon fibre), and a better product in the form of a lighter bicycle. The mixture of direct materials actually used compared to the standard mix is reflected in the direct materials mix variance.

The absolute amount of materials required to produce a frame can also change, depending on the mix of carbon fibre and aluminium. As more carbon fibre is added, a smaller total quantity of material is required (therefore there is a better yield from a standard costing perspective). The number of bicycles yielded by the production process, given the standard mix of direct materials, is reflected in the direct materials yield variance.

Together the direct materials **mix variance** and the direct materials **yield variance** make up the direct materials usage variance, which we have already dealt with in the chapter.

principles of management accounting

The same logic applies to direct labour where one or more types of labour are interchangeable. In such circumstances, the direct labour efficiency variance can be split into a direct labour mix and a direct labour yield variance.

Appendix example 13.3

This example follows from the previous examples:

The Saneone XXI is produced from a mix of carbon fibre and aluminium. The standard is that each frame should be manufactured using 1 metre of carbon fibre and 2 metres of aluminium, but the two materials are interchangeable to some extent. Carbon fibre is available at a standard cost of R400 per metre, while the standard cost of aluminium is R100 per metre.

The division used 1,5 metres of carbon fibre and 1 metre of aluminium per frame in October. The carbon fibre was purchased at a cost of R410 per metre, and the aluminium at a cost of R85 per metre.

Specialised Cycles budgeted to sell 500 Saneone XXI bicycles and actually produced and sold 900.

Required:
Calculate the direct raw materials price and efficiency variances, and split the efficiency variance into its mix and yield components for the Saneone XXI.

Exhibit 13.24 Direct materials price and usage variances

	Actual price	Actual quantity		Standard price	Actual quantity		Standard price	Standard quantity	
Carbon fibre	R410	× 1 350	= R553 500	R400	× 1 350	= R540 000	R400	× 900	= R360 000
Aluminium	R85	× 900	= R76 500	R100	× 900	= R90 000	R100	× 1 800	= R180 000
			R630 000			R630 000			R540 000

Price variance = R0

Usage variance = R90 000 U

Total materials variance = R90 000 U

The actual quantities above are obtained by multiplying the actual number of units by the actual number of metres used (900 units × 1,5 m and 900 units × 1 m). The standard quantities are obtained by determining how much should have been used to produce 900 bicycles (900 units × 1 m and 900 units × 2 m). Note that, although carbon fibre had a negative price variance of R13 500 (R553 500 – R540 000), this was cancelled out by a positive price variance of R13 500 (R90 000 – R76 500) for aluminium.

The direct raw materials usage variance is unfavourable because the actual total quantity at the standard price (R630 000) exceeded the standard quantity at the standard price (R540 000).

Direct materials mix variance

The materials mix variance arises when the mix of raw materials varies from the standard pre-determined mix of 1m of carbon fibre to 2m of aluminium. The Saneone XXI product line produced a higher specification bicycle by increasing the quantity of carbon fibre relative to aluminium in the mixture. The raw materials mix variance for the Saneone XXI can be calculated as follows (notice the similarities to the sales mix variance calculation):

Exhibit 13.25 Direct materials mix variance for the Saneone XXI product line

	Standard price	Actual mix		Actual quantity			Standard price	Standard mix		Actual quantity		Raw materials mix variance
Carbon fibre	R400	× 1,5 / 2,5 m	× 2 250	= R540 000	less	R400	× 1 / 3 m	× 2 250	= R300 000	= R240 000 U
Aluminium	R100	× 1 / 2,5 m	× 2 250	= R90 000	less	R100	× 2 / 3 m	× 2 250	= R150 000	= (R60 000) F
Total				R630 000					R450 000	R180 000 U

The mix variance is unfavourable because relatively more of the expensive carbon fibre was used than planned (1,5/2,5 metres or 60 per cent instead of $\frac{1}{3}$ metre or 33,33 per cent).

The variance therefore indicates that the mix of raw materials changed, as more carbon fibre was used, resulting in an unfavourable variance of R240 000. Less aluminium was required as a result, but the saving reflected in the R60 000 favourable variance was not sufficient to offset the additional cost of the more expensive raw materials, resulting in an overall unfavourable variance of R180 000. It should be noted that mix variances are calculated using standard prices to ensure that any price effect is removed from the calculation. An additional advantage of the change in the mix of raw materials is an increase in quality, in the form of a lighter bicycle, which would presumably be more marketable, possibly resulting in favourable sales variances for the product line. When interpreting the variance, we therefore need to compare the effect of the unfavourable mix variance to the benefit gained from any additional sales as a result of the increased quality. We also need to consider any other effects of the change on the business (for example, in this case, sales of the Madone XXI were impacted negatively by the growth in sales of the Saneone XXI.) This effect needs to be taken into consideration when considering the total effect of the change on the entire firm.

Direct materials yield variance

The materials yield variance arises from the difference between the total materials used (at the standard mix) and the total materials that should have been used (at the standard mix), given the output achieved. Specialised Cycles has a standard input of 3 metres of total raw materials to produce one Saneone XXI frame, with a standard mix of 1 metre of carbon fibre to 2 metres aluminium. The October actual results reflected an actual total raw materials input of only 2,5 metres of raw materials to produce one frame (lower by 0,5 metres), in the proportion of 1,5 metres of carbon fibre to 1 metre of aluminium. We therefore expect a favourable yield variance, as less input was required to yield a bicycle.

principles of management accounting

The direct materials yield variance is calculated as follows:

Exhibit 13.26 Direct materials yield variance

	Standard price	Standard mix	Actual quantity			Standard price	Standard mix	Standard quantity		Raw materials yield variance
Carbon fibre	R400	× 1 / 3 m	× 2 250	= R300 000	less	R400	× 1 / 3 m	× 2 700	= R360 000	= (R60 000) F
Aluminium	R100	× 2 / 3 m	× 2 250	= R150 000	less	R100	× 2 / 3 m	× 2 700	= R180 000	= (R30 000) F
Total				R450 000					R540 000	= (R90 000) F

The yield variance is favourable because less material was used than planned in October.

Notice how the sum of the direct materials mix and yield variances equals the direct materials usage variance (R180 000 U + R90 000 F = R90 000 U).

Notice also that, although we calculated the price and usage variance (and its mix and yield components) in total here, we could also calculate the variances for only one of the materials at a time. For example, we could read off the exhibits that the usage variance for carbon fibre specifically is R180 000 unfavourable (R360 000 − R540 000), consisting of a R240 000 unfavourable mix variance and a R60 000 favourable yield variance.

Labour variances: mix and yield

Where direct labour is interchangeable (for example, if the Saneone XXI makes use of both semi-skilled and skilled labourers and they can to a certain extent perform each other's work), the direct labour efficiency variance can be split into direct labour mix and yield variances in the same manner as shown above for direct materials.

Labour variances: idle time

Key term: idle time variance

There are various reasons that were discussed in the chapter for unfavourable labour variances. For example, quality of staff, experience levels, the learning curve effect, capacity, relationship factors and the work environment are all possible reasons for the existence of labour variances.

Another possible factor that could affect labour variances is how much of labourers' time at work are spent actively working. For example, we may expect that labourers should spend 80 per cent of a working day physically working on the product or service. This expectation could be based on, for example, past experience, industry norms or time-and-motion studies. Of course, we can hardly expect labourers to spend 100 per cent of a work-day physically working, as this would mean that labourers never stop for lunch or comfort breaks, or that there is no down time or expected stoppages in the factory whatsoever.

However, although we may expect labourers to spend, say, 80 per cent of their clocked hours working, unexpected stoppages, strikes, inefficiencies, down time and go-slows that had not been originally anticipated may occur, with the result that labourers may possibly spend less than 80 per cent of the work-day actively working.

The difference between the hours that we expect labourers to work actively, and the hours that they actually work actively, is called idle time. It is possible to measure the rand value of how much this idle time costs an organisation, by calculating an **idle time variance**. It is expressed in terms of the standard rate for labour.

Note that the idle time variance is a sub-component of the labour efficiency variance, and is thus also an example of a planning variance, in that it splits out from the total labour efficiency variance that portion of the variance which is related to labourers' idle time. The balance of the labour efficiency variance (after removing the idle time variance) would thus be attributed to factors other than labour idleness.

The operating labour efficiency variance is therefore 2 431 hours (2 860h – 429h), and ((2 431h – 2 600h) × 150) gives a R25 350 favourable variance. Together with the R64 350 unfavourable idle time planning variance, this gives the R39 000 unfavourable total labour efficiency variance (example 13.6).

Appendix example 13.4

Assume that the information is the same as in the chapter examples for Specialised Cycles.

Semi-skilled labour is used in the manufacturing process, and four hours of labour are required at a cost of R125 per hour. Skilled labour is then used to fit all of the components onto the frame, and to apply final finishes to the bicycle. Two hours of skilled labour are required, at a standard cost of R150 per hour.

Assume that all workers are expected to spend 80 per cent of their time at the factory actively working. This is considered normal for the industry. However, because of lower than expected salary increases, skilled labourers went on a 'go-slow' in protest strike action for a few days during October, resulting in the fact that only 65 per cent of the total hours clocked by the skilled labourers were spent actually working on the bicycles.

Required:
Calculate and interpret the idle time variance that may exist for October.

You should remember from the previous examples in the chapter that, in total, the skilled labourers clocked 2 860 hours in October. The expected number of hours that these labourers should have actively worked is therefore 2 288 (2 860 x 80%). However, because of the strike action, the skilled labourers actively worked for only 65 per cent of the hours clocked, which is 1 859 hours (2 860 x 65%). In other words, the labourers were idle for 429 total hours (2 288 – 1 859).

If we express these hours at the standard wage rate of skilled labourers, being R150 per hour, we can conclude that the 429 hours of idle time cost the organisation R64 350 (R150 x 429) in total. This is the idle time variance.

> *Note:* There is some debate around the rate that should be used when calculating the idle time variance. In this example, we used R150 per hour being the standard rate per hour for skilled labour. Some argue that because the 429 hours represents idle labour hours, that is, hours that the labourers were not physically working on the product even though they were expected to be, the rate that should be used should be a rate that labourers are paid per non-idle hour. The R150 is a rate per clocked hour, which means that they are paid R150 for each hour clocked while at work whether they are physically working or not. Therefore, those in support of this view say that the rate to be used should rather be R187,50/hour (R150/80%) which reflects the standard rate of how much labourers should be paid for each hour they are expected to be physically working. The amount of R187,50 can also be calculated as total budgeted labour cost (R300 000) divided by expected active working hours for October (2 000 budgeted labour hours x 80% = 1 600 active working hours) = R187,50/hour.

principles of management accounting

Basic questions

BQ 1

Source: Adapted from CIMA P1

Operation B in a factory has a standard time of 15 minutes. The standard rate of pay for operatives is R10 per hour. The budget for a period was based on carrying out the operation 350 times. It was subsequently realised that the standard time for Operation B included in the budget did not incorporate expected time savings from the use of new machinery from the start of the period. The standard time should have been reduced to 12 minutes.

Operation B was actually carried out 370 times in the period in a total of 80 hours. The operatives were paid R850.

What is the operational labour efficiency variance?

a) R60 adverse
b) R75 favourable
c) R100 adverse
d) R125 adverse

BQ 2

Source: Adapted from CIMA P1 – Management Accounting – Performance Evaluation

Which of the following describes a flexible budget?
a) A budget which, by recognising different cost behaviour patterns, is designed to change as volume of activity changes.
b) A budget for a twelve month period which includes planned revenues, expenses, assets and liabilities.
c) A budget which is prepared for a rolling period which is reviewed monthly, and updated accordingly.
d) A budget for semi-variable overhead costs only.

BQ 3

Source: Adapted from CIMA P1 Pilot paper

The following data have been extracted from the budget working papers of WR Limited:

Activity (machine hours)	Overhead cost R
10 000	13 468
12 000	14 162
16 000	15 549
18 000	16 242

In November the actual activity level was 13 780 machine hours and the actual overhead cost incurred was R14 521.

What is the total overhead expenditure variance for November?

BQ 4

Source: Adapted from CIMA P1 Pilot paper

SW manufactures a product known as the TRD100 by mixing two materials. The standard materials cost per unit of the TRD100 is as follows:

| Material X | 12 litres @ R2,50 = R30 |
| Material Y | 18 litres @ R3,00 = R54 |

In October the actual mix used was 984 litres of X and 1 230 litres of Y. The actual output was 72 units of TRD100.

What is the total materials mix variance for October?

BQ 5

Source: Adapted from CIMA P1 Pilot paper

Refer to the information given in BQ 4 above.

What is the total materials yield variance for October?

BQ 6

Source: Adapted from CIMA P1 – Management Accounting – Performance Evaluation

X Ltd operates a standard costing system and absorbs fixed overheads on the basis of machine hours. Details of budgeted and actual figures are as follows:

	Budget	Actual
Fixed overheads	R2 500 000	R2 010 000
Output	500 000 units	440 000 units
Machine hours	1 000 000 hours	900 000 hours

i) What is the fixed overhead expenditure variance?
   a) R190 000 favourable
   b) R250 000 adverse
   c) R300 000 adverse
   d) R490 000 favourable

ii) What is the fixed overhead volume variance?
   a) R190 000 favourable
   b) R250 000 adverse
   c) R300 000 adverse
   d) R490 000 favourable

BQ 7

Source: Adapted from CIMA P1

D Limited manufactures and sells musical instruments, and uses a standard cost system. The budget for production and sale of one particular drum for April was 600 units at a selling price of R72 each. When the sales director reviewed the results for April in the light of the market conditions that had been experienced during the month, she believed that D Limited should have sold 600 units of this drum at a price of R82 each. The actual sales achieved were 600 units at R86 per unit.

What are the following variances for this particular drum in April?
a) Sales price planning variance
b) Sales price operating variance

BQ 8

Source: Adapted from CIMA P1 – Management Accounting – Performance Evaluation

PQR Ltd operates a standard absorption costing system. Details of budgeted and actual figures are as follows:

	Budget	Actual
Sales volume (units)	100 000	110 000
Selling price per unit	R10	R9,50
Variable cost per unit	R5	R5,25
Total cost per unit	R8	R8,30

a) What is the sales price variance?
b) What is the sales volume variance at profit level?

BQ 9

Why is there no production volume variance for fixed costs in a variable costing system?

BQ 10

The section of the chapter entitled 'Criticism of standard costing' includes the following sentence:

> 'When manufacturing complexity increases, the investigation of and assignment of responsibility for variances become very difficult and require a great deal of diligence and care.'

Why is it so important that variances should be assigned to the correct person, and why is this not a straightforward task?

Long questions

LQ 1 – Intermediate (30 marks; 54 minutes)

Source: Adapted from CIMA P1 – Management Accounting – Performance Evaluation

The newly-appointed Managing Director of FX has received the variance report for Month 6, which is shown below:

Month 6 variance report:

Output and sales for Month 6: Budget: 1 000 units. Actual: 1 200 units.

	R	R	R
Budgeted contribution			90 000
Budgeted fixed costs			70 000
Budgeted profit			**20 000**
Volume variance			18 000
Expected profit on actual sales			**38 000**
Sales price variance			12 000
Production variances	**Favourable**	**Adverse**	
Materials price		6 300	
Materials usage		6 000	
Labour rate	5 040		
Labour efficiency		2 400	
Variable overhead expenditure		–	
Variable overhead efficiency		1 200	
Fixed overhead		4 000	
	5 040	19 900	14 860
Actual profit			**11 140**

Background information (not seen by the managing director):
The report did not include any other information. Details relating to the company and the product that it makes are given below:
- FX produces one type of product. It operates a variable costing system.

The standard unit cost and price of the product is as follows:

	R	R
Selling price		250
Direct materials (5 kg at R20/kg)	100	
Direct labour (4 hours at R10/h)	40	
Variable overheads (4 hours at R5/h)	20	160
Contribution		90

- The variable overhead absorption rate is based on direct labour hours.
- The company has budgeted fixed overheads of R70 000 per month.
- Budgeted sales and production levels are 1 000 units per month.

Month 6:
The company has just completed Month 6 of its operations. Extracts from its records show:
- 1 200 units were produced and sold.
- The actual direct materials purchased and used were 6 300 kg, costing R132 300.
- The actual direct labour hours worked were 5 040 hours.

principles of management accounting

REQUIRED		Marks
(a)	Prepare a report for the managing director of FX that explains and interprets the Month 6 variance report. The managing director has recently joined the company and has very little previous financial experience.	17
The managing director was concerned about the materials price variance and its cause. He discovered that a shortage of materials had caused the market price to rise to R23 per kg.		
(b)	In view of this additional information, calculate for direct materials: (i) The total variance (ii) The planning variance (iii) The two operational variances.	7
(c)	Discuss the advantages and disadvantages of reporting planning and operational variances. Your answer should refer, where appropriate, to the variances you calculated in (b) above.	6
TOTAL MARKS		**30**

LQ 2 – Intermediate (30 marks; 54 minutes)

Source: Adapted from CIMA P1 – Management Accounting – Performance Evaluation

WC is a company that installs kitchens and bathrooms for customers who are renovating their houses. The installations are either pre-designed 'off the shelf' packages or highly-customised designs for specific jobs.

The company operates with three divisions: Kitchens, Bathrooms and Central Services. The Kitchens and Bathrooms divisions are profit centres but the Central Services division is a cost centre. The costs of the Central Services division, which are thought to be predominantly fixed, include those incurred by the design, administration and finance departments. The Central Services costs are charged to the other divisions based on the budgeted Central Services costs and the budgeted number of jobs to be undertaken by the other two divisions.

The budgeting and reporting system of WC is not very sophisticated and does not provide much detail for the directors of the company.

Budget details
The budgeted details for last year were:

	Kitchens	Bathrooms
Number of jobs	4 000	2 000
	R	R
Average price per job	10 000	7 000
Average direct costs per job	5 500	3 000
Central services recharge per job	2 500	2 500
Average profit per job	2 000	1 500

Actual details

The actual results were as follows:

	Kitchens	Bathrooms
Number of jobs	2 600	2 500
	R	R
Average price per job	13 000	6 100
Average direct costs per job	8 000	2 700
Central Services recharge per job	2 500	2 500
Average profit per job	2 500	900

The actual costs for the Central Services division were R17,5 million.

REQUIRED		Marks
(a)	Calculate the budgeted and actual profits for each of the profit centres and for the whole company for the year.	4
(b)	Calculate the sales price variances and the sales mix profit and sales quantity profit variances.	6
(c)	Prepare a statement that reconciles the budgeted and actual profits and shows appropriate variances in as much detail as possible.	10
(d)	Using the statement that you prepared in part (c) above, discuss (i) the performance of the company for the year; and (ii) potential changes to the budgeting and reporting system that would improve performance evaluation within the company.	10
TOTAL MARKS		30

LQ 3 – Advanced (40 marks; 72 minutes)

Source: Adapted from University of Johannesburg Archive

You are the financial director of Electro Motors Ltd, which manufactures cooling motor systems for the local and export markets. The company was established in 1978 and has since established itself as a high quality supplier of many large fridge and freezer manufacturers.

Current position

Since 2XX2, the company has experienced a decline in demand for their motors. Management has categorically stated that the main reason for the lower demand is the depressed world economy. The decline in demand continues and the profitablilty and cash flows of Electro Motors Ltd has been put under increasing pressure.

principles of management accounting

The actual results for September 2XX4 were as follows:

	R
Sales	7 263 500
Less: Cost of sales	6 240 900
Material	2 925 000
Labour	393 600
Variable manufacturing overheads	272 300
Fixed manufacturing overheads	2 650 000
Gross profit	1 022 600
Variable non-manufacturing overheads	(466 800)
Fixed non-manufacturing overheads	(1 209 500)
Actual loss	(653 700)

The variance analysis for September 2XX4 was as follows:

Materials	Price	375 000	(U)
	Usage	173 000	(F)
Labour	Rate	120 000	(F)
	Efficiency	420 000	(F)
Variable overheads	Expenditure	–	
	Efficiency	–	
Fixed manufacturing costs	Spending	250 000	(U)
	Volume	1 233 000	(U)
Sales	Price	456 000	(F)
	Volume (Sales value basis)	1 400 000	(U)
Fixed administration costs	Spending	429 500	(U)

Additional information:
- Standard selling price   R175
- Normal (budgeted) production capacity   80 000 units
- Material, labour, variable and fixed manufacturing costs are allocated on a per unit basis.

	REQUIRED	Marks
(a)	Prepare a standard income statement as well as a budgeted income statement for September 2XX4.	15
(b)	Analyse and discuss the results of Electro Motors Ltd. Also, advise the directors of Electro Motors as to possible steps that they can take to improve their financial performance.	15
(c)	Journalise the complete accounting entries with regard to the following cost elements: (i) Materials (ii) Labour (iii) Fixed manufacturing costs (iv) Variable non-manufacturing costs (v) Fixed administration costs.	10
	Note: The journals for the write-down of the variances to the income statement are not required.	
	TOTAL MARKS	**40**

LQ 4 – Advanced (50 marks; 90 minutes)

Source: Adapted from UCT

AgriProducts is a divisionalised organisation that produces a wide range of agricultural products. One of the divisions, AgriDrums, manufactures a range of plastic drums designed for holding either water or chemicals. The drums are different sizes and range from holding 1 m^3 to 12 m^3 of liquid. The drums designed for chemicals are made of a thicker, more robust plastic compound that cannot be eroded by petrol, oil and other chemicals used by the agricultural sector. A standard absorption costing system is used for planning and control purposes, organisation-wide.

One of the most popular drums produced by AgriDrums is a dark green 5 m^3 reinforced drum suitable for holding chemicals, and this drum accounts for a significant portion of the division's total sales. Information regarding this dark green drum is presented below.

AgriDrums expects to produce and sell 1 700 of these drums per quarter for the foreseeable future. The standard selling price of 1 drum is R4 800, which results in the division earning a standard gross profit of R520 per drum.

The company uses the FIFO method of inventory valuation.

Total costs for the last quarter, based on the assumption of producing 1 700 drums, were originally budgeted to be the following:

	R	Standard price per input
Plastic (litres)	1 700 000	R20 per litre
HD6 (litres)	1 487 500	R35 per litre
Colourant (litres)	986 000	R58 per litre
Valve and seal set	340 000	R200 per set (1 set is required per drum)
Direct labour (hours)	1 062 500	R25 per labour hour
Variable overheads	637 500	60% of the total labour cost
Fixed overheads	1 062 500	R25 per labour hour

The actual costs incurred during the last quarter, as well as information regarding those costs and resources used, are as follows:

	R	Note
Plastic	1 696 000	2
HD6	1 306 400	2
Colourant	969 600	3
Valve and seal set	0	1
Direct labour	940 800	4
Variable overhead	660 000	
Fixed overhead	1 070 000	

General note:

Actual production of drums amounted to 1 600 drums for the period. Production was cut in response to reduced demand in the last quarter of 2XX6. The general market for drums was 8 per cent smaller than anticipated at the time of drafting the budget for the last quarter due to unusually good summer rains in the Western

principles of management accounting

Cape, which lead to a reduction in chemical usage (it is futile to spray crops in rainy periods as the chemical is washed off). Unfortunately the decrease in production was not perfectly matched to the decline in demand, which resulted in AgriDrums' inventory of drums (of this type) increasing by 250 units. All drums sold were at the standard price of R4 800 per drum, except for 100 drums which were sold at a discount of R150 per drum.

Notes:
1. There was neither opening nor closing inventory of raw materials for the quarter, other than the valve and seal sets. AgriDrums had 2 000 sets on hand at the beginning of the quarter, and 390 sets on hand at the end of the quarter. One set is used per drum. Any faulty sets are returned to the supplier for a full refund. Ten sets were returned to the supplier this quarter. AgriDrums orders its stock quarterly, and the stock for the next quarter (January to March 2XX7) has yet to arrive. The budgeted cost of R200 per set was based on the price at which the sets were purchased (this is known, since the sets are purchased in advance). The purchase price for the current order, delivery of which is expected on 2 January 2XX7, is 8 per cent higher, which reflects the unexpectedly high CPI figures for October 2XX6. Every set that left inventory is accounted for – it was either successfully fixed to a drum, or returned to the supplier.
2. Plastic and HD6 (a very tough plastic-like compound) are both required for all plastic drums that the organisation produces. The proportion in which the plastic and HD6 are mixed to make the body of the drums varies, depending on how tough the drum is required to be. The tougher the drum needs to be, the higher the proportion of HD6 to plastic. These materials are both purchased in litres and the organisation paid R20 and R35,50 per litre for plastic and HD6 respectively.
3. The colourant was purchased at 3 per cent more per litre than anticipated.
4. AgriDrums budgeted on paying an average of R25 per labour hour to its staff. They hired a number of new junior workers during the period, with the result that the average wage per hour decreased. On average 28 hours were worked per drum.

The directors of AgriProducts wish to evaluate the performance of the manager of AgriDrums, and a variance analysis as regards the 5 m^3 reinforced drum is required in order to provide insights into the management of the division.

REQUIRED		Marks
(a)	Calculate all variances necessary to identify any deviation of actual profit from that which was originally budgeted. Variances should be further analysed in as much detail as is useful to provide meaningful information and insight into the management of AgriDrums.	32
(b)	Given the results of your analysis and the information provided in the question, discuss whether the division (including both the production and sale of drums) has been well – or poorly – managed.	8
(c)	Calculate the total value of the closing finished goods inventory using standard costs and show the journal entry required in order to record finished goods inventory at a valuation which is consistent with GAAP (IAS2). You may assume that all the variances are considered to be material and that none of the variances reflects any abnormal amounts of waste.	10
TOTAL MARKS		**50**

LQ 5 – Advanced (40 marks; 72 minutes)

Source: Adapted from SAICA QE1

Signs-for-Africa (Pty) Ltd ('Signs-for-Africa') manufactures durable, low-cost, plastic road warning signs at its factory situated in Rosslyn, Tshwane. The company has historically exclusively focused on export markets but changed its focus to the South African market in 2XX6 because of the growth opportunities locally. The South African National Roads Agency Ltd (SANRAL) and local authorities in South Africa decided in 2XX6 to replace gradually all the existing metal road warning signs with plastic signage. The main reasons for this change are that plastic signs are less likely to be stolen and are safer in the event of collisions.

Signs-for-Africa manufactures two kinds of signs, namely standard road warning signs (SRWS) and electronic road warning signs (ERWS). The only material used to manufacture SRWS is plastic, whereas ERWS are fitted with one solar panel driven warning light, which is purchased from a supplier based in Japan. The warning light is fitted by skilled electricians during the production process. Apart from this, the ERWS are identical to SRWS and manufactured in the same process as SRWS.

Signs-for-Africa has operated a standard costing system for many years. The Manufacturing, Procurement and Sales divisions are all involved in setting standards on an annual basis. Their inputs are collectively incorporated into the company budget for the forthcoming financial years. The Procurement division is responsible for the ordering of materials, negotiating prices with suppliers, logistics relating to the receipt of materials and ongoing liaison with suppliers and potential suppliers. The Manufacturing division is responsible for all production matters including recruiting and managing all labourers involved in the production process.

The budget for the year ended 31 December 2XX7 was approved by the board of directors of Signs-for-Africa in early January 2XX7. The budget included the following relevant information and assumptions relating to planned sales and manufacturing volumes, and standard costs:

Signs-for-Africa (Pty) Ltd
Budget for the year ended 31 December 2XX7

	Quantity	R
Revenue		
SRWS	6 000 units	2 100 000
ERWS	12 000 units	6 600 000
Material costs		
Plastic	144 000 kg	(1 872 000)
Solar panel driven warning lights	12 000 units	(1 440 000)
Labour costs		
Type A labourers	18 000 hours	(450 000)
Electricians	12 000 clock hours	(420 000)
Variable manufacturing overheads		(270 000)
Fixed manufacturing overheads		(90 000)
Patent costs		(60 000)
Non-manufacturing overheads		(2 600 000)
Budgeted profit		**1 498 000**

Notes:
- The standard quantity of plastic used in the manufacturing process is 8 kg for each warning sign manufactured.
- All inventories are accounted for at standard cost.
- Type A labourers were budgeted to be paid a standard rate of R25 per hour, and the manufacturing standard is one hour of type A labour for each manufactured product.
- Electricians were expected to operate at a productivity level of 90 per cent and 54 minutes of electrician time was budgeted for each ERWS product. Electricians were budgeted to be paid R35 per standard clock hour.
- Variable manufacturing overheads were budgeted at R5 per machine hour and every product takes a standard time of three machine hours to complete.
- Fixed manufacturing overheads are allocated to the manufacturing cost of products based on machine hours.
- Signs-for-Africa is required to pay a standard patent fee of R5 per ERWS product sold, to its Japanese supplier.

There was no opening inventory of materials or finished products at the start of the 2XX7 financial year. No inventories of work-in-progress existed at the start or end of the financial year; nor had any been budgeted for.

The actual results for the year ended 31 December 2XX7 are summarised below:

Signs-for-Africa (Pty) Ltd
Results for year ended 31 December 2XX7

	Quantity	R
Revenue		
SRWS	5 000 units	1 800 000
ERWS	7 500 units	3 750 000
Manufacturing volumes		
SRWS	6 160 units	
ERWS	9 240 units	
Materials		
Plastic purchased	150 000 kg	(1 500 000)
Plastic used in the manufacturing process	138 600 kg	
Solar panel driven warning lights	9 240 units	(1 155 000)
Labour		
Type A labourers	12 320 hours	(332 640)
Electricians	8 662,5 clock hours	(346 500)
Variable manufacturing overheads		(207 900)
Fixed manufacturing overheads		(95 480)
Patent costs		(45 000)
Non-manufacturing overheads		(2 680 000)

Notes:
- Machine hours amounted to 38 500 in 2XX7.
- Signs-for-Africa calculates sales volume variances on the gross profit basis.
- Non-manufacturing overheads are fixed in nature.

The divisional managers responsible for the Manufacturing, Procurement and Sales divisions believe that the change of focus to the South African market has adversely affected the profitability of Signs-for-Africa. In their opinion SANRAL and local authorities did not plan the rollout of plastic road warning signs properly and tend to place orders on an ad hoc basis. The ERWS product range has also not taken off because of the higher price of the product compared to the SRWS range, despite the vastly superior visibility of ERWS to motorists.

Additional information
The schedule set out below contains the list of variances which the company normally calculates. The management accountant has already calculated some of these variances. His calculations are correct.

Signs-for-Africa (Pty) Ltd
Schedule of variances for the year ended 31 December 2XX7

	Adverse variances	Favourable variances
	R	R
Revenue		
Sales price variance:		
SRWS		50 000
ERWS	375 000	
Sales margin mix variance:		
SRWS		
ERWS		
Sales margin quantity variance:		
SRWS		
ERWS		
Expenses		
Material price variance:		
Plastic material		
Solar panels	46 200	
Material usage variance:		
Plastic material		
Solar panels		Nil
Labour rate variance:		
Type A	24 640	
Electricians		

Expenses (continued)		
Labour efficiency variance: Type A		77 000
Electricians		
Variable overhead expenditure variance		
Variable overhead efficiency variance		
Fixed overhead expenditure variance		
Fixed overhead volume variance:		
Fixed overhead capacity variance		
Fixed overhead efficiency variance		
Patent expenditure variance		
Patent volume variance		
Non-manufacturing overheads expenditure variance	80 000	

	REQUIRED	Marks
(a)	Calculate all the possible variances for the year ended 31 December 2XX7 not yet calculated by the management accountant. Using your calculated variances and those of the management accountant, reconcile budgeted profit to actual profit or loss for the year.	22
(b)	Based on the variances calculated in part (a) and other information provided: (i) Identify and discuss the key reason(s) for lower than expected profitability of Signs-for-Africa (Pty) Ltd in the 2XX7 financial year, and (ii) Provide positive feedback, if any, and negative feedback, if any, on the performances of the Manufacturing, Procurement and Sales divisions.	3 8
(c)	Calculate the number of units of standard road warning signs and electronic road warning signs that Signs-for-Africa (Pty) Ltd needed to sell in 2XX7 in order to break even based on the actual results for the year ended 31 December 2XX7. Assume that the actual sales mix by product achieved in 2XX7 remains constant.	7
	TOTAL MARKS	**40**

References

Acorn Industries. 2010. *Standard costing and variance analysis*. [Online] Available <http://www.financedoctors.net/Notes/133.pdf> [22 June 2010].

SAICA. 2010. Statements of Generally Accepted Accounting Practice: IAS 2 (AC 108), *Inventories (revised January 2010)*. Johannesburg: SAICA.

Volition. 2005. *Case studies. Client: Murray & Roberts Foundries Group*. [Online]. Available <www.volition.co.za/downloads/Case_Study_Murray_Roberts_Foundries.pdf> [22 January 2008].

Advanced reading Integration section: Chapters 10 to 13

Shelley-Anne Roos

> The aim of this section is to integrate students' knowledge of Chapters 10 to 13, and to move students toward a more advanced, high-level understanding of the topics, the relationships between them, and the exam technique required.

Chapter 10, *Relevant costs for decision-making* is one of the most important chapters in this book. If you look back at Chapter 1, *Introduction to management accounting*, you will notice that the very thing that sets management accounting apart from financial accounting, is the fact that the information supplied by a management accounting system depends on the purpose for which the information is required. In other words, we ask, 'What information is *relevant* for the specific decision that we face?' Providing relevant information is what management accounting professionals do, and it follows that management accounting is impossible without a thorough understanding of relevance. It should not surprise you, then, to discover that relevant costing features in many high-level management accounting exams. Even when the topic is not specifically examined, it tends to find itself into the questions via other topics, because almost all of them require a grasp of the principles of relevance.

Consider that as early as Chapter 2, *Cost classification*, you had to understand that a given cost may be fixed in the short-term, but variable when a longer time horizon is considered (it may therefore be irrelevant to some decisions, but relevant to others). As late in the book as Chapter 17, *Competitive advantage*, we will discuss techniques and practices that may help to reduce certain costs in given circumstances, but may be expensive to implement (we therefore consider the relevant cost of implementing such changes). Although relevant costing questions usually require calculations to arrive at a specific numerical answer, advanced questions frequently also require that you consider non-financial and qualitative factors as part of the decision.

The concept of relevance also forms the cornerstone of Chapter 11, *Decision-making under operational constraints*. This chapter focuses specifically on situations where resources are limited, and where decisions have to be taken regarding the optimal use of such limited resources. Again, the topic lends itself well to calculations that result in clear-cut numerical answers, but once you have mastered the chapter, it should not be difficult to perform such calculations. In an advanced question, the examiner is likely to sketch a scenario and require the consideration of multiple factors in your decision, including scenario-specific non-financial and qualitative factors.

Chapter 12, *Budgets, planning and control* introduces another topic that – like relevant costing – can be integrated with many other topics. Cost behaviour, for example, has to be thoroughly understood in order to draw up a budget. Budgeting is also integral to performance management, especially when it comes to the motivational impact of budgets and the effect of budget variances on performance assessment. Furthermore, a thorough understanding of the concepts underlying

principles of management accounting

budgeting and variance analysis is particularly important in order to understand standard costing.

Chapter 13, *Standard costing* builds on the concepts of budgeting and variance analysis. Standard costing introduces numerical calculations that students often find intimidating in their earlier studies. However, once you understand that each additional variance calculated merely aims to split the variance between the budget and the actual results into further detail, it becomes apparent that there is a clear pattern to the calculation of variances. Rather, it is the interpretation of these variances that calls for a higher level of insight into the topic. Advanced questions could ask students to interpret variances in the particular context of a given organisational scenario, instead of merely requiring a list of possible generic causes for the variances.

What follows is a question that tests some of the material covered in Chapters 10 to 13. Although the question has been adapted for purposes of this section, it originates from Part 1 of the SAICA qualifying exam. The suggested exam technique for attempting advanced questions such as this one is to follow these steps:

- Read the question requirements first, to focus your thoughts on what will be required of you.
- Read the scenario and plan all of your answers.
- Answer the requirements in the given order, starting with requirement (a). The order may be important, because long questions are sometimes set in such a way that thinking through the earlier answers leads you to the later answers.
- *Apply* your answers to the scenario by making sure that you are considering the specific circumstances of the particular organisation throughout.

Integrated question: African Business School

African Business School (Pty) Ltd ('ABS') is a registered training organisation that operates from three training sites in Irene (close to Pretoria), Magaliesburg and Randburg. ABS focuses on providing one- to three-day courses on managerial development topics to middle and senior management personnel. Courses are held on weekdays, and facilities are closed over weekends. ABS leases the three training sites.

The Irene and Randburg training sites can accommodate a maximum of 30 people per day and the Magaliesburg site 40 people per day. Standard course rates are charged per person per day and there is no difference in the daily prices for one-, two- and three-day courses.

The Magaliesburg training site is situated on the outskirts of the town of Magaliesburg, within a small game reserve. The facility includes a lodge that can accommodate training course attendees overnight. Attendees on two- and three-day courses stay over at the lodge, and all meals are included in the course rates. This site currently charges such attendees an extra R400 per night for meals and accommodation. The land on which the lodge and training site are situated is leased from the owners of the game reserve. The lease has recently been renewed for a further ten years.

The head office of ABS is responsible for scheduling of courses, marketing, finance and administration. The head office is situated on the Randburg site, and the allocation of rent and related fixed overheads is based on the relative floor space occupied by the head office and the Randburg training facility. Salient information regarding the operational and financial performance of the three training sites and the lodge for the year ended 28 February 2XX6 is summarised below:

Integration section: Chapters 10 to 13

African Business School (Pty) Ltd
Financial information for the year ended 28 February 2XX6

	Notes	Irene training site	Randburg training site	Magaliesburg Training site	Magaliesburg Lodge
		R	R	R	R
Revenue		1 215 000	2 025 000	2 160 000	1 052 000
Course fees	1	1 215 000	2 025 000	2 160 000	0
Accommodation and meals		0	0	0	800 000
Bar revenue	2	0	0	0	252 000
Operating costs		(1 322 488)	(1 760 980)	(1 670 645)	(1 225 887)
Variable expenses	3	(172 125)	(273 375)	(360 000)	(397 500)
Fixed costs	4	(925 000)	(1 112 000)	(910 000)	(680 000)
Head office costs	5	(225 363)	(375 605)	(400 645)	(148 387)
Operating profit/(loss)		**(107 488)**	**264 020**	**489 355**	**(173 887)**

Notes:

1 The course fee per person per day during the 2XX6 financial year was R600 at all ABS training venues. The number of people who attended courses during 2XX6 and site capacities are set out below:

	Irene training site	Randburg training site	Magaliesburg training site
Maximum number of days available for training in the 2XX6 financial year	225	225	225
Maximum number of people who could have attended one-day courses in 2XX6	6 750	6 750	9 000
Actual number of people attending courses:			
One-day courses	1 425	1 695	240
Two-day courses	150	420	720
Three-day courses	100	280	640

2 The lodge marks up alcohol and beverages sold in its bar by 60%.
3 Variable costs at the training sites include costs of hiring external presenters, course materials and refreshments served during courses. ABS employs a limited number of presenters at each training site on a permanent basis and contracts with external presenters for specific courses as required. Variable costs at the lodge comprise the costs of alcohol and beverages, and catering costs.

principles of management accounting

4 Fixed costs in the 2XX6 financial year were made up as follows:

	Irene training site	Randburg training site	Magaliesburg Training site	Magaliesburg Lodge	Head office
	R	R	R	R	R
Administration and finance costs	0	0	0	0	680 000
Cleaning costs	90 000	95 000	85 000	165 000	75 000
Kitchen staff salaries and overheads	0	0	0	275 000	0
Bar staff salaries	0	0	0	60 000	0
Marketing expenses	0	0	0	0	80 000
Rental of premises	215 000	235 000	115 000	105 000	85 000
Presenter salaries	450 000	510 000	590 000	0	0
Scheduling costs	0	0	0	0	230 000
Other fixed costs	170 000	272 000	120 000	75 000	0
	925 000	1 112 000	910 000	680 000	1 150 000

5 Head office costs were fully allocated to each training site and the lodge in 2XX6 based on each site's revenue (excluding bar revenue) as a percentage of total ABS revenue.

ABS has been under pressure from the shareholders because of the performance of the company over the last three years. At the last shareholders' meeting, management was requested to identify and explore ways to improve the financial performance of the company. Management has subsequently identified the following three options for improving profitability:
- Closing the Irene training venue, or
- Outsourcing the catering at the Magaliesburg training facility, or
- Implementing zero-base budgeting throughout the company to save costs.

Option 1: Closing the Irene training venue
As the Irene site seems to be the least profitable, management is investigating the implications of closing this training facility, based on two possibilities: The first is to close the facility completely, and the second is that the University of Pretoria (UP) operate the facility on behalf of ABS.

Courses currently offered at Irene could be offered at the Randburg site if the Irene site were closed down, and initial feedback indicates that 75 per cent of ABS clients would attend courses at Randburg if the Irene site were closed.

Other relevant information relating to the potential closure of the Irene training facility:
- The presenters currently employed in Irene could be offered positions at Randburg;
- The rental agreement for the Irene premises expires on 28 February 2XX7;
- The estimated costs of retrenching employees at Irene, excluding presenters, would be R200 000; and
- Other site closure costs would amount to R75 000.

Alternatively, the UP has offered to operate the Irene training site on behalf of ABS. UP will assume full operational responsibility for the site including marketing, course scheduling, finance and administration. In addition, UP will pay all operational expenses associated with the site, except for head office charges, and will collect course fees directly from attendees. Apart from course presenters, the current Irene employees will be employed by UP. ABS will retrench the presenters at Irene at a total cost of R350 000.

Essentially ABS will provide course material to UP and allow them to operate the training site as an ABS facility. In return, UP will pay ABS a fee amounting to 5% of course revenue. UP has undertaken to charge the same course fee per person per day as is charged at other ABS sites.

Option 2: Outsourcing of the catering at Magaliesburg Lodge
Management also investigated the possibility of outsourcing the catering at the lodge. Though the catering is of a very high standard and receives mostly positive comments on course evaluations, management is of the opinion that the costs of providing this service are too high.

Brilliant Catering has made the following proposal for taking over the catering and bar functions on an exclusive basis at the lodge:

- Existing kitchen and bar staff will be offered employment by Brilliant Catering. Employees who refuse the offer will be retrenched by ABS. If no employee accepts the Brilliant Catering offer, the estimated retrenchment cost will amount to R230 000.
- Accommodation functions at the lodge will remain the responsibility of ABS.
- If Brilliant Catering takes over the catering and the bar, and kitchen and bar staff elect to join Brilliant Catering, the fixed costs at the lodge payable by ABS will decrease by an estimated R325 000 per annum.
- ABS will continue to pay rental for the premises as well as the fixed overheads associated with provision of accommodation facilities.
- Brilliant Catering will charge ABS a fixed fee of R125 per person per day for meals provided. Brilliant Catering will operate the bar for profit and amounts spent by attendees on alcohol and beverages will be recovered from ABS, who in turn will recover it from attendees.

Option 3: Implementing zero-base budgeting in ABS to save costs in future
ABS regards itself as a rather small and manageable company, and as a result has never made too much fuss about its budgeting process. However, in order to improve profitability, it is now considering implementing zero-base budgeting throughout the company as a means of saving costs.

	REQUIRED	Marks
(a)	Advise the management of ABS, with reasons, on the most appropriate strategy with regard to the Irene training site namely: • To continue operating the Irene training site on the current basis, • To close the site, or • To outsource the operations to the University of Pretoria. Round off to the nearest rand.	15
(b)	Evaluate and provide an initial recommendation as to whether outsourcing the catering at the lodge to Brilliant Catering will improve the profitability of ABS. List any additional aspects that should be considered before a final decision is taken.	8
(c)	Discuss, with reasons, whether you think the use of zero-base budgeting is a viable option to improve the profitability of ABS.	5

principles of management accounting

(d)	For ABS, course presenters are a valuable resource. Calculate the shadow price of course presenters at the Randburg training site and explain your answer.	3
(e)	Evaluate to what extent it would be possible and useful to implement a standard costing system for ABS' training activities.	4
	TOTAL MARKS	**35**

Discussion

A suggested solution to the question can be found at the back of the book. Once you have attempted the question and checked the solution, you may find the following discussion useful.

The case study in the question focuses on an organisation in the services sector, namely one that provides business education. Sadly, there are many students who seemingly disregard such an important fact when they first attempt advanced questions. If you were not astutely aware of the specific services sector scenario when you answered this question, check through your answer for any tell-tale signs that you may not have thoroughly absorbed the information (such as, for example, inappropriate references to manufacturing or related wording that may indicate to the examiner that you did not grasp the context of an educational services provider). The more advanced the question, the more important the scenario – in a high-level question the purpose is to determine whether you can apply your knowledge (even knowledge that you may have studied in the more classic context of a manufacturing scenario) to a specific case study that could be very different from what you expected. The examiner and the professional body that you aspire to join do not attempt to guess at what kind of organisation you and your fellow students will likely end up working in during your career. On the contrary, they know that students are likely to work in a wide variety of sectors (private, public and not-for-profit), in a variety of industries, and that each individual may make several career changes during his or her lifetime. Exam questions therefore test your ability to adapt to whatever scenario you are presented with – a true test of your understanding of the principles of management accounting.

Parts (a) and (b) of this question require a thorough understanding of relevant income, relevant costs and related relevant facts – we can say that an understanding of relevant *information* is required, as is often the case in advanced questions. Your answer to parts (a) and (b) may not necessarily be presented in the same format as those on the suggested solution. The more advanced the question, the less likely it is that there is a single 'correct' answer, and the more observant the marker has to be in order to award marks for the logic applied to the scenario. In parts (a) and (b), marks would be awarded only if either the 'total' or the 'incremental' approach to relevant costing were consistently applied in order to present a logical answer, and if the discussion points were valid and relevant to the scenario (even if they differed from those in suggested solution).

> If you are concerned about how marks are awarded in professional exams, where each student's answer may be different, you should work through a few past exams to understand how marks are awarded. SAICA publishes its past exam papers on its website, together with suggested solutions which include mark plans. It also publishes a separate document which discusses how students scored in the exam, and gives feedback on each question. CIMA publishes what it calls 'post exam guides' on its website, which feature comments from the examiner, common errors, and an indication of how marks were awarded. The respective websites are <www.saica.co.za> and <www.cimaglobal.com>.

Notice that in neither part (a) nor part (b) of the question was it sufficient simply to *calculate* relevant revenues and costs. To give an informed opinion, you also had to identify and discuss the non-financial and qualitative aspects of the decisions. Some financial and quantitative factors also needed discussion, namely those where incomplete information was given. For example, in part (a) we knew that the Irene lease would run out only on 28 February 2XX7, and we could therefore deduce that ABS would probably be held responsible for another year's lease payments. However, the exact amount of the lease payments (after considering escalation clauses) is not known – we can merely identify and discuss it as yet another factor that would influence the decision.

Two further trends in advanced questions are therefore highlighted in the previous paragraphs:
- The more advanced the question, the less likely it is to have one specific, clear-cut answer, and
- The more advanced the question, the more likely that uncertain outcomes, assumptions and estimates will feature as part of the scenario.

The reason for both of these trends is that advanced questions mimic real-life management accounting scenarios more closely than basic, theoretical questions do.

> A number of common characteristics of advanced questions are introduced and discussed in the integration sections in this book. For a summary of all of them, see the integration section at the end of the book that deals with Chapters 14 to 17.

After the ABS question was featured in the Qualifying Exam, SAICA remarked in its feedback that some students lost marks because they had erroneously included answers to part (b) in part (a). Did you do this in your answer? You would not have if you had followed the suggested approach, because you would have read through all of the requirements first, and would have planned all your answers before starting to write them out.

The last important aspect of requirements (a) and (b) that we need to emphasise is that both requirements asked for your advice, but neither specifically stated that you should also consider non-financial and qualitative factors. This is because, at an advanced level, you are expected to *know* that your advice would be of limited use if you considered only financial and quantitative aspects – in practice, management decisions are based on the entire set of relevant circumstances.

Part (c) requires no calculation, and tests your understanding of zero-base budgeting. Notice how the suggested solution does not list any generic advantages and disadvantages of zero-base budgeting, because these would have taken up valuable time and would not have earned marks. Rather, the entire discussion is *applied* to the scenario. In advanced work, the question is usually not whether suggestion X seems like a good idea in theory when you read a textbook, but rather whether suggestion X may be a good idea at a *specific point* in time for a *specific organisation*, given its unique circumstances (in this case, whether zero-base budgeting may be of benefit to ABS in the 2XX7 year).

You may feel that part (d) was a trick question. Why would you be asked to calculate a shadow price if there isn't one? Because it tests the most important part of your understanding of the topic, namely whether you really know what a shadow price is. It does so by considering the concept in an unusual context. For students who understood the nature of shadow prices and could explain it on paper, part (d) was a giveaway. Also notice the benefit of answering the requirements in the given order – in part (d) you can use the capacity calculations that you have already performed in part (a).

Part (e) counts for only four marks, and you have to make sure that what you write is relevant. As always, read the requirement very carefully: you are not required to deal with the lodge (the requirement refers to training activities only), and you are required to discuss to what extent it would be *possible* and *useful* to implement standard costing. The obvious way to plan your four-mark answer would be to make at least two well-illustrated arguments about the possibility of implementation, and two well-illustrated arguments about the usefulness of standard costing – both parts, of course, *specifically applied* to ABS.

Performance management

chapter 14

Shelley-Anne Roos

LEARNING OBJECTIVES
By the end of this chapter, you should be able to:
1 Explain the conceptual aspects of performance measurement.
2 Distinguish between cost centres (standard cost centres and discretionary cost centres), revenue centres, profit centres and investment centres.
3 Discuss the concepts of controllability and traceability, and apply these concepts in the performance evaluation of units and managers.
4 Distinguish between centralised and decentralised management responsibility and control structures, and discuss their relative advantages and disadvantages.
5 Explain and calculate return on investment, residual income, economic value added (EVA®) and return on sales, and discuss the advantages and disadvantages of each.
6 Discuss the value-based management concepts of shareholder value analysis and market value added.
7 Discuss the balanced scorecard and formulate performance measures for each of its four perspectives.
8 Discuss the considerations in setting performance targets and designing reward structures, and advise on these matters in given circumstances.

Aspen Pharmacare and performance management

Aspen Pharmacare is a manufacturer of pharmaceuticals and a supplier of pharmaceutical, consumer and nutritional products. In its annual report, it states that its South African operations contributed more half of revenue and profits over the year under review. The South African results were boosted by the pharmaceutical division, which increased its revenue by 34 per cent in a market characterised by 'robust volume growth'. However, 'testing market conditions' prevailed in the depressed retail sector, and Aspen is therefore pleased that its consumer division managed 16 per cent revenue growth. Commenting on a year in which the company as a whole grew strongly, the Group Chief Executive mentions the competence and commitment of its employees who contributed to the success.

Source: Aspen 2009

Aspen evaluates the performance of its divisions and employees to determine how they contribute to the overall success of the company. This assessment also enables Aspen to manage its future performance. Chapter 14 focuses on the principles of performance management as they apply to units and employees within an organisational structure.

14.1 Introduction

Every organisation is established for a purpose. A retail chain such as Woolworths may strive for excellence as a passionate, committed South African retail brand, while a state hospital such as the Tygerberg Hospital wishes to provide affordable, quality health care to patients. Irrespective of the kind of organisation or the activities in which it is involved, the need arises to measure how well each organisation has performed in pursuit of its purpose. Woolworths Holdings' shareholders, for example, may wish to use information such as the quoted share price, reported earnings per share and dividend information in order to establish how well the company as a whole has performed from an equity investor's perspective. The Department of Health may be interested in Tygerberg Hospital's patient care statistics in order to form an opinion on how well the state hospital is performing.

For an organisation as a whole to perform well, its parts need to perform well. For this reason, senior managers evaluate the performance of parts of an organisation. In both Woolworths and Tygerberg Hospital, managers evaluate the performance of different units within the organisation (such as the accounting department) and the performance of the staff within each of the units.

14.1.1 Performance management and objectives

> **Key terms:** objectives, performance evaluation, performance management, performance measure

Performance evaluation can be described as 'backward-looking': it assesses something that has already happened. Managers, however, need not only to evaluate past performance, but also to manage future performance.

The evaluation of past performance can provide valuable information for the management of future performance. For example, when the performance of a particular retail store branch is evaluated, managers may notice that its low profits are largely due to excessive shoplifting. Based on this information, they could decide to install an improved security system to address the problem and ensure higher future profits for the branch.

Apart from using 'backward-looking' performance evaluation information to manage future performance, managers can also use another very powerful tool to improve future performance. By communicating how performance will be evaluated and rewarded in a future period, managers can send a strong signal that conveys what is expected of units and individuals within the organisation. In fact, the careful formulation of performance evaluation criteria for future periods is one of the best ways for managers to ensure that units and individuals within the organisation perform in the way that managers would like them to perform.

Performance management aims to eliminate undesirable actions and to encourage desirable actions by units and individuals. This raises the question of what constitutes desirable action in an organisation, and what aspects of performance should be emphasised. Woolworths' customers, for example, are often happy to spend time browsing through the store without the personal assistance of a staff member. In Tygerberg Hospital's trauma centre, however, it is crucial that staff personally attend to patients as quickly as possible. The reason that organisations may choose to highlight different aspects of performance stems from the nature and purpose of the organisation itself. Organisations often formulate a vision or a mission statement. Woolworths aspires to being a 'passionate, committed' retailer, while Tygerberg Hospital wants 'to provide affordable, world-class quality health

care …'. From these broad statements of intent, organisations may formulate a number of objectives to indicate more specifically what they would like to achieve. Performance evaluation criteria are designed to measure the achievement of these objectives. If properly formulated, performance evaluation criteria help managers to manage the performance of the organisation in terms of the fulfilment of its objectives. When performance evaluation criteria are formulated based on **objectives**:
1. The organisation focuses its performance management on the important aspects that are addressed in its objectives, and
2. Performance evaluation criteria are considered for each objective, so that all of the prioritised objectives receive attention.

14.1.2 Information for performance evaluation

Key term: performance measure

Remember that, as part of the management of performance, past performance is evaluated. During performance evaluation an opinion has to be formed on how well a unit or individual has performed. To form this opinion, performance is measured (in other words, a **performance measure** such as return on investment is used) and the result is compared to a yardstick. This is an important point to note when answering a question on the work covered in this chapter. One cannot fairly evaluate whether, say, a 12 per cent per annum return on investment is 'good' or 'unacceptable' for a given unit in a specific situation without the use of a yardstick. The yardstick in this example could be a similar unit or an indicator (for example, 'Compared to unit B's 15 per cent per annum return on investment and the industry average of 14,5 per cent per annum, unit A has performed poorly'), a specific target that has been set (for example, 'Compared to the target return on investment of 10 per cent per annum, unit A has performed well'), or a prior period (for example, 'Unit A has improved its return on investment from 11 per cent per annum in 2XX8 to 12 per cent per annum in 2XX9').

Care should be taken whenever one unit or individual is compared with another, as no two have identical characteristics and circumstances. Ideally, either appropriate adjustments should be made to performance results in an attempt to neutralise known differences in as far as is practical, or different yardsticks should be applied to the entities. Particular care is required when a unit within an organisation is compared to another independent organisation in the same industry. A unit receives benefits from the central organisation (for example, legal advice or public relations) that may not be comprehensively recorded at unit level, while an independent organisation has to fund all of these by itself.

14.1.3 Management accounting information

Accounting students know that organisations have to keep financial records in order to prepare financial statements, calculate taxes, and comply with other legal and management requirements. For the purpose of performance management, however, financial accounting information alone may not be sufficient. Information internal to the organisation, which may not necessarily be reported externally or may not be of a financial nature, is also required to manage the performance of units and individuals inside the organisation. The information used for managing performance inside an organisation falls within the domain of management accounting: it forms part of the information that managers need in order to perform their tasks.

14.2 Responsibility accounting

> **Key terms:** cost centre, investment centre, profit centre, responsibility centre, revenue centre

A **responsibility centre** is responsible for specific activities, and its performance is the responsibility of a specific manager. Nedbank's Helderberg Business Bank branch could, for example, be seen as a responsibility centre within Nedbank. The branch itself also consists of other, smaller responsibility centres (such as the sales team and the credit team), and forms part of a larger responsibility centre (Nedbank Business Bank, Winelands Region).

Responsibility accounting is used to manage the performance of responsibility centres. There are four main types of responsibility centres in organisations:

1. *A cost centre is held responsible for its costs only.* Performance management in a **cost centre** focuses primarily on minimising cost. There are two types of cost centres. In a standard cost centre there is a clear relationship between inputs and outputs. Production departments are sometimes classified as standard cost centres. Performance can be measured by comparing actual costs to standards. In a discretionary cost centre there is no clear relationship between inputs and outputs. Research and development departments are sometimes classified as discretionary cost centres. Performance management is difficult in these types of centres, as low spending may imply insufficient effort while high spending may imply wastage. The absence of an input/output relationship poses a significant performance management challenge.

2. *A revenue centre is held responsible for its revenues only.* Sales departments that directly generate sales income are sometimes classified as revenue centres. Performance management in a **revenue centre** focuses primarily on maximising revenues. Sometimes revenue centres are also held responsible for marketing-related costs.

3. *A profit centre is held responsible for its costs and revenues.* A local branch of an organisation is sometimes classified as a **profit centre**, and is thereby held responsible for both the revenues that it generates and the costs that it incurs. Performance management in a profit centre focuses primarily on maximising profit.

4. *An investment centre is held responsible for its costs and revenues, as well as for investments in the centre.* A local branch of an organisation may be classified as an **investment centre**, and thereby be held responsible for the revenues that it generates, the costs that it incurs, and the money that is invested in, and by, the branch. Performance management in an investment centre focuses primarily on maximising profit per rand invested.

Keep in mind that in management accounting there are no fixed 'rules' (such as the international financial reporting standards that apply to financial accounting) that prescribe, for example, in which circumstances a unit should be classified as a cost, revenue, profit or investment centre. Rather, the goal is to choose the option that will provide the best possible management information and induce the most appropriate behaviour under the circumstances.

14.2.1 Performance of units and managers

> **Key terms:** controllability, traceable

A distinction needs to be made between the performance of a *unit* in an organisation, and the performance of the *manager* in charge of that unit. An excellent manager may, for example, be in charge of an ailing unit, or an ineffective manager may prevent a flourishing unit from achieving even greater success. *Unit* performance evaluation assists senior management in deciding on the allocation of scarce resources between units. Ideally, the performance evaluation of a *manager* should be based on those aspects over which the manager has had control. The following example serves as an illustration.

Example 14.1

On 1 January 2XX8, James was appointed manager of the West Coast branch of StayRSA, a company that leases self-catering cottages to tourists. The following is an extract of actual results from the management accounts of the West Coast branch for the year ended 31 December 2XX8:

	Note	2XX8	2XX7	% change
Revenue from cottage rentals	1	R1 200 000	R810 000	48,1%
Administration (including salaries and wages)		(R382 000)	(R362 500)	5,4%
Municipal charges (including water and electricity)		(R57 500)	(R50 000)	15%
Maintenance	2	(R190 000)	(R15 000)	1 167%
Marketing	3	(R95 000)	(R1 000)	9 400%
Repairs due to storm damage	4	(R75 500)	–	–
Fixed head office reservation administration costs	5	(R70 000)	(R10 000)	600%
Branch income		R330 000	R371 500	(11,2%)

Notes:
1. In 2XX8 the West Coast branch charged R480 per cottage per night, irrespective of the season and the number of occupants. The corresponding rate in 2XX7 was R450 per night. Cottages can be rented 365 days a year. The branch has 10 cottages.
2. James is of the opinion that inadequate maintenance had been performed on most cottages in the years prior to his appointment.
3. James marketed the West Coast cottages at trade fairs in July and August.
4. A winter storm caused extensive damage to some buildings. The amount of R75 500 was not covered by the insurance policy. All insurance matters are administered by StayRSA's head office.
5. The actual cost of central reservation administration incurred at head office is allocated to branches based on their usage of head office reservation resources. On budgeted costs the allocations would have been R50 000 in 2XX8 and R8 000 in 2XX7. It appears that the budget overruns were due to poor cost control at head office.

Required:
Comment on the performance of the West Coast branch and its manager in 2XX8.

principles of management accounting

At first glance it seems that the West Coast branch and its manager have performed poorly – the branch income has declined by 11,2 per cent. However, the information should be properly analysed before conclusions are drawn.

- In 2XX8 revenue was received for 2 500 nights (R1 200 000 / R480), an average of 250 nights per cottage (2 500 nights / 10 cottages). This implies a 68,5 per cent occupancy rate (250 nights occupied / 365 nights in a year). In 2XX7, 1 800 nights' income was received (R810 000 / R450), an average of 180 nights per cottage (1 800 nights / 10 cottages). This implies a 49,3 per cent occupancy rate (180 nights / 365 nights). Revenue has increased as a result of not only inflation (as reflected in the price increase), but also much higher occupancy. *The branch and its manager have significantly improved the occupancy rate despite a price increase from R450 to R480 per night.*
- The increases in administration and municipal expenses are small in comparison with the increase in revenue. Because some of the expenses, such as electricity, are likely to increase with higher occupancy, these comparatively modest increases may indicate successful cost management efforts. Another way of analysing the improvement would be to calculate that these expense categories equal 36,6 per cent of revenue in 2XX8 ([R382 000 + R57 500] / R1 200 000), while they equal a comparatively larger 50,9 per cent of revenue in 2XX7 ([R362 500 + R50 000] / R810 000). *The branch and its manager seem to have improved control over costs in these categories, as the expenses have declined relative to revenues.*
- Significantly more was spent on maintenance in 2XX8 compared to 2XX7. The average maintenance expense of R102 500 over the two years ([R190 000 + R15 000] / 2) equals 10,2 per cent of the average revenue (R102 500 / [R1 200 000 + R810 000] / 2]). StayRSA could compare this percentage to that of its other branches to determine whether the average expenditure was acceptable. However, it is possible that maintenance may have been neglected even before 2XX7, which would make the large 2XX8 expense even more defensible. *Head office may have preferred a more even spread over time in the branch's accounts. James believes that some of the cottages were poorly maintained upon his arrival. If head office agrees with this view, he will be able to justify the large expense.* Managers are often tempted, in the same way as James's predecessor, to postpone expenses such as maintenance in order to improve short-term results. In the longer term, such a policy is clearly not sustainable.
- The arguments related to maintenance apply equally to marketing. In addition, it is often difficult to assess precisely the impact of a particular marketing campaign on revenue. In this case it is possible that some of the increased revenue of 2XX8 may have resulted from the increased marketing effort. The marketing may also hold a longer-term future benefit. It may be wise to consider tracing revenue to marketing campaigns by, for example, offering a discount if a voucher is shown on check-in or if customers quote a reference number from an advertisement. *Head office might have preferred a more even spread over time in the branch's accounts, but the increased expenditure seems to have paid off. James is spending more on marketing than his predecessor, and seems to be reaping impressive returns.*
- The storm damage is a result of the geographical location of the branch. If the property, for example, were to face regular losses owing to natural disasters, this would influence decisions made by head office managers regarding the future viability of the branch. James, on the other hand, could control neither the storm nor the fact that the insurance policy did not cover all the damage (insurance policies are controlled at head office). Had he been appointed manager of another branch unaffected by the storm, he would not have

incurred this expense. *The branch's performance evaluation should take the repair expense into account. However, unless head office managers are of the opinion that James has overpaid for the repair work, the entire R75 500 should be disregarded in his performance evaluation.*
- Head office reservation administration costs have been allocated to the branch based on its usage of head office resources. Had the branch been an independent organisation, it would have had to incur these additional reservation expenses. The budget overruns should, however, affect the performance evaluation of head office and not the branch, as the cause seems to be poor cost control at head office. *In the performance evaluation of the branch and James, only R50 000 (the budgeted amount) should be subtracted from income. James had control over how much use the branch made of head office reservation resources, but no control over head office's actual spending overruns.*

Evaluating managers' performance based on those aspects over which they have control is often called the '**controllability** concept'. Conceptually, the approach is defensible. Some organisations choose, however, to include uncontrollable aspects in managers' performance evaluation. This can be for a variety of reasons, such as the practical difficulties encountered in separating controllable from uncontrollable costs, or the fact that they wish to draw managers' attention to expenses beyond their control and the need for them to be recovered. In the latter case, it may be sufficient merely to show uncontrollable costs on the performance evaluation report, without taking them into account in managers' performance evaluation.

When unit performance is evaluated, allocated amounts are usually subtracted from income to the extent that they are **traceable** to the unit. In our example, head office reservation administration costs were traced based on the branches' usage of head office reservation resources (we assume that this was measured in an appropriate activity-based manner). However, not all costs are traceable to units. Consider, as an example, the cost of employing staff at head office to administer VAT and income tax returns for the company. These cannot be traced to the West Coast branch, because the costs would have existed even if there had been no branch on the West Coast. Still, as is the case with the controllability concept described above, many organisations choose to subtract non-traceable allocated amounts when evaluating unit performance. This practice has merit in that the unit would have had to incur such costs even if it had not formed part of a larger organisation.

14.3 Centralised and decentralised organisational structures

> **Key terms:** autonomous, centralisation, decentralisation, strategic business units, sub-optimal decisions

As organisational structures vary, management responsibility and control may be assigned differently within organisations. In the context of performance management, **centralisation** versus **decentralisation** refers to the extent of delegation of decision-making responsibility to lower organisational levels.

Where an organisation's senior managers retain extensive control over strategic and operational decisions at all levels of the organisation, the structure is said to be one of centralised management control. Conversely, where the senior managers delegate vast decision-making responsibilities to lower levels, a decentralised structure is said to exist and the units are said to be '**autonomous**'. When autonomous units are responsible for developing and marketing their own products or services, they are called '**strategic business units**'. Each organisation lies somewhere on the continuum between the theoretical extremes of centralised and decentralised structures. Also, within a single organisation, certain aspects may be decentralised while others could remain centralised. Many organisations start off with a centralised control structure and become increasingly decentralised as they grow. The optimal extent of decentralisation changes as the organisation and its environment change.

14.3.1 Potential benefits from decentralisation

1. *Greater responsiveness to needs at lower levels.* Lower level managers have the freedom to make decisions about the units that they are responsible for. These managers are likely to have the best understanding of the unique characteristics and needs of the units under their control.
2. *Faster decision-making.* Because decisions are taken at unit level instead of at organisational level, each manager can respond to local needs swiftly and without the delays associated with having to wait for senior management response.
3. *Increased motivation.* Managers control their own units, and are held responsible for their decisions by way of performance evaluation. Because managers have the freedom to manage units according to their own judgement, increased motivation and entrepreneurial spirit are likely.
4. *Improved senior management focus.* Senior managers spend less time and effort managing lower organisational levels, and can pay more attention to strategic issues.
5. *Division into manageable size.* One of the main reasons for the decentralisation is that modern organisations are often so large that senior managers have no choice but to delegate authority. Decentralisation divides the organisation into units of manageable size, run by unit managers.
6. *Management development.* Increased responsibility provides lower level managers with the opportunity to develop and refine management skills. This ensures that the organisation has a pool of managers at lower levels with adequate experience to move into more senior positions as required.
7. *Elimination of internal inefficiencies.* In a decentralised management structure internal inefficiencies are often eliminated in transferring units, as managers of receiving units have the freedom to purchase the goods and services needed from external organisations rather than being forced to accept internal transfers. Chapter 15, *Transfer pricing* explores this further.

14.3.2 Potential negative consequences of decentralisation

1. *Increased risk of acting against the best interest of the organisation as a whole.* In a decentralised structure, managers may be tempted to make decisions with the best interest of the unit under their control in mind, at the exclusion of other considerations. In instances where the best interest of the unit conflicts with the best interest of the organisation as a whole, '**sub-optimal' decisions** may be taken. This means that lower-level managers may not take the decision that is best for the organisation as a whole – a situation that is clearly undesirable.
2. *Undesirable duplication of assets and activities.* Centralisation of decision-making power enables senior managers to prevent undesirable duplication of assets and activities within the organisation. In a decentralised structure, lower level

managers have the freedom to take decisions for their own units, which could lead to undesirable duplication.
3. *Risk of competition between units rather than co-operation.* In a decentralised structure units commonly compete with each other for organisational resources, which are often distributed based on performance evaluation results. This may lead to a culture among individuals of loyalty to the unit to the extent that valuable opportunities for co-operation and information sharing between units may be lost.
4. *Higher information management costs.* Decentralised organisations incur higher costs in monitoring and controlling the activities of units and managers, and suffer an increased likelihood of having to perform complex procedures to agree transfer prices. Higher information management costs include direct financial costs as well as the cost of all the resources consumed by the process such as time, staff and office space.
5. *Loss of control and knowledge by senior management.* The fact that unit managers take decisions may in effect shield top management from having to maintain adequate control over and knowledge of unit activities.

14.3.3 Prerequisites for successful decentralisation

Key term: goal congruence, independent, interdependent

Successful decentralisation occurs where the potential negative consequences of decentralisation are addressed without compromising the potential benefits from decentralisation.

For autonomous units in an organisation to work well together, something that strategists refer to as **goal congruence** is required. Goal congruence in an organisation means that individuals and units take actions that are in their self-interest and simultaneously also in the best interest of the organisation as a whole. This is primarily achieved through the careful planning of the organisation's performance management system. The ideal performance management system is designed in such a way that each individual and each unit within the organisation prefers to act in the best interest of the organisation as a whole at all times, because they are simultaneously acting in their own best interests (such as when the individual receives a bonus based, in part, on the organisation's overall performance). Complete goal congruence remains an ideal rather than a practically attainable organisational state, and organisations strive towards it as best they can.

Notice how goal congruence counteracts numbers 1 to 3 of the potential negative consequences of decentralisation. In a goal-congruent system, managers (1) act in the best interest of the organisation as a whole; (2) do not duplicate resources if doing so conflicts with the organisation's best interests; and (3) are not loyal to the unit at the expense of the organisation as a whole. Furthermore, goal congruence suggests that managers (4) will not allow information management costs to increase to the extent that they eradicate the benefits of decentralisation. However, with advances in information technology, the cost of information management is reduced, and this aspect is increasingly less of a concern.

The potential loss of control and knowledge by senior management (5) may be more of a concern in organisations where units perform related operations that need to be closely co-ordinated. In such a case, units are said to be **interdependent**. If, on the other hand, units undertake very different activities, such units are referred to as **independent**. A decentralised structure works well in organisations with independent units. In practice the relationship between the units may lie

principles of management accounting

somewhere on the continuum between the extremes of complete interdependence and total independence.

14.4 Financial performance measures

Key terms: Du Pont analysis, economic value added, residual income, return on investment, return on sales

Example 14.2 illustrates the performance measures of **return on investment, residual income, return on sales,** and **economic value added**. Bear in mind that the choice of performance measures is likely to influence behaviour: if units and individuals know in advance how their performance will be measured, they are likely to act in a manner that will result in a positive evaluation based on the measures in question.

Example 14.2

Apart from the West Coast branch, StayRSA also operates an East Coast branch and a South Coast branch. All three branches let self-catering cottages to guests. Branch managers enjoy a large degree of autonomy in decision-making, and the branches are managed as investment centres. Below is an extract of actual results from the management accounts for the year ended 31 December 2XX8. Recall from example 14.1 that only R50 000 (not R70 000) of the fixed head office reservation administration costs are subtracted to arrive at the West Coast branch's income – the correct income to use is therefore R350 000.

	West Coast	East Coast	South Coast
Branch revenue	R1 200 000	R2 200 000	R3 300 000
Branch expenses	(R850 000)	(R1 600 000)	(R1 800 000)
Branch income	R350 000	R600 000	R1 500 000
Branch long-term assets	R3 450 000	R5 900 000	R9 700 000
Branch current assets	R50 000	R100 000	R300 000
Total branch assets	R3 500 000	R6 000 000	R10 000 000
Branch current liabilities	R300 000	R400 000	R500 000

Required:
Evaluate the performance of the West Coast branch using financial performance measures.

Based on branch income, the West Coast branch was the worst performer, followed by the East Coast branch. The South Coast branch performed best. However, the assets and liabilities indicate that the West Coast branch also has less money invested in it than the other two branches. Organisations are interested in knowing how well their units and managers perform given the resources at their disposal, because this indicates whether the funds could have been invested more wisely elsewhere. Several performance measures have been developed to this end.

14.4.1 Return on investment

Return on investment (ROI) is a popular financial performance measure based on accounting information, and is expressed as a percentage. The formula is:

> **Return on investment = Income / Investment**

A higher ROI is preferred to a lower ROI – the higher the ROI, the more income generated per rand invested. The ROI for each of StayRSA's three branches is as follows:

	West Coast	East Coast	South Coast
Branch income	R350 000	R600 000	R1 500 000
Divided by total branch assets	R3 500 000	R6 000 000	R10 000 000
Return on investment	10%	10%	15%

Based on ROI, the West Coast and East Coast branches performed equally in 2XX8, while the South Coast branch performed better than the other two.

As early as 1918 the Du Pont company further analysed ROI to provide managers with more detailed performance information. Du Pont used the following formula, known as the **Du Pont analysis**, to investigate the relationship between revenues, income and investment:

> **Income / Investment (or ROI) =**
> **Revenue / Investment × Income / Revenue**

The first part of this formula focuses on the revenue generated per rand invested and is often called 'asset turnover'. The second part of the formula expresses income generated per rand of revenue, and is known as 'return on sales'. ROI can therefore be improved by either earning more revenue in relation to the investment base, or by retaining a larger part of revenue as income. The ROI of each of StayRSA's three branches can be further analysed as follows:

	West Coast	East Coast	South Coast
Branch revenue	R1 200 000	R2 200 000	R3 300 000
Divided by total branch assets	R3 500 000	R6 000 000	R10 000 000
Asset turnover	34,3%	36,7%	33%
Branch income	R350 000	R600 000	R1 500 000
Divided by branch revenue	R1 200 000	R2 200 000	R3 300 000
Return on sales	29,2%	27,3%	45,5%
Asset turnover × Return on sales	34,3% × 29,2%	36,7% × 27,3%	33% × 45,5%
Return on investment	10%	10%	15%

When the ROI is further analysed, it is apparent that the South Coast branch had a high ROI because of its very high return on sales. Its asset turnover was lower than that of the other two branches. The East Coast branch had the best asset turnover, but the lowest return on sales. Note that one can also make a very good case for subtracting current liabilities to arrive at the 'investment' figures used in the calculations. The definition of 'investment' is discussed more fully later in the chapter.

principles of management accounting

Return on investment has the following advantages:
- ROI is easy to calculate and to interpret, because it has a simple formula for which the inputs are readily available in organisations' financial information systems.
- Because ROI relates income generated to the size of the investment in assets, managers are encouraged to use assets productively.
- Because ROI is expressed in percentage terms, a unit's ROI can easily be compared to that of other entities and to indicators such as the cost of capital, prime interest rate, or bond yields.

Return on investment has the following potential disadvantages:
- *ROI may lead to goal incongruence.* As an example, assume that the South Coast branch is considering investing R2 000 000 in a project that is likely to yield operating income of R260 000 in the first year. Because the project has a 13 per cent ROI (R260 000 / R2 000 000), it would likely be in the interest of StayRSA to invest in the project if StayRSA's overall ROI is less than 13 per cent. However, if the South Coast branch's performance is evaluated based on ROI, the branch is unlikely to invest in the project. This is because the South Coast branch is earning a 15 per cent ROI. A project that earns 13 per cent decreases the South Coast branch's ROI ((R1 500 000 + R260 000) / (R10 000 000 + R2 000 000) = 14,7 per cent). The project will likely be rejected by the branch, even if investing in the project would have been in the best interest of StayRSA as a whole.
- *ROI is calculated using accounting information.* Students of management accounting know that future cash flows, not accounting figures, should be used in decision-making. Because managers strive for a positive performance evaluation result, managers whose actions are measured in terms of ROI could focus their efforts on improving reported accounting figures at the expense of future cash flows.
- *ROI is a short-term measure based on historical results.* It reflects only the return earned over the period for which it is measured, at the exclusion of all potential future results. If the East Coast branch, for example, considered building a restaurant on its premises and were evaluated based on ROI alone, it could decide against the project if building the restaurant would increase assets without a sufficient accompanying increase in income in the short term. Even if the restaurant is projected to make healthy profits in later years, the branch manager might not be willing to risk the poor performance evaluation results in the short term.
- It may be difficult to determine what 'investment' and 'income' to use under the circumstances.

14.4.2 Residual income

Residual income (RI) is a financial performance measure based on accounting information, and is expressed in monetary terms. The formula is:

> **Residual income = Income − (Required rate of return x Investment)**

Study the formula carefully – essentially it asks 'how much *more* income was earned than what was required, given the level of investment?' A higher RI is preferred to a lower RI, while a negative RI is undesirable as it means less than the required income was earned. Keep in mind that the required rate of return that the organisation chooses to use in this formula will to a large extent reflect the level of risk associated with the unit being measured. If the formula returns a negative answer, it indicates that the income earned was too low, given the level of risk and the organisation's requirements.

If we assume StayRSA uses a required rate of 11 per cent per annum in RI calculations, the RI for each of StayRSA's three branches is as follows:

	West Coast	East Coast	South Coast
Branch operating income	R350 000	R600 000	R1 500 000
Less required rate of return × total branch assets	(11% × R3 500 000)	(11% × R6 000 000)	(11% × R10 000 000)
Residual income	(R35 000)	(R60 000)	R400 000

Measured in terms of RI, the South Coast branch is performing best, while the East Coast branch has the largest negative RI and is the worst performer. Again, one can make a very good case for subtracting current liabilities to arrive at the 'investment' figures used in the calculations. The definition of 'investment' is further discussed later in the chapter.

Residual income has the following advantages:
- A different required rate of return can be used in the calculation of each unit's RI. For example, the RI of a unit that is involved in more risky projects can be calculated using a higher required rate. This would reflect the relationship between risk and return.
- RI is not subject to the same potential goal congruence problem as ROI. Again, assume that the South Coast branch is considering a R2 000 000 investment that is likely to yield operating income of R260 000 in the first year. Had the branch's performance been measured based on ROI, it would have rejected the 13 per cent return because it is lower than its present 15 per cent ROI. However, if the branch's performance were evaluated based on RI, the project would increase the branch's RI by R40 000 (R260 000 – [R2 000 000 × 11%]). Goal congruence is achieved, as the South Coast branch is likely to invest in the project because it improves its own RI, while simultaneously acting in the best interest of StayRSA. This is because the ROI formula results in a unit's ROI being the *weighted average* of the ROIs of its investments, while the RI formula results in the RI of a unit being the *sum* of the RIs of its investments.

Residual income has the following disadvantages:
- Because RI is expressed in rand terms instead of in percentage terms, it is more difficult to interpret than ROI. ROI relates income to the size of the investment and allows for easy comparison with other entities or indicators. RI, on the other hand, is affected by size – it tends to be larger for larger units. This problem may be addressed by setting RI targets instead of comparing absolute amounts between units.
- As is the case with ROI, RI is calculated using accounting information. Managers whose actions are measured in terms of RI could focus their efforts on improving reported accounting figures at the expense of future cash flows.
- As is the case with ROI, RI is a short-term measure based on historical results. It reflects only the return that has been earned over the period for which it is measured, to the exclusion of all potential future results.

principles of management accounting

- It may be difficult to determine what 'investment', 'required rate of return' and 'income' to use under the circumstances.

14.4.3 Economic value added

Economic value added (EVA®) is a financial performance measure based on accounting information that takes the organisation's weighted average cost of capital into account, and is expressed in monetary terms. The consulting firm Stern Stewart & Co pioneered the development of EVA®.

The formula is:

> **EVA® = Adjusted operating income before deducting interest on long-term liabilities, after tax − (Weighted average cost of capital x [Total adjusted assets − current liabilities])**

Notice that EVA® is the RI formula rewritten, but using specific definitions of the terms 'income' (namely adjusted operating income before interest, after tax), 'required rate of return' (namely the weighted average cost of capital) and 'investment' (namely total adjusted assets less current liabilities). EVA® aims to concentrate managers' efforts on delivering shareholder value. The 'adjustments' that are made to income and assets are attempts to eliminate undesirable accounting conventions. These may include revaluing assets at replacement cost, and treating items such as research and development (R&D) and marketing as depreciable assets. As with RI, a higher EVA® is preferred to a lower EVA®, while a negative EVA® is undesirable as it means too little income is earned in relation to the risk.

Assume that StayRSA's after-tax weighted average cost of capital calculated at its target capital structure (that is, the rate recommended for use as a discount rate in net present value calculations when potential investments are evaluated) is 10 per cent. Furthermore, assume that the necessary adjustments to income and assets have been calculated as given below. The EVA® for each of StayRSA's three branches is as follows:

	West Coast	East Coast	South Coast
Branch income	R350 000	R600 000	R1 500 000
Adjustments (assume)	R70 000	R110 000	R300 000
	R420 000	R710 000	R1 800 000
Less tax at 28%	(R117 600)	(R198 800)	(R504 000)
After-tax branch income	R302 400	R511 200	R1 296 000
Total branch assets	R3 500 000	R6 000 000	R10 000 000
Adjustments (assume)	R88 200	R110 000	R600 000
Branch current liabilities	(R300 000)	(R400 000)	(R500 000)
'Investment' for EVA®	R3 288 200	R5 710 000	R10 100 000

West Coast branch: R302 400 − (10% × R3 288 200) = (R26 420)
East Coast branch: R511 200 − (10% × R5 710 000) = (R59 800)
South Coast branch: R1 296 000 − (10% × R10 100 000) = R286 000

Based on EVA®, the South Coast branch is performing best, while the West Coast and East Coast branches are both destroying economic value.

EVA® has the same advantages and disadvantages as RI, except for (i) the fact that the difficulty of choosing definitions for 'investment', 'required rate of return' and 'income' is addressed by the EVA® formula, and (ii) the accounting information has been restated to reflect economic reality more closely. However, EVA® has an additional disadvantage in that, in order to make the necessary adjustments to income and assets, assets on the statement of financial position usually have to be restated at replacement cost, and intangibles have to be valued and their useful lives estimated. These are often difficult quantifications to make, and the resulting adjustments may be seen as arbitrary.

Notice that whether ROI, RI or EVA® is used as the performance measure, there are generally three ways in which performance can be improved: increase income without investing more, make investments that yield more than the target return, or sell investments that yield less than the target return.

14.4.4 Return on sales

Recall that ROI can be further analysed into 'asset turnover' (Revenue/Investment) and 'return on sales' or ROS (Income / Revenue). ROS is often used as a performance measure. As calculated in section 14.4.1, the East Coast branch of StayRSA performed worst in terms of ROS (27,3 per cent), with the South Coast branch performing best (45,5 per cent).

Return on sales has the following advantages:
- ROS is easy to calculate and to interpret, because it has a simple formula for which the inputs are readily available in organisations' financial information systems.
- Because ROS is expressed in percentage terms, a unit's ROS can easily be compared to that of other entities.

Return on sales has the following disadvantages:
- It does not indicate whether assets have been used productively.
- ROS is calculated using accounting information. Managers whose actions are measured in terms of ROS could focus their efforts on improving reported accounting figures at the expense of future cash flows.
- ROS is yet another short-term measure based on historical results. It only reflects the return that has been earned over the period for which it is measured, at the exclusion of all potential future results.
- It may be difficult to determine what 'income' to use under the circumstances.

14.4.5 Determining 'investment'

An important potential problem with the calculation of many popular performance measures such as ROI and RI is to know what figure to use as the 'investment' – different investment figures yield different formula results. Three problems arise: how investment should be defined, how investment should be measured, and whether depreciation should be subtracted from assets.

Definition of investment

When managers are evaluated, the income under their control is taken into account. Likewise, only the assets under their control should be used as the investment base, less the current liabilities under their control. When units are evaluated, it is best to apply a wider definition of 'investment', as many assets not controlled by the unit's manager may nevertheless be necessary for the unit to operate. The following definitions may be appropriate for unit performance evaluation:

1. *Total assets held*. This includes all the assets held by the unit. This definition was used in the ROI and RI examples for StayRSA. Note that one can make a case for also including intangible assets that are not usually recorded in the same manner as physical assets, such as investment in research and development. The difficulty in objectively measuring these intangibles often prevents them from being included in the 'investment' figure. Remember that EVA® specifically requires that intangibles should be treated as assets.
2. *Total assets employed*. Only assets that are currently in use are included. Idle assets and assets held for future use are excluded. This definition is useful where, for example, senior management dictates that certain unproductive assets are to be held by units. This definition was not used in the ROI and RI examples for StayRSA, because no information on idle assets was given.
3. *Total assets less current liabilities*. One could recalculate the ROI and RI examples for StayRSA using this definition, which acknowledges branches' performance in optimising the use of current liabilities as a source of funding. Remember that the EVA® formula requires current liabilities to be subtracted from total assets.

The Chartered Institute of Management Accountants (CIMA) defines a specific form of return on investment, namely return on capital employed (ROCE). The formula is:

> **Return on capital employed**
> **= Profit before interest and tax / Average capital employed**

Again, as with the term 'investment', the exact meaning of 'capital employed' may vary according to the definitions above. Notice, however, that the denominator is calculated as the average capital employed at the beginning and end of the period. Furthermore, CIMA envisages that, where there are 'problems of seasonality, new capital introduced or other factors' it could even be necessary to use the average capital employed over a number of periods within the period of measurement.

Remember that one way of improving ROI, RI and EVA® is to reduce assets that do not produce the desired level of income. This implies that better management of working capital improves results: better debtors' collection, for example, improves ROI, RI and EVA® because the value of debtors included in 'investment' is reduced, while 'income' may remain largely unaffected.

Measurement of investment

Investment can be measured in the following ways (which may render very different values for long-term assets):

1. *Historic cost*. This is the original cost of assets at the time of acquisition. Although readily obtainable and easy to interpret, this approach is conceptually flawed. In the ROI, RI and EVA® formulae, the 'income' figure relates to the period under review, and is therefore a current figure that implicitly incorporates inflation and other relevant factors. However, if the 'investment' part of the formula is measured at historic cost, this figure does not take into account inflation or other relevant factors after the date of acquisition of the assets. This timing inconsistency is an important drawback of using a historic cost measurement.
2. *Current cost*. This is the cost, at the present time, of acquiring an asset that is closely comparable to the asset in question. Where such a comparable asset cannot be found, current cost can be estimated as the present value of acquiring services closely comparable to the services rendered by the asset in

question. Current cost does not cause the same timing inconsistency as the historic cost measurement, and is conceptually superior. A potential problem is that current cost may be difficult to obtain, and that extensive calculations using current cost indices may be necessary to estimate current costs. Further calculations are necessary to adjust the depreciation subtracted from 'income' to also reflect current cost.

Depreciation

The question arises whether gross carrying amounts (the value of assets before subtracting accumulated depreciation) or net carrying amounts (the value of assets after subtracting accumulated depreciation) should be used.

Example 14.3

Assume that, in addition to the branches already introduced, StayRSA also operates a Drakensberg branch and a Karoo branch. Assume that cottages and cottage furnishings are the only assets held by these two branches, and that they are individually depreciated over their estimated useful lives. The following is an extract of actual results from the management accounts for the year ended 31 December 2XX8:

	Drakensberg	Karoo
Branch income	R2 040 000	R400 000
Age of branch cottages and cottage furnishings	2 years	7 years
Net carrying amount of total branch assets at historic cost	R10 200 000	R1 600 000
Gross carrying amount of total branch assets at historic cost	R11 000 000	R3 300 000

Required:
Calculate the return on investment of the Drakensberg and the Karoo branches, using the net and gross carrying amounts of assets respectively.

ROI based on net and gross carrying amounts respectively is calculated as follows (similar calculations can be made for RI and EVA®).

	Drakensberg	Karoo
ROI based on net carrying amount	R2 040 000 / R10 200 000	R400 000 / R1 600 000
	= 20%	= 25%
ROI based on gross carrying amount	R2 040 000 / R11 000 000	R400 000 / R3 300 000
	= 18,5%	= 12,1%

Based on net carrying amounts, the Karoo branch performs best. The Karoo branch is 5 years older than the Drakensberg branch, and has had more years' depreciation subtracted from its assets. As assets get older, their net carrying amount decreases and the return on investment increases (even if no extra income is generated), simply because more depreciation is subtracted from the assets each year. The use of net carrying amounts can be deceptive, as it favours branches with older assets.

Based on gross carrying amounts, the Drakensberg branch performs best. This is not unexpected, as its newer assets are likely to have a higher income-generating ability. The use of gross carrying amounts highlights the fact that the Karoo branch – with its older cottages and furnishings that have not been replaced in seven years – is generating less income per rand invested. Critics argue that the decrease over time in income earning capability of assets is ignored when gross carrying amounts are used.

14.4.6 Determining 'required rate of return'

A required rate of return has to be determined if the RI formula is used. In the EVA® formula, which is an adaptation of RI, the weighted average cost of capital is used as the required rate of return. This is conceptually correct, as it is the same rate used to determine the desirability of potential investments and therefore promotes goal-congruence. This required rate should, as previously stated, be adjusted to reflect the risk profile of the unit if necessary. Furthermore, two things have to be kept in mind to ensure consistency within the formula:

- The length of the period reflected in 'income' should correspond to the length of period reflected in the required rate. If, for example, a year's worth of 'income' is used, the rate should also be the rate of return required per year.
- If the weighted average cost of capital is used for calculating RI (or a rate derived from it, but adjusted for the unit's risk profile), the rate is after tax. 'Income' should therefore also be after tax (as prescribed by the EVA® formula).

14.4.7 Determining 'income'

The EVA® formula requires the use of after-tax operating income. An important potential problem with the use of ROI, RI and ROS is that an appropriate definition for 'income' has to be sought.

- The conceptually correct definition is usually 'income before interest on long-term liabilities, after tax'. Note that this is the definition used in the EVA® formula. This means that tax, which is an operating cost, is subtracted from the unit's income. The argument is that managers of autonomous units should seek to minimise the tax liability as part of operational performance, and their performance should therefore be measured after tax. Interest on long-term liabilities, on the other hand, is not an operating cost but rather a cost of finance. It is conceptually correct to use income before interest on long-term liabilities, as the amount of debt in the capital structure should not influence the calculation of the return earned. This also provides for consistency in the formula: long-term liabilities are not subtracted from 'investment', so the interest on them should not be subtracted from 'income'. Where sufficient detail is available, it would be correct to subtract interest on current liabilities from 'income' if current liabilities are subtracted from 'investment'.
- There may be circumstances where the performance results of units that operate under different tax laws need to be compared. 'Income before interest and tax' is useful here, as the effect of tax on earnings is not taken into account. Organisations may prefer to use income before tax in any case, simply because tax may not be recorded in the unit income statements. Notice that the ROCE formula in section 14.4.5 uses profit before tax.

Once 'income' has been determined, it is important that the required rate of return used when a residual income calculation is performed should be consistent with this choice. In other words, the required rate of return should also be an after-tax rate if after-tax income is used. Similarly, the required rate of return should be before tax if income before tax is used. Note that the EVA® formula is consistent in this regard: it prescribes after-tax income and uses the WACC (an after-tax rate) as its required rate of return.

Throughout this chapter 'income' is taken after subtracting depreciation, even where the gross value of assets is used to determine 'investment'. Some organisations may choose to add back depreciation when calculating 'income'.

Where units have investments not only in operating assets, but also other non-operating assets (such as shares in another company or property earning rental income), income from such assets is very often *excluded* from 'income', and the value of such investments excluded from 'investment'. The result indicates the unit's own operating performance at the exclusion of the performance of its external investments. Where units and managers are free to make their own non-operating investment decisions, it does, however, make sense also to recalculate the performance measures *including* the income from, and investment in, non-operating assets. The required rate of return used in a residual income calculation should then also reflect the risk profile of the unit, including its non-operating assets.

It is apparent that, because management accounting aims to provide the best possible management information given the circumstances, there is no single 'correct' way to calculate performance measures. Instead, what is fundamental is that calculations should suit the circumstances, should be internally consistent, and that they should be thoroughly understood for them to be correctly interpreted in performance evaluation. Generally, the 'income' and 'investment' used to measure a unit's performance should take into account all aspects that can fairly be traced to the unit, and should disregard all untraceable aspects. Similarly, the 'income' and 'investment' used to measure a manager's performance should take into account all aspects that can fairly be deemed controllable by the manager, and should disregard all uncontrollable aspects.

14.4.8 Multinational considerations

When organisations operate in multiple countries, comparing the performance of units becomes more complex. Not only are political, economic, social and technological conditions generally different in different countries, but units may also conduct business in different currencies.

If StayRSA had a branch in Botswana and wanted to use ROI, RI, EVA® and ROS to compare its performance with that of the South African branches, it would have to decide whether to convert the Botswana branch's results to rands before calculating the performance measures, or whether to use Botswana pula in the calculations. StayRSA would find that it would be wiser to convert the Botswana pula to rands before performing the calculations. This is because the differences in economic factors such as inflation are addressed when the currency conversion is made. In theory, the difference in exchange rates between the countries compensates for the relative inflation levels. The performance of the Botswana branch can therefore more fairly be compared to that of the South African branches if the Botswana pula are converted to rands. Income is converted at the average exchange rate for the period under review, while investment is converted at relevant historic exchange rates if the historic cost measurement is used. StayRSA still has to take care to ensure that it understands properly all the unique factors that have impacted the Botswana branch's performance before drawing conclusions on its relative performance.

14.5 Value-based management

Value-based management (VBM) is the management of all aspects of a company with the aim of maximising shareholder wealth.

14.5.1 Shareholder value analysis

Key term: shareholder value analysis

It is the responsibility of management to create value for shareholders. Financial statements are usually not sufficient to form an opinion of shareholder value. **Shareholder value analysis** (SVA) is a performance measure linked to the concept of value-based management. Rappaport (1998) defines the value of a company as follows:

> **Value of the company = Present value of free cash flows from operations + value of marketable securities**

When the market value of debt is deducted from the value of the company, the result is shareholder value. Based on the calculation of shareholder value, Rappaport identified seven 'value drivers' in a company. These represent the variables used to calculate the present value of free cash flows in the formula above.

The higher each of the following value drivers, the higher the shareholder value:
- Sales growth rate
- Operating profit margin
- Planning period.

The higher each of the following value drivers, the lower the shareholder value:
- Cash income taxes
- Investment in fixed assets
- Investment in working capital
- Cost of capital.

SVA can be performed on the company as a whole or on individual units. It can also be used to calculate what Rappaport calls the 'threshold margin' – the minimum operating profit margin required to maintain shareholder value. Because cash flows differ from period to period, SVA is usually not suitable as a performance measure for a single period and is rather used for valuation and planning purposes.

14.5.2 Market value added

Key term: market value added

Market value added (MVA) is another performance measure linked to value-based management. It is an external measure indicating how shareholders have been affected by the actions taken by management. The formula is as follows:

> **MVA = Increase in market capitalisation during the period – increase in capital invested during the period (including retained income)**

The period over which MVA is measured depends on the purpose of the evaluation. One could, for example, choose to measure the value added since a new management team took over, or the value added since the acquisition of a subsidiary.

Example 14.4

Since Sarah was appointed CEO of Johannesburg Ltd, the market value of the company has increased by R55 000 000. Over the same time period, new capital of R15 000 000 was invested in the company and retained income increased by R10 000 000.

Required:
Calculate the market value added since Sarah's appointment as CEO.

The market value added since Sarah's appointment as CEO is R30 000 000 (R55 000 000 − R15 000 000 − R10 000 000).

Like economic value added (EVA®), MVA was developed by the consulting firm Stern Stewart, and the two concepts are closely related. Theoretically, MVA is the present value of all future EVA®s. The following further illustrates the relationship and distinction between the two concepts:
- EVA® is a historical measure, while MVA introduces the forward-looking aspect (it theoretically measures the company's ability to add value in future).
- EVA® measures one historical period (usually a year), while MVA discounts all future EVA®s.
- EVA® is an internal performance measure that encourages managers to deliver a good MVA, while MVA is an external measure used by investors.
- EVA® can be calculated for individual units, while MVA can only be calculated for the company as a whole.

The disadvantages of MVA overlap with those of EVA® to some extent, as they form part of the same concept. The disadvantages of MVA are as follows:
- Various adjustments have to be made to accounting figures before they can be used.
- Adjustments are often arbitrary.
- Because MVA gives an absolute value instead of a percentage, it does not consider the relative size of the company.
- Market sentiment also impacts the share price.
- As MVA receives so much publicity, it may be a self-fulfilling prophecy. If enough investors believe that the technique is important, companies that indicate that they use MVA will likely experience a growth in share price.
- Dividends are not taken into account. If two companies have the same MVA, the one that also paid a good dividend was a better investment. This will not be reflected in the MVA.

In addition to the disadvantages above, value-based management (including both SVA and MVA) may be criticised for its singular focus on the wealth of shareholders. It is increasingly believed that performance should be measured with the interests of all stakeholders in mind, not only that of shareholders.

14.6 Multidimensional performance measures

Key term: stakeholder, triple bottom line

After the widely publicised collapse in 2001 of the US energy company, Enron, and several accounting scandals in other firms, professionals across the fields of accounting posed questions as to how such corporate demises could be avoided. Management accountants focused in particular on the fact that the modern corporate world has a tendency to over-emphasise financial performance measures that were designed to measure short-term shareholder benefit. In a briefing published in 2002, the Chartered Institute of Management Accountants (CIMA) writes that Enron was seemingly 'laser-focused' on maximising earnings per share (CIMA 2002:3). Performance measurement, by its very nature, has always been at risk of encouraging unethical behaviour. Unethical actions can range from misrepresenting results to deliberately setting low targets in order to exceed them with greater ease. Today management accountants and other professionals work to find ways to measure and manage performance in a more balanced manner. They wish to address the traditional overemphasis on financial measures, short-term measures and shareholder interests (Roos 2005:12). Good performance management systems are increasingly designed to include the following:

- *Financial measures* (that which is measured in monetary terms, such as earnings per share); *non-financial measures* (that which is not measured in monetary terms, such as the number of defects per 1 000 units produced); *quantitative measures* (that which is measured using numbers, either financially such as earnings per share, or non-financially such as the number of defects per 1 000 units produced); and *qualitative measures* (that which is measured without numbers, such as the attractiveness of a product's packaging). A mix of these different types of measures is used so that they supplement each other.

- *Long-term as well as short-term measures.* If, for example, quarterly performance evaluation is carried out based solely on ROI, managers may be more likely to take decisions that go against the organisation's long-term best interests in order to deliver satisfactory short-term performance. A longer-term orientation can be gained by evaluating performance based on the ROI over multiple periods, for example by monitoring the ROI over a three-year period. Incorporating measures with a longer-term focus, such as measuring the efforts made towards product innovation, would also encourage a more balanced management effort. Organisations should not, however, disregard short-term performance to the extent that long-term survival is threatened: a cash flow crisis could, for example, threaten the existence of the organisation if it is not quickly identified by short-term financial performance measures and rectified. Care should therefore be taken that performance feedback is delivered at optimal intervals. Performance evaluation periods should not be so short that they impose an unnecessary administrative burden and encourage an excessive short-term focus, but should also not be so long that the benefit of timely feedback and intervention is lost. The nature of a performance measure often dictates the ideal frequency for reporting that particular measure.

- *Measures that focus on the interests of stakeholders who are not shareholders.* A **stakeholder** is any group or individual with a legitimate interest in the activities of an organisation. John Elkington advocates that performance should be managed on three fronts known as the **'triple bottom line'**, referring to an organisation's performance in terms of economic prosperity, environmental quality and social justice.

14.6.1 Balanced scorecard

Key term: balanced scorecard

A widely used modern multidimensional performance management system is the **balanced scorecard**, developed by Kaplan and Norton (1996). Objectives are set for each of four perspectives suggested by the authors: financial, customer, internal business process, and learning and growth. The authors suggest what kinds of objectives could be set in each perspective:

- *Financial* objectives for revenue growth, productivity improvement and cost reduction, asset utilisation, and risk management. The financial perspective summarises the readily measurable economic consequences of actions already taken.
- *Customer* objectives for product and service, customer relationship, and image and reputation attributes. The customer perspective measures performance in the customer and market segments in which the organisation competes.
- *Internal business process* objectives for operations, innovation and post-sale service processes. The internal-business-process perspective focuses on the critical internal processes in which the organisation must excel.
- *Learning and growth* objectives for employees, systems and organisational alignment of procedures. The learning-and-growth perspective addresses the infrastructure that the organisation must build to create long-term growth and improvement.

Performance is measured for each perspective according to objectives set, establishing a link between strategy (the setting of objectives) and performance measurement. Traditionally organisations tended to focus on financial performance measures (that measure past success), often neglecting the other three perspectives (that build future success). The balanced scorecard steers organisations towards a balance between different perspectives on performance (that include financial and non-financial aspects), different stakeholder interests, and performance over different time horizons.

Many modern performance management systems use multiple performance measures, preferably from different categories. This is to avoid a situation where, for example, a unit is measured almost exclusively with reference to ROI and is likely to focus its efforts on maximising ROI at the expense of all other important performance areas. Unfortunately there is often a trade-off to be made between results. If, for example, an organisation focuses its attention on learning and growth (often a long-term investment with few tangible short-term financial benefits) in a particular period, the financial results in that period may be adversely affected. Where there is a trade-off to be made, strategic considerations may dictate which performance areas receive more attention and resources in a particular period.

14.7 Agreeing on targets and rewarding performance

Performance management systems enable managers to send signals to employees, indicating what actions and behaviour are expected of them. Frequently the results of performance evaluations are used to reward units and individuals for achievements in past periods. Reward systems serve as an incentive to improve performance.

In the interest of fairness, motivation and participation, many researchers believe that units and individuals should be, at least to some extent, involved in setting their own performance evaluation targets prior to the start of a performance period. This ensures that targets are not set 'from the top down' by managers who may be unaware of the unique challenges in a given environment or situation. During target-setting units or individuals can, for example, explain why particular levels of performance may not be realistically achievable. Furthermore, units and individuals know the exact performance targets (which they have themselves agreed to) in advance. They have a fair opportunity to work towards the targets throughout the period, and can justifiably be held accountable if targets are not achieved. Some of the dangers of employee involvement in target-setting is the fact that targets may be deliberately set too low so that actual performance easily looks impressive in comparison, or the fact that particular employees may in some circumstances be inclined to perform better when working towards stringent 'top-down' targets.

Favourable performance by individuals can be rewarded in different ways, such as through increased remuneration, promotion to higher status, or non-financial benefits such as superior physical workplace features. Remuneration may consist of cash and non-cash components. Senior managers, for example, often receive share options in addition to cash benefits. Share incentive schemes work on the principal that managers are likely to act in the interest of shareholders, because they themselves are shareholders (or hold options that entitle them to become shareholders). If the company performs well and its share price increases, managers' shares are worth more. The schemes do not, however, directly encourage managers to work in the interest of other stakeholders. The following should be noted in relation to share incentive schemes:

- Share incentives are often more likely to be given to more senior employees, because seniority often determines an employee's ability to influence a company's share price (the controllability principle).
- Options to purchase shares at a future date at a particular exercise price are often given, rather than the shares themselves. A condition may apply that the option can only be exercised if the individual is still employed by the company at that time. This encourages individuals who are regarded as valuable employees to remain attached to the company, at least until the options may be exercised.

Cash remuneration itself may also consist of different elements. Consider a hairdresser who applies for a position at a salon. She is offered a salary, commission, and the possibility of a performance bonus based on the salon's annual income. The fixed element of the offer is the salary, while the commission and bonus elements are variable. The higher the fixed salary in relation to the variable elements, the more risk is borne by the salon: it has to pay the salary even when profits are low, but is better off if profits are high. Conversely, the higher the variable elements in relation to the fixed salary, the more risk is borne by the hairdresser: she is assured of little income if she performs poorly, but high income if she performs well.

14.8 Not-for-profit and public sector organisations

> **Key terms:** not-for-profit organisation, public sector organisation

The principles of performance management apply not only to profit-seeking organisations, but also to not-for-profit and public sector organisations. These organisations do, however, have unique characteristics that have to be considered in designing a performance management system. Achieving optimal performance management in not-for-profit and public sector organisations poses an interesting challenge to management accountants' skills.

The primary purpose of a **not-for-profit organisation** is not one of profit maximisation, although it may – to a limited extent – engage in economic activity in pursuit of its primary purpose. The Animal Welfare Society of South Africa is an example of a not-for-profit organisation. The purpose of a **public sector organisation** is to serve the public, and it is funded by the government. An example of a public sector organisation, the Tygerberg Hospital, was introduced at the beginning of this chapter.

The demand for goods and services provided by private sector, profit-seeking organisations is limited by how much the market can absorb. Not-for-profit and public sector organisations, on the other hand, face the problem of having to address what seemingly approximates unlimited demand, but with limited resources at their disposal. In these organisations performance is often managed with reference to what is commonly known as the 'three Es':

- *Economy.* Performance is economical when the least possible money is spent.
- *Efficiency.* Performance is efficient when minimum resources are consumed.
- *Effectiveness.* Performance is effective when objectives are achieved.

Economy and efficiency are usually comparatively easy to measure, and are therefore often measured by performance management systems. Effectiveness is often more difficult to measure: how, for example, does one know that the Tygerberg Hospital has given the best quality health care to the most patients that it could possibly have assisted? Effectiveness is also the most important of the 'three Es': if objectives are not achieved, the level of economy and efficiency with which they are not achieved are comparatively unimportant. Not-for-profit and public sector organisations should therefore take great care in managing the effectiveness of their performance, in addition to controlling the economy and efficiency thereof.

14.9 Summary

Organisations measure performance in order to evaluate the past achievements of managers and organisational units. They also communicate how performance will be measured in future in order to manage the performance of individuals and units in periods in the future. Performance is measured in line with the organisation's overall objectives, and is compared to an appropriate yardstick to make it possible to draw meaningful conclusions.

Under responsibility accounting, individuals are held responsible for specified revenues, costs, assets and liabilities. As a basic point of departure, managers are ideally held accountable for those items which are within their control, while the performance of units is measured based on that which is traceable to the unit.

In highly decentralised organisational structures, unit managers have a large degree of freedom when it comes to decision-making. Decentralisation should, however, be executed in such a manner as to ensure goal congruence: the performance management system should ensure that individuals automatically act in the best interest of the organisation as a whole while pursuing their own self-interest.

Popular financial performance measures include return on investment, residual income, economic value added (EVA®) and return on sales. The relative advantages and disadvantages of these measures give rise to the fact that ideally none of them should be used in isolation, but that they should rather form part of a balanced portfolio of performance measures. The precise definitions of the input variables used to calculate the measures should be chosen carefully: the 'investment', 'required rate of return' and 'income' used in the formulae should be appropriate under the circumstances.

Value-based management is focused on maximising shareholder wealth, and includes concepts such as shareholder value analysis and market value added.

These days, multidimensional performance measures, most notably the balanced scorecard, are particularly prominent in that they take a balanced view of what ought to be achieved in an organisation. Performance measures should ideally not focus exclusively on financial performance, should not over-emphasise the short term, and should take a stakeholder rather than merely a shareholder view.

Conclusion: Performance management and other topics in this book

As a conclusion to performance management, it is important to note how large a part of management accounting it comprises. Topics such as standard costing, benchmarking, budgeting, continuous improvement, costing systems and cost allocation can all be directly linked to performance management, because they deal with ways in which objectives are set, results are recorded and performance is measured. As the topics do not exist in isolation, performance management principles are applicable throughout the field of management accounting.

Tutorial case study: Stellenbosch University

The main campus of *Stellenbosch University* is located in the town of Stellenbosch in the Western Cape. It also has a presence in some other locations – for example, its Business School is on a separate campus in the city of Bellville, its Military Academy is located in Saldanha, and Tygerberg Hospital in Parow is the teaching hospital for its Health Sciences faculty. The University's mission is 'to create and sustain, in commitment to the academic ideal of excellent scholarly and scientific practice, an environment within which knowledge can be shared, and can be applied to the benefit of the community'.

Source: Stellenbosch University 2010

Although the case study information relates specifically to Stellenbosch University, knowledge of the tertiary institution through which you study may prove helpful in answering the following questions.

1. Indicate whether the university can best be described as a profit-orientated private sector organisation, a not-for-profit organisation, or a public sector organisation.
2. Explain what objectives you think the university may set for itself.

3 Indicate along what lines you think the university may divide itself into units and sub-units.
4 Give one example of each of the following, and explain the reasons for your choices: A unit within the university that you think the university management may wish to classify as:
   a) A cost centre
   b) A revenue centre
   c) A profit centre
   d) An investment centre.
5 Give two examples of financial performance measures and two examples of non-financial performance measures for each of the units you named in response to question 4.
6 For each of the financial performance measures formulated in response to question 5, explain what yardsticks could be used to evaluate how well the units have performed.
7 For one of the units named in response to question 4, explain by way of example how the performance measurement of the manager of the unit may differ from the performance measurement of the unit.
8 Discuss whether you would recommend a largely centralised or a more decentralised management control structure for the university. Also indicate whether you think the same extent of decentralisation should be applied throughout the university.
9 Give examples of how the performance management system of the university could promote goal congruence where units have a large degree of autonomy.
10 Discuss whether shareholder value analysis and the calculation of market value added are relevant to the university.
11 Discuss whether the balanced scorecard could be of value to the university in designing its performance management system.

Basic questions

BQ 1

A transport company operates a number of divisions. One of the divisions, the Trucking Division, has just submitted its management accounts for the financial year ended 31 July 2XX6 to head office. The Trucking Division reported a return on investment of 12 per cent and operating income of R1 000 000 for the year ended 31 July 2XX6. How did the division perform in terms of return on investment and operating income during the year ended 31 July 2XX6, or what additional information would you need before evaluating its performance?

BQ 2

The Copy department of a University photocopies course material for students. Below are three scenarios explaining the performance measurement of the department.
- *Scenario A*: Detailed records are kept of the cost of paper, ink and other operating expenses attributable to the department. These are compared to the budget on a monthly basis, and all negative budget variances greater than 5 per cent are investigated.
- *Scenario B*: As in scenario A, detailed records of costs are kept. The department charges academic and other service departments 12 cents per page requested.

principles of management accounting

This is recorded as income in the department's accounts, and costs are subtracted from the income. Income and costs are compared to the budget on a monthly basis, and all negative budget variances greater than 5 per cent are investigated.
- *Scenario C*: As in scenario B, detailed records of costs are kept, and the department charges other departments 12 cents per page requested. The manager of the department uses his own discretion in the purchase and sale of capital equipment. The performance of the department is measured with reference to 'profit' generated relative to assets employed.

What kind of responsibility centre is likely to apply in each of scenarios A, B and C?

BQ 3

Head office costs of R662 000 have been allocated to the Cape Town hotel, which is part of a hotel group. The costs comprise R600 000 in head office administration costs allocated and R62 000 in respect of wine supplied by head office with the hotel logo on the bottle.
- Head office administration costs are allocated equally among the hotels in the group. The budget corresponds to the actual head office administration costs for the year.
- Hotels in the group can order wine bottles with the hotel logo from the head office. The budgeted cost per bottle has been set at R300. In her budget for the year the Cape Town hotel's manager, Thandi, made provision for 150 such bottles, but ended up ordering 200.
- An error occurred at head office, and as a result the bottles were initially incorrectly labelled. The supplier had to be paid to remove and replace the incorrect labels. The actual cost per bottle was R310, as a result of this blunder.

How should the item 'head office costs allocated' be taken into account in Thandi's performance evaluation?

BQ 4

Treesaver is a not-for-profit organisation that was established in the Garden Route a year ago and aims to save trees of particular historic interest. After a successful year, it is already considering establishing branches in other parts of the country where important trees grow. However, the founding members find the idea of managing organisational branches that are so far apart a daunting task. After some deliberation, they conclude that it may be in their best interest to exercise extensive control over the activities of the branches, and that all significant decisions taken at branch level should be approved by themselves before being implemented. What are the potential relative advantages and disadvantages for Treesaver of implementing the management control structure envisaged?

BQ 5

Two of the divisions of a large retail organisation have approached the central management team to resolve a dispute between them. The Security division is tasked with providing effective, visible security at the organisation's retail outlets. The primary objectives of the security division are to prevent shoplifting and to protect the safety of customers and staff. In doing so, they insist on searching an increasing number of bags and other personal effects of customers to detect shoplifting. The Sales division is furious about the constant security checks. They can prove that they are losing revenue to competitor organisations where the public can shop without security interference. The primary measure used to evaluate the performance of the Security division is the percentage increase or decrease in the absolute value of losses as a result of shoplifting. The following figures were recorded in 2XX5 and 2XX6 respectively:

	2XX6	2XX5
Total sales income	R315 000 000	R300 000 000
Losses resulting from shoplifting	R40 000 000	R39 000 000

Keeping goal congruence in mind, how can a change in the way performance is measured help to resolve the conflict?

BQ 6

The following is an extract from the accounting records of Company C:

Item	2XX2	2XX1
Total assets	R67 675 000	R65 730 000
Net income before interest, after tax	R8 130 000	R10 140 000
Revenue	R64 555 000	R59 590 000

Company C calculates return on investment based on the average investment. Its return on investment for 2XX2 has been calculated as 12,2 per cent. The directors are very disappointed, as they were expecting a 15 per cent return. What can be learnt about Company C's return on investment if the Du Pont analysis is applied?

BQ 7

Produ (Pty) Ltd has several factories and a highly decentralised management structure. Each factory's performance is primarily evaluated based on return on investment. The weighted average cost of capital of the company is 11 per cent per annum. Alice, the Cape Town factory manager, is considering selling machinery worth R200 000. She estimates that the machinery generates annual after-tax operating income of R24 000. In the previous financial year the Cape Town factory's return on investment was 14 per cent per annum. The risk profile of the Cape Town factory is in line with that of the company. Why may Alice possibly be contemplating the sale of the machinery? Would it be in the best interest of Produ (Pty) Ltd to sell the machinery?

BQ 8

The following applies to a company with no long-term liabilities in respect of the 2XX7 year:

Sales	R3 000 000
Operating expenses (fixed and variable)	(R2 000 000)
Income	R1 000 000
Assets	R8 000 000

principles of management accounting

For purposes of the residual income formula, management requires a return of 10 per cent per annum. Similar companies yield a return on investment of 11 per cent per annum, and a return on sales of 30 per cent per annum. How well did the company perform financially, especially with reference to return on investment, residual income, and return on sales?

BQ 9

Peter has calculated the following performance measure of the company he works for:

> Income less (required rate of return × assets)
> = R1 368 000 − (12% × R10 500 000)
> = R108 000

The manager he reports to has subsequently asked him to state whether he had performed a calculation of Economic Value Added (EVA®). Peter explained that he had intended to calculate residual income, but that the same calculation might just as well be seen as a calculation of EVA®. To calculate 'assets', Peter used total assets less current liabilities. Do you agree that a residual income calculation could just as well pass for a calculation of EVA®? What questions would you ask Peter in order to assess whether his calculation does indeed constitute a calculation of EVA®?

BQ 10

The Global Company's shares are presently trading at R30 per share, and traded at R25 per share three years ago. The carrying amount of the company's equity presently stands at R800 000 000, while it was R750 000 000 three years ago. The number of issued shares has remained 25 000 000 throughout. A new management team took over exactly three years ago, and claims to have improved the wealth of shareholders significantly. What is the market value added since the new management team took over?

Long questions

LQ 1 − Intermediate (15 marks; 27 minutes)

Source: Adapted from CIMA P1

This year's profit for a multinational group of companies was significantly below expectations. Concern has been expressed about the reporting and performance measurement systems used by the group. A review of the performance measures currently used by the group has been carried out and has identified a number of issues:
- Return on Investment (ROI) is used throughout the group to evaluate the performance of the managers of the subsidiaries.
- Performance measures are predominantly of a financial nature.
- The number of customer complaints in some subsidiaries had increased significantly during the year. This had not been reported to the parent company.

Chapter 14 Performance management

REQUIRED		Marks
(a)	Discuss three problems that could occur as a result of using Return on Investment to evaluate the performance of managers.	5
(b)	Explain three reasons why a performance measurement system based solely on financial measures may not be effective in evaluating the long term performance of companies.	5
(c)	(i) Discuss how the use of a balanced scorecard could have helped to avoid the customer complaint issues. (ii) List four performance measures which could be used to monitor customer satisfaction.	3 2
TOTAL MARKS		15

LQ 2 – Intermediate (10 marks; 18 minutes)

Source: Adapted from CIMA P2

A firm of attorneys is using budgetary control during 20X0. The senior partner estimated the demand for the year for each of the firm's four divisions: Civil, Criminal, Corporate, and Property. A separate partner is responsible for each division.

Each divisional partner then prepared a cost budget based on the senior partner's demand estimate for the division. These budgets were then submitted to the senior partner for his approval. He then amended them as he thought appropriate before issuing each divisional partner with the final budget for the division. He did not discuss these amendments with the respective divisional partners. Actual performance is measured against the final budgets for each month, and each divisional partner's performance is appraised by asking the divisional partner to explain the reasons for any variances that occur.

The corporate partner has been asked to explain why her staff costs exceeded the budgeted costs for last month while the chargeable time was less than budgeted. Her reply is below:

> 'My own original estimate of staff costs was higher than the final budgeted costs shown on my divisional performance report. In my own cost budget I allowed for time to be spent developing new services for the firm's corporate clients and improving the clients' access to their own case files. This would improve the quality of our services to clients and therefore increase client satisfaction. The trouble with our present system is that it focuses on financial performance and ignores the other performance indicators found in modern performance management systems.'

REQUIRED		Marks
(a)	Discuss the present budgeting system and its likely effect on divisional partner motivation.	6
(b)	Explain two non-financial performance indicators (other than client satisfaction and service quality) that could be used by the firm.	4
TOTAL MARKS		10

LQ 3 – Advanced (29 marks; 52 minutes)

Source: Adapted from ACCA P5

The Health and Fitness Group (HFG), which is privately owned, operates three centres in the country of Mayland. Each centre offers dietary plans and fitness programmes to clients under the supervision of dieticians and fitness trainers. Residential accommodation is also available at each centre. The centres are located in the towns of Ayetown, Beetown and Ceetown.

principles of management accounting

The following information is available:
i) Summary of financial data for HFG in respect of the year ended 31 May 2XX8.

	Ayetown	Beetown	Ceetown	Total
	R'000	R'000	R'000	R'000
Revenue:				
Fees received	1 800	2 100	4 500	8 400
Variable costs	(468)	(567)	(1 395)	(2 430)
Contribution	1 332	1 533	3 105	5 970
Fixed costs	(936)	(1 092)	(2 402)	(4 430)
Operating profit	396	441	703	1 540
Interest costs on long-term debt at 10%				(180)
Profit before tax				1 360
Income tax expense				(408)
Profit for the year				952
Average book values for 2008:				
Assets				
Non-current assets	1 000	2 500	3 300	6 800
Current assets	800	900	1 000	2 700
Total assets	1 800	3 400	4 300	9 500
Equity and liabilities:				
Share capital				2 500
Retained earnings				4 400
Total equity				6 900
Non-current liabilities				
Long-term borrowings				1 800
Total non-current liabilities				1 800
Current liabilities	80	240	480	800
Total current liabilities	80	240	480	800
Total liabilities				2 600
Total equity and liabilities				9 500

ii) HFG defines residual income (RI) for each centre as operating profit minus a required rate of return of 12 per cent of the total assets of each centre.
iii) At present HFG does not allocate the long-term borrowings of the group to the three separate centres.
iv) Each centre faces similar risks.
v) Tax is payable at a rate of 30 per cent.
vi) The market value of the equity capital of HFG is R9 million. The cost of equity of HFG is 15 per cent.
vii) The market value of the long-term borrowings of HFG is equal to the carrying amount.
viii) The directors are concerned about the return on investment (ROI) generated by the Beetown centre and they are considering using sensitivity analysis in order to show how a target ROI of 20 per cent may be achieved.

ix) The marketing director stated at a recent board meeting:

'The Group's success depends on the quality of service provided to our clients. In my opinion, we need only to concern ourselves with the number of complaints received from clients during each period as this is the most important performance measure for our business. The number of complaints received from clients is a perfect performance measure. As long as the number of complaints received from clients is not increasing from period to period, then we can be confident about our future prospects.'

REQUIRED	Marks
The directors of HFG have asked you, as management accountant, to prepare a report providing them with explanations as to the following:	
(i) Which of the three centres is the most 'successful'? Your report should include a commentary on return on investment (ROI), residual income (RI), and economic value added (EVA®) as measures of financial performance. Detailed calculations regarding each of these three measures must be included as part of your report. (Note: A maximum of seven marks is available for detailed calculations.)	14
(ii) The percentage change in revenue, total costs and net assets during the year ended 31 May 2XX8 that would have been required in order to have achieved a target ROI of 20% by the Beetown centre. Your answer should consider each of these three variables in isolation. State any assumptions that you make.	6
(iii) Whether or not you agree with the statement of the marketing director in note (ix) above.	5
Professional marks for appropriateness of format, style and structure of the report.	4
TOTAL MARKS	29

LQ 4 – Advanced (25 marks; 45 minutes)

Source: Adapted from ACCA P5

The Superior Software House (SSH) commenced trading on 1 December 2XX2 in the country of Bonlandia. SSH develops custom-made software packages on behalf of clients. When requested to do so, SSH also provides training to clients' staff in the use of these software packages.

On 1 December 2XX6, the directors of SSH established a similar semi-autonomous operation in Karendia. All software packages are produced in Bonlandia and transferred to Karendia at cost plus attributable overheads (that is, there is no mark-up on the software packages transferred from Bonlandia to Karendia).

Karendia is a country in which the structure of industry has changed during recent years. There has been a major shift from traditional manufacturing businesses to service-orientated businesses which place a far greater emphasis on the use of business software.

The operational managers in both Bonlandia and Karendia have no control over company policies in respect of acquisitions and financing. The operational manager of Bonlandia receives a bonus of 40 per cent of his basic salary for meeting all client delivery deadlines in respect of Karendia. At a recent meeting he instructed his staff: 'Instal client software by the due date, and we'll worry about fixing any software problems after it's been installed. After all, we always fix software problems eventually.' He also stated: 'It is of vital importance that we grow our revenues in Karendia as quickly as possible. Our clients in Karendia may complain, but they have spent a lot of money on our software products and will not be able to go to any of our competitors once we have installed our software, as all their businesses would suffer large-scale disruption.'

principles of management accounting

Financial data (all stated on an actual basis) in respect of the two divisions for the two years ended 30 November 2XX7 and 2XX8 are shown below:

Summary income statements

	Bonlandia 2008 R'000	Karendia 2008 R'000	Combined 2008 R'000	Bonlandia 2007 R'000	Karendia 2007 R'000	Combined 2007 R'000
Revenue	14 600	2 800	17 400	14 000	2 000	16 000
Salaries	4 340	1 248	5 588	4 000	1 200	5 200
Software and consumables	2 040	486	2 526	2 000	450	2 450
Other operating costs	2 880	654	3 534	2 800	600	3 400
	9 260	2 388	11 648	8 800	2 250	11 050
Marketing	2 392	600	2 992	2 100	400	2 500
Interest (Group)			850			900
Depreciation and amortisation	400	160	560	400	100	500
	2 792	760	4 402	2 500	500	3 900
Total costs	12 052	3 148	16 050	11 300	2 750	14 950
Profit/(loss) for the period	2 548	(348)	1 350	2 700	(750)	1 050

Statements of financial position

	Bonlandia 2008 R'000	Karendia 2008 R'000	Combined 2008 R'000	Bonlandia 2007 R'000	Karendia 2007 R'000	Combined 2007 R'000
Assets						
Non-current assets	9 000	1 600	10 600	8 000	1 000	9 000
Current assets	4 550	1 000	5 550	5 000	800	5 800
Total assets	13 550	2 600	16 150	13 000	1 800	14 800
Equity and liabilities						
Share capital and reserves			9 150			7 800
Non-current liabilities						
Long-term borrowings			4 000			4 500
Current liabilities	2 400	600	3 000	2 000	500	2 500
Total equity and liabilities			16 150			14 800

REQUIRED		Marks
(a)	Assess the financial performance of SSH and its operations in Bonlandia and Karendia during the years ended 30 November 2XX7 and 2XX8. (*Note:* You should highlight additional information that would be required in order to provide a more comprehensive assessment of the financial performance of each operation.)	14
(b)	Discuss the statements of the operational manager of Bonlandia and assess their implications for SSH.	4
(c)	Assess the likely criteria which would need to be satisfied for software to be regarded as 'quality software'.	4
(d)	Suggest a set of SIX performance measures which the directors of SSH could use in order to assess the quality of service provided to its clients.	3
TOTAL MARKS		**25**

LQ 5 – Advanced (30 marks; 54 minutes)

Source: Adapted from ACCA P5

The Benjamin Education College (BEC), which is partially government funded, is a well-established provider of professional courses for students of accounting, law and marketing in the country of Brightland.

Its mission statement states that the college 'is committed to providing high quality education to all students'. BEC provides education to private fee-paying students as well as to students who are funded by the government.

The Jackson Business Centre (JBC), which commenced trading during 2XX4, is also a provider of professional courses for students of accounting, law and marketing in the country of Brightland. It is a privately owned college and all its students are responsible for the payment of their own fees.

Relevant operating data for BEC and JBC for the year ended 30 November 2XX9 are as follows:

i) Both BEC and JBC offer a range of courses in accounting, law and marketing on a twice per annum basis.

ii) Fees (budget and actual) payable to BEC and JBC in respect of each student who enrolled for a course

	BEC	BEC	JBC
	Privately-funded students	Government-funded students	Privately-funded students
Course type:	R	R	R
Accounting	1 200	900	1 000
Law	1 000	750	1 200
Marketing	800	600	1 200

iii) Salary costs per staff member were payable as follows:

	BEC	BEC	JBC
	Budget	Actual	Actual
	R	R	R
Lecturer	50 000	52 000	55 000
Administrative	20 000	20 800	22 000

principles of management accounting

iv) Budgeted costs for the year based on 8 000 students per annum for BEC were as follows:

	R	Variable cost (%)	Fixed cost (%)
Tuition materials	720 000	100	–
Catering	100 000	80	20
Cleaning	40 000	25	75
Other operating costs	600 000	20	80
Depreciation	40 000	–	100

Variable costs vary according to the number of students attending courses at BEC.

v) Actual costs (other than salary costs) incurred during the year:

	BEC R	JBC R
Tuition materials	741 600	730 000
Catering	95 680	110 000
Cleaning	40 950	40 000
Other operating costs (including costs of freelance staff)	646 800	645 000
Depreciation	40 000	60 000

vi) The management of JBC is considering introducing on-line tuition support by its lecturing staff.
vii) Both BEC and JBC operated a policy which aimed to employ 60 lecturers throughout the year.
viii) The appendix below shows budget and actual statistics for BEC and actual statistics for JBC.

Sundry statistics for the year ended 30 November 2XX9

	BEC Budget	BEC Actual	JBC Actual
Number of students:			
Accounting	3 600	3 800	4 000
Law	1 500	1 400	1 560
Marketing	1 800	2 000	2 000
Student mix (%) for each course type:			
Privately funded	80	70	100
Government funded	20	30	
Number of enquiries received:			
Accounting	4 800	4 750	5 000
Law	2 000	2 800	2 000
Marketing	2 400	2 500	2 400
Number of lecturers employed throughout the year	60	60	60
Number of lecturers recruited during the year:			
Accounting	2	6	1
Law	1	3	–
Marketing	1	3	–
Number of administrative staff employed throughout the year	10	10	8
Number of administrative staff recruited during the year	2	8	–
Number of times freelance lecturing staff were used	–	–	20
Number of new courses under development	–	–	4

REQUIRED	Marks
The senior management team of BEC has asked you, as management accountant, to prepare a report providing them with the following:	
(i) A statement which shows actual and budgeted income statements of BEC and an actual income statement for JBC in respect of the year ended 30 November 2XX9 on a comparable basis.	10
(ii) An assessment of the performance of BEC and JBC using both financial and non-financial measures based on the information contained in the question. You should identify other measures of performance which you consider relevant to BEC.	10
(iii) A discussion of the issues that might restrict the extent to which a performance measurement system is accepted and supported by management and employees.	6
Professional marks will be awarded for appropriateness of format, style and structure of the report.	4
TOTAL MARKS	**30**

References

Aspen Pharmacare. 2009. *Aspen Pharmacare Holdings Limited annual report 2009*. [Online]. Available: <http://financialresults.co.za/aspen_ar2009/downloads.htm > [29 June 2010].

Cape Gateway. 2010. *Tygerberg and dental hospitals: overview*. [Online]. Available: <www.capegateway.gov.za/eng/your_gov/5987/> [29 June 2010].

CIMA (Chartered Institute of Management Accountants). 2002. 'Business transparency in a post-Enron world'. *Executive Briefing*, August. London: CIMA.

Eaton, G. 2005. *Management accounting official terminology*. London: CIMA Publishing.

Elkington, J. 1998. *Cannibals with forks: the triple bottom line of 21st century business*. Gabriola Island, BC: New Society.

Johnson, HT & Kaplan, RS. 1987. *Relevance lost – the rise and fall of management accounting*. Boston, MA: Harvard Business School.

Kaplan, RS & Norton, DP. 1996. *The balanced scorecard*. Boston, MA: Harvard Business School. 14, 25, 26, 28, 61, 85, 115–116.

Rappaport, A. 1998. *Creating shareholder value: a guide for managers and investors*, Revised edition. New York: Free Press.

Roos, S. 2005. 'Involving the management accountant in external reporting to prevent corporate accounting scandals'. *Southern African Business Review*, 9(2):12–21.

Stellenbosch University. 2010. *Mission*. [Online]. Available: <www.sun.ac.za/university/StratPlan/stratdocs.htm> [30 June 2010].

Stern Stewart & Co. 2010. [Online]. Available: </www.sternstewart.com> [30 June 2010].

Woolworths Holdings. 2010. *Corporate profile*. [Online]. Available: <http://www.woolworthsholdings.co.za/corporate/overview.asp> [29 June 2010].

Transfer pricing

chapter 15

Shelley-Anne Roos

LEARNING OBJECTIVES
By the end of this chapter, you should be able to:
1. Explain the conceptual aspects of transfer pricing.
2. Explain the need for transfer pricing within an organisation.
3. Calculate and discuss the level of internal transfers and the level of external sales that result in the best outcome for the organisation as a whole.
4. Calculate and discuss market price-based and cost-based transfer prices.
5. Calculate and discuss transfer prices where the transferring and receiving units respectively operate in both perfect and imperfect markets (see Appendix 15.1).
6. Discuss methods of resolving transfer pricing problems, including prorating the difference according to variable costs, supplementing the transfer price by a recurring fee, dual pricing, supplementary performance measures, and additional unofficial accounting records.
7. Discuss and calculate transfer prices for international transfers.
8. Discuss the strategic and ethical considerations relevant to transfers and transfer pricing.

Sasol and transfer pricing

A number of businesses and divisions form part of the *Sasol* group of companies, and some of them trade with each other. Sasol Mining, for example, supplies coal to Sasol Synfuels. Sasol Synfuels, in turn, supplies methane-rich gas to Sasol Gas. Sasol Financing centrally manages the group's treasury matters, and acts as a business partner to Sasol's businesses on specialised financing arrangements.

Source: Sasol 2009

Although Sasol's units all work together to earn profits for the group as a whole, performance of the individual units also needs to be managed. A number of transfer pricing issues arise, for example:
- What would be a reasonable price for Sasol Mining to charge for the coal it supplies to Sasol Synfuels?
- What would be a reasonable price for Sasol Synfuels to charge for the gas it supplies to Sasol Gas?
- Does Sasol Mining have to pay for the services it receives from Sasol Financing? If so, should it pay the same price that Sasol Synfuels and Sasol Gas pay for the services that they receive from Sasol Financing?

Chapter 15 explores the issues that organisations face when determining transfer prices.

15.1 Introduction

> **Key term:** transfer price

Chapter 14, *Performance management* explained the need for managing the performance of units within an organisation. Where units transact with each other, transfer pricing is necessary to enable units to record internal transactions in their financial records, and for the measurement, evaluation and management of financial performance of units. Transfer pricing in effect allocates profits to units, and can support the autonomy of units in a decentralised organisational structure. Transfer pricing can also be used as a means of promoting goal congruence in an organisation. These aims of transfer pricing will be discussed in more detail in this chapter.

The term 'unit', as used here, means any part of an organisation whose performance is separately recorded and evaluated. Some organisations may refer to such units as branches, departments or divisions. A unit may even be a company that forms part of a larger group of companies. Transfer pricing issues arise when such units transact with each other – a **transfer price** is the price at which goods or services are transferred between different units of the same organisation.

Example 15.1

Unit A of the Paper Company manufactures A4-size blank paper sheets for use in printers and copiers. Unit A incurs variable costs of R65 in manufacturing each standard box of paper. Unit B of the Paper Company operates a large warehouse and distributes the paper throughout South Africa. Unit B incurs incremental costs of R20 per box of paper. Stationery retail stores pay the Paper Company R100 per box of paper.

Required:
Indicate how the contribution earned could be shared between units A and B.

The Paper Company earns a contribution of R15 (R100 – R65 – R20) per box of paper. How this is divided between the two units depends on how much Unit A charges Unit B for the paper transferred (in other words, it depends on the transfer price). If Unit A charges R80 per box, Unit B will earn no contribution: Unit B will 'purchase' each box of paper for R80, incur further costs of R20 and sell it for R100. The entire contribution that the company earns, namely R15 per box, will be recorded in the books of Unit A (R80 – R65). The reverse is true if Unit A charges R65 per box. Unit A will earn no contribution, while the entire R15 company contribution is recorded in the books of Unit B (R100 – R65 – R20). It seems that a transfer price of between R65 and R80 is desirable – one that fairly allocates a portion of the contribution to each unit.

The need to establish transfer prices often arises from the need to manage the performance of units within an organisation – the transferring division records a 'sale' while the receiving division records a 'purchase'. This allows managers to keep an internal set of accounts for each unit within the company, which can be used to assess the performance of units and their managers. Note that the transfer price that units A and B finally agree on in example 15.1 is not recorded in the annual financial statements of the Paper Company and does not impact on the contribution recorded by the Paper Company as a whole. This is because, in the books of the company as a whole, the 'sale' by Unit A is cancelled out by the 'purchase' by Unit B. The Paper Company records a contribution of R15 per box of paper, irrespective of the transfer price agreed upon.

Where units take the form of separate legal entities, such as companies that form part of a larger group, each company records transfer prices paid or received in its own annual financial statements. Related party disclosure has to be supplied in the annual financial statements in accordance with IAS 24. Upon consolidation of the group results, intra-group transactions cancel each other out and only the net result (equivalent to the R15 contribution in example 15.1) is recorded in the consolidated accounts. Where units are legal entities and have goods for transfer on hand at the end of the financial year, care has to be taken that the value placed on such inventory items complies with the requirements of IAS 2. Even where units are not legal entities but are significant segments of a company, the company may have to produce segment reports in accordance with IFRS 8.

15.2 Decentralisation and transfer pricing

Key terms: autonomous units, decentralised organisations

By their very nature, transfer prices occur only in organisations that consist of different units for which performance is separately recorded. Such organisations often have some degree of decentralised management control, which means that decision-making responsibility is to some extent delegated to unit managers. While some organisations may prescribe transfer prices or set transfer price boundaries, highly **decentralised organisations** (where units are said to be **autonomous units**) allow transfer prices to be determined through negotiation between the units concerned.

Decentralisation and negotiation of transfer prices often result in very favourable outcomes for an organisation, as units are encouraged to aggressively develop ways of conducting business efficiently in order to secure internal sales. However, transfer prices can potentially be a source of great conflict between units, as they directly affect the performance measurement results of the units concerned. Even a highly decentralised organisation's central management may sometimes wish to intervene in negotiations that cause undesirable levels of conflict or unacceptable outcomes, through the setting of transfer prices or transfer price boundaries.

15.3 Principles of transfer pricing

Key term: goal congruence

Complicated transfer pricing issues can arise in organisations with a decentralised management control structure. Although the delegation of authority has substantial potential advantages, as discussed in Chapter 14, *Performance management*, particular care has to be taken to avoid the setting of transfer prices that conflict with the best interests of the organisation as a whole.

> ### Example 15.2
>
> The same information as in example 15.1 applies, but with the following additional points:
> - Unit A's manufacturing capacity is limited to 20 000 boxes of paper per month.
> - Units A and B have agreed on a transfer price of R72,50 per box of paper.
> - AfriWrite, a stationery warehousing and distribution company, has now offered to purchase all the paper boxes from Unit A each month for distribution in neighbouring countries.
> - AfriWrite has agreed to pay R75 per box of paper.
>
> **Required:**
> Determine whether Unit A should agree to sell paper to AfriWrite.

AfriWrite is willing to pay Unit A R2,50 more per box of paper than the internal transfer price. This means that Unit A can increase its monthly contribution by R50 000 (20 000 boxes × R2,50). However, if Unit A supplies to AfriWrite, it will be acting in its own best interest but not in the best interest of the Paper Company as a whole. The Paper Company earns a contribution of R15 (R100 – R65 – R20) per box of paper on internal transfers to Unit B, but only R10 (R75 – R65) per box of paper sold to AfriWrite. The transfer price of R72,50 per box will have to be revised, as it encourages Unit A to act against the best interest of the organisation as a whole.

Chapter 14, *Performance management* discussed the concept of **goal congruence**. Goal congruence means that individuals and units take actions that are in their self-interest and simultaneously also in the best interest of the organisation as a whole. The ideal performance management system, which includes the transfer pricing system, is designed in such a way that each individual and each unit within the organisation prefers to act in the best interest of the organisation as a whole at all times because they are simultaneously acting in their own best interests. The overriding requirement for a transfer pricing system is therefore that it should ensure that transfer prices encourage unit managers to act in the best interest of the organisation as a whole. In example 15.2, this can be achieved by setting a transfer price of between R75 and R80. Because Unit A will now earn at least R75 per box of paper transferred, the sub-optimal decision to sell paper to AfriWrite will not be taken.

Note that, in example 15.1, the acceptable range of transfer prices was R65 to R80. In example 15.2 the minimum transfer price has increased to R75, owing to the presence of AfriWrite in the market.

Apart from encouraging goal congruence, a transfer pricing system should also be effective and efficient. A transfer pricing system is *effective* when its objectives are achieved – an effective system, for example, ensures that the performance of units is accurately and fairly recorded. An *efficient* transfer pricing system consumes the minimum resources in the achievement of its objectives, in other words it does not place an unnecessary financial or administrative burden on the organisation.

15.4 Market price-based transfer prices

> **Key terms:** intermediate product or service, perfectly competitive market

An **intermediate product or service** is the product or service that is transferred from one unit of an organisation to another unit in the same organisation. If the transferring unit can sell the intermediate product or service externally in a perfectly competitive market, the market price may be the ideal transfer price. A **perfectly competitive market** exists when a homogeneous product or service with equal buying and selling prices is sold in a market where individual buyers and sellers cannot affect prices by their own actions.

Example 15.3

The same information as in example 15.1 applies, but with the following additional points:
- Paper manufacturers sell standard A4-sized paper for use in printers and copiers to stationery warehousing and distribution companies in the open market at R75 per box.
- There is a large number of sellers and buyers.
- A perfectly competitive market exists.

Required:
Recommend a transfer price per box of paper transferred from Unit A to Unit B.

In this case the market price of R75 per box is the ideal transfer price. Unit A can sell its paper in the open market for R75 per box and Unit B can purchase paper in the open market at R75 per box. A transfer price of R75 per box will leave both units no worse off if an internal transfer takes place. However, should there be any cost savings associated with an internal transfer, there is more room for negotiation. Assume that it costs Unit A R1 per box to have the paper delivered at the premises of an external paper warehousing and distribution company. Unit A incurs no such cost when it transfers paper to Unit B, as Unit A's factory is on the same premises as Unit B's primary warehouse. Unit A effectively earns only R74 (R75 – R1) per box when it sells paper externally. Unit B can purchase paper externally at R75 per box. A transfer price of between R74 and R75 should therefore be negotiated.

Practical examples of savings that frequently occur on internal transfers include not only transport costs, as in the example above, but also savings in marketing costs (entertainment, for example) and financing costs (if the external purchaser buys the product on credit).

In example 15.3 we have assumed that all manufacturers produce standard, identically-packaged paper. In practice there may be variations in aspects such as the quality, packaging, service levels offered or discounts granted, meaning that an accurate market price for the exact product or service may not be available.

15.5 Cost-based transfer prices

One way of setting a transfer price is for the organisation's central management to decide to calculate transfer prices based on the cost of the intermediate product or service. Organisations sometimes choose to add a specified mark-up percentage to the cost-base.

Example 15.4

The same information as in example 15.1 applies, but with the following additional points:
Unit A's fixed costs amount to R5 per box of paper, while Unit B's fixed costs are R1 per box of paper.

Required:
Calculate the transfer price per box of paper if the Paper Company's central management stipulates that all boxes of paper should be transferred to Unit B at a transfer price of (a) variable cost plus 20 per cent and (b) full cost plus 20 per cent.

The transfer prices are as follows:
a) Based on variable cost: R65 plus 20 per cent = R78
b) Based on full cost: (R65 plus R5) plus 20 per cent = R84.

Cost-based transfer prices can lead to sub-optimal decisions if the organisation's units are autonomous. Assume that Unit B can purchase paper from another manufacturer, Pulp World, at R75 per box. If Unit B has the autonomy to purchase paper either from Unit A or from an external supplier, Unit B will rather purchase externally than receive a transfer from Unit A under both scenarios (a) and (b) above. However, the Paper Company's best interest would not be served by such a decision. The company earns a contribution of R15 (R100 – R65 – R20) per box on internal transfers, but a contribution of only R5 (R100 – R75 – R20) per box if Unit B buys paper from Pulp World.

If a transfer price based on variable cost without any mark-up is used, the disadvantage is that the transferring division does not recover its fixed costs. Transfer prices based on full cost, on the other hand, have the disadvantage that indirect costs could be questionably allocated owing to the use of inappropriate cost pools, cost drivers, or allocation bases.

Whenever the transfer price is set higher than the transferring unit's incremental cost, as in example 15.4 above, receiving divisions reimburse transferring divisions for more than just the cost of supplying the product or service. The longer the chain of intra-company transfers (in other words Unit A supplies to Unit B, which supplies to Unit C, and so forth), the more internal profit is added on top of profits already recorded by preceding divisions. The process increases the danger of units taking decisions that conflict with the best interest of the company as a whole.

An additional point to remember is that, to prevent any cost inefficiencies in the transferring unit from being carried over to the receiving unit, the transfer price should be based on standard costs or budgeted costs rather than actual costs.

15.6 Negotiated transfer prices

Where units are highly autonomous, transfer prices are agreed through negotiation. In order to ensure that the transfer price does not lead to decisions that conflict with the best interest of the company as a whole, a range of goal-congruent transfer prices can first be determined. A final transfer price is then negotiated within this range. The following steps apply:
1 Establish the level of internal transfers (to other units in the organisation) and the level of external sales (to other organisations) that will result in the best outcome for the organisation as a whole.
2 Determine the minimum and the maximum transfer prices that will result in autonomous units choosing to operate at the level determined in step 1.

15.6.1 General guidelines

> **Key terms:** autonomous receiving unit, autonomous transferring unit, maximum transfer price, minimum transfer price

In order to carry out step 2 above, a minimum and a maximum transfer price have to be determined that will lead autonomous units to act in a goal-congruent manner.

> The **minimum transfer price** is the smallest amount an **autonomous transferring unit** would be willing to receive and still choose to act in the best interest of the organisation as a whole. The **maximum transfer price** is the largest amount an **autonomous receiving unit** would be willing to pay and still choose to act in the best interest of the organisation as a whole.

The minimum transfer price should at least cover the transferring unit's incremental cost of producing the product or service. Where opportunity cost is incurred owing to the transfer of the product or service, the minimum price should also ensure that the transferring unit is compensated for revenue forgone. This may be the case where, for example, there is an external market for the intermediate product or service and revenue from external sales are forgone, or where the transfer of the product or service has an impact on the sale of other products or services. The minimum price should therefore be the transferring unit's incremental cost per unit of product or service, plus opportunity cost per unit of product or service. This guideline ensures that where there is no external market and no other kind of revenue forgone (in other words the opportunity cost is zero), the minimum price is simply the incremental cost per unit of product or service.

To ensure that the receiving unit earns some contribution, the maximum transfer price should not exceed the incremental contribution the receiving unit earns per unit of product or service. However, should the receiving unit be able to purchase on the intermediate market at an even lower price, the maximum transfer price should be limited to the intermediate market price. This prevents the receiving unit from purchasing externally when an internal transfer is in the best interest of the organisation as a whole.

The general guidelines can be summarised as follows.

The minimum transfer price per unit of product or service is:
- The transferring unit's incremental cost per unit of product or service
- *Plus* the transferring unit's opportunity cost per unit of product or service.

The maximum transfer price per unit of product or service is the lesser of:
- The receiving unit's incremental contribution per unit of product or service (before subtracting the transfer price) *
- The market price at which the receiving unit can purchase each unit of product or service from an external supplier.

> * If a single batch of transfers takes place at a contracted price, the receiving unit's cumulative contribution per unit of product or service (before subtracting the transfer price) is used here instead. This is an advanced aspect and is dealt with in the appendix to this chapter.

principles of management accounting

The examples contained in the appendix to this chapter are advanced and illustrate the above general guidelines in complex situations. Students are advised to confirm with their lecturers whether knowledge of the examples in the appendix is required in the specific course that they are registered for.

Example 15.5 below, which expands on the Paper Company examples, illustrates the application of the general guidelines in a simple yet comprehensive scenario.

Example 15.5

Unit A of the Paper Company manufactures A4-size blank paper sheets for use in printers and copiers. Unit A incurs variable costs of R65 in manufacturing each standard box of paper. Unit B of the Paper Company operates a large warehouse and distributes the paper throughout South Africa. Unit B incurs incremental costs of R20 per box of paper. Stationery retail stores pay the Paper Company R100 per box of paper.

Unit A's manufacturing capacity is limited to 20 000 boxes of paper per month. AfriWrite, a stationery warehousing and distribution company, has now offered to purchase 60% of Unit A's capacity (12 000 paper boxes) from Unit A each month for distribution to neighbouring countries. AfriWrite has agreed to pay R81 per box of paper. Unit B can also purchase paper on the open market at R81 per box of paper, but will then have to incur transport costs of R1 per box.

Required:
Suggest an appropriate transfer pricing strategy for the Paper Company.

Step 1: Establish the level of internal transfers and the level of external sales that will result in the best outcome for the organisation as a whole.

The Paper Company earns a contribution of R15 (R100 – R65 – R20) per box of paper on internal transfers. The company earns R16 (R81 – R65) in contribution per box of paper sold to AfriWrite. Based on financial considerations alone, the company should therefore sell as many boxes of paper as possible to AfriWrite, and transfer the remaining boxes of paper internally.

It is not viable for Unit B to purchase paper on the open market, as the company would earn a negative contribution of R2 per box of paper (R100 – R81 – R1 – R20).

The optimal plan is therefore:
- Sell 12 000 boxes of paper per month to AfriWrite
- Transfer 8 000 boxes of paper (20 000 – 12 000 boxes) per month internally to Unit B.

Step 2: Determine the minimum and the maximum transfer prices that will result in autonomous units choosing to operate at the level determined in step 1.

The minimum transfer price is:
- *Unit A's incremental cost.* Unit A incurs incremental costs of R65 per unit
- *Plus Unit A's opportunity cost.* On the first 12 000 boxes of paper Unit A could earn R16 contribution (R81 – R65) per box. The remaining 8 000 boxes cannot be sold in the open market, and carry no opportunity cost.

The minimum transfer price for the first 12 000 boxes of paper is therefore R81 (R65 + R16), and the minimum price for the remaining 8 000 boxes of paper is R65 (R65 + R0).

The maximum transfer price is the lesser of:
- *Unit B's incremental contribution per box of paper (before subtracting the transfer price).* Unit B can sell the paper at R100 per box, and incurs R20 in incremental costs. Its incremental contribution is therefore R80 (before subtracting the transfer price).
- *The market price at which Unit B can purchase from an external supplier.* Unit B can purchase paper in the open market at R81 per box, plus R1 in additional transport costs.

The maximum transfer price is therefore the lesser figure of R80 per box of paper for all 20 000 boxes.

The optimal transfer price for the first 12 000 boxes of paper per month is between R81 (minimum price) and R80 (maximum price). The minimum transfer price exceeds the maximum transfer price, and the transfer will not take place. This is the correct result, as the first 12 000 boxes of paper should rather be sold to AfriWrite.

The optimal transfer price for the remaining 8 000 boxes of paper is between R65 and R80. These boxes should be transferred, and Units A and B should negotiate a final price within this range.

15.6.2 Transfer pricing and shadow prices

Key term: shadow price

Linear programming (refer to Chapter 11, *Decision-making under operational constraints*) is sometimes used to determine the optimal product or service mix in organisations where there is a scarcity of resources. Where a linear programming problem is combined with a transfer pricing problem, the receiving unit's incremental contribution per unit of product or service, as used in determining the maximum transfer price, is the shadow price per unit of product or service. As discussed in Chapter 11, the **shadow price** is the value which would be created by having available one additional unit of a limiting resource at its original cost.

15.7 Resolving transfer pricing problems

Key term: dual pricing

There may be instances, most notably where there is no intermediate market for the product or service, where the transferring unit is in a weak negotiating position and is unlikely to secure a transfer price in excess of incremental cost. In such situations it should be considered whether the transferring unit should in future be operated as a cost centre rather than a profit or investment centre. Chapter 14, *Performance management* discussed different types of responsibility centres and explained that a cost centre is held responsible for its costs only. It follows that, where the transferring unit is a cost centre, there is no need to establish a transfer price that allocates a portion of the contribution to it. A transfer price that reimburses the cost centre for costs incurred will therefore be sufficient. Another option to consider is whether the transferring and receiving units should perhaps be merged.

The examples in this chapter have illustrated that there is often a range of goal-congruent transfer prices within which autonomous units can negotiate a final transfer price. The final transfer price depends on many factors, such as the relative strengths on the units' negotiating positions and the negotiation skills of unit managers. Units may choose to calculate the transfer price on another basis (such as a straightforward cost basis) in order to use the figure as a starting point for negotiations. The following are some ways in which transfer pricing negotiations or a transfer pricing dispute may be resolved.

Option one: prorating the difference according to variable costs

Example 15.6

Units A and B of a company have to negotiate a transfer price of between R40 and R52 for components transferred from Unit A to Unit B. Unit A's variable costs are R30 per component, while Unit B's variable costs are R60 per final product.

Required:
Suggest an appropriate transfer price by prorating the difference between the minimum and maximum transfer prices according to variable costs.

Unit B's variable costs are twice that of Unit A. Of the R12 (R52 – R40) spread between the minimum and maximum price, one-third (30 / [60+30]) should be allocated to Unit A and two thirds (60 / [60+30]) to Unit B. The transfer price is therefore set at the minimum price plus one third of the spread: R40 + (R12 / 3) = R44. Alternatively it can be calculated as the maximum price minus two thirds of the spread: R52 – (R12 / 3 x 2) = R44.

A disadvantage of prorating the difference according to variable costs is the fact that both divisions have an incentive to overstate and/or not properly control variable costs.

Option two: supplementing the transfer price by a recurring fee

In addition to agreeing on a transfer price per unit of product or service, the receiving unit may also be held liable to pay the transferring unit a recurring fee per period (for example, a fixed fee of R10 000 per month). This means that the transferring unit has two sources of internal revenue: the transfer price received and the recurring fee received. This is a particularly useful solution in situations where there is no external market for the intermediate product (in other words the minimum transfer price is the transferring unit's incremental cost) and there is a need for the transferring unit to recover its fixed costs.

Kaplan and Cooper (1998) use activity-based costing to determine the optimal transfer price and recurring fee. The incremental cost used to determine the transfer price is the sum of unit level and batch level costs. The recurring fee is made up of product-sustaining and facility-sustaining costs, and reflects the percentage use that the receiving unit makes of the transferring unit's capacity (for the same reasons as stated before, standard or budgeted costs are again preferred to actual costs). If the receiving unit, for example, intends to purchase 40 per cent of the products in a specific product line and intends to use 30 per cent of the capacity of the transferring unit, the recurring fee should be 40 per cent of the relevant product sustaining costs plus 30 per cent of the transferring unit's facility sustaining costs. The capacity that has been paid for is then reserved for the receiving unit. Paying for reserved capacity provides a good incentive for the receiving unit not to overestimate the capacity that the transferring unit should reserve for it. If inappropriate estimates were made, the receiving unit and other customers that purchase the intermediate product can 'rent' excess capacity in the transferring unit from each other as required.

(Chapter 6, *Overhead allocation* describes the classification of costs into unit level, batch level, product-sustaining costs, and facility-sustaining costs.)

Option three: dual pricing

Where transfer pricing disputes cannot be resolved, a **dual pricing** system may be employed in order to satisfy both the transferring and the receiving unit. Under dual pricing:
- The transferring unit is credited with a transfer price that is deemed to be a fair representation of the revenue it should receive
- The receiving unit is debited with a transfer price that is deemed to be a fair representation of the price it should pay (the price at which the receiving unit records the purchase does not have to be the same as the price at which the transferring unit recorded the sale)
- The difference between the selling price recorded by the transferring unit and the purchase price recorded by the receiving unit is recorded in a central company account.

Dual pricing is not an ideal solution to transfer pricing problems, as it creates an artificial environment in which unit managers are shielded from market forces and effective negotiation. This conflicts with the rationale behind the establishment of autonomous organisational units.

Option four: supplementary performance measures

Performance measures other than those based on a unit's profit may be used in order to encourage internal transfers that are in the best interest of the organisation as a whole, but unattractive from a unit perspective. A company may, for example, specifically reward managers for internal transfers made, or may base part of the bonus of the manager responsible for the transferring unit on the profit of the receiving unit.

Option five: additional unofficial accounting records

Where the transfer price that is in the best interest of the organisation as a whole is unfair towards individual units (as is the case in example 15.8 below), an additional, separate set of unofficial accounting records can be kept in which a transfer price is recorded that is more appropriate for internal performance management purposes. Transfers then take place at the price that is best for the organisation as a whole, but the unofficial records are used for performance management.

15.8 Transfer of self-constructed assets

IAS 16, *Property, plant and equipment* determines that, where a product is constructed by one unit of an organisation and transferred to another unit where it is treated as a fixed asset, internal profits are not regarded as part of the cost of the asset. If the transferring unit manufactures similar products for sale in the normal course of business, the cost at which the transferred product is recorded in the books of the receiving unit is therefore usually the same as the cost of constructing products that were sold externally.

Example 15.7

Unit A manufactures machines at a cost of R20 000 each. One of the machines is transferred to Unit B of the same company, where the machine is used in the production process. Units A and B agree on a transfer price of R23 000 for the machine.

Required:
Give the amount at which the machine should be recorded in the company's financial statements according to GAAP.

The cost to manufacture the machine was R20 000, and this is the cost of the asset in the company's accounts. The internal profit of R3 000 is not regarded as part of the cost.

15.9 International transfers

It has already been stated that the need to establish transfer prices often arises from the need to manage the performance of units within an organisation. However, where the organisation's units are located across international boundaries, legal requirements in the respective countries also require transfers to be valued. Most notably, taxation laws and customs requirements in most countries require that the value of transferred goods and services be declared.

Organisations which transfer goods or services across international borders are inclined to favour transfer prices that minimise the tax, duties and levies payable by the organisation as a whole. As in any other transfer pricing problem, the first step in setting transfer prices in such organisations should be to determine the range of prices that will serve the best interests of the organisation as a whole. The following aspects in particular should be kept in mind:

- Income tax
- Value-added tax or general sales tax
- Import/export duties
- Customs requirements
- Anti-dumping legislation (legislation that protects local industries by preventing companies from transferring goods into the country at prices below market value).

In addition to the above, some countries may place restrictions on the repatriation of dividends. This means that the host government does not allow unlimited funds to leave the country in the form of dividends paid to foreign shareholders, as it may be seen as an exploitation of the host country's resources. In such cases a company may consider lowering the price of transfers out of such a country (or increasing the price of transfers into such a country), as this offers an alternative way of taking funds out of the country. However, many countries' income tax laws contain measures to prevent this potential loophole from being exploited.

Section 31(2) of the South African Income Tax Act 58 of 1962 discourages companies from exploiting South African resources and recording excessive profits in foreign countries. It does so by granting the Commissioner of the South African Revenue Service the right to amend the value placed on goods or services transferred between related parties for income tax purposes. Where the value is not market related, the Commissioner may tax the parties as if the market value had been used (that is, the price that would have been set in an 'arm's length' transaction if the transaction had taken place in the open market between unrelated parties).

Example 15.8

A company has a manufacturing unit located in Country U which transfers finished products to the company's retail unit located in Country V. The full cost of manufacturing each product is R400. In country U, similar products sell in the open market at R500 each. The retail unit incurs additional costs of R50 per unit and sells the products at R550 each in Country V. The tax authorities in Country U retain the right to amend the tax value placed on goods or services transferred between related parties in order to bring it in line with the market value of the goods or services. The company income tax rate in Country U is 28 per cent. The company income tax rate in Country V is 15 per cent.

Required:
Recommend an appropriate transfer price.

The company as a whole makes a profit of R100 (R550 − R400 − R50) per product. The company should try to record as much as possible of the R100 income in Country V instead of Country U, as Country V's tax rate is significantly lower. This means that the transfer price has to be kept as close to the minimum as possible, namely R400 per product. However, if a transfer price of R400 is chosen, the tax authorities in Country U will deem the value to be R500 for income tax purposes. Income tax of R28 [(R500 − R400) × 28%] is due in Country U and R15 [(R550 − R50 − R400) × 15%] in Country V.

The best solution in this case is therefore to set the transfer price at market price. If the market price of R500 is used, tax in Country V is avoided [(R550 − R50 − R500) × 15% = R0]. The total income tax liability is R28 payable in Country U.

In the above example, a transfer price of R500 was in the best interest of the organisation as a whole, but resulted in the receiving unit recording zero income, which is problematic from a performance measurement perspective. Options three, four and five discussed in section 15.7 of this chapter may be appropriate in overcoming this problem.

When working with transfers across international borders, the issue of exchange rates may arise. Fluctuations in exchange rates may have a positive or negative impact on the profits of an organisation's individual units. However, unless exchange rate fluctuations lead to changes in behaviour (such as setting a transfer price outside the goal-congruent range), they should not impact the profits of the organisation as a whole at intermediate product-level because internal 'sales' and 'purchases' cancel each other out.

15.10 Strategic and ethical considerations

> **Key terms:** strategic and ethical considerations

Transfer pricing calculations can become quite complex, and a high level of technical skill is required to solve advanced transfer pricing problems. When so much effort is directed at mastering calculations, the qualitative and non-financial aspects of the topic are often overlooked. **Strategic and ethical considerations** could, however, dictate that a different transfer price should be used.

A company may, for example, for *strategic* reasons set transfer prices in such a manner that low profits are recorded in a specific business unit in order to make the market appear unattractive to potential competitors.

Ethical considerations become particularly prominent when transfers are made across international borders. If a company, for example, conducts mining operations in a developing country and transfers all goods to a developed country at a very low transfer price, the company may be seen as exploiting a developing nation's resources without due compensation. Even if the minimum transfer price is the correct transfer price to use from a financial perspective, and even if the host country's tax and other laws do not discourage or prohibit such an action, the company could be doing irreparable damage to its corporate image. The triple bottom line, as introduced in Chapter 14, *Performance management*, should be kept in mind: modern organisations are expected to strive simultaneously for economic prosperity, environmental quality and social justice (Elkington 1998:2).

15.11 Summary

A transfer price is the price at which goods or services are transferred between different units of the same organisation. Because it impacts on the performance evaluation of the units involved, transfer pricing can potentially cause goal-congruence problems in decentralised organisations.

Transfer prices may be based on market prices or costs, as deemed appropriate, but the final price is often negotiated between units in a decentralised organisation. In order to ensure goal congruence, negotiations ought to take place between the minimum transfer price (the smallest amount the transferring unit would be willing to receive while still choosing to act in the best interest of the organisation as a whole) and the maximum transfer price (the largest amount the receiving unit would be willing to pay while still choosing to act in the best interest of the organisation as a whole). These limits are influenced by the particular circumstances, such as whether there is a market for the intermediate product, and whether the intermediate and final products are sold on perfect or imperfect markets (see the appendix for advanced examples).

Because transfer pricing scenarios are often complex, a straightforward, universally-acceptable transfer price may not always be found. A number of options are available to resolve transfer pricing problems. Other issues such as tax implications and legislation, strategic factors and ethical considerations further affect the transfer price chosen.

Conclusion: Transfer pricing and other chapters in this book

As the need to manage the performance of units within an organisation is often one of the primary reasons for establishing transfer prices, this chapter should be studied together with Chapter 14, *Performance management*.

Other topic links include the following: standard or budgeted costs should be used instead of actual costs in the setting of transfer prices. The use of transfer prices and shadow prices was discussed in section 15.6.2, while the use of transfer pricing with activity-based costing was discussed in section 15.7.

Tutorial case study: Sappi Group

The *Sappi Group* has three divisions: Sappi Fine Paper, Sappi Forest Products and Sappi Trading. Sappi Fine Paper produces paper in manufacturing facilities in North America, Europe and South Africa. Sappi Forest Products consists of three business units – Sappi Saiccor produces chemical cellulose, Sappi Kraft manufactures kraft pulp and packaging and newsprint items, and Sappi Forests produces plantation timber. Sappi Trading's head office is in Hong Kong, and it sells the group's products outside the home markets of the operating divisions.

Source: Sappi 2010

1. Discuss whether and why it may be necessary for the Sappi group to make use of transfer pricing.
2. Explain what the main principle should be that guides all of the Sappi group's transfer pricing decisions.
3. Discuss the characteristics that a transfer pricing system in Sappi may have in order for it to be regarded as goal congruent, effective and efficient.
4. Identify one intermediate product in the Sappi group, and discuss whether or not Sappi Trading's main business can be regarded as an intermediate service.
5. Discuss the possible disadvantages of using a cost-based transfer price when pulp is transferred from Sappi Forest Products to Sappi Fine Paper.
6. Explain whether Sappi Fine Paper would favour the minimum or the maximum transfer price when pulp is transferred from Sappi Forest Products to Sappi Fine Paper.
7. Explain whether Sappi Forest Products would favour the minimum or the maximum transfer price when pulp is transferred from Sappi Forest Products to Sappi Fine Paper.
8. Discuss three ways in which the Sappi group may resolve a transfer pricing dispute.
9. Identify the major factors related to international transfers that the Sappi group should take into account when setting a transfer pricing policy.
10. Explain how the South African Income Tax Act 58 of 1962 discourages Sappi Forest Products from transferring pulp to Sappi Fine Paper's manufacturing facilities in Europe at a transfer price that is below the market value of the pulp.
11. Give reasons, other than the tax implications discussed in question 10, why it may not be desirable for the Sappi group to transfer pulp from Sappi Forest Products to Sappi Fine Paper's manufacturing facilities in Europe at a price that is below the market value of the pulp.

principles of management accounting

Appendix 15.1 Determining transfer prices in perfect and imperfect markets

This appendix contains three examples which illustrate how transfer prices are determined under different intermediate and final market conditions where units are highly decentralised. For the sake of consistency, the steps set out in this chapter are followed throughout. This appendix is an advanced section of the chapter which contains highly technical calculations. Care should be taken not to lose sight of the basic principles of transfer pricing, as illustrated in the body of the chapter. Notice how, in each case, the optimal number of units that should be transferred in order to act in the best interest of the organisation as a whole is determined first. Thereafter the minimum and maximum prices are set in such a way that the transferring and receiving units respectively choose to transfer the optimal number of units.

Appendix example 15.1

Transferring unit has no external market, and receiving unit sells on an imperfect market

Unit A of a company manufactures Component X, which is transferred to Unit B, where it is used to manufacture Product Y. There is no external market for Component X. Unit B sells the final product, Product Y, on an imperfect market (the imperfection of the market is illustrated by the fact that different quantities sold command different prices, as can be seen in the table below). One Component X is used in the manufacture of each Product Y. Unit A incurs variable costs of R10 per Component X, as well as fixed costs of R50 000 per month that are unavoidable in the short term. Unit B incurs variable costs of R5 per Product Y and R30 000 worth of fixed costs per month that are unavoidable in the short term. Unit B can sell Product Y as follows:

Selling price of Product Y	Quantity sold in units per month
R50	10 000
R38	20 000
R25	30 000

A consultant has suggested a transfer price of R22 per Component X.

Required:
Determine whether a transfer price of R22 per Component X is appropriate and, if not, suggest an appropriate range of transfer prices for Component X.

At a transfer price of R22 per Component X, Unit A's outlook is as follows:

Quantity X	Incremental quantity	Revenue from transfers	Variable costs (R10 per unit)	Contribution for Unit A
10 000	10 000	R220 000	R100 000	R120 000
20 000	10 000	R440 000	R200 000	R240 000
30 000	10 000	R660 000	R300 000	R360 000

As the schedule indicates, Unit A will choose to transfer the maximum number of components.

At a transfer price of R22 per Component X, Unit B's outlook is as follows:

Quantity Y	Revenue from sales	Transfers received	Variable costs (R5 per unit)	Contribution for Unit B
10 000	R500 000	R220 000	R50 000	R230 000
20 000	R760 000	R440 000	R100 000	R220 000
30 000	R750 000	R660 000	R150 000	(R60 000)

As the schedule indicates, Unit B will choose to sell 10 000 of Product Y if the transfer price is R22.

The outlook for the company as a whole is as follows (note that the internal transfer is ignored here, as the 'selling' and 'purchasing' of transferred components cancel each other out):

Quantity Y	Revenue from sales	Total variable costs (R10 p/u + R5 p/u)	Contribution for the company
10 000	R500 000	R150 000	R350 000
20 000	R760 000	R300 000	R460 000
30 000	R750 000	R450 000	R300 000

It is in the best interest of the company as a whole to sell 20 000 of Product Y, so 20 000 of Component X must be transferred from Unit A to Unit B. However, the transfer price of R22 causes Unit B to order only 10 000 of Component X, and is therefore inappropriate.

In order to suggest a more appropriate transfer price, the steps are as follows:
- *Step 1*: Establish the level of internal transfers and the level of external sales that will result in the best outcome for the organisation as a whole. It has been calculated that 20 000 of Component X should be transferred.
- *Step 2*: Determine the minimum and the maximum transfer prices that will result in autonomous units choosing to operate at the level determined in step 1.

The minimum transfer price is:
- Unit A's *incremental cost*. In this example incremental cost equals variable cost, and amounts to R10 per Component X.
- Plus Unit A's *opportunity cost*. There is no intermediate market for Component X. The opportunity cost is zero.

The minimum transfer price is R10 per Component X.

The maximum transfer price is the lesser of:
- Unit B's *incremental contribution (before subtracting the transfer price)*. See the schedule below. At a sales level of 20 000 Unit B's contribution is R660 000, while it is R450 000 at the lower sales level of 10 000. At the optimal sales level of 20 000, the incremental contribution per Product Y is R21 calculated as (R210 000 / 10 000) or ([R660 000 − R450 000] / [20 000 − 10 000]).

principles of management accounting

Quantity Y	Incremental quantity	Revenue	Variable cost for Unit B (R5 p/u)	Contribution for Unit B	Incremental contribution	Incremental contribution per product	Cumulative contribution per product
10 000	10 000	R500 000	R50 000	R450 000	R450 000	R45	R45
20 000	10 000	R760 000	R100 000	R660 000	R210 000	R21	R33
30 000	10 000	R750 000	R150 000	R600 000	(R60 000)	(R6)	R20

- *The market price at which Unit B can purchase from an external supplier.* There is no intermediate market for Component X, so there is no such option.

The maximum transfer price is R21 per Component X.

Units A and B should negotiate a transfer price of between R10 and R21 per Component X. That price range will ensure that, if individual units of Component X are transferred from Unit A to Unit B, both units will prefer to continue with such transfers until 20 000 components have been transferred. Each Component X will be transferred at no more than R21, ensuring that Unit B will choose to purchase 20 000 components. The maximum price of R21 prevents Unit B from ceasing orders after the first 10 000 transfers have been received.

However, a situation could arise where the two units enter into a contract in which they agree in advance to transfer 20 000 components. This increases the maximum transfer price. Now, instead of considering Unit B's incremental contribution per Product Y in formulating the maximum price, the correct value to consider is Unit B's cumulative contribution per Product Y. At a sales level of 20 000, Unit B's cumulative contribution is R33 per component (R660 000/20 000). The maximum is higher in case of a contracted transfer of 20 000 components, because the contribution is evenly spread over the components. A transfer price of between R200 000 (R10 × 20 000) and R660 000 is appropriate for a contracted transfer (in case of such a transfer, the consultant's suggested R22 per component transfer price falls within the goal-congruent range – the consultant may have been working on this assumption).

Range of transfer prices

Assume that any number of individual components can be transferred at a time, and that a transfer price of R20 is negotiated (which falls within the goal-congruent R10 to R21 range). Unit A will choose to transfer as many of Component X as possible to increase its own contribution. Unit B, however, will order 20 000 components and thereby ensure that the company's best interests are served. This is because Unit B will earn a contribution of R260 000 ([R38 – R20 – R5] × 20 000) at a sales level of 20 000, compared to a contribution of R250 000 ([R50 – R20 – R5] × 10 000) at a level of 10 000 and R0 ([R25 – R20 – R5] × 30 000) at a level of 30 000.

The following proves that the transfer price range divides the contribution earned by the company between the two units:

Company contribution with optimal transfer level of 20 000 units (see company schedule)	R460 000
Contribution divided between Units A and B: R660 000 – (R10 × 20 000)	R460 000

Appendix example 15.2

Transferring unit has an imperfect intermediate market, and receiving unit sells on a perfect market

Unit A of a company manufactures Component S, which is transferred to Unit B where it is used to manufacture Product T. Unit B sells the final product, Product T, on a perfect market at a selling price of R160 (the perfect market is illustrated by the fact that there is only one price per unit, regardless of the number sold). One Component S is used in the manufacture of each Product T. Unit A can produce a maximum of 15 000 components per month. Unit A incurs variable costs of R55 per Component S. Unit B incurs variable costs of R90 per Product T. Unit A can also sell Component S as follows:

Selling price of Component S	Quantity sold in units per month
R116	5 000
R86	10 000
R73	15 000

Required:
Suggest an appropriate range of transfer prices for Component S.

Step 1: Establish the level of internal transfers and the level of external sales that will result in the best outcome for the organisation as a whole.

Unit A will attempt to maximise the profit gained from external sales.

Quantity S	Incremental quantity	Revenue from external sales	Cost for Unit A (R55 per unit)	Contribution for Unit A
5 000	5 000	R580 000	R275 000	R305 000
10 000	5 000	R860 000	R550 000	R310 000
15 000	5 000	R1 095 000	R825 000	R270 000

Unit A maximises its contribution if it sells 10 000 of Component S externally. Unit A will therefore be willing to transfer the remaining 5 000 components it can manufacture at any transfer price above incremental cost, because there is no opportunity cost associated with the components that Unit A does not wish to sell externally. Unit B sells Product T on a perfect market, and will prefer to sell as many of them as possible in order to maximise its contribution.

The outlook for the company as a whole is as follows:

Quantity S sold externally	Quantity T sold	Revenue from selling S	Revenue from selling T	Cost for Unit A (R55 p/u)	Cost for Unit B (R90 p/u)	Contribution for the company
0	15 000	R0	R2 400 000	R825 000	R1 350 000	R225 000
5 000	10 000	R580 000	R1 600 000	R825 000	R900 000	R455 000
10 000	5 000	R860 000	R800 000	R825 000	R450 000	R385 000
15 000	0	R1 095 000	R0	R825 000	R0	R270 000

505

principles of management accounting

The company's contribution is maximised when Unit A sells 5 000 of Component S externally, transfers 10 000 components to Unit B, and Unit B sells 10 000 of Product T. Unit A therefore has to be convinced to transfer 10 000 components per month to Unit B, instead of selling 10 000 externally and transferring just 5 000. However, for Unit A to be willing to transfer an additional 5 000 components per month, Unit B will have to compensate Unit A for the contribution lost (in other words, for the opportunity cost of transferring the components instead of selling them externally).

Step 2: Determine the minimum and the maximum transfer prices that will result in autonomous units choosing to operate at the level determined in step 1.

The minimum transfer price is:
- Unit A's incremental cost. In this example, incremental cost equals variable cost, and amounts to R55 per Component S.
- Plus Unit A's opportunity cost. For 5 000 of the components there is no incremental revenue lost, as Unit A would not have chosen to sell them externally. For the other 5 000 of the components contribution from external sales is lost, namely the difference in Unit A's contribution between when it sells 10 000 components externally, and when it sells only 5 000 components externally. The contribution forgone per component (see the schedule for Unit A) is R5 000 (R310 000 – R305 000) divided by the incremental quantity of 5 000, therefore R1.

The minimum transfer price for 5 000 of the components is R55, while the minimum price for the other 5 000 components is R56 (R55 + R1) per Component S.

The maximum transfer price is the lesser of:
- Unit B's incremental contribution (before subtracting the transfer price). See the schedule below. At the optimal sales level of 10 000 products, the incremental contribution per Product T is R70.

Quantity T	Incremental quantity	Revenue	Cost for Unit B (R90 per unit)	Contribution for Unit B	Incremental contribution	Incremental contribution per product	Cumulative contribution per product
5 000	5 000	R800 000	R450 000	R350 000	R350 000	R70	R70
10 000	5 000	R1 600 000	R900 000	R700 000	R350 000	R70	R70
15 000	5 000	R2 400 000	R1 350 000	R1 050 000	R350 000	R70	R70

- The market price at which Unit B can purchase from an external supplier. Considering Unit A's market information, the market price could range from R73 to R116 per Component S. However, because the market is imperfect, it is difficult to predict the price that an external supplier would quote in the absence of further information.

The maximum transfer price for the 10 000 components is R70 each.

This means that 5 000 components should be transferred at a price of between R55 and R70 each. The remaining 5 000 components should be transferred at a price of between R56 and R70 each.

Chapter 15 Transfer pricing

If the parties enter into a contract for the transfer of 10 000 components, Unit B's cumulative contribution per Product T has to be considered. At a sales level of 10 000, Unit B's cumulative contribution is R70 (see the schedule). In this example it is the same as the maximum already determined. The contract price should be between R555 000 [(R55 × 5 000) + (R56 × 5 000)] and R700 000 (R70 × 10 000).

The following proves that the transfer price range divides the contribution earned by the company between the two units:

Company contribution with optimal transfer of 10 000 units (see company schedule)	R455 000
Maximum contribution that could be earned by Unit A in the external market	(R310 000)
Contribution gained through optimal transfer arrangement	R145 000
Contribution divided between Units A and B: R700 000 – (R55 × 5 000) – (R56 × 5 000)	R145 000

Appendix example 15.3

Both units sell on imperfect markets

Unit A of a company manufactures Component G, which is transferred to Unit B, where it is used to manufacture Product H. Unit B sells the final product, Product H, on an imperfect market. One Component G is used in the manufacture of each Product H. Unit A can produce a maximum of 60 000 components per month. Unit A incurs variable costs of R9 per Component G. Unit B incurs variable costs of R36 per Product H, as well as fixed costs of R100 000 per month that are unavoidable in the short term. Unit A can also sell Component G on an imperfect intermediate market. The sales levels and corresponding external market prices for Units A and B are as follows:

Selling price of Component G	Selling price of Product H	Quantity sold in units per month
R40	R65	20 000
R29	R60	40 000
R22	R57	60 000

Required:
Suggest an appropriate range of transfer prices for Component G.

Step 1: Establish the level of internal transfers and the level of external sales that will result in the best outcome for the organisation as a whole.

Unit A will attempt to maximise the profit gained from external sales.

Quantity G	Incremental quantity	Revenue from external sales	Cost for Unit A (R9 per unit)	Contribution for Unit A
20 000	20 000	R800 000	R180 000	R620 000
40 000	20 000	R1 160 000	R360 000	R800 000
60 000	20 000	R1 320 000	R540 000	R780 000

Unit A maximises its contribution if it sells 40 000 of Component G externally. Unit A will therefore be willing to transfer the remaining 20 000 components that it can

principles of management accounting

manufacture at any transfer price above incremental cost, because there is no opportunity cost associated with the components that Unit A does not wish to sell externally.

The outlook for the company as a whole is as follows:

Quantity G sold externally	Quantity H sold	Revenue from selling G	Revenue from selling H	Cost for Unit A (R9 p/u)	Cost for Unit B (R36 p/u)	Contribution for the company
0	60 000	R0	R3 420 000	R540 000	R2 160 000	R720 000
20 000	40 000	R800 000	R2 400 000	R540 000	R1 440 000	R1 220 000
40 000	20 000	R1 160 000	R1 300 000	R540 000	R720 000	R1 200 000
60 000	0	R1 320 000	R0	R540 000	R0	R780 000

The company's contribution is maximised when Unit A sells 20 000 of Component G externally, transfers 40 000 components to Unit B, and Unit B sells 40 000 of Product H. Unit A therefore has to be convinced to transfer 40 000 components per month to Unit B, instead of transferring just 20 000. However, for Unit A to be willing to transfer an additional 20 000 components per month, Unit B will have to compensate Unit A for the contribution lost (in other words, for the opportunity cost of transferring the components instead of selling them externally).

Step 2: Determine the minimum and the maximum transfer prices that will result in autonomous units choosing to operate at the level determined in step 1.

The minimum transfer price is:
- Unit A's incremental cost. In this example incremental cost equals variable cost, and amounts to R9 per Component G.
- Plus Unit A's opportunity cost. For 20 000 of the components there is no incremental revenue, as Unit A would not have chosen to sell them externally. For the other 20 000 of the components, contribution from external sales is lost, namely the difference between Unit A's contribution when it sells 40 000 components externally, and when it sells 20 000 components externally. The contribution forgone per component (see the schedule for Unit A) is R180 000 (R800 000 – R620 000) divided by the incremental quantity of 20 000, and is therefore R9.

The minimum transfer price for 20 000 of the components is R9, while the minimum price for the other 20 000 components is R18 (R9 + R9) per Component G.

The maximum transfer price is the lesser of:
- Unit B's incremental contribution (before subtracting the transfer price). See the schedule below. At the optimal sales level of 40 000 products, the incremental contribution per Product H is R19.

Quantity H	Incremental quantity	Revenue	Cost for Unit B (R36 p/u)	Contribution for Unit B	Incremental contribution	Incremental contribution per product	Cumulative contribution per product
20 000	20 000	R1 300 000	R720 000	R580 000	R580 000	R29	R29
40 000	20 000	R2 400 000	R1 440 000	R960 000	R380 000	R19	R24
60 000	20 000	R3 420 000	R2 160 000	R1 260 000	R300 000	R15	R21

- The market price at which Unit B can purchase from an external supplier. Considering Unit A's market information, the market price could range from R22 to R40 per Component G. However, because the market is imperfect, it is difficult to predict the price that an external supplier would quote in the absence of further information.

The maximum transfer price for the 40 000 components is R19. This means that 20 000 components should be transferred at a price of between R9 and R19 each. The remaining 20 000 components should be transferred at a price of between R18 and R19.

If the parties enter into a contract for the transfer of 40 000 components, Unit B's *cumulative* contribution per Product H has to be considered. At a sales level of 40 000, Unit B's cumulative contribution is R24 per component (see the schedule). A transfer price of between R540 000 ((R9 × 20 000) + (R18 × 20 000)) and R960 000 (R24 × 40 000) is appropriate for a contracted transfer.

The following proves that the transfer price range divides the contribution earned by the company between the two units:

Company contribution with optimal transfer level of 40 000 units (see company schedule)	R1 220 000
Maximum contribution that could be earned by Unit A in the external market	(R800 000)
Contribution gained through optimal transfer arrangement	R420 000
Contribution divided between Units A and B: R960 000 − (R9 × 20 000) − (R18 × 20 000)	R420 000

Basic questions

BQ 1

The baking division of the Pie Company bakes ready-to-eat pies for distribution to the Pie Company's 25 retail outlets. The retail outlets charge R8 per pie sold, and incur variable costs of R1 per pie. It costs the baking division R4 (variable costs) to bake each pie. The manager of the baking division and those of the retail outlets all have vast decision-making responsibilities within their units, but pies may not be sold to or purchased from external suppliers. The units are not separate legal entities. Is there a need for transfer pricing within the Pie Company? What transfer price should be used (a) for transfers between units; (b) in the statutory, audited income statement of the Pie Company?

BQ 2

What are the merits and demerits of negotiation between unit managers as a means of arriving at a transfer price?

BQ 3

Every year Unit A of a company transfers 5 per cent of its output to Unit B of the same company. Five years ago the two unit managers negotiated a formula to arrive at a transfer price which they both regarded as fair, and every year since then they have merely substituted the formula inputs with the latest available information. A consultant recently investigated the transfer price and found that, although the price is goal congruent, there was room for improving the formula. Should the consultant be appointed to carry out a more thorough investigation, the classification of fixed and variable costs could possibly be revised and improved, and this might result in a slightly different and more accurate transfer price. Should a thorough investigation of the transfer price be requested?

BQ 4

The farming division of AgriFarms is located in the Eastern Cape and produces eggs, which are transferred to AgriFarms' marketing division. The marketing division packages the eggs in attractive packaging and sells them to upmarket retail outlets in Gauteng. The eggs are all 'jumbo' size, and divisional managers are free to transact with external parties as they please. Would market price be an appropriate transfer price for the transfer of eggs from the farming division to the marketing division?

BQ 5

Division One of a company transfers manufactured components to Division Two of the same company. Division Two pays Division One the incremental cost per unit, plus a fixed fee of R20 000 per year for the usage of Division One's capacity. Division One incurs an incremental cost of R10 on each unit that it manufactures. In the year 2XX3 Division One transferred a total of 10 000 components to Division Two. What was the total transfer price (expressed as a price per unit) in 2XX3?

BQ 6

Division A and Division B are highly decentralised units of Company C. Division A incurs an incremental cost of R12 per unit manufactured. Some of Division A's manufactured units are transferred to Division B. Division B can purchase products that are almost identical to the ones manufactured by Division A at a cost of R14 per unit in the open market. One of Company C's financial managers recently made the following remark: 'It is company policy to place a mark-up of 20% of incremental cost on all products sold. I don't see why this should not also apply to transfers from Division A to Division B.' Assuming that it is in the best interest of the company as a whole that the internal transfers should take place, do you agree with the financial manager? If not, what transfer price would you suggest?

BQ 7

What is meant by a 'range of goal-congruent transfer prices'?

BQ 8

Liquichem has a division that manufactures a chemical powder and transfers it to another division of Liquichem, where a liquid chemical is manufactured. The powder costs R200 per gram to manufacture (all variable costs), and 25 grams of powder is required per 100 millilitres of liquid chemical. The liquid costs R300 per 100 millilitres to manufacture (all variable costs). The powder can be sold to another company at R220 per gram. There is also a third party manufacturer that can supply Liquichem with powder at a cost of R230 per gram, but the properties of the powder are such that only 20 grams of powder are required per 100 millilitres of liquid chemical. Should powder be internally transferred and, if so, what would be an appropriate transfer price?

BQ 9

Unit A of a company transfers products to Unit B of the same company. The optimal transfer price is between R50 and R100 per unit, and the optimal production plan is for Unit A to transfer 100 000 units of the product to Unit B every month. Unit A manufactures 200 000 units per month, its variable costs are R50 per unit, and it incurs fixed costs (in the nature of product- and facility-sustaining costs) of R800 000 per month. Unit B's variable costs are also R50 per product received from Unit A. The managers of Unit A and Unit B have reached a deadlock in their negotiations to decide on a final transfer price. How may the transfer pricing dispute be resolved?

BQ 10

A company's manufacturing division is located in South Africa, while its sales division is located in Asia. The manufacturing division transfers 100 000 units of product to the sales division each year. The manufacturing division incurs variable costs of R15 per unit. The sales division incurs variable costs of R5 per unit, and sells the product at R30 per unit.

a) What is the most appropriate transfer price per unit for transfers from the manufacturing division to the sales division under each of the following circumstances? For purposes of part (a), regard the income tax rate as the only relevant tax issue:
   i) The tax rate in South Africa is 28 per cent and in the relevant Asian country it is 15 per cent.
   ii) The tax rate in South Africa is 28 per cent and in the relevant Asian country it is 35 per cent.
b) What other tax considerations, apart from the income tax rate, should be taken into account in setting the transfer price?

Long questions

LQ 1 – Intermediate (12 marks; 22 minutes)

Source: Adapted from ACCA P5

The Better Agriculture Group (BAG), which has a divisional structure, produces a range of products for the farming industry. Divisions B and C are two of its divisions. Division B sells a fertiliser product (BF) to customers external to BAG. Division C produces a chemical (CC) which it could transfer to Division B for use in the manufacture of its product BF. However, Division C could also sell some of its output of chemical CC to external customers of BAG.

An independent external supplier to The Better Agriculture Group has offered to supply Division B with a chemical which is equivalent to component CC. The independent supplier has a maximum spare capacity of 60 000 kilograms of the chemical which it is willing to make available (in total or in part) to Division B at a special price of R55 per kilogram.

Forecast information for the forthcoming period is as follows:

Division B:
- Production and sales of 360 000 litres of BF at a selling price of R120 per litre. Variable conversion costs of BF will amount to R15 per litre.
- Fixed costs are estimated at R18 000 000.
- Chemical (CC) is used at the rate of 1 kilogram of CC per 4 litres of product BF.

principles of management accounting

Division C:
- Total production capacity of 100 000 kilograms of chemical CC. Variable costs will be R50 per kilogram of CC.
- Fixed costs are estimated at R2 000 000.

Market research suggests that external customers of BAG are willing to take up sales of 40 000 kilograms of CC at a price of R105 per kilogram. The remaining 60 000 kilograms of CC could be transferred to Division B for use in product BF. Currently no other market external to BAG is available for the 60 000 kilograms of CC.

	REQUIRED	Marks
(a)	State the price/prices per kilogram at which Division C should offer to transfer chemical CC to Division B in order that the maximisation of BAG profit would occur if Division B management implement rational sourcing decisions based on purely financial grounds.	6
(b)	Division C is considering a decision to lower its selling price to customers external to the group to R95 per kilogram. If implemented, this decision is expected to increase sales to external customers to 70 000 kilograms. For *both* the current selling price of CC of R105 per kilogram and the proposed selling price of R95 per kilogram, prepare a detailed analysis of revenue, costs and profits or loss of BAG. (*Note:* In addition, comment on other considerations that should be taken into account before this selling price change is implemented.)	6
	TOTAL MARKS	**12**

LQ 2 – Intermediate (18 marks; 32 minutes)

Source: Adapted from CIMA P1

The G Group has a divisionalised structure. One of the divisions manufactures engines and one of the other divisions assembles motor cycles. The performance of the divisional managers, and consequently their bonuses, is based on the return on capital employed (ROCE) of their individual divisions. Both of these divisions operate in highly competitive markets.

Motor cycle division

A key component in a motor cycle is the engine. Engines are readily available on the open market but the division currently buys 3 600 engines each year internally from the Engines division for R1 375 per engine. The manager has just received the following message from the Manager of the Engines division.

Engine prices: As a result of recent cost increases, the price per engine will now be R1 600.

On receiving the message, the manager of the Motor cycle division contacted several external manufacturers and found one that would supply the required engines at R1 375 per engine. However she has since received a directive from the managing director of the Group that states that she must buy the engines internally.

Engines division

Following the recent cost increases, the full absorption cost of a motor cycle engine is R1 450. This includes R400 for fixed production overheads. This type of motor cycle engine is one of many different engines produced by the division.

The manager of the Engines division is aware of the competitive external market that he faces and knows that it will be difficult for him to charge external customers more than R1 375 per engine. However, he is also aware that the rising costs will have an impact on his bonus. He is trying to protect his bonus by passing these costs on to the Motorcycle division. He is keen to make as much profit as he can from these internal sales because the division is currently working below capacity.

The Engines division has now developed a new 'lean burn' car engine that is sold exclusively to external customers. The production of this engine will utilise the spare capacity of the division and will earn the division a contribution of R40 per machine hour. The demand is so high for the car engines that their production could also use 9 000 machine hours that are currently used to make 1 000 of the motorcycle engines which are transferred to the motor cycle division.

REQUIRED		Marks
(a)	Calculate the impact on the annual profits of each of the two divisions and the G Group as a whole of the directive that the engines must be purchased internally for R1 600 per engine instead of from the external supplier.	6
(b)	Explain, with supporting calculations, the minimum and maximum transfer prices that could now be charged for the motorcycle engines.	7
(c)	Briefly explain three aims of a transfer pricing system.	5
TOTAL MARKS		18

LQ 3 – Advanced (25 marks; 45 minutes)

Source: Adapted from CIMA P2 Pilot paper

DEF is a trading company that is divided into three divisions: D, E and F. Each division maintains its own accounting records and prepares an annual summary of its results. These performance summaries are shown below for the year ended 30 September 2XX9.

Division	D	E	F
	R'000	R'000	R'000
Sales (net of returns)	150	200	400
Variable production costs	50	70	230
Fixed production costs	60	50	80
Administration costs	30	25	40
Profit	10	55	50
Capital employed	400	550	415

The following additional information is available:
i) Divisions are free to trade with each other without any interference from Head Office. The managers of the respective divisions negotiate transfer prices between themselves. During the year and included in the above costs and revenues are the following transactions:
  • Division D sold goods for R20 000 to Division E. The price negotiated was agreed on a unit basis between the managers of the two divisions. The variable production cost of these items in Division D was R18 000. Division D was operating under capacity and agreed to a transfer price that was little more than its own variable cost.
  • Division F sold goods for R15 000 to Division E. The price negotiated was agreed on a unit basis between the managers of the two divisions.

principles of management accounting

The variable production cost of these items in Division F was R9 000. Division F was operating under capacity and negotiated a transfer price based on its total production cost.

ii) Included in the administration costs for each division are the following management charges from Head Office:

    D: R10 000   E: R8 000   F: R15 000

iii) At the start of each year Head Office sets each division a target return on capital employed. The target depends on their nature of the work and their industry sector. For the year ended 30 September 2XX9 these targets were:

    D: 6%   E: 3%   F: 15%

REQUIRED		Marks
(a)	Discuss the shortcomings of the above performance summaries when measuring the performance of each division.	5
(b)	Discuss the potential problems of negotiated transfer pricing, and how these have impacted on the performance of each of Divisions D, E, and F for the year ended 30 September 2XX9.	6
(c)	Prepare an alternative statement that is more useful for measuring and reporting the performance of Divisions D, E, and F.	8
(d)	Discuss how the use of 'dual' transfer prices could affect the measurement of divisional performance within DEF. Illustrate your answer with suggested dual prices.	6
TOTAL MARKS		**25**

LQ 4 – Advanced (30 marks; 54 minutes)

Source: Adapted from CIMA P1

A multi-national sports equipment manufacturer has a number of autonomous divisions throughout the world. Two of the divisions are in America, one on the west coast and one on the east coast. The west coast division manufactures cycle frames and assembles them into complete cycles using bought-in components. The east coast division produces wheels that are very similar to the wheel sets that are used by the Frames Division but it currently sells them only to external customers. Details of the two divisions are given below.

Frames division (west coast)

The Frames division buys the wheels that it needs from a local supplier. It has negotiated a price of R870 per set (there are two wheels in a set). This price includes a bulk purchase discount which is awarded if the division purchases 15 000 sets per year. The production budget shows that 15 000 sets will be needed next year.

Wheels division (east coast)

The Wheels division has a capacity of 35 000 sets per year. Details of the budget for the forthcoming year are as follows:

Sales	30 sets	
Per set		R
Selling price		950
Variable costs		650

The fixed costs of the division at the budgeted output of 30 000 sets are R8m per year but they would rise to R9m if output exceeded 31 000 sets.

Note: The maximum external demand is 30 000 sets per year and there are no other uses for the current spare capacity.

Group directive

The managing director of the group has reviewed the budgets of the divisions and has decided that in order to improve the profitability of the group the Wheels division should supply wheel sets to the Frames division. She is also thinking of linking the salaries of the divisional managers to the performance of their divisions but is unsure which performance measure to use. Two measures that she is considering are 'profit' and the 'return on assets consumed' (where the annual fixed costs would be used as the 'assets consumed').

The manager of the Wheels division has offered to supply wheel sets to the Frames division at a price of R900 per set. He has offered this price because it would earn the same contribution per set that is earned on external sales (this is after adjusting for distribution and packaging costs).

REQUIRED		Marks
(a)	Assume that the 15 000 wheel sets are supplied by the Wheels division at a transfer price of R900 per set. Calculate the impact on the profits of each of the divisions and the group.	5
(b)	Calculate the minimum price at which the manager of the Wheels division would be willing to transfer the 15 000 sets to the Frames division if his performance is to be measured against maintaining: (i) The profit of the division (currently R1m) (ii) The return on assets consumed by the division (currently 12,5%).	9
(c)	Produce a report to the managing director of the group that: (i) Explains the problems that may arise from the directive and the introduction of performance measures (ii) Explains how the problems could be resolved. (*Note:* You should use your answers to parts (a) and (b) and other relevant calculations, where appropriate, to illustrate points in your report.)	10 6
TOTAL MARKS		**30**

LQ 5 – Advanced (20 marks; 36 minutes)

Source: Adapted from ACCA P5

You are the management accountant of the SSA Group which manufactures an innovative range of products to provide support for injuries to various joints in the body. The group has adopted a divisional structure. Each division is encouraged to maximise its reported profit.

Division A, which is based in a country called Nearland, manufactures joint-support appliances which incorporate a one-size-fits-all-people feature. A different appliance is manufactured for each of knee, ankle, elbow and wrist joints. Budget information in respect of Division A for the year ended 31 December 20X0 is as follows:

principles of management accounting

	Support appliance			
	Knee	Ankle	Elbow	Wrist
Sales units (000s)	20	50	20	60
Selling price per unit (R)	24	15	18	9
Total variable cost of sales (R'000)	200	350	160	240

Each of the four support products uses the same quantity of manufacturing capacity. This gives Division A management the flexibility to alter the product mix as desired. During the year to 31 December 20X0 it is estimated that a maximum of 160 000 support products could be manufactured.

The following information relates to Division B which is also part of the SSA group and is based in Distantland:
i) Division B purchases products from various sources, including from other divisions in SSA group, for subsequent resale to customers.
ii) The management of Division B has requested two alternative quotations from Division A in respect of the year ended 31 December 20X0 as follows:
- Quotation 1 – Purchase of 10 000 ankle supports
- Quotation 2 – Purchase of 18 000 ankle supports

The management of the SSA Group has decided that a minimum of 50 000 ankle supports must be reserved for customers in Nearland in order to ensure that customer demand can be satisfied and the product's competitive position is maintained in the Nearland market.

The management of the SSA Group is willing, if necessary, to reduce the budgeted sales quantities of other types of joint support in order to satisfy the requirements of Division B for ankle supports. They wish, however, to minimise the loss of contribution to the Group.

The management of Division B is aware of another joint support product, which is produced in Distantland, that competes with the Division A version of the ankle support and which could be purchased at a local currency price that is equivalent to R9 per support. SSA Group policy is that all divisions are allowed autonomy to set transfer prices and purchase from whatever sources they choose. The management of Division A intends to use market price less 30% as the basis for each of quotations 1 and 2.

REQUIRED			Marks
(a)	(i)	The management of the SSA Group have asked you to advise them regarding the appropriateness of the decision by the management of Division A to use an adjusted market price as the basis for the preparation of each quotation and the implications of the likely sourcing decision by the management of Division B.	
		Your answer should cite relevant quantitative data and incorporate your recommendation of the prices that should be quoted by Division A for the ankle supports in respect of quotations 1 and 2 which will ensure that the profitability of SSA Group as a whole is not adversely affected by the decision of the management of Division B.	8
	(ii)	Advise the management of Divisions A and B regarding the basis of transfer pricing which should be employed in order to ensure that the profit of the SSA Group is maximised.	4

(b)	After considerable internal discussion concerning Quotation 2 by the management of SSA Group, Division A is not prepared to supply 18 000 ankle supports to Division B at any price lower than 30% below market price. All profits in Distantland are subject to taxation at a rate of 20%. Division A pays tax in Nearland at a rate of 40% on all profits.	
	Advise the management of SSA Group whether the management of Division B should be directed to purchase the ankle supports from Division A, or to purchase a similar product from a local supplier in Distantland. Supporting calculations should be provided.	8
TOTAL MARKS		**20**

References

Eaton, G. 2005. *Management accounting official terminology*. London: CIMA Publishing.

Elkington, J. 1998. *Cannibals with forks: the triple bottom line of 21st century business*. Gabriola Island, BC: New Society.

Kaplan, RS & Cooper, R. 1998. *Cost and effect: using integrated cost systems to drive profitability and performance*. Boston, MA: Harvard Business School Press.

SAICA (South African Institute of Chartered Accountants). 2009. *IAS 2 Inventories (issued January 2009)*. Johannesburg: SAICA

SAICA (South African Institute of Chartered Accountants). 2009. *IFRS 8 Operating Segments (issued January 2009)*. Johannesburg: SAICA

SAICA (South African Institute of Chartered Accountants). 2009. *IAS 16 Property, plant and equipment (issued January 2009)*. Johannesburg: SAICA

SAICA (South African Institute of Chartered Accountants). 2010. *IAS 24 Related party disclosures (issued January 2010)*. Johannesburg: SAICA

SAPPI. 2010. *Divisional overview*. [Online]. Available: <http://www.sappi.com/SappiWeb/About+Sappi/Divisional+overview/Divisional+overview.htm> [5 July 2010].

SASOL. 2009. *Positive actions – annual review and summarized financial information 2009*. Johannesburg: Sasol.

Contemporary management accounting concepts

chapter 16

Richard Chivaka and Shelley-Anne Roos

LEARNING OBJECTIVES

By the end of this chapter, you should be able to:
1. Define and discuss the Theory of Constraints.
2. Explain and apply the steps outlined in the Theory of Constraints.
3. Explain how the Theory of Constraints differs from and complements activity-based costing in product-profitability decisions.
4. Explain materials requirement planning and enterprise resource planning.
5. Explain how a just-in-time system operates.
6. Explain the concept of benchmarking.

> **Skills shortages in the tool, die and mould-making industry**
>
> By 2010, South Africa was experiencing a critical shortage of technically skilled people in the tool, die and mould-making sector, which negatively impacted South African manufacturing companies' performance and their global competitiveness. *Tool, die and mould-making* is the process of equipment manufacture that aids in the conversion of raw materials (such as hard metals, aluminium and plastics) into a shape. According to the industry, there were too few professionals in this industry specialising in production, engineering and design to meet the needs of South African manufacturers. In response, the industry launched the National Tooling Initiative Programme, an apprenticeship programme for aspiring tool, die and mould makers.
>
> Source: Skillsportal 2011

Manufacturers – such as the manufacturers affected by the shortage of skills in the tool, die and mould-making (TDM) industry sometimes experience short-term constraints which prevent them from producing enough inventory to meet market demand. The Theory of Constraints (TOC) helps organisations to deal with the short-term problem by maximising the throughput of the constrained resource. This means, among other things, that some product lines are given preference over others in order to best utilise the scarce resource. TOC then leads the organisation to search for long-term solutions (as manufacturing organisations affected by the TDM skills shortage collectively did by establishing the apprenticeship programme) to alleviate the constraint. The theory stipulates that the organisation should then identify and turn its attention to the next constraint.

principles of management accounting

This chapter discusses TOC, after which it gives a brief overview of the concepts of materials requirement planning and enterprise resource planning. In the final parts of the chapter, two other contemporary concepts, just-in-time and benchmarking, are discussed.

16.1 Introduction

In the face of globalisation, advances in technology, and increasingly discerning customers, among other factors, organisations these days have to modernise the production and information assimilation techniques they have traditionally applied. We start our discussion with the Theory of Constraints.

> **A note about this chapter:**
> The concepts in this chapter were originally developed in a manufacturing environment, and are therefore best understood when explained in the context of a factory. Once you understand the concepts, you may wish to consider how these concepts, in adapted form, could benefit other organisations, including those in the services sector.

16.2 Theory of Constraints

Key term: bottlenecks, Theory of Constraints

The **Theory of Constraints** holds that a system's achievements are limited by a small number of constraints, and that there is always at least one constraint. It focuses on factors such as **bottlenecks**, which act as constraints to the maximisation of the throughput from the system.

The Theory of Constraints originated from the work done by Goldratt, which started in the 1970s. He was interested in rectifying scheduling problems after realising that there were shortcomings in the materials requirement planning (MRP) technique which assumed that production capacity in a factory was either available or could easily be created (MRP is explained later in this chapter). Such an assumption was not valid in practice as a result of so-called bottlenecks in the production system.

A bottleneck is an activity in the production process where a constraint is experienced. The example below is used to illustrate the concept.

Example 16.1

There are two activities in a factory: manufacturing and assembly. The manufacturing staff are able to manufacture 100 units of the product per day, but owing to a skills shortage, only two assemblers work in the factory at any given time. The assemblers are able to assemble only 50 units per day. The market demand for the product is 200 units per day.

Required:
Identify the bottleneck activity and calculate how many units of the product the factory can produce per day.

In this example, assembly is experiencing the most critical capacity constraint, and it is therefore the factory's bottleneck activity. Notice that irrespective of how hard the manufacturing staff work, the factory is not able to produce more than 50 units per day because the units have to pass through the bottleneck activity (assembly) *after* they have been manufactured. We can generalise that the output of other activities that occur in a process (manufacturing in this example) is limited to the number of units that can be processed by the bottleneck activity.

Because in practice factories deal with limited production capacities, it is important to focus on the management of bottlenecks. In the example above, management would have to focus their attention on assembly if they wanted to increase the factory's daily production output.

16.2.1 Constraints

> **Key terms:** external constraints, internal constraints, inventory, operating expenses, throughput, throughput accounting, throughput ratio

In later work, Goldratt broadened the scope of his work from focusing on production bottlenecks only, to studying any factor that limits the ability of a system to perform in line with the goal of the organisation. Such a factor is referred to as a 'constraint'. Goldratt called the theory he devised in order to address these constraints the 'Theory of Constraints'.

Constraints can be either internal or external. **Internal constraints** arise from the internal operations of an organisation, such as insufficient staff training, or inadequate machine capacity. **External constraints** arise from the environment within which an organisation operates and on which it relies in order to achieve its goals. Examples of external constraints would be insufficient supply of inputs and lack of customer orders. In order to achieve improved profitability, it is important for a factory to manage the constraints as a way of enhancing throughput, while at the same time keeping inventory and operating expenses to the minimum. The three terms 'throughput', 'inventory' and 'operating expenses' as used here have very specific meanings in the context of the Theory of Constraints, and are discussed below.

Throughput is the rate at which money is generated. To calculate throughput, we deduct the money paid to suppliers (for direct materials and direct services) from the money obtained from customers (in the form of sales). Notice that labour expenses are not deducted from sales when throughput is calculated.

While throughput should be maximised, every attempt should be made to minimise inventory and operating expenses.

Inventory, for the purposes of the Theory of Constraints, is the sum of direct materials inventory, work-in-progress inventory, finished goods inventory (all of which are valued only at the amount paid to suppliers in respect thereof), research and development cost, plant and machinery, and buildings. **Operating expenses** in this context include all operating costs (other than direct materials and direct services) incurred to generate throughput. They include labour costs, whether direct or indirect, and both idle time and operating time. They also include expenses such as rent, electricity and depreciation.

The management accounting technique that focuses on achieving the maximum return per unit of constrained activity is called **throughput accounting**.

One of the main ratios calculated when throughput accounting is applied is the **throughput ratio**. It is calculated as the throughput per unit of constrained activity, divided by the operating expenses per unit of constrained activity. In example 16.1 above, the constrained activity would be assembly hours. If more than one product were manufactured, the throughput ratio for each product could be calculated and the products could be ranked accordingly.

principles of management accounting

> ### Example 16.2
> The same information applies as in example 16.1. The factory manufactures two products, A and B. It takes 16,8 minutes to assemble each unit. Product A sells for R500 per unit and its direct materials cost R400 per unit. Product B sells for R450 per unit and its direct materials cost R300 per unit, while it also consumes direct services of R70 per unit. Each day the factory as a whole spends R1 000 on wages and R800 on overheads.
>
> **Required:**
> Determine whether the production of Product A or Product B should be favoured, using a throughput accounting approach.

Product A's throughput is R100 (R500 – R400), while Product B's throughput is R80 (R450 – R300 – R70). Throughput per assembly minute is therefore R5,95 (R100/16,8 minutes) for Product A and R4,76 (R80/16,8 minutes) for Product B.

Operational expenses per day of R1 800 (R1 000 + R800) divided by the total assembly minutes available per day of 840 (16,8 minutes × 50 units, given in example 16.1) gives a cost per assembly minute of R2,14.

The throughput ratio for Product A is 2,78 (R5,95/R2,14), and it is 2,22 (R4,76 / R2,14) for Product B. Product A should therefore be favoured over Product B, as it has a higher throughput ratio. Notice that both ratios are greater than one, which means the factory is gaining money by producing the products (the revenue earned per unit of constrained activity is proportionately greater than the cost per unit of constrained activity).

The product ranking obtained when throughput accounting is applied, could potentially differ from that obtained if variable costing is used (refer to Chapter 5, *Absorption versus variable costing*). This is because costs are classified differently under the two approaches: variable costing would deduct all manufacturing variable costs from sales to obtain the contribution, and the ranking would then be made according to the highest contribution per limiting factor (as explained in Chapter 11, *Decision-making under operational constraints*).

16.2.2 Steps in the Theory of Constraints

> **Key term:** drum-buffer-rope

The Theory of Constraints argues that managers should focus their attention on the management of constraints within the factory's system, rather than on cutting costs. Focusing on the constraint enables the factory to streamline its operations and make it more efficient.

The Theory of Constraints lists a series of chronological steps that should be followed. The steps are designed with the objective of maximising throughput for the entire factory, and are as follows:

Figure 16.1 Series of steps in implementing TOC

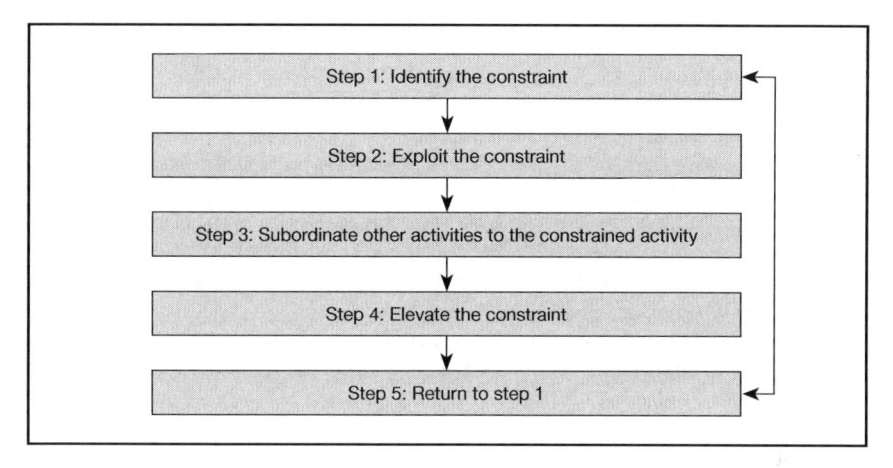

```
Step 1: Identify the constraint
          ↓
Step 2: Exploit the constraint
          ↓
Step 3: Subordinate other activities to the constrained activity
          ↓
Step 4: Elevate the constraint
          ↓
Step 5: Return to step 1
```

Step 1: Identify the constraint

We have defined a constraint as any factor that limits the ability of a system to perform in line with the goal of the organisation. The Theory of Constraints identifies and resolves one constraint at a time.

In a profit-driven organisation, one of the principal goals is usually to maximise profit. In a factory we may assume that this profit motive will translate into a desire to produce sufficient output to meet market demand. In example 16.1 above, we have identified the assembly activity as the constraint that needs to be addressed first – it is presently the most serious inhibiting factor that is preventing the factory from meeting the demand for its products.

In practice, the identification of constraints can be done in a number of ways. In a manufacturing environment the identification of an internal constraint can involve the detection of the accumulation of work-in-progress inventories. A constrained activity in a production line may cause work-in-progress to accumulate in front of it. This indicates to managers that there is a constraint impacting negatively on throughput. The identification of an internal constraint can also be achieved by the comparison of the resource needs against the availability of those resources. In this case managers compare, for example, the hours available for each class of labour with the hours required for each class of labour. The same can be done for resources such as machine capacity and storage. In the case of external constraints, managers investigate both the supply side as well as the demand side to identify constraints. On the supply side, managers can compare the required materials inputs against the inputs that suppliers are able to provide. On the demand side, the market intake of the products being produced (as indicated by customer orders) provides the parameters that govern the extent to which other resources should be committed in the system.

Step 2: Exploit the constraint

The next step is to make sure that the constraint is 'exploited' to the full by operating at maximum capacity. In other words, the aim is to ensure that the maximum throughput is gained per unit of constraint. Because of its limited capabilities that are inhibiting the throughput of the factory as a whole, the organisation cannot afford any sub-optimal performance in the constrained activity.

A constraint can, for example, be used to its maximum capacity by ensuring that inputs are inspected *before* being processed through the activity to make sure that the capacity of the limited resource is not wasted in processing defective inputs. In addition, inventory 'buffers' (extra units that are ready to go through the activity) can be located ahead of the constrained activity to ensure that it is never starved of work. Where multiple products are manufactured, the product mix can be altered in order to ensure that the product that provides the highest throughput per unit of constrained activity is favoured.

The constraint in examples 16.1 and 16.2 in this chapter is the bottleneck experienced at the assembly activity. In step 2 the aim should be to maximise the throughput per assembly labour hour. Based on the ideas above, management could do the following:

- *Insert an inspection point* before the assembly activity, where units can be inspected to ensure that no time is wasted in processing faulty units.
- *Keep buffer inventory:* A number of units that have already been manufactured may be placed in the assembly area to make sure assemblers are never idle while they wait for units to be manufactured. Note, however, that because the manufacturing activity can work at much greater speed than the assembly activity, manufactured units are likely to pile up here in great numbers awaiting assembly. This should be avoided by slowing down the rate at which the manufacturing staff work (see step 3 below). Only a small buffer inventory should be kept.
- *The product mix* can be altered as was illustrated in example 16.2.

Step 3: Subordinate other activities to the constrained activity

To harmonise the system and to avoid producing excess inventory, the management of the constrained activity should be coupled with the management of the non-constrained activities. It is important that the factory should not create excess work-in-progress inventory by allowing the non-constrained activities to produce more units than the constraint can process. In other words, all activities that are not in short supply should be aligned with the activity that is in short supply. This ensures that costs are reduced (particularly those related to inventory), as resources are not 'stockpiled' but are drawn into the system in synch with the constrained activity.

Refer again to example 16.1. The manufacturing activity should not be allowed to produce 100 units per day, as the assembly activity can process only 50 units per day. If the manufacturing activity continues to produce 100 units per day this does not increase the output of the factory – instead, it results in piles of work-in-progress inventory that ties up valuable funds, takes up space on the factory floor, may need to be moved around and stored at extra cost, has to be covered by insurance, and (depending on the nature of the product) may spoil, be damaged or become obsolete with age. The manufacturing activity should produce only 50 units per day until the constraint in the assembly activity has been removed. There should, however, be a small number of manufactured units in need of assembly (work-in-progress units) that are kept as buffer inventory to make sure the assembly activity never runs out of work (see step 2 above).

Note that, in order for other activities to be subordinated, the performance measures that are traditionally used to measure the results of those activities should also be subordinated to the performance measures of the Theory of Constraints. For example, in the factory in example 16.1, management cannot continue to measure the efficiency of workers in the manufacturing activity in the same way that they did before. These workers will now be required to produce fewer units per day and should not be penalised for it.

Step 3 comes with its own set of terminology. The tool that is used to subordinate activities for the purposes of the Theory of Constraints is called **drum-buffer-rope** (DBR). The constrained activity is referred to as the 'drum' – it dictates the 'beat' to which all the other activities should perform. The 'buffer' is the work-in-progress inventory units that are kept on hand and act as a buffer to the drum to protect the constrained activity from running out of work. The buffer is measured in terms of time rather than physical units (in other words, X minutes' worth of inventory is kept as a buffer). The activities before the constrained activity are called the 'rope'. They pull units towards the constrained activity when required, and the rope is slack when units are not required.

In example 16.1 the assembly activity is the drum, the work-in-progress product units kept on hand to keep the assembly unit busy are the buffer, and the manufacturing activity is the rope.

Step 4: Elevate the constraint

The steps that have been taken so far have helped to address the immediate short-term problem of dealing with the constraint. In the long term, however, the factory does not merely have to accept the existence of the constraint. It can take active steps to remove or 'elevate' the constraint. Elevating the constraint means transforming the constraint into a non-constraint.

In example 16.1, management may wish to fund a training programme to equip more workers with the skills to assemble the product. Once these workers are ready to start working in the assembly activity on the factory floor, the constraint has been elevated and a longer-term solution (more comprehensive than the short-term measures taken in step 3) has been found.

Step 5: Return to step 1

Following the steps in the Theory of Constraints is a repetitive process. As soon as one constraint has been elevated, the next factor that limits the ability of the factory to perform in line with its goals is identified.

Let's assume that, for the assembly activity constraint illustrated in example 16.1, step 4 of the Theory of Constraints resulted in additional workers being trained to assemble the product and that the factory is now able to assemble 150 units per day. Next the attention will be focused on the manufacturing activity where it is presently possible to produce only 100 units per day although the market demand is 200 units per day. The steps of the Theory of Constraints are repeated – this time with the manufacturing activity as the constraint. Once this constraint has also been elevated, the assembly activity in this example will once again become a constraint, as it is now producing 150 units per day – still short of the required 200 units per day.

16.2.3 Theory of Constraints reports

Theory of Constraints reports should be produced in order to provide useful insights to management about the improvements or otherwise in the process. These reports should clearly highlight throughput margins as well as throughput margins per unit of the constraint. It places management in a position to evaluate the real benefits of the effort expended in applying the Theory of Constraints.

16.2.4 Theory of Constraints and activity-based costing

Both TOC and activity-based costing (ABC) to some extent provide information regarding the profitability of products and services. However, they have fundamental differences in terms of (1) time horizons and (2) the nature of profitability decisions.

TOC works with a very short-term horizon, because it focuses on exploiting constraints to address an immediate problem. In the long term, these constraints are elevated (step 4). The short-term horizon explains the conflict between throughput accounting and variable costing, because in the very short term, only direct materials and direct services are truly variable costs. ABC, on the other hand, takes an even longer-term perspective by accumulating almost all costs (as discussed in Chapter 6, *Overhead allocation*).

Furthermore, TOC plays a unique role in profitability decisions in that it emphasises the benefit realised from using a scarce resource in the production process. The nature of profitability decisions that TOC can support therefore involves short-term product-mix decisions based on the maximisation of throughput per unit of a constrained resource. ABC cannot be used for such decisions owing to its emphasis on accurate product costs and cost driver analysis, both of which support strategic decisions such as pricing.

Despite the differences highlighted above, TOC and ABC can be used in conjunction. TOC supports short-term profitability decisions and as such can be used to enhance the profit of an organisation in the short term. ABC, on the other hand, takes a long-term perspective and therefore supports long-term profitability decisions such as pricing and profit planning.

16.3 Materials requirement planning (MRP)

> **Key terms:** bill of materials file, inventory file, master parts file, master production schedule, materials requirement planning, pull system, push-through system

Manufacturing organisations operate in complex environments in which the ordering of materials has to be co-ordinated in such a way that disruptions to production are minimised. Usually sales are forecast, a decision is taken regarding the desired inventory levels, and then production planning and inventory control (abbreviated as PPIC) is instituted. One approach used to co-ordinate the planning and use of materials in production is known as **materials requirement planning** (MRP).

CIMA defines materials requirement planning as a 'system that converts a production schedule into a listing of the materials and components required to meet that schedule, so that adequate [inventory] levels are maintained and items are available when needed'.

The idea behind MRP is that the estimated output in a given period should determine the timing and quantity of materials that should be ordered for that period. The main objective of MRP is to achieve a planned and co-ordinated schedule of materials requirements in a given period for each item. In order to achieve this objective, the materials requirement decision takes into account (1) scheduled materials receipts, (2) projected target inventory levels and (3) materials items already allocated to production but not yet drawn from inventory (Drury 2004:1090).

An MRP system includes the preparation of:
- A **master production schedule** that details demand forecasts for the finished product
- A **bill of materials file** that details the quantity, type and quality of each of the materials required for each final product
- A **master parts file** which details all the account lead times of purchasing materials and the manufacture of components
- An **inventory file** that specifies exactly when and how many units of each of the materials should be purchased, taking into account lead times of purchasing materials and the manufacture of components.

MRP is regarded as a so-called **push-through system** because as production starts, the output of one production section is 'pushed' to the next section, regardless of whether or not the receiving section is ready for the input. This stands in contrast to the just-in-time (JIT) system (see section 16.5 below), where each workstation starts work only once the next workstation on the production line requires it to do so, and where materials are ordered only once the first workstation requires them (this is a so-called **pull system**). An important disadvantage of an MRP system is therefore that, unlike in a JIT system, inventory can accumulate in workstations which receive such inventory before they are ready to process it.

In light of the paragraph above, it may also now be clear why Goldratt's frustration with the MRP system led him to formulate the Theory of Constraints, as mentioned in the beginning of the chapter. MRP assumes that production capacity in a factory is always either available or can easily be created – therefore it simply 'pushes' inventory units through the process according to its output targets. This results in excess production by non-constrained activities and therefore excessive work-in-progress inventory (which adds no value to the organisation), rather than in increased sales.

MRP has developed from the time it was introduced in the 1960s. First, it was expanded into a system called manufacturing resource planning, often referred to as MRPII. MRPII uses the same principles, but extends their application to include the planning and scheduling of other resources such as finance, logistics, engineering and marketing.

Thereafter the system was further expanded to integrate all the planning steps up to MRP, and to include other corporate functions as well. It became what is now known as enterprise resource planning (ERP).

16.4 Enterprise resource planning (ERP)

Key term: enterprise resource planning

Enterprise resource planning (ERP) may be defined as:

> '... an integrated suite of application software modules that provides operational, managerial and strategic information for enterprises to improve productivity, quality and competitiveness' (Siriginidi 2000:3).

Enterprise resource planning (ERP) is aimed at balancing the utilisation of all the resources of an organisation. An ERP system treats organisational transactions in an integrated fashion, which means that all transactions are part of the inter-linked processes that make up the business (Gupta 2000:114). ERP is an all-encompassing approach that includes all the different organisational functions.

Using software, organisations are able to integrate different elements of the business into a single database system. This brings all key enterprise activities into a single software system to enhance management decisions. While MRP uses a 'push' approach, ERP uses a 'pull' approach based on a time-phased order-release system which schedules and releases work and purchase orders as and when they are required in the production system (Siriginidi 2000:3). ERP therefore improves on the major weakness of MRP – the 'push' approach, which invariably leads to inventory accumulation. In addition, ERP now includes a wide variety of both back office and front office functions. The scope of the current ERP systems encompasses the entire value chain of an organisation (see Chapter 17, *Competitive advantage* for a discussion of the value chain) to provide an end-to-end view of the business.

Gupta (2000:114) gives an example of how an ERP system treats a purchase transaction. A purchase order that is entered into the order entry module passes the order to a manufacturing application, which in turn sends a materials request to the supply chain module. The supply chain module then makes the necessary order from suppliers and uses the logistics module to get the materials inputs to the factory. The purchase transaction is simultaneously revealed in the finance module (general ledger module).

ERP is supportive of the just-in-time philosophy (see section 16.5 below). The high level of integration in the ERP modules ensures that management has immediate access to key information with which to manage global business needs of an integrated and networked enterprise (Siriginidi 2000:3).

16.5 Just-in-time systems

Key terms: just-in-time system, manufacturing cells

Just-in-time (JIT) is a management philosophy rather than merely a production technique, and focuses the organisation's efforts on performing value-adding activities on demand while minimising waste. Activities that add value to a product are those that increase the value of the product in the eyes of the customer. Although vehicle manufacturers (most notably Toyota of Japan) are largely credited with the origination thereof, just-in-time principles these days enjoy widespread popularity.

A pull system is at the heart of the **just-in-time system** – in other words, products are produced only once they are required by a customer. In turn, materials to produce the products are procured only once required by the production process. This stands in contrast to the more traditional manufacturing systems (such as that envisaged by MRP), where demand is projected and products are produced accordingly and kept in inventory until they are sold. The traditional system is one of 'pushing' product units through the factory and thereby increasing output, while preventing idle time.

In a traditional system, inventory units act as buffers between the different parts of the system, such as procurement, production and sales. In contrast, in a just-in-time system, a work station works on a unit only once it has received a formal request to do so from the next station in the production line.

Just-in-time systems aim to minimise non-value adding activities. Keeping inventory is seen as such an activity. The costs related to the storage, transport, insurance, protection and handling of excess inventory items has traditionally been underestimated – just-in-time manufacturers save money by minimising these expenses and gain customer goodwill by efficiently 'pulling' requested products through the factory and delivering the items on demand.

Just-in-time systems also aim to eliminate all activities related to the production of units of poor quality. Just as the costs related to excess inventory are minimised, the internal and external failure costs related to poor quality are minimised. Internal failure costs are costs associated with defective units discovered inside the factory, for example the cost of re-working or scrapping defective units. External failure costs are the costs related to defective units that have left the factory before their defects were discovered, and include the cost of honouring warranties as well as the opportunity cost of sales lost because of a damaged reputation. Just-in-time principles place the emphasis on prevention costs (such as purchasing materials of a high quality from a reliable supplier) and inspection costs (to ensure that defects are prevented). Total quality management is discussed more fully in Chapter 17, *Competitive advantage*.

While it is unacceptable in a just-in-time environment for any units to be defective (just-in-time factories usually aim for zero defects), it is just as unacceptable for production machines to break down. Because just-in-time systems are usually employed in highly mechanised factories where a relatively small portion of the work is performed manually, the proper maintenance of machines is an important objective. Maintenance work is usually performed by the worker who uses that particular machine, and in a just-in-time system it is usually not difficult for him to find the time to carry out preventative maintenance. Where traditional manufacturing systems 'push' as many inventory units through the factory as possible and aim to keep workers and machines busy, workers and machines in a just-in-time system are often purposefully kept idle while they wait for the next work station to place an 'order' for another unit. This idle time is spent on preventative machine maintenance.

Although every effort is made to prevent defective units and machine breakages, both of which take up production time, these could still occur on occasion. In traditional factories the effect of such errors and stoppages is minimised by having enough work-in-progress inventory units on the factory floor to continue work on them. In a just-in-time system, however, where each unit is produced only when needed and where on-time delivery to the next work station and eventually to the customer are paramount, any errors or stoppages are a major cause for concern. Yet no effort is made to negate the effects of these events – the factory is brought to a standstill until the problem has been resolved. This amplifies the error, emphasises quality, and highlights the unacceptability of defects in product units and machines, resulting in an absolute dedication to eliminating a repeat of the problem.

Just-in-time factories have a unique layout. They usually have U-shaped work stations known as **manufacturing 'cells'**. Each product group is, as far as practical, produced within such a cell, so that minimal movement of work-in-progress inventory is required (because moving inventory does not add value to the product). Workers are said to be multi-skilled – each worker is trained to operate and maintain all of the machines within the cell. Furthermore, units are said to be produced in 'batch sizes of one'. This means that, unlike in traditional factories, where large batches of identical units are produced before the machines are reset to produce a different type of unit, each individual unit is regarded as a batch that justifies machine set-up. Traditional factories reduce set-up costs by reducing the number of machine set-ups, and one would be inclined to assume that just-in-time systems would also aim to minimise machine set-ups because of the non-value-adding nature of the activity. However, the system does not allow for the advance production of any product units that will end up in inventory, and therefore rather directs efforts at automating the set-up process through advanced technology, to the extent that the cost of resetting machines is minimal. Furthermore, products are designed in such a way as to minimise the number of set-ups needed.

16.5.1 The just-in-time environment

Just-in-time factories do not exist in isolation – they operate inside a just-in-time supply chain. More than traditional factories, just-in-time factories need their suppliers to help them run their operations smoothly. For materials to be purchased on a just-in-time basis (in other words, only the exact number of units are purchased once they are already required in production), suppliers have to make frequent deliveries of small quantities of materials. Because the supply function is so crucial to the success of the system, just-in-time factories do not 'shop around' for the cheapest materials or regularly switch between suppliers. The costs incurred by traditional factories in sourcing the cheapest supplier for each batch of materials to be delivered are saved in a just-in-time system. A long-term relationship is established with a reliable, punctual supplier; the quality of materials and the reputation of the supplier are more important than the price of the materials. Suppliers often have representatives stationed at the factory itself to ensure that a seamless and defect-free passage of goods from the supplier to the factory floor takes place. Automation, fast response times, and cost savings on activities that do not add value are central to a just-in-time system, and orders are therefore usually placed to the supplier electronically and automatically through an electronic data interchange system.

16.5.2 Performance measurement in a just-in-time environment

Because just-in-time systems in many respects represent a significant move away from traditional manufacturing philosophies, some of the management accounting techniques that were developed in a traditional setting are less appropriate or even harmful in a just-in-time environment. The most notable is standard costing (refer to Chapter 13, *Standard costing*). In a standard costing system, variances are calculated and unfavourable variances that are deemed to be significant are investigated and acted upon. A negative direct materials price variance, for example, would indicate to management that cheaper materials should have been sourced, or that materials should have been purchased in bulk in order to be charged at a lower unit price. Both of these actions work against the just-in-time philosophy which strives for quality over price when it comes to materials, and opposes the stockpiling of materials not yet required by production. Similarly, the direct labour efficiency variance inspires incorrect action. It measures how 'busy' workers have been in producing maximum inventory, while the just-in-time system would prefer them to keep idle or attend to machine maintenance instead of producing unneeded units.

Just-in-time systems are better served by performance measures that work in harmony with the philosophy of the system. Non-financial measures are emphasised in a just-in-time environment. For example, management is likely to be more interested in the number of defects per 1 000 units produced, than in the rand value of materials purchased for the month.

When a decision has to be taken regarding the possible implementation of a just-in-time system, relevant costing principles (see Chapter 10, *Relevant costs for decision-making*) are applied to perform a quantitative analysis (this will compare the cost of implementing the system with the savings obtained in eliminating non-value-adding activities including those related to excess inventory, poor quality, and manual work where automation is possible). Qualitative factors are then also considered in weighing the costs and benefits of implementing the system.

16.6 Benchmarking

Key term: benchmarking

How long should it take from the time you call to place an order for a pizza, to the time it is delivered to your home? How long should a bank take to approve a student loan? What is a reasonable amount of paper and ink to be used when an invoice is printed? When you need to answer such questions, the first point of departure is usually to think of a company that you have some knowledge of. You may try to recall how long Debonairs took to deliver a pizza the last time you ordered one, you may remember how long you waited for the approval of your student loan, and you may count how many pages and estimate how much ink was used in the last invoice you received from Telkom. These departure points are likely to form the basis of your answers, because you know that 'it has been done that way before, and therefore the answer is reasonable'. Organisations constantly ask themselves similar questions about their own performance. Debonairs, for example, may have enough data on their own operations to be able to calculate the average time it takes them to deliver a pizza, but how do they know whether this should be good enough for them? When these questions arise, organisations look for data that show them how the same operation is performed elsewhere, through a process called **benchmarking**. Benchmarking is about measuring relative performance levels.

Organisations that perform benchmarking are usually interested in two main sets of data: they would like to know the average performance of other entities, as well as the performance of the entity that is presently achieving the best results in that particular field. In both cases, they compare their own performance against these benchmarks and take corrective action as needed.

There are four main types of benchmarking:
- *Competitive benchmarking* compares the performance of one organisation to that of a direct competitor. Debonairs could, for example, compare its pizza delivery time to that of St. Elmo's.
- *Internal benchmarking* compares the performance of one unit of an organisation to that of another unit inside the same organisation. The student loan division of a bank could, for example, compare its loan application turnaround time to that of the vehicle finance division of the same bank.
- *Functional benchmarking* compares the performance of one function of an organisation to the same function of another organisation, regardless of whether they operate in the same field of business. Telkom could, for example, compare the amount of paper and ink used per customer invoice to that used in the customer invoices of Foschini.
- *Strategic benchmarking* is aimed at strategic action and organisational change. An organisation could investigate the strategies employed by a competitor, and model its own strategies on those.

Competitive benchmarking poses a unique problem: how does one get hold of the relevant data from competitors? Where competition is intense, organisations are unlikely to exchange freely information that could potentially help the other party. Organisations sometimes use 'reverse engineering' (analysing a competitor's product by taking it apart and studying it) to obtain benchmarks related to the physical product. For other issues, the answer lies in third party organisations (usually consulting firms) which specialise in gathering and analysing industry data. Organisations in a particular industry are invited to submit their own data according to relevant performance categories, and in turn receive a report from the third party detailing the data submitted by all industry players. The data are made available to all participants, but the names are usually kept anonymous. Although this kind of benchmarking is often done, some care has to be exercised in interpreting results. All organisations in the industry do not necessarily record their performance results and costs in exactly the same manner, which could result in misleading points of comparison. Furthermore, no two organisations operate under exactly the same circumstances, and environmental factors could affect them in different ways.

In the case of internal and functional benchmarking it is theoretically more likely that information will be shared freely by the parties involved, as the competitive threat is absent. However, where internal benchmarking is performed in an organisation which actively compares the relative performance of its units and models its reward structure accordingly, there is a danger that managers may be unwilling to co-operate and assist each other in a benchmarking exercise.

The primary advantage of setting targets through benchmarking is that, no matter how difficult they may seem to achieve, one is assured that the targets are realistic, because they have already been achieved by others. Many uncontrollable factors, such as general economic conditions or national power supply issues, may affect entities more or less equally and therefore do not have to be taken into account in interpreting the results. On the negative side, benchmarking has a number of disadvantages. Apart from the security risk in sharing information and the cost of carrying out a benchmarking exercise, it is also often criticised for stifling creativity because it is essentially a catching-up exercise aimed at copying others. Furthermore, benchmarking tends to focus attention on efficiency (employing the minimum resources in carrying out a task), while effectiveness should actually take precedence (ensuring that the stated goal is obtained). In other words, benchmarking may encourage doing things as efficiently as possible rather than questioning whether the right things are being done at all.

16.7 Summary

Some production and information assimilation techniques have gained prominence in modern factories. These may even, in adapted form, be useful in non-manufacturing organisations. A number of these techniques were discussed in this chapter, because management accountants need an understanding of the concepts in order to add value in providing information and making decisions where such techniques have been implemented.

The Theory of Constraints (TOC) identifies and addresses the problems that occur in the short term when manufacturing constraints result in bottlenecks. Throughput accounting is used to optimise production by focusing on direct materials and direct service costs in calculating throughput, as they are the only costs that are variable within a very short-term time horizon. Once the immediate bottleneck situation has been dealt with, TOC then seeks to alleviate the constraints in the longer term.

Materials requirement planning (MRP) is a production scheduling technique that was later further developed into manufacturing resource planning (MRPII), a technique that extends to planning and scheduling other resources such as finance, logistics, engineering and marketing. Both of these are regarded as 'push' techniques because they estimate demand and schedule production accordingly. Units are therefore manufactured whether or not they are immediately required by customers.

Enterprise resource planning (ERP) differs from MRP in that it is an even more integrated type of software system, and because it follows a 'pull' approach. It triggers production only when required, and is therefore in harmony with a just-in-time system.

Just-in-time systems focus organisations' efforts on performing value-adding activities on demand while minimising waste. This implies, among other things, dramatically reducing inventory levels and placing a strong emphasis on quality and on-time delivery. Just-in-time fits well with the contemporary feel of this chapter – it is characterised by extensive automation and by its exploitation of modern advances in information technology.

Benchmarking is a way in which organisations can compare their performance to current best practices. It therefore implicitly sets targets that are realistic and attainable.

Conclusion: Contemporary management accounting concepts and other topics in this book

The modern environment in which organisations find themselves, as addressed in this chapter, gives rise to the need for organisations to seek competitive advantage. This is further explored in Chapter 17, *Competitive advantage*.

In the section on the Theory of Constraints it was pointed out that throughput accounting calculates a throughput contribution which is different from the contribution calculated in Chapter 5, *Absorption versus variable costing* and in Chapter 11, *Decision-making under operational constraints*. This is because throughput accounting works with a shorter time horizon within which fewer costs are truly variable, a principle which is best understood after Chapter 10, *Relevant costs for decision-making* has been studied. The section on TOC also contrasted the concept with activity-based costing, as discussed in Chapter 6, *Overhead allocation*.

Some modern techniques conflict with traditional management accounting techniques. Most notably, the just-in-time philosophy (a 'pull' technique) is at odds with standard costing, which discourages idle time and potentially encourages producing excess units, keeping excess materials, purchasing cheaper materials, and so forth. Standard costing and its variance calculations are discussed in Chapter 13, *Standard costing*.

With the application of all of the concepts discussed in this chapter it is of great importance that the performance measures employed by the organisation should be in harmony with the objectives of the system. In the case of benchmarking the technique can, in itself, be regarded as a form of performance measurement. The principles studied in Chapter 14, *Performance management* are therefore relevant here.

Volkswagen Group South Africa

Volkswagen South Africa is located in Uitenhage, an industrial town some 35 kilometres from Port Elizabeth in the Eastern Cape. The Eastern Cape is home to the largest automotive cluster in South Africa. The uniquely South African Volkswagen Polo Vivo was the number one selling passenger car brand in this country in 2010 – 23 297 units were sold. The Polo Vivo is, however, by no means Volkswagen South Africa's only product – more than a dozen different models of cars are produced.

Source: Volkswagen South Africa 2011

1. Explain and describe five steps that Volkswagen South Africa might follow if it found that a production constraint at its Uitenhage plant was preventing it from manufacturing the number of Polo Vivos that it strives to supply.
2. Contrast the benefits that Volkswagen South Africa might gain from using a materials requirement planning system in its production plant, with the benefits it might gain from implementing enterprise resource planning.
3. Recommend and justify whether you think it would be feasible for Volkswagen South Africa to follow the just-in-time approach at its Uitenhage plant.
4. List five performance areas related to production that Volkswagen South Africa could wish to benchmark against its local rival, the Ford Motor Company of Southern Africa, which also operates a factory near Port Elizabeth.

Basic questions

BQ 1

Source: Adapted from CIMA P1

The following data relate to a manufacturing company. At the beginning of August there was no inventory. During August 2 000 units of Product X were produced, but only 1 750 units were sold. The financial data for Product X for August were as follows:

Materials	R40 000
Labour	R12 600
Variable production overheads	R9 400
Fixed production overheads	R22 500
Variable selling costs	R6 000
Fixed selling costs	R19 300
Total costs for X for August	R109 800

Which of the values below was the value of inventory of X at 31 August using a throughput accounting approach, as would be used when applying the Theory of Constraints?
a) R5 000
b) R 6 175
c) R6 575
d) R13 725

BQ 2

Source: Adapted from CIMA P1

How does throughput accounting (as used when the Theory of Constraints is employed), differ from variable costing?

BQ 3

Source: Adapted from CIMA P1

JJ Ltd manufactures three products: W, X and Y. The products use a series of different machines but there is a common machine that creates a bottleneck.

The standard selling price and standard cost per unit for each product for the forthcoming period are as follows:

	W	X	Y
Selling price	R200	R150	R150
Cost:			
Direct materials	(R41)	(R20)	(R30)
Labour	(R30)	(R20)	(R36)
Overheads	(R60)	(R40)	(R50)
Profit	R69	R70	R34
Bottleneck machine – minutes per unit	9	10	7

Forty per cent of the overhead cost is classified as variable.

Using a throughput accounting approach, what would be the ranking of the products to allow for best use of the bottleneck?

BQ 4

The production manager of Manufacturing4Africa recently made the following remark:

> 'We have a real problem in the factory. Our two newest production machines, the MHP2008 and the ExpressRT, are not performing as well as we had hoped. Unfortunately our product has to pass through both of them. At least the ExpressRT should be able to produce about 300 000 units per month, but the MHP2008 has been turning out only 250 000 units each month. The sales team is really angry – they say we're holding them back. The product is very popular and they could easily sell much more, if only we could manufacture enough!'

What steps should the production manager follow in order to address the problem, and how do they apply to Manufacturing4Africa?

principles of management accounting

BQ 5

Source: Adapted from CIMA P1

Two definitions are as follows:

Definition A: 'An approach to production management which aims to maximise sales revenue less materials'

Definition B: 'A system whose objective is to produce or procure products or components as they are required by a customer or for use, rather than for inventory'

Which of the following pairs of terms correctly matches the definitions in A and B above?

	Definition A	Definition B
a)	Manufacturing resource planning	Just-in-time
b)	Enterprise resource planning	Materials requirements planning
c)	Theory of constraints	Enterprise resource planning
d)	Theory of constraints	Just-in-time

BQ 6

Source: Adapted from CIMA P1

Two definitions are as follows:

Definition 1: 'A system that converts a production schedule into a listing of materials and components required to meet the schedule so that items are available when needed'

Definition 2: 'An accounting system that focuses on ways by which the maximum return per unit of bottleneck activity can be achieved'

Which of the following pairs of terms correctly matches definitions 1 and 2 above?

	Definition 1	Definition 2
a)	Manufacturing resource planning (MRPII)	Just-in-time
b)	Materials requirement planning (MRP)	Throughput accounting
c)	Materials requirement planning (MRP)	Theory of constraints
d)	Benchmarking	Throughput accounting

BQ 7

Source: Adapted from CIMA P1

Which of the following definitions are correct?
i) Just-in-time systems are designed to produce or procure products or components as they are required for a customer or for use, rather than for inventory.
ii) Materials requirement planning (MRP) systems are computer-based systems that integrate all aspects of a business so that the planning and scheduling of production ensures components are available when needed.

a) None
b) (i) only
c) (ii) only
d) (i) and (ii)

BQ 8

Source: Adapted from ACCA Paper 3.3

CSIX Ltd manufactures fuel pumps using a just-in-time manufacturing system. The transactions during the month of November were as follows:

Purchase of raw materials	R 5 575 000
Conversion costs incurred:	
Labour	R1 735 000
Overheads	R3 148 000
Finished goods completed (units)	210 000
Sales for the month (units)	206 000

Can the just-in-time system operated by CSIX Ltd be regarded as 'perfect'? What are the reasons for your answer?

BQ 9

Source: Adapted from CIMA P1

T Ltd is a large insurance company. The Claims Department deals with claims from policy holders who have suffered a loss that is covered by their insurance policy. Policy holders can claim, for example, for damage to property, or for household items stolen in a burglary. The Claims Department staff investigate each claim and determine what, if any, payment should be made to the claimant.

The manager of the Claims Department has decided to benchmark the performance of the department and has chosen two areas to benchmark:
- The detection of false claims
- The speed of processing claims.

For each of the above two areas:
a) What would be an appropriate performance measure?
b) How could the relevant benchmarking data be gathered?

BQ 10

Source: Adapted from ACCA Paper 3.3

Academic studies argue that the annual budget model may be seen as acting as a barrier to the effective implementation of alternative models for use in the accomplishment of strategic change.

In what way(s) may the traditional budgeting process be seen as a barrier to the achievement of the aims of benchmarking?

Long questions

LQ 1 – Intermediate (9 marks; 16 minutes)
Source: Adapted from CIMA P1 Pilot paper

A company produces three products using three different machines. No other products are made on these particular machines. The following data are available for December:

Product	A	B	C
Throughput contribution per unit	R36	R28	R18
Machine hours required per unit:			
Machine 1	5	2	1,5
Machine 2	5	5,5	1,5
Machine 3	2,5	1	0,5
Estimated sales demand (units)	50	50	60

Maximum machine capacity in December will be 400 hours per machine.

	REQUIRED	Marks
(a)	Calculate the machine utilisation rates for each machine for December.	2
(b)	Identify which of the machines is the bottleneck machine.	2
(c)	State the recommended procedure given by Goldratt in his Theory of Constraints for dealing with a bottleneck activity.	2
(d)	Calculate the optimum allocation of the bottleneck machine hours to the three products.	3
	TOTAL MARKS	**9**

LQ 2 – Intermediate (9 marks; 16 minutes)
Source: Adapted from CIMA P1

SM makes two products, Z1 and Z2. Its machines can work on only one product at a time. The two products are worked on in two departments by differing grades of labour. The labour requirements for the two products are as follow:

	Minutes per unit of product	
	Z1	Z2
Department 1	12	16
Department 2	20	15

There is currently a shortage of labour and the maximum time available each day in Departments 1 and 2 is 480 minutes and 840 minutes, respectively.

The current selling prices and costs for the two products are shown below:

	Z1	Z2
	R per unit	R per unit
Selling price	50,00	65,00
Direct materials	(10,00)	(15,00)
Direct labour	(10,40)	(6,20)
Variable overheads	(6,40)	(9,20)
Fixed overheads	(12,80)	(18,40)
Profit per unit	10,40	16,20

As part of the budget-setting process, SM needs to know the optimum output levels. All output is sold.

REQUIRED		Marks
(a)	Calculate the maximum number of each product that could be produced each day, and identify the limiting factor/bottleneck.	3
(b)	Using traditional contribution analysis, calculate the 'profit-maximising' output each day, and the contribution at this level of output.	3
(c)	Using a throughput approach, calculate the 'throughput-maximising' output each day, and the 'throughput contribution' at this level of output.	3
TOTAL MARKS		9

LQ 3 – Advanced (20 marks; 36 minutes)

Source: Adapted from ACCA Paper 3.3

Ride Ltd is engaged in the manufacturing and marketing of bicycles. Two bicycles are produced. These are the 'Roadster', which is designed for use on roads, and the 'Everest', which is a bicycle designed for use in mountainous areas. The following information relates to the year ending 31 December:
i) Unit selling price and cost data are as follows:

	Roadster	Everest
	R	R
Selling price	200	280
Materials cost	80	100
Variable production conversion costs	20	60

ii) Fixed production overheads attributable to the manufacture of the bicycles will amount to R4 050 000.
iii) Expected demand is as follows:
Roadster   150 000 units
Everest   70 000 units
iv) Each bicycle is completed in the finishing department. The number of each type of bicycle that can be completed in one hour in the finishing department is as follows:
Roadster   6,25
Everest   5,00
There is a total of 30 000 hours available within the finishing department.
v) Ride Ltd operates a just-in-time (JIT) manufacturing system with regard to the manufacture of bicycles and aims to hold very little work-in-progress and no finished goods inventory whatsoever.

principles of management accounting

	REQUIRED	Marks
(a)	Using variable costing principles, calculate the mix (units) of each type of bicycle which will maximise profit and state the value of that profit.	6
(b)	Calculate the throughput accounting ratio for each type of bicycle and briefly discuss when it is worth producing a product where throughput accounting principles are in operation. Your answer should assume that the variable overhead cost amounting to R4 800 000 incurred as a result of the chosen product mix in part (a) is fixed in the short term.	5
(c)	Using throughput accounting principles, advise management of the quantities of each type of bicycle that should be manufactured which will maximise profit and prepare a projection of the net profit that would be earned by Ride Ltd in the year ending 31 December.	5
(d)	Explain two aspects in which the concept of 'contribution' in throughput accounting differs from its use in variable costing.	4
	TOTAL MARKS	20

LQ 4 – Advanced (10 marks; 18 minutes)

Source: Adapted from CIMA P2

The X Group is a well-established manufacturing group that operates a number of companies using similar production and inventory-holding policies. All of the companies are in the same country, although there are considerable distances between them.

The group has traditionally operated a constant production system whereby the same volume of output is produced each week, even though the demand for the group's products is subject to seasonal fluctuations. As a result there is always finished goods inventory in the group's warehouses waiting for customer orders. This inventory will include a safety inventory equal to two weeks' production.

Raw materials inventories are ordered from suppliers using the Economic Order Quantity (EOQ) model in conjunction with a computerised inventory control system which identifies the need to place an order when the re-order level is reached. The purchasing department is centralised for the group. On receiving a notification from the computerised inventory control system that an order is to be placed, a series of quotation enquiries are issued to prospective suppliers so that the best price and delivery terms are obtained for each order. This practice has resulted in there being a large number of suppliers to the X group. Each supplier delivers directly to the company that requires the materials.

The managing director of the X group has recently returned from a conference on world class manufacturing and was particularly interested in the possible use of just-in-time (JIT) within the X group.

REQUIRED	Marks
Write a report, addressed to the managing director of the X group, that explains how the adoption of JIT may affect its profitability.	10
TOTAL MARKS	10

LQ 5 – Advanced (25 marks; 45 minutes)

Source: Adapted from CIMA P6

E5E is a charity concerned with heart disease. Its mission statement is:

To fund world class research into the biology and the causes of heart disease.
To develop effective treatments and improve the quality of life for patients.
To reduce the number of people suffering from heart disease.
To provide authoritative information on heart disease.

E5E obtains funding from voluntary donations from both private individuals and companies, together with government grants. Much of the work it does, in all departments, could not be achieved without the large number of voluntary workers who give their time to the organisation and who make up approximately 80 per cent of the workforce.

E5E does not employ any scientific researchers directly, but funds research by making grants to individual medical experts employed within universities and hospitals. In addition to providing policy advice to government departments, the charity's advisors give health educational talks to employers and other groups.

The Board recognises the need to become more professional in the management of the organisation. It feels that this can be best achieved by conducting a benchmarking exercise. However, it recognises that the introduction of this process may make some members of the organisation, particularly the volunteers, unhappy.

REQUIRED		Marks
As financial controller:		
(a)	Discuss the advantages and disadvantages of benchmarking for E5E.	8
(b)	Provide advice on the stages in conducting a benchmarking exercise in the context of E5E.	13
(c)	Provide advice on how those implementing the exercise should deal with the concerns of the staff, particularly the volunteers.	4
TOTAL MARKS		**25**

References

Blocher, EJ, Chen, KH, Cokins, G & Lin, TW. 2007. *Cost management: a strategic emphasis*, Third (International) Edition. New York: McGraw-Hill.

Blocher, E, Stout, DE, Cokins, G & Chen, K. 2008. *Cost management: a strategic emphasis*, Fourth edition. New York: McGraw-Hill.

Eaton, G. 2005. *Management accounting official terminology*. London: CIMA Publishing.

Goldratt, EM & Cox, J. 1986. *The goal: a process of ongoing improvement*, Second edition. Great Barrington, MA: North River Press.

Gupta, A. 2000. 'Enterprise resource planning: the emerging organisational value systems'. *Industrial Management & Data Systems*, 100(3):114–118.

Reeve, JM. 2003. *Readings and issues in cost management*, Second edition. New York: Thomson Learning.

Shehab, EM, Sharp, MW, Supramaniam, L & Spedding, TA. 2004. 'Enterprise resource planning: An integrative view'. *Business Process Management Journal*, 10(4):359–386.

Siriginidi, SR. 2000. 'Enterprise resource planning in reengineering business'. *Business Process Management Journal*, 6(5):376–391.

Skillsportal. 2011. *Apprenticeship programme for aspiring tool, die and mould makers*. [Online]. Available: <http://www.skillsportal.co.za/page/skills-development/825588-Apprenticeship-programme-for-aspiring-tool-die-and-mould-makers> [24 January 2011]

Volkswagen South Africa. 2011. *Strong finish to new passenger car market in 2010*. [Online]. Available: <http://www.vw.co.za/news/article/276/> [24 January 2011].

Competitive advantage

chapter 17

Richard Chivaka and Shelley-Anne Roos

LEARNING OBJECTIVES

By the end of this chapter, you should be able to:
1. Describe, from a management accounting perspective, the following techniques, practices and philosophies which support competitive advantage:
   - Porter's generic strategies
   - Activity-based management
   - Total quality management
   - Target costing
   - Life-cycle costing
   - Supply chain management
   - Value chain analysis.

Ford's Puma engine

Ford Motor Company of Southern Africa (FMCSA) has invested R3 billion to prepare its Silverton assembly plant in Pretoria for the production of the new-generation Ford Ranger compact pick-up, and to ready its Struandale engine plant in Port Elizabeth to produce the new-generation Puma diesel engines that are used in the Ranger. As from April 2011, the Struandale plant manufactures 220 000 component sets (engine head, cylinder block and crankshaft) annually.

The Struandale plant had to compete with numerous top-ranked plants around the world to win the contract to produce the high-tech Puma engine. Employees received extensive training, and best-in-class quality initiatives were implemented.

The CEO of FMCSA views the awarding of the contract as a high-level recognition of FMCSA's efficiency and skill, and an entrenchment of the South African company as a key player in the global Ford network. 'The production of the new Ranger and the Puma engines in South Africa confirms the world-class status of the Silverton and Struandale plants, allied to the quality and professionalism of our valued supplier partners,' he said.

Like FMCSA, companies increasingly find themselves pitched against competitors from around the world. In order for companies to survive and thrive in an environment of global competition, they have to ensure that they are equipped with the necessary skills and strategies.

Source: Business Link Magazine 2010

17.1 Introduction

This chapter is concerned with the role of management accounting in supporting business strategy in the context of the intense competition in the global economic environment.

Given ever-increasing global competition, the survival of profit-seeking organisations depends on their ability to reconfigure business strategies, supported by relevant information such as that supplied by the management accounting system. Once fashioned in the context of a set of internal and external challenges that a company faces at a particular point in time, a business strategy evolves in synch with the changing global economic environment. Management accounting should support an organisation's strategy by employing relevant tools and practices. Gaining competitive advantage requires an organisation to outperform its competitors in terms of quality, cost, price, functionality and customer service. Given that attaining competitive advantage is a function of a number of variables, it follows that management accounting needs to apply different tools to achieve satisfactory results. Some techniques, practices and philosophies that have been suggested as being potentially useful in supporting business strategy in the current global environment include Porter's generic strategies, activity-based management, total quality management, target costing, life-cycle costing, supply chain management, and value chain analysis.

> The concepts discussed in this chapter are large, complex topics and have been the subjects of in-depth research by numerous academics and business practitioners. This chapter aims to provide the management accounting student with a basic background to these topics. However, if students are interested in learning more about these topics, there is a wealth of resources available today that elaborate on their theory, importance and application.

17.2 Porter's generic strategies

Key term: generic strategies

The turbulent global business environment, which culminated in the 2008 to 2009 recession, brought challenges that threatened the survival of businesses. Recession ushered in a two-pronged problem for business:
1 A significant drop in growth on the one hand, and
2 A change in the way customers spend their money, given the tight budgetary constraints brought about by falling income levels.

As such, the need to create real value for the customer as measured in terms of quality, cost, functionality and customer service has again been brought to the fore in company boardroom agendas.

Strategy formulation is a very important process which determines, among other things, how an organisation competes, given the forces that determine success in its chosen industry. Porter (1979) identifies five forces that determine the nature and intensity of competition in any industry, namely:
1 The risk of entry by potential competitors
2 The bargaining power of suppliers
3 The bargaining power of customers,
4 The threat of substitute products or services, and
5 The intensity of rivalry among established firms in the industry.

In order to compete favourably and add to shareholder value, a company must not only understand the dynamics of these forces, but also take into account the implications of the cause-and-effect relationship among them when designing and implementing its own strategy. This entails decisions about positioning: identifying areas where a company can effectively deploy its capabilities and defend itself against known and understood causes of industry competitive forces. Porter (1985) advocates that, in order to compete effectively, each organisation has to choose one of three **generic strategies**. The three options are as follows:

- *Cost leadership*. When an organisation chooses a cost leadership strategy, it aims to be the lowest-cost producer in the industry. The cost leader is often a large, well-established organisation that can exploit economies of scale. Once cost leadership has been achieved, the organisation can earn higher profits owing to its low input costs. However, it may choose to match its low cost with a low selling price, thereby undercutting competitor prices and dominating the market.
- *Differentiation*. There can be only one cost leader in each industry, as only one organisation can truly be the industry's lowest-cost producer at any given time. Organisations therefore need to distinguish their products or services from those offered by competitors by differentiating them – by making them different in the eyes of the customer. This can be done in a number of ways, for example, by offering unique features or superior customer service, exploiting unique distribution channels, using attractive packaging, and other similar means. One of the most frequently-encountered ways in which organisations differentiate their products or services is by attaching a brand name to it in order to signify its uniqueness.
- *Focus*. There are two types of focus strategy:
  - Cost leadership focus
  - Differentiation focus.

A focus strategy (also sometimes called a 'niche' strategy) applies either cost leadership or differentiation, as discussed above, to a specific niche within the market. In other words, instead of serving the whole market, the market is divided up into segments by the organisation, and the strategy is applied to only a specific part or part(s) of the market on which the organisation chooses to focus. Market segmentation takes place based on criteria deemed appropriate by the organisation. For example, one organisation may choose to segment its market based on the age of customers, and decide to strive for, say, cost leadership in the market segment that serves customers over the age of 60. Another may choose to segment its market based on gender, and employ a differentiation strategy which targets female customers.

Porter contends that every organisation has to choose one of these three generic strategies in order to determine the basis on which it will compete.

17.3 Activity-based management

Key terms: activity-based management, operational ABM, strategic ABM

Activity-based management (ABM) utilises the same activity and cost information as an activity-based costing system (see Chapter 6, *Overhead allocation*) to support operational and strategic management decisions. Using ABM, organisations are able to realise the goals that management wishes to achieve, but can do so using fewer resources (Cooper & Kaplan 1999). ABM focuses management's attention on activities as a way of improving the value that customers receive as well as the profit realised by an organisation. ABM's main focus is on the efficiency and effectiveness with which organisational activities are undertaken to generate the maximum benefit from resources utilised. Owing to its focus on activities performed in product and service delivery, ABM helps management to concentrate on the organisational key success factors which in turn enhance competitive advantage.

ABM identifies the major activities that take place in the organisation and determines the cost driver of each such activity. This allows for the effective management of the activities, because managers now understand what causes costs to be incurred. If the organisation then wishes to make use of activity-based costing, it proceeds to assign the cost of the activities to products or services based on their consumption of the respective cost driver resources.

ABM facilitates the identification of process improvement opportunities and the deployment of strategies to reduce and/or eliminate waste in processes. The elimination of waste results in the provision of products and services at lower cost. Furthermore, by creating activity visibility in organisational processes, management can examine the real contribution of each of the activities in meeting customer needs. ABM is applied at both the operational and strategic levels of organisations.

Operational ABM assumes that the demand for organisational activities is reasonable, and the challenge for management is to meet this demand with fewer human, equipment and working capital resources. Operational ABM does not question why activities are being performed; it takes these as given and strives to perform them with fewer organisational resources. This means that operational ABM is based on the principle of *efficiency*, in other words, doing things right. Operational ABM is therefore concerned with management actions that are aimed at increasing efficiency, lowering costs, and enhancing asset utilisation (Cooper and Kaplan, 1999).

The application of operational ABM generates benefits to organisations in a number of ways. Due to better resource utilisation, organisations are able to achieve higher profits. Operational ABM supports cost management by enabling organisations to avoid additional investment in personnel and fixed assets. This is achieved by increasing the efficiency in resource utilisation, in other words, achieving more output with the same resource quantity and quality. Operational ABM also generates cost savings for organisations via lower expenditure on resources. Operational ABM uses a number of process improvement tools such as cost driver analysis, activity analysis, and performance management. Cost driver analysis involves all efforts expended in examining, quantifying and explaining the effect of cost drivers on the cost of activities. Activity analysis is the process of assessing each of the main activities performed within a company.

Performance management ensures a maintained focus on the key goals of the organisation.

Strategic ABM is based on the principle of *effectiveness*, in other words, doing the right things. It assumes that the efficiency levels within the organisation are given, and management's task is to make sure that organisational resources are being used on opportunities that generate the maximum benefits. The information generated by an ABC costing system gives management a better picture of the profitability of different products and services. Through strategic ABM, management takes this

information and directs organisational attention towards more profitable products and services. This is achieved by shifting the activity mix away from unprofitable products and services to more profitable ones (Cooper and Kaplan, 1999:277). As such, strategic ABM includes decisions such as:
- Product/service design
- Product/service development
- Product-line and customer mix
- Customer relationships (covering issues such as order size, delivery, packaging, and pricing)
- Supplier relationships (covering issues such as supplier cost analysis, on-time delivery and quality)
- Distribution channel analysis, and
- Market segmentation.

Operational and strategic ABM work together to ensure that organisations perform a given quantity of activities with fewer resources (operational ABM), and at the same time shift the organisational activity mix to more profitable products, services, processes and customers (strategic ABM) (Cooper & Kaplan 1999).

One of the most prominent applications of ABM is customer profitability analysis, whereby customers or customer groups are regarded as cost objects and the cost of serving them is analysed in an activity-based manner.

17.4 Total quality management

Key term: total quality management

The survival of organisations in the global economic environment depends on, among other things, their ability to make quality products or provide quality services. Because of the dismantling of trade barriers in the global village, coupled with readily available information about competing products and services, customers have a wide variety of products and services to choose from. As such, they are increasingly demanding their money's worth from products and services. This has brought to the fore the need to produce quality products and provide quality services, and has resulted in the application of **total quality management** as a technique which manages and controls those processes.

17.4.1 Definition of quality

Key term: quality

Quality is defined as the extent to which a product or service meets customer expectations by conforming to the required design or specifications at the price customers are willing to pay. It is important to note that the definition and measures of quality come from the market and not from boardrooms. The point here is that if organisations are to provide quality products and services, it is not the organisations themselves that judge whether the quality is acceptable or not. Quality should therefore be regarded as an external measure of the attributes of products and services.

17.4.2 Dimensions of quality

Quality is not a one-dimensional measure of the degree of acceptability of a product or service. It is a composite measure of a number of attributes that customers desire and demand in a product or service. Table 17.1 below shows some of the key facets of quality that collectively make up what customers would deem a quality product or service (Hoque 2005:242):

Table 17.1 Dimensions of quality

Performance	How well and consistently a product or service functions
Aesthetics	The appearance of a physical product, that is, how appealing it is in the eyes of the customer
Serviceability	How easily a product can be maintained or repaired
Features	The characteristics of a product that differentiate it from functionally similar products
Reliability	The probability of a product performing its intended function for a specified length of time
Durability	The length of time that the product functions in the hands of the customer
Conformance	How well a product meets the specifications set during the development stage
Fitness of use	The suitability of the product to carry out its advertised functions

17.4.3 Elements of total quality management

Total quality management (TQM) is a customer-centric approach premised on the principle of *'get it right first time'*. TQM is the unyielding and continuous effort expended by everyone in the organisation to understand, meet and exceed the expectations of customers (Blocher et al 2005:681). It emphasises preventative measures. The aim is therefore to design and build quality in (rather than to inspect units in order to assess quality) by focusing on the causes rather than the symptoms of poor quality (Drury 2004:958). In the quest for TQM, quality-related costs are identified and reduced.

TQM elements include the following (Lord 1999):
- Eliminating or reducing non-value-adding activities (such as setting up machines and ordering materials)
- Reducing inventories, lead times and defects
- Streamlining production flow
- Co-operating with suppliers and synchronising production plans with supplier delivery schedules
- Increasing flexibility and productivity of the workforce
- Encouraging operators to maintain their own equipment, and to detect, record, and solve their own problems.

The above are all aimed at producing and delivering quality products and services to customers at the lowest cost possible. For TQM to be successful, it should be regarded as a 'culture' that permeates every structure, process and activity performed in the organisation.

Figure 17.1 Critical total quality management success factors

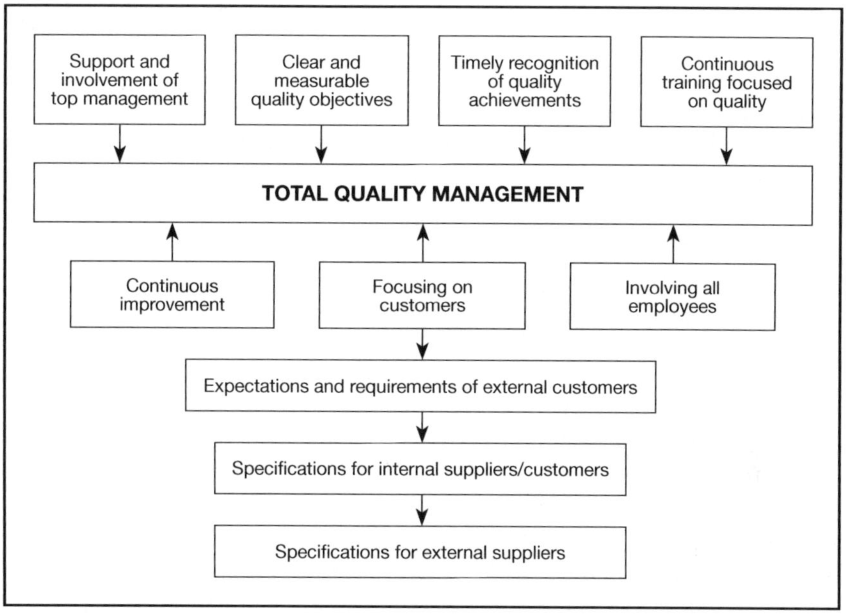

```
┌─────────────┐  ┌─────────────┐  ┌─────────────┐  ┌─────────────┐
│ Support and │  │  Clear and  │  │   Timely    │  │ Continuous  │
│involvement of│  │ measurable  │  │ recognition │  │training focused│
│top management│  │  quality    │  │ of quality  │  │ on quality  │
│             │  │ objectives  │  │achievements │  │             │
└──────┬──────┘  └──────┬──────┘  └──────┬──────┘  └──────┬──────┘
       ▼                ▼                ▼                ▼
┌─────────────────────────────────────────────────────────────────┐
│                    TOTAL QUALITY MANAGEMENT                     │
└──────▲─────────────────────▲─────────────────────▲──────────────┘
       │                     │                     │
┌──────┴──────┐       ┌──────┴──────┐       ┌──────┴──────┐
│ Continuous  │       │ Focusing on │       │ Involving all│
│ improvement │       │  customers  │       │  employees   │
└─────────────┘       └──────┬──────┘       └──────────────┘
                             │
            ┌────────────────┴────────────────────────┐
            │ Expectations and requirements of         │
            │         external customers               │
            └────────────────┬─────────────────────────┘
                             ▼
            ┌──────────────────────────────────────────┐
            │ Specifications for internal              │
            │          suppliers/customers             │
            └────────────────┬─────────────────────────┘
                             ▼
            ┌──────────────────────────────────────────┐
            │ Specifications for external suppliers    │
            └──────────────────────────────────────────┘
```

Source: Blocher et al 2005

If organisations are to benefit from TQM, it is necessary to set targets for continuous quality improvement and cost reduction (see 'Kaizen costing' in section 17.5.5). Such targets are supposed to be in the context of a well-understood quality-improvement programme, the aim of which is to better the previous period's quality level. In other words, quality is not a static measure that can be achieved by an event. It needs to be improved all the time if organisations are to sustain their competitive advantage. Consequently, continuous improvement involves setting new targets that push the frontiers of quality levels.

17.4.4 Cost of quality

> **Key terms:** cost of quality, prevention costs, appraisal costs, internal failure costs, external failure costs, cost of quality report

Cost of quality is the sum of the costs that arise from 'activities associated with prevention, identification, repair, and rectification of poor quality and opportunity costs from lost production time and lost sales as a result of poor quality' (Blocher et al 2005:691).

Costs of quality are generally classified into four broad categories as follows (Juran 1974):
- Prevention costs
- Appraisal costs
- Internal failure costs
- External failure costs.

Prevention costs

Prevention costs arise from initiatives aimed at preventing the production of defective products. The principle behind initiatives that give rise to these costs is *'prevention is better than cure'*. Prevention costs occur before production in order to eliminate or reduce the chances of producing defective products. Product design and quality training are examples of preventative activities that give rise to prevention costs.

Appraisal costs

> **Key term:** appraisal costs

Appraisal costs arise from activities that are performed to detect, measure and analyse data to ensure that products and services conform to specifications. These costs occur during production but before products are delivered to the customers. Examples of activities undertaken to detect quality problems include inspection and quality audits.

Internal failure costs

> **Key term:** internal failure costs

The appraisal function generates useful feedback about the quality-related problems that exist despite the preventive measures put in place. Activities aimed at the rectification of defective products and services gives rise to **internal failure costs**. These costs are called internal failure costs because they occur before the product leaves the premises of the organisation. Examples of activities that incur internal failure costs include re-work and re-inspection of products.

External failure costs

> **Key term:** external failure costs

The measures put in place to prevent, detect and rectify defective products and services sometimes fail to eliminate the production and delivery of unacceptable products and service to end-use customers. When that happens, the defects in the products and services are detected and experienced by customers. In other words, in the case of **external failure costs**, the quality problems are detected outside the boundaries of the organisation. Examples of external failure costs include the cost of repairing units already delivered, replacement costs, and product recall. A very expensive (although difficult to quantify in practice) external failure cost is the opportunity cost of sales lost as a result of a damaged reputation.

Cost of quality report

Key term: cost of quality report

A **cost of quality report** shows the various categories of quality costs expressed as a percentage of sales or turnover (Hoque 2005). Table 17.2 below gives examples of the components of quality costs.

Table 17.2 Components of quality costs

Cost of quality category	Examples
Prevention costs	<ul><li>Quality engineering</li><li>Quality training programmes</li><li>Quality planning</li><li>Product design</li><li>Quality circles or cells</li><li>Supplier selection and evaluation</li></ul>
Appraisal costs	<ul><li>Raw materials inspection and testing</li><li>Work-in-progress inspection</li><li>Finished goods inspection</li><li>Packaging inspection</li><li>Test equipment (acquisition, maintenance, salaries and wages)</li></ul>
Internal failure costs	<ul><li>Rework</li><li>Scrap</li><li>Loss as a result of downgrades</li><li>Re-inspection</li><li>Retesting</li><li>Loss due to work interruptions</li><li>Design changes</li></ul>
External failure costs	<ul><li>Cost of recalls</li><li>Sales returns and allowances due to quality deficiency</li><li>Repairs</li><li>Product liability</li><li>Warranty costs</li><li>Contribution lost (from cancelled orders owing to poor quality and to perceived poor quality)</li></ul>

Source: Adapted from Hoque 2005:245; Blocher et al 2005:692; Wang et al 1998

The cost of quality increases as one moves down the order of prevention, appraisal, internal failure and external failure costs. The total cost of quality is minimised when more emphasis is placed on the earlier categories. This implies that more money ought to be spent early on, such as on designing a quality product and purchasing quality materials. Organisations that achieve and sustain competitive advantage using TQM therefore focus on prevention and appraisal in order to eliminate internal and especially external failure.

You will recall from Chapter 16, *Contemporary management accounting concepts* that modern manufacturers may employ a just-in-time (JIT) system which minimises inventory and relies on the prompt delivery of goods to the factory, and ultimately to customers. Quality is essential in a JIT system, as there is no excess inventory on hand to replace units with quality problems, and no room for error. In such scenarios the timeliness with which goods are delivered is often also seen as an additional dimension of quality.

17.4.5 Lean systems

Key terms: lean systems, Six Sigma

The latest thinking around issues of achieving competitive advantage through improved operations is encapsulated in the principles underlying **lean systems** and **Six Sigma**. Focusing on individual products and services and their respective value chains (see section 17.8 below), lean philosophy aims to eliminate all waste in all areas and functions of the business by adopting an enterprise-wide perspective that identifies seven forms of waste, namely:

- Over-production
- Defects
- Unnecessary inventory
- Inappropriate processing
- Excessive transportation
- Waiting, and
- Unnecessary motion.

> By taking into account the current state and the desired future state of process performance throughout the enterprise, the lean philosophy assists organisations to develop improved operational strategies, for example, parallel working and flexibility through multi-skilling employees (Pepper & Spedding 2009). Improved operational performance in turn impacts positively on business performance, resulting in the attainment of competitive advantage.

17.4.6 Six Sigma

In conjunction with the emergence of lean systems, Six Sigma supports operational excellence through reducing variation in all organisational processes, both manufacturing and administrative. The term 'Six Sigma' refers to a statistical measure related to the capability of the process to produce non-defective products (Klefsjö et al 2001). Six Sigma provides organisations with a structured approach to process improvement through a five stage cycle: define, measure, analyse, improve, and control. The structured and systematic methodology to process improvement is guided by a specific target – a reduced defect rate of 3,4 defects for every one million opportunities. Each of the five stages is supported by a number of relevant tools and techniques such as statistical process control and Kaizen costing (see section 7.5.5) in order to measure, analyse and improve critical processes with a view to bringing the system under control (Pepper & Spedding 2009). Six Sigma creates competitive advantage through improved product quality.

17.5 Target costing

Given the somewhat conflicting objectives of providing innovative products and services at a lower cost than one's competitors, and at the same time ensuring the profitability of the organisation, cost management is a key element in the survival of organisations.

17.5.1 Definition of target costing

Key terms: reverse costing, target costing

Target costing is a way of reducing the costs of future products by concentrating on cost management during product development. It is an approach that entails the establishment of allowable product cost by subtracting an organisation's desired profit margin from the estimated selling price (which is to a large extent determined by estimating what customers would be willing to pay). Also known as **reverse costing**, target costing uses a market-driven approach to determine the allowable cost (target cost) of a product during the product's design and development. Target costing is therefore concerned with addressing the question *'what may a product cost?'* rather than *'what does a product cost?'*, in order to ensure that products designed and developed by an organisation are commercially viable in the market.

17.5.2 Establishing a selling price

Establishing the selling price of the proposed product is done in such a way that it takes into account expected market conditions at the time of launching the product. In addition, the proposed product selling price should take into account certain internal and external factors. Internal factors worth considering include the position of the product in the organisation's product portfolio, strategies, and profitability goals of top management. This process is important because the proposed product has to fit within the broader product strategies of the organisation, as well as the required return on investment as determined by shareholder needs.

External factors that are considered in setting a target selling price include:
- The organisation's image in the market
- The level of customer loyalty in the product's market
- The product's expected quality level, functionality, and price compared to competing products.

In addition, the organisation's expected market share in the targeted market is taken into account to make sure that the organisation does not price itself out of the market.

17.5.3 Determining the desired profit margin

The desired profit margin applied in establishing a product's target cost is determined by taking into account, among other things, stakeholder needs and funding for future research and development of new products. It is important therefore to remember that not only is the desired profit margin influenced by the required return of investment (as determined by shareholders), but that the organisation's future financial needs for developing products are also an influencing factor.

17.5.4 Product-level target cost

Key term: product-level target cost

When satisfied with the proposed selling price and the desired profit margin set, the difference between the two results is what is known as the **product-level target cost**. From Figure 17.2, we can see that the product-level target costing process involves comparing the theoretical product-level target cost and the actual cost of the product prototype (shown as 'current cost'). This process often shows the current product cost to be higher than the product-level target cost. This then brings about a strategic cost reduction challenge, where the organisation has to determine how to reduce the prototype cost (current cost) to a level that is equal to or below the product-level target cost. This requires breaking down the product-level target cost into component-level target costs.

Figure 17.2 Product-level target costing processes

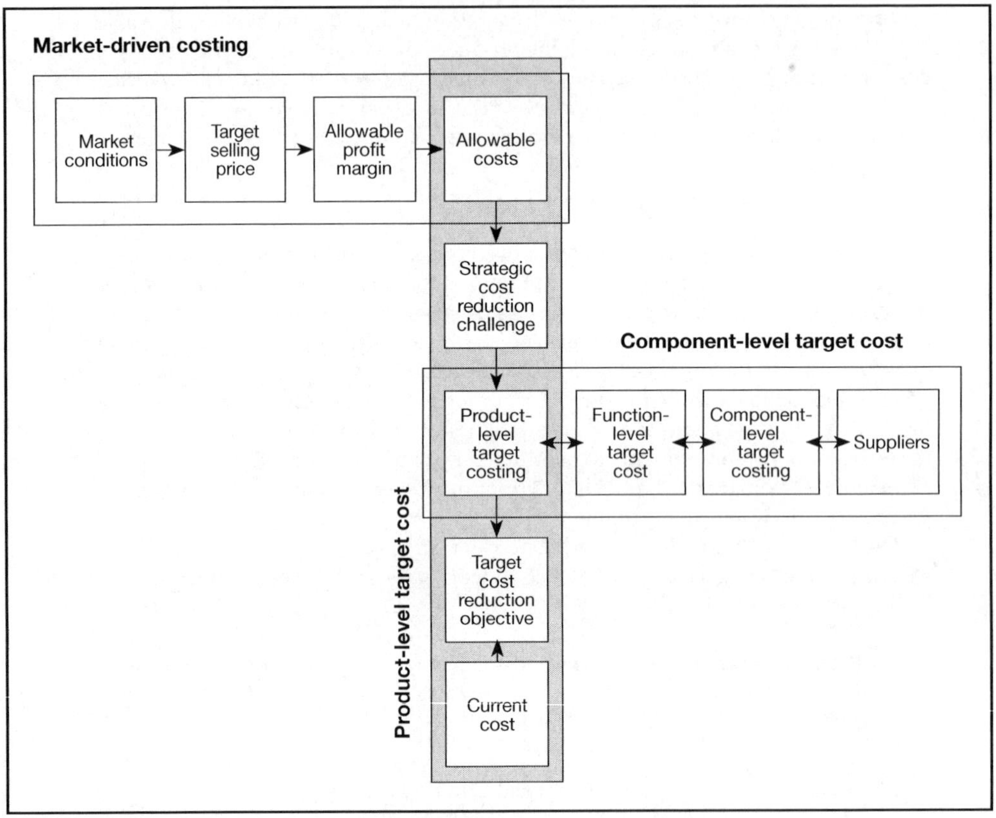

Source: Adapted from Cooper and Slagmulder 1999:32

17.5.5 Component-level target costs

Key terms: component-level target costs, kaizen costing

The product-level target cost is further broken down into **component-level target costs**, which are communicated to all key players within the organisation. The component-level target costs are also communicated to all suppliers to design and manufacture components or inputs that meet the required functionality and quality at the specified costs. Therefore, the process of setting a product's target cost takes place at two levels (product and component level), as shown in Figure 17.2 above.

Even once production of the new product line has started, the target cost may still be below the initial cost of producing the units. However, the target cost is expected to be achieved by the time the product reaches the 'mature' stage.

Chapter 17 *Competitive advantage*

> **Kaizen costing**
> While most of the cost reductions are realised during product design, incremental cost reductions can be effected during product or component manufacture. **Kaizen costing** (a Japanese term) is used when an organisation strives for continuous improvement. It is a deliberate programme that is in synch with the organisation's strategic objectives and is designed to support the cost management efforts inherent in target costing. It involves a clearly-understood plan of how the cost reductions are to be achieved, in addition to a feedback loop that tells the organisation the extent to which the cost reduction objectives have been realised.

17.6 Life-cycle costing

Key term: life-cycle costing

Life-cycle costing (LCC) is the maintenance of cost records that accumulate the costs incurred over the lifespan of a product, service or physical asset. Making useful decisions that result in attaining competitive advantage requires adequate visibility of costs at each stage of the life-cycle. The following sections discuss each of these stages.

17.6.1 Pre-production costs

Research has shown that the bulk (up to 80 per cent) of a product's total life-cycle costs is committed during the research, development and engineering cycle (Monden & Hamada 1991; Kaplan & Atkinson 1998; Dekker & Smidt 2003; Atkinson et al 2004). Committed costs are costs that arise from the product features that have been included in the product prototype, the production processes designed, and any specialised tooling required for the manufacture of the product. From an LCC point of view, the decisions that product designers, engineers and managers make during this stage are critical in saving money in the next two stages. It is therefore advisable to spend adequate money on pre-production activities such as research and development in order to ensure a lower total LCC for the product.

Notice that the adoption of LCC means that pre-production costs such as research and development costs need to be allocated to specific product lines. This may not previously have been done in many organisations.

17.6.2 Production costs

Production commences once a product has been declared commercially viable after the pre-production stage. From a cost management point of view, once the production cycle starts, there is little room for design changes because they would have been set in the previous stage. As such, cost savings that can be achieved during this stage are limited to the opportunities presented by the actual production methods that an organisation uses. Organisations can still achieve some cost savings in the production stage, for example, by employing activity-based management, continuous improvement, kaizen costing and just-in-time manufacturing (see Chapter 16, *Contemporary management accounting concepts*).

During the production stage itself, costs are not evenly incurred over the time during which a particular product line is manufactured, as is often assumed in simplified calculations in management accounting. The product life-cycle model contends that every product and service has a life-cycle. The product goes through an introductory stage (where costs are typically high and sales grow rapidly), a maturity stage (where costs and sales have stabilised and healthy cash inflows are achieved), and a decline stage (where the market has become saturated, and where a point is eventually reached where it is no longer viable to produce the product). If we focus only on costs, we can appreciate that per-unit costs are often logically higher in the introductory stage of the life-cycle, before economies of scale, learning curves and other efficiencies have set in. By the time the maturity stage is reached, the organisation has usually been able to lower the per-unit costs owing to larger volumes and the experience and efficiencies gained through the passage of time.

Figure 17.3 Life-cycle costs of a product or service

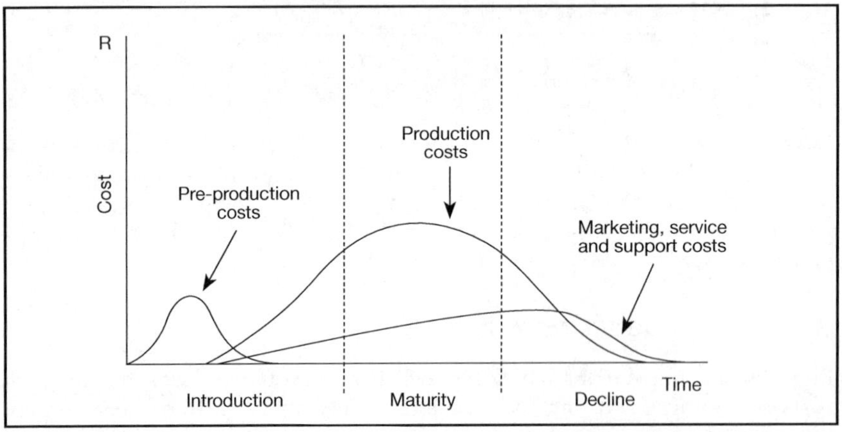

Source: CIMA 2000:36

17.6.3 Marketing, service and support costs

Most of the costs incurred in this stage result from product design and production in terms of quality, form and functionality. These costs include marketing costs (allocated to specific product lines) and repairs and maintenance costs as well as warranty costs.

In terms of achieving and sustainable competitive advantage, it is important to remember that the lower the LCC of a product that an organisation manufactures and sells, the better the organisation's competitive advantage.

The opening sentence of this section on LCC introduced the concept as one that can be applied not only to products that are manufactured or services that are delivered by an organisation (as discussed above), but also to physical assets held by the organisation, such as plant and machinery. This means that all the costs relating to the asset that are incurred in the time during which the asset is held are accumulated. This includes the costs incurred by the organisation in disposing of the asset. When the LCC concept is applied to physical assets such as plant and machinery, the estimated LCC of the asset can be considered when the investment decision is taken, instead of focusing exclusively on the purchase price.

17.7 Supply chain management

Key terms: supply chain, supply chain management

Christopher and Ryals (1999:3) define the supply chain as:

'[t]he network of organisations that are involved, through upstream and downstream linkages, in the different processes and activities that produce value in the form of products and services in the hands of the ultimate customer'.

Supply chain management (SCM) involves the flows of materials, information, and finance in a network con-sisting of customers, suppliers, manufacturers, and distributors. Organisations co-ordinate their individual activities to satisfy the end-use customer and ensure the profitability of the entire supply chain. A **supply chain** can be seen as a synchronised flow of products, information, processes, and cash – from raw materials to end customers – that optimises the profitability of the entire chain, from the suppliers' suppliers to the customers' customers, and the individual business partners that make up the chain (Cap Gemini 2000). Organisations constituting a supply chain work together beyond the boundaries of their own businesses.

The 1990s saw customers becoming very demanding, expecting higher levels of product and service performance. As a result of the globalisation of many industries, customers had access to competitive products and better alternatives, which made them expect greater product and service customisation, and at the same time they became used to a constant stream of innovations in the goods and services they use. There has as a result been a change in supply-chain strategy as organisations have realised that the purpose of supply-chain integration is not solely to reduce costs. Instead, organisations regard SCM as a catalyst for value creation by achieving higher levels of customer satisfaction as a way of creating long-term relationships that impact positively on their profitability. SCM strategy has therefore changed from being internally focused with the objective of cost reduction, to being externally focused with the objective of achieving greater customer satisfaction, as a way of creating value for all supply chain partners. Consequently, the mid-1990s saw organisations establishing tightly integrated or synchronised supply chains, where information technology and the Internet were the key enablers of the supply chain innovative strategy.

Logistics and SCM are not synonymous. SCM goes beyond the scope of logistics to include the establishment of long-lasting, trust-based collaborative relationships between organisations within a supply chain, who treat each other as partners. Consequently SCM involves sharing information about new product development, which includes marketing for the concept, research and development for the actual design, manufacturing, finance and logistics.

Consider Figure 17.4, which shows the supply chain of a fictional organisation, SA Manufacturers. SA Manufacturers purchases the components that it uses in the manufacturing process from SA Components. SA Components buys its input materials from SA Raw Materials. SA Manufacturers sells its product to SA Distributors. Notice the arrows between the blocks representing the various organisations in the sketch. If we want to draw a highly-integrated supply chain, we can shorten the distance between the organisations and place the blocks right next to each other (or even show them overlapping) to indicate the level of co-operation and integration that has been achieved through optimal supply chain management.

Figure 17.4 The supply chain of SA Manufacturers

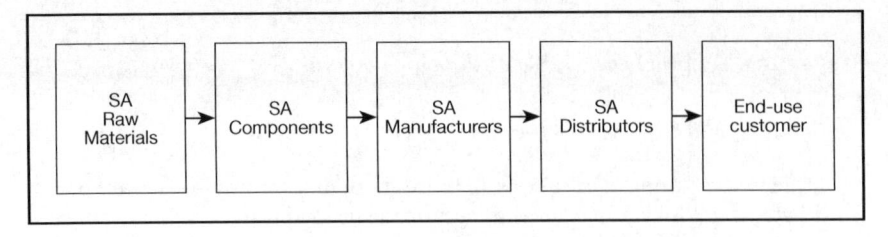

SA Raw Materials → SA Components → SA Manufacturers → SA Distributors → End-use customer

17.7.1 How supply chain management confers competitive advantage

In order to achieve strategic fit and attain competitive advantage, key players across the supply chain must first understand the customer needs in the targeted segment that the supply chain wants to satisfy. Once this is done, the next step is to understand the supply chain capabilities. When the two aspects match and are combined, a strategic fit is achieved.

Organisations that form part of an integrated supply chain are able to meet customers' needs more quickly and more efficiently than where organisations have an arm's-length relationship. Focus and specialisation in a tightly co-ordinated supply chain enable organisations to collect comprehensive, accurate and timely information that is critical in satisfying their end-use customers. The nature of competition has changed to the extent that, increasingly, entire supply chains compete against each other (instead of individual organisations competing against each other).

Information is critical to all the operations of a supply chain. An information system such as management accounting is therefore expected to play an important role in supporting the strategic intent of the entire supply chain, which is the creation of competitive advantage for all supply chain partners through cost reduction and improved customer service. Organisations across the supply chain require the contribution of ideas and information from management accounting.

17.8 Value chain analysis

Key terms: internal value chain, value chain, value chain analysis, value system

A **value chain** is defined by CIMA as the sequence of business activities by which, in the perspective of the end user, value is added to the products or services produced by an organisation.

Value chain analysis is a tool that organisations can use to attain competitive advantage. This is realised by disaggregating an organisation into its strategically relevant activities so as to understand cost behaviour as well as existing and potential sources of differentiation. Gaining competitive advantage therefore arises from the ability of an organisation to execute the value-creating activities in a better and more cost-effective way than an organisation's competitors are able to. For an organisation to realise the benefits arising from its **internal value chain**, it is necessary to understand all the activities within the organisation that create competitive advantage. Once these activities have been identified, they should be managed in a more effective and efficient way compared to competitors' activities.

Figure 17.5 shows the generic internal value chain for an organisation as depicted by Porter. Each organisation's primary activities consist of:
- Inbound logistics (receipt and handling of inputs)
- Operations (transforming of the inputs)
- Outbound logistics (handling and distributing outputs)
- Marketing and sales (of outputs), and
- Service (post-sales service to customers).

There are also four support activities, namely firm infrastructure (where, among others, the accounting function would be classified), technology development, human resource management, and procurement. The 'margin' in Porter's sketch shows the value that has been created by the value chain – that amount by which the value of outputs exceeds the value of inputs.

Figure 17.5 Porter's value chain

Firm infrastructure					MARGIN
Technology development				
Human resource management				
Procurement				
Inbound logistics	Operations	Outbound logistics	Marketing and sales	Service

Source: Porter 1998

Using our knowledge of supply chain management from the previous section, we can contend that an organisation's internal value chain does not operate in isolation – it forms part of an industry value chain or a 'value system' (the term used by Porter). The **value system** is made up of all the value-creating activities within the supply chain, starting with the basic raw materials and ending with the delivery of the final product into the hands of the end-use customer.

Figure 17.6 Porter's value system

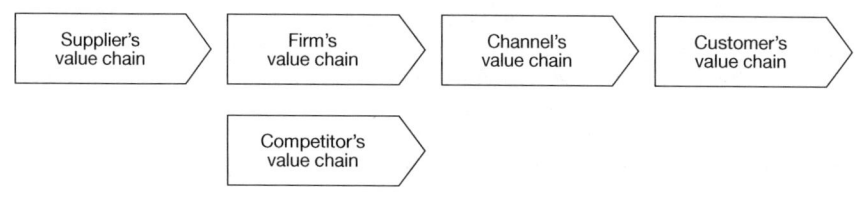

Supplier's value chain → Firm's value chain → Channel's value chain → Customer's value chain

Competitor's value chain

Source: Porter 1998

The value chain shows the relationship between activities (described as the 'linkages') and recognises that activities are interdependent. Donelan and Kaplan (1998) argue that an organisation's value chain activities are interrelated in such a way that no activity should be managed independently without due regard to the potential impact on all other activities. Achieving competitive advantage by using value chain analysis involves the management of value chain activities and the exploitation of linkages (for example, in a just-in-time system, an electronic input of an order by a sales clerk seamlessly triggers production). Adequate resources should be devoted to value chain activities that confer the maximum benefits to the organisation. Other activities should be streamlined, reduced or outsourced in order to ensure that the organisation's efforts are geared towards activities that have the greatest impact on its ability to achieve and sustain competitive advantage.

17.9 Summary

This chapter has dealt with a number of techniques, practices and philosophies that enable organisations to build and maintain competitive advantage in today's highly competitive, global economy.

Porter contends that organisations should choose one of three generic strategies that will enable them to lay the foundation for how they see themselves competing in the global market place. All other decisions and actions taken then ought to be in line with the chosen strategy.

Activity-based management is a technique that requires mangers to identify and manage the underlying activities that cause costs to be incurred. Where activity-based costing uses this knowledge to determine accurately the cost of products and services, activity-based management improves the organisation's competitive position by studying which activities are necessary and how they can be managed most efficiently.

Total quality management comes from the realisation that, in today's global economy, delivering a quality product or service to customers is crucial to the survival of the organisation. Quality has many dimensions, all of which depend on how the customer perceives the product or service. At the heart of total quality management is a realisation that it is better (and in total, cheaper) to rather spend money early on to ensure quality, instead of delivering a product or service of poor quality.

Most accounting students, when asked to recommend a selling price for a product, would be inclined to perform a detailed cost calculation and add a mark-up percentage to arrive at the selling price. Target costing challenges this view: it simply contends that the selling price should be what the customer is willing to pay. When a desired profit is deducted from this price, the target cost is known. The product is then designed in such a way that the target cost will be achievable. Once production has started, the kaizen costing technique, which aims to drive production costs down steadily in each period, may be employed to help reach the target cost level. Organisations that make use of target costing are usually willing to accept losses in the short-term, but are likely to gain market share and customer loyalty early on because the product is priced just right for its market.

Life-cycle costing is a way of making sure managers see all the costs that a product or service has incurred during its entire life-cycle. It keeps a cost record per product line, which aggregates all the costs from the pre-production stage up until the product line is discontinued.

In these modern times of intense competition, organisations can no longer afford to focus inwardly exclusively when attempting to find competitive advantage. They are increasingly realising that co-operation between organisations in the supply chain is key: suppliers and customers along the length of the supply chain are moving closer together and finding ways to improve the competitive position of the chain as a whole.

Value chain analysis allows managers to group organisational activities into categories (such as those supplied by Porter's value chain) in order to get a clear view of how value is added by the organisation. This knowledge is then further exploited to improve competitive advantage, for example, by investigating how key activities can be linked to each other more efficiently, and to see which activities may not be necessary at all.

Conclusion: Competitive advantage and other chapters in this book

Various management accounting topics and techniques have been discussed in this book. All of the techniques, when applied in the private sector in profit-seeking organisations, assume a viable and functioning organisation, and then focus on aspects such as planning, control and decision-making within the organisation. However, owing to increasing competition and increasingly demanding customers, the very survival of many modern organisations is threatened. This chapter has explored ways in which competitive advantage is achieved and sustained in the contemporary business environment.

Some of the concepts in this chapter specifically tie in with the just-in-time manufacturing philosophy discussed in Chapter 16, *Contemporary management accounting concepts*. Activity-based management is closely linked to activity-based costing, which was discussed in Chapter 6, *Overhead allocation*.

Finally, it is crucial that performance should be managed (see Chapter 14, *Performance management*) in a way that supports the strategy that was chosen to pursue competitive advantage. For example, if the organisation strives for the elimination of waste, an emphasis on quality, and tight links with suppliers and customers, performance measures should focus on these goals in order to encourage their achievement.

Tutorial case study: Distell Group

The *Distell Group Limited* produces and markets wine, spirits, ciders and ready-to-drink lines. Its wine brands include Nederburg, Tassenberg and Durbanville Hills. Well-known spirit brands are Amarula Cream, Klipdrift, and Mainstay, while ciders and ready-to-drink brands such as Hunters, Savannah, Bernini and Esprit are also manufactured. Distell is listed on the JSE.

Distell's 2010 financial statements were negatively impacted by adverse economic conditions. After the 2010 annual report was released, the managing director remarked that, looking ahead, the company did not anticipate a marked improvement in trading conditions. 'Unemployment and limited disposable income are likely to continue to impact adversely on consumer spending. We expect the trading environment to remain extremely competitive, both domestically and internationally.'

Source: Distell 2010

1 Three years earlier, in its 2007 annual report, Distell mentioned that it had 'cost leadership goals'. Explain what is meant by 'cost leadership', and how this may provide a competitive advantage in the difficult economic times Distell now faces.
2 Describe a number of main activities that you think may be identified in the manufacturing process if Distell were to implement activity-based management.
3 Describe one cost of quality that may form part of each of the following cost of quality categories in Distell: prevention cost, appraisal cost, internal failure cost, and external failure cost.

> 4 Describe to what extent target costing may be a suitable technique for Distell to employ in its wine production operations.
> 5 Discuss the impact of the design of the glass bottle itself on the costs that would be incurred during the total life-cycle of a product produced by Distell.
> 6 Identify the organisations that would form part of Distell's supply chain. You are not required to name specific organisations, but rather the types of organisations (for example 'farmer').
> 7 Apply Porter's value chain to Distell by identifying the activities that would likely represent each type of primary activity.

Basic questions

BQ 1

What is the difference between activity-based costing (ABC) and activity-based management (ABM)?

BQ 2

Source: Adapted from CIMA P1

Note: This question assumes that you have already studied JIT in Chapter 16, *Contemporary management accounting concepts*.

Why is the adoption of Total Quality Management (TQM) particularly important within a just-in-time (JIT) production environment?

BQ 3

Would Kaizen costing ordinarily be applied during the product design stage? Explain your answer.

BQ 4

What are the basic steps in determining a product's (or a service's) target cost?

BQ 5

A manager recently said: 'In the time during which we produced this product, we sold 50 000 units of it, bringing in total revenue of R5 million. It cost us only R80 per unit to manufacture (which includes materials, labour and overheads), so we made a lot of money.' What do you think of his statement from a life-cycle costing point of view?

BQ 6

How do you think Porter would describe the generic strategies followed by some of South African Airways' local rival airline services such as 1Time, kulula.com and Mango?

BQ 7

When supply chain management is practised, does this necessarily mean that an organisation will work together more closely with its suppliers? Explain why.

BQ 8

In Porter's sketch of the generic internal value chain of an organisation, will each organisation necessarily have a 'margin'? Give a reason(s) for your answer.

BQ 9

To what extent is knowledge of an organisation's supply chain necessary in order to perform value chain analysis?

BQ 10

How has the modern business environment become so competitive that organisations now all strive to attain some form of competitive advantage?

Long questions

LQ 1 – Intermediate (5 marks; 9 minutes)

Source: Adapted from ACCA Paper 3.3 Performance Management

Quicklink Ltd operates in the distribution and haulage industry and has achieved significant growth since its formation in 1997. Its main activities comprise the door-to-door delivery of mail, parcels and industrial machinery. The board of directors agreed to purchase Celer Transport, an unincorporated business. Celer Transport has main activities comprising the delivery of mail, parcels, and processed food.

REQUIRED	Marks
Discuss the main benefits that might accrue from the successful implementation of a Total Quality Management programme by the management of the combined entity.	5
TOTAL MARKS	5

LQ 2 – Intermediate (8 marks; 14 minutes)

Source: Adapted from ACCA Paper 2.4 Financial Management and Control

Sassone (Pty) Ltd is a medium-sized profitable organisation that manufactures engineering products. One of its stated objectives is to maximise shareholder wealth. The directors of Sassone need to increase capacity to meet expected demand for a new product, Product G, which is to be used in the manufacture of new-generation computers. Product G cannot be manufactured on existing machines. The directors have identified two machines which can manufacture Product G, each with a capacity of 60 000 units per year.

REQUIRED	Marks
Discuss how life-cycle costing and target costing may assist Sassone in controlling costs and pricing engineering products.	8
TOTAL MARKS	8

LQ 3 – Advanced (8 marks; 14 minutes)

Source: Adapted from ACCA Paper 3.5 Strategic Business Planning and Development

Good Sports Limited is an independent sports goods retailer owned and operated by two partners, Alan and Bob. The sports retailing business has undergone a major change over the past ten years. First of all, the supply side has been transformed by the emergence of a few global manufacturers of the core sports products, such as training shoes and football shirts. This consolidation has made them increasingly unwilling to provide good service to the independent sportswear retailers too small to buy in sufficiently large quantities. These independent retailers can hold popular global brands in inventory, but have to order using the Internet and have no opportunity to meet the manufacturer's sales representatives. Secondly, sportswear retailing has undergone significant structural change with the rapid growth of a small number of national retail chains with the buying power to offset the power of the global manufacturers. These retail chains hold a limited range of high-volume branded products in inventory and charge low prices which the independent retailer cannot hope to match.

Good Sports has survived by becoming a specialist niche retailer catering for team sports such as cricket, hockey and rugby. They are able to offer specialist advice and keep a supply of the goods that their customers want.

Increasingly since 2XX0 Good Sports had become aware of the growing impact of e-business in general and e-retailing in particular. They employed a specialist website designer and created an online purchasing facility for their customers. The results were less than impressive, with the Internet search engines not picking up the organisation's website. The seasonal nature of Good Sports' business, together with the variations in sizes and colours needed to meet an individual customer's needs, meant that the sales volumes were insufficient to justify the costs of running the site.

Bob, however, is convinced that developing an e-business strategy suited to the needs of the independent sports retailer such as Good Sports is integral to business survival. He has been encouraged by the growing interest of customers in other countries in the service and product range they offer. He is also aware of the need to integrate an e-business strategy with their current marketing, which to date has been limited to the sponsorship of local sports teams and advertisements taken in specialist sports magazines. Above all, he wants to avoid head-on competition with the national retailers and their emphasis on popular branded sportswear sold at retail prices that are below the cost price at which Good Sports can buy the goods.

REQUIRED	Marks
Good Sports Limited has successfully followed a niche (or focus) strategy to date. Assess the extent to which an appropriate e-business strategy could help support such a niche strategy.	8
TOTAL MARKS	8

LQ 4 – Advanced (25 marks; 45 minutes)

Source: Adapted from ACCA Paper P3 Business Analysis Pilot paper

DRB Electronic Services is located in X, a developed country, and imports electronic products from the Republic of Korea. It re-brands and re-packages them as DRB products and then sells them to business and domestic customers in the local geographical region. Its only current source of supply is ISAS electronics, based in a factory on the outskirts of Seoul, the capital of the Republic of Korea. DRB regularly places orders for ISAS products through the ISAS website, and pays for them by credit card. As soon as the payment is confirmed, ISAS automatically e-mails DRB a confirmation of order, an order reference number, and a likely shipping date. When the order is actually despatched, ISAS sends DRB a notice of despatch e-mail and a container reference number.

ISAS currently organises all the shipping of the products. The products are sent in containers and then trans-shipped to EIF, the logistics organisation used by ISAS to distribute its products. EIF then delivers the products to the DRB factory. Once they arrive, they are quality inspected, and products that pass the inspection are re-branded as DRB products (by adding appropriate logos) and packaged in specially-made DRB boxes. These products are then stored ready for sale. All customer sales are from inventory. Products that fail the inspection are returned to ISAS.

Currently 60 per cent of sales are made to domestic customers and 40 per cent to business customers. Most domestic customers pick up their products from DRB and set them up themselves. In contrast, most business customers ask DRB to set up the electronic equipment at their offices, for which DRB makes a small charge. DRB currently advertises its products in local and regional newspapers. DRB also has a website which provides product details. Potential customers can enquire about the specification and availability of products through an e-mail facility on the website. DRB then e-mails an appropriate response directly to the person making the enquiry. Payment for products cannot currently be made through the website.

Feedback from existing customers suggests that they particularly value the installation and support offered by the organisation. The organisation employs specialist technicians who (for a fee) will instal equipment in both homes and offices. They will also come out and troubleshoot problems with equipment that is still under warranty. DRB also offer a helpline and a back-to-base facility for customers whose products are out of warranty. Feedback from current customers suggests that this support is highly valued. One commented that 'it contrasts favourably with your large competitors, who offer support through impersonal off-shore call centres and a time-consuming returns policy'. Customers can also pay for technicians to come on-site to sort out problems with out-of-warranty equipment.

DRB now plans to increase its product range and market share. It plans to grow from its current turnover of R5m per annum to R12m per annum in two years' time. Dilip Masood, the owner of DRB, believes that DRB must change its business model if it is to achieve this growth. He believes that these changes will also have to tackle problems associated with

- *Missing, or potentially missing, shipments:* Shipments can be tracked only through contacting the shipment account holder, ISAS, and on occasions they have been reluctant or unable to help. The trans-shipment to EIF has also caused problems, and this has usually been identified as the point where goods have been lost. ISAS does not appear to be able to track reliably the relationship between the container shipment and the waybills used in the EIF system.
- *The likely delivery dates of orders, the progress of orders and the progress of shipments is poorly specified and monitored.* Deliveries are therefore relatively unpredictable, and this can cause congestion problems in the delivery bay.

Dilip also recognises that growth will mean that the organisation has to sell more products outside its region and that the technical installation and support so valued by local customers will be difficult to maintain. He is also adamant that DRB will continue to import only fully-configured products. It is not interested in importing components and assembling them. DRB also does not wish to build or invest in assembly plants overseas or to commit to a long-term contract with one supplier.

principles of management accounting

REQUIRED		Marks
(a)	Draw the primary activities of DRB on a value chain. Comment on the significance of each of these activities and the value that they offer to customers.	9
(b)	Explain how DRB might re-structure its upstream supply chain to achieve the growth required by DRB and to tackle the problems that Dilip Masood has identified.	10
(c)	Explain how DRB might re-structure its downstream supply chain to achieve the growth required.	6
TOTAL MARKS		**25**

LQ5 – Advanced (25 marks; 45 minutes)

Source: CIMA P6

2B is a medium-sized retailer of sports equipment and leisure clothing. It was established in 1987, and currently operates from three retail shops in town centre locations.

The management team of 2B is very careful about how it recruits staff. In addition to the specific skills required to do the job, any applicant must also have a passion for sport. This has resulted in 2B's gaining a reputation for excellent customer service and enthusiastic staff. A large proportion of staff time is also devoted to training, both on the product range and customer service techniques. According to a recent survey conducted by the store managers, the customers believe that 2B employees are helpful and knowledgeable. The customers also praised the 2B shops for being well designed, and said that it was very easy to find what they were looking for.

Another feature of 2B that is appreciated by the customers is the range of goods in inventory. By developing close relationships with the major manufacturers of sports goods and clothing, 2B is able to keep in inventory a far wider range of items than its rivals. Control of this inventory was made easier last year by the development of a sophisticated computerised inventory control system. Using the system, any member of staff can locate any item of inventory in any of the shops or the warehouse. If the required item is not in inventory at 2B, it is also possible to check automatically the availability of inventory with the manufacturer.

At a recent management meeting, one of the store managers suggested that 2B consider developing its very basic website into one capable of e-retailing. At present, the website gives only the location of stores and some very basic details of the range of inventory carried. Although the development of the website would be expensive, the managers have decided to give the suggestion serious consideration.

REQUIRED		Marks
(a)	Using the value chain model, explain those activities that add value in the 2B organisation, BEFORE the e-retail investment.	10
(b)	Identify those activities in the value chain of 2B that may be affected by the e-retail investment, explaining whether the value added by each of them may increase or decrease as a result of the e-retail investment.	15
TOTAL MARKS		**25**

References

Atkinson, AA, Kaplan, RS & Young, SM. 2004. *Management accounting*, Fourth edition. Upper Saddle River, New Jersey: Pearson Prentice Hall.

Blocher, EJ, Chen, KH, Cokins, G & Lin, TW. 2005. *Cost management: a strategic emphasis*, Third edition (International edition). New York: McGraw-Hill/Irwin.

Business Link Magazine. 2010. *All-new Ford Ranger a significant milestone for Ford in South Africa*. [Online]. Available: <www.businesslinkmagazine.co.za/blog/news-views/news-views-blog-articles/all-new-ford-ranger-a-significant-milestone-for-ford-in-south-africa/> [14 February 2011].

Cokins, G. 2001. *Activity-based cost management: an executive guide*. New York: John Wiley & Sons.

Cap Gemini, Ernst & Young & IndustryWeek. 2000. *High performance value chains: charting the course for synergy in the connected economy*. [Online]. Available: <www.capgemini.com> [28 March 2008].

Chivaka, R. 2002. 'The role of management accountants in value creation through improved supply chain management: a case study of the South African retail sector'. Supply Chain Management & E-business Conference, Sheffield, UK. 1–29.

Chivaka, R. 2003. *Value creation through strategic cost management along the supply chain*. Published PhD thesis, University of Cape Town. 1–376.

Chivaka, R. 2005. 'Cost management along the supply chain – methodological implications'. In *Research methodologies in supply chain management*. Heidelberg, Germany: Physica.

Chivaka, R. 2006. 'Cost management using target costing methodology across the supply chain: a transaction cost economics perspective'. Paper presented at the 29th Congress of the European Accounting Association, Dublin, Ireland. 1–29.

Christopher, M & Ryals, L. 1999. 'Supply chain strategy: its impact on shareholder value'. The International Journal of Logistics Management, 10(1):3.

Cooper, R & Kaplan, RS. 1999. *The design of cost management systems: text and cases*, Second edition. Upper Saddle River, New Jersey: Prentice Hall.

Cooper, R & Slagmulder, R. 1999. 'Develop profitable new products with target costing'. *Sloan Management Review*, Vol. 40(4):23–33, Summer.

Dekker, H & Smidt, P. 2003. 'A survey of the adoption and use of target costing in Dutch firms'. *International Journal of Production Economics*, 84:293–305.

Distell. 2010. *Distell undeterred by current market, focuses on future fitness*. [Online]. Available: <www.distell.co.za/RunTime/POPContentRun.aspx?pageidref=2489> [10 February 2011].

Donelan, JG & Kaplan, EA. 1998. 'Value chain analysis: a strategic approach to cost management'. *Cost Management*, March/April.

Drury, C. 2004. *Management and cost accounting*, Sixth edition. London, UK: Business Press, Thompson Learning.

Hoque, Z (ed). 2005. 'Quality costing: concepts and processes'. In *Handbook of cost and management accounting*. London, UK: Spiramus Press.

Juran, JM. 1974. *Quality control handbook*, Third edition. Dallas, Texas: McGraw-Hill.

Kaplan, RS & Atkinson, AA. 1998. *Advanced management accounting*, Third edition. Upper Saddle River, New Jersey: Prentice Hall International Inc.

Klefsjö, B, Wiklund, H & Edgeman, R L. 2001. 'Six Sigma as a methodology for total quality management'. *Measuring Business Excellence*, 5(1):31–35.

Lord, BR. 1999. 'Key performance indicators in a total quality management environment: a case study'. *Cost Management*, May/June.

Monden, Y & Hamada, K. 1991. 'Target costing and kaizen costing in Japanese automobile companies'. *Journal of Management Accounting Research*, 16–34, Fall.

Pepper, MPJ & Spedding, TA. (2009) 'The evolution of lean six sigma'. *International Journal of Quality & Reliability Management*, 27(2):138–155.

Porter, M. 1979. *Competitive advantage: creating and sustaining superior performance*. New York: Free Press, a division of Simon and Schuster Adult Publishing Group.

Porter, M. 1985. *Competitive advantage: creating and sustaining superior performance*. New York: Free Press, a division of Simon and Schuster Adult Publishing Group.

Porter, M. 1998. *Competitive advantage: creating and sustaining superior performance.* New York: Free Press, a division of Simon and Schuster Adult Publishing Group.

Wang, G, Gao, Z & Lin, TW. 1998. 'Integrating the quality cost report and TQM tools to achieve competitive advantage'. *Cost Management*, 42–47, January/February.

Advanced reading Integration section: Chapters 14 to 17

Shelley-Anne Roos

> The aim of this section is to integrate students' knowledge of Chapters 14 to 17, and to move students toward a more advanced, high-level understanding of the topics, the relationships between them, and the exam technique required.

Performance management forms a large and important part of management accounting syllabi. It is a topic that builds on the principles of management accounting theory – one needs an in-depth understanding of costs and revenues in order to appropriately analyse the performance of an organisation. When considering financial information with the purpose of assessing performance, it is necessary to understand how costs were classified, how they would behave (both individually and in relation to each other), how they were recorded (for example, absorption costing was applied for financial accounting purposes), and what techniques were used to assign costs to cost objects (for example, how overheads were allocated, whether job or process costing was used, whether standard costing techniques were employed). Performance assessment requires one to analyse a set of information, to apply judgement to form an opinion, and to communicate findings in a convincing manner. It follows that performance management is an ideal theme for examiners to use in advanced questions that integrate a number of management accounting topics in a single case study scenario. For this reason you will find that many questions in advanced courses, as well as professional exam questions, feature this important topic.

Transfer pricing could potentially require intricate numerical calculations and pose many technical difficulties, although advanced exam questions often prefer to test students' understanding of the topic together with other related topics. A potentially complex topic such as transfer pricing is one that is best mastered when focusing on the basic underlying principles. It is important to understand that transfer pricing results in intra-organisational entries, in other words, the transactions between different units within an organisation cancel each other out and do not affect the results of the organisation as a whole. However, should an organisation's units be autonomous (meaning that unit managers have a great degree of decision-making power), the *decisions* that managers make based on transfer prices may indeed affect the results of the organisation as a whole. The management accountant should assess the transfer price and determine whether it leads to optimal decision-making within the organisation. The reason that unit managers may take sub-optimal decisions based on inappropriate transfer prices is that transfer pricing affects the performance assessment of the unit. Your understanding of transfer pricing should therefore be informed by your knowledge of performance management.

One of the biggest growth areas in the field of management accounting is strategic management. Increasingly, management accounting syllabi include theories on strategy, and high-level management accounting questions are set in the form of case studies where the answers have to be *applied* in the context of the strategy and circumstances of *the particular scenario* in the question. The topics dealt with in Chapters 16 and 17 of this book are likely to feature in such case study scenarios, interwoven with background information on the organisation and financial as well as qualitative facts. It is imperative to understand that decisions are based on the information supplied by a management accounting system, and that those decisions have to be in line with the strategic direction that the organisation wishes to take. Strategy impacts on management accounting, and in turn, management accounting information informs strategy. For example, how performance is managed in an organisation depends on the organisation's strategy (an organisation that has, say, decided to place strategic emphasis on customer retention ought to build prominent customer retention measures into its performance management and reward system). But, in turn, the results of performance measurement in this organisation may have indicated that it is particularly good at retaining customers, which may have informed the decision to direct strategic focus at this core competence in the first place.

> Now that you have studied all the chapters and the integration sections in this book, you should spend some time reflecting on how to prepare for advanced questions in management accounting.

As you progress through your studies of management accounting, you will likely find the questions that you have to answer moving increasingly in the following directions as the work becomes more advanced:

- Questions require more reading, as an increasingly detailed scenario is sketched as background to the question requirements.
- More and more topics are combined within a single question, and the topics are increasingly interwoven to test your understanding of the situation as a whole.
- Answers require more writing, while a smaller portion of the answer is made up of purely numerical calculations. Many management accounting students have strong numerical skills and find this intimidating. However, consider that your high-level understanding of topics can be tested only if you are asked to discuss, comment, analyse, interpret and recommend (as you would be asked to do when employed in a senior management position).
- Questions become less likely to have one specific, clear-cut answer. In the previous point it was mentioned that more discussion is required, which makes it less likely that candidates' answers will be similar. Even where the answer requires calculation, the advanced nature of the question may allow for multiple answers, as long as each answer is internally consistent in its logic.
- You are likely to have to consider uncertain outcomes, assumptions and estimates. In practice, management cannot be certain, for example, that 50 000 units of a product will be sold in the first year. At best they can estimate sales at 50 000 units – when decisions are based on this figure, they need to take into account that they are working with an estimate. Advanced questions mimic real-life problems more closely.
- Fewer marks are awarded for stating facts or performing calculations that could have been memorised. While it is important to study the theory and master the calculations in your early studies, advanced studies require that you apply this knowledge to a particular scenario. If, for example, you are asked whether a given transfer pricing policy would be appropriate, you do not receive marks for discussing the general advantages and disadvantages of the policy. Only advantages and disadvantages that flow from the specific scenario would be valid. Because these are specific to the scenario, the fact that you can identify them illustrates that you understand both the topic and the case study.

What follows is a question that tests some of the material covered in Chapters 14 to 17. Read the question requirements first (to focus your thoughts on what will be required of you), then read the scenario and plan all of your answers. Answer the requirements in the given order (starting with requirement (a)), just in case the question was set in such a way that thinking through the earlier answers leads you to the later answers. Be sure to apply your answers to the scenario as much as possible.

Integrated question: Outdoor Africa

Outdoor Africa operates a retail store on premises of 4 000 square metres in the Limpopo province. The company consists of three divisions that are all located on the same premises. The Garden division sells plants, garden decorations and garden implements, while the Furniture division sells outdoor furniture. The third division is the Cafeteria, where clients can enjoy light meals. Outdoor Africa is open every day of the year, including weekends and public holidays.

Outdoor Africa's head office, which houses senior management and administrative staff, is at a different location.

Results: year ended 29 February 2XX8

The following information is available in respect of the financial year ended 29 February 2XX8:

	Garden division	Furniture division	Cafeteria
Sales	R5 800 000	R2 400 000	R1 500 000
Gross profit percentage added to cost of sales	45%	50%	100%
Floor space occupied	2 000 square metres	1 500 square metres	500 square metres

Numerous permanent staff members worked at Outdoor Africa's retail premises during the year. Each of the three divisions has a manager which earned a total salary package of R100 000 per annum. Furthermore, the Garden division and the Furniture division each have one assistant per 250 metres of floor space, each of whom received a total salary package of R60 000 for the year. A total of nine permanent waiters and kitchen staff members work in the cafeteria, each of whom received a total salary package of R50 000 for the year.

Indirect costs are apportioned to divisions as follows:

	Amount	Allocation base
Rent, electricity and cleaning services	R720 000	Floor space
Advertisements*	R210 000	Divided equally

* From time to time Outdoor Africa places a standard advertisement in local newspapers. The advertisement features contact details and a map to the premises – individual products are not advertised.

Other expenses not allocated to divisions amounted to R750 000.

Staff meals

A group of Outdoor Africa employees complained to the managing director in late February 2XX8 that it was expected of them to take lunch to work at their own expense, while there is a cafeteria on the premises. He asked the management accountant to investigate the possibility of providing meals to staff at the cafeteria at the expense of their own divisions, starting from March 2XX8. The management accountant has gathered the following information:

principles of management accounting

- All staff members working at Outdoor Africa's trade premises would be interested in having free lunches at the cafeteria. It is important to management that all workers enjoy the same benefits, regardless of the division they work for.
- The cafeteria has 25 tables, and four persons can sit at each table.
- The cafeteria's busiest time is between 13h00 and 14h00. Should staff meals be served, staff will not be allowed to eat during this rush hour. The staff of each division will be divided up so that Outdoor Africa's staff members eat in two equal groups: one group will eat in the hour before the lunchtime rush hour, while the other group will eat in the hour after the lunchtime rush hour. There will therefore be staff available in each division to proceed with normal tasks while their colleagues have lunch.
- The variable cost per lunch per staff member will be R25 for a standard meal, as approved by management. Staff will not order from the existing menu.
- Staff will be seated at specific, reserved tables in order to cause the least possible disruption to clients.
- The cafeteria's divisional manager has the authority to refuse the supply of lunches to Outdoor Africa's staff, even if the managing director decides that all staff should be given lunch. In such an instance staff will have lunch at the expense of their divisions at the restaurant across the street, at a cost of R35 per lunch per staff member.
- All staff members have to enjoy the same meals, in other words it is not permissible for some of Outdoor Africa's staff members to eat in the cafeteria and for others to eat across the street.
- The following statistics could be gathered from information extracted from the cafeteria's point-of-sale software:

	Average number of tables occupied by clients	Average rand value per table spent by clients
12h00 to 13h00	22	R100
13h00 to 14h00	25	R120
14h00 to 15h00	20	R100

Suggestions for change

Although everyone who works for Outdoor Africa generally gets along well, some employees have become quite annoyed with Charles, the son of the company's founder. Charles does not officially work for the company, but claims to read management accounting material in his spare time and is quick to make suggestions to any employee he comes across. Some recent incidents that have fuelled the irritation of employees are the following:

1. Charles called the procurement clerk in the Garden division an 'ignorant fool' for still not having implemented a just-in-time system, as he 'should have done years ago'.
2. Charles tore up a copy of the August 2XX7 monthly management accounts at Outdoor Africa's head office, shouting, 'These accounts are useless for performance assessment – clearly the only way to get quality information is to benchmark the Garden division against the Furniture division!'
3. He was overheard saying that the company 'will go out of business if it doesn't change its pricing policy from cost-plus pricing to target costing'.
4. In December 2XX7 a routine meeting took place between the manager of the Garden division and its main supplier, a prominent local nursery. Charles showed up unannounced and told the supplier's representative that he wouldn't be doing business with Outdoor Africa for much longer, because 'proper supply chain management dictates that the company should rather start its own nursery'.

Integration section: Chapters 14 to 17

	REQUIRED	Marks
(a)	Draft a basic income statement for the year ended 29 February 2XX8 for each of the three divisions and for Outdoor Africa as a whole. Use a table format with a column for each.	6
(b)	Comment comprehensively on the relative performance of the three divisions for the year ended 29 February 2XX8, and recommend how Outdoor Africa could improve its profitability.	15
(c)	Determine the impact on the annual profit of Outdoor Africa as a whole of the proposal to provide lunch to staff members at the cafeteria.	6
(d)	Assuming that the managing director requests that lunch indeed be provided to staff members in future, calculate the price per lunch per staff member that the Garden division and the Furniture division ought to pay to the Cafeteria.	6
(e)	Give your reasoned opinion as to the validity, from a management accounting perspective, of Charles's views reflected in the four recent incidents described (use the numbers 1 to 4 to discuss each incident in turn).	12
(f)	Discuss whether the Cafeteria is likely to follow a cost leadership strategy or a differentiation strategy (as identified by Porter), based on the limited information available.	5
	Ignore tax throughout.	
	TOTAL MARKS	**50**

Discussion

A suggested solution to the question can be found at the back of the book. Once you have attempted the question and checked the solution, you may find the following discussion useful.

Part (a) should be straightforward for most students. Advanced scenario questions often start with a rather basic first requirement to ease you into the question. Part (a) requires you to set out the information in an orderly format, which helps you to interpret it further. You should make sure that you score well in part (a). Notice that part (b) follows part (a), so this is an example of a question where it is important to attempt the requirements in the correct order.

Part (b) is typical of an advanced question in management accounting. It asks you to comment on the relative performance of the divisions. Notice that you are not able to comply with this requirement if you either perform calculations only (because then you have not commented), or offer a narrative discussion only (because then you would have very little to discuss – you need to do a substantial number of calculations on which to base your comments). It is also important to note that part (b) asks you to perform two tasks. You first have to comment on the performance, and then you have to make recommendations based on your comments. This is an example of the importance of reading the requirements very thoroughly before writing your answer. If you had followed the suggested technique, you would have read through the requirements before reading through the scenario, so you would have been alert to information that could be useful in your answer. You would also have planned the answer to part (b) before starting to write, by making two headings (one for comments, and one for recommendations, to make sure you address both parts of the requirement). In an advanced question, the examiner is unlikely to allow you to gain anywhere near full marks for a requirement if you have addressed only part of the tasks (in part (b) it is likely that a 'ceiling' or maximum mark will apply for commenting, and another maximum mark for recommending).

There are a number of common errors that you may have made in your answer to part (b). Firstly, make sure you know that an organisation cannot improve its profits by allocating its expenses differently between divisions. The only scenario in which this would be possible requires a long and carefully-worded explanation. If Outdoor Africa were to allocate its expenses more equitably for purposes of performance evaluation of divisions, you may argue that divisional workers could feel more motivated by the improved performance measurement system. If improved motivation then actually led to their working more effectively, the division's results could improve because of this (which would then mean more total profit for Outdoor Africa). It is therefore incorrect simply to write as part of your recommendations that Outdoor Africa would improve its profit through better cost allocation. Allocation can, however, impact on the relative performance of the divisions (the first part of requirement (b)), but to earn marks for this, performance should be evaluated *before* the incorrectly-allocated expense.

If you look at the suggested solution to part (b), you may find that it is easy, even though you may not have scored as well as you had hoped. The information given in the question should be used to assess performance (for example, floor space, income statement information, and so on), rather than forcing pre-conceived theoretical ideas (for example, ROI or RI) on a scenario where they could not be applied.

You may have been tempted to make some generic recommendations in your answer, for example, that the company should 'try to increase sales by advertising more' or 'try to cut costs'. Such recommendations are not specific to your understanding of the scenario and your analysis of the performance of the respective divisions, and are unlikely to earn marks.

Lastly, it is important to notice that the suggested solution to part (b) could be worth much more than 15 marks, although only 15 marks were available. Furthermore, the suggested solution is by no means comprehensive, and you could have made many other valid remarks. The more advanced a question, the less likely it is to have a single, correct, model answer. To score well, you need to have the confidence to write what you find appropriate – a confidence that comes from understanding the material and being sure that you are interpreting the question correctly.

Part (c) is a relevant costing question, and a good example of how transfer pricing (see part (d)) requires an understanding of relevant costing. Again, you needed to answer part (c) first before moving on to part (d). It is not necessary to recognise part (c) consciously as a relevant costing question in order to score full marks – all that is necessary is to read the requirement thoroughly and to apply logic to arrive at the answer.

Part (d) is a good example of a transfer pricing requirement that requires you to think logically and apply the basic principles, as it is often examined in advanced questions. It gives the examiner the opportunity to distinguish between students who understand the principles and those who do not, without repetitive calculations or setting aside a large number of marks at the expense of other topics. If you scored well in part (d), this is a good indication that you grasp the topic.

Part (e) is a rather advanced question. It tests some knowledge from Chapters 16 and 17, but in a context where you have to apply it very carefully to the scenario. As for most advanced requirements, the suggested solution is by no means comprehensive, but it does indicate the main issues that you should have discussed. The suggested solution to part (e) may help you to gain further insight into the topics if you did not master them fully when you studied the text.

Part (f) is difficult to answer because of a deliberate lack of information in the scenario, and because it requires the application of Porter's theory to a single division within a company. You could, however, gain the basic marks by showing that you understand the meaning of the theories, using the case study to illustrate the concepts. From there, some speculation and discussion is needed to gain further marks.

Suggested solutions to integration section questions

Integration section: Chapters 1 to 5

Part (a)(i)

The budget was drawn up using absorption costing. From the information we can see that opening and closing inventory, as well as cost of sales, were calculated after adding ('absorbing') fixed manufacturing costs to the value of inventory.

Inventory increased from zero finished pumps (only components in the form of 24 casings were in opening inventory) to 30 finished pumps in closing inventory. The increase would have had a positive effect on the absorption costing profit, because fixed costs are included in closing inventory. This has created the false impression that the division's position has improved. The actual position is even worse than suggested by the loss of R142 620.

A better understanding of the budget can be gained if the variable costing approach is used. For this analysis the variable costs need to be separated from the fixed costs.

The division's variable and fixed costs can be summarised as follows:

Variable costs per pump	R
Pipe connector (one per pump)*	20,00
Casing (one per pump)*	230,00
Impellers (one set per pump)	250,00
Shaft**	15,00
Electric motor	450,00
Labour: shaft cutting, casings & impellers – all fixed	0,00
Labour: assembly (R50 per hour × 2 hours)	100,00
Sales and administration costs***	38,25
Head office costs****	14,00
Total variable cost	**R1 117,25**

*   To determine the future profitability of the division, we are looking for the best estimate of the costs that will be incurred to manufacture pumps during the next few months. Our best indication of what a pipe connector is likely to cost is R20. The replacement cost is the best indication of what a casing is likely to cost (rather than the R205 cost price and the modification costs that apply only to the 24 units in inventory).
** *Shafts:* Fixed costs allocated to shafts are R160 000/1 000 units = R160 per unit. We divide by 1 000 units because the normal production capacity of the division is 1 000 pumps per month (refer to the second paragraph of the question). The variable cost is therefore R175 – R160 = R15 per shaft.
*** *Sales and administration costs:* R37 100 (R148 400 × 25%) is variable. This is R38,25 per pump sold (R37 100/970 pumps sold).

principles of management accounting

**** The portion of head office costs relating to the patent is directly attributable to the division and is variable per pump sold. This amount therefore needs to be included here. To determine the variable portion, the high-low method is used. April is the 'high' month and information for the 'low' month is given. Therefore [R173 580 (April) – R171 900 (lowest month)]/(970 units – 850 units) = R14 per pump sold.

Fixed costs

The total production cost is given as R1 622 000 in the budgeted income statement, and relates to the production of 1 000 pumps during the month. Therefore each unit was assigned a cost of R1 622 (R1 622 000/1 000 pumps) under the absorption costing system.

To determine the fixed costs assigned to each unit, we need to deduct the variable costs that would have been included in this amount. All variable manufacturing costs would have been included.

R1 622 total cost – R20 (connector) – R230 (casing) – R250 (impellers) – R15 (shaft) – R450 (electric motor) – R100 (labour: assembly) = R557 fixed costs allocated per pump.

This means the total fixed cost of production is estimated as R557 000 (R557 × 1 000 pumps) per month. Note that no under- or over-allocation is included in the income statement; therefore the allocated fixed cost is equal to the incurred fixed cost of production.

The fixed portion of sales and administration cost is R148 400 × 75% = R111 300.

The fixed portion of allocated head office costs is (R173 580 – R14 variable cost × 970 pumps sold) = R160 000. These costs should be deducted from divisional profits in our analysis, because the head office does some work for the division and therefore these central costs would theoretically have been incurred if the division had been a stand-alone company (on the assumption that the allocation is fair). *Do not worry too much if you made an error here: this principle is dealt with later in the book (Chapter 14,* Performance management*).*

Total fixed costs per month for the division are R557 000 (fixed production cost) + R111 300 (fixed sales and administration cost) + R160 000 (fixed head office cost allocated to the division) = R828 300.

The insurance income is a once-off item – it is non-recurring and therefore it does not help us to project the future profitability of the division. The income should be ignored for purposes of this analysis.

Break-even point

The selling price per pump is R1 703 320/970 pumps sold = R1 756.

The contribution per pump is therefore R1 756 – R1 117,25 (variable cost per pump as calculated) = R638,75.

The break-even point is R828 300 (total fixed costs of the division)/R638,75 (contribution per pump) = 1 296,75 pumps.

The contribution that could be earned from selling excess impellers is not taken into account. This is because the break-even point for pumps calculated above is 1 297 pumps while only 1 150 sets of impellers can be manufactured every month. Pumpworks will use the limited number of impellers to manufacture pumps rather than to sell them, because Pumpworks earns a higher contribution per pump than the R120 (R370 − R250) it can earn from selling impellers. In other words, at the break-even point there will be no spare impellers to sell.

This brings us to the next question: can the Pumpworks division manufacture 1 297 pumps per month? From the information we see that it can manufacture only 1 150 sets of impellers and 1 100 shafts per month. Furthermore, labour information points to the fact that there are 13 workers in the casings department that each work 160 hours per month and it takes 2 hours to manufacture one casing. This means only 1 040 casings (13 workers × 160 hours/2 hours) can be manufactured per month. The capacity of the Pumpworks division is therefore limited to the smallest of these capacity constraints, namely the casings labour. A maximum of 1 040 pumps can be manufactured per month, because a maximum of 1 040 casings can be manufactured per month.

The break-even point of 1 297 is in excess of the capacity of 1 040. This means, given the present production capacity, the Pumpworks division cannot break even. The picture is much bleaker than what the manager of the Pumpworks division has alleged it to be. Given the present production capacity and projected demand level for April (sales of only 970 units), the division cannot break even. Unless significant changes are made very soon, the division cannot reach the break-even point in five months' time.

Part (a)(ii)

If we look at how a break-even point is calculated, we can see that there are three factors that could result in a lower break-even point: (i) fixed costs can be reduced, or contribution can be improved, meaning that either (ii) variable costs are reduced or (iii) the selling price is increased.

These would therefore be the three areas that we would want to focus on in order to improve the profitability of Pumpworks. An improvement in any of the three, or in a combination of the three factors, would lower the break-even units and make the target easier to attain.

(i) and (ii): At normal capacity the total variable costs are R1 117 250 (R1 117,25 per unit × 1 000 units). Total costs are therefore R1 945 550 (R1 117 250 variable + R828 300 fixed). Variable costs represent 57,4 per cent of total costs at normal capacity. It follows that a saving in variable costs could have a significant impact on total costs. Pumpworks could, for example, investigate the possibility of manufacturing the bought-in connectors and/or electric motors itself if practical. Alternatively, other suppliers or a price re-negotiation with existing suppliers could be explored. Pumpworks could also investigate the productivity of its labour force – the fact that the manager of the Pumpworks division asked a junior financial clerk to look into this may suggest that the manager already suspects labour is an area where costs can be saved. Only a small portion of the cost of labour is variable – the fixed component of labour cannot be saved in the short term and we would therefore rather seek to improve labour efficiency (however, keep in mind that if labour manufactures more units per hour, a market for these additional units has to exist).

(iii) We can calculate by how much the selling price would have to be increased in order to break even if all other factors remain constant:

Unit sales is presently 327 units (1 297 – 970) below the break-even point. This means there is a shortfall in contribution of R208 871 (327 units × R638,75 contribution per unit). The price increase required is therefore R215,33 per unit (R208 871/970 units). This represents a 12 per cent price increase (R215,33/R1 756). This may be regarded as a significant increase, and we would have to determine whether the market would accept this. Furthermore, a price increase may cause a decrease in demand.

In addition to the above, there are some other factors specific to the Pumpworks division that could help it to improve its performance:

- If capacity is increased, the problem of having a break-even point in excess of maximum production capacity will be addressed. This means that the capacity of labour in the casings department would have to be addressed first. *This principle is emphasised in Chapter 16,* Contemporary management accounting concepts, *where the Theory of Constraints holds that the bottleneck activity which restricts the capacity of the factory should be identified and addressed. However, no knowledge of Chapter 16 was required in order to answer this question.*
- It would be of little use if capacity were increased without a corresponding increase in demand. Methods of stimulating demand will therefore have to be explored so that the full monthly production capacity can be sold.
- Alternatively, if demand cannot be increased, the division could explore alternative uses for any spare capacity. For example, the opening sentence of the case study mentions another division in the company: perhaps there is a possibility of supplying agricultural pumps to the Agri-water division.

Part (b)

The notion is untrue. Although direct labour in a factory may often be variable according to the number of hours worked, this is not necessarily always the case. We can discuss the problematic nature of the statement as follows:

1 When we say that a cost is variable, we should understand *in relation to what* it is variable. Does it vary according to the number of units produced, the number of hours (which is often the case with labour, and which can be closely related to the number of units produced if units are very similar), or some other cost driver? Each cost in each organisation is unique, and we should specifically investigate and determine the cost/cost driver relationship.
2 This leads us to the next problem: the generalisation of the statement. The terms 'in a factory' and 'always' show us that the clerk has never considered the uniqueness of each organisation. It appears that he may have attempted to formulate a 'rule' for himself, with no regard for the actual situation at hand.
3 If we look at the labour information that we have on Pumpworks, we can see that only a small portion of labour costs are, in fact, variable per unit (2 assembly hours per unit). All other labour costs are fixed *in the short term* (see the next point).
4 The distinction between variable and fixed costs has a time aspect to it. In the very long term, no cost is 'fixed'. The labour costs that we regard as 'fixed' for purposes of this solution are fixed for our planning horizon. In part (a), we re-drafted the budget for one month only (April 2XX5), and we made projections on the possibility of returning the division to profitability within the next five months. It is within this short planning horizon that we were comfortable to assume that the portion of labour which we classified as fixed would remain constant.

Integration section: Chapters 6 to 9

Part (a)

Closing inventory of finished goods can be calculated as 35 000 litres (planned production) less 33 000 litres (planned sales) = 2 000 litres. Closing inventory of work-in-progress is given in note 3 – it is also 2 000 litres.

We start this suggested solution by re-tracing how closing inventory was valued in the draft budget. Note 2 in the question explains that only the cost of raw materials was taken into account in the value of closing inventory. Raw materials cost R200 per litre of raw materials added to the process. But 1,1 litres of raw materials are needed to produce one litre of output. This means that, to produce 2 000 litres of finished goods, 2 000 × 1,1 = 2 200 litres of raw materials are added. Valued at the raw materials cost of R200, this gives the value of closing inventory in the draft budget of R440 000 in respect of finished goods.

Because raw materials are added at the beginning of the process, the 2 000 litres of closing work-in-progress would also have used 2 200 litres of raw materials. Again, 2 200 litres × R200 gives the value of closing inventory in the draft budget: work-in-progress is also valued at R440 000.

Absorption costing now needs to be employed in order to re-value the finished goods and re-calculate the profit before interest and tax. In this particular question, we need to make use of process costing to arrive at the answer.

Equivalent production statement				
Input units		**Output units**		
		Total	Materials	Conversion
40 700	Started (35' + 2') × 1,1			
	Completed	35 000	35 000	35 000
	Normal loss (35' + 2') × 0,1	3 700	3 700	0
	Closing work-in-progress	2 000	2 000	1 000
40 700		40 700	40 700	36 000

Unit cost statement	Total (R)	Materials (R)	Conversion (R)
Direct materials ('raw materials')	8 140 000	8 140 000	
Direct labour ('labour')	3 060 000		3 060 000
Manufacturing overhead cost*	8 280 000		8 280 000
	19 480 000	8 140 000	11 340 000
Per unit	515	200	315

Production cost statement		R	R
Finished goods (25 000 units × R515) + (35 000 × 0,1 × 2 000) (normal loss)**			18 725 000
Work-in-progress:			755 000
Materials (2 000 units × R200) + (2000 × 0,1 × R300)		440 000	
Conversion (1 000 units × R315) (normal loss)		315 000	
			19 480 000

581

principles of management accounting

* Manufacturing overhead cost has to be calculated. This will include both variable and fixed overheads, because absorption costing is used. Only costs relevant to the valuation of inventory are to be included (the company wants to prepare the accounts on a basis consistent with that used in the annual financial statements). The relevant costs from the draft budget are as follows:
R1 080 000 (variable water and electricity) + R1 800 000 (variable waste disposal costs) + R1 260 000 (other variable overhead costs) + R1 450 000 (fixed depreciation on plant and machinery) + R1 820 000 (fixed repairs and maintenance of plant) + R870 000 (other fixed overheads) = R8 280 000.
** At year-end only 2 000 units of the 35 000 units are still on hand, and their value amounts to R1 070 000 (R18 725 000/35 000 units × 2 000 units).

We can now re-calculate the budgeted profit before interest and tax:

Existing profit before interest and tax	R2 574 000
Less: Existing value of closing inventory	(R880 000)
Add: Revalued closing inventory:	
Finished goods	R1 070 000
Work-in-progress	R755 000
Recalculated profit before interest and tax	R3 519 000

Part (b)

The liquid fertiliser and the other useful product result from a joint process that yields more than one product. If the sales value of R50 per litre is regarded as significant, the two products would be regarded as *joint products*. The sales value of liquid fertiliser is R820 per litre (R27 060 000/33 000 litres). It is therefore also possible that the other useful product may be regarded as a *by-product* instead of a joint product (if one takes the view that R50 is not significant in relation to R820).

If the products are regarded as joint products, the joint costs (those that are incurred before the split-off point) are to be allocated between the two joint products. This can be done on the basis of physical measures, market values at the split-off point, net realisable values, or constant gross profit percentage.

If the other product is regarded as a by-product, an amount of R50 per litre (less any further processing costs) is to be deducted from the cost of producing liquid fertiliser. In other words, the cost of producing liquid fertiliser is now lower because the income earned from the other product is set off against the cost.

To summarise the effect of the new scenario on the value of liquid fertiliser:
- If the products are regarded as joint products, liquid fertiliser will have a lower value per litre because some of the joint costs are allocated to the other product.
- If the other product is regarded as a by-product, liquid fertiliser will have a lower value per litre because the R50 sales value (less any further processing costs) will be deducted from the cost of producing liquid fertiliser.
- In both instances, the waste disposal costs of R1 800 000 relating to effluent water no longer exist in the new scenario, lowering the value of liquid fertiliser even further because this cost is no longer part of the valuation.

Part (c)

The system used in part (a) to apply absorption costing to the liquid fertiliser is process costing. The proposed new venture is one in which Chem (Pty) Ltd (Chem) will transport the liquid fertiliser directly from the factory to the clients' farms, and will apply the product to the soil. The problem with using process costing in this new venture is not the fact that we are dealing with a service instead of a product. Process costing is applicable where a large number of identical products move through the same process and consume identical resources. In a situation where one can merely substitute the words 'identical products' with 'identical services', process costing would still be applicable. That, however, is not the case here. To start with, a different travelling distance (distance over which the fertiliser is transported) would apply each time, resulting in an uneven consumption of resources. Furthermore, the information states that 'The optimal application of the fertiliser is very dependent on the type of crop to be cultivated, as well as on the specific soil and weather conditions'. We can therefore say that each instance in which such a service is delivered, is a 'job' on its own. Each job requires a unique mix of transportation, materials, time and labour. Job costing is therefore the appropriate costing system to be used. Chapter 7, *Job costing*, features examples of scenarios where job costing would be appropriate: a manufacturer of custom-made kitchen cupboards, a vehicle repair shop, and a manufacturer of aircraft where the customers (airlines) stipulate custom specifications. We can recognise this new service proposed by Chem as one that fits well with those examples, because each job is unique. The financial manager is concerned that it would be 'too confusing and time consuming' to have two costing systems within the same company. He or she is correct in that implementation decisions should be subjected to a cost/benefit analysis – if the 'cost' (both in rand terms as well as in terms of qualitative negative factors) outweighs the likely benefits to be gained, the system should not be implemented. However, in this case, using the appropriate costing system (job costing) will result in accurate management information, which is the core purpose of a management accounting system. Forcing the inappropriate process costing system onto this new service simply because it is used elsewhere in the company, would lead to incorrect costing which is inappropriate for all types of management decisions, including the pricing of the jobs (clearly, each job should be individually priced). The benefits of using job costing therefore outweigh the rather unconvin-cing qualitative costs that have been mentioned.

[What could be relevant here is a combination of job costing and standard costing – it may be possible to set realistic standard costs for, say, each kilometre travelled, each different application technique used, and so on. Standard costing is described in a later chapter in this book, Chapter 13.]

Part (d)

Activity-based costing (ABC) is a sophisticated way of allocating overhead costs (those which are not directly traceable) to cost objects. Of course, under ABC direct costs are allocated to cost objects as well, but these would have been allocated in the same way regardless of whether ABC was used. ABC is appropriate where a more sophisticated allocation of overhead costs would increase the quality of the costing information beyond the costs involved in implementing the new system (a cost/benefit analysis).

If we consider the available information, we find that:
- Chem does have overhead costs that are classified 'fixed' in the draft budget, and
- These overhead costs may be considered significant. In the draft budget there is an amount of R5 440 000 labelled as 'fixed manufactured overheads'.

However, ABC is about allocating overheads to the products and/or services that the company produces. At the moment Chem produces one product only – liquid fertiliser. The opening paragraph of the scenario confirms that there are no other products, because the company 'is highly specialised and manufactures only one finished product' (one could also have confirmed this by looking back at the answer to part (a), where all inventory costs have been accounted for after considering only liquid fertiliser). We can therefore safely say that – at present – no allocation is necessary because all of the overheads can be 100% attributed to the manufacture of the single product, liquid fertiliser. Process costing is applied because each litre of liquid fertiliser consumes an identical amount of resources – after we have re-calculated the costs on an absorption costing basis in part (a), each litre now carries the same amount of overhead costs.

Chem, however, is planning a possible new venture, the delivery and application of liquid fertiliser to farmers' crops. Once this service is introduced, Chem will have both a product and a service that consume company resources. Examples of possible shared overheads could be the cost of transportation and labour. Both the product and the service's 'jobs' should now carry an appropriate allocation of overhead costs. Activity-based costing could be useful once the new agricultural service is offered, providing that the cost of implementing the system (both in terms of rands as well as qualitative factors) does not outweigh the benefits gained.

Integration section: Chapters 10 to 13

Part (a)

The analysis has to be based on the 2XX6 information, as only this information is available in the scenario.

Option 1 for Irene: Retain the Irene training site
The Irene training site is making a contribution towards head office costs. If you add back the head office costs of R225 363, you can see that there was an operating profit of R117 875 which helped to absorb head office costs (after head office costs, the loss at Irene is R107 488).

Option 2 for Irene: Close down the Irene site
We need to calculate whether Randburg has enough capacity to absorb the expected increase in the number of students if Irene is closed down.
- In 2XX6 3 375 students attended at Randburg (1 695 one-day courses + (420 two-day courses × 2) + (280 three-day courses × 3)).
- Randburg therefore operated at 50 per cent capacity (3 375/6 750 training days available).
- In 2XX6 2 025 students attended at Irene (1 425 one-day courses + (150 two-day courses × 2) + (100 three-day courses × 3)).
- If 75 per cent of the 2 025 Irene students moved to Randburg, Randburg would have 3 375 + 1 519 = 4 894 students, which is only 72,5 per cent of its capacity.
- It follows that the Randburg site appears to have enough capacity to absorb the increase in students at the venue.

ABS will lose 25 per cent of its Irene students, so R1 215 000 × 25 per cent = R303 750 in lost revenue.

Irene's 2XX6 contribution was R1 215 000 – R172 125 variable costs = R1 042 875.
- The contribution percentage is therefore R1 042 875/R1 215 000 = 86 per cent.
- ABS will therefore lose a contribution of R303 750 × 86 per cent = R260 719.

The relevant income and costs of closure are as follows:

Lost contribution	R260 719
Save rent	(R215 000)
Save cleaning costs	(R90 000)
Save other fixed costs	(R170 000)
Annual saving if site is closed	R214 281

This should be compared to the current R117 875 operating profit before head office allocation. However, R275 000 in once-off costs will be incurred (R200 000 retrenchment costs + R75 000 other costs). Furthermore, the rental lease only expires at 28 February 2XX7, so it seems that another year's rental will have to be paid. We are not sure what the rental amount is, but it is likely to be at least R215 000 (the 2XX6 figure).

Apart from the above financial considerations, you should keep in mind that the company will no longer have a training facility near Pretoria if Irene is closed down. ABS's management are basing their estimate of 75 per cent of students moving to Randburg on 'initial feedback', but this does not mean that so many students will indeed end up travelling to Randburg. You should also consider that – although Randburg apparently has enough capacity to take in the additional Irene students – there may be an unanticipated increase in fixed costs at Randburg that management may not presently be aware of. On the other hand, there may be decreases in ABS's overall costs (head office costs) when the size of the company is significantly reduced by closing the Irene site. Lastly, our annual savings calculation assumed that all of the Irene presenters would move to Randburg because they were offered positions there. If one or more of them chose not to move, additional retrenchment costs may be incurred.

Option 3 for Irene: Outsourcing to UP
ABS will receive additional revenue in the form of the fee paid by UP to ABS of R1 215 000 × 5 per cent = R60 750. No other recurring revenue will be received or costs incurred. Therefore this amount is compared to the R117 875 operating income before head office costs.

ABS will incur a once-off retrenchment cost of R350 000.

There may be concern among some lecturers that UP will have access to ABS's intellectual property (training material), which could create competition for ABS.

In the education sector it is also important to note that the quality of presenters plays a large role in the quality of the education – the quality of presenters (UP versus ex-Irene presenters relocated to Randburg) should be considered.

Conclusion
When the alternatives are compared, while outsourcing is the least attractive, it seems that closing down the Irene site may be the most financially attractive option. However, we have already discussed some assumptions and uncertainties regarding the calculation – these should be kept in mind. ABS also needs to consider that its reputation may potentially suffer if it became known that one of its three sites was closed down. The closure will also significantly reduce ABS's total training capacity (by 6 750 one-day students per year).

It is important to note that improving the profitability of the Irene site was not considered here – there may be other options (better marketing, acquiring superior presenters, and so on) that may steer the site back to profitability.

principles of management accounting

It is also important to note that the calculations were based on 2XX6 financial information, which may change in future.

Part (b)

The charge payable to Brilliant Catering is R125 per person per day for meals provided. Only attendees who attend two and three day courses stay over at the lodge, and they are charged R400 per night for meals and accommodation. We can deduce that a student on a two day course stays over for one night, and a student on a three day course stays for two nights. The total charge payable to Brilliant Catering is therefore R125 × (720 + 640 × 2) = R250 000. This can also be calculated as R800 000/R400 × R125.

Revenue in 2XX6 (assume attendees will still be charged R400)	R800 000
Brilliant Catering charge	(R250 000)
Fixed costs of the lodge	(R680 000)
Annual savings in fixed costs	R325 000
Annual profit from the lodge	R195 000

The above is positive in light of the fact that the lodge operated at a loss of R25 500 before head office costs in 2XX6 (R173 887 – R148 387).

However, ABS should question whether Brilliant Catering will make a profit on the arrangement. If not, the arrangement is not likely to be sustainable in the long run.

Revenue (charge paid by ABS)	R250 000
Bar profits (R252 000/160 × 60)	R94 500
Costs taken over	(R325 000)
Brilliant Catering profit	R19 500

What is not taken into account in the calculation above is that Brilliant Catering will likely conduct business differently from ABS and may be able to save some costs or increase bar revenue (it is difficult to assess from the information to what extent increasing the mark-up on drinks is viable).

Conclusion

From the analysis it seems to be a good idea to outsource the catering, provided that Brilliant Catering will continue with the arrangement in the long run (which is likely only if it is financially viable for them, too). It should be kept in mind that as much as a R230 000 once-off retrenchment cost may be incurred if the staff members do not take up Brilliant Catering's employment offer. Another problem is that the quality of the food is presently very good – the quality will no longer be directly controlled by ABS if outsourcing takes place. Food and service quality can impact heavily on course attendees' overall impression of the course.

Before coming to a final conclusion, it may be worthwhile to find out whether any other outsourcing alternatives have been considered (other options which may be differently structured, or offered by a different caterer).

Part (c)

We need to consider whether zero-base budgeting could lead to material cost savings in the company. Zero-base budgeting involves starting with a 'clean sheet', in other words, not referring back to previous periods' budgets as a starting point.

Instead, each line item has to be deliberately included in the new budget, and the amount budgeted has to be justified from scratch.

The *process* of zero-base budgeting is therefore usually much more resource intensive than that of incremental budgeting, so there are unlikely to be any potential cost savings in the budgeting process itself. The potential cost savings come from using zero-base budgeting to draw up a budget that may look leaner in that it makes provision for fewer cost items or lower charges per item, or both. If the process is properly carried out, the budget ought still to be realistic and attainable.

Of course, drawing up a new budget with a leaner cost structure does not result in cost savings on its own. But aligning the performance measurement of managers and divisions (including the training sites and lodge) to the budget will motivate individuals to attain the targets that were set. This will be particularly viable if a negotiated style of budgeting was incorporated during the zero-base budgeting exercise (in other words, if managers were asked to help prepare the zero-base budget).

It is, however, very difficult to anticipate – with the limited information at our disposal – whether any significant cost savings will result in ABS because of the implementation of zero-base budgeting. To decide whether it should be implemented, we should keep the following in mind:

- Consultants are often hired to implement zero-base budgeting. Consulting fees can be expensive, so one has to be sure it would result in substantial savings.
- Management has identified three options to improve profitability, one of which is the implementation of zero-base budgeting. They are unlikely to have included this as an option if there wasn't some reason for them to believe that it had the potential to make a significant difference.
- Management time will be consumed by the exercise – if management can afford to focus on this now, it may be a viable option.
- This option is certainly not a mutually-exclusive alternative to the other two profit-improvement options that are being considered (closing Irene and outsourcing catering at Magaliesburg). In other words, zero-base budgeting can be implemented to save costs if it is considered desirable, *and* one or both of the other options can also be pursued. In total the improvement in profitability may then be significant.

Part (d)

The shadow price of a resource is the increase in value which would be created by having available one additional unit of the resource at its original cost. In the case of course presenters at the Randburg training site, this would mean the value created by having one additional course presenter available.

The shadow price is zero, because from the information it is apparent that zero value would be created if another lecturer were available at Randburg. Randburg has the capacity to accommodate 6 750 one-day attendees. We assume that this capacity figure takes into account seating in the lecture halls as well as course presenter capacity and other capacity issues. We have already calculated in part (a) that Randburg operated at 50 per cent of its capacity in 2XX6. Even if Irene were to be closed down and 75 per cent of its students moved to Randburg, Randburg would still have spare capacity (see part (a)).

For a resource to have a shadow price greater than zero, it has to be a *scarce or limited* resource.

Part (e)

Standard costing was originally developed in the manufacturing industry and is used where masses of similar items move through a repetitive process. The purpose is to identify and investigate variances from standards, and in doing so to measure performance and improve future performance.

Standard costing can, however, be used in the services industry. ABS could theoretically set standard 'selling prices' for its courses – in fact, there already seems to be a standard course fee per person per day at all ABS training venues (in 2XX6 this amount was R600). There could also be standards for course expenses e.g. the cost course material per student per course offered – such standards could also quite realistically be set. The equivalent of 'direct labour' in ABS's scenario will be the cost of course presenters, yet another standard that is easily set.

Rather, in the case of ABS, the question is whether a standard costing system would add any significant value beyond that which is already provided by ABS's existing budgeting system. Because the training operations seem to be quite straight forward and standardised in any case, one may ask whether the analysis of standard costing variances would provide further useful management information beyond the analysis of budget-versus-actual variances that one assumes is already taking place. A standard costing system can be expensive to implement and time consuming to maintain and operate, so a cost/benefit approach needs to be followed in determining whether such a system is indeed necessary. In practice it is unusual to find standard costing systems in the education provision industry – perhaps with good reason.

It is therefore theoretically possible to implement a standard costing system, but one has to question the ability of the system to add value to ABS in terms of improved management information.

The advantage relating to inventory valuation that is experienced in the traditional standard costing setting of the manufacturing industry – namely that inventory is carried at standard cost – is also largely irrelevant in the education industry.

Integration section: Chapters 14 to 17

Part (a)

	Garden division	Furniture division	Cafeteria	Outdoor Africa
Sales	R5 800 000	R2 400 000	R1 500 000	R9 700 000
Cost of sales	R4 000 000	R1 600 000	R750 000	R6 350 000
Gross profit	R1 800 000	R800 000	R750 000	R3 350 000
Managers	R100 000	R100 000	R100 000	R300 000
Assistants	R480 000	R360 000	R450 000	R1 290 000
Rent	R360 000	R270 000	R90 000	R720 000
Advertisements	R70 000	R70 000	R70 000	R210 000
Profit	R790 000	R0	R40 000	R830 000
Other expenses				R750 000
				R80 000

Part (b)

Performance analysis
Some facts that are apparent from the analysis in part (a) are the following:
- Measured on absolute turnover, the Garden division performs best, followed by the Furniture division and the Cafeteria.
- Measured on absolute gross profit, the Garden division again performs best, followed by the Furniture division and the Cafeteria.
- Measured on absolute profit, the Garden division again performs best, followed by the Cafeteria and the Furniture division.
- Measured on gross profit percentage, the Cafeteria performs best, followed by the Furniture division and the Garden division.
- The Garden division therefore relies on volume rather than on a large mark-up percentage to ensure its profitability.

Further calculations:

	Garden division	Furniture division	Cafeteria
Profit as % of turnover	13,62%	–	2,67%
Profit before advertisements, as % of turnover	14,83%	2,92%	7,33%
Salaries as % of turnover	10,00%	19,17%	36,67%
Sales/floor space	R2 900 per sq metre	R1 600 per sq metre	R3 000 per sq metre
Profit/floor space	R395 per sq metre	–	R80 per sq metre
Profit before advertisement/ floor space	R430 per sq metre	R47 per sq metre	R220 per sq metre
Sales per staff member	R644 444	R342 857	R150 000
Profit per staff member	R87 778	–	R4 000
Sales per assistant	R725 000	R400 000	R166 667
Profit per assistant	R98 750	–	R4 444

In some of the above calculations, advertisements were specifically left out, as it could be argued that, on the facts, they should not be allocated to divisions.

Some of the findings from the further calculations are as follows:
- It is clear that the Garden division is the largest in all respects and in absolute terms the most profitable.
- The Garden division is also the one with the highest profit percentage, and therefore performs best financially.
- The Cafeteria, however, has the smallest floor space but generates the highest turnover per square metre.
- However, as soon as profit is considered, the Cafeteria does not perform well. The problem with the Cafeteria is its large salary bill.
- Further evidence of the above is that the Cafeteria performs relatively poorly per staff member/assistant.
- The Furniture division performs worst throughout.

Recommendations
The following recommendations flow from the performance analysis carried out.
- Outdoor Africa can improve profitability by concentrating on the garden division.

- The Cafeteria can be more profitable if smaller salaries were paid. It should be considered whether all the staff members are necessary.
- As the Cafeteria performs well per square metre, the expansion of the Cafeteria (greater floor space) could be considered. This may enable more clients to be served if the staff-lunch proposal is accepted in 2XX8/2XX9.
- Especially since the Cafeteria earns the highest gross profit percentage, it would be in Outdoor Africa's interest to expand this division so that its sales may increase.
- The floor space of the Furniture division could possibly be reduced. Outdoor Africa should, however, be careful in deciding to close the Furniture division altogether – there may be cross-selling between the divisions in this type of organisation (in other words more people may visit the premises because everything is sold under one roof – if one division closes, it could have a negative impact on the profitability of the remaining divisions).

Outdoor Africa could consider establishing a new division that is related to the existing divisions (e.g. swimming pool equipment, water fountains, paint or paving) that could possibly bring further cross-selling opportunities and may turn a higher profit on part of the Furniture division's floor space. A problem with scaling down the Furniture division without closing it, however, is the fact that furniture items by their very nature take up a lot of space.

Part (c)

- There are 26 staff members at Outdoor Africa's retail premises (head office staff, including the managing director, do not work at the premises and are excluded from this calculation).
    (3 Divisional managers + 8 assistants in the Garden division + 6 assistants in the furniture division + 9 in the Cafeteria = 26)
- Meals will cost Outdoor Africa 26 × R25 = R650 per day, therefore R650 × 365 days in the year to 28/2/2XX9 = R237 250 per annum.
- Staff occupy during each sitting 26 persons/2 groups/4 chairs = 3,25 tables. They therefore occupy four tables.
- Between 12h00 and 13h00, 22 of the 25 tables are already occupied. There is therefore one table short. This represents an opportunity cost of R50 contribution × 365 days = R18 250 per annum.
- Between 14h00 and 15h00 there is enough spare capacity to release 4 tables.

Total impact on Outdoor Africa:
R237 250 + R18 250 = R255 500 smaller profit for the year.

Tip: Work with opportunity cost per table (we cannot prove, for example, that there were four clients sitting at a table on average, and we also don't need income per client). Furthermore, it is wrong to assume that clients' meals cost R25 each – they order from the menu. Rather work backwards from R100 per table to calculate opportunity cost, because gross profit mark-up is known.

Part (d)

It is in the best interest of Outdoor Africa as a whole rather to lose R255 500 on internal Cafeteria meals, instead of paying 26 × R35 × 365 = R332 150 across the street.

Minimum price
The divisions should pay R25 per lunch per staff member, plus opportunity cost.

Between 12h00 and 13h00 there is opportunity cost for one table. A table brings in R100 in sales; therefore (at a gross profit percentage of 100 per cent) the contribution is R50. This R50 has to be spread across all 26 staff members; therefore the minimum price is R25 + R1,92 = R26,92.

Alternative: Calculate separate prices for morning and afternoon sittings. Then the minimum price is R25 + (R50/13) R3,85 = R28,85 in the morning and R25 in the afternoon.
(Proof that it amounts to the same as the above: (R28,85 × 13) + (R25 × 13) = R700 and R700/26 = R26,92)

Maximum price
The maximum price is R35 per lunch per staff member.

A price of between R26,92 and R35 is acceptable.

Notice that Cafeteria employees also eat. By charging the above price per staff member to the other two divisions, it is implied that the Cafeteria carries the cost of its own staff lunches.

Alternative for minimum price: If the assumption is made that the Cafeteria manager demands that opportunity cost be carried by the other two divisions in full (because there are enough tables available if only his own staff were to eat there), the minimum price changes to: R25 + (R50/16) = R28,13, or R25 + (R50/8) = R31,25 in the morning and R25 in the afternoon.

Part (e)

Charles's views are typical of someone who has a little bit of knowledge of the topics, but who lacks an in-depth understanding of the theory underlying the concepts. In particular, Charles's insight is hampered by the fact that he is not officially employed by Outdoor Africa. As an outsider, he is attempting to bring superficial 'textbook' knowledge into a practical situation where it may not necessarily be appropriate (this is the equivalent of answering an advanced management accounting question without considering the scenario!). There is therefore some validity in some of his statements, but the application of his ideas has not been properly thought through. Each incident is now discussed in turn.

Incident 1
It appears that Charles has heard of the benefits of just-in-time systems, which are indeed valid. Many modern organisations benefit greatly from such a system. However, there are a number of problems with this comment, all of which relate to Charles's lack of consideration for the particular environment.
- His comment was directed at the procurement clerk of the Garden division. Charles does not appreciate that just-in-time is an all-encompassing system that has to be implemented throughout an organisation. In fact, for the system to work, the entire supply chain ought to operate in a just-in-time fashion. The clerk certainly cannot, to name but one example, decide on his own to order plants 'just-in-time' if the supplier cannot deliver according to these demands.
- The Garden division sells plants, which is an unlikely product to subject to a just-in-time system. Plants take time to nurture and grow, and an optimal

balance has to be found between the amount of time spent in the nursery (at the supplier's premises) and at the retail store. This is a unique scenario which is not anticipated by classic just-in-time theory (which was developed in the manufacturing sector and is particularly relevant in highly automated factories).
- Flowing from the previous point, one should consider that – although the retail sector could benefit greatly from the just-in-time philosophy – many of the aspects of just-in-time were specifically developed for and are applicable to the manufacturing sector (again, specifically highly automated modern factories).
- A cost-benefit analysis should be carried out before any system change is recommended, but in this case a just-in-time system is likely to be ruled inappropriate before it is necessary to consider such detail. Perhaps whatever is bothering Charles about the procurement process in the Garden division can be better addressed through optimised supply chain management, as discussed under incident 4.
- Just-in-time has indeed been practised and well-documented, for a number of years (hence Charles's wording 'years ago'), but the fact that it is a tried-and-tested popular business philosophy does not render it appropriate regardless of the circumstances.

Incident 2
Charles is correct in that the two divisions could indeed be benchmarked against each other for performance assessment purposes, at least to some extent. In many circumstances benchmarking is a useful tool – this is an example of internal benchmarking (where two divisions within the same organisation are compared). Performance measures such as the divisions' respective returns per square metre, costs per employee, and the like could be compared (part (b) of this solution gives examples). The relevant information appears to be obtainable from the present information system, and (although part (b) of the question works with annual figures) it would be possible to perform such a benchmarking exercise on a monthly basis. However, there are again a number of problems with Charles's remark.
- The divisions can be benchmarked against each other only to the extent that they are in fact comparable. They sell different products and are exposed to different external factors which should be kept in mind (both in the type of measures that are benchmarked, as well as in the interpretation of the results).
- Monthly management accounts should strike the optimal balance between comprehensiveness and brevity. An informed decision should be taken as to what information would be the most useful for managers to receive on a monthly basis, and the report should focus on that.
- It is incorrect that benchmarking the two divisions against each other is 'the only way' to perform proper performance assessment of the divisions. Many other types of information could also be relevant. Even as far as benchmarking itself is concerned, Outdoor Africa may wish to consider benchmarking the company as a whole against a competitor instead, or benchmarking the individual divisions against those of competitors (although comparable information would be more difficult to find).
- It seems that Charles is suggesting that the entire contents of the monthly management accounts should be the benchmarking of the Garden and the Furniture divisions. This, of course, is not optimal, as it does not address the performance of the Cafeteria, the head office, or Outdoor Africa as a whole. It also does not consider qualitative factors.

- The most important aspect that Charles should remember is that management accounting information is supplied according to the needs of management. One therefore first has to find out what information will lead to optimal management decisions, and then work backwards to discover how such information can best be supplied. Benchmarking should not be forced purely for the sake of benchmarking.

Incident 3
Charles's third comment is problematic. Increasingly, we get the impression that Charles becomes aware of techniques that he seems impressed by, but then he tries to force them onto situations where they are not applicable.
- Target costing is not a straight-forward alternative to cost-plus pricing, because target costing is not merely a pricing technique. Target costing does start by assessing what selling price the market would absorb (in other words, what customers are likely to be willing to pay for a specific product). This is the only part of target costing that may be relevant to Outdoor Africa, but it would be very difficult and costly in practice to research such a price for each plant, implement, piece of furniture and cafeteria meal.
- Target costing then proceeds to design the product in such a manner that – over time – costs will be low enough to make a satisfactory profit at the target selling price. This implies that it is applicable in a manufacturing environment and should be carried out at the product design and development stage. These are irrelevant in the context of Outdoor Africa.
- Outdoor Africa is a retail business that sells a wide range of plants and related products, furniture and cafeteria meals. The practical pricing policy for Outdoor Africa to follow would be a cost-plus approach, tempered by qualitative factors. For example, it could decide to forgo some profit on specific product lines each week in order to offer specials that attract customers to the store (in order to cross-sell other items, or turn new customers into repeat customers).

Incident 4
There is ample research evidence that suggests tighter linkages within a supply chain lead to improved profits for the organisations within the chain. Charles seems to believe that Outdoor Africa should pay attention to proper supply chain management, which is a valid recommendation. It is also true that one way of tightening a supply chain would be to integrate the organisations inside the supply chain. If Outdoor Africa started 'its own nursery' as he suggested, this could indeed lead to a more optimised value chain because both the supply of plants and the retail thereof would be controlled by the company. However, vertically combining organisations inside the chain is not the only way to optimise a supply chain, and there are a number of factors that Charles may not have considered before he made the comment.
- Even if Outdoor Africa started 'its own nursery' it would still need supply chain management. The suppliers to the nursery are companies that manufacture pesticides, packaging, compost, seeds and a host of other inputs. Outdoor Africa would also still have a 'downstream' supply chain (its own customers) that needs to be managed.
- Starting a nursery to supply the Garden division with plants is a major expansion decision that has to be taken on strategic and financial grounds. It is unclear whether Outdoor Africa has the expertise, capital, and other resources to undertake this, and whether this is part of the strategic direction that the company would like to take. If Outdoor Africa were thinking along

those lines, it would also have to consider the option of taking over an existing supplier instead of starting a nursery from scratch (in which case Charles may just have made an enemy of yet another future employee of Outdoor Africa).

In general, relating to all the incidents, one could comment that Charles's behaviour is inappropriate and unlikely to have a positive impact on Outdoor Africa. He is alienating employees and suppliers, shouting, tearing up reports, showing up at meetings unannounced, and insulting people. (We do not elaborate on these issues here, as the requirement specifically asks us to focus on the management accounting aspects.)

Part (f)

Porter identified three generic strategies: cost leadership (being the lowest cost producer in the industry), differentiation (making the product or service desirable by offering something different) and focus (finding a niche market and applying either cost leadership or differentiation within that market). The requirement asks us to consider only the first two strategies.

In this scenario, cost leadership would mean that Outdoor Africa's cafeteria would have the ability to prepare meals at the lowest cost in the industry. The difficult aspect to consider here is what we mean by 'industry'. If we look at the restaurant and fast foods industry as a whole, it is unlikely that the cafeteria can produce meals at a lower cost than, say, McDonalds which enjoys economies of scale. In fact, even if we define the 'industry' more narrowly as sit-down restaurants in the Limpopo province only (excluding fast food outlets), Outdoor Africa's cafeteria may be unlikely to enjoy the kind of economies of scale that would cause it to be the cost leader.

Outdoor Africa's cafeteria is, however, likely to be different from most other industry players. It is located on the premises of a large garden and outdoor store – even based on the very limited information that we have about the cafeteria, we can surmise that it is at least differentiated from most other restaurants in terms of its *location*.

The likely answer would therefore be to say that the cafeteria is differentiated based on its location, and that it could choose to differentiate itself even further (by, say, offering a playground for children, or exotic meals named after plant species that are sold by the Garden division). However, should one define the 'industry' as narrowly as 'cafeterias located in plant retail outlets in the Limpopo province', we would again have to consider whether it might be the cost leader. What is therefore clear from this discussion is the importance of the definition of 'industry' in applying Porter's theory. (The real benefit, however, of applying the theory is the fact that it forces us to think through these strategic issues in order to decide on how the cafeteria could position itself in the market.)

Glossary

Note: Only the page(s) where a concept is defined are referred to below.

A

abnormal gains: occur where actual losses in the production process are less than the planned losses; reflected separately in the production cost statement 217

abnormal losses: arise where actual losses in the production process exceed the anticipated (budgeted or planned) losses; reflected separately in the production cost statement 217

absorption costing: a costing system which is useful for internal reporting and decision-making purposes, fixed manufacturing overheads are treated as a product cost, resulting in a portion of these overheads being included in any inventory balances; involves the accumulation and reporting of cost information within a format which is consistent with the accounting standards underlying financial accounting, which is aligned with the principle of matching income with expenses 27, 78, 102

accountant's model: an approach to CVP analysis which recognises that total fixed costs remain constant and variable costs per unit remain constant, and have a linear or straight-line relationship with levels of activity 77

achievable standards: these are not too slack, but represent normal working conditions and allow for a certain level of expected spoilage and inefficiency under normal conditions 378

activity-based costing (ABC): a system used for tracing indirect (overhead) costs to cost objects such as products, services, customers, business units, and related organisational elements, based on the activities that cause the overhead costs to be incurred and which drive those costs 159

activity-based management (ABM): utilises the same activity and cost information as that supplied by an activity-based costing system to support operational and strategic management decisions; focuses management's attention on activities as a way of improving the value that customers receive as well as the profit realised by an organisation 545

administrative costs: costs involved in administering the business of an organisation 15, 23

analytical review: an auditing procedure frequently used to review income statements 17

assignment: the actual relationship between what causes the cost to be incurred and the cost objects (products, services, divisions, contracts, investments, and so on) to which costs are to be assigned; tracing of costs to cost objects; concerned with identifying the relationship between the cost and the object for which the total cost is calculated 8

B

balanced scorecard: widely-used modern multidimensional performance management system 471

benchmarking: measures *relative* performance levels. Organisations compare their own performance against benchmarks in industry and take corrective action as needed 531

best fit line: the line that reduces the sum of the squares of regression errors 44

bill of materials file: (in relation to MRP) details the quantity, type and quality of each of the materials required for each final product 526

break-even chart: depicts the break-even point graphically *81*
break-even point: represents the level of activity where neither a profit nor a loss is made, being the level of activity where total sales revenue equals total costs *79*
budgetary slack: an allowance built into a budget when a manager intentionally over-estimates expenses or under-estimates expected income in order to meet set targets more easily *365*

C

cash budget: reflects cash flow items where the period in which the transaction is recorded is the period in which the cash flow takes place *351*
clock card or **time sheet:** used to record the presence of employees at work *191*
constraint: *see* limiting factor
continuous budget: *see* rolling budget
controllability concept: evaluating managers' performance based on those aspects over which they have control *455*
correlation: degree of association between two variables such as cost and activity, which may be either positive or negative *362*
cost-benefit model: an approach to problem areas where management determines the cost of investigating a specific variance, measured against the benefit that is likely to be obtained from taking corrective action *397*
cost behaviour: volatility of costs and revenues with respect to changes in sales and production levels *8*
cost driver: the factor that causes costs to be incurred *38*
cost object: the item to which the cost is to be traced *17*
cost of quality: the sum of the costs that arise from activities associated with prevention, identification, repair, and rectification of poor quality, and opportunity costs from lost production time and lost sales as a result of poor quality *549*
cost to company: total budgeted cost *191*
cost-volume-profit (CVP) analysis: interrelationship between activity levels, costs and an organisation's profits, analysing how cost behaviour, production levels and sales volumes impact an organisation's profit *76*

D

decision package: a discrete, stand-alone organisational activity *356*
departmental rate: an overhead rate is determined for each department in an organisation *149*
differential cost: a cost that differs between two alternatives *22*
direct cost: a cost which it is economically feasible to trace to the cost object *17*
direct labour costs: costs where it is economically feasible to trace the amount of labour that is physically expended on a product *23*
direct materials: physical inputs that can be traced in an economically feasible manner to the product that is manufactured *23*
drum-buffer-rope (DBR): the tool used to subordinate activities for the purposes of the Theory of Constraints *525*
dual pricing system: may be employed in order to satisfy both the transferring and the receiving unit where transfer pricing disputes cannot be resolved *497*
duration driver: amount of time spent on an activity *52*

E

economic value added (EVA®): a financial performance measure based on accounting information that takes the organisation's weighted average cost of capital into account, expressed in monetary terms *462*
economist's model: an approach to CVP analysis which recognises that the rate of change in total costs and total revenue is unlikely to remain constant as volumes change *76*

enterprise resource planning (ERP): an integrated suite of application software modules that provides operational, managerial and strategic information for enterprises to improve productivity, quality and competitiveness 527

external constraints: arise from the environment within which an organisation operates and on which it relies in order to achieve its goals 521

F

FIFO (first-in-first out): method of determining the cost of materials which assumes that materials are issued in the sequence in which they were ordered, and assigns an issue price accordingly 188

fixed budget: drawn up for a specific activity level, and used to gain an overall picture of the business plan 363

fixed cost: a cost that in total is unresponsive to a change in activity 12

fixed manufacturing overheads: fixed amounts paid on a regular basis in a manufacturing environment; costs incurred in converting materials into finished goods 103

flexed budget: prepared by separating expected fixed costs from expected variable costs, and adjusted when there are fluctuations in costs 364

flexed budget variance: variance between the profit as shown in the flexed budget and the actual profit as a result of changes in the expected price or quantity of the underlying inputs 380

function: classification of costs in the financial statements in accordance with the function of the cost 22

G

generic strategies: consist of three main strategies: cost leadership, differentiation and focus 545

goal congruence: individuals and units take actions that are in their self-interest and simultaneously also in the best interest of the organisation as a whole 457

H

high-low method: a mathematical approach which involves calculating the equation of a line to split a mixed cost into its variable and fixed components 42

I

ideal standards: represent perfect working conditions, with no allowance for spoilage or inefficiency; often seen as unattainable 378

incremental budgeting: the term used for the traditional approach to budgeting, where the previous year's results are used as a basis for unit costs, which are then adjusted for inflationary increases as well as increases and decreases in budgeted volumes to determine expected income and expenditure for the following year 355

independent (units): undertaking very different activities (with a minimum of managerial supervision or intervention) 457

indirect cost: a cost which it is impossible or not economically feasible to trace to the cost object 17

integrated accounting system: a costing system which is fully integrated with the financial accounting system, making use of a number of control accounts and/or subsidiary ledger accounts for this purpose 195

intensity driver: measure of the amount of demand on resources 52

interdependent (units): performing similar operations that need to be closely co-ordinated 457

interlocking accounting system: comprises two entirely separate accounting systems, running side-by-side, with only one control account linking the two systems 195

intermediate product or service: a product or service that is transferred from one unit of an organisation to another unit in the same organisation *490*

internal constraints: arise from the internal operations of an organisation, such as insufficient staff training, or inadequate machine capacity *521*

internal reporting: involves a combination of past information, together with future-orientated information, such as forecasts and budgets, to enable management to perform their duties of planning, control and decision-making *4*

inventoriable cost: the kind of cost that is included in inventory for financial accounting purposes *22*

inventory: (in relation to the Theory of Constraints) the sum of direct materials inventory, work-in-progress inventory, finished goods inventory, research and development cost, plant and machinery, and buildings *521*

inventory file: (in relation to MRP) specifies exactly when and how many units of each of the materials should be purchased, taking into account lead times of purchasing materials and the manufacture of components *527*

J

job card: record of materials and their costs in relation to a particular job *187*

job-costing system: a system designed to deal with the calculation of the cost of jobs, each of which is unique, requiring an input of differing quantities of material, labour and allocated overhead cost *186*

just-in-time (JIT): a management philosophy rather than merely a production technique; focuses the organisation's efforts on performing value-adding activities on demand while minimising waste *528*

K

kaizen costing: used when an organisation strives for continuous improvement, designed to support the cost management efforts inherent in target costing *555*

key performance indicator (KPI): a metric used to quantify the performance an organisation aims to achieve *355*

L

least squares method: *see* linear regression analysis

least squares regression: a statistical approach to establishing the equation of the line that best fits all of the data points provided *44*

life-cycle costing (LCC): the maintenance of cost records that accumulate the costs incurred over the lifespan of a product, service or physical asset *555*

limiting factor (constraint): a scarce resource of which there is a limited supply and which affects the ability of the organisation to earn profits *316*

linear regression analysis: fitting historical information into a formula whereby it is possible to distinguish between variable and fixed portions; used to assist in forecasting what the total cost will be when there is a new level of activity in the future. Also known as the least squares method *360*

M

make-or-buy decision (outsourcing decision): entails evaluating the costs of manufacturing a component internally in contrast to acquiring it from an external party *285*

manufacturing 'cells': (usually) U-shaped work stations in just-in-time factories, where each product group is, as far as practical, produced within the cell to minimise movement of work-in-progress inventory *529*

manufacturing costs: inventoriable costs relating to manufacturing *23*

market value added (MVA): a performance measure linked to value based management; an external measure indicating how shareholders have been affected by the actions taken by management *468*

master budget: summary of all the functional budgets and the cash budget, providing an overall picture of the planned performance for the budget period; culminates in budgeted financial statements *350*

master parts file: (in relation to MRP) details all the account lead times of purchasing materials and the manufacture of components *527*

master production schedule: (in relation to MRP) details demand forecasts for finished products *527*

materials requirement planning (MRP): a system that converts a production schedule into a listing of the materials and components required to meet that schedule, so that adequate [inventory] levels are maintained and items are available when needed *526*

mixed cost: a cost that consists of two components, usually a variable and a fixed component *14*

N

non-inventoriable costs: those costs that are not included in inventory for financial accounting purposes; other operating costs, often subdivided into selling costs and administrative costs *23*

normal distribution table: a table illustrating for statistical purposes the normal range within which one can be confident, at a certain level of probability (although never 100 per cent), that the true value lies. It also shows the standard deviations to be added or subtracted for a certain probability level *51*

normal losses: losses which are expected or anticipated and arise when the process is running according to plan, provided for by incorporating budgeted losses into the normal cost of production *217*

not-for-profit organisation: an organisation the primary purpose of which is not profit maximisation, although it may – to a limited extent – engage in economic activity in pursuit of its primary purpose *473*

O

operating expenses: (in relation to the Theory of Constraints) include all operating costs (other than direct materials and direct services) incurred to generate throughput, including labour costs, whether direct or indirect, and including both idle time and operating time. They also include expenses such as rent, electricity and depreciation *521*

operational budget: a budget prepared for a single financial period, usually a year or less, to control normal operating costs *347*

opportunity cost: the best benefit forgone by taking the proposed course of action, arising only when capacity constraints exist, which means that additional capacity is scarce *21*

outsourcing decision: *see* make-or-buy decision

P

perfectly competitive market: exists when a homogeneous product or service with equal buying and selling prices is sold in a market where individual buyers and sellers cannot affect prices by their own actions *491*

performance evaluation: assesses something that has already happened; necessary for the management of future performance *450*

performance management: aims to eliminate undesirable actions and to encourage desirable actions by units and individuals *450*

performance measure: an opinion formed, using a yardstick, on how well a unit or individual has performed *451*

period cost: a cost that is recognised as an expense immediately on being incurred *27*

principles of management accounting

plant-wide rate: a single overhead rate for an organisation in its entirety; determined by accumulating the total overheads incurred across the organisation, and dividing that by the allocation base determined as the most suitable for the enterprise *149*

principal budgeting factor: a limiting factor in relation to budgeting, among which are sales demand, availability of raw materials, machine capacity, and availability of cash and sources of funding *348*

probability theory: concept of expected values which may be used for budgeting where there is a great degree of uncertainty about future events *358*

process costing: a system used to determine the cost of a large number of identical product units produced in a continuous process *210*

product cost: a cost that is absorbed in inventory and deferred until the inventory is sold *27*

product-level target cost: the difference between the proposed selling price and the desired profit margin *553*

production volume variance: represents the difference between the budgeted fixed overhead and the fixed overhead allocated to products or services *393*

productive hours: used to calculate the hourly direct labour rate *192*

projection: an expected future trend pattern obtained by extrapolation, based on the notion that past events can serve as an indication of what will happen in the future *359*

public sector organisation: an organisation the purpose of which is to serve the public; funded by the government *473*

pull system: a system whereby each workstation starts work only once the next workstation on the production line requires it to do so, and where materials are ordered only once the first workstation requires them; based on a time-phased order-release system which schedules and releases work and purchase orders as and when they are required in the production system *527*

push-through system: a system whereby, as production starts, the output of one production section is 'pushed' to the next section, regardless of whether or not the receiving section is ready for the input *527*

R

regression error: the distance between the line and the point where the points do not sit exactly on the line in a graph illustrating a linear relationship *45*

relative sales values: *see* value-based overhead allocation system

relevance: the incremental effect on costs and revenues of the actions of management *9*

relevant cost: a differential future cash flow *20*

relevant range: defines the range of activity over which the assumptions made concerning the behaviour of costs and revenue remain valid *78*

residual income (RI): a financial performance measure based on accounting information, expressed in monetary terms *460*

responsibility centre: a centre(s) responsible for specific activities, the performance of which is the responsibility of a specific manager; usually divided into cost, revenue, profit, and investment centres *452*

return on investment (ROI): a popular financial performance measure based on accounting information; a short-term measure based on historical results, reflecting the return earned over the period for which it is measured, to the exclusion of all potential future results; expressed as a percentage *459*

return on sales (ROS): a short-term measure based on historical results, reflecting the return earned over the period for which it is measured, to the exclusion of all potential future results; calculated as income divided by revenue, and expressed as a percentage *463*

reverse costing: *see* target costing

S

rolling budget (continuous budget): prepared on a regular basis for the next year or other short-term period, and where the existing budget is continuously updated, as in the case of cash budgets 357

rule of thumb model: a subjective process used to identify problem areas, where previous experience and knowledge of the business assist in the process 397

S

sales mix: the proportion in which an organisation's products and services are sold or delivered 89

scatter graph or diagram: a graphical method of cost estimation that plots various observations of aggregate costs against the activity level 40

shadow price: an increase in value created by having available one additional unit of a limiting resource at the original cost 324

shareholder value analysis (SVA): a performance measure linked to the concept of value-based management 468

slack variable: represents the amount of a constraining resource or item that is left unused after the optimal production mix has been achieved 331

stakeholder: any group or individual with a legitimate interest in the activities of an organisation 471

standard cost: a cost used instead of the actual purchase cost and which remains constant throughout a period 190

static budget variance: represents the difference between the profit or loss as originally planned at a fixed level of output, and the profit or loss actually made 379

step cost: a cost that is available only in fixed allotments. It varies with the activity level in a stepwise manner, not a linear fashion 13

strategic budget: a long-term budget, set up for a period usually between three and 15 years, and where the scope is much less detailed than in the case of an operational budget 347

strategic business units: autonomous units responsible for planning, developing, producing and marketing their own products 456

sunk cost: a cost that has already been incurred and consequently cannot be altered by, and is therefore not relevant to, the decision 22

supply chain management (SCM): a network of organisations involved in the different processes and activities which produce value in the form of products and services 557

T

target costing (reverse costing): a way of reducing the costs of future products by concentrating on cost management during product development 553

Theory of Constraints: an approach to production management which aims to maximise sales revenue less material and variable overhead costs, focusing on factors such as bottlenecks, which act as constraints to maximisation 520

throughput: (in relation to the Theory of Constraints) the rate at which money is generated, calculated by deducting the money paid to suppliers (for direct materials and direct services) from the money obtained from customers (in the form of sales), without deducting labour expenses from sales 521

throughput ratio: calculated as the throughput per unit of constrained activity, divided by the operating expenses per unit of constrained activity **521**

timing: relates to the date and time period when a cost or cash flow is recognised in the income statement 9

total quality management (TQM): a customer-centric approach premised on the principle of *'get it right first time'*; emphasises preventative measures 548

traditional overhead allocation system: a volume- or value-based overhead allocation system 141

transaction driver: measures the number of times an activity is performed 52

transfer price: the price at which goods or services are transferred between different units of the same organisation *488*

***t*-statistic or *t*-stat:** compares the size of the standard error of the coefficient to the size of the coefficient itself, in order to provide an understanding of the relative size of the standard error *51*

V

value chain: the sequence of business activities by which value is added to the products or services produced by an organisation *558*

value chain analysis: used by organisations to attain competitive advantage by breaking down an organisation into its strategically relevant activities so as to understand cost behaviour as well as sources of existing and potential differentiation *558*

value-based management (VBM): the management of all aspects of a company with the aim of maximising shareholder wealth *468*

value-based overhead allocation system: a method of allocating overhead costs where overheads are allocated in proportion to the selling prices of products (also known as 'relative sales values') *141*

variable costing: involves the accumulation and reporting of cost information within a format that enables short-term planning, control, and decision-making *102*

variable costing system: requires all fixed costs to be recognised as an expense in the period in which they are incurred *28*

variable costs: costs which increase (or decrease) in proportion with increases (or decreases) in the level of activity, or which may change in relation to another activity *9*

variable manufacturing overheads: overheads which vary in proportion to production changes *23*

variable overhead variance: calculated as the difference between the total actual costs of variable overhead and the standard cost of variable overhead, as reflected in the flexed budget *391*

volume variance: variance between the flexed budget profit and the static budget profit as a result of the difference between planned and actual production levels *380*

volume-based overhead allocation system: refers to any method of allocating overhead costs that is based on some measure related to production or service volumes *141*

W

weighted average: method of determining the cost of materials which prices the inventory at an average price which is re-calculated each time materials are received *189*

work-in-progress (WIP): partially completed units at the end of a costing period in a process costing system, where additional costs will be incurred in the following period to complete the units *212*

Z

zero-base budgeting (ZBB): an approach to budgeting which rejects the principle of incremental budgeting and advocates that a budget should be prepared from 'scratch', or zero, and that every item in a budget has to be specifically justified in order to be included *356*

Index

Page numbers in **bold** refer to figures and tables.

A

ABB [*see* activity-based budgeting (ABB)]
ABC [*see* activity-based costing (ABC)]
ABM [*see* activity-based management (ABM)]
absorption costing 27, 28, 92, 93, 103–107, 134, 168, 269, 270, 288, 302, 382, 386, 392, 393–396, 406, 416, 419, 569, 577, 578, 581, 582, 584
   strengths and weaknesses 121
   versus variable costing 78, 101–132
accounting entries 402–410
accuracy 142–151
activity-based budgeting (ABB) 167, 168
activity-based costing (ABC) 92, 149, 159–167, **166**, 168, 188, 267, 271, 304, 414, 496, 501, 526, 533, 545, 546, 561, 583, 584
   compared with traditional allocation systems **166**
   limitations 166–167
   Theory of Constraints 526
activity-based management (ABM) 167, 168, 416, 544, 545–547, 555, 560, 561
   operational 546, 547
   strategic 546–547
activity rates, calculation of 161
administrative expenditure 350
analytical review 17
assignment 8–9, 17–19
assignment of costs 8, 17, 140, 159, 161–166, 167, 168, 267, 547, 569
Association of Chartered Certified Accountants (ACCA) 1
autonomous
   receiving unit 493
   transferring unit 493
   units 456, 457, 466, 489, 492, 493, 495, 497, 503, 506, 508, 569

B

balanced scorecard 471, 474
   objectives 471
batch-level activities 159, **160**
benchmarking 415, 474, 520, 531–532, 533, 592–593
   competitive 531, 532
   disadvantages 532
   functional 531, 532
   internal 531, 532
   standard costing 415
   strategic 531
best fit line 44
Beyond Budgeting® 368
   Round Table 368
bill of materials file 527
bottlenecks 76, 520–521, 524, 532, 580
break-even analysis 79–82, 121
   with multiple products 89–91
break-even chart 81–82, **81**, 93
break-even point 79, 80, 81, 82, 89, 90, 91, 92, 93, 137, 138, 578, 579, 580
budget committee 347
budget manual 347
budget process
   role of management accountant 368
   role of ratio analysis and KPIs 355
budgetary control 363, 366, 368, 375,
budgetary slack 365
budgeting
   alternative approaches 355–358
   determining principal factor 348
   impact on motivation of managers 365–366
   incremental 355–356, 356–357
   linear programming 334
   negotiated style 367
   probability theory 358–359
   zero-base [*see* zero-base budgeting]
budgets 345–374
   administrative expenditure 350
   capital expenditure 350
   cash 350, 351–354, **354**, 355, 357, 369
   continuous 357
   cost centre **348**
   fixed 363–364
   flexed [*see* flexed budgets]
   general overheads costs 349
   human resources **348**
   imposed 366–367
   interrelationship with standards 376–377
   master 350, 355
   materials purchases **348**
   objectives 346–347
   operational 347
   participative 366–367
   production **348**, 349, 350–351
   raw materials purchases 349, 350, 351
   responsibility for 347–348, **348**
   rolling 357–358, 369
   sales 346, **348**, 349

sequence in preparation 349–350
strategic 347
tactical 347
by-product costing 247–271, **248**
by-products 250–251
costing 247–271, **248**

C

capacity 93, 104, 122, 164, 165, 167, 194, 256, 282, 283, 316, 322, 361, 400, 426, 497
constraints 277, 278, 316, 520
fixed overhead variance 395
idle 161, 294
machine 316, 348, 521, 523
maximum 11, 13, 523, 524
normal 104, 161
practical 161
production 93, 135, 280, 348, 350, **354**, 520
safety 285
spare 122, 256, 277, 279, 281, 282, 283, 285, 295, 296
capital expenditure 350
budget 346, 350
postponement **354**
capital investments 274
appraisal 334
case studies 6, 29, 55, 94, 123, 168, 200, 233, 258, 306, 336, 369, 416, 474, 501, 534, 561
cash **354**, 557
availability 348
differential flow 274
flow 20, 21, 301, 351, 369, 468, 470, 556
flow statement 350, 355
future flow 8, 19, 20, 21, 22, 460, 461, 463
income taxes 468
remuneration 472
cash budget 350, 351–354, 355, 357, 369
drawing up 351–353
management action based on 354, **354**
centralisation 455, 456
centralised organisational structures 455–458
certainty 51, 296, 305
decisions under conditions of 278–292
Chartered Institute of Management Accountants (CIMA) 1, 3, 210, 298, 359, 446, 464, 470, 526, 558
clock cards 191
closing-down decisions 274, 278, 288–292
qualitative issues 291–292
quantitative issues 289–291
simple approach 291
coefficient of determination **50**
competitive advantage 415, 533, 543–568
components 404
computer packages for linear programming 335

consecutive processes 233–234, **234**
constant gross profit percentage 254–255
constraints 521–522, **523**
capacity 277, 278, 316, 520
elevation **523**, 525
establishment of, for linear programming 331
exploitation 523–524, **523**
external 521, 523
identification 523, **523**
internal 521, 523
subordination of other activities **523**, 524–525
continuous feedback on performance 367–368
contribution 79–81
contribution margin formula 80–81
control 345–374
controllability principle 455, 472
conversion costs 210, **210**, 211, 214, 216, 218, 219, 220, 222, 223, 225, 228, 230, 231, 235, 236, 248, 267
correlation 362
correlation coefficient **50**
cost accounting 1, 2
concepts 102–109
integrating with financial accounting 195–199
joint costs, treatment of 249–255, **250**
problems 248
records 190
standards 403
cost behaviour 8, 9–17, 37, 54, 76, 102, 441, 558
application of principles 16–17
means of predicting 53
cost-benefit models 397
cost centre **150**, **166**, 452, 495
budgets 348
discretionary 452
managers 348
standard 452
cost classification 7–36
cost drivers 19, 38–39, 40, 41, 42, 43, 44, 45, 46, **50**, 51, 52, 53, 54, 55, 57, 79, 159, **166**, 166, 167, 187, 188, 193, 194, 349, 360, 392, 492, 526, 546
determination of total cost 39
identification of 160–161
impact of 414
plausibility 39
cost elements, basic
application of concept of relevance to 292–296
labour 294–296
materials 292–294
cost estimation 37–74
factors affecting accuracy 52–53

cost objects 376
    assignment of costs 8, 17, 140, 159, 161–166, 167, 168, 267, 547, 569
cost of labour 376, 382, 390
    determining 191–193, 267
cost of quality 549–552
    categories **551**
    components **551**
    report 551
cost pools 159–160, 267
    batch-level activities 159, **160**
    facility-sustaining activities 159, **160**
    inappropriate 492
    product-level activities 159, **160**
    total cost per activity 161
    unit-level activities 159, **160**
cost standards, determination of 377–378
cost to company 191
cost-plus pricing 301, 302–303, 304
cost-volume-profit (CVP) analysis
    accountant's models 76–78, **77**
    assumptions and limitations 92–93
    economist's models 76–78, **76**
    relevant range 78, **78**
cost-volume-profit (CVP) relationships 75–100
costing
    direct 107
    integration with financial accounting systems 195–199
    kaizen 549, 552, 555, 560
    life-cycle 544, 555–556, 560
    marginal 107
    relevant 19, 20, 22, 133, 274, 319, 321, **441**, 446, 530
    reverse 553
    standard [*see* standard costing]
    target [*see* target costing]
    variable [*see* variable costing]
cost(s)
    allocating 17, 102
    appraisal 550, **551**
    conversion 210, **210**, 211, 214, 216, 218, 219, 220, 222, 223, 225, 228, 230, 231, 235, 236, 248, 267
    current 286, 464, 465
    delivery 27
    differential 20, 22
    direct 17, 18, **18**, 19, 108, 140, 149, 186, 210, 267
    expired 121–122
    external failure 529, 549, 550, **551**, 551
    fixed [*see* fixed costs]
    future [*see* future cost]
    historic 464, 467
    indirect 17, 18, **18**, 28, 140, 146, 147, 149, 186, 187, 197, 210, 267, 492
    internal failure 529, 549, 550, **551**, 551

inventoriable 22, 102
labour [*see* cost of labour]
manufacturing 23, 27, 104, 107, 109, 111, 114, 115, 117, 118, 119, **120**, 120, 122, 148, 377, 403
materials 187–191, 195, 200, 211, 214, 216, 225, 228, 231, 235, 248, 267
means of estimating 53
mixed 8, 9, 14–16, **15**, 37, 38, 42, 44, 53, 54
non-inventoriable 22
non-manufacturing 27, 107, 109, 111, 115, 119, 122, 146, 148, 377
opportunity [*see* opportunity cost]
overhead 9, 18, 57, 140, 141, 142, 149, 151, 153, 159, 160, 161, **166**, 166, 167, 186, 187, 193, 194, 195, 200, 210, 211, 214, 236, 267, 304, 349, 377, 392, 405, 406
packaging 28
period 27, 78, 107, 108, 109, 114, 121, 123, 146, 161, 192, 193, 215, 217, 223, 226, 228, 231, 252, 382, 392, 406, 410
per unit 556
prevention 529, 549, 550, **551**
product 27, 28, 78, 145, 147, 161, 164, 167, 301, 302, 526, 553, 554
relevant 19, 20–21, 121, 159, 168, 236, 257, **277**, 285, 287, 291, 292, 303, 305, 441, 446
[*see also* decision-making]
step 9, 13–14, **14**, 18, 77
sunk 20, 22, **275**, 276, 279
target 301, 302–303, 552–555, 560
total 8, 9, **10**, 11, **12**, **14**, **15**, 39, 40, **41**, 41, **42**, 43, **44**, **45**, 46, 48, **50**, 51, 52, 53, 54, **76**, 76, **77**, 77, 79, **81**, 82, 92, 103, 145, 149, 152, 161, 191, 193, 194, 210, 211, 214, 216, 218, 219, 228, 232, 234, 254, 255, 304, 360, 361, 364, 387, 551
variable [*see* variable costs]
creditors' payment period 355
CVP analysis
    accountant's models 76–78, **77**
    assumptions and limitations 92–93
    economist's models 76–78, **76**
    relevant range 78, **78**

D

debtors' collection period 355
decentralisation 474
    potential benefits 456
    potential negative consequences 456–457
    prerequisites for successful 457–458
    transfer pricing 489
decentralised organisational structures 455–458, 474

principles of management accounting

decision package 356, 357
decision trees 299–301, **300**
decision-making 9, 20, 28, 38, 58, 78, 89, 93, 102, 103, 109, 121, 122, 140, 142, 168, 200, 227, 234–236, 347, 376, 406, 416, 455, 456, 460, 474, 489, 561, 569
   in relation to joint costs 249, 255–257
   management 2, 22, 28, 133, 402
   operational constraints 315–343
   relevance of variable costing 121
   relevant information 273–314
   short-term 93, 102, 103, 107, 167
   strategic/long-term 2, 5, **166**, 167
decisions
   closing-down 274, 278, 288–292
   make-or-buy 274, 278, 285–288
   outsourcing 285, 322
   pricing 301–305, 402
   special order 278–285, 292, 303
   sub-optimal 456, 490, 492, 569
   under conditions of certainty 278–292
   under conditions of uncertainty 296–301
delivery costs 27
departmental rate 149–151
depreciation 20, 23, 27, 33, 133, 179, 194, 195, 196, 197, 351, 463, 465–466, 467, 521, 582
detail 142–151
differential cash flow 274
differential cost 20, 22
difficulty, level of 378
direct costing 107
direct labour 23, 52, 54, 57, 113, 114, 117, 187, 194, 195, **195**, 197, 200, 210, **210**, 236, 256, 267, 376, 412, 414, 417, 424
   productive hours available 192–193
   total cost 191–192
   variance 389–391, **390**, 426, 530
direct materials 23, 113, 114, 187, **195**, 197, 210, **210**, 214, 216, **234**, 256, 364, 391, 413, 417, 521, 526, 532
direct materials variance 387–389, **388**, 401, **424**
   mix 423, 424–425, **424**, **425**, 426
   negative 530
   yield 423, 425–426, **426**
drum-buffer-rope (DBR) 522, 525
dual pricing 497
Du Pont analysis 459
duration driver 52, 160–161

E

economic value added (EVA™) 458, 462–463, 469, 474
economy 473
effectiveness 473
efficiency 473
engineering studies 378

enterprise resource planning (ERP) 520, 527–528, 533
equation of a line
   computerised approach using Microsoft Excel® 47–51, **48–50**
   manual approach 45–47
equivalent production statement 211, **212**, **213**, 214, 216, **216**, 218, **219**, 220, **221**, **222**, **223**, 226, **227**, 227, 228, **229**, 231, **232**, **233**, **236**
equivalent units 211, 214, 215, 227, 228, **236**
expected values 298–299
experience curve 57
experience levels 400

F

facility-sustaining activities 159, **160**
feasible region
   derivation of, for linear programming 332
   establishment 325, 328
   interpretation of, for linear programming 332–333
final tableau
   establishment of, for linear programming 326, 331
financial accounting 20, 22, 28, 102, 103, 106, 107, 122, 123, 134, 146, 161, 168, 188, 191, 194, 217, 227, 234, 253, 395, 396, 402, 451, 452, 569
   integrating with cost accounting 195–199
   matching principle 119
   objective 148
   reports 102
   requirements 22, 140
   statement 148
   versus management accounting 2, 3, 4, **4**, 134, 441
financial accounting systems 5
   integrating with costing 195–199
financial performance measures 458–467
   determining income 466–467
   determining investment 463–466
   determining required rate of return 466
   economic value added (EVA™) 462–463
   multinational considerations 467
   residual income (RI) 460–462
   return on investment (ROI) 459–460
   return on sales (ROS) 463
financial measures 470
first-in-first-out (FIFO) method 214
   process costing using 227–233
fixed costs 9, 12–13, **12**, 15, 18, 19, 28, 40, 41, 42, 44, 45, 47, 52, 54, **77**, 77, 78, 79, 80, 81, **81**, 82, 83, 84, 85, 87, 88, 89, 90, 93, 102, 103, 104, 107, 108, 109, 111, 114, 115, 118, 119, 120, 121, 122, 123, 133, 134, 159, 161, 167, 194, 210, 256, 294, 296, 302, 303, 356, 360, 361, 364, 392, 395, 412, 492, 496

importance of 121
fixed overhead
  expenses 194–195, 392–396, 406
  variances 392–396, **395**
fixed overhead expenses 194–195, 392–396, 406
fixed overhead variances 392–396, **395**
flexed budgets 363–364
  preparation of 364–365
  revenue **367**
  variance 379–385
function 9, 22–27
funding, sources of 348
future cash flows 8, 19, 20, 21, 22, 460, 461, 463
future cost 20
  versus opportunity cost 277

G

gains 217–233
  abnormal 225–227
generic strategies
  cost leadership 545
  differentiation 545
  focus 545
  Porter's 544–545
goal congruence 457, 461, 474, 488, 490, 500
graphical method of linear programming 325–329
  feasible region 328
  limiting factors 326–328
  objective function 326
  optimal production mix 328–329
  steps in 325–329
  variables 326

H

high-low method 38, 42–44, 47, 54, 134, 364
  preparation of projections using 359–360
  shortcomings **44**
historic cost data 53
historic data
  preparing projections using 359–362
historical records 377–378

I

imposed budgets 366–367
  bottom-up 413
  relative advantage over participative budgets 366–367
  relative disadvantage compared with participative budgets 367
  top-down 367, 413
income
  determining 466–467
  statement costs **25–27**
incremental budgeting 355–356, 356–357
independent units 457

indirect labour costs 23, 187, 193, 194
  allocation **195**
inflationary effects on variances 399
integrated accounting system
  accounting entries 195–196, **195**
  T accounts **197–198**
intensity driver 52, 161
interdependent units 457
interlocking job-costing system
  accounting entries 196–199
  T accounts **199**
intermediate product or service 490
International Accounting Standards 22, 249
  IAS 1 22
  IAS 2 22, 27, 103, 104, 105, 121, 122, 140, 146, 148, 218, 227, 253, 255, 377, 489
  IAS 16 498
  IAS 24 489
  joint costs 255
International Financial Reporting Standards (IFRS) 4, **4**, 27, 377, 402, 403, 452
  IFRS 8 489
international transfers 498–499
inventory
  closing 106, 107, 110, 111, 115–119, **120**, 120, 122, 190, 191, 349, 351, 353, 389, 402, 403
  file 527
  management 400
  none 109–112
  opening 107, 110, 111, 112–115, 117, 118, 119, **120**, 120, 122, 189, 349, 351, 353
  valuation 121
  [*see also* inventory valuation]
inventory levels, changes in impact on profit 109–121, **120**
inventory losses 399
inventory valuation 121
  FIFO method 188–189
  specific identification 189–190
  standard costing 377
  standard costs 190–191
  weighted average method 189
investment
  centre 452, 495
  definition 463–464
  determining 463–466
  measurement 464–465
investor ratios 355
irrelevant information
  elements 276–277
  versus relevant information 275–276, **275**

J

job card 187
job costing 185–207
  objectives 186

607

job-costing system
  elements of cost 186–195
Johannesburg Securities Exchange (JSE) 4
  regulations 4
joint costing 247–271, **248**
joint costs
  cost accounting treatment of 249–255, **250**
  decision-making 255–257
  International Accounting Standards 255
joint process **250**
joint products 252–255
  constant gross profit percentage 254–255
  market values at split-off point 253
  net realisable value 253–254
  physical measures 252–253
just-in-time environment 530
  performance measurement 530–531
just-in-time (JIT) systems 528–531

K
kaizen costing 549, 552, 555, 560
key performance indicators (KPIs)
  role in budgeting process 355

L
labour 27, 55, **195**, 196, 200, **250**, 292, 294–296, 327, 335, 349, 377, 402, 427
  determining cost 191–195
  direct [*see* direct labour]
  efficiency 52, 55, 399, 400, 413
  equation 327
  fixed 295–296
  indirect [*see* indirect labour costs]
  -related effects 400
  shadow price 329, **330**, 330
  skilled 234, 296, 316, 334, 383, 391
  time/hours 39, 55, **56**, 56, 57, 141, 142, 147, 148, **150**, 151, 163, 193, 194, 195, 267, 320, 321, 322, 324, 325, 327, 328, 329, 330, 331, 332, 333, 349, 376, 392, 394, 404–405, 406, 414, 523, 530
  total costs 55, 195, 210, 211, 214, 267, 287, 334, 376, 382, 387, 521
  variable 294–295
labour variances 395, 399, 400, 413, 416
  idle time 426–427
  mix and yield 426
labour-related effects on variances 400
lean systems 552
learning curves 55–67, **56**
  cumulative average–time learning model 57–58, **64**
  cumulative average time per unit **56**
  cumulative doubling approach 59–60
  cumulative total labour hours **56**
  graph/schedule approach 61–63
  incremental unit–time learning model 57–58, **64**
  mathematical approach 63–67
learning tempo 56
least squares regression 44–52
life-cycle costing (LCC) 555–556, **556**
  marketing, service and support costs 556, **556**
  pre-production costs 555, **556**
  production costs 555–556, **556**
limiting factors 316–322, 325
  determination of rank and contribution for linear programming 327
  establishment of, for linear programming 325, 326–327
  graphing of, for linear programming 328, **328**
  multiple 319–322
  shadow prices 324
  single 316–319
linear programming
  budgeting 334
  calculation of shadow prices 329–330
  capital investment appraisal 334
  computer packages 335
  graphical method 324–329
  limitations 335
  maximum payment for additional resources 334
  practical application 334–335
  simplex method 331–334
  steps in 325–329
linear regression analysis 360–362
linear relationship 11, 40, 42, 43, 45, 46, **50**, 52, 54, 55, 77
liquidity 355
long-term pricing 303–304
losses 217–233
  abnormal 221–224, 225
  identified before end of process 219–221
  normal 218–219, 224–225
  normal and abnormal units sold as scrap 224–227
loss leader 304

M
machine capacity 316, 348, 521, 523
make-or-buy decisions 274, 278, 285–288
  qualitative issues 287–288
  quantitative issues 286–287
  scarce resources 322–323
management
  activity-based [*see* activity-based management]
  total quality [*see* total quality management]
  value-based 468–469, 474

Index

management accountants 1, 2, 5, 6, 13, 102, 133, 134, 188, 274, 301, 305, 395, 398, 470, 473, 532, 569
   role in budget process 368
management accounting 1–3
   contemporary concepts 519–542
   definition 1–3
   information 451
   introduction 1–6
   modern 5–6
   versus financial accounting 2, 3, 4, 4, 134, 441
management action
   based on cash flow 354, **354**
management information, levels 5
   operational 5
   strategic 5
   tactical 5
manager(s) 3, 4, 5, 6, 8, 9, 17, 28, 81, 84, 85, 88, 89, 91, 93, 122, 134, 167, 346, 348, 357, 368, 378, 379, 396, 397, 398, 399, 412, 413, 415, 450, 451, 456, 457, 458, 459, 460, 461, 462, 463, 466, 467, 469, 470, 472, 473, 474, 488, 489, 490, 496, 497, 522, 523, 532, 546, 555, 560, 569
   cost centre **348**
   functional 348, **348**
   human resources **348**
   impact of budgeting on motivation 365–366
   line 366, 367, 368
   non-financial 83
   performance of 453–455
   production **348**, 413
   purchasing **348**
   sales **348**
manufacturing cells 529
manufacturing costs 23, 27, 104, 107, 109, 111, 114, 115, 117, 118, 119, **120**, 120, 122, 148, 377, 403
manufacturing overheads 23–27, **104**, 145, 146, 148, 151, 165, **210**
   fixed 23, 78, 103–104, **104**, 106, 107, 108, 111, 113, 114, 115, 117, 119, 121, 122, 377, 382, 392, 393, 416
   non- 103, **104**, 114, 146, 165, 382
   total 144
   variable 23, 113, 114, 117, 377
margin of safety 85–86
marginal costing 107
market value added (MVA) 468–469
market values
   of joint products at split-off point 253
master budget 350, 355
master parts file 527
master production schedule 527
matching principle 119

materials 23, 103, 104, 186, 187, 192, 194, 195, **195**, 200, 217, 222, 223, 230, 231, 292–294, 376, 377, 383, 413, 528, 529, 530, 533, 548, 557
   costs 9, 187–191, 195, 200, 211, 214, 216, 225, 228, 231, 235, 248, 267
   direct 23, 113, 114, 187, **195**, 197, 210, **210**, 214, 216, **234**, 256, 364, 391, 413, 417, 521, 526, 532
   direct variance 387–389, **388**, 401, 423, 424–425, **424**, **425**, **426**, 530
   quality 399, 551
   raw [*see* raw materials]
   -related effects 399–400
   relevance 296
   variance 395, 416
materials ordering and handling system **187**
materials purchases **348**
materials requirement planning (MRP) 520, 526–527, 533
materials-related effects on variances 399–400
McDonaldisation 414
mixed costs 8, 9, 14–16, **15**, 37, 38, 42, 44, 53, 54
modern mechanised environments
   variance analysis in 414
multidimensional performance measures 470–471
multiple regression 52

N

net realisable value 252, 253–254, 255, 257, 403
non-financial measures 470, 530
non-manufacturing costs 27, 107, 109, 111, 115, 119, 122, 146, 148, 377
non-manufacturing overheads 103, **104**, 114, 146, 165, 382
normal distribution table 51
not-for-profit organisations 1, 3, 9, 473

O

objective function
   establishment of, for linear programming 326, 331
   expressing as equation for linear programming 332
objectives 450–451
operating expenses 521
operational constraints
   decision-making under 315–343
opportunity cost 21–22, 226, **275**, 282, 283, 284, 285, 296, 493, 494, 503, 505, 506, 508, 529, 550
   calculation of 294
   versus future cost 277–278, 282

optimal production mix
    determination of, for linear programming 328–329
organisational structures
    centralised 455–458
    decentralised 455–458, 474
organisations
    not-for-profit 1, 3, 9, 473
    public sector 3, 9, 473
overhead absorption rates 349
overhead allocation 139–183
    traditional system 141
    value-based system 142
    volume-based system 141–142
overhead expenses 27, 193–195
    fixed 194–195, 392–396, 406
    variable 194, 391–392, 405–406

P

packaging costs 28
participation 366–367
participative budgets 366–367
    relative advantage over imposed budgets 367
    relative disadvantage compared with participative budgets 366–367
penetration pricing 304
perfectly competitive market 491
performance
    continuous feedback 367–368
    evaluation 366–367, 451
    measurement 122, 530–531
    rewarding 472
performance evaluation 8, 28, 58, 346, 347, 366–367, 376, 379, 450, 451, 453, 455, 456, 457, 458, 460, 463, 467, 470, 472, 500, 574
    criteria 450, 451
    information for 451
performance management 449–486
performance measures 451
    financial 458–467
    multidimensional 470, 471, 474
physical measures method 252–253, 255, 257, 260
planning 345–374
plant-wide rate 149–151
Porter's generic strategies 544–545
Porter's value chain 559, **559**, 560
practical capacity 161
premium pricing 304
price
    elasticity 302
    setters 301–302
    skimming 304
    takers 301–302
    variance 384, 385, **386**, 386, 387, 389, 391, 392, 393, 398, 399, 400, 401, **401**, 402, 403, 404, 413, **424**, 424, 530

price elasticity 302
price skimming 304
pricing
    cost-plus 301, 302–303, 304
    dual 497
    long-term 303–304
    penetration 304
    premium 304
    short-term 281, 303
    strategies 304
    transfer 487–517
pricing decisions 301–305, 402
    cost-plus pricing versus target costing 302–303
    long-term pricing 303–304
    price elasticity 302
    price takers versus price setters 301–302
    pricing strategies 304–305
    short-term pricing 303
pricing strategies 304–305
    loss leader 304
    penetration pricing 304
    premium pricing 304
    price skimming 304
    product bundling/optional extras 305
    product differentiation 305
principal budgeting factor 348, 349, 350
probabilities 296–298, 300, 301, 359, 397
probability theory
    budgeting 358–359
process costing 209–246
    calculations 211–233
    first-in-first-out (FIFO) method 227–233
    simple system, flow of costs in **210**
product
    bundling 305
    differentiation 305
product-level activities 159, **160**
production budget **348**, 349, 350–351
production cost 356, 364
    statement 211, 212, **212**, **213**, 214, 215, 216, **216**, 217, 218, **219**, 219, 220, **221**, 222, **223**, 223, 224, **225**, 225, 226, **227**, 228, **229**, 230, 231, 232, **232**
production departments 151, 152, **166**, 452
production variance
    mix 423–424
    yield 423–424
profit
    actual 91, 379, 380, 381, 383, 396
    amount given level of activity 83
    centre 452, 495
    formula 79–80
    impact of changes in inventory levels 109–121, **120**
    impact of variable costing 122
    reconciliation of actual to standard 396
    standard 386, 396

target 84–85
profitability 9, 167, 253, 301, 304, 347, 350, 355, 412, 417, 421, 521, 526, 546, 547, 552, 553, 557
profit margin 302, 303, 553
　allowable **554**
　determining desired 553
　gross 355
　operating 468
projecting sales 362–363
projections
　high-low method 359–360
　linear regression analysis 359–362
　preparing using historic data 359–362
　regression 362–363
public sector organisations 3, 9, 473
pull system 413, 527, 528
push-through system 527

Q

qualitative measures 470
quality
　cost of 549–552, **551**
　definition 547
　dimensions 548, **548**
quantitative measures 470

R

ratio analysis
　role in budgeting process 355
ratios
　current 355
　debt 355
　gearing 355
　quick 355
raw materials 27, 161, 234, 249, **250**, 316, 317, 325, 327, 328, 329, **330**, 331, 332, 333, 334, 335, 346, 391, 399, 402, 403–404, 425, **551**, 559
　availability 348
　purchases budget 349, 350, 351
recurring fee
　supplementing transfer price 496–497
regression
　and projections 362–363
regression analysis 51, 362, 363
　linear 360–362
regression error 44, **45**, **50**, 51
relationship factors 400
relevance 9, 19–22, **275**
　application to basic cost elements 292–296
　definition 274–278
　understanding concept of 274–278
relevant cost 19, 20–21, 121, 159, 168, 236, 257, 277, 285, 287, 291, 292, 303, 305, 441, 446
relevant costing 19, 20, 22, 133, 274, 319, 321, 441, 446, 530

relevant information
　elements 276–277
　versus irrelevant information 275–276, **275**
required rate of return 350, 460, 461, 462, 463, 467, 474
　determining 466
residual income (RI) 458, 460–462, 466, 467, 474
responsibility accounting 346, 369, 452, 473
responsibility centre 346, 452, 495
return on capital employed (ROCE) 355, 464
return on investment (ROI) 451, 458, 459–460, 464, 465, 474, 553
return on sales (ROS) 458, 459, 463, 474
revenue 406–410
　centre 452
revenue variance 385–387
　sales mix 417–421, **420**
　sales quantity 417–421, **421**
rolling budgets 357–358, 369
rule of thumb models 397

S

sales
　demand 317, 319, 348, 349
　mix 89, 90, 91, 92, 93, 318, 387, 417, 418
　mix variance 91, 417–421, **420**, 425
　price variance 385, **386**, 386, 387, 398, **419**, 419, 420
　projecting 362–363
　quantity variance 387, 417–421, **421**, 422, 423
sales mix variance 417–421, **420**
sales quantity variance 417–421, **421**
sales volume
　reduction in selling price to increase 87–89
　required to cover additional costs 87
　variance 386, 387, 398, 417, 418, 419, **419**, **420**, 420, 421
scarce resources
　make-or-buy decisions 322–323
scatter diagrams 362
scatter graph 40–42, **41**, **42**
scrap 236, 249, **250**, 251, 252, 255, 349, **551**
　normal and abnormal loss units sold as 224–227
self-constructed assets, transfer of 498
selling price 76, 77, 79, 80, 81, 83, 84, 85, 86, 87, 88, 142, 147, 253, 254, 255, 256, 281, 301, 302, 303, 304, 406, 497, 545, 553, 560
　establishing 553
　target **554**
sensitivity analysis 82–89, 93, 333
service organisations
　standard costing in 415

shadow prices 495
   calculation 329–330
   labour 329, **330**, 330
   limiting factors 324
   linear programming 329–330
shareholder value analysis 468
short-term
   measures 460, 461, 463
   pricing 303
simplex method of linear
   programming 331–334
   constraints 331
   final tableau 332–333
   objective function 331, 332
   principles 331–334
   purchase of additional
      resources 333–334
   sensitivity analysis 333
   slack variables 331–332
   variables 331
Six Sigma 552
skilled labour 234, 296, 316, 334, 383, 391, 405, 426
   [*see also* unskilled labour]
   semi- 296, 391, 392, 394, 404–405, 411, 412, 426
slack 329
slack variables
   introduction of, for linear
      programming 331–332
solvency 355
South African Institute of Chartered Accountants (SAICA) 1, 2
special order decisions 278–285, 292, 303
   qualitative issues 285
   quantitative issues 279–284
   simple approach 284–285
split-off point 249, 250, **250**, 252, 257
   market value of joint products 253, 256, 257
staff quality 400
stakeholders 1, 2, 3, 4, 6, 28, 469, 471, 472
standard costing 190, 214, 375–440, 474, 530, 533, 569
   advanced concepts 417–427
   benchmarking 415
   benefits 413
   criticisms 412–413
   inventory valuation 377
   reconciliation 396, **396**
   service organisations 415
standard error **50**, 51, 52
standards
   achievable 378
   basic 378
   ideal 378
   interrelationship with budgets 376–377
   revision of 402

statement of cash flows 350, 355
   cash flow 20, 21, 301, 351, 369, 468, 470, 556
   differential cash flow 274
   future cash flow 8, 19, 20, 21, 22, 460, 461, 463
static budget
   revenue **387**
   variances 379–385, 387, 393, 394, 395
statistical models 397
step costs 9, 13–14, **14**, 18, 77
strategic business units 456
sub-optimal decisions 456, 490, 492, 569
sunk cost 20, 22, **275**, 276, 279
supply chain 557, **558**
   management (SCM) 557–558
support service departments
   allocation of costs 151–158
   direct approach 152, **155**
   repeated distribution approach 152–153, **156–157**
   simultaneous equation approach 153–154, **153**, **158**
   step down approach 152, **155–156**

T

target cost 303, 560
   component level 554–555, **554**
   product level 553–554
   product-level process **554**
target costing 301, 302–303, 552–555, 560
   definition 553
targets 368, 482, 527
   agreeing on 472
   failure to meet 347, 365
   setting 365, 366, 369, 461, 470, 532, 533, 549, 587
Theory of Constraints (TOC) 413, 519, 520–526, 527, 532, 533, 580
   activity-based costing 526
   reports 525
   steps 522–525, **523**
three Es 473
throughput 482, 516, 520, 521, 522, 523, 524, 525, 526, 533
   accounting 521, 522, 526, 532, 533
   calculation 521, 532
   ratio 521, 522
time sheets 191
timing 9, 27–28
total assets
   employed 464
   held 464
   less current liabilities 464
total cost 8, 9, **10**, 11, **12**, **14**, **15**, 39, 40, **41**, 41, **42**, 43, **44**, **45**, 46, 48, **50**, 51, 52, 53, 54, 76, **76**, 77, **77**, 79, **81**, 82, 92, 103, 145, 149, 152, 161, 191, 193, 194, 210, 211, 214, 216,

218, 219, 228, 232, 234, 254, 255, 304, 360, 361, 364, 387, 551
total quality management 547–552, **549**
   critical success factors **549**
   elements 549–550
traceability 18, 140, 267, 455, 467, 473, 583
traditional allocation systems 141
   compared with ABC **166**
transaction driver 52, 160
transfer
   international 498–499
   self-constructed assets 498
transfer prices
   cost-based 491–492
   determining in perfect and imperfect markets 502–509
   market price-based 490–491
   maximum 492, 493, 494, 495, 500, 503, 504, 506, 508
   minimum 490, 493, 494, 495, 496, 500, 503, 506, 508
   negotiated 492–495
transfer pricing 487–517
   decentralisation 489
   principles 489–490
   resolving problems 495–497
   strategic and ethical considerations 500
triple bottom line 471, 500
t-stat **50**, 51–52
turnover
   asset 355, 459, 463
   growth in 355
   inventory 355

U

uncertainty 85, 89, 278, 299, 358
   decisions under conditions of 278, 296–301
unit cost 210, 211, 214, 215, 216, 225, 230, 231, 233, 236, 247, 252, 253
   statement, 211, 212, **212**, **213**, 214, 216, **216**, 218, **219**, 220, **221**, 222, **223**, 223, 224, **225**, 226, **227**, 227, 228, **229**, 230, 231, 232, **232**
unit-level activities 159, **160**
units
   performance 453–455
unskilled labour 234, 296, 383

V

value-based management 468–469
   market value added 468–469
   shareholder value analysis 468
value-based allocation system 142
value-based techniques, 140, 141–142
value chain 378, 528, 552, 558, 593
   analysis 416, 544, 558–560
   internal 558

Porter's 559, **559**, 560
value drivers 468
value system 559
   Porter's **559**
variable costing 28, 78, 79, 92, 93, 107–109, 134, 288, 336, 386, 392–393, 394, 419, 420, 522, 526
   impact on profit 122
   relevance to decision-making 121
   strengths and weaknesses 121–122
   versus absorption costing 78, 101–132
variable costs 9–11, **10**, **11**, 12, 15, 18, 19, 22, 38, 41, 42, 43, 44, 45, 46, 55, 77, 78, 79, 80, **81**, 82, 83, 84, 87, 88, 92, 93, 102, 103, 107, 108, 109, 111, 122, 235, 280, 282, 283, **284**, 356, 364, 382, 392, 522, 526
   pro-rating difference 496
variable overheads 23, 57, 194, 200, 391–392, 405–406
   expenses 194, 391–392, 405–406
   variances 387, 391–392, **391**, 414
variables
   definition of, in linear programming 326, 331
   slack 331–332
variance accounts
   balances in 410–412
variance analysis 376
   in modern mechanised environments 414
variances
   calculation 379–396
   cost 386, 387, 393, 397, 399, 406, 412
   direct labour 389–391, **390**, 426, 530
   direct materials 387–389, **388**, **424**, 424–425, **425**, **426**
   efficiency 389, 391, 393, 398, 399, 400, 411, 412, 413, 414, 416, 424, 426, 427, 530
   flexed budget 379–385
   idle time 426–427
   interpretation 397–399
   investigation 397
   labour 426–427
   market share 422–423, **422**
   market size 422–423, **423**
   mix 423–424, 424–425, 426
   operating 400–401
   planning 400–401
   possible causes of 399–400
   price 384, 385, **386**, 386, 387, 389, 391, 392, 393, 398, 399, 400, 401, **401**, 402, 403, 404, 413, **424**, 424, 530
   production 423–424
   production volume 393, 394, 395
   quantity 384, 385, 387, 388, 389, 391, 392, 393, 394, 398, 403
   rate 389, 400, 405, 411, 412
   revenue 385–387, 399
   sales **387**

sales mix 91, 417–421, **420**, 425
sales price 385, **386**, 386, 387, 398, **419**, 419, 420
sales quantity 387, 417–421, **421**, 422, 423
sales volume 386, **386**, 387, 398, 417, 418, 419, **419**, **420**, 420, 421
spending 391, 392, 393, 394, 395, 405, 406
static budget 379–385
variable overhead 387, 391–392, **391**, 414
volume 379–385, 423
yield 423–424, 425–426
volume-based allocation system 141–142
volume-based techniques 141–142

W
wage system 191–192
waste 249, **250**, 251–252, 255, 257
weighted average
    cost of capital 462, 466
    method of inventory valuation 188, 189, **214**, 215, 267

method of process costing 227, 230, 231, **232**, 233,236
return on investment 461
unit contribution margin 89, 90, 91, 93
work environment 400, 426
work-in-progress (WIP) 197, 211, 212–217, 220, 403, 404, 407, 410, 411, 521, 523, 524, 525, 527, **551**
    balances 234
    closing 212–214, 219, 221–224, 225, 228, 236
    opening 214–217, 221–224, 227, 228, 231, 232, 236

Z
zero-base budgeting 356, 369, 378, 444, 445, 447, 586, 587
    advantages over incremental budgeting 356–357
    disadvantages compared with incremental budgeting 357